THE OXFORD HANDBOOK OF

THE ENGLISH
REVOLUTION

THE OXFORD HANDBOOK OF

THE ENGLISH

REVOLUTION

Edited by

MICHAEL J. BRADDICK

OXFORD

UNIVERSITY PRESS

OXFORD
UNIVERSITY PRESS

Great Clarendon Street, Oxford, OX2 6DP,
United Kingdom

Oxford University Press is a department of the University of Oxford.
It furthers the University's objective of excellence in research, scholarship,
and education by publishing worldwide. Oxford is a registered trade mark of
Oxford University Press in the UK and in certain other countries

© Oxford University Press 2015

The moral rights of the author have been asserted

First Edition published in 2015
Impression: 1

Published in the United States of America by Oxford University Press
198 Madison Avenue, New York, NY 10016, United States of America

British Library Cataloguing in Publication Data
Data available

Library of Congress Control Number: 2015930593

ISBN 978–0–19–969589–8

Printed and bound by
CPI Group (UK) Ltd, Croydon, CR0 4YY

Cover image: Map of the British Isles with battle ships in the North Sea,
and a view of Prague and the Battle of the White Mountain of 1620, comparing
the English and Bohemian Civil Wars. Etching by Wenceslaus Hollar c. 1659
© The Trustees of the British Museum

CONTENTS

PART III INSTITUTIONS AND ACTORS

PART IV PARTIES, IDEAS, AND PEOPLE

PART V WIDER PERSPECTIVES

List of Illustrations

Notes on Contributors

Philip Baker is a Research Fellow at the History of Parliament Trust, London, and Senior Research Fellow in the Humanities Research Institute, University of Buckingham. He is the editor of *The Levellers: the Putney Debates* (2007), the co-editor of *The Agreements of the People, the Levellers, and the Constitutional Crisis of the English Revolution* (2012), and the author of a number of articles and essays on the civil war period and the history of early modern London.

Toby Barnard emeritus fellow of Hertford College, Oxford, is the author of *Cromwellian Ireland* (reprinted, 2000); *A New Anatomy of Ireland* (2003) and *Improving Ireland?* (2008).

Michael J. Braddick is Professor of History at the University of Sheffield. He has published extensively on state formation, popular politics and the English civil war. His most recent book is *God's Fury, England's Fire: A New History of the English Civil Wars* (2008).

John Coffey is Professor of Early Modern History at the University of Leicester. He has published widely on Puritan thought in the English Revolution. He is also the author of *Persecution and Toleration in Protestant England, 1558–1689* (2000), and *Exodus and Liberation: Deliverance Politics from John Calvin to Martin Luther King Jr* (2013) and co-editor of *The Cambridge Companion to Puritanism* (2008). With Neil Keeble, Tim Cooper, and Thomas Charlton he is currently working on a critical edition of Baxter's memoir, *Reliquiae Baxterianae*, for Oxford University Press.

Joseph Cope is Professor and Chair of the Department of History at the State University of New York at Geneseo, where he has taught since 2001. He is the author of *England and the 1641 Irish Rebellion* (2009) and is currently working on a study of faith healers in during the mid-seventeenth century.

Alan Cromartie is Professor of the History of Political Thought at the University of Reading. He is author of *The Constitutionalist Revolution: An Essay on the History of England* (2006).

Richard Cust is Professor of Early Modern History at the University of Birmingham. He has published a number of books and articles on early Stuart politics, including *Charles I. A Political Life* (2005) and *Charles I and the Aristocracy, 1625–1642* (2013).

J. C. Davis is Emeritus Professor of History, University of East Anglia and the author of an analytical study of Oliver Cromwell's reputation (2001) as well as an influential essay on Cromwell's religion. He has also written extensively on political thought, especially its radical varieties, in early modern England and, more generally, on the history of utopian thought.

Rachel Foxley lectures in early modern history at the University of Reading and is the author of *The Levellers: Radical Political Thought in the English Revolution* (2013).

Julian Goodare is Reader in History, University of Edinburgh. He is the author of *State and Society in Early Modern Scotland* (1999) and *The Government of Scotland, 1560–1625* (2004). He is an Associate Editor of the *Oxford Dictionary of National Biography*.

Tim Harris has taught at Brown University since 1986, where he is currently Munro-Goodwin-Wilkinson Professor in European History. His books include *London Crowds in the Reign of Charles II* (1987), *Politics under the Later Stuarts* (1993), *Restoration: Charles II and his Kingdoms, 1660–1685* (2005), *Revolution: The Great Crisis of the British Monarchy, 1685–1720* (2006), and *Rebellion: Britain's First Stuart Kings, 1567–1642* (2014).

Derek Hirst is William Eliot Smith Professor of History at Washington University, St Louis. During more than three decades in St Louis he has broadened his early focus on early Stuart politics. His recent publications include *Dominion: England and its Island Neighbours c.1500–1707* (2012) and the co-authored *Andrew Marvell, Orphan of the Hurricane* (2012).

Andrew Hopper is Senior Lecturer in the Centre for English Local History at the University of Leicester and the author of *'Black Tom': Sir Thomas Fairfax and the English Revolution* (2007), and *Turncoats and Renegadoes: Changing Sides during the English Civil Wars* (2012).

Ann Hughes is Professor Emerita at Keele where she was Professor of Early Modern History until 2014. She is the author of many books and articles about the English Revolution, most recently *Gender and the English Revolution* (2011) and co-editor with Thomas Corns and David Loewenstein, *The Complete Works of Gerrard Winstanley* (2009).

Mark Knights is Professor of History at Warwick University and has published extensively on early modern political culture, particularly in the late seventeenth and early eighteenth centuries. His most recent book is *The Devil in Disguise: Delusion, Deception and Fanaticism in the Early English Enlightenment* (2011) and he is now working on a study of early modern corruption, from Reformation to Reform.

Laura Lunger Knoppers is Professor of English at the University of Notre Dame. She has published widely on seventeenth-century British literature, politics, religion, and visual culture, especially the works of John Milton. Most recently, she is the author of *Politicizing Domesticity from Henrietta Maria to Milton's Eve* (2011) and editor of the *Oxford Handbook of Literature and the English Revolution* (2012).

Peter Lake is Distinguished University Professor of English history at Vanderbilt University. He has just completed a study of Shakespeare's history plays and the politics of the 1590s and (with Isaac Stephens) a book on religious identity in pre-civil war Northamptonshire. He is also turning his 2011 Ford lectures into a book.

John Miller is Emeritus Professor of History at Queen Mary University of London. He has published extensively on late seventeenth-century English History, including more recently *Cities Divided: Politics and Religion in English Provincial Towns 1660–1722* (2007); and *A Brief History of the English Civil Wars* (2009).

John Morrill was Professor of British and Irish History at the University of Cambridge 1998–2013 and he is a Life Fellow of Selwyn College Cambridge. He is the author of more than 100 books and essays on many aspects of early modern state formation, the politics of religion in the long seventeenth century, and on the life and faith of Oliver Cromwell.

Micheál Ó Siochrú is Associate Professor of History at Trinity College Dublin. He is the author of numerous books and articles on seventeenth-century Ireland, including *God's Executioner: Oliver Cromwell and the Conquest of Ireland* (2009). He is currently working on a new edition of Oliver Cromwell's letters and papers for Oxford University Press.

Jason Peacey is Professor of Early Modern British History at University College London. He is the editor of *The Regicides and the Execution of Charles I* (2001), and the author of *Politicians and Pamphleteers* (2004), and of *Print and Public Politics in the English Revolution* (2013).

Stephen K. Roberts is Editor of the House of Commons 1640–1660 Section of the History of Parliament. He has written extensively on aspects of regional government and society in England and Wales in this period, and is joint editor of *Midland History* and general editor of the Worcestershire Historical Society.

David L. Smith is Fellow and Director of Studies in History at Selwyn College, Cambridge. His books include *Constitutional Royalism and the Search for Settlement, c. 1640–1649* (1994), *A History of the Modern British Isles, 1603–1707: The Double Crown* (1998), *The Stuart Parliaments, 1603–1689* (1999), and (with Patrick Little) *Parliaments and Politics during the Cromwellian Protectorate* (2007).

R. Scott Spurlock is Lecturer in Religious Studies at the University of Glasgow. He is co-editor of the Palgrave Macmillan book series 'Christianities in the trans-Atlantic World, 1500–1800' and editor of *The Records of the Scottish Church History Society*.

Laura A. M. Stewart is Senior Lecturer in Early Modern British History at Birkbeck, University of London, and has published widely on many aspects of early modern

Scottish and British history. She has recently completed her second book, *Rethinking the Scottish Revolution*, which will be published by Oxford University Press in 2015.

Ted Vallance is Professor of Early Modern British Political Culture at the University of Roehampton. He is the author of several books including *Revolutionary England and the National Covenant* (2005). He is currently working on a monograph on public opinion and loyal addressing in late Stuart and early Hanoverian England.

John Walter is Research Professor of History at the University of Essex. He has published widely on early modern protest and popular political culture, including *Understanding Popular Violence in the English Revolution* (1999) and *Crowds and Popular Politics in Early Modern England* (2006). He is currently completing a book on state oaths in the English revolution, to be published by Oxford University Press.

Timothy Wilks is Professor of Cultural History at Southampton Solent University. His research interests include the patronage of artists, the history of collecting, and European court cultures. His recent publications include a biography of a lesser favourite of the early Stuart Court, Lord Dingwall, and a study of art plunder in the Thirty Years' War.

Peter H. Wilson is G.F. Grant Distinguished Professor of History at the University of Hull, having previously worked at Newcastle and Sunderland universities. His book *Europe's Tragedy. The Thirty Years War* won the Society for Military History's Distinguish Book Award in 2011. He is currently writing a general history of the Holy Roman Empire for Penguin and Harvard University Press.

Phil Withington is Professor of History at the University of Sheffield. He has published extensively on urban citizenship and popular politics during the early modern era. His current research includes a project on intoxicants and early modernity and a book about the social history of the Renaissance.

Steven N. Zwicker is Stanley Elkin Professor in the Humanities and Professor of English at Washington University, St Louis. He has written widely on seventeenth-century politics and literature including *Dryden's Political Poetry* (1972), *Politics and Language in Dryden's Poetry* (2014), *Lines of Authority: Politics and English Literary Culture, 1649–1689* (1996), and, with Derek Hirst, *Andrew Marvell, Orphan of the Hurricane* (2012); in addition he has edited Dryden's poetry for Penguin Books, and several volumes of interdisciplinary essays with Kevin Sharpe.

ACKNOWLEDGEMENTS

I am grateful to all the contributors for their work on this book. For much of the time it was taking shape I was a Pro Vice Chancellor at the University of Sheffield. Without the help of Suzanne Hubbard and Gary Rivett I would have found it impossible to make progress with it and I am very grateful to them both. I would also like to thank my Vice Chancellor, Sir Keith Burnett, for his wholehearted support of my scholarly work while I was in that post. In the latter stages I benefited greatly from the advice of Karen Harvey, Simon Middleton, and Jason Peacey. I am also deeply grateful to Cora and Melissa who showed their customary level of interest, which was very refreshing.

PART I

INTRODUCTION

CHAPTER 1

....

CIVIL WAR AND REVOLUTION IN ENGLAND, SCOTLAND, AND IRELAND

....

MICHAEL J. BRADDICK

SINCE the 1970s there has been a sustained reaction against progressive accounts of the English Revolution that were broadly characterized by 'revisionist' historians as Marxist or Whig. They were said to be both teleological (assuming an inevitable direction to events) and anachronistic (describing ideas, attitudes, and social and political groups in our terms rather than those appropriate to the period). Those that located the causes of events in underlying structural changes were also said to be deterministic (paying little or no attention to individual subjectivities, self-understanding, choices, or agency).[1] These historiographical concerns were shared much more widely, of course, and in other fields were important in stimulating new departures such as the new cultural history or the history of marginal and excluded social groups. In the historiography of early modern England this tended to reinforce a separation of political and other kinds of history. While political histories concentrated more closely on narrative, the new social history began to look elsewhere for the political lives of the humble and poor, and the struggles that gave meaning to their lives: early modern social and cultural history has flourished but largely independently of the historiography of the Revolution with which influential historians had once tried to link it.[2]

The methodological critique of progressive histories also led to sharp criticism of many of their key conclusions. The English Revolution was for a time routinely presented as a paradigm case of the transition to modernity, and a phenomenon around which social, political, intellectual, and cultural histories could be focused. As specialists began to dismantle this view so the study of the Revolution seemed to take an inward turn: the conclusions being proposed were more often seen as particular to this sub-field rather than crucial for understanding the broader sweep of human history. At the same time, as historical writing diversified, the Revolution ceased to be such an important focus for teaching and writing about sixteenth- and seventeenth-century England more broadly.

Indeed, work on early modern England that has been influential in other fields in recent years has often paid little or no attention to the Revolution. Each of the leading revision-ists is in fact associated with arguments about long-term or comparative significance: Mark Kishlansky with the rise of partisan and majoritarian politics; John Morrill with the revolt of the provinces, Wars of Religion, and the British problem; Conrad Russell with the functional breakdown of the English state and the crisis of the multiple kingdoms.[3] But these have been much less influential than the analysis of the 'first modern society' had been.[4] Much of this has been implicitly accepted in the field and in particular the crit-ics of revisionism tended to concentrate their fire on revisionists' conclusions rather than on their methodological critique of progressive writing. Post-revisionists have certainly been critical of revisionism's methodological claims (sometimes sharply so), but it has not been in defence of the methods of progressive histories.[5]

Revisionism is now being historicized, however, and much of the heat has gone out of these debates. This volume takes the opportunity to reflect on some of the deeper issues at stake in these arguments, and in the interpretation of the Revolution—in particu-lar how its historians now see the relationship between structures and events, how they approach the rich intellectual and cultural products of the period, and how they address its comparative and long-term significance.

One key legacy of the close attention to the political dynamics of the crisis has been an acceptance that exclusive concentration on England is unsustainable.[6] As a result, the title of this book is more problematic than it would once have been. However, related terms such as the War(s) of the Three Kingdoms have little currency outside academic circles and in any case do not cover some of the most interesting aspects of the period for many readers: revolutionary radicalism in England for example, which is largely a post-war and more narrowly English phenomenon. This terminological confusion reflects a more fundamental fact: although the crisis was shared, and the fates of the Three Kingdoms were obviously and crucially intertwined, the experience and signifi-cance of that crisis were very different in each national context. The starting point for this book is, therefore, the most familiar perspective—that of the English Revolution—but the chapters here explore how those events grew out of, and resonated in, the politics of each of the Three Kingdoms, and in their interactions. To that extent it is as much an exercise in comparative history as an account of a shared history, and the treatment here often serves to sharpen our sense of the differing significance of events and outcomes in England, Scotland, and Ireland.

EVENTS

The recent attention to the dynamics of politics stands in marked contrast to older struc-tural accounts of the Revolution. Stone's classic work, for example, ended the analysis of the 'causes of the English Revolution' in 1642, but more recent work has emphasized how far there was to travel from the battle of Edgehill to the execution of the king.[7] As these chapters show, however, the return to narrative has not come entirely at the expense of attempts to understand structures and transformations in them, and does not imply that there is nothing to study beyond events and contingency.

Some of the most important work on the period before the civil war now empha-sizes the frameworks, intellectual and practical, in which events unfolded. Peter Lake's chapter discusses some of the key features of political culture and practice on which 'events' impacted. Since the 1530s, politicians in England had been tempted to take reli-gious and political issues outside the institutions of government in order to influence decisions within them. Political rumour, circulating manuscripts, and, increasingly, pamphlets, helped create, cumulatively, a public for national politics, but one that was not easily controlled: a post-Reformation public sphere. It resulted from practical deci-sions and tactical manoeuvres, but constituted an ongoing framework for future politi-cal action. Control was quickly lost in the multiple crises of the late 1630s and a chaotic public debate broke out. This was in itself a breach of accepted norms, making negotia-tion more difficult, and bringing an end to this public polemic became for some peo-ple a political end in itself.[8] Alan Cromartie has analysed the development of political thought between 1480 and 1642 in a similar way: not seeking origins for the party posi-tions in 1642 so much as reconstructing the frames of reference and traditions of inter-pretation on which events impacted.[9] These features of political life do not explain why war broke out, but we cannot understand the crisis without understanding them.

Julian Goodare's point of departure is the fluidity of politics in the Covenanting cri-sis: how did a series of events initially seen as a fairly limited problem of law and order become a revolution? His answer is partly to do with the capacity for self-organization in Scottish society, particularly in religious affairs. But there is also a significant role for contingency—the slow response of the Scottish privy council and its own divisions over the new Prayer Book, and the effects of the decisions Charles himself took, and failed to take. A more pragmatic man might have withdrawn the Book and disgraced a key adviser in order to buy off opposition, but Charles stuck to his guns. It was this inflexibil-ity which, in Goodare's view, prompted the creation of the National Covenant.

English government, in dealing with this crisis, depended on a high degree of volun-tary local participation which could not be taken for granted.[10] England in 1637 was at peace, although it was not free of political tensions. These tensions coalesced into pow-erful opposition, argues Richard Cust, as a result of contingent, external events—first in Scotland and then in Ireland. English military failure, and the political failure of the Short Parliament, allowed a 'junto' led by disaffected peers to mobilize support for a settlement very different from that intended by Charles, and this struggle was at the heart of English politics. In the aftermath of the Irish rising, Charles made a series of 'grotesque miscalculations' prompting a backlash that drove him from his capital. This made civil war likely, and was a devastating blow to his prospects in fighting it. How things turned out, then, was the product of chance and external events—the rising in Ireland, Charles's political judgements, and how his opponents chose to see them—but these events were framed by ideas, institutions, and practices whose distinctiveness we can trace back before the war.

The Irish rising now assumes a central importance in explaining the collapse of royal authority in England. Joseph Cope shows that how it was reported, and how Charles seemed to respond, confirmed fears about the political and religious future in Scotland and England. But the rising was also, in part, prompted by events in England and Scotland: Wentworth's enemies in Ireland were given an opportunity by attacks on him in England. The English reaction to the Irish rising—horrified, credulous, and hostile anti-popery—helped foster unity among Irish Catholics previously divided by other cultural distinctions. As in England and Scotland, the impact of events elsewhere was very significant, but so too was local chance—for example, the disastrous political consequences of forging a royal commission from Charles as a legitimation for the rising. And how events unfolded depended very much on immediate local conditions—reflecting histories of local grievance and neighbourly conflict.[11]

Under the pressure of events, actions were taken which gave rise to new arguments, practices, institutions, and relationships: actions taken for a particular purpose established practices and precepts which in turn shaped future action. For example, as Goodare shows, the Covenanting crisis led to the articulation of a remarkable national document, the focus for a 'constitutionalist, anti-absolutist movement'. Laura Stewart is equally alert to the rapidly shifting ground of politics but also emphasizes the lasting significance of the measures and arguments used to make sense of the crisis: for example, fiscal-military reform or the new force given to the idea of a covenanted society, which broadened the range of people managing Scotland's political fate. My own chapter explores how partisans in England mobilized men, resources, and political support, in a process of armed negotiation. As their political demands escalated, and as the scale and destructiveness of the war increased, differences emerged about war aims and what would constitute a just peace. Building and sustaining support in these conditions prompted new forms of political argument, new sources of disagreement, and new alliances. The interaction of military and political mobilization was therefore central to political innovation and to the development of the political debate. Exploring mobilization combines sensitivity to the fluidity of politics with exploration of the origins of political innovation.

In a similar way, Micheál Ó Siochrú shows how twelve years of war in Ireland, in which 25% of the population died in multi-faceted military conflicts of bewildering complexity, gave rise to a sustained exercise in Catholic self-government. As Ireland was torn asunder by internal conflicts and foreign intervention, the Confederacy sought out an inclusive and constructive definition of Irishness, on which to re-establish a stable social and political order. While it was undercut by political divisions which were exacerbated by reactions to a constantly and rapidly shifting political scene, this was an experiment of some durability and of much greater historical importance: a significant product of political calculations made in a messy, complex, and shifting crisis.

These essays also show that the conflict grew out of and ramified in the politics of each of the Three Kingdoms in distinctive ways. As a result, when Charles was defeated in England in 1646, the settlement reached with him there was not simply of local significance, but would fundamentally shape Irish and Scottish politics. As Philip Baker shows, political debate in England during the 1640s created the possibility of discussion of regicide, but there is very little evidence of a concerted attempt by a group of any substance to achieve that. He has reservations about the strongest statements that the regicide was largely contingent but he finds little evidence of a settled desire to bring about Charles's death. As a result of these hesitations, guesses about what foreign powers might intend became significant: for example that there might be an Irish invasion. For Baker the regicide manifested the failure of peace-making in all Three Kingdoms rather than a long-planned constitutional revolution or conscious act of state-building. For the latter we might look at developments taking place across the previous decade.[12]

Although the events of the 1640s had independent significance in each of the Three Kingdoms, they also tied their fates together. Charles I's son, the future Charles II, was proclaimed in Scotland not just as King of Scotland but also of Great Britain and Ireland, and as long as Ireland was under Catholic control it would remain a base for royalism. Whatever higher aspirations English parliamentary leaders may have had for Scotland and Ireland after the regicide, the pressing need for military security dominated their actions. The end result was conquest and subordination. Derek Hirst finds few positive achievements to commend in these English interventions, secondary as they always were to the imperative need to establish military control. Hopes for legal and social reform in Scotland were not realized and the authority of kirk and nobility was gradually reasserted, while in Ireland, despite the massive spoils available to the conquerors through confiscations, it was the pre-existing Protestant interest that won out.

Military imperatives also underlay fundamental tensions in England. As David Smith shows, the 1650s were punctuated by military interventions—in 1648/9 of course, but also in 1653, 1654, and in the period of direct military rule between 1655 and 1657. Oliver Cromwell was crucial to holding the regime together, as the events following his death seem to demonstrate. Army officers once more at odds with civilian politicians played a crucial role in the Restoration. That, as Tim Harris shows, was a Britannic event. The end of the Protectoral regime grew out of a military intervention coordinated in Ireland, Scotland, and England. It too was unpredictable, and it is not at all clear at what point the restoration of the monarchy became the clear purpose of Monck's intervention. Although it was widely welcomed, the Restoration was never universally popular and, just as importantly, it was embraced by different groups for different reasons. The settlements in each of the Three Kingdoms were unsatisfactory in different ways—the Restoration had not been born of consensus, and the settlement did not establish consensus. The complex interconnections of politics in the Three Kingdoms continued to drive political instability throughout the later seventeenth century.[13]

INSTITUTIONS AND ACTORS

The second part of the book explores more explicitly some of the structures of political life which shaped and were shaped by the crisis, as well as the interconnections between the Three Kingdoms and their comparative histories.

The fates of the Three Kingdoms were connected by the careers of Charles I and Oliver Cromwell. As we have seen, Charles I's political judgements and preferences, and even his personality, are identified by many historians as crucial to an understanding of how events played out. His handling of the Prayer Book rebellion in Scotland, or of his parliamentary critics in England in late 1641 and early 1642, his conduct of peace negotiations after 1646 or at his trial—these all seem to be crucial moments at which events might have taken a different course had Charles behaved differently. In fact Charles has often been blamed not just for the way events played out, but also for provoking conflict in the first place by refusing to let sleeping dogs lie, or by the stubborn pursuit of unrealizable or insensitive policies, often in a high-handed way. More recently, Kevin Sharpe and Mark Kishlansky have mounted vigorous defences of the coherence of Charles's views and of his political tactics, while pointing up the unreasonableness of his opponents. The debate continues,[14] but it is clear that exploring how Charles approached politics in each of his kingdoms is another way of understanding their connected but divergent experiences: to the Irish he was the best defence against the often hysterical anti-popery of the English parliament; in Scotland the best hope for the Presbyterian settlement; and in England the bulwark of the balanced constitution and episcopal authority. How he appeared to his supporters reveals the divergent issues that were at stake in each of his kingdoms, and the complexity of his task in trying to govern them as a single inheritance.

Cromwell's memory is perhaps more contested than that of any other British political figure—sometimes celebrated for his contribution to the rise of parliament and, later, democracy; decried by others for the suppression of more radical figures; and almost unanimously condemned for his conduct in Ireland. We know surprisingly little about him at crucial points in his life, and there are wide divergences of opinion as to how to interpret his apparent indecision at crisis points: was he a calculating hypocrite who said what needed to be said in order to achieve power, or a religious bigot whose mask regularly slipped?[15] Colin Davis suggests we see him instead as engaged in perpetual negotiation, seeking continually to build alliances and coalitions. That was made more difficult by the complex interactions between events and opinions in England, Scotland, and Ireland. Davis offers a view of a man with core principles—'red lines' which could not be crossed—but whose normal mode was a kind of patient coalition-building suited to the political culture of early modern English government.[16] He had fewer potential allies in Scotland and virtually none in Ireland, with the result that negotiation yielded far less.

David Smith reveals connections between the development of representative institutions in the Three Kingdoms, but also points up their differing trajectories. They took on more routine responsibility everywhere, achieving in the process greater independence from royal command as well as creating more elaborate committee structures. There was borrowing in both areas—the Long Parliament's Triennial Act and committee structures, for example, owed something to Covenanting practice. The Confederate's General Assembly was a much more novel experiment—it was necessarily a far more powerful organ of government than the Irish parliament had been, despite its continued loyalty to the crown. These developments were the fruits of the 1640s however, and mostly fell victim to the military needs of the republican regime in England, eventually being replaced by institutions representing Britain as a whole. With the Restoration came a return of an English parliament with the clock set back to 1641 and a Scottish parliament set at 1633. In Ireland the restored parliament was an instrument of the broader settlement, securing the Protestant interest and English authority. The development of these institutions reveals a shared experience, and indeed a connected history, but also a comparative history. Andrew Hopper offers a similar analysis of the armies. Within a shared crisis they acted differently as vehicles of political education and engagement, prompting different forms of institutional innovation (state formation) and playing different political roles.

Aristocratic networks—'knots' of aristocrats, as John Morrill terms them—also connected events in the Three Kingdoms.[17] The history of the English crisis was for a time written with the nobility largely left out, and even as a manifestation of a crisis in their authority.[18] This no longer seems to bear scrutiny. John Adamson has argued that leading aristocrats made much of the political running, even (contrary to common expectation) on the parliamentary side. While there has been criticism of how far he has pushed the argument, it is clear that the English aristocracy were crucial players in the crisis.[19] And as John Miller makes clear, noble power remained an important feature of English political life after the Restoration.[20] Recent work has demonstrated how the nobilities of Scotland and Ireland also adjusted to, and weathered, political change, and in those Kingdoms too, the aristocracy were crucial in shaping how the crises unfolded.[21]

The persistence of noble power has been emphasized as part of a broader critique of attempts to link political conflict directly to the effects of changes in social structure. A sophisticated debate about popular political allegiance has built on the tradition of making the connection in this way, but even in a much-refined form it remains very controversial.[22] The social history of politics has more recently been written around the history of political communication, and forms of communal and popular politics. In these areas many historians now see evidence in England of broader and more intensive political engagement in and as a consequence of the Revolution. Jason Peacey explores the role of print in that context. The collapse of pre-publication licensing was associated with a massive qualitative change in what was printed in England—new kinds of authors, often producing cheap titles reporting and commenting on the news. This intensified public debate and encouraged active, regular, and detailed participation among a reading public. It increased the transparency of politics, and encouraged comment on particular individuals, rather than more general processes or issues, in languages that could be appropriated. It proved a mixed blessing for governments, and its importance is reflected in the attempts of successive regimes to re-establish control. Peacey is tempted to refer to this as a public sphere.[23]

We cannot tell very accurately who was able to enter this new realm, or on what terms. There is general evidence about price, distribution, and the size of print runs, but it is very difficult to know how widely and where any particular publication circulated. But print is not the only evidence we have of deepening political engagement in the English crisis. Stephen Roberts argues that the greatly increased burden of the state—particularly the financial burden—was associated with a regularization of local government. There is no scholarly consensus about whether participation in local government was more broadened socially than narrowed politically in these years. There is evidence that the net was cast wide for committee membership, but also that active membership was a rather different thing, and that it was inflected by a partisan insistence on 'honesty'. This in itself, of course, reflects the deeper penetration of national politics into local life. Attempts to make these committees accountable and the use of juries helped establish a representative element in local government. Despite examples of breaches of due process and the use of martial law, we can discern a general process of greater integration of institutions, and political languages, between national politics and local life.

The growth of partisan political communication and accelerating political engagement are also important themes of recent work. Crucial in that sense were England's urban citizens. Phil Withington shows how, over the previous three generations, the 'urban system' developed considerably: a much larger number of corporations, integrated more closely into national life by a quickening commercial economy, active in Reformation politics and self-activating in local government informed by ideals of Renaissance humanism. Urban citizens elected the majority of MPs (who were of course at the heart of the crisis) and often played a crucial role in the outbreak of the war—mobilizing partisan support, and delivering control of key strong points or military stores. The institutions and values of the urban citizenry created a 'field of conflict' in which political differences were fought out, and an arena in which decisive actions could be taken. The urban system was crucial in framing the crisis, and its citizens were often key actors in the unfolding drama, while the language of citizenship was also important in framing political argument. Attempts after the Restoration to control corporations reflect the significance attached to them by seventeenth-century governments.[24]

The crisis in England impinged on a society in which groups below the gentry were active in the routines of government, and in which there was considerable shared ground between the political languages of elite and commoner. John Walter shows how crowd actions might jog or influence authorities, while sixteenth-century rebellions demonstrated a considerable capacity for active engagement in politics. More routinely, libels and gossip were potentially powerful ways of embarrassing and restraining governors. In the early 1640s crowds pursued agrarian grievances, and continued to do so, but as the crisis unfolded other kinds of partisan politics emerged—the use of committees against social superiors on political grounds, or direct actions intended to foster religious reformation and street politics, particularly in London. Petitioning and national oath-taking engaged large constituencies with the detail of national politics. Taken together, the Revolution created a new space for popular politics, which became more divided and partisan, and this was to persist.[25]

Ann Hughes shows how gendered conceptions of social order shaped perceptions of the crisis, but also how they were challenged by it. Disorder was diagnosed and decried in gendered terms, and the languages of insult and threat were profoundly shaped by such fundamental assumptions about how the world ought to work. At the same time, women had new opportunities to act in military and political roles, albeit justified in relation to their conventional household roles and responsibilities. As Levellers or as prophets, for example, women made directly ideological claims. It is also clear that much polemic, self-presentation, and critique centred on notions of manhood. This was not a revolution in gender roles—no one argued for formal political rights for women and it is difficult to point to long-term changes in such a complex set of relationships—but this approach demonstrates how allegiance was profoundly influenced by 'matters of interest, imagination, and emotion'.[26] Equipped with a sensitivity to how the experience was shaped and mediated by social structures, beliefs, and practices, we understand the crisis better; but we can also see early modern English society through its revolution.

It is difficult to reproduce this kind of thematic analysis for Ireland and Scotland, partly for archival reasons but mainly because the secondary literature is simply not as abundant. But Scott Spurlock shows how the Covenanting revolution deepened the engagement of a broad public with national politics, in ways that persisted after the Restoration. The experience of the Covenant may also have been important for the consciousness of individual Scots, encouraging them to be more active, but also more self-critical, political subjects. The proliferation of committees transformed local government, and during the 1650s more regular local courts led to a fuller engagement with the institutions of government. As Smith also notes, there was a significant legacy in greater parliamentary independence, something like a legislative revolution.[27] Scottish politics were becoming more institutionalized through the national government—manifest in the further decline of the feud, for example. While the Covenanters were defeated, and there was no permanent change in the composition of the Scottish elite, therefore, this period did mark a break in Scottish history. And of course, the defeat of the Covenanting movement had profound importance for Scottish religious life.

The Confederates in Ireland suffered a catastrophic military defeat that was also a total defeat for their religious and political ideals. As a consequence, this period has often been treated as decisive for Ireland's future, with Cromwell as its architect: the contrast with English perceptions of Cromwell has often been very sharp. As Cope shows, the memory of this period in Ireland was dominated by an arc of Protestant celebration, with no very powerful counter-narrative, and Ó Siochrú's work has in one sense sought to remedy the defect by emphasizing the significance of this experiment in Catholic self-government.[28] Toby Barnard takes a more moderate view of Cromwell, both as a military commander and as a driving force behind the settlement. In the latter context, in fact, Cromwell followed rather than led an established English view of Ireland. In other ways too, the measures of the 1640s and 1650s accelerated developments that were longer in the making, and took longer to complete, than a concentration on the formal measures taken would suggest, but the positive achievements were few. It was a 'formative decade. . . . What was guaranteed by the grim events of 1649–53 was that Ireland did not break free of English control, at least not for more than two centuries.'[29] It was formative for what it ruled out, rather than for what it created.

PARTIES, IDEAS, AND PEOPLE

Dynamic politics also gave rise to remarkable intellectual and artistic creativity. One of the key claims of revisionism was that progressive histories distorted or ignored the views of the majority of people—royalists, neutrals, and conservatives were given far less attention than 'radicals', a category that was in itself highly anachronistic, while the conflation of 'radical' and 'popular' distorted the aspirations and experience of the broader population. More recent work has taken a much broader view of the creativity of revolutionary thinking, and has tended to see it as emerging in dialogue with events, rather than narrating the course of events as a battle between radicals and their opponents.

For Alan Cromartie royalism was a product of the crisis not one of its causes, taking shape in defence of threatened institutions and values, and then persisting. It was not a coherent position or programme before the war—in fact it centred on the political settlement reached in 1641, which Charles I himself found fairly repugnant. As it took shape, though, it laid claim to terms that secured its longevity—honour, civility, learning, and, in some eyes, liberty. Royalists did not defend Charles I so much as the constitutional role of the monarch, and in so doing exposed tensions in an opposition view that was also essentially monarchist. Royalists also defended religious order and decency, drawing on stereotypes of puritanism of very long standing, and so managed to present their aggressive episcopalianism as a moderate alternative. The cultural representation of royalism embodied defence of conventional values of all kinds, and in the absence of a social revolution the hold of these values among elite groups allowed this emergent royalism to weather the upheavals. It had crystallized out of the fluid politics of the period, though, and became something of an embarrassment to the restored monarch, who like his father would have liked to have stood for other things.

Rachel Foxley shows that parliamentarianism was also an evolving commitment, as people arrived at support for parliament by a variety of routes and at different times. Motivated by differing religious, political, or more immediate concerns, they were united in an immediate aim and at a particular point, rather than by an ideological platform, like the Scottish National Covenant. Their cause rested on a retrospective account of the failings of Charles I's government rather than a unified view of what the future should hold, and because their retrospective accounts differed, so too did their suggested remedies. There was further fragmentation as the crisis unfolded, giving rise to fluid alliances and conditional individual loyalties. One consequence of this fluidity and lack of clarity was radicalization, although we need to recognize that people were pushed in new directions by different forces and for different reasons, so that there was no unitary radicalism either. From all this emerged some distinctive new positions, however—notably a parliamentary absolutism regarded with some hostility by a more popular radicalism.

This was also a crucial period in the development of formally articulated political theory: indeed to J. G. A. Pocock these were the 'epic years' in the history of English political thought[30] and behind the pressure of immediate choices and the rough and tumble of partisan politics lay more profound debates. For Ted Vallance much of this can be read as an argument about how to secure liberty. He shows how differing conceptions of liberty lay behind the radically different responses to the policies of Charles I's personal rule, between for example Hobbes and Filmer on one hand, and Scott and Parker on the other. The same issue later informed the position of radical critics of the parliamentary position too, notably the Levellers, and framed the way the hopes (and failings) of successive regimes were discussed during the 1650s. It was these issues, rather than more strictly constitutional questions, which underlay the deepest divisions. In a similar way, John Coffey detects a series of conceptual developments of great significance for the future of Protestantism. The reaction against Laudianism fostered an attempt to define Calvinist orthodoxy in the Westminster Assembly. This attempt failed, and in fact helped to unleash a chaotic religious debate in which, for example, aspects of Laudianism were assimilated to radical critiques of Calvinism. The legacy was more positive than the 'failure' of Calvinist orthodoxy, however. These debates were crucial for the future of Protestantism and the Westminster Confession, for example, is an 'official statement of faith' for millions of Presbyterians. Similarly, the impulse to explore the natural world, the better to understand creation, gave rise to insights of lasting significance.

The appeal to broader publics was an essential feature of politics; it was done in overlapping and contested terms, for quite different purposes; and that prompted innovative forms of political argument, and new ways of understanding. Laid bare by the crisis, views on some fundamental issues were articulated with great clarity and originality. The resultant creativity produced not just radicalism as conventionally defined but innovative royalism, as well as the remarkable but alien millenarianism of the Hartlib circle, or the enterprising use of astrology.[31]

Creativity in that sense has also been an important theme of recent scholarship on literature and the arts. Steven Zwicker evokes the creative profusion of the literary production of these decades—of authors and genres, and experiment—and shows how individuals moved across this terrain in unpredictable ways. Literary work was deeply marked by the polemical environment: a lush and fertile world in which many writers moved with great freedom, and out of it came some masterpieces. For Zwicker the genius of this work, epitomized in some ways by Marvell's 'Upon Appleton House', lies in its handling of ambivalence, ambiguity, and uncertainty. The fluidity and dynamism emphasized in recent historical treatments of political life helps to contextualize some of the period's most enduring literary works and to impose taxonomies or to categorize too closely is to distort this rich literary field.

There were creative developments in the visual arts and architecture too. Timothy Wilks shows that a once-conventional emphasis on puritan iconophobia is inadequate. Some of the parliamentary aristocrats were serious patrons—Essex, Warwick, Northumberland, and Pembroke—and even in wartime Oxford some promising artists such as Dobson could make their way for a while with royalist patronage. Much devotional art was destroyed, of course, and there was an exodus of talented artists, but there was also movement in the other direction—notably of Peter Lely and Wenceslas Hollar—and the regimes of the 1650s were serious about the projection of a public image. Similar arguments hold for architecture. The war brought an end to the building boom of the 1630s but building resumed after 1646. Town rebuilding along planned lines and a less ornamented classicism were features of the period that (to a contested extent), were consistent with the longer-term development of seventeenth-century architectural taste. A key feature of artistic patronage in this period, however, was how surprising were the aesthetic tastes of some prominent politicians—Lambert, for example. There was sectarian hostility to the image, and to ostentation more generally perhaps, but it is difficult to read off aesthetic tastes from political positions, and certainly mistaken to assume that artistic creativity was crushed by militant parliamentarianism.

WIDER PERSPECTIVES

The crisis gave rise to changed patterns of political engagement, state formation, and religious and political thought, transformations that were prompted in differing ways and with different consequences in each of the Three Kingdoms. Clearly, emphasis on the dynamism of politics does not rule out attention to long-term changes in the institutional and intellectual frameworks through which political life was articulated.

Progressive histories had presented the Revolution as a key moment in the resolution of structural social tensions arising from fundamental economic change, and crucial to England's path to modernity. That connection has been a casualty of revisionism, and perhaps also of the separate path taken by economic and social history since the 1970s: social structural and economic change is now generally accepted to have moved to a separate rhythm. The effects of war and military mobilization, rather than the aspirations of the Revolution, now carry more weight in explaining the course of social and economic change. Following this trend, John Miller downplays the effects on the relative power of different social groups in England and although there were economic changes in this period that were of long-term, and indeed global, significance, their relationship to the political crisis is unclear. English naval growth and the navigation system, which bound an increasingly large part of the global trade into an English network, had clear political origins, and there was a rapid growth in the financial sector too, which clearly intertwined with institutional changes arising from the crisis. The underlying demographic trends shifted too—population growth levelled off, and rising middle incomes supported a consumer boom. Although the threat of famine receded, poverty persisted, stimulating the institutionalization of the Poor Law, which was to persist into the nineteenth century and represented a significant regularization of local government activity. But these changes are not easy to relate to the mid-century crisis and it is clear that many of them worked out independently of the political crisis. There was, though, a marked growth of religious diversity and political partisanship, institutionalized in cities and towns, and dividing the ruling elite: here the Revolution crisis had enduring effects on social relations.[32]

There was a literary and artistic legacy[33] but Laura Knoppers's subject is the legacy of these events as a *subject* of literary and artistic work, focusing on the nineteenth century, when debate about the legacy of the seventeenth-century revolutions was prominent, and affected by the long shadow of the French Revolution. She shows how Delaroche's famous painting of *Cromwell and Charles I* (1831) and Victor Hugo's play *Cromwell* (1827) offered an 'open-ended representation that calls for an active reader'. Walter Scott's earlier novel, *Woodstock* (1824), had also invited such an engagement with the issues, in a way that echoes in some ways Zwicker's view of literary and artistic responses at the time of the crisis. These works manifest a more general legacy in our cultural life: the representation not 'of any particular political message, but almost the opposite: a kind of open-endedness and need for interpretation'.[34]

Developments in this period retain their place in accounts of state formation. The British state that emerged over the following 80 years was, Mark Knights argues, deeply marked by a revolutionary process that extended well into the eighteenth century. Changes in political practices and institutions, and in ways of thinking about these things, transformed the state, political culture, and political discourse. A state emerged with radically transformed fiscal-military capacity, a plural religious culture, and a steadily expanding territorial reach; but there was also a counter-pressure from a country Whig position committed to resistance to executive tyranny and court corruption. Partisanship was institutionalized in frequent elections, an increasingly vibrant public sphere, and transformed practices of petitioning. We can also identify a distinctively post-civil war discourse—a revolutionary emphasis on popular sovereignty and the right to resist tyrants and religious toleration was opposed by a counter-discourse dedicated to the defence of the monarchy and the church. The memory of the civil war remained important in animating these debates long after 1660.

The emergent British state was also deeply marked by the patterns of interaction between the Three Kingdoms consolidated during the crisis. In John Morrill's analysis the English parliament did not look beyond England, even when executing Charles I, whereas the Scots were acutely aware that the best hope of securing their aims was in concert with an English settlement. Irish aspirations to establish Catholicism ran directly counter to a settled English view that popery must be extirpated not just in England but also in Ireland. This cemented the political subordination of the Irish kingdom. How particular English localities experienced the war was clearly inflected by their proximity to the other kingdoms but English perceptions of the war were narrower than in Scotland and Ireland. These asymmetries were also manifest in patterns of marriage and landholding among the interconnected aristocracies of the Three Kingdoms. Each of the Three Kingdoms had a civil war, but there were also wars between them. After 1649 even the English parliamentary leaders saw that, but incorporation had failed and the search would continue 'for a stable state system that would never be fully a British state, with one law, one church, and one sense of nationhood'.[35]

This was a crucial period too, as Knights and others note, for the development of the British empire and for the Atlantic world. The Revolution was closely associated with the increasing fiscal and military power of the English state, the quickening of overseas trade and the increasing will and capacity to regulate it through the navigation system.[36] Colonies of overseas settlement took root at an accelerating rate after mid-century, and from the 1660s English merchants could handle and protect a slave trade that was of fundamental importance for the future of the Atlantic. Links around the Atlantic were also forged, and colonies and merchants came to a new understanding of their relationship with the crown. While there is no doubt that the Revolution was important for the future of the Atlantic,[37] it is less clear that the developing Atlantic world was important to the origins or course of the Revolution. Robert Brenner has traced the relationship between particular merchant interests and particular political programmes and others have shown links between opponents of Charles I and Atlantic ventures, without in the latter case suggesting that it is their Atlantic interests which determined their political views.[38] New England polemicists such as Roger Williams and returning exiles such as Hugh Peter played an important role in the radicalization of English politics, but it seems easier to say that their radicalism had led to their exile rather than that the very nascent Atlantic world was exerting a significant pull on English politics. This was to change rapidly after 1650, however, and by the 1690s it is clear that Atlantic and Imperial interests had developed a fundamental importance for English politics (and for the relationships between the Three Kingdoms).[39]

The connection with wider European politics by contrast has been a very neglected theme in recent writing, although there are clear connections between the course of events in England and, for example, in Germany.[40] The Solemn League and Covenant envisaged the possibility that other Protestant powers might join and as Hirst points out, the English republic had military concerns that were European-wide—it was the hostility of the French, Spanish, and Dutch as much as of the Scottish and Irish that fed them. Peter Wilson does not seek to offer a general, comparative, explanation for conflict in this period, nor a consideration of the interconnectedness of the British and Imperial conflicts. Instead he outlines key interpretative issues in the Imperial context that might inform thinking about other European conflicts. The empire had a civil war, in which foreign powers intervened for discrete purposes, with defined interests, separated from their other conflicts, and directed at securing the Imperial settlement most helpful to their own interests. For Wilson the German crisis was one of a number of regional conflicts rather than part of a general European crisis, but this does not rule out the possibility of fruitful comparison and contrast. This return to a broader canvas, and the significance of these events in a comparative and more transhistorical context, is re-emerging as an historiographical possibility.[41]

Conclusions

No single significance can be attributed to these events on the basis of this rich and diverse historical literature: instead, like Delaroche, it invites an active reader to make up their own mind, and to explore in it the issues that concern them. This does not imply a refusal to draw any meaning from these events but rather a refusal to impose a single cause or meaning on complex and diverse experiences. This historiography provides the material and opportunity to reflect on many issues of political salience—for example, the importance of gender for understanding politics, the relationship between religious toleration and social order, the relationship between political instability and intellectual creativity, the emergence of the institutions of the British state and its empire, and many others. The field has not abandoned the attempt to find meaning in these events but has opened up to a more diverse range of questions.

It is also clear that an emphasis on fluidity and dynamism has not ruled out attention to what shaped and framed the crisis, and how the crisis transformed political and social life in the longer term. The actions of individuals or groups reproduce the structures and practices of political life, but also create and shape them for the future. Ideas have recently been given more prominence than material interests in explaining the course of events, but they are seen as developing in dialogue with events, not simply driving them: there is no simple retreat from materialism to idealism. There is a developing connection with a broader social history around the history of political communication and engagement, and the cultural history of *mentalités*, rather than of social structural change and economic transformation. These events have significance in understanding political development in each of the Three Kingdoms, and their relationships with one another, as well as of their religious, intellectual, literary, and artistic lives, and this comparative history is increasingly open to wider comparison too. Rather than a lurch from one pole to another—from interests to ideas or from structures to contingency—the centre of gravity now seems to reside in the relationships between these things. There is much more to be done, of course, and in particular the potential of the Revolution to illuminate the social and cultural life of early modern society has barely been tapped. But with the heated debate prompted by revisionism now largely burned out, the time is ripe for a more concerted discussion of these core issues.

Notes

1. Glenn Burgess, 'On Revisionism: An Analysis of Early Stuart Historiography in the 1970s and 1980s', *Historical Journal*, 33.3 (1990): 609–27.
2. See, for example, the foundational texts by Peter Laslett, *The World We Have Lost—Further Explored*, 3rd edition (London, 1983), esp. chap. 8; and Keith Wrightson, *English Society, 1580–1680* (London, 1982).
3. Mark Kishlansky, *Parliamentary Selection: Social and Political Choice in Early Modern England* (Cambridge, 1986); John Morrill, *The Nature of the English Revolution: Essays by John Morrill* (London, 1993), Morrill, 'The British Problem, c.1534–1707', in Brendan Bradshaw and John Morrill (eds.), *The British Problem c.1534–1707: State Formation in the Atlantic Archipelago* (Basingstoke, 1996), 1–38; Conrad Russell, *The Causes of the English Civil War* (Oxford, 1990).
4. A. L. Beier, David Cannadine, and James A. Rosenheim (eds.), *The First Modern Society: Essays in English History in Honour of Lawrence Stone* (Cambridge, 1989). These essays, of course, deal with much more than the English Revolution.

5. For more on revisionism and its critics see the further reading at the end of this chapter.

6. Russell, *Causes*; Morrill, 'British Problem'.

7. Lawrence Stone, *The Causes of the English Revolution, 1529-1642* (London, 1972).

8. The 'explosion of print' in the early 1640s was not an insular English phenomenon. It had Scottish origins and grew out of European connections: Joad Raymond, *Pamphlets and Pamphleteering in Early Modern Britain* (Cambridge, 2003), chap. 5.

9. Alan Cromartie, *The Constitutionalist Revolution: An Essay on the History of England, 1450-1642* (Cambridge, 2006).

10. See also Michael Braddick, *God's Fury, England's Fire: A New History of the English Civil Wars* (London, 2008), chap. 2.

11. See, for comparison, John Walter, *Understanding Popular Violence in the English Revolution: The Colchester Plunderers* (Cambridge, 1999).

12. See chapters by Smith and Roberts.

13. See Tim Harris, *Restoration: Charles II and His Kingdoms, 1660-1685* (London, 2006); and Harris, *Revolution: The Great Crisis of the British Monarchy, 1685-1720* (London, 2007).

14. Kevin Sharpe, *The Personal Rule of Charles I* (London, 1992); Mark Kishlansky, 'Charles I: A Case of Mistaken Identity', *P&P*, 189 (2005): 41-80, and the ensuing debate with Clive Holmes, Julian Goodare, and Richard Cust, *P&P*, 205 (2009): 175-237. See also Mark Kishlansky, *Charles I: An Abbreviated Life* (London, 2014).

15. Hirst also notes his strategic indecision as a military commander, p. 181.

16. For a similar view of Charles I see Richard Cust, *Charles I: A Political Life* (Harlow, 2005).

17. p. 565.

18. Stone, *Causes*, 72-6.

19. John Adamson, *The Noble Revolt: The Overthrow of Charles I* (London, 2007); Richard Cust, *Charles I and the Aristocracy, 1625-1641* (Cambridge, 2013).

20. Miller; for the revisionist implications of the persistence of the Old Regime see Jonathan Clark, *English Society, 1660-1832*, 2nd edition (Cambridge, 2000).

21. Adamson, *Noble Revolt*; Cust, *Charles I and the Aristocracy*; Keith Brown, *Noble Power in Scotland from the Reformation to the Revolution* (Edinburgh, 2013); Jane Ohlmeyer, *Making Ireland English: The Irish Aristocracy in the Seventeenth Century* (London, 2012).

22. David Underdown, *Revel, Riot and Rebellion: Popular Politics and Culture in England, 1603-1660* (Oxford, 1985); Mark Stoyle, *Loyalty and Locality: Popular Allegiance in Devon During the English Civil War* (Exeter, 1994). See the debate between Underdown and Morrill in *Journal of British Studies*, 26 (1987): 451-79.

23. For the influence of Habermas see Peter Lake and Steven C. A. Pincus (eds.), *The Politics of the Public Sphere in Early Modern England* (Manchester, 2007).

24. Paul D. Halliday, *Dismembering the Body Politic: Partisan Politics in England's Towns, 1650-1730* (Cambridge, 1998); John Miller, *Cities Divided: Politics and Religion in English Provincial Towns, 1660-1722* (Oxford, 2007).

25. On this theme see also Tom Leng, ' "Citizens at the door": Mobilising against the Enemy in Civil War London', *Journal of Historical Sociology* (forthcoming 2015). For examples of partisan engagement see David Cressy, *Dangerous Talk: Scandalous, Seditious and Treasonable Speech in Pre-Modern England* (Oxford, 2010).

26. p. 360.

27. p. 248-9.

28. See the chapters in this volume by Cope and Ó Siochrú.

29. p. 390.

30. J. C. Davis, '"Epic Years": The English Revolution and J. G. A. Pocock's Approach to the History of Political Thought', *History of Political Thought*, 29.3 (2008): 519–42.

31. For the term creativity as preferable to radicalism see Mike Braddick, 'Mobilisation, Anxiety and Creativity in England During the 1640s', in John Morrow and Jonathan Scott (eds.), *Liberty, Authority, Formality: Political Ideas and Culture, 1600–1900* (Exeter, 2008), 175–94.

32. For further thoughts on this theme see Michael J. Braddick, 'Loyauté Partisane Durant la Guerre Civile et Histoire des Relations Sociales en Angleterre', in Laurent Bourquin, Philippe Hamon, Pierre Karila-Cohen, and Cédric Michon (eds.), *Conflits, Opinion(s) et Politicization de la Fin du Moyen Âge au Début du xxe Siècle* (Rennes, 2011), 95–114.

33. Explored in detail in Laura Lunger Knoppers (ed.), *The Oxford Handbook of Literature and the English Revolution* (Oxford, 2012).

34. Quotations at pp. 543, 550.

35. p. 573.

36. Michael J. Braddick, *State Formation in Early Modern England, 1550–1700* (Cambridge, 2000), chaps. 5, 6, 8, and 9; James Scott Wheeler, *The Making of a World Power* (Stroud, 1999).

37. Carla Gardina Pestana, *The English Atlantic in an Age of Revolution, 1640–1661* (Cambridge, MA, 2007).

38. Robert Brenner, *Merchants and Revolution: Commercial Change, Political Conflict and London's Overseas Traders, 1550–1653* (Cambridge, 1993); Karen O. Kupperman, *Providence Island, 1630–1641: The Other Puritan Colony* (Cambridge, 1995). Brenner has been sharply criticized. See, for example, John Morrill, 'Conflict Probable or Inevitable', *New Left Review*, 1.207 (1994): 113–23; and Richard Grassby's review in the *William and Mary Quarterly*, 50.4 (1993): 808–12.

39. Steve Pincus, *1688: The First Modern Revolution* (London, 2009).

40. This was once an important theme in the literature, now revived on a bolder scale by Geoffrey Parker, *Global Crisis: War, Climate Change and Catastrophe in the Seventeenth Century* (New Haven, 2013).

41. See, for example, Jonathan Scott, *England's Troubles: Seventeenth-Century English Political Instability in European Context* (Cambridge, 2000); Diarmaid MacCulloch, *Reformation: Europe's House Divided, 1490–1700* (London, 2004).

Further Reading

Adamson, John, 'Introduction: High Roads and Blind Alleys: The English Civil War and its Historiography', in John Adamson (ed.), *The English Civil War: Conflict and Contexts, 1640–49* (Basingstoke, 2009), 1–35.

Burgess, Glenn, 'On Revisionism: An Analysis of Early Stuart Historiography in the 1970s and 1980s', *Historical Journal*, 33.3 (1990): 609–627.

Cogswell, Thomas, Richard Cust, and Peter Lake, 'Revisionism and its Legacies: The Work of Conrad Russell', in Thomas Cogswell, Richard Cust, and Peter Lake (eds.), *Politics, Religion and Popularity in Early Stuart Britain: Essays in Honour of Conrad Russell* (Cambridge, 2002), 1–17.

Hughes, Ann, *The Causes of the English Civil War*, 2nd edition (Basingstoke, 1998).

MacLachlan, Alastair, *The Rise and Fall of Revolutionary England: An Essay on the Fabrication of Seventeenth-Century History* (Basingstoke, 1996).

Morrill, John, *The Nature of the English Revolution: Essays by John Morrill* (London, 1993).

Russell, Conrad, *The Causes of the English Civil War* (Oxford, 1990).

Stone, Lawrence, *The Causes of the English Revolution, 1529–1642* (London, 1972).

Worden, Blair, *Roundhead Reputations: The English Civil Wars and the Passions of Posterity* (London, 2001).

CHAPTER 2

POST-REFORMATION POLITICS, OR ON NOT LOOKING FOR THE LONG-TERM CAUSES OF THE ENGLISH CIVIL WAR

PETER LAKE

THIS chapter describes certain changes in what we might term the political culture, in the ways in which 'politics' were conceived and conducted, in the post-Reformation period. The claim being made here is not that these changes caused the civil war, but rather that they ensured that when a series of linked political crises in three kingdoms came together to produce the events formerly known as the English revolution, the resulting crisis took on forms very different from anything that had come before and they did so because of a distinctively post-Reformation political world.

POST-REFORMATION POLITICS

The advent of heretical ideas (subsequently known as 'protestant') in the 1520s and 1530s, and the subsequent course of the English Reformation/s, put disputes about the nature of true religion and the locus of spiritual and ecclesiastical authority at the centre of events. A number of different groups thereby acquired an interest in using a variety of media to spread their view of the situation to a variety of publics, while denouncing their opponents of the moment as some sort of subversive/heretical or deviant threat to 'order'. Initially these contests took the fairly straightforward form of show-down between an orthodox ('Catholic') establishment and some sort of hereti-cal, 'Lutheran' or later 'sacramentarian' opposition. But very rapidly the course of the king's divorce and the breach with Rome meant that what was involved was a series of conflicts between different elements within or around the regime. John Fisher may have started off orchestrating, on behalf of an ultra orthodox king, an official defence of 'orthodoxy' against the heresies of Luther, but he rapidly became a rabid opponent of, and author of a variety of manuscript tracts against, the king's divorce and ended up as a martyr for the papal primacy.[1] Thomas More underwent a similar pilgrimage from defender of the establishment against heresy to opponent of royal policy, aider and abetter of the nun of Kent, and a form of (deeply ambivalent) 'Catholic' martyrdom.

From the outset recourse to a range of public media, to print, the pulpit, various sorts of show trial and performance was as much a tactic of members of the establishment, as it was of an insurgent 'reforming opposition'. Throughout the 1530s recourse to that full range of public media, up to and including the popular stage, was to remain a central feature of the Henrician regime as it was forged and run by Thomas Cromwell. Indeed, from the very outset, it would not be going too far to locate the origins of 'the post-Reformation public sphere' rather more in the activities of central members of the establishment than their various opponents.[2] Of course, both reformers located well outside the mainstream and outright opponents of the Henrician Reformation attempted, in a variety of ways, to go public; using rumour, circulating manuscript and the pulpit, as well of course, as print, to make their case before a variety of audiences and/or readerships. But, throughout, the innovatory and contested nature of Henrician reform ensured that it was elements within the regime who often made the running; justifying (often rather radical) change, attempting to gloss events and official policies in their own sense and interest, while responding to, and indeed exploiting for their own reformist purposes, outbreaks of resistance and dissent.

We might think that the resulting public sphere would therefore be centrally concerned with 'religion', that is to say, structured around an emergently confessional opposition between the 'gospel' and its popish enemies, or viewed from the other side, between various ('Catholic') versions of 'orthodoxy' and their heretical others. And so, to a certain extent, it was. But because of the form that the Henrician Reformation took, because at its core, or at least in its origins, it was a struggle for jurisdiction and power between crown and papacy, religious questions of idolatry and right worship, of superstition and true belief, became inextricably bound up with (quintessentially political) questions of allegiance and treason. The ideological hybridity of the master category—popery—through which the resulting divisions and tensions were mediated showed this only too well. For as the word itself implies, as well as being a nexus of religious error and superstitious trumpery, at bottom, popery was all about loyalty to the pope, its adherents characterized by a residual hankering after the papal primacy.

As a result, at certain crucial moments, the proponents of what we might see as rather radical religious change were able to cast themselves as the defenders of order and royal authority, while outing their rivals and opponents, the defenders of traditional religion, as subversives, bent, not on defending central features of the religious status quo, but rather on disobeying their prince and undoing the Royal Supremacy. For their part, the opponents of further religious change had recourse to the language of evil counsel, picturing a king misled by low-born and heretical evil counsellors into disastrous policies from which he needed to be recalled, either by the plaints and petitions of his subjects (the Pilgrims of Grace) or by the sharply worded admonitions of his ex-clients and favourites (Reginald Pole).[3]

By the late 1530s and 1540s, the result was a struggle for power under, and influence over, the crown, conducted in terms of two opposed rhetorics: one centred on the threat of popery, conceived as a question of political loyalty and obedience, but with obvious (but also intensely contested) religious connotations; the second on the threat of heresy, and of sacramentarianism, in particular, a religious phenomenon which—because of the king's personal insistence on the doctrine of transubstantiation as a sine qua non of orthodoxy—brought with it connotations of disobedience and sedition. The fall of Cromwell might well be seen as the triumph of the latter over the former, but that triumph was anything but complete and the two discursive positions, and the groups and individuals who deployed them, continued to jockey for position throughout the 1540s.[4]

Henry VIII self-consciously exploited a rhetoric of moderation and the mean in order to maintain, indeed to maximize, his position as the ultimate arbiter of the nature of order and of orthodoxy and of the relative seriousness of the threats with which his rule was confronted. But this placed the royal person and the workings of the royal will and conscience at the eye of the ideological storm, since, in a period characterized by various sorts of religious division, attempts to display and vindicate the royal conscience, even of the most intentionally univocal, non-dialogic sort, tended to become, if not an invitation, then certainly, a provocation to debate.[5]

The official ideology of the Edwardian regimes and Reformation was framed in precisely the same terms. Popery retained its political elements, of course, but its role as a nexus of religious error, of superstition and idolatry, of trickery and trumpery, as indeed the mystery of iniquity, the religion of Antichrist, and thus as a world historical force with a major role to play in God's providential plan for the triumph of his true church, now came to the fore.[6] As Henrician texts like Bales's play *King Johan* show,[7] this was not a novel view of popery but it was now placed front and centre in the public discourse of the national church, a church whose claims to orthodoxy were now vindicated by solidarity with the foreign reformed churches and a common crusade against the linked (and similarly Antichristian) forces of popery, on the one hand, and Anabaptist and sectarian radicalism, on the other. Here, then, were recognizable but by no means identical, versions of the limiting extremes that had been used to define the Henrician mean. But they were now being adopted to legitimate not a Henrician compromise that had satisfied no one other than Henry VIII, but rather a version of the English church as part of a wider reformed cause, what Diarmaid McCulloch has termed the Strasbourg–St Gall connection.[8]

Elizabeth's Reign and the Rise
of Anti-Puritanism

And that Edwardian view of the world started out as the framework within which the Elizabethan church was conceptualized and defended by its first apologists. The great innovation of Elizabeth's reign was what we might term the internalization of anti-sectarian rhetoric, as anti-puritanism. In Edward's reign that language had been used to associate the English church with the foreign reformed churches in the common defence of an emergent reformed orthodoxy. Now it was introjected, to precisely opposite effect, into the conduct of intra-Protestant debates between defenders of the ecclesiastical status quo and proponents of various styles and modes of further reformation. The central figure here was John Whitgift who, in an extended exchange with the leading presbyterian ideologue of the day, Thomas Cartwright, deployed the Edwardian version of the two extremes used to define the *via media* of the English church, popery, and Anabaptism, to exclude, as he hoped, the likes of Cartwright and his ilk, from the charmed circle of English Protestant respectability. True to the spirit of his Edwardian forebears, Whitgift sought to assimilate Cartwright and his associates both to popery and to Anabaptism, using what he took to be their ultra-scripturalism and populism to associate them with the latter and what he took to be their clericalist opposition to the Royal Supremacy to associate them with the former.

Ostensibly a form of religious polemic, Whitgift's anti-puritanism was also inherently political. It dealt with issues of governance and jurisdiction and stressed heavily the extent of direct royal authority over ecclesiastical affairs. In so doing it encoded within itself a set of (intensely monarchical) political values, defined against what he took to be the 'popularity' inscribed within presbyterian theory and puritan political practice. By popularity Whitgift meant a commitment to theories of government in which the role of the people was expanded. But he also used the term to refer to the political methods used by the supporters of the discipline to put their case to a variety of more or less popular publics through the pulpit and the press, and through the circulation of manuscripts and of rumours and a variety of petitioning campaigns, some of them aimed at the parliament rather than at the prince.[9]

Thus by the early 1570s the dual threats of puritanism and of popularity had been equated the one with the other, and the sinister influence of the lay patrons of the puritan movement identified as operating in and through both. Anti-populist and anti-puritan reaction played a crucial role in the fall of Archbishop Grindal and the subsequent rise of Whitgift, and when, in 1583–4, Whitgift sought to enforce subscription on the clergy at a moment when popery seemed to be on the march this produced a clash, in parliament, in the council, and at court, between two agendas, the one dominated by the threat of puritanism and the other by that of popery. The consequent show-down ended in something of a tie. But the Whitgiftian offensive provoked a revival of the presbyterian agitation, a revival which first culminated in, and then broke apart over, the

Marprelate affair, an outbreak of populist pamphleteering that enabled Whitgift and his ally Sir Christopher Hatton to move definitively against the presbyterian movement. Lord Burghley, who had never signed on to the Whitgiftian anti-puritan agenda, persisted with a view of the current conjuncture centred on the linked threats of popery and Habsburg universal monarchy, a view to which he committed the queen and realm in a rabidly anti-Catholic and anti-Spanish proclamation of 1591.[10]

On the extremes, and at moments of high tension, anti-puritanism and anti-popery were opposed discourses. While the godly maintained that the puritan threat was a fabrication, that those accused of puritanism were simply the most zealous and reliable of the queen's subjects and that the real threat came from popery, various Catholics and crypto-Catholics maintained that most English Catholics were entirely loyal subjects and that the real threat came from the puritans. But for anyone within or attached to the regime it became essential to balance the discourse of anti-popery with that of anti-puritanism. The conventional view—certainly Burghley and Leicester's view—was that irritating and irresponsible as some of the more obstreperous of the puritans could be, the threat from popery was incomparably the greater, and that, all in all, given the severity of the popish threat, the puritans, so called, were best viewed as a part, indeed as rather a big part, of the solution rather than as any part of the problem.[11] The claim advanced by the likes of Whitgift, his client and henchman Bancroft, and his ally Sir Christopher Hatton, that popery and puritanism were equivalent threats was thus both novel and deeply disruptive of the structuring assumptions that had underpinned the high Elizabethan regime. However, by the 1590s, that view—which was also the queen's—was becoming widespread.[12]

So, in many ways from the later 1530s, and certainly from the early 1570s, we have two rival accounts of the major religio-political threats to the regime in play, one centred on popery and the other on puritanism. The resultant discourses were, in an obvious sense of the word, 'religious', but they were also inherently 'political', not only because they dealt with questions of government and jurisdiction, but also because they encapsulated a variety of political values and principles about the nature of popularity, of tyranny, about the right ways in which crucial truths of right religion ought to be communicated to the people and defended from the proponents of error.

Polemic, Conspiracy Theory, and the Public Sphere

And this was a practical as well as a theoretical or ideological issue, since in both cases, the truth had to be publicly defended. Both presbyterians and the papists claimed (and very probably believed) that if they could be allowed to present their cases in public before prince and people, the truth of their cause would be vindicated, the prince converted, and right religion, as they understood it, established. The presbyterians repeatedly made that claim and the famous mission of Campion and Parsons of 1580 was in many ways organized around it. Now the authorities never quite gave in to such demands, but they did feel called upon, repeatedly in print, and in the pulpit and the university disputation, to refute, at great length, the arguments of the other side.[13]

As the thousands of pages of formal polemic launched by various, often officially sponsored, defenders of the English church against both the presbyterians and the papists show, there was a widespread sense that such challenges could be neither ignored nor simply suppressed. They had to be answered, and seen to be answered, in public. Divines of all stripes acknowledged that the refutation of error was a crucial means whereby God's truth could be vindicated and disseminated. Such assumptions had been a feature of the theological and cultural scene since at least the beginning of the Reformation in England. There was thus a straight line to be drawn from the efforts of Fisher and More against Tyndale and his ilk, to the vast tomes of anti-papal polemic produced, under Elizabeth, by the likes of Jewel, Fulke, and Whitaker and the equally voluminous works of anti-presbyterian polemic produced, during the same period, by Whitgift and Bridges, Cooper and Bancroft, Saravia, Sutcliffe, and Hooker.

Much of the time, these debates and exchanges were of the most recondite sort and must have engaged the attention only of the most learned of audiences. But these disputes were also conducted at far more demotic levels, through cheap print and performance, designed to reach promiscuously mixed, indeed popular, audiences.[14] The result was the repeated conduct, before a variety of differently constituted audiences, of some of the central religio-political debates of the age, and the dissemination, at a number of cultural and social levels, of the discourses of both anti-popery and anti-puritanism.

The assumption of the inherent, scripturally based righteousness of their own cause prompted nearly all of the parties to have recourse to various sorts of conspiracy theory to explain the failure of their cause to prevail, and in particular the failure of the monarch of the moment to see things their way. Confronted by the confounding capacity of their king serially to defend the cause and course of reformation, Henrician conservatives had had recourse to evil counsellor theory; a view of the matter whereby often low-born evil counsellors, motivated either by heretical zeal or, more often, by private ambition and the will to power, had misled the king into supporting the cause of heresy and error, by playing on and enabling his weaknesses and passions.

Confronted by the refusal of Queen Elizabeth to see things their way, both puritans and Catholics had recourse to similar conspiracy theories. Puritans saw the queen misled by a corrupt episcopal faction, who, determined to preserve their own position, denounced the puritans to the queen as enemies to all order in church and state, while telling the godly that they were really on their side, if only they could get the queen to come round.

The Catholics told an altogether more interesting and complicated tale, whereby Elizabeth had fallen victim to a tight clique of low-born machiavels and atheists, who persuaded her that only by repudiating the power of the papacy could she secure the crown. They then used the fact of religious change as the pretext to exclude from her counsels the largely Catholic ancient nobility and to expel Catholics from the church, creating a pool of patronage through which they could secure a monopoly of power under and around the crown and build factional support in church and state. By virtually inventing a popish threat, where none in fact existed, this clique had managed to persuade Elizabeth that only they and their creatures could protect her from the machinations of her (popish) enemies, both at home and abroad. Central to their schemes had been the succession. First, they had persuaded Elizabeth not to marry, and then sought to alienate her from her natural heir, Mary Stuart, whom they portrayed, not as Elizabeth's natural successor, and thus as the ultimate bulwark against sedition and disorder, but rather as her greatest enemy. Their ultimate aim, having deprived Elizabeth of an heir of her body and of her next successor, was to move against the queen herself and, having removed her from the scene, to divert the succession in their own interest.[15]

These commentaries on the contemporary scene were written and produced, for the most part, by religious *engagés*. But despite that, these texts affected to be largely devoid of confessional *parti pris* and propagated an entirely secular vision of politics, in which the only role for religion was to provide a cover for political manoeuvre. Power was the protagonists' only God and 'policy' their means to achieve that wholly secular end. The templates these tracts used, and to which they referred their readers, to understand the current conjuncture were often historical, taken from the history of pagan Rome and of high and late medieval England, in particular from the Wars of the Roses. The tracts thus operated as exercises in politick history, applying lessons and templates derived from the past to the present and the immediate future in an effort to decode just what was happening now and what was likely to happen next.[16]

In its later iterations this Catholic critique contained an account of the regime as a veritable protection racket, the participants in which, in the queen's name, but in their own interests, were oppressing and bilking the subject to fund their endless war with Spain and to line their own pockets and those of their clients and hangers-on. Abusing the legal system to defend their own interests, they appropriated and abused the prerogative powers of the crown in the pursuit, not of the public good, but of their own, private, interests. Misleading the queen about the real condition of her realm, they patronized and protected their own puritan followers, while persecuting the queen's entirely loyal Catholic subjects, whose treatment at the hands of the regime stood as a synecdoche for its wider attitude towards the subject and the commonweal.

Recourse to this sort of libellous secret history had first been made not by some group of embittered and defeated outs, but by members of the regime itself, desperate to discredit Mary Stuart after her deposition in Scotland, flight to England, and projected match with the duke of Norfolk. Indeed, the first recourse to this mode of argument by the Catholics, in *The treatise of treasons*, had been in response to that initial (pseudo-official) assault upon Mary.

Rather than confer credibility on these libels by attempting directly to refute them (tempted though Burghley certainly was), the regime and its creatures told stories about the 'real life' conspiracies of the papists themselves, bringing before the public a succession of Catholic plots to kill the queen and replace her with Mary Stuart. The result was a propaganda war prosecuted through all the available media; various sorts of performance, show trials and executions, through the pulpit, through rumour and a variety of different sorts of print, proclamations, official or pseudo-official tracts and squibs, and printed sermons.[17]

A CLIMACTIC POINT? THE 1590S

By the final decade of Elizabeth's reign, three widely canvassed, alternative, but by no means always incompatible, conspiracy theories were available for the analysis and conduct of politics; the anti-popish, the anti-puritan, and one centred on evil counsel, court corruption, and the pursuit by the powerful of private, rather than public, interests. While the first two were 'religious'—in the case of anti-popery, based on an intensely eschatological reading of history—they encoded crucial political assumptions and values. If the third was entirely secular it had been produced and deployed in the course of, and in order to interpret, the intensely confessional dynastic politics of Elizabeth's reign. Moreover, it was easily spliced together with one or other of the other two narrative templates, since the corrupt evil counsellors at hand could be outed either as puritans or, rather more often, as papists, their manoeuvres designed not merely to further their private material interests and ambitions but also the cause of (false) religion, which of course, in its turn, served to legitimate and enable their own further pursuit of profit and power.

Each of these narratives had been canvassed and contested, repeatedly, in public. The conduct of such disputes was always intermittent, crisis-related, and intensely contested; that is to say, the broaching of such issues before a variety of promiscuously uncontrolled publics never became anything like either licit or quotidian. However, the exigencies which prompted such behaviour, even in some of the most powerful and well-connected persons in the kingdom, as well as the regime's leading critics and opponents—that is to say in Burghley and Essex, in Whitgift and Bancroft, as much as in Thomas Cartwright, John Field, or Robert Parsons—were frequent and pressing enough for this to have become a settled, albeit never a normative, feature of the religio-political scene, and a familiar, and even necessary, part of the toolkit of many of the leading political players and ideologues of the day.

These discourses—anti-popery, anti-puritanism, and the politique analysis of evil counsel—have been identified by many historians as crucial to the ways contemporaries viewed, and sought to act upon, the events that led to the English civil war. And we have found them to be established features of the political and discursive scene by the 1590s, which, since the English civil war did not, in fact, start in the 1590s, means that, on their own, they can hardly figure as causes of that war.

Nor was there anything intrinsically radical, or even necessarily oppositional, in any of these discourses. Both anti-popery and anti-puritanism had claims to something like official status; certainly they were used by supporters of (various versions of) the status quo to defend it against differently conceived sources of danger. Nor was there anything radical about the ideal of service to the commonweal or about the idea that political virtue was best defined as the pursuit of the public, rather than of private, interest. Evil counsel was merely the binary opposite, the defining other, of good counsel, the 'public', the defining other of the 'private', and 'corruption' the inevitable result of the pursuit of the latter rather than of the former. These were commonplaces, even clichés, obvious truths to which virtually everyone would assent. The same was true, of course, about both popery and puritanism, which were, after all, terms of opprobrium and thus, as often as not, to be found in the eye of the beholder. As the Catholic critiques of the Elizabethan regime had shown, one person's epitome of Ciceronian virtue and true religion could be another's evil counsellor, machiavel, and practical atheist. And, thus, all of these discourses only became controversial in the application; that is to say, when it became time to decide just who was a puritan or who a papist or indeed an evil, as opposed to a virtuous, counsellor.

For the most part, under Elizabeth, the potential within these discourses for generating internecine, intra-Protestant, dispute had been kept under control. From the late 1560s until the 1590s popery remained public enemy number one as a childless and unmarried queen confronted an uncertain future, her nearest heir a papist, and protracted conflict with Spain. Moreover, the need to maintain a unified front against the popish foe constituted a real constraint on the conduct of internal political argument. Thus, with the notable exception of certain presbyterian and radical puritan critiques of the bishops, arguments about evil counsel and court corruption remained the preserve of Catholic polemicists.[18]

However, in the later 1590s, the ideological materials long held in place by this political force field began to shift. That decade saw the final crackdown on the puritan movement, followed by the Archpriest Controversy, in which a Catholic faction, the so-called appellants, sponsored by Bancroft and Robert Cecil, attempted to expand the logic of anti-puritanism to encompass (Calvinist) doctrine in order to establish their loyalist credentials. They did this by harping on what they portrayed as the *equally* subversive threats represented by the Jesuits and the puritans, and on their support for James VI as the next monarch of England.[19]

Amongst the more radical puritans all this elicited not merely an upsurge of separatist activity, but a strand of political critique which associated episcopacy, and the current ecclesiastical policies of the regime, with an assault on both the religious and legal liberties of the subject, an assault akin to popish tyranny.[20] But perhaps most spectacularly, in the run-up to the Essex rebellion both the earl himself and James VI can be found applying the basic tenets of the Catholic evil counsellor narrative to the doings of the inner circle of the regime, whom they suspected of doing a deal with Spain over both the peace and the succession, the better to perpetuate their own hold on power. Not only that but, after the debacle of the earl's 'rebellion', the regime sought to turn precisely the same claims against Essex; now he was the one dealing with the enemy and making eyes at the papists—and in the Bye and Main plot precisely the same sort of claim and counter-claim continued to figure in the high politics of regime change, even after the accession of King James.[21]

ALL CHANGE? THE EARLY STUART POLITICAL SCENE

Certainly, James's accession both removed the threat of a popish succession and ended the war with Spain. That, together with his status as Mary Stuart's son, raised Catholic hopes for some sort of toleration and his reign opened with a bout of public petitioning and positioning, as both Catholics and puritans agitated for religious change in their favour. The Gunpowder Plot, though, seemingly reinstantiated popery as a unifying and univocal other but James refused fully to exploit the anti-papal card. Instead, he preferred to use the oath of allegiance to highlight his own views of Christian kingship and, following the logic of Richard Bancroft's earlier sponsorship of the appellant clergy, to divide and rule English Catholics, while maintaining the (Elizabethan) claim that English Catholics were only punished for their political disloyalty and disobedience rather than for their religious beliefs.[22]

Moreover, over the long haul, James's accession meant the return to court of various Catholic and crypto-Catholic interests and individuals, clustered around certain foreign Catholic ambassadors, like the notorious Gondomar; around James's wife—Ann of Denmark—and also around the ex-Marian and crypto-Catholic, Henry Howard, earl of Northampton, now, after years in the political wilderness under Elizabeth, elevated to prominent positions at court and on the council.

The presence of such Catholic elements was a function of James's self-consciously absolutist style of kingcraft, which, as both an ideology and a rhetorical strategy, tended to equate presbyterian-puritan and Jesuit(ed)-papist threats to the (absolute) powers of princes and the national churches over which, by divine right, they presided.[23] James saw the careful balancing of different confessional and factional groupings, and the exploitation of the fault lines between 'radical' and 'moderate' papists and puritans, as the essence of successful kingship and he rated very highly his own practice of the necessary political arts. Jacobean kingcraft required the presence of various sorts of Catholic at court.[24]

Moreover, as Michael Questier has shown, the influence of such 'papists' increased, or at least appeared to increase, at those moments when a Catholic match for either of James's two sons hove into view, as the balance of both James's ecclesiastical and foreign policies required that it should.[25] When we add James's capacity, when it suited him, to play the anti-puritan card—although here, as a number of scholars have observed, his bark was always considerably worse than his bite and anyway everything turned (as always) on just who was included under that term—we can appreciate, at certain crucial moments, just how bad things could look from a puritan perspective and how easy it was to have recourse to the language of anti-popery and evil counsel to explain what was happening or, worse still, what might be about to happen next.[26]

At the same time, the financial exigencies of the regime, compounded both by James's notorious personal extravagance, the presence at court of various Scots office-holders and hangers-on, and latterly by his propensity to shower offices and money upon pretty young men, virtually invited critiques of court-based corruption and even evil counsel; critiques which fitted all too well with existing patterns of anti-popery. Freed from the constraints operative under Elizabeth, anti-popery thus became available as a means to critique central aspects of the regime. This represented a very considerable sea-change from the reign of Elizabeth.

Partly in reaction to such developments, the analysis of puritan popularity came to be applied to the activities of the critics of the regime, who were increasingly portrayed as subversive 'tribuni plebis', ambitious and unscrupulous men, who, by posing before the people as champions of various sorts of 'liberty', and protectors of the Commonwealth from various sorts of corruption, sought to enhance their own status and power at the expense of the just prerogatives of the crown and the authority of its officers. Here was the equivalent of evil-counsellor speak, a code through which the actions and attitudes of men who regarded themselves as quintessentially loyal subjects of the crown and zealous servants of the Commonwealth could be redescribed in the most virulently hostile and denunciatory of terms, their defence of the public good turned into the pursuit of private advantage, and what they regarded as their attempts to redress the grievances of the subject into so much rabble-rousing self-promotion.[27]

Just as with the critiques of court corruption and evil counsel, there were more (or less) secular versions of popularity. Just as much as those organized around evil counsel and court corruption, narrative templates centred on 'popularity' had roots in a variety of (secular) historical and classical texts. Thus, 'popularity' did not have to be associated with puritans, any more than court 'corruption' or evil counsel had to be associated with 'papists'. But those elisions and equivalences were very often either assumed or asserted, in ways that underline yet again how ostensibly religious ideologies—in this case, anti-popery and anti-puritanism—also encoded and expressed a series of political values and judgements. All of which enabled those ideologies to be mixed and matched with other, more obviously secular and politique, strands of analysis and argument, and applied, as explanatory tools, to the course of (what might appear to a modern eye to be almost wholly 'political') events.[28]

This extension of the internal logic of anti-puritanism was not limited to the realm of secular politics, however. It also underlay the sea-change in religious policy commonly known as 'the rise of Arminianism' or 'Laudianism'. This fundamental shift operated at a number of distinct but related levels—formal theology, liturgical practice and worship, personal and collective piety. It encoded a distinctive vision of the relations between the sacred and the profane, the nature of God's presence in the world, of the relationship of the English church to its Catholic past and to other contemporary churches, both Catholic and reformed, of the Christian community, of the visible church, and of the role of the priesthood in both, not to mention in the wider political and social orders; all of which was defined against a vision of puritan disorder, deviance, and error. Crucial here was an attempt to label as deviant and 'puritan' certain 'Calvinist' doctrines, which their adherents regarded as not only, in some general sense, 'orthodox' but also as the official doctrine of the national church. Central predestinarian doctrines and beliefs were denounced as radically disintegrative of the Christian community and as subversively antinomian in their impact on Christian conversation and therefore as utterly incompatible with monarchical rule.[29]

While the polemical or ideological logic at work here was plain enough, the political and polemical stakes were very high. Both Whitgift and Cartwright had accepted the assumption that the church of England's doctrine had been, in some fundamental sense, reformed. This had been an organizing principle of the high Elizabethan and Jacobean establishments and a key factor in the continuing attachment of even quite radical puritans to the national church. Both times the discourse of anti-puritanism had been extended to attack Calvinist theology—first in the 1590s and then in the 1620s—it had been done on the back of an outbreak of virulently political anti-puritanism; the first occasioned by the final assault on the presbyterian movement of the early 1590s, the second by the vocal opposition to the prospect of a Spanish match in the late 1610s and early 1620s. While the first attempt failed, the second succeeded, culminating, after a prolonged period of ambivalence and indecision, in the later 1620s, in the Laudianism of the Caroline church.[30]

These changes destabilized crucial terms like popery and puritanism, making them available for application, not merely to various, differently constituted, external threats, but to disputes and controversies conducted within what had been the mainstream of English Protestantism. The result was that, by the 1620s and 1630s, members of the same episcopal bench could be outed, by different groups, as either papists or puritans, and, while some could find popery operating at the very centre of the royal court, others claimed to detect puritanism at work amongst self-professedly conformist clergy or the most zealously active of the local gentry.[31]

The 1590s and the 1620s were in many ways remarkably comparable decades. Both were dominated by wars waged against the great Catholic power of the age. Both were marred by economic crises, caused by plague and, in the case of the 1590s, dearth, and of the 1620s, trade depression. Both featured increasingly polarized and bitter court politics, centred on a beleaguered royal favourite and a seemingly dysfunctional war effort. Both contained increasingly bitter religious disputes and an attempt to extend an existing rhetoric of anti-puritanism to the realm of doctrine. In both decades, fiscal strains consequent upon the prosecution of the war produced complaints about the costs of war and the perversion of the prerogative powers of the crown. But in the 1620s, tropes and accusations, narrative techniques and polemical moves, that, under Elizabeth, had been limited to the Catholic or radical puritan fringe invaded mainstream intra-Protestant political and religious argument. On the political side of the ledger, we have the rhetoric of evil counsel, a tendency to see the regime as dominated by a narrow clique of often low-born favourites, and in the puritan version of the story, of ambitious prelates, battening off the patronage of the crown, misleading the monarch into disastrous policies both at home and abroad, while lining their own pockets, favouring their own cronies and creatures, and oppressing the subject. On the religious side, we have a tendency to characterize the dominant position of the English church as, in some narrowly sectarian sense of the word, 'Calvinist', to see Protestants and puritans as adherents of different religions and to cast puritans as inherently subversive enemies of all monarchical authority. Such claims had been central to Catholic attacks on the Elizabethan regime as a conspiracy of evil counsel, attacks which, by the early 1590s, were presenting the abuses and oppressions of the regime—imprisonment without trial amongst them—as a tyrannical assault upon an ancient legal and constitutional status quo.

To take two examples, the claim that James I had been poisoned by the duke of Buckingham, upon which much of the impeachment proceedings against the duke turned, was a direct product of *The forerunner of revenge*, a tract by one Dr Eglisham, who was by that point a Catholic exile in Flanders, where his screed was printed. Here was a classic (Catholic) exercise in libellous secret history being directly introduced, without difficulty or demur, into mainstream English political discourse.[32] Again, when Charles I imprisoned the five knights, without trial, for their refusal to pay the forced loan of 1626, he was doing no more to them than the Elizabethan regime had done to countless refractory Catholics. This time, however, the result was not the acquiescence of the Protestant political nation in the customary exercise, for the common good, of widely accepted extralegal royal powers, but rather a replication, on the floor of the House of Commons, of the cries of foul with which at least some English Catholics had greeted their treatment at the hands of the Elizabethan regime. This was followed by the petition of right, an attempt legally to reinstantiate precisely the ancient rights and liberties that various Catholics had accused the Elizabethan regime of infringing, and which, by the 1620s, many of his Protestant subjects thought needed uncompromising reassertion in the face of the recent conduct of their king.[33]

Moreover, by the 1620s, the practice of politics as a form of 'popularity', the deployment before various publics of these three narratives, had become entirely self-conscious. Again, this was a long-term trend, with its roots in the later sixteenth century. Francis Bacon, who, along with the likes of John Williams, proffered his services to James and the duke as an expert in such things, was a crucial figure linking the two periods, and indeed those two, oft-compared, popular favourites, Essex and Buckingham, together.[34] Moreover, throughout the 1620s, even Buckingham, whose power as a royal favourite originated almost entirely at court, played the game of popularity before a range of audiences, with both pertinacity and skill. Even Charles I felt the need at crucial moments to explain himself to his people, often at considerable length.[35]

Not only was this being done self-consciously within the closed circles of the regime; contemporaries, in a number of venues, reflected and commented upon that process, perhaps most notably in the public theatre, where famously *A game at chess* staged the vision of politics as a game of move and counter-move, in the course of which the conspiracies and duplicities of one's opponents had to be seen through and countered. In *The staple of news* Ben Jonson responded to these impulses. In a series of plays, both comedies and political tragedies, Jonson fed off and played with the absurdities and duplicities of contemporary politico-religious discourse, both commenting upon and enlisting to his own purposes the anti-Catholic, and particularly the anti-puritan, stereotypes and narratives of the day, all the while satirizing the attempts of outsiders to penetrate within the claims and counter-claims about what was really happening that made up so much of the contemporary political scene and animated so much of contemporary 'news culture'. As for Buckingham, in August 1628, at the climactic point of his career, he was quite prepared to resort to the popular stage to send messages about his current condition and future plans, and indeed to perform his own political virtue, before a promiscuously mixed, 'popular' audience.[36]

NOT THE CAUSES OF THE ENGLISH CIVIL WAR; THE 'POST-REFORMATION PUBLIC SPHERE' AND THE SHAPING OF CIVIL WAR POLITICS

In short, in twenty or so years the constraints placed upon the discourse of anti-puritanism, anti-popery, and evil counsel under Elizabeth had completely broken down. But, of course, since the civil war did not start in the 1620s, we are still not talking about the causes of said civil war. But when the civil war did start, or rather in the period immediately before it started, these were the discourses, the interpretative modes and narrative tropes, through which contemporaries viewed the political process and in terms of which various groups pitched for wider support. And those pitches were made through printed forms and performances, show trials, and public executions, sermons (publicly sanctioned and spontaneous, performed and printed), various types of religious polemic and disputation (again both performed and printed), and, of course, through myriad petitions. All of which forms of communicative practice and political positioning would have made no sense, would, indeed, have been entirely unavailable, without the preceding decades of post-Reformation politicking.

Even at this late date, though, it would be hard to argue that the availability of such interpretative modes and communicative practices 'caused' the 'civil war'. What preceded the war itself was an extended cold (propaganda) war. The 'junto' and their godly supporters made their pitch for support against a popish conspiracy of evil counsel surrounding the king, and argued for further reformation of both church and state to defeat that conspiracy and defend true religion. The king appealed to a variety of constituencies by picturing central figures in the junto as, in effect, evil counsellors, machiavels and politiques, popular spirits and firebrands, determined to undermine the powers of the monarch and seize power for themselves. He and his partisans conjured a puritan threat to all order in church, state, and society, which centred on puritan attempts to abolish episcopacy, which would undo one of the basic elements in the fabric of both church and state, and unleash populist impulses that might well not stop at the abolition of bishops. Those rival visions of the very recent past, present, and likely future were, of course, canvassed, by both sides, through a greatly expanded public realm of print, preaching, demonstration, petitioning, and a burgeoning news culture.[37]

What was novel was not the existence of these modes of action, but the speed and intensity, and the sheer volume of the material, in and through which they were conducted.[38] But none of this rendered inevitable the outbreak of civil war. For as a number of historians have recently argued,[39] there were moments when Charles's attempts to mobilize anti-puritan, anti-Scots, pro-episcopal opinion, to make himself the head of a body of newly conservative opinion, alienated by the seeming radicalism of the junto and their godly allies, and profoundly disturbed by the tyranny that events like the execution of Strafford seemed to presage, looked as though they might succeed, enabling Charles to regain the political initiative without recourse to arms. The reasons that did not happen might be thought to turn on the fine detail of political manoeuvre, of the judgement and misjudgement, the good and bad timing, not to mention the good and bad luck, of the major players. Even here, therefore, we may not be dealing with 'the causes of the civil war'. However, while the modes of political and communicative action which contemporaries had learned to use in the century or so following the English Reformation to interpret and act upon political events may not have caused the war, they did profoundly shape the sort of crisis or series of crises that it was or became.

Notes

1. Richard Rex, 'The English Campaign against Luther in the 1520s', *Transactions of the Royal Historical Society [TRHS]*, 5th ser., 39 (1989): 85–106; Alexandra da Costa, *Reforming Printing: Syon Abbey's Defence of Orthodoxy, 1525–1534* (Oxford, 2012); Brad Pardue, *Printing, Power and Piety: Appeals to the Public During the Early Years of the English Reformation* (Leiden, 2012).

2. On the 'post-Reformation public sphere' see Peter Lake and Steven Pincus (eds.), *The Politics of the Public Sphere in Early Modern England* (Manchester, 2007).

3. G. R. Elton, *Reform and Renewal: Thomas Cromwell and the Common Weal* (Cambridge, 1972); Ethan Shagan, 'Confronting Compromise: The Schism and its Legacy in Mid-Tudor England', in Shagan (ed.), *Catholics and the 'Protestant Nation': Religious Politics and Identity in Early Modern England* (Manchester, 2005); Shagan, 'The Pilgrimage of Grace and the Public Sphere?', in Lake and Pincus (eds.), *Public Sphere*, 31–58; Shagan, *The Rule of Moderation* (Cambridge, 2011), chap. 2.

4. G. R. Elton, 'Thomas Cromwell's Decline and Fall', *Cambridge Historical Journal*, 10 (1951): 150–85.

5. Shagan, *Rule of Moderation*, 107–10; Kevin Sharpe, *Selling the Tudor Monarchy* (London, 2009).

6. Catharine Davies, *A Religion of the Word: The Defence of the Reformation in the Reign of Edward VI* (Manchester, 2002), esp. chaps. 1–2.

7. Bale's play, *King Johann*, illustrates the presence of a certain strand of virulent anti-popery in almost its fully formed state in the late 1530s, its deployment in the course of a bitter faction struggle, and also taken to the street: Greg Walker, *Plays of Persuasion: Drama and Politics at the Court of Henry VIII* (Cambridge, 1991), chap. 6.

8. Diarmaid MacCulloch, *Thomas Cranmer* (New Haven, 1996), 174f.; also see his 'Putting the English Reformation on the Map', *TRHS*, 15 (2005): 75–95.

9. Peter Lake, *Anglicans and Puritans? Presbyterianism and English Conformist Thought from Whitgift to Hooker* (London, 1988), chap. 1 and Lake, 'Puritanism, (Monarchical) Republicanism, and Monarchy; or John Whitgift, Anti-Puritanism and the Invention of "Popularity"', *Journal of Medieval and Early Modern Studies*, 40 (2010): 463–95.

10. Patrick Collinson, *The Elizabethan Puritan Movement* (London, 1967), *passim* but esp. parts 4, 5, and 8.

11. For an exposition of that view written as it were in Burghley's name see Francis Bacon's 'Certain observations upon a libel' in Alan Stewart and Harriet Knight (eds.), *The Oxford Francis Bacon, Early Writings, 1584–1596* (Oxford, 2012), 343–424, esp. 365–8.

12. Peter Lake, 'Matthew Hutton: A Puritan Bishop?', *History*, 64 (1979): 182–204; Patrick Collinson, *Richard Bancroft and Elizabethan Anti-Puritanism* (Cambridge, 2013).

13. Peter Lake and Michael Questier, 'Puritans, Papists and the "Public Sphere" in Early Modern England', *Journal of Modern History*, 72 (2000): 587–627.

14. The most obvious example of this was, of course, the Marprelate tracts and the reaction thereto sponsored by Bancroft. On which see Joseph Black (ed.), *The Martin Marprelate Tracts* (Cambridge, 2008); also see Peter Lake and Michael Questier, *The Antichrist's Lewd Hat: Protestants, Papists and Players in Post-Reformation England* (New Haven, 2002), chaps. 12 and 13. More generally see Antoinjina Bevan-Zlatar, *Reformation Fictions: Polemical Protestant Dialogues in Elizabethan England* (Oxford, 2011).

15. Peter Lake, 'The "Monarchical Republic of Elizabeth I" Revisited (by its victims) as a Conspiracy', in Barry Coward and Julian Swann (eds.), *Conspiracies and Conspiracy Theory in Early Modern Europe* (Aldershot, 2004), 87–111; Lake, 'From *Leicester his Commonwealth* to *Sejanus his Fall*: Ben Jonson and the Politics of Roman (Catholic) Virtue', in Shagan (ed.), *Catholics and the 'Protestant Nation'*, 128–61.

16. I hope to discuss the role of the stage and in particular of the history play in popularizing this attitude to both 'history' and 'politics' and its interpretation in a book on Shakespeare's history plays and the confessional, dynastic, and factional politics of the 1590s.

17. I summarize here the argument of my Ford lectures of 2011, of which I hope to publish an expanded version under the (provisional) title of *Bad Queen Bess? Libelous Politics and Secret Histories in an Age of Confessional Conflict*.

18. Patrick Collinson, 'The Elizabethan Exclusion Crisis and the Elizabethan Polity', *Proceedings of the British Academy*, 84 (1994): 51–92. For the wider point about anti-popery ceasing to be a centripetal and becoming an at least potentially centrifugal force see Carol Z. Weiner, 'The Beleaguered Isle: A Study of Elizabethan and Early Jacobean Anti-Catholicism', *Past and Present*, 51 (1971): 27–62.

19. Peter Lake and Michael Questier, 'Taking it to the Street? The Archpriest Controversy and the Issue of the Succession' (forthcoming).

20. Michael Winship, 'Freeborn (Puritan) English Men and Slavish Subjection: Popish Tyranny and Puritan Constitutionalism, c.1570–1602', *English Historical Review* [*EHR*], 124 (2000): 1050–60; also see Winship, *Godly Republicanism* (Cambridge, MA, 2012), chaps. 2 and 3.

21. Arnold Hunt, 'Tuning the Pulpits: The Religious Context of the Essex Revolt', in Lori-Anne Ferrell and Peter McCollough (eds.), *The English Sermon Revised* (Manchester, 2001), 86–114; Mark Nichols, 'Sir Walter Raleigh's Treason: A Prosecution Document', *EHR*, 110 (1995): 902–24; Nichols, 'Two Winchester Trials: Henry Lord Cobham and Thomas, Lord Grey of Wilton, 1603', *Historical Research* [*Hist. Res.*], 68 (1995): 26–48.

22. Michael Questier, 'Loyalty, Religion and State Power in Early Modern England: English Romanism and the Jacobean Oath of Allegiance', *Historical Journal* [*HJ*], 40 (1997): 311–29. For a different view see Johann Sommerville, 'Papalist Political Thought and the Controversy over the Jacobean Oath of Allegiance', in Shagan (ed.), *Catholics and the 'Protestant Nation'*, 162–84.

23. Peter Lake, 'The King (the Queen) and the Jesuit: James Stuart's *True law of free monarchies* in context/s', *TRHS*, 6th ser., 14 (2004): 243–60.

24. Kenneth Fincham and Peter Lake, 'The Ecclesiastical Policy of James I', *Journal of British Studies* [*JBS*], 24 (1985): 169–207.

25. Michael Questier, *Stuart Dynastic Policy and Religious Politics 1621–1625* (Cambridge, 2005); Thomas Cogswell, 'England and the Spanish Match', in Richard Cust and Ann Hughes, *Conflict in Early Stuart England* (London, 1989), 107–23.

26. Peter Lake, 'Constitutional Consensus and Puritan Opposition in the 1620s: Thomas Scott and the Spanish Match', *HJ*, 25 (1982): 805–25.

27. Richard Cust, 'The Public Man in Late Tudor and Early Stuart England', in Lake and Pincus (eds.), *Public Sphere*, 116–143; Cust, 'Charles I and Popularity', in Thomas Cogswell, Richard Cust, and Peter Lake (eds.), *Politics, Religion and Popularity in Early Stuart Britain* (Cambridge, 2002), 235–58; Cust, ' "Patriots" and "Popular Spirits": Narratives of Conflict in Early Stuart Politics', in Nicholas Tyacke (ed.), *The English Revolution c.1590–1720* (Manchester, 2007), 43–61.

28. Noah Millstone's research on manuscript separates will transform our knowledge of these topics by documenting in extraordinary detail the sheer scale of the production of, and the breadth of the demand for, such separates, and by demonstrating their role in disseminating a politique vision of politics, in which the central political narrative and the claims advanced by major players had to be decoded if they were to be properly understood. This disseminated much more widely techniques of hermeneutic suspicion previously something of a monopoly of Catholic critics. Millstone's work opens up a new field of enquiry into how contemporaries actually thought about politics, as opposed to how they played the game of 'Political Thought'. I should like to thank Dr Millstone for many discussions of these and related subjects, which have played a major role in formulating the position laid out in this chapter.

29. Peter Lake, 'The Laudian Style', in Kenneth Fincham (ed.), *The Early Stuart Church, 1603–1642* (Basingstoke, 1993), 161–85 and Anthony Milton, *Catholic and Reformed: The Roman and Protestant Churches in English Protestant Thought, 1600–1640* (Cambridge, 1994).

30. Peter Lake, 'The "Anglican Moment"? Richard Hooker and the Ideological Watershed of the 1590s', in Stephen Platten (ed.), *Anglicanism and the Western Christian Tradition* (Norwich, 2003), 90–121, 229–33.

31. Kenneth Fincham and Peter Lake, 'Popularity, Prelacy and Puritanism in the 1630s: Joseph Hall Explains Himself', *EHR*, 1 (1996): 856–81.

32. The 'poisoning of James I' is the subject of important new work by Alastair Bellany and Tom Cogswell, whom I would like to thank for many conversations on this topic. See Thomas Cogswell, 'The Return of the Dead Alive: The Earl of Bristol and Dr Eglisham in the Parliament of 1626 and in Caroline Political Culture', *EHR*, 128 (2013): 535–70.

33. Cf. Mark Kishlansky, 'Tyranny Denied: Charles I, Attorney General Heath, and the Five Knights Case', *HJ*, 42 (1999): 53–83.

34. James's regime was confronted with the choice of whether or not to play the anti-popish card to explain away the Overbury scandal and Bacon played a crucial role in persuading

James to do no such thing, on which see Alastair Bellany's seminal book, *The Politics of Court Scandal in Early Modern England* (Cambridge, 2002). My thinking on this topic has been much influenced by a sadly unfinished thesis by a former student of mine, Sandeep Kaushik, who did excellent work on Bishop Williams as a sort of self-proclaimed expert in the politics of popularity.

35. Thomas Cogswell, 'The People's Love: The Duke of Buckingham and Popularity', in Cogswell, Cust, and Lake (eds.), *Politics, Religion and Popularity*, 211–34; Cogswell, 'The Politics of Propaganda: Charles I and the People in the 1620s', *JBS*, 29 (1990): 187–215; Cogswell, ' "Published by authority": Newsbooks and the Duke of Buckingham's Expedition to the Ile of Rhé', *Huntington Library Quarterly*, 67 (2004): 1–25; Alistair Bellany, ' "Naught but illusion"? Buckingham's Painted Selves', in Kevin Sharpe and Steven Zwicker (eds.), *Writing Lives: Biography and Textuality, Identity and Representation in Early Modern England* (Oxford, 2008), 127–60; Bellany, 'Buckingham Engraved: Politics, Print Images and the Royal Favourite in the 1620s', in Michael Hunter (ed.), *Printed Images in Early Modern Britain* (Farnham, 2010), 215–35; Richard Cust, 'Charles I and a Draft Declaration for the 1628 Parliament', *Hist. Res.*, 63 (1990): 143–61.

36. Thomas Cogswell and Peter Lake, 'Buckingham Does the Globe: Henry VIII and the Politics of Popularity in the 1620s', *Shakespeare Quarterly*, 60 (2009): 253–78.

37. For petitioning see Anthony Fletcher, *The Outbreak of the English Civil War* (London, 1981). For the ideological cacophony of 1641–2 see David Cressy, *England on Edge: Crisis and Revolution, 1640–1642* (Oxford, 2006).

38. For a case study of petitions and pamphlets ricocheting between the centre and the localities, illustrating that this was no more a monopoly of the puritan, 'oppositionist', side of the argument than had it been in the 1520s see Peter Lake, 'Puritans, Popularity and Petitions: Local Politics in National Context, Cheshire, 1641', in Cogswell, Cust, and Lake (eds.), *Politics, Religion and Popularity*, 259–89.

39. Richard Cust, *Charles I: A Political Life* (Harlow, 2005), chap. 5.

FURTHER READING

Bellany, Alastair, *The Politics of Court Scandal in Early Modern England* (Cambridge, 2002).

Braddick, Michael J., 'Mobilisation, Anxiety and Creativity in England during the 1640s', in John Morrow and Jonathan Scott (eds.), *Liberty, Authority, Formality: Political Ideas and Culture, 1600–1900* (Exeter, 2008), 175–193.

Cogswell, Thomas, 'The People's Love: The Duke of Buckingham and Popularity', in Thomas Cogswell, Richard Cust, and Peter Lake (eds.), *Politics, Religion and Popularity in Early Stuart Britain* (Cambridge, 2002), 211–234.

Cogswell, Thomas, 'The Politics of Propaganda: Charles I and the People in the 1620s', *Journal of British Studies*, 29 (1990): 187–215.

Cust, Richard, 'Charles I and Popularity', in Thomas Cogswell, Richard Cust, and Peter Lake (eds.), *Politics, Religion and Popularity in Early Stuart Britain* (Cambridge, 2002), 235–258.

Cust, Richard, ' "Patriots" and "Popular Spirits": Narratives of Conflict in Early Stuart Politics', in Nicholas Tyacke (ed.), *The English Revolution c.1590–1720* (Manchester, 2007), 43–61.

Lake, Peter, *Bad Queen Bess? Libelous Politics and Secret Histories in an Age of Confessional Conflict* (forthcoming).

Lake, Peter and Steve Pincus (eds.), *The Politics of the Public Sphere in Early Modern England* (Manchester, 2007).

Lake, Peter and Michael Questier, 'Puritans, Papists and the "Public Sphere" in Early Modern England', *Journal of Modern History*, 72 (2000): 587–627.

Peacey, Jason, *Print and Public Politics in the English Revolution* (Cambridge, 2013).

Questier, Michael, 'Loyalty, Religion and State Power in Early Modern England: English Romanism and the Jacobean Oath of Allegiance', *Historical Journal*, 40 (1997): 311–329.

Zaret, David, *The Origins of Democratic Culture: Printing, Petitions, and the Public Sphere in Early-Modern England* (Princeton, 2000).

PART II

EVENTS

CHAPTER 3

....

THE RISE OF THE
COVENANTERS, 1637–1644

....

JULIAN GOODARE

'It is not a revolt, it is a revolution!'

THIS is what the duc de Liancourt reportedly told Louis XVI at the time of the storming of the Bastille in 1789. Whether accurately reported or not, the remark has been much quoted because it encapsulates the way in which participants in great events come gradually to realize their significance.

For the Scottish Revolution, the equivalent to the storming of the Bastille was the riot in St Giles' Cathedral, Edinburgh, against Charles I's new Prayer Book, on 23 July 1637. Initially, the authorities saw it as little more than a temporary law and order problem. When petitions against the Prayer Book began to pour in, it gradually became clear that something serious was afoot. Still, it took some time for all concerned to realize that the protests were a revolt. And after that, how much longer did it take them to realize that it was a revolution? Especially since the concept of 'revolution' was not as clear in the 1630s as it was in 1789, this latter question will be harder to answer.

FROM REVOLT TO REVOLUTION

....

It used to be conventional to ascribe the Scottish revolt to 'absentee monarchy', with the king unable to control the situation because he was 'absent'. But letters took only about four days between Edinburgh and London—and the authorities on the spot were just as out of touch. The prayer book riot took place on 23 July. The privy council issued a proclamation on the 24th ordering people to behave themselves, and talked to the magistrates of Edinburgh, who held responsibility for law and order in the town. They did not write to the king until the 26th. Yet Charles acted quickly in response. He wrote to the council on the 30th, ordering them to punish the rioters and assist the bishops in 'setling' the Prayer Book.[1] This letter was written even before Charles received the council's letter; presumably he had received an earlier letter from the Scottish bishops. At any rate, Charles could hardly have acted more quickly. And his response, though uncompromising, was also unsurprising, given that he was told that the problem was one of law and order.

From late July to early September, the authorities in Edinburgh and London did not behave as if they thought they were dealing with a revolt, let alone a revolution. They treated the prayer book riot as a problem of law and order within Edinburgh itself. Yet the authorities in Edinburgh were divided. The privy council contained several bishops, but was dominated by lay councillors who tended to resent the bishops' influence. The council told the king that the problem had been caused by the bishops' unseemly haste in introducing the Prayer Book; the bishops instead complained of a failure by the lay authorities to back them up. There was constant buck-passing between the privy council, the burgh magistrates, and the bishop and ministers of Edinburgh, none of whom wanted to take responsibility for arresting the rioters or preventing future riots.

Meanwhile, however, protest against the Prayer Book was spreading widely. Initially this took the form of petitions by parish ministers, protesting against the government's order for them to buy and use the book. But nobles, lairds, and others began to send supporting petitions. Protesters held local meetings, and hundreds of 'supplicants' gathered ominously in Edinburgh. The question for the government was no longer who was going to take responsibility for the Prayer Book, but who was going to respond to the 'supplicants'.

The main difference between the various authorities was that some of them—Charles, Archbishop Laud, and some of the Scottish bishops—really wanted the Prayer Book; others—the Scottish lay councillors and the Edinburgh magistrates—did not. The privy council 'suspended' the Prayer Book, but saw no need to advise Charles explicitly that he should withdraw it. The earl of Traquair, the treasurer and usual leader of the lay councillors, seems to have assumed that the Prayer Book would soon be abandoned, and that the episode would discredit its promoters. Its most prominent Scottish promoter, John Maxwell, bishop of Ross, was a man whom Traquair had outmanoeuvred in 1636 to become treasurer, and Traquair probably hoped to use the Prayer Book fiasco to press home his advantage. To do that, at first he mainly needed to wait while the Prayer Book's promoters dug themselves into a hole. He even advised the petitioners on how to make one of their petitions more acceptable to the king. As opposition mounted, the Prayer Book would inevitably be withdrawn, Maxwell would be disgraced, and Traquair himself would emerge as the saviour of the day.

If Charles had wanted to compromise, he could have withdrawn the Prayer Book, duly disgracing some advisers such as Maxwell. Some historians have criticized Charles for refusing to take this course, apparently assuming that it would have returned things to the *status quo ante*. However, this would be a naive assumption. Once Charles had been forced by public protest to abandon his flagship policy, he would have purchased stability at the price of conceding credibility to his critics. Next time he wanted something, he would have had to make further concessions. For instance, parliamentary taxation had to be renewed every four or six years. The most recent tax had been voted in 1633, with the last instalment due for collection in 1639; another parliament would be required to renew it. It is improbable that such a parliament would have been amenable to the royal wishes. The regime's most determined critics, as their actions in 1638 would show, would not have been satisfied with a mere return to the *status quo ante* 1637. The concessions necessary to mollify them would have been sweeping indeed.

So it is perhaps not surprising that throughout 1637, Charles and Laud were more receptive to Maxwell's advice, repeatedly ordering the privy council to enforce the Prayer Book and to arrest the ringleaders of sedition. Unfortunately for them, this was impractical. One intransigent royal proclamation, on 17 October, led next day to a bigger riot in Edinburgh than the initial July one. The magistrates of Edinburgh had joined the protesters in September, and after October's riot, the privy council could not meet in the town. The king had lost control of his Scottish capital, much as he would later lose his English one.

In November, the protesters stepped up their organization. They claimed that some councillors had encouraged them to elect commissioners to represent their case to the government—ostensibly to disperse the threatening mass of petitioners in Edinburgh. Whatever the truth of this, the king's advocate, Sir Thomas Hope, soon endorsed their action. At any rate, the protesters created a nationwide network of committees, cementing their power locally and centrally. By the spring of 1638 this committee structure became known as the 'Tables'. There were committees in every shire, sending representatives to four coordinating committees in Edinburgh. These four committees, or 'Tables', comprised nobles, shire commissioners, burgh commissioners, and ministers. These in turn elected representatives to a 'fifth Table', which coordinated the whole movement. Despite the careful informality of the term 'Table', the 'fifth Table' was poised to become a provisional government.

Faced by continued governmental intransigence (and continued governmental dithering), the protesters launched the National Covenant. It was first signed by leading nobles in Greyfriars Church, Edinburgh, on 28 February 1638. The National Covenant was to become the manifesto of the Scottish Revolution. It was even described at the time as a 'presbyterian manifesto'.[2] In form it was mainly an agreement between the Scottish people and God, but it was also an agreement between the signatories collectively. It claimed to be no innovation—it was the king who was the innovator—but a renewal of a covenant previously made in 1581 and 1590. The text began with the so-called 'Negative Confession' of 1581, an anti-Catholic statement issued by James VI and his council which was now taken to constitute a 'covenant' on the model of the covenants made between God and the Israelites in the Old Testament. The National Covenant then rehearsed a large number of acts of parliament in favour of 'true' religion, and concluded with a bond among the signatories committing them to stand together to maintain that religion and to oppose anyone who tried to change it. The Covenant also committed the signatories to uphold the king's authority, but everyone understood that this did not involve obedience to the commands of an ill-advised king.

The Covenanters demanded 'free assemblies and parliaments' to deal with the innovations and those responsible.

This was thus a constitutionalist, anti-absolutist, movement. The National Covenant's authors, Alexander Henderson, minister of Leuchars, and Archibald Johnstone of Wariston, an Edinburgh lawyer, were both influenced by the great theorist of Dutch resistance, Johannes Althusius.[3] The sixteenth-century Scottish thinker George Buchanan was also important. The National Covenant could be interpreted in various ways, and the precise relationship between a religious covenant (between God and people) and a secular contract (between king and people) was less important than the general sense that political and religious authority arose from the community rather than descending from the king. The Covenant was a unifying force rather than a divisive one.

It was also a broad-based social movement. The Covenant was signed by everyone who mattered—nobles, lairds, ministers, and burgh councillors—and, in many parishes, by every adult male householder. Naturally the Covenanters sought noble leadership. Early on, prominent roles were taken by those whom Wariston called 'the pryme foor noblemen': the earl of Rothes, and Lords Lindsay, Balmerino, and Loudoun.[4] None of these were great magnates, but they were backed by the earl of Argyll, who was.

Charles insisted correctly that this was not simply a 'religious' revolt. The issue of royal and state authority was bound up with it. The Covenanters had many religious objections to the Prayer Book, but one additional objection was crucial: it was not warranted by 'law', as expressed in acts of the General Assembly and acts of parliament. Their demand for a 'free' General Assembly and a 'free' parliament—'free' meaning not controlled by the king—was thus about who controlled these bodies, and indeed about who controlled Scotland. General Assembly and parliament, and in the meantime the 'fifth Table', would rule. With hindsight, we can see that this was, by now, a revolution.

But this was not clear at the time. Charles had lost control of Scotland for the time being, but surely a compromise settlement was near? Or perhaps the king would choose a more confrontational military option? Advice of all kinds reached him. He chose to pursue conciliation for the time being, but always with the proviso that he would crush the 'rebels' if they did not submit. Charles's chosen conciliator was the marquis of Hamilton, a Scottish magnate who had pursued a career as a courtier and who was associated with the Protestant cause on the Continent. Hamilton was commissioned to negotiate with the Covenanters, and to get them to surrender the covenant in return for vague concessions. However, Charles knew that they were unlikely to do so, and he was already planning a military solution if they did not.

Hamilton's visit to Scotland lasted from June until December. He did his best in the negotiations, and advised the king that he should make further concessions in order to reach a settlement. If the king withdrew the Prayer Book, accepted the National Covenant as legal, and summoned a General Assembly and parliament to sort out the Covenanters' grievances, royal authority might be recovered. It has been suggested that Hamilton himself was more committed to this policy than to the military alternative that the king was pursuing, though this may be only because at the time it was his job to negotiate. He continued in the king's active service once the military option came to the fore, and some of his later advice definitely favoured that option.

Once the king rejected Hamilton's suggested concessions, which he did within days, the negotiations were bound to fail—but Hamilton spun them out as long as possible, since the royal forces would not be ready to march until early 1639. He even persuaded the king to agree to the Covenanters' demand for a General Assembly, by pointing out that if he refused, the Covenanters would hold an assembly anyway. The General Assembly took place in November and December 1638, and made a clean sweep of the crown's recent innovations, as well as some less recent ones, as we shall see.

COVENANTING GRIEVANCES

How had Charles's government managed to provoke such strong and united opposition? The Covenanters' grievances proved to be widespread, manifold, and deep-rooted. This revolt was about far more than the Prayer Book, and indeed about more than religion. It is possible to divide the Covenanters' grievances into three categories: religious, economic, and constitutional. These to some extent overlapped, and different groups emphasized different aspects, but the National Covenant came to symbolize all three.

In religion, the leading Covenanters were committed *iure divino* presbyterians. Bishops had been reintroduced in Scotland by James VI and I, and commanded little support; debate at the 1638 General Assembly was about whether episcopacy should just be 'removed' or whether it should also be 'abjured', implying that it was fundamentally unlawful. The decision went in favour of abjuration, and that line was maintained thereafter. Presbyterianism required parity of ministers, and also called for government of the church by committees of ministers. While the former principle was unquestioned, the latter was sometimes tempered by tendencies that if found in England might have been called 'independency'. General assemblies of 1640, 1641, and 1642 all saw arguments about 'conventicles'—unofficial religious services. In August 1642, those against conventicles were persuaded not to press the matter 'for eschewing offence to the good people of England that favoured those ways'.[5]

One of the biggest grievances, and one that the 1638 General Assembly took care to remove, had been introduced in 1618 by James VI and I. This was the Five Articles of Perth, a group of ceremonies in church worship, of which the most inflammatory was a requirement to kneel at communion. Committed presbyterians regarded kneeling as idolatrous. In seeking to maintain their preferred form of communion service, they had brought into being an underground network of dissident ministers and lay people. Even before Charles's accession in 1625, religious dissent had become organized.

Once the Caroline regime began to unravel, a wide spectrum of economic grievances emerged. These were articulated most clearly in the demands made by the shire commissioners and burgh commissioners—lesser landlords, merchants, and craftsmen—to the parliament of 1639.[6] These demands barely mentioned religion. No doubt religion was thought already to have been taken care of, but the economic grievances were nevertheless real.

The crown had issued numerous monopolies in recent decades, mostly to courtiers and court-connected adventurers; the commercial classes objected strongly to them. Both shire and burgh commissioners wanted all monopolies discharged, and added lists of particularly hated monopolies (tobacco and tanning of leather featured in both groups' lists). The demand for 'ane commissioun for introduceing of manufactories with seting up of forrane and domestik tradis' pointed towards the commercial policy that the Covenanters themselves would develop: a framework of statutory regulation for all those engaged in a given enterprise, with fiscal privileges for enterprises in favoured areas.

Taxation was no more than a muted grievance; Scotland had hitherto been lightly taxed (and the Covenanters were about to introduce sweeping tax increases). One demand, 'That nae taxatioun may be grantit bot in parliament', was constitutional as much as economic. Shire and burgh commissioners also wanted action to facilitate the collection of debts. Aristocratic indebtedness had become prominent in recent decades, and the privy council had tended to protect noble debtors from their creditors. Now the voice of the creditors' lobby could be heard.

One notable economic grievance was absent from the shires' and burghs' demands: Charles I's revocation scheme. This scheme to restructure land tenure was controversial and far-reaching, and many accounts of the Scottish Revolution simply treat the revocation and the Prayer Book as the Covenanters' two main grievances. However, although there is no doubt that the revocation contributed to the Scottish Revolution, care is needed in assessing whose grievance it was. Charles in 1625 had issued a 'revocation' claiming the right to confiscate lands and other rights of church and crown that had been alienated in recent decades, or in some cases at any past date. As well as lands, 'teinds' (tithes) were also significant. The crown had no intention of actually confiscating the lands it claimed, but it did want to use the royal claim as a lever with which to engineer three changes. Firstly, landlords should agree to provide higher stipends for ministers. Secondly, since tithes had become a second form of rent, landlords would be empowered to buy out the rights of tithe-holders in order to simplify landlord–tenant relations. Thirdly, the crown would obtain a 6% annuity from surrendered tithes.

Tithe commutation was a desirable and forward-looking reform; the English did not achieve it for another two centuries. The machinery that the revocation established for this continued to operate until 1925, and the Covenanters had no objection to it; nor did they object to ministers' stipends. Much of the problem with the revocation was not the principle, but the complexities of implementation. Various interest groups stood to gain or lose, and outcomes could vary widely depending on operational decisions such as rates of compulsory purchase. Many aspects of the revocation were seen as desirable in principle, but people were unwilling to trust Charles's government with the practical arrangements. They had to begin by surrendering their possessions to the crown and hoping that they would get them back undamaged.

The Covenanters, nevertheless, did take policy on landholding in some new directions. The revocation had attempted to revive the traditional land tenure of ward and relief (roughly equivalent to knight service in England), which would have facilitated a revival of fiscal feudalism. Instead, after the revolution, landlords were enabled to convert their tenures to feu-ferme, a tenure closer to absolute proprietorship.

In constitutional matters, the Covenanters used representative assemblies—parliament and the General Assembly of the church—to remedy their grievances. Their precocious use of parliament followed the precocious way in which the kings of the early seventeenth century had used their prerogative. Even the earliest petitions against the Prayer Book complained that the book had not been sanctioned by parliament or the General Assembly. In November 1637, Wariston was 'collecting togither a note of the most remarquable acts of Parlement for thir defective tymes', and studying 'the poynt of the Kings praerogative—the kitlest [i.e. trickiest] poynt eyther *in jure* or *facto*, in kirk or staite disputes'.[7] The more intransigent the king became, the more they needed constitutional checks to prevent him returning to his previous policies.

It is sometimes thought that the Covenanters differed from English parliamentarians in believing in the theory of two kingdoms, by which the civil government and church were separately governed and the former did not control the latter. In fact the Covenanters were happy for parliament to govern the church; the National Covenant itself listed many acts of parliament in favour of religion, back to the acts of the Reformation Parliament of 1560. Their objection to episcopacy was combined with an objection to the royal supremacy over the church, which they saw as related and as 'Erastian'; unlike in England, there was no Scottish tradition of using the royal supremacy as a reforming tool. However, Anglo-Scottish differences here were modest; the Scots did believe in *parliamentary* supremacy, which is what mattered to (for instance) English puritans in the Long Parliament.

THE BISHOPS' WARS

Military planning began at court in January 1638, when the earl of Antrim proposed an Irish attack on Scotland. Soon after that, the earl of Nithsdale outlined a broad plan for an Anglo-Irish attack similar to that attempted in 1639 and 1640.[8] This became a mainstream plan with news of the National Covenant, when Charles realized that he had lost control of Scotland—that the Scottish problem was at least a revolt, if not a revolution. He began sending arms to the Scottish royal castles. It was soon realized that English forces could not be mustered before 1639; in the meantime, Hamilton was sent to Scotland at least partly to gain time.

This does not mean that Hamilton's mission was entirely insincere. Throughout, Charles pursued a range of options, from the conciliatory to the aggressive. The latter ideas tended to envisage the punishment of the entire Scottish nation for its disobedience. Among the schemes discussed in Charles's presence in 1638 were to govern

Scotland by a viceroy, as in Ireland (Wentworth's idea), or even to partition the country, annexing the southern counties to England.[9]

Charles's main idea, though military, was less aggressively anti-Scottish. He assumed that if he turned up at the Scottish border with a large enough army, most Scots would recognize that their duty lay in obedience to the king. Resistance would melt away with little or no actual fighting, and it would be possible to isolate and punish the ringleaders of sedition. The king's strategists worked out in detail how their armies would reach Scotland, but did not make plans for the conquest or occupation of Scottish territory.

As for the Covenanters themselves, they were well aware of the king's intentions. They were prepared to fight in their own defence, but they knew from the start that their hopes lay in forging links with sympathetic Englishmen, so as to undermine the English war effort. Wariston wrote a pamphlet appealing to the English people, and specifically to a future English parliament, over the king's head. It was published as war loomed on 4 February 1639, but the Covenanters had already commissioned him to write this 'Information for Ingland' on 10 July 1638.[10] It was soon followed by a 'Remonstrance', published both in English and in Dutch; the argument was becoming international.[11]

The Covenanters also mobilized for war. The Scottish state had not fought any wars for a long time; there was no standing army, no navy, and no royal guard. One or two royal castles were sometimes important, but the king failed to garrison Edinburgh Castle properly in 1639, and the Covenanters captured it without firing a shot. (Restored to the king in the pacification, the Castle was then given a royalist garrison that would inconvenience the Covenanters throughout the fighting of 1640.) In the Lowlands at least, Scottish noblemen no longer had military retinues. A militia existed on paper, but, unlike in England, little had been done to organize or equip it.

However, in other ways, Scotland was well placed to begin military mobilization. The country had long exported fighting men to the Continent—not only common soldiers, but also officers. The officers usually retained links with their homeland, and with the prospect of warfare at home, many experienced officers returned to take part. Some were simply mercenaries pursuing their careers; others were committed Protestants who saw the covenanting wars as an extension of the Continental struggles in which they had fought—often in Swedish service. These men knew how to raise, train, and equip modern regiments, not traditional retinues.

The Scottish state funded the war through rapidly modernizing its fiscal capability. The heaviest taxes would come in 1644, with military intervention in England; this period also saw a completely new tax, the excise. But the groundwork for fiscal revolution was laid in 1639, when a revaluation of landed estates was undertaken, allowing a new direct tax (the 'monthly maintenance') to be collected on current valuations. Previous rulers had sought this fundamental reform in vain.[12] With this financial capability, weapons could be bought on credit. Scotland had a strong mercantile community and a large merchant fleet, with close trading links with the Netherlands, the main suppliers of armaments. The Covenanters spent the latter part of 1638 importing vast amounts of weapons. They had to ship their supplies from the Continent past the king's navy. A few Scottish ships were seized, but the royal blockade seems to have been largely ineffective.

The Covenanters' revolt was of international interest. They themselves could not approach foreign powers officially, but they made numerous informal contacts (including an approach to France in 1639). The Netherlands and Sweden favoured them. Christian IV of Denmark sometimes seemed to favour his nephew Charles, but he allowed ships laden with weapons for Scotland to pass through the Sound. In 1640, Charles offered to pawn Orkney and Shetland to Christian, but Christian was uninterested, taking the view that Charles no longer controlled the islands.[13] The Swiss Protestant churches wrote letters encouraging the Covenanters and reproving Laud for oppressing them.[14]

There were two 'Bishops' Wars'—or perhaps two phases of a single conflict, since both sides recognized the intervening truce as temporary. The Covenanters began open military activity in February 1639—not at the Anglo-Scottish border, but in the north-east of Scotland, where royalist supporters were mobilizing under the nominal leadership of the marquis of Huntly. Huntly was soon captured, and the royalists eventually recognized that their position was hopeless. Most of these manoeuvres were bloodless, but on 10 May, Sir George Gordon of Gight and other royalists attempted to seize Towie House, held by the covenanting Lord Fraser and master of Forbes. David Prat, Gordon's servant, was shot and killed—the first person to die in the wars that would soon engulf all three kingdoms.[15]

Another potential military theatre was the west of Scotland, where the Gaelic-speaking Highland clans were more organized for war than Lowland nobles (though only lightly armed). The two most powerful clans, the Campbells and MacDonalds, had long been rivals. The Campbells, led by the earls of Argyll, had allied themselves with the Lowland government and gained numerous territories from the disunited MacDonalds. One branch of the MacDonalds, meanwhile, had established themselves in nearby Ulster, where they were led by the earl of Antrim. Antrim's father had made several attempts to recover some of the family's Scottish properties, and throughout the western Highlands there were resentful MacDonalds who would welcome an opportunity to humble the Campbells. However, instead of mobilizing them, Antrim tried with little success to raise a more conventional Irish army in 1639, while in 1640 his efforts were supplemented by an army raised by the viceroy, Strafford. These armies never reached Scotland, but they forced the Covenanters to retain troops in the west, and confirmed the Campbells as firm supporters of the Covenant. They also led the Covenanters to contemplate pre-emptive invasion of Ireland—something that would soon become a reality.

The Covenanters assembled their main army in the eastern Borders in May 1639. From their base at Duns Law they could command the invasion routes from the south. But the invasion never came; the royal forces were not up to it. Throughout both Bishops' Wars, the Covenanters had better morale, better strategy, and better intelligence. They had weaknesses, sometimes serious, of recruitment and supply, but they successfully masked these from the royalists, and even persuaded them that Scottish forces were larger than they were. An eclipse of the sun on 22 May was said to be God's warning against continuing the war, but the main reason why Charles agreed to negotiate in June was that his demoralized commanders feared defeat. The resulting 'pacification of Berwick' (18 June) held for the rest of the year, but both sides expected fighting to resume.

Before war broke out again, though, two parliaments were held. In England, the 'Short Parliament' (13 April to 5 May 1640) refused Charles's demands for war finance. In Scotland, the Covenanters' parliament was even shorter (2–11 June 1640), but dramatically successful. It assembled despite the king's attempts to forbid it to do so, and enacted a sweeping and revolutionary constitutional programme. The religious settlement of 1638–9 was confirmed. A 'triennial act' (soon to be copied by the English) enacted that parliaments were to be held every three years at least, whether the king wished it or not. A committee of estates—twelve members from each of the three estates, plus three judges from the court of session—was established to coordinate the executive government of the country in between meetings of parliament. This standing body effectively replaced the privy council. Finally, the 1640 parliament made military preparations.

The fighting in the summer of 1640 was more serious than in 1639. Both sides sought a decisive victory. The royal army, however, assembled tardily in Yorkshire, far south of the Scottish border, and showed no sign of invading Scotland. The Covenanters thus took a daring decision. Until now they had presented their war as defensive, and insisted that they had no quarrel with England. But they could not keep their army together indefinitely. Negotiations with the king early in 1640 had enabled them to make contact with dissident English politicians, who encouraged them to believe that Charles's English regime would collapse internally if discredited. Indeed, the fiasco of the Short Parliament had already revealed Charles's English unpopularity. So the Covenanters' army boldly invaded England on 20 August. On the 28th the Scots stormed across the River Tyne at Newburn, driving away an English force that tried to bar their crossing. As the English retreated, the triumphant Scots captured Newcastle on the 30th.

The royal defeat in the Bishops' Wars was comprehensive, and twofold. One aspect of it was simply that the Scots had not submitted to the king. Confronted by a royal army, the more reluctant Covenanters should have defected from the 'rebel' cause, leaving the ringleaders isolated; at least, that had been Charles's hope. Yet the Covenanters had remained united and uncompromising. They had faced their king in arms, and had got away with it.

The other aspect of the royal defeat was that even once the Scots had clearly invaded English territory, the English had not rallied to the crown. Instead the Scots succeeded in winning more open friends among Charles's English opponents. After the capture of Newcastle, this led the Covenanters to take another daring decision. They established their army in the town—the main supply port for London's coal—and made clear that they were staying until they achieved a favourable settlement. Londoners would have a cold winter unless the Scots were accommodated.

In negotiations at Ripon (2–26 October), Scottish and English commissioners agreed a temporary cessation of hostilities, and that England would pay the Scottish army £850 sterling per day from 16 October until a full settlement was reached. Since such a settlement would take time, and since Charles did not have £850 per day, this necessitated an English parliament that could authorize taxation. Charles had already (on 24 September) issued the summons for what became the 'Long Parliament', and it assembled on 3 November; the Scottish victory meant that he could not dissolve this parliament until he had satisfied the Scots. They would take some satisfying.

THE TREATY OF LONDON

From a Scottish point of view, the opening months of England's Long Parliament were taken up with negotiating the peace settlement that became known as the Treaty of London. Previous negotiations had been between king and Covenanters; this time, the Covenanters insisted on negotiating with English parliamentary commissioners, thus formally involving the English parliament. They demanded royal confirmation of their religious and constitutional settlement of 1638–40, reparations for war damage, punishment of so-called 'incendiaries', and arrangements for ensuring that the settlement would be a lasting one. This last point, necessarily vague, entailed Anglo-Scottish measures to ensure that the king would no longer be able to use England to attack Scotland. Effectively the Covenanters aimed to use the negotiations, and their army's continued presence, to entrench the power of the king's English opponents.

After protracted negotiations, the Treaty of London was settled in the summer of 1641. The king agreed to publish the acts of the 1640 Scottish parliament in his own name, thus accepting its radical settlement. This also indicated that the royal *assent* was no longer required to acts of parliament; Scotland henceforth would be governed by parliament, with the king lacking even a veto power. The Scots received financial reparations (called 'brotherly assistance'). A standing Anglo-Scottish parliamentary commission, the conservators of the peace, was established to coordinate the two realms and prevent disputes between them. The Scots' vague demand for a lasting settlement gradually turned into a set of proposals for far-reaching changes in England—especially for unity of religion with Scotland—and they did not achieve this, nor did they get the 'incendiaries' punished (a lower priority for them). Nor did they obtain free trade between Scotland and England—a demand added to their original ones. Eventually ratified by both sides in July and August, the treaty was thus a genuine compromise between differing interests. Following it, the army occupying Newcastle returned to Scotland in August, most of it being then disbanded.

Charles himself continued his wooing of the Covenanters in April by announcing a visit to Scotland in person; he eventually arrived in August and stayed until October. The most optimistic scenario for the king's visit was that he would persuade the Covenanters to support him in overthrowing the English parliament, since they had seen in the Treaty of London that English parliamentarians, even radical ones, did not share the whole of the Covenanters' religious agenda. This was unlikely, of course, and it did not happen. What was slightly more likely was that the visit would win *some* friends in Scotland, and that this would split the Covenanters or at least distract them from further interference in England. Charles already envisaged civil war in England, and it was imperative for him to prevent the Covenanters' military machine from swinging into action on parliament's side.

During this visit, Charles made some of the concessions that he had not made in the Treaty of London. His first task was to attend a parliament that was ostentatiously stage-managed by the Covenanters. Particularly damaging for royal power was the introduction of parliamentary control over appointments of officers of state, privy councillors, and judges in the court of session. Charles argued against this for a month but had to give in. His bargaining strength was further weakened by a plot among royalist army officers to arrest the leading Covenanters; the 'Incident', as it became known when discovered in October, made it harder for moderate Covenanters to trust the king.

In October, news arrived of the outbreak of rebellion in Ireland. One of the few things on which king and Covenanters agreed was that a Scottish army should be sent to counter the rebellion and to defend the Anglo-Scottish 'plantation' in Ulster. Negotiations took until July 1642, partly because the English parliament was involved as well as the king, but the Covenanters eventually sent an army to Ulster, and the English parliament agreed to pay for it. The fortunes of the Scottish Revolution now depended on Irish developments as well as English ones.

THE SOLEMN LEAGUE AND COVENANT

By virtually surrendering Scotland to the Covenanters, Charles had hoped to avoid provoking them to throw in their lot with the English parliament. With the outbreak of the English Civil War in August 1642, his strategy may have seemed successful; the Covenanters busied themselves with their Ulster army but did not seek to intervene in England. However, after the battle of Edgehill (23 October), the English parliament began to feel more need of Scottish help. They sent an agent to Scotland in November, setting off a long and complex Scottish debate. With hindsight, the logic of the Covenanters' actions is clear: if they let the king win in England, he would attack them next. But the Covenanters had been so successful that this was less clear at the time; the king's friends could argue that he had accepted their revolution in 1641. Moreover, the terms of any intervention remained to be discussed.

The 1641 settlement had done one thing for Scottish royalists: it had revived the privy council, with leading Covenanters being given positions on it. However, Hamilton and several of his friends were also on the council, and Hamilton now used his position to play a series of delaying cards. In January 1643, he and Traquair organized the so-called 'Cross Petition', professing to support the National Covenant but opposing intervention in England. This gathered enough support to distract the Covenanters for some time. Hamilton was constructing a group of moderate Covenanters satisfied with the 1641 settlement and moderate royalists prepared to acquiesce in that settlement, excluding more notorious royalists like Huntly.

However, Hamilton had too few supporters to sustain this effort for long. Eventually, on 12 May, the Covenanters summoned a convention of estates—a parliament in almost all but name, and with the advantage of assembling quickly. It met on 22 June. In between these two dates, Hamilton's coalition-building efforts were blown away by the revelation of the Antrim Plot, a scheme to invade Scotland from Antrim's Irish estates. Hamilton's manoeuvres had had some success, and he may even have stopped the Covenanters sending an army into England in the autumn of 1643, but he could do no more than delay the inevitable.

The convention made clear within days that it was ready to negotiate a treaty with the English parliament. Negotiations began then in earnest, and took until August. The English had seen in the Treaty of London that the Scots had ideas about how to reform England. Some of these ideas were welcome—the Scottish army in Newcastle had purged the notorious Arminian decorations from Durham Cathedral—but others were, at best, divisive within England—not all the English wanted to abolish episcopacy. However, that was not the Scots' problem at this stage.

The main part of the treaty that emerged was called the Solemn League and Covenant. This took the form of a declaration by the citizens of England, Scotland, and Ireland. They would preserve the church of Scotland, and reform the churches of England and Ireland 'according to the Word of God, and the example of the best reformed Churches' (this example was understood to mean Scotland). This reform would include the abolition of episcopacy. They would uphold the 'rights and privileges of the Parliaments, and the liberties of the kingdoms', and 'preserve and defend the King's Majesty's person and authority'. Along with this declaration, which was adopted by the Scottish and English parliaments, the two parliaments made a military and financial agreement by which the Scots would send an army to England and the English parliament would pay for it.

In a much-quoted phrase, Robert Baillie wrote: 'The English were for a civill League, we for a religious Covenant.'[16] This has often been used to explain why the Solemn League and Covenant failed (assuming we think that it did fail—but that is another question), the idea being that the two parties' expectations differed. However, Baillie's remark is more useful in focusing attention on their different *needs*. The English needed a Scottish army: the Scots needed guarantees that their army would be used to establish a congenial regime. Both sides understood this. The 'civill League' provided the army: the 'religious Covenant' provided the necessary ideological guarantees. The Solemn League and Covenant was a compromise, partly between different English interests, but not an unworkable one.

In September 1643, the Covenanters sent a Scottish garrison to Berwick, the first instalment of their military assistance to the English parliament. Meanwhile, the royalists were in disarray. Hamilton and other royalists met at Kelso but decided that prospects for an uprising were hopeless. Hamilton himself, and his brother the earl of Lanark, returned to England in December, only for the king to arrest them for insufficient zeal in the royal cause. Lanark soon escaped—and would spend the next two years work-ing for the Covenanters. The Solemn League and Covenant was thus almost as consen-sual, at least in Scotland, as the National Covenant. It did not divide the politicians into two camps, in the way that (for instance) the Grand Remonstrance of 1641 had done in England. When the Army of the Solemn League and Covenant finally crossed the border into England in January 1644, its march had the support of most politically active Scots.

CONCLUSIONS

An assessment of the Scottish Revolution may begin with the problem of allegiance. This in turn raises a second problem: there has been little attempt to understand *royal-ist* allegiance. There have been numerous works explaining the Covenanters, beginning with the unsurpassed narrative of David Stevenson;[17] but these have usually taken royal-ist failure for granted. An analysis of royalist failure may in fact shed light on covenant-ing success also.

Scottish royalists seem largely to have been nobles of one kind or another.[18] This impression may be modified by future research, but those lower down the social scale—lairds and especially burgesses—seem more generally to have been committed Covenanters.[19] Since lairds were landlords with similar interests to nobles, the greater royalism of the latter may be explicable through their closer connections with the royal court.[20]

Royalist nobles displayed a range of attitudes. Hamilton, the moderate coalition-builder, has received more attention than some.[21] Along with him, Traquair was essen-tially a fixer rather than an ideologue. Huntly was the magnate of the north-east, which used to be seen as a 'royalist' area—but the north-east was divided, in the manner of most English counties, so that Huntly could never control it outright.[22] And Hamilton and Huntly were not the only kinds of royalist. We should pay more attention to people like Nithsdale, a Catholic courtier who had risen to favour as an associate of Buckingham. He regularly urged drastic action against the Covenanters, and, as we have seen, first conceived the strategy of the Bishops' Wars.

These various 'royalists' could hardly ever work together. Royalist disunity was exacer-bated by the defection to the king of the earl of Montrose, a flamboyant early covenanter who became an open royalist by at least 1642. Unlike Nithsdale, whose Catholicism put him firmly at odds with the Covenanters' religious stance, Montrose always insisted that he accepted the National Covenant and opposed episcopacy. Nevertheless he became a militant royalist, arguing constantly against Hamilton's serpentine dealings. When the Hamiltons were arrested in December 1643, it was at Montrose's prompting.[23] By early 1644, the future of Scottish royalism lay with Montrose—not that this was much of a future.

Royalist problems in Scotland can partly be explained by the exigencies of royal-ist strategy. The king was usually either attacking Scotland from outside—in 1639 and

1640—or conciliating the Covenanters—in 1638, and again from September 1640 to June 1643, when his wish to re-establish control of England took priority over his aims for Scotland. Attacking Scotland from outside made it difficult to provide leadership for indigenous royalists. Conciliating the Covenanters was never more than a temporary objective, but it usually took precedence over rallying royalists. Hamilton's efforts at coalition-building were hampered by the fact (of which he was well aware) that such a coalition was rarely more than a plan B. He could not rally royalists openly, because it was imperative not to provoke the Covenanters.

Royalist disunity contrasts strongly with covenanting unity. The Covenanters formed a successful coalition, with moderates like the earl of Dunfermline (a gentleman of the royal bedchamber) able to work with radicals like Balmerino or Wariston. The unity of the coalition held, from its beginnings in 1637, into 1644 and beyond. A commitment to presbyterianism, coupled with a commitment to parliamentary government, underpinned the movement's unity; the movement could also accommodate sectional interests like the burghs' wish for congenial commercial policies.

Much of the foregoing analysis has been influenced by a 'three kingdoms' perspective. However, if not used with care, 'three kingdoms' analysis tends to divide the participants into 'the Scots', 'the English', and 'the Irish'. Yet some Scots had more in common with some English (for instance) than they did with other Scots. And the agendas that they pursued were rarely simply national. The Covenanters' English and Irish policies were not 'foreign' policies, but extensions of their aims at home. An understanding of the Covenanters' English strategy, in particular, depends on a realization that not all of their programme was equally urgent; they could be flexible about some of it. They had a broad international vision. The final clause of the Solemn League and Covenant envisaged that other godly nations might join it—perhaps the United Netherlands or Sweden—and that it might be a means to aid other oppressed Protestants—Baillie mentioned concern for 'the Bohemians and Palatines'.[24] These matters were important, but they could wait. In 1644, the Covenanters' hopes were high, and it remained to be seen how much of their broader programme they could achieve.

NOTES

1. *Register of the Privy Council of Scotland*, 2nd ser., VI, 483–4, 509; Sir Thomas Hope of Craighall, *Diary, 1633–1645*, ed. Thomas Thomson (Bannatyne Club, 1843), 64.
2. James Gordon, *History of Scots Affairs, 1637–1641*, 3 vols., ed. Joseph Robertson and George Grub (Spalding Club, 1841), I, 81.
3. Edward J. Cowan, 'The Making of the National Covenant', in John Morrill (ed.), *The Scottish National Covenant in its British Context* (Edinburgh, 1990), 68–89, at 78–82.
4. Sir Archibald Johnston of Wariston, *Diary, 1632–1639*, ed. George M. Paul (Scottish History Society, 1911), 318.
5. David Stevenson, *The Scottish Revolution, 1637–1644: The Triumph of the Covenanters* (Newton Abbot, 1973; reprinted Edinburgh, 2003), 251.
6. *Aberdeen Council Letters*, II (1634–1644), ed. Louise B. Taylor (Oxford, 1950), 140–8. All quotations are from this passage.

7. Wariston, *Diary*, 275.
8. Peter Donald, *An Uncounselled King: Charles I and the Scottish Troubles, 1637–1641* (Cambridge, 1990), 71.
9. Stevenson, *Scottish Revolution*, 100.
10. Wariston, *Diary*, 361; [Archibald Johnstone of Wariston,] *An Information to All Good Christians Within the Kingdome of England* (Edinburgh, 1639; STC (2nd edn.) 21905).
11. Donald, *Uncounselled King*, 131.
12. Laura A. M. Stewart, 'Fiscal Revolution and State Formation in Mid-Seventeenth-Century Scotland', *Historical Research*, 84 (2011): 443–69.
13. Steve Murdoch, 'Scotland, Scandinavia and the Bishops' Wars, 1638–40', in Allan I. Macinnes and Jane Ohlmeyer (eds.), *The Stuart Kingdoms in the Seventeenth Century: Awkward Neighbours* (Dublin, 2002), 113–34.
14. James K. Cameron, 'The Swiss and the Covenant', in G. W. S. Barrow (ed.), *The Scottish Tradition* (Edinburgh, 1974), 155–63.
15. Stevenson, *Scottish Revolution*, 147.
16. Robert Baillie, *Letters and Journals, 1637–1662*, 3 vols., ed. David Laing (Bannatyne Club, 1841–2), II, 90.
17. Stevenson, *Scottish Revolution*. For recent overviews see David Stevenson, 'Charles I, the Covenants and Cromwell, 1625–1660', in Bob Harris and Alan R. MacDonald (eds.), *Scotland: The Making and Unmaking of the Nation, c.1100–1707*, vol. II: *Early Modern Scotland, c.1500–1707* (Dundee, 2007), 36–55; Julian Goodare, 'The Scottish Revolution', in Sharon Adams and Julian Goodare (eds.), *Scotland in the Age of Two Revolutions* (Woodbridge, 2014), 79–96; Allan I. Macinnes, 'The "Scottish Moment", 1638–1645', in J. S. A. Adamson (ed.), *The English Civil War: Conflict and Contexts, 1640–1649* (Basingstoke, 2009), 125–52.
18. Keith M. Brown, 'Courtiers and Cavaliers: Service, Anglicization and Loyalty among the Royalist Nobility', in Morrill (ed.), *Scottish National Covenant*, 155–192.
19. John R. Young, 'The Scottish Parliament and the Covenanting Revolution: The Emergence of a Scottish Commons', in John R. Young (ed.), *Celtic Dimensions of the British Civil Wars* (Edinburgh, 1997), 164–184; David Stevenson, 'The Burghs and the Scottish Revolution', in Michael Lynch (ed.), *The Early Modern Town in Scotland* (London, 1987), 167–91.
20. For a study making this point from allegiance in 1621 see Julian Goodare, 'The Scottish Parliament of 1621', *Historical Journal*, 38 (1995): 29–51.
21. John Scally, 'Counsel in Crisis: James, Third Marquis of Hamilton and the Bishops' Wars, 1638–1640', in Young (ed.), *Celtic Dimensions of the British Civil Wars*, 18–34; Donald, *Uncounselled King*, chap. 3.
22. Barry Robertson, 'The Covenanting North of Scotland, 1638–1647', *Innes Review*, 61 (2010): 24–51.
23. Edward J. Cowan, *Montrose: For Covenant and King* (London, 1977), 144.
24. Baillie, *Letters and Journals*, II, 82.

FURTHER READING

Adams, Sharon and Julian Goodare (eds.), *Scotland in the Age of Two Revolutions* (Woodbridge, 2014).

Cowan, Edward J., *Montrose: For Covenant and King* (London, 1977).

Donald, Peter, *An Uncounselled King: Charles I and the Scottish Troubles, 1637–1641* (Cambridge, 1990).

Furgol, Edward M., *A Regimental History of the Covenanting Armies, 1639–1651* (Edinburgh, 1990).

Goodare, Julian, *State and Society in Early Modern Scotland* (Oxford, 1999).

Lee, Maurice, *The Road to Revolution: Scotland under Charles I, 1635–1637* (Urbana, IL, 1985).

Macinnes, Allan I., *The British Confederate: Archibald Campbell, Marquess of Argyll, c.1607–1661* (Edinburgh, 2011).

Macinnes, Allan I., 'The 'Scottish Moment', 1638–1645', in J. S. A. Adamson (ed.), *The English Civil War: Conflict and Contexts, 1640–1649* (Basingstoke, 2009), 125–152.

Makey, Walter, *The Church of the Covenant, 1637–1651* (Edinburgh, 1979).

Morrill, John (ed.), *The Scottish National Covenant in its British Context* (Edinburgh, 1990).

Stevenson, David, *Scottish Covenanters and Irish Confederates* (Belfast, 1981).

Stevenson, David, *The Scottish Revolution, 1637–1644: The Triumph of the Covenanters* (Newton Abbot, 1973; reprinted Edinburgh, 2003).

Stevenson, David, *Union, Revolution, and Religion in 17th-Century Scotland* (Aldershot, 1997).

Stewart, Laura A. M., 'Fiscal Revolution and State Formation in Mid-Seventeenth-Century Scotland', *Historical Research*, 84 (2011): 443–469.

Stewart, Laura A. M., *Urban Politics and the British Civil Wars: Edinburgh, 1617–1653* (Leiden, 2006).

Young, John R., *The Scottish Parliament, 1639–1661: A Political and Constitutional Analysis* (Edinburgh, 1996).

CHAPTER 4

....

THE COLLAPSE OF ROYAL POWER IN ENGLAND, 1637–1642

....

RICHARD CUST

ENGLAND IN 1637

ENGLAND in 1637 did not look like a country which was on the brink of civil war.[1] It had a settled, well-established monarchical regime and, in contrast to much of continental Europe which was blighted by the Thirty Years War, it appeared to be an oasis of peace and order. The nation had been involved in the war between 1624 and 1629, and this brought with it all the expense and disruption that wars at this time incurred, particularly those which were unsuccessful. But in 1629 Charles had signed peace treaties with France and Spain, and since then had stuck steadfastly to a policy of peace, in spite of continuing pressures to re-enter the war on the Protestant side. With peace had come the end of parliaments. At first this appeared to be an interim measure, as the crown sought to defuse the political opposition and popular discontents which had surfaced in the House of Commons in 1629. But gradually the king's determination not to summon another parliament until it could be demonstrated that the 'ill affected spirits' had been removed hardened into a settled conviction that he was better advised to rule without it. Ministers became wary of raising the possibility lest they antagonize him. Lord Keeper Coventry who was unwise enough to do so in 1633 was said to have been 'so rattled' by Charles 'that he is now the most pliable man in England and all thoughts of parliament are quite out of his pate'.[2] At a time when summoning and dissolving parliaments was entirely at royal discretion there seemed to be little prospect that another one would meet in Charles I's lifetime. The Personal Rule had already lasted for eight years and it appeared unlikely that it would end any time soon.

The policies adopted by the crown during the Personal Rule were often unpopular but not to the point where they seemed likely to bring about the collapse of royal government. As Conrad Russell has remarked, the *State Papers Domestic*, which collected together much of the government's correspondence, is 'not the record of a regime which was sitting on a powder keg'.[3] There is evidence of foot-dragging and discontent over government directives, and exasperation at the unwillingness of puritans to comply with Laudian reforms in the church; but, in general, it gives the appearance of a government in relatively good working order. The collection of ship money, the most contentious tax of the period, is a case in point. It provoked a good deal of grumbling and discontent, but most of this was focused, ostensibly, on the ways in which the tax was rated at a local level. Few were prepared to express open opposition to the principle of the king collecting a tax without the consent of parliament, at least before the split judgment in Hampden's case, early in 1638, made such expressions more acceptable. However, even after this, over 90% of the money assessed was still eventually collected, a success rate which compared very favourably with most early modern taxes.[4] The willingness of local gentry to continue to cooperate with the privy council in keeping the wheels of government turning was epitomized in the appointment of Oliver Cromwell as a justice of the peace for the Isle of Ely in 1638.[5] Cromwell was a puritan and no lover of the crown's policies; but he acknowledged that in the interests of order and stability it was important for gentlemen to cooperate in the processes of government, and that in doing so they gained a good deal in terms of personal honour and reputation.

In matters of religion and the church there was always much greater potential for the open expression of opposition because many puritans saw it as an article of faith that they should speak out against policies which they considered 'popish' and ungodly. There was plenty for them to protest against. From the late 1620s, Charles, in alliance with Archbishop Laud and a group of anti-Calvinist bishops, had been reforming the Church of England to remove Calvinist and puritan practices and steer it in a high-church, 'Anglican', direction. The afternoon sermons and lectures favoured by the godly had come under attack; puritan Sabbath observance had been challenged by the Book of Sports; St Paul's and other cathedral churches had been refurbished to emphasize 'the Beauty of Holiness'; and by 1637, in many dioceses, communion tables were being moved to the east end of parish churches and railed off to emphasize the authority of priesthood and the importance of sacramental religion. There was plenty of opposition to these measures, but it was fragmented and disorganized and the regime was generally able to silence it with harsh, well-publicized punishments. By 1637 some puritans were beginning to despair altogether of changing the direction of policy and contemplating emigration to the more congenial religious surroundings of New England. These included peers like Viscount Saye and Sele and Lord Brooke, whose readiness to give up their estates and political power in England was a measure of their alienation from the regime.[6]

The systematic opposition to many of the government's policies mounted by individuals like Saye and Brooke demonstrated that the appearance of general acquiescence in the Personal Rule was deceptive. Where it is possible to eavesdrop on the private thoughts and opinions of contemporaries, in a source like the diary of the puritan steward of Northampton, Robert Woodford, there is plenty of evidence that support for the regime was already being hollowed out. Woodford was particularly alarmed by the Laudian altar policy which he saw as the symptom of a spiritual malaise which threatened to bring God's providential judgements down upon the nation. He was also beginning to harbour even more damaging doubts as to whether the king, surrounded by Laudian bishops and 'evil counsellors', was still firm in his commitment to the Protestant religion.[7] Others were similarly apprehensive of the influence of Charles's Catholic queen, Henrietta Maria, and popish advisers at court, of the failure to re-enter the Thirty Years War in support of the Protestant cause and of the disregard of traditional 'liberties' and the rule of law. Above all there was a general desire for a meeting of parliament, which could give voice to these discontents and carry out its traditional role of counselling the king and securing the redress of grievances. However, while Charles persisted in his determination to rule without it, there was little that could be done. Most Englishmen regarded a parliament as the only legitimate forum for expressing open discontent with the crown's policies. Anything else risked being construed as resistance or rebellion which they had been brought up to believe was a sin against God and the ultimate danger to the settled monarchical government which was the main guarantor of order and stability. Without a parliament it would be very hard for opposition to find a focus or secure general acceptance.

THE PRAYER BOOK REBELLION
AND THE BISHOPS' WARS

What transformed the situation was not events in England, but in Scotland. It was the Covenanter rebellion in 1638, prompted by the introduction of an English-style Prayer Book which ultimately left Charles I with no alternative but to summon parliament and bring to an end his Personal Rule. The origins and course of the Scottish rebellion have been discussed in Julian Goodare's essay in this volume. Here it is worth evaluating the contribution made to the crisis by Charles's own mistakes and political misjudgements, which were to be recurring themes in the events leading to the outbreak of civil war in England in 1642.

The formal introduction of a new English-style Prayer Book in Scotland in July 1637, on the advice of Archbishop Laud and the Scottish bishops, took place against a background of widespread alienation from Charles's rule and led to bitter protests. But the king's own interventions made the situation considerably worse. His refusal to acknowledge that there was anything in the Prayer Book that was contrary to 'true religion' hamstrung the efforts of his Scottish councillors to broker a compromise; while his determination to see Scottish resistance as a humiliating rejection of his monarchical authority—on one occasion telling his chief Scottish adviser the marquis of Hamilton that while the National Covenant was in force 'I have no more power in Scotland than a duke of Venice, which I will rather die than suffer'—raised the stakes to the point at which armed conflict became almost inevitable. The impact of his political incompetence was, perhaps, best summed up in the proclamation he issued in February 1638, declaring that he, and not his bishops or councillors, was responsible for the Prayer Book and that anyone who opposed it would be regarded as a traitor. This led directly to the signing of the National Covenant because it forced opponents of the Prayer Book to recognize that they were now challenging their monarch directly, and that for reasons of self-preservation they must attempt to unite the nation behind them. The consequence of Charles's interventions, then, was to turn a limited protest into a full-blown rebellion.[8]

His management of the Bishops' Wars was equally unsuccessful. The king lost his best chance of defeating the Scots when he was tricked out of giving them battle at Kelso on 4–5 June 1639. He probably had the larger and better-equipped army, but the Scots were able to bluff him into retreating by drawing up their forces in shallow formation, with extra sets of colours, to convince him that their force was much bigger than was actually the case.[9] The Treaty of Berwick which followed gave the Scots time to organize themselves militarily and consolidate their support inside England with some astute appeals to public opinion.

The most momentous political event in England at this time was the summoning of the Short Parliament in April 1640. This was a straightforward consequence of the king's determination to continue the war against the Scots. Charles himself was still unenthusiastic about a parliament; but his councillors, including the earl of Strafford who was now in charge of the war effort, were adamant that this was the only way to raise the requisite funds and secure a political mandate to demonstrate that the nation was behind the war. However, the parliament completely failed to deliver. MPs came to Westminster determined to secure redress of grievances and if the crown was to secure supply it would have to make substantial concessions. But Charles stuck stubbornly to the view that, in the face of rebellion in his northern kingdom, his subjects were duty bound to assist him. The first two weeks of the assembly produced stalemate, as the Commons insisted on putting redress before supply and Charles tried to kick-start discussion of subsidies by introducing the supply motion in the House of Lords. It was not until early May that he came up with the concrete offer of concessions that MPs sought, a proposal for abandoning ship money in return for twelve subsidies. But this was too little too late. The Commons, egged on by a small group of MPs led by John Pym, who had been engaged in treasonable collaboration with the Scots, had gone past the point at which it was willing to compromise. Negotiations collapsed and the parliament was dissolved.[10]

The failure of the Short Parliament left the war effort against the Scots in disarray. The lack of funds and failure to secure a political mandate ensured that the English army which assembled in the north in August 1640 was divided and poorly equipped, with many of the pressed levies on the verge of mutiny. It succumbed to a better organized and more united Scottish force at the first taste of action, in the battle of Newburn on 28 August. The Scots then rapidly occupied Durham and Northumberland and at the Treaty of Ripon negotiated a payment of £850 a day to support their forces. With defeat in battle Charles had failed what was still regarded as the ultimate test of a monarch. Bereft of political support and with his finances in a state of collapse, he had little alternative but to summon the Long Parliament.

THE LONG PARLIAMENT AND THE COLLAPSE OF ROYAL POWER IN ENGLAND

Scottish victory in the Bishops Wars and the meeting of another parliament transformed English politics. The most significant change was that a rebellion had taken place against the monarch and had succeeded. This broke the taboo on armed resistance to the monarch which was one of the most significant constraints operating in favour of the status quo. The very fact of success destroyed the belief, assiduously cultivated by the Tudors, that rebellion always failed. Moreover the Scots had rebelled in the name of religion and conscience and had apparently met with divine approval for their actions. All this served to promote armed resistance as a legitimate response to dealing with a tyrannical ruler thus opening up a whole range of new political possibilities.

The other critical consequence of the Scots victory was to provide the king's opponents with a coercive power which they had previously lacked. Since the decline of baronial affinities in the early sixteenth century those who sought to challenge royal policy had not possessed the means to take on the monarch in armed conflict. They could put pressure on him by withholding supply and attacking his ministers in parliament, and they could bring influence to bear at court; but, in the last resort, they could not force him to do anything. This situation was changed by the presence of the Scots, in control of what was unquestionably the most potent military force in Britain and willing to use it to promote the interests of their English allies. In the short term this deprived Charles of the power to dissolve parliament at will which had long been one of the monarch's greatest political assets. If he did not like the way things were developing in a parliament he could simply call off the game and start again. Often the mere threat of this was enough to curtail a parliament's freedom of action. But now, with the Scots threatening to march south unless the king kept up payments of £850 a day, dissolution was no longer an option.[11]

In the longer term the Scots army guaranteed the security of their English allies and gave them the room to manoeuvre for a settlement on their terms. This group, which soon became known as 'the Junto', had come to the fore in the immediate aftermath of the Bishops Wars when they sponsored the Twelve Peers Petition which condemned the policies of the 1630s and called for a parliament to remedy the nation's ills. Led by Pym in the Commons and his allies Saye and Brooke, and the earls of Bedford, Essex, and Warwick in the Lords, this became the most dynamic force in English politics over the following months. Their collusion with the Scots during 1639 and 1640 left them wide open to a charge of treason and there was every likelihood that if Charles could turn the tables he would move against them. This forced them into a high-stakes political game in which they sought to impose a political settlement which would guarantee their personal security. In the terminology used by John Adamson in his ground-breaking study of 'the Noble Revolt', they sought to 'Venetianize' the king by removing his power to appoint councillors, to summon or dissolve parliament, or to veto legislation. They also sought to bring about radical reform in the church by removing the bishops, partly to appease their Scots allies who blamed bishops for the Prayer Book and partly to promote their own puritan agenda. Charles was never likely to accept such reforms willingly, as his bitter observations on the authority of a 'duke of Venice' indicated. But the Junto could not afford to back down and over the following months national politics revolved around the struggle to make their settlement stick.[12]

In these circumstances, the options open to Charles were extremely limited. His one major asset was that he could not be removed. The Junto would probably have liked to depose him had this been feasible; but there was no obvious candidate to replace him which meant that any final solution to the crisis would have to involve the king which gave him the power of veto over its terms.[13] In other respects, however, his position was very weak. His loss of military power and the power to dissolve parliament left him with only two serious possibilities if he wanted to regain the political initiative.

The first of these was to mount some sort of coup against the parliamentary leadership. This certainly appealed to him. He had few qualms about using force in dealing with those he regarded as traitors and rebels; and his whole analysis of the crisis was posited on the assumption that the 'multitude' had been led astray by a few 'malignant spirits' whose removal would herald a return to normality. In practical terms it was also viable. If he could secure control of the Tower of London this would give him command of London, and he still had the remnants of an army in the north. As we shall see, he was tempted to try this option on more than one occasion during the Long Parliament.

The alternative was to endeavour to divide his enemies and build his own royal party. With most of the political nation united against the Scots war and the policies of the Personal Rule this may not have looked viable in late 1640. But once the Junto started to implement their reforms there was always the likelihood of a royalist backlash. The Great Council of Peers which had met at York in September–October 1640 to negotiate a way out of the Scottish crisis had revealed that a majority of noblemen felt some sympathy for Charles's plight and were determined to maintain the traditional status quo. Any measures to unduly restrict the royal prerogative or interfere with the structures of the Church of England were likely to meet with their disapproval. The other main element in the political equation, public opinion and the engagement of the gentry and middling sort, was similarly volatile. For the time being they were united in favour of reform and backed the Junto's agenda to the hilt. But as the implications of this started to become apparent, particularly with the upsurge in radical puritanism, divisions would inevitably emerge. There was fertile ground, then, on which Charles could build a royalist party. However, this would require a degree of political skill, restraint, and judgement on his part that during the Scottish crisis had been singularly lacking.[14]

The story of the collapse of royal power in England up to the outbreak of civil war in the summer of 1642 was largely the story of the struggle between the king and his opponents in the Junto to make their version of a political settlement stick. Both sought to draw on the support of wider constituencies: the peers in the House of Lords, Commons MPs and the wider publics of local gentry and the politically informed middling sort, and, indeed, the Scots who from the spring of 1641 also started to divide. For much of the time the peerage also sought to perform its traditional role of building bridges between crown and people. But the heart of the process was the contest between the crown and the Junto.

During the early months of the Long Parliament, up to March 1641, the Junto and their Scots allies were clearly in the ascendancy. After a failed attempt at a coup against the Junto leadership in late November, as a result of which Charles's most forceful counsellor, the earl of Strafford, was imprisoned, the king was pushed to the margins of the political process. Negotiations went ahead for a full-scale peace treaty with the Scots and work began on dismantling the machinery of the personal rule and bringing its leading architects to account. By mid-January 1641 it appeared that, with the encouragement of his moderate councillors, Charles himself had been co-opted to the process of reform. It was reported at court that he was 'brought to a dislike of those counsels that he hath formerly followed and therefore resolves to steer another course'. Bedford and Saye were appointed to the privy council and there were strong rumours that Pym would take over the crucial financial post of chancellor of the exchequer. The king also gave his blessing to the Triennial Act which prevented a re-run of the Personal Rule by guaranteeing that a parliament would be summoned at least once every three years. As a *quid pro quo* negotiations began with the Junto over providing the crown with an adequate basis for the royal finances and achieving a compromise over Strafford. All this appeared to hold out the prospect of settlement on terms that were just about acceptable to Charles. But from late February this began to recede as he began looking for opportunities to reassert his authority.[15]

The first signs began to emerge publicly of the long-anticipated resentment at the Scots occupation of the northern counties and both within parliament and at a local level there was growing opposition to the 'root and branch' reform of episcopacy. But the major preoccupation of the king at this time was to try to save Strafford. His impeachment was effectively putting on trial the policies of the Personal Rule. The Commons' charges against him were drawn up in such a way that if they could be made to stick this would provide a powerful demonstration that the authoritarian politics that he symbolized was no longer permissible. Charles could have taken much of the force out of their attack by making concessions and going along with a compromise scheme to simply strip him of his offices; but this was something he deliberately chose not to do. He was determined that the earl should face down his accusers and vindicate the crown's policies. In late February he appeared in the Lords when the charges were being read and delivered his opinion that in most respects there was no case to answer; and when the trial opened in March Strafford presented a robust and effective defence of his actions. As a result, the Junto leadership introduced a bill of attainder which declared that Strafford was guilty as charged and therefore liable to execution for treason. This high-handed procedure did not command universal support. Several MPs and peers were alarmed about the morality of a measure which was tantamount to judicial murder, and the indications were that it would fail to pass through the Lords who had already expressed misgivings about the strength of the Commons' case. There was also growing alarm about the threat from the 'popular multitude' as crowds of Londoners, encouraged by Pym and the Junto leadership, gathered around the parliament house and intimidated MPs and peers with calls for the earl's execution. By the end of April the nascent royalist party was growing in strength and the balance of political advantage appeared to be tilting towards the king. At the start of May, however, Charles's party-building strategy was blown apart by revelations about the Army Plot.[16]

The plot initially involved the king's northern army marching on London, seizing the Tower, releasing Strafford and then dissolving parliament. When the army officers refused to countenance this, Sir John Suckling, the courtier-poet, went ahead and recruited a band of mercenaries who attempted to occupy the Tower on 3 May. Charles kept his distance from the detailed planning, but there is little doubt that he gave the plot his blessing and regarded it as a legitimate response to the traitorous activities of his enemies. The effect of the plot was to destroy completely the political advantage that had been accruing to him during March and April. Revelations about the attempt to seize the Tower, and other details of the plot, created a frenetic atmosphere in parliament and led to the passage of several measures which severely damaged the king's chances of reimposing his authority. The Commons thrashed around for ways of expressing their abhorrence and safeguarding themselves against a coup, and came up with the Protestation. This was an oath of association which bound those who took it to defend king, parliament, the Protestant religion, and laws and liberties 'against all popery and popish innovations'. In the coming months it was to be a powerful device for rallying support for parliament. During the same period the Commons also passed a bill providing that the existing parliament should not be dissolved without its own consent which was to severely restrict the king's freedom of action. The Lords, recognizing that in this crisis Charles could not be relied on to act responsibly, went even further and for a few days effectively took over the reins of government, issuing a proclamation to arrest the plotters, calling out the militia and asking him to change various lord lieutenancies. One can see in this the furtherance of the process of taking authority out of the king's hands and securing control over his appointment of officers. But in the short term the most important effect was to sweep away the king's moderate support and seal Strafford's fate. The bill of attainder reached the Lords on 4 May, the day after the revelations about the plot and the passage of the Protestation oath. This served to frighten off much of the earl's potential support and the bill passed its third reading, leaving Charles to face an agonizing decision over signing the earl's death warrant.[17]

The Army Plot and the events of early May 1641 marked an important watershed in relations between the king and the Junto. They demonstrated clearly that the king could not be trusted to abide by the undertakings that he gave and confirmed the Junto leadership in their belief that their only hope of security was to complete the process of 'Venetianization'. They had made a start on this by eliminating the counsellor who posed the biggest threat to their survival, removing the king's power to summon and dissolve parliament, interfering with his choice of crown officers, and temporarily taking control of the executive. Over the following months these intrusions into the royal prerogative became more pronounced as they recognized the urgency of removing Charles's power to do them harm. On the king's part, the feeling that he had been coerced, against his conscience, into agreeing to Strafford's execution increased his bitterness towards his enemies. To his resentment at the way in which he was steadily being stripped of his authority was added a sense that to make further concessions which went against God's wishes could only bring down divine disapproval. On top of this, the death of the earl of Bedford in May removed the Junto leader best equipped to negotiate a compromise between the two sides and divisions over Strafford's attainder had begun to break up the consensus and determination to seek the political middle ground that had largely prevailed in the House of Lords. National politics was becoming markedly more polarized.[18]

The two sides spent the summer months of 1641 jockeying for position and building up support. The Junto pressed on with reform and exploited further revelations about army plotting to press the king to remove 'evil counsellors'. In other respects, however, they were on the defensive. The Scots finally decided to end their occupation which removed their most effective means of coercing the king. They also began to experience the unpopularity which went with exercising power. The abolition of episcopacy was encountering wide resistance; the poll tax to pay for the disbandment of the two armies was generally resented; and stories began to circulate about the ambition and arrogance of the Junto leadership, with the epithet 'King Pym' entering general usage by the autumn. Out of this, Charles made considerable headway in building a royalist party. He took a bold decision to travel to Scotland in August 1641, ostensibly to oversee the completion of the treaty with the Scots, but also to exploit the divisions emerging in the Covenanter ranks to build support north of the border. An increasingly vocal and effective royalist party was emerging in the Commons, not yet large enough to command a majority, but able to restrict the Junto's freedom of action and subject its policies to searching criticism. His strongest support, however, was in the Lords where resistance to the exclusion of bishops was combined with a sense of the need to preserve the royal prerogative in order to maintain the traditional constitutional balance. From October onwards a discernible loyalist party voted *en bloc* to stymie further Junto moves towards reform. Charles himself was also successful in presenting a moderate front, and for many in the country it had come to seem that, whatever his faults, at least he stood for the maintenance of the status quo.[19]

At the time of the king's return from Scotland, on 25 November 1641, the political balance appeared to be tilting once more in his favour. He had been damaged by his failure to respond positively to news of the Catholic Rebellion in Ireland in October. This revived fears of 'popish plots', particularly those associated with the queen; and it prompted proposals by the Junto to take control of the military force needed to suppress the rebellion. But in other respects his prospects appeared relatively encouraging. He had managed to use his majority in the Lords to block the Junto's militia bill which would have deprived him of control of the army; and he was particularly effective at promoting himself as the main defender of a traditional, Jacobean style, Church of England. Moreover, if a proclamation instructing all absentee members of the Commons and the Lords to attend by 12 January 1642 produced results, there was the distinct possibility that he could command a majority in both houses and persuade them to dissolve themselves.[20] In late December, however, he threw away these advantages with a series of grotesque political misjudgements.

The first of these was the decision to replace Sir William Balfour, the lieutenant of the Tower who had held out against the army plotters in May with a notoriously unscrupulous Catholic 'swordsman', Thomas Lunsford. This provoked demonstrations and protests on the streets of London, prompted the Commons to accuse two of his leading counsellors, Bristol and Digby, of treason and led to open talk of civil war, with the labels 'cavalier' and 'roundhead' being applied for the first time.[21]

Charles's second mistake was to encourage a protest by the bishops. During the post-Christmas demonstrations Archbishop Williams had been jostled by a crowd of apprentices and this had frightened most of the other bishops into absenting themselves from the Lords. The peers responded by asking the Commons to join them in a declaration against riotous assemblies and, when they refused, to debate a motion by Digby, that because of the pressure from the mob the parliament was no longer free. At last there seemed a possibility of the adjournment that Charles had long been angling for. A resolution that parliament was acting under duress could be held to override the statute against dissolving without its own consent. On 28 December, however, the upper house voted by a bare majority that parliament was free and could continue sitting. At this point the king seriously overplayed his hand. Hoping to capitalize on the Lords' alarm over the mob, he approved a protest drawn up by Williams in the name of twelve of the bishops declaring that since they could find neither 'redress or protection' from parliament all proceedings in their absence should be declared null and void. This would have invalidated the vote that parliament was free and reopened the possibility of adjournment. But when the Lords discussed it on the 30th they showed considerable irritation over the contradicting of their earlier vote and the Junto were able to push through a resolution that the protest entrenched on parliament's fundamental privileges. Ten of the twelve bishops were incarcerated in the Tower and the number of the king's natural supporters in the house significantly reduced.[22]

The mistakes over Lunsford and the bishops, however, were as nothing compared with the folly of the attempted coup against the Junto leadership. This was a policy that Charles had been considering on and off ever since Strafford had first suggested it in November 1640; however, the final decision to go ahead seems to have been taken suddenly on 1–2 January 1642. Apparently urged on by Digby and the queen, he was persuaded that the rejection of the bishops' protest had been a temporary aberration and that, given a clear lead, the majority of the Lords would still be firmly behind him. Only this can explain the huge gamble of preferring treason charges. However, when the attorney general read out the charges in the upper house on 3 January, against five members of the Commons and Lord Mandeville, the peers showed themselves in no mood to countenance such naked political aggression. Instead of moving to examine witnesses, as Charles had anticipated, they appointed a committee to decide whether the charges were 'a regular proceeding according to the law' and voted to join the Commons in requesting an armed guard. The next day the king took the fateful decision to go in person with three hundred armed men to arrest the Five Members.[23] The MPs were forewarned and escaped by the river. Charles was left in the hugely embarrassing position of arriving at the Commons to demand their surrender only to find that they had already departed.[24]

The king's actions in late December 1641 and early January 1642 provoked a reaction which lost him his capital. The Lords and Commons passed a series of resolutions which effectively gave military control of London to the parliament. The sheriff was empowered to raise a *posse comitatus* for parliament's safety, and the city's forces were put under the command of Sergeant Major Skippon, an ally of the Junto. There was also a widespread popular reaction against Charles as news of his actions spread. Huge crowds came out on to the streets to escort the Commons back to Westminster when they decided it was safe to return to their house, with the city bandsmen carrying copies of the Protestation stuck onto their pikes. By this stage the king had had enough. On the 10th he took his family and fled to Hampton Court, effectively surrendering control of London to his enemies. What had begun as an attempted coup ended as a counter coup against him.[25]

THE FORMATION OF AN ENGLISH ROYALIST PARTY

These events were arguably the most critical of Charles's reign. They ensured that civil war was now not just possible, but highly probable. Both sides had taken up positions from which it was very difficult to retreat and by withdrawing from London the king had physically separated them into two camps. The confrontations of the period had also introduced a crucial element of violence which made the final resort to armed force less unthinkable. If this had happened anywhere else the French ambassador observed, 'la ville seroit a feu et sang dans 24 heures'. In England there was still the restraining influence of deeply rooted traditions of unity and legality; however, the leadership on both sides was getting close to the point of no return. As Conrad Russell has explained, Charles had effectively been deprived of his capital by a rebel insurrection and if he now 'wanted civil war . . . he was only doing the obvious thing for a king in his position to do'.[26] Meanwhile the Junto, having been publicly accused of treason, were unlikely to feel secure in any undertaking given by the person who had brought the charges. What held back the final confrontation at this stage was largely the king's sense that he was not yet strong enough to win a civil war. The story of the following months was, in many respects, the story of how he was able to gather enough support to fight.

Following his departure from London, Charles embarked on a dual strategy. In public he made every effort to present himself as moderate and accommodating. His chief adviser in this was Sir Edward Hyde who took on the role of chief draftsman for the spate of royal declarations that were published in the spring and summer of 1642. The tone of these was summed up in the advice that Hyde gave to Charles as he headed towards York in March. The king must strive to quell rumours about 'designs of immediate force' and avoid 'giving the least hint to your people that you rely upon any thing but the strength of your laws and their obedience'.[27]

On the other hand, behind the scenes, Charles was preparing for war. Egged on by Henrietta Maria, who by early 1642 had established herself as his most influential counsellor, he developed a plan to set up his court in York, take control of Hull as a base for recruiting a royalist army, start purchasing weapons in the Netherlands and finally coerce parliament into backing down and acknowledging obedience to their monarch. There seems little doubt that Charles favoured this more aggressive option. He was still profoundly resentful at the way in which the Junto were steadily stripping him of his royal authority and was convinced, as he told the Dutch ambassador, that no matter how much he conceded, his opponents would never be satisfied. Striking back against them seemed not only the most attractive, but also the most viable option. What held him back was lack of political allies.[28]

In the aftermath of his departure from London in January 1642 his main source of strength lay in the House of Lords. In spite of the removal of the bishops, there was still a royalist majority which was powerful enough to block the Junto's efforts to take control of the militia or confirm the exclusion of bishops. Charles, with Bristol's advice, made a number of conciliatory moves which bolstered his credentials as the main bulwark of the legal and constitutional status quo and helped to drive a wedge between Lords and Commons. On 28 January, the duke of Richmond attempted to exploit this by again proposing an adjournment of the parliament. But, as had happened a month earlier, this backfired disastrously. Richmond was fortunate to escape imprisonment and royalist peers found themselves pilloried in petitions and pamphlets as members of 'the malignant party'. As intimidation increased from the crowds thronging round Westminster, their attendance in the Lords declined. During February the Junto were finally able to secure majority support for bishops' exclusion and the passage of the Militia Ordinance. Charles had lost what influence he had had over proceedings in parliament.[29]

Nonetheless during the first half of 1642 it was the king who continued to make the political weather. It was his determination to secure the means to punish his opponents and his progressive withdrawal to the north which largely dictated the shape and pace of events. But it took two sides to fight a civil war and just as important was the attitude of the Junto leadership. Their strategy at this time was basically to prepare for war while giving every appearance of wishing to preserve the peace. Having been accused of treason, Pym and the other leaders recognized that their only security lay in emasculating Charles to a degree that he could not possibly find acceptable. This made any resolution of the conflict short of civil war highly improbable. However, if they did have to fight, the Junto needed to carry with them the bulk of the Commons and a substantial part of the political nation which, given the deeply ingrained traditions of non-resistance and the desire for peace, was never going to be easy. This was why Pym had to go on giving the appearance of seeking accommodation, while, as Russell puts it, trying to 'needle the king into beginning a civil war himself'.[30] It was a difficult balancing act, but he largely carried it off, with Charles's willing cooperation.

The king's decision to head north seemed to confirm all the Junto's dire warnings about his aggressive intent. Pym responded by pushing through the Commons a 'declaration of fears and jealousies' which raised the stakes by making an alarming reference to rumours of the king's 'great designs' for 'breaking the neck of your parliament'. The Junto also took further steps to mobilize its greatest asset, the level of popular support that parliament enjoyed in the country. There was a new round of parliament-sponsored subscription to the Protestation; petitioning from the shires was stepped up, often accompanied by parades of local support in London; and the first moves were made in getting parliament-appointed lord lieutenants to take control of the county militias.[31]

Charles, in the meantime, began the process of building enough support to fight a civil war. When he arrived at York in late March he was almost bereft of allies. The expected rally to him by the northern gentry did not materialize and his attendance consisted of two of his most loyal peers, Richmond and Newcastle, and a few household officers and guards. In default of any possibility of being able to take more aggressive action he fell back on Hyde's advice and staked a claim to the political and moral high ground by presenting himself as the aggrieved party. His attempt to take Hull in April was an important part of this strategy. It was preceded by a series of pamphlet exchanges in which he accused parliament of usurping his right to appoint the town's governor and contravening the Petition of Right by billeting soldiers there. He then conducted a series of elaborately theatrical negotiations with Governor Hotham in front of the town walls which were aimed as much at provoking his enemies as actually securing the town. When Hotham remained defiant he was able to brand him a traitor and insist that parliament's defence of his actions amounted to 'actual war levied against us'.[32]

The episode at Hull and parliament's order to execute the Militia Ordinance gave the king considerable leverage as the paper war intensified in May. He now had a powerful case for arguing that defiance of his authority was tantamount to a rejection of the rule of law and the constitutional status quo; and his case was beginning to find support in the localities. The criticisms of the Junto leadership and puritan religious policy, which had surfaced intermittently during 1641, were coming together and were linked with a growing acceptance of the king's portrayal of himself as the guardian of tradition. In Herefordshire a group of leading justices subscribed to an open letter which described the constitution as bound together by a 'triple cord', comprising king, Lords, and Commons: 'Every one of the three has a negative voice and if any should have the power of binding it should be thought rather the king than the Commons.'[33] The different strands of royalism were coalescing to provide a coherent platform for the formation of a royalist party. But until the king was able to gather a credible body of political and military support at York there was little prospect that he would actually be able to fight a civil war. In these circumstances, Charles demonstrated to the full his qualities as a party leader. He combined the personal conviction and determination needed to drive his cause forward, and rally committed royalists, with sufficient tactical awareness to reach out to the middle ground and reassure those who might be wavering in their loyalty. This enabled him to retrieve a situation in which most commentators saw him as simply too weak to mount an effective challenge to parliament.

The turning point came late in May 1642 when he finally managed to persuade a substantial number of peers to join him in the north. He did this by means of a personal summons to each of them, 'on their allegiance', to attend him at York to provide counsel concerning 'affairs much importing the peace and good of the kingdom'. Peers had a very strong sense of their obligations of personal service to the king and, also, of their duty to counsel their monarch in time of need; so this was a summons that they found very hard to resist. By mid-June some forty of them had rallied to the king, considerably outnumbering those who remained at Westminster. His prospects were almost immediately transformed. Their presence gave his proceedings a political credibility that they had lacked before and provided a powerful focus for rallying political and military support. He was able to persuade the peers to sign an 'Engagement', pledging themselves to defend his person and 'just and legal prerogative', and explicitly rejecting the Militia Ordinance. These peers also began pledging money and backing for military action, initially with personal subscriptions to raise two thousand cavalry, then by accepting office under the royal Commissions of Array, which were Charles's response to the Militia Ordinance. Parliament reacted by ordering their lord lieutenants to start mustering local troops and impeaching some of the peers who had joined the king.[34] As both sides appeared to be gearing up for war, there was a widespread reaction in the country which found its most tangible expression in a series of county-wide petitions calling for settlement. This produced the final attempt to broker a peace.

The driving force behind this came from a group of peers who assumed their traditional responsibility for building bridges between the king and his people. It took the form of the Nineteen Propositions which emerged out of a bi-partisan initiative led by Bristol and Northumberland. The original aim appears to have been 'to set down all the things in difference between the king and the subject, with the most probable ways of reconciling them'. But the propositions which emerged from the Lords in late May were much less accommodating than originally intended, with the Junto-led committee taking as their guiding principles parliament's right to dictate the king's choice of councillors and the requirement that he accept the Militia Ordinance. In spite of the uncompromising tone of the Nineteen Propositions, the peers involved in the drafting believed that they would at least provide the opportunity to open a dialogue with the king, and there were plenty of peers at York prepared to urge this on him. However, Charles was unimpressed. In his published *Answer to the XIX Propositions* their effect was described as being to turn him into 'but the outside, but the picture, but the sign of a king', and this was something he would never agree to.[35]

The king's answer was debated in the Commons in late June and there was considerable support from an emerging 'peace party' for toning down some of the original propositions. But such moves were soon overtaken by the escalating military preparations. As parliament stepped up the execution of the Militia Ordinance and began recruiting an army under the earl of Essex, Charles issued instructions to the Commissioners of Array and began raising his own force. The first clash took place in Leicestershire at the end of June when the royalist commissioner, Henry Hastings, was resisted in his attempt to take control of the county magazine. The outbreak of actual fighting was still delayed, but by early July the civil war was to all intents and purposes under way.

CONCLUSION

The collapse of royal authority to the point at which civil war broke out in 1642 was, at its core, a story about the power struggle between the king and the Junto. For Charles maintaining his authority as a monarch, and punishing those who sought to strip him of it, was very much a matter of personal honour, a test of his resolve and manhood, as his wife repeatedly told him. For the Junto anything short of a settlement which effectively 'Venetianized' the king under the direction of a parliamentary commonwealth would leave them exposed to treason charges as soon as he regained the initiative. Neither side felt that it could settle for anything less than what it regarded as clear-cut victory. This explains why efforts to broker a compromise in the summer of 1642, which had the support of the majority of the political nation, came to nothing. Ultimately neither of the main protagonists felt it could afford to allow this to happen.

This is not to say, however, that it was politics at the centre which alone explains the outbreak of civil war. The combustible mix of circumstances which produced this outcome was rooted in a complex variety of structural faults and broader social, cultural, and political developments. The so-called 'British problem', created by the Stuart monarchy's efforts to rule over England, Scotland, and Ireland, with their very divergent political and religious cultures, produced tensions which continually threatened to destabilize the government of all three kingdoms.[36] The divided religious legacy of the Reformation led to conflict between 'puritan' and 'Anglican' visions of the true church, and a continuing fear of 'popery', which created spiritual antagonisms over which many contemporaries felt they could not afford to compromise. And the emergence of a 'public sphere' of politics in which broad swathes of the gentry and middling sort became engaged in political debate and controversy created constituencies to which both the main protagonists continually sought to pitch their appeals and, ultimately, provided them with the means to fight the war.[37] These factors and others—such as the contingencies which produced a rebellion in Ireland in October 1641 and stoked up fears of 'popery' in England—created the context in which civil war became possible after 1637.

However, in the final analysis, it was the clash of the main political actors which turned potential into reality. And—because in early modern monarchical states it was kings who largely made the political running—the course of events was shaped, above all, by Charles. It was his crass handling of the Scottish crisis which turned local protest into full-blown, and successful, rebellion; his determination not to agree terms which he saw as personally humiliating which stymied efforts at settlement; and his repeated attempts to resolve his problems by a dramatic coup, rather than patiently building political support, which handed the initiative back to his opponents when he appeared to be gaining the upper hand. Charles's mistakes and misjudgements brought royal authority almost to the point of collapse after he abandoned London in January 1642. However, had he simply been incompetent he would never have been able to rally sufficient support to fight a civil war. In the end it was his capacity and resolve as a party leader, demonstrated most clearly in the way he retrieved an apparently hopeless situation to form a credible royalist party in May and June, that finally ignited the conflict. At the end of his masterly analysis of the causes of the civil war, Conrad Russell concluded that while these were complex and multifarious, without Charles a civil war is 'almost impossible to imagine'.[38] This is a verdict that it is hard to dispute.

Notes

1. For an assessment of England in 1637, see Conrad Russell, *The Fall of the British Monarchies, 1637–1642* (Oxford, 1991), chap.1.
2. *The Earl of Strafforde's Letters and Dispatches*, ed. W. Knowler, 2 vols. (1729), I, 141.
3. Russell, *Fall*, 1.
4. Kevin Sharpe, *The Personal Rule of Charles I* (London, 1992), 587–8.
5. Russell, *Fall*, 2.
6. Richard Cust, *Charles I: A Political Life* (Harlow, 2005), 133–47; Ann Hughes, 'Robert Greville, Second Baron Brooke of Beauchamps Court (1607–1643)', *Oxford Dictionary of National Biography* (2004).
7. John Fielding, 'Opposition to the Personal Rule of Charles I: The Diary of Robert Woodford, 1637–1641', *Historical Journal*, 31 (1988): 769–88.
8. David Stevenson, *The Scottish Revolution, 1637–1644: The Triumph of the Covenanters* (Newton Abbot, 1973; reprinted Edinburgh, 2003), chap. 2; Cust, *Charles I*, 210–43.
9. John Adamson, 'England without Cromwell: What if Charles I had Avoided the Civil War?', in Niall Ferguson (ed.), *Virtual History: Alternatives and Counterfactuals* (London, 1997), 95–101.
10. Russell, *Fall*, 90–123; Clive Holmes, *Seventeenth-Century Lincolnshire* (Lincoln, 1980), 138.
11. Conrad Russell, 'The Scottish Party in English Parliaments, 1640–2 or the Myth of the English Revolution', *Historical Research*, 66 (1993): 39.
12. John Adamson, *The Noble Revolt: The Overthrow of Charles I* (London, 2007).
13. Russell, *Fall*, 279.
14. Cust, *Charles I*, 262–73.
15. Adamson, *Noble Revolt*, chaps. 3–6; Cust, *Charles I*, 274–7.
16. Cust, *Charles I*, 277–83.
17. Conrad Russell, 'The First Army Plot of 1641', *Transactions of the Royal Historical Society*, 5th ser., 38 (1988): 85–106; Russell, *Fall*, 296–7.
18. Adamson, *Noble Revolt*, chaps. 10–12; Richard Cust, 'Charles I and Providence', in Kenneth Fincham and Peter Lake (eds.), *Religious Politics in Post-Reformation England* (Woodbridge, 2006), 195–9.
19. Adamson, *Noble Revolt*, chaps. 13–14; Richard Cust, *Charles I and the English Aristocracy, 1625–1642* (Cambridge, 2013), chap. 5, pt. II.
20. Adamson, *Noble Revolt*, chap. 15; Cust, *Charles I*, 310–17.
21. Cust, *Charles I*, 317–18; Russell, *Fall*, 439–41; Anthony Fletcher, *The Outbreak of the English Civil War* (London, 1981), 171–3, 176.

22. Russell, *Fall*, 442–4; Adamson, *Noble Revolt*, 476–84.
23. Adamson, *Noble Revolt*, 488–94; Russell, *Fall*, 448–9.
24. Adamson, *Noble Revolt*, 494–7.
25. Russell, *Fall*, 450–1; Fletcher, *Outbreak of the Civil War*, 182–4.
26. Russell, *Fall*, 454.
27. *State Papers Collected by the Earl of Clarendon*, 2 vols. (Oxford, 1767), II, 138–9.
28. Cust, *Charles I*, 332–3.
29. Cust, *Charles I and the Aristocracy*, chap. 5, pt. III.
30. Russell, *Fall*, 459–62.
31. Russell, *Fall*, 478–50; Cust, *Charles I*, 334–5.
32. Cust, *Charles I*, 337–41.
33. Jacqueline Eales, *Puritans and Roundheads: The Harleys of Brampton Bryan and the Outbreak of the English Civil War* (Cambridge, 1990), 132–135; Fletcher, *Outbreak of the Civil War*, 283–9, 302–5.
34. Cust, *Charles I and the Aristocracy*, chap. 5, pt. III.
35. Russell, *Fall*, 513–16; Cust, *Charles I and the Aristocracy*, chap. 5, pt. III.
36. Conrad Russell, 'The British Problem and the English Civil War', *History*, 72 (1987): 395–415.
37. Peter Lake and Steven Pincus (eds.), *The Politics of the Public Sphere in Early Modern England* (Manchester, 2007).
38. Conrad Russell, *The Causes of the English Civil War* (Oxford, 1990), 209–11.

FURTHER READING

Adamson, John, *The Noble Revolt: The Overthrow of Charles I* (London, 2007).
Cust, Richard, *Charles I and the Aristocracy, 1625–1642* (Cambridge, 2013).
Cust, Richard, *Charles I: A Political Life* (Harlow, 2005).
Fletcher, Anthony, *The Outbreak of the English Civil War* (London, 1981).
Russell, Conrad, *The Causes of the English Civil War* (Oxford, 1990).
Russell, Conrad, *The Fall of the British Monarchies, 1637–1642* (Oxford, 1991).
Sharpe, Kevin, *The Personal Rule of Charles I* (London, 1992).
Stevenson, David, *The Scottish Revolution, 1637–1644: The Triumph of the Covenanters* (Newton Abbot, 1973; reprinted Edinburgh, 2003).

CHAPTER 5

....

THE IRISH RISING

....

JOSEPH COPE

THE outbreak of the Irish rebellion in October 1641 represents a fundamentally important episode on the road to revolution. Primed with anti-popish fears stirred up in the early months of 1641, the rising could be interpreted as solid proof of the dangers that many perceived in Charles I's kingdoms. In the 1660s, Edward Hyde, first earl of Clarendon, reflected on the significance of the rising, recalling that when news of the crisis reached the House of Commons on 1 November 1641, 'there was a deep silence in the House . . . and a kind of consternation, most men's heads having been intoxicated, from their first meeting in Parliament, with imaginations of plots and treasonable designs through the three kingdoms'.[1] The letters announcing the rising sent to the English parliament from Dublin Castle presented the crisis in stark and simple terms, characterizing it as a 'wicked and damnable conspiracy plotted and contrived . . . by some evil affected papists here'.[2]

In contrast to this simple reading of the rebellion, the 1641 rising exposed multiple fractures between and within Ireland's diverse ethnic and religious groups. Focusing on the period between the 1641 fall of Charles I's Lord Deputy Thomas Wentworth, first earl of Strafford, and the conclusion of the Cessation between Charles I and the Confederate Catholics in September 1643, it is possible to map out the reconfiguration of loyalties and the disintegration of pre-rebellion communities. As with the English civil war and revolution generally, historians must account for the long-term tensions that came to the surface during the conflict and the short-term and contingent factors that led to the initial outbreak of hostilities in October 1641. Source materials, particularly the 1641 depositions, preserve ample evidence of grievances dating at least as far back as the early seventeenth-century plantations. More immediate concerns arising from the destabilizing policies of Thomas Wentworth's tenure as Lord Deputy in the 1630s also played an important role in driving the Irish crisis of 1641.[3] But the conflict in Ireland cannot be neatly separated from the other mid-century crises within Charles I's composite monarchy. Wentworth's policies during the Scottish wars, the radicalization of English politics in 1641, and the crown's furtive negotiations with the Confederate Catholics in 1643 underscore the importance of taking a broad British approach to the rising.

It is at the same time important to balance the British dimensions of the rising against other perspectives. Within the past several decades, scholars have increasingly looked at the local contexts of the rebellion through research in the archive of contemporary testimony commonly known as the 1641 depositions.[4] Microhistorical studies of the depositions reveal regional differences, local tensions, and interpersonal disputes. Moving in the opposite direction, some scholars have sought to internationalize understandings of the rising by drawing out parallels to the disintegrating composite monarchies elsewhere in Europe.[5] England's panicked response to the 1641 rising must be understood in an international context, with anti-popery providing a conceptual framework for making sense of the conflict.

Finally, it is also necessary to be mindful of fragmentation within the various ethnic and religious interests in Ireland. Obviously the split between Catholics and Protestants loomed large in the mid-seventeenth century, as did the divisions between native Irish, Old English, New English, and Scots-Irish communities. Within these groups, however, historians have begun to map out significant tensions. Among Ireland's Roman Catholic population, friction emerged between predominantly native Irish partisans in the rising and Old English elites who tried to distance themselves from the rebellion. As the conflict evolved, these tensions contributed to factionalism within the Catholic Confederacy, which worsened when Irish veterans of military service on the Continent returned to Ireland in 1642. Likewise among Ireland's Protestants, the outbreak of the rising revealed deep fissures between New English and Scots-Irish planters. As the conflict wore on, evidence of internal fragmentation also appeared within the New English segment of the population, especially when it became necessary to take a side in the English civil war.

Mid-seventeenth-century Irish politics can thus be conceptualized as a complex dance between various parties on constantly shifting ground. In order to understand the tensions that led to the 1641 rising, it is necessary to be mindful of the simmering resentment caused by the displacement of native Irish and Old English elites by New English during the late sixteenth and early seventeenth centuries. The forces that accelerated the fragmentation of Irish society and created the specific catalysts for the rebellion, however, must be understood within the contingencies of the late 1630s and 1640s.

IRISH POLITICS AND THE FALL
OF STRAFFORD

Charles I's appointment of Sir Thomas Wentworth as Lord Deputy of Ireland in 1632 forms the starting point for a discussion of the 1641 rising. As Lord Deputy, Wentworth had the responsibility to manage a religiously and ethnically diverse nation. The Irish population maintained the Gaelic language and other distinct cultural traditions and remained solidly connected to the Roman Catholic Church. The Old English, descendants of the twelfth-century Norman conquerors, saw themselves as distinct from the

Irish population. However, by the seventeenth century, intermarriage and other cultural interactions and a common experience of marginalization by the Tudor church and state had eroded many of these distinctions. The New English represented late arrivals, appearing at the vanguard of Tudor policies aimed at centralizing power. Often the beneficiaries of sixteenth- and seventeenth-century plantation schemes, which wrested power and land from Irish and Old English interests, the New English were a minority and almost exclusively Protestant population. Finally, Ulster housed a large Scottish population. In part this reflected traditional patterns of migration between Ulster and the Scottish isles. However, the Scots-Irish population had grown significantly in the early seventeenth century when James I, in an effort to broaden the 'British' base population in the north allowed Scots to take up land in the Ulster plantation.

Thomas Wentworth arrived in Dublin with a mandate to resolve the crown's financial woes in the kingdom, but achieving fiscal solvency put the Lord Deputy on a collision course with many entrenched interests in Ireland. Wentworth explored an expansion of the English plantations in Connacht and various means of wringing money and land out of existing landowners and new settlers. These policies successively alienated segments of the Irish, Old English, and New English populations.[6]

The Old English and Irish had ample cause to be suspicious of Dublin Castle. The Tudor and Stuart plantations in general reflected anti-popish and ethnocentric assumptions. The prescriptions for the plantation of Ulster imposed fundamental changes in land use and rural economy, mandated settlement by New English and Scottish migrants, and envisioned a new landscape dominated by fortified estates, English-style towns, and Protestant churches.[7] In reality, few of the early modern plantations completely reflected the prescribed conditions. However, the plantations fundamentally realigned political and economic power and played an important symbolic role in communicating the state's hostility to Irish customs and the Roman Catholic religion. By the early 1630s, elements within the New English administration at Dublin Castle appeared ready to extend the attack on Roman Catholicism. In the period immediately preceding Wentworth's appointment, acting Lord Justices Adam Loftus and Richard Boyle, first earl of Cork, made no secret of their hostility towards popery and presided over a period of assault on Catholic interests and religious practices. Wentworth's regime moderated some of these policies, but the long-term anxieties remained. The Lord Deputy's advocacy of expanded plantations in Connacht, which would have adversely affected Irish and Old English interests, added to these concerns.

Wentworth's policies in the 1630s badly strained his ties with his New English and Protestant constituencies. In a general sense the appointment of a stranger as Lord Deputy could be interpreted as a repudiation of New English leadership in Ireland. Wentworth made these problems worse through the pursuit of religious policies that upset the delicate working arrangement that had been achieved within the Church of Ireland in the decades before his arrival. In the minority in Ireland, many Protestants ascribed to an aggressively anti-popish worldview and perceived Catholicism as an existential threat.[8] These anti-popish assumptions led to deep suspicion of Wentworth's motives when, in the mid-1630s, anti-Calvinist bishops supported by the Lord Deputy gained prominence and fashioned policies that imposed greater conformity on the Church of Ireland. In the aftermath of the Scottish prayer book controversy in 1637, Wentworth's government increased this pressure, using the Irish court of high commission to root out Covenanter sympathizers.

As Wentworth pushed for conformity among Irish Protestants, the state's perceived inattention to policing recusancy fed fears that the Lord Deputy planned to extend full toleration to Roman Catholics. The failed negotiations between Wentworth and the Old English magnates over 'the Graces'—which would have firmed up uncertain Catholic land titles and eliminated some of the legal restrictions on the Catholic population—enhanced these fears. The fact that negotiations over the Graces failed proved doubly damaging to Wentworth, as the Lord Deputy found himself simultaneously alienated from New English who saw the Graces as a betrayal of the Protestant interest and Old English Catholics who felt that Wentworth had negotiated in bad faith.

Wentworth's actions during the Bishops' Wars reflected how badly the Lord Deputy misunderstood his position in Ireland. Wentworth operated within a true British context in 1639–41, shuttling back and forth between London and Dublin several times while offering advice to the English privy council. Ironically, the Lord Deputy's entanglements in a three kingdoms context opened the door to collaboration among a diverse range of otherwise mutually antagonistic players in Ireland.

Wentworth arrived in England at Charles I's request in September 1639 and played a key role in planning the king's campaign to break the stalemate with the Scots. Confident about his command of the political landscape in Ireland, Wentworth, elevated to the English peerage as first earl of Strafford in January 1640, returned to Ireland in March 1640 with a plan for raising an army in Ireland for service in a summer campaign against the Covenanters. Initially, this plan worked well. The pliant Irish parliament that assembled in Dublin in March and April 1640 voted in favour of four subsidies and passed a declaration condemning the Covenanters.

The collapse of the Short Parliament in the spring of 1640, however, opened up opportunities for the Lord Deputy's enemies in Ireland to act. During the second session of the Irish parliament in June 1640, foes on all sides—New English who had seen their local authority challenged by Strafford's regime, committed Protestants angry about the direction of the Irish church, and Old English Catholics disgruntled over the Lord Deputy's vacillations on religious liberty and ominous overtures on land tenure—assailed Wentworth's authority. Within the Irish parliament, a coalition of men united by little more than their loathing of the Lord Deputy successfully stalled the subsidy to the extent that, when the Scots soundly beat Charles I's forces at Newburn in August 1640, Wentworth's much-touted Irish army had barely mobilized. During the third session of the Irish Parliament, which convened on 1 October 1640, the Irish parliament drafted a far-reaching condemnation of Strafford's tenure as Lord Deputy. Reflecting its origins in a coalition of actors, the grievances outlined in the 'Humble and Just Remonstrance' largely focused on issues that transcended the confessional divide, particularly economic and constitutional issues. With the exception of complaints about the court of high commission and the failed negotiations over the Graces, Wentworth's religious policies remained marginal to the case articulated in the Irish parliament.[9]

In contrast to the Irish parliament's proceedings, when the Long Parliament took up the case against Wentworth, religion framed much of the discussion. In a speech on 7 November 1640 before a committee of both houses, Sir John Clotworthy, a planter in county Antrim and sitting MP for Bossiney, Cornwall, claimed that Wentworth had perverted religion, abetted corruption, and turned a blind eye to the proliferation of popery. Wentworth's intrusion into the Scottish conflict revealed his sinister potential, Clotworthy warned, as the Lord Deputy now had in arms 8,000–10,000 'papists, ready to march where I know not'.[10] The articles of treason drawn up by the English House of Commons against Strafford in late January 1641 seized upon these points and even more emphatically tied the Lord Deputy to shadowy plots, presenting the Irish army as a force 'of papists, his dependents ... which he might employ to reduce this kingdom'.[11]

During the English Parliament's proceedings against Wentworth, anxiety about the Lord Deputy's actions spread beyond the halls of Westminster. Large-scale and tense public protests occurred throughout the trial and during debate over the Bill of Attainder against Strafford. The Lord Deputy's execution on 12 May 1641 drew out a crowd estimated by contemporaries as numbering 100,000.[12] What had begun as an Irish parliamentary protest against Wentworth's overreaching had become an opportunity for anti-popish politicking in the English parliament and mass demonstrations in London. The fears of a popish plot that had been stirred up during this period in many respects structured English understandings of the events in Ireland for the next several years.

In Ireland, the evolution of the case against Wentworth in the Long Parliament, combined with Charles I's apparent inability or unwillingness to prevent the execution of one of his closest advisers, frightened many Old English and Irish lords and gentry. Since 1495, Irish politics operated under Poyning's Law, which established the Irish Parliament's subordination to the English Privy Council. The English Parliament's claims to possess jurisdiction over the Lord Deputy now pointed to a significant expansion of Westminster's role in Irish policies. With Wentworth out of the picture, anti-popery a driving force in English popular and parliamentary politics, and the constitutional arrangements uncertain, Ireland's Catholics found themselves in a suddenly vulnerable position.

DISINTEGRATION: THE 1641 CRISIS

In the face of a feared crackdown on popery originating from the English Commons, two parallel and largely insulated strategies emerged among Irish Catholic elites. Within the Irish parliament, members pressed for a constitutional settlement, taking advantage of the power vacuum to try to roll back the policies of the 1630s. More aggressively, some also saw the elimination of Wentworth as an opportunity for the Irish parliament to assert its autonomy and revise the operations of Poyning's Law.[13] Disgruntled leaders of the most powerful native Irish families, however, began to explore a very different response to the anxieties stirred up by the Wentworth trial. Among the Irish, Connor, Lord Maguire, and Rory O'More took on early leadership roles in the summer of 1641, networking with prominent families in Ulster, including the Maguires in county Fermanagh, the O'Neills in county Armagh and county Monaghan, the O'Reillys in county Cavan, and the McMahons in county Monaghan. They also connected with officers of Wentworth's Irish army at Carrickfergus and with Irish officers serving overseas in the Spanish army, most notably Owen Roe O'Neill. Although the chief Old English families were not directly involved in the plotting of the rebellion, this confederacy had at least some contact with prominent Palesmen including Colonel Richard Plunkett and Nicholas Preston, Lord Gormanston.

The Irish plotters of the 1641 rising had ample cause for discontent and fear. Although the peace that concluded the Nine Years War in 1603 had allowed Irish lords to maintain significant landholdings and local power, the early years of James I's reign witnessed growing pressure on Irish and Catholic interests. In the face of this, in 1607 two of the most powerful Ulster magnates—Hugh O'Neill, earl of Tyrone, and Rory O'Donnell, earl of Tyrconnell—and their followers abandoned Ireland for the Continent. Their departure cleared a path for the crown to seize and redistribute massive landholdings in the modern counties of Armagh, Cavan, Donegal, Fermanagh, Londonderry, and Tyrone.

The flight of the earls and the subsequent Stuart plantations had been devastating for those Irish who stayed behind. Research on prominent Irish families in Ulster on the eve of the rebellion presents a grim picture of resentment, anxiety, economic dislocation, and indebtedness.[14] In contrast to those Old English who sought constitutional change through the Irish parliament, many Irish elites seem to have felt much less optimistic about their future in post-Wentworth Ireland. One index to the depths of this pessimism may be found in the fact that a number of Irish gentry who served English legal and political institutions participated in plotting the rising. Sir Phelim O'Neill, who had been an MP and a justice of the peace, perhaps best embodies this, but similar examples can be found among the O'Rourkes in county Leitrim, the O'Farrells in county Longford, and the O'Reillys in county Cavan. These men had stakes in the existing political order and yet threw their lot in with rebellion.[15]

According to the conspirators' plan, the rising would include two main components. Lord Maguire and Hugh MacMahon gathered a body of armed men in Dublin with plans to take the Castle by surprise on the night of 22 October 1641. As this Dublin stratagem unfolded, gentry-led Irish in Ulster would rise up and disarm settlers in key plantation settlements. Effectively decapitating the state, the seizure of Dublin would prevent a coordinated response to these loosely coordinated local risings.

In the event, the plot did not proceed as planned. The campaign against Dublin Castle disintegrated on the evening of 22 October when Owen O'Connolly, a kinsman of one of the Dublin leaders, revealed details of the engagement to Sir William Parsons, one of the two acting Lord Justices. In Ulster, however, the rebels found greater success. The lead conspirators targeted strategically significant settlements and disarmed New English

planters and garrisons. Over the next several days, Phelim O'Neill disarmed British settlers from an arc of territory in central Ulster extending from Dungannon to Newry;
forces under Rory Maguire in county Fermanagh and the O'Reillys in county Cavan
found similar success within the first week of the rising.

Even at this early stage of the rising, it is possible to discern a constitutional motive.
On 4 November, Phelim O'Neill issued a declaration from Newry purporting to possess
a commission from Charles I authorizing attacks on English settlers.[16] The forged commission presented justification for the rising in constitutional terms, complaining of the
English parliament's intrusion on royal prerogative and warning that the king feared 'these
storms blow aloft and are very likely to be carried by the vehemency of the Protestant party
into our kingdom of Ireland and endanger our royal power there'.[17] The O'Reillys in county
Cavan likewise asserted a 'great cause of fear in the proceedings of our neighbour nations'
and signalled a desire to negotiate with Charles I over Catholic grievances including the
failed Graces.[18] The depositions preserve similar evidence, as well as accounts of participants in the rising citing the Scottish Covenanters' evolving relationship to the crown as
a template for Irish aims.[19] These references suggest a rough understanding of how the
constitutional relationship between the Irish parliament, the English parliament, and the
crown had evolved. Fears of the Long Parliament's agenda played an integral role in this
framing of the rising, but at least some partisans in the rising also seem to have believed
that the British crisis of the 1640s had opened the door to a radical reconstruction of the
constitutional relationship between Charles I and his Irish subjects.[20]

Over the past two decades, scholarship on the social history of the 1641 rebellion has
proliferated, in large measure thanks to historians' rehabilitation of the 1641 depositions. Consisting of a disparate collection of accounts taken primarily from despoiled
settlers in the 1640s and early 1650s and archived at Trinity College Dublin, the 1641
depositions provide a rich source of evidence, not least about the differing regional
manifestations of the rebellion and local and individual experiences with violence and
survival.

Deposition evidence suggests that as the traditional structures of authority disintegrated in October and November 1641, a popular rebellion emerged. The violence of the
early weeks of the rising reflected inequalities that had been created and sustained by
the Stuart plantations, with evidence suggesting that participants pursued grievances
arising from economic hardship and debt. Likewise, rebel references to perceived New
English abuses of the law suggest resentment over the loss of political power and social
prestige.[21] It is also clear that some violence simply arose from opportunistic attacks on
dispersed and disorganized settlers.[22]

In some cases, the depositions allow a close look at specific attacks and the interpersonal dynamics that informed violence. For example, in an article on the murder of
Arthur Champion, a New English planter in Fermanagh, Raymond Gillespie, finds that
the outbreak of the rising presented an opportunity to avenge a history of bad neighbourly behaviour and a generally quarrelsome disposition.[23] The depositions also shed
light on social dynamics in local communities. The failure of English planters to mobilize for self-defence, the refusal of Scots planters to join with English neighbours against

the rebels, and examples of New English Protestants renouncing their religion suggest isolation, fragmentation, and mistrust within the settler population. On the other hand, microhistorical evidence demonstrates how some newcomers had been able to build community relationships across confessional and ethnic lines. In county Cavan, the experience of the Scottish minister George Creichton demonstrates how ties of charity, neighbourhood, and kinship could assist an endangered settler during the rising.[24]

Deposition evidence also reveals divisions between Scottish and English settlers during the first weeks of the rising. Whereas English planters seemed unable to respond collectively to the outbreak of the rising in Ulster, the Scots proved much more capable of organizing for self-defence. At Killeshandra in county Cavan, Sir James Hamilton and Sir James Craig organized a garrison that held out against the rebels until the summer of 1642.[25] In the Laggan valley, Sir William Stewart and Sir Robert Stewart organized a militia force that remained active in north-west Ulster throughout the 1640s.[26] This partially reflects the fact that the rebels focused their attention on English settlers during the first weeks of the rising, largely avoiding conflict with the Scots. The fact that the Scottish plantations tended to be more ethnically homogeneous and organized around kinship ties also proved significant.

There are numerous references to rebel partisans who claimed that they had no intention of attacking their Scottish neighbours, and the depositions reflect some accommodation between the rebels and Scottish planters in the north, including a handful of cases in which deponents alleged that Scots took pleasure in witnessing and sometimes participated in attacks on English settlers.[27] The presence of Scottish Catholics should also not be overlooked. In the early months of 1642, for example, the earl of Antrim's Scottish tenants joined with the Irish rebels. This material also suggests a significant ethnic component to the rising, which connects to repeated assertions in the depositions that Irish rebels waged symbolic attacks on English cultural artefacts, for example massacring English breeds of livestock.[28]

A growing number of local studies of the rising based on the depositions point to significant regional differences. For example, references to acts of violence appear more commonly in central Ulster than in depositions from the south and east. The rebellion manifested itself in Munster and Leinster gradually, giving settlers time to prepare for self-defence or flight. Depositions from the Munster plantations also suggest a great deal of interaction between various religious and ethnic constituents, including intermarriage and bilingualism, which may have mediated some local tensions.

FRAMING THE REBELLION: THE 1641 RISING AND THE CRISIS OF THE THREE KINGDOMS

In contrast to the complexities evident on the ground in Ireland, English observers found it easy to make sense of the rising. In the spring of 1641, the architects of Wentworth's trial had framed the Lord Deputy's actions as part of a broader popish plot.

The rising confirmed these fears and widespread print coverage played an important role in further disseminating anti-popish anxieties. As much as one-third of England's total print output in October 1641–March 1642 dealt in some manner with the rising.[29]

Much of the English print coverage of the rising stressed atrocity and asserted that Irish Catholics waged a war of extermination against Protestants and Englishmen. Typically short and cheap, pamphlets and tracts on the rebellion contained many sensationalized elements, including graphic and melodramatic scenes of arbitrary violence. A tract entitled *Treason in Ireland*, for example, described the murder of Protestant children, the massacre of twenty families in a plantation town, the rape of a virgin in the presence of her captive parents, the decapitation and mutilation of an aged woman, and an incident in which Irish Catholics sexually assaulted an English maiden and then drowned her in a hot cauldron.[30] Texts with lurid titles such as *Bloody News from Ireland, The Rebels' Turkish Tyranny, The Tears of Ireland*, and *Worse and Worse News From Ireland* repeated similar accusations.[31] Explicitly, a number of these works also connected the rebellion to Catholic interests on the Continent. For example, in his 1642 work entitled *A Remonstrance of Diverse Remarkable Passages Concerning the Church and Kingdom of Ireland*, Henry Jones, dean of Kilmore and chief collector of the 1641 depositions asserted 'that from Spain they did expect an army. . . . From France also they looked for aid. Being in all this further encouraged by bulls from Rome.'[32]

Whereas atrocities and popish intrigue took centre stage in print, in general, the depositions tended to focus on theft and the destruction of property. Even in parts of Ulster where violence was significant, the evidence from the depositions is anything but clear. Close readings of particular acts of atrocity suggest significant differences in accounts, problems with chronology and coherence, and cross-fertilization as deponents failed to differentiate between events that they had witnessed directly and those that they had heard about from other settlers.[33] Interpreting other kinds of violence can be equally difficult. For example, English pamphlets repeatedly asserted episodes of rape, but references to these crimes are almost non-existent in the depositions.[34]

English printed material provides evidence of growing mistrust of Charles I's conduct. Although no pamphlet went so far as to assert the king's participation in the rising, cheap print did publicize rebel claims about royal support for their actions, often framing these accounts as examples of Irish treachery. Henry Jones's *Remonstrance*, for example, dwelled upon the forged commission, reported on rebel rumours that Charles was present in Ulster, and repeated rebel boasts that the queen had played a key role in directing the rising.[35]

The English parliament participated directly in the process of connecting the rebellion to popish plots. Within days of receiving news of the rising in November 1641, John Pym renewed discussion of the Grand Remonstrance in the Commons. This document reiterated suspicions of Wentworth's conduct and connected generic anti-popish fears to the outbreak of the rebellion. In Ireland, the Grand Remonstrance asserted, 'they have had time and opportunity to mold and prepare their work' and only divine providence had stopped them from having 'totally subverted the government of it, routed out religion, and destroyed all the Protestants.'[36]

Reconstruction of reader response to this material is difficult, but the evidence from crowd protests in London and petitioning campaigns in the provinces suggests that this synthesis of recent Irish events found a sympathetic audience. The last week of December 1641 proved especially intense in the metropolis, with the Commons accepting several petitions from diverse constituencies of Londoners who connected the Irish rebellion to calls for reform of the Church of England and self-defence against popish enemies. Outside London, the rising also had a destabilizing effect. Settlers fleeing from the Irish conflict began appearing in English and Scottish ports in December and January, bringing with them tales of misery and woe. Panics, although not common, also occasionally broke out in 1642 as local communities responded with fear to the movements of persons displaced from Ireland as a result of war.[37]

In Ireland, the English characterization of the rising as a popish plot played an important role in forcing together mutually suspicious Irish and Old English Catholics. The Lord Justices' proclamation of 23 October 1641 presented the rising as the work of 'evil affected Irish papists' and this underlying sentiment characterized Dublin Castle's response to the rising.[38] Over the winter of 1641–2, the state organized raids out of the city and commanders like Sir Charles Coote often failed to differentiate between loyal and rebellious Catholics. For Old English Catholics who had attempted to separate themselves from the rebellion, the state's crackdown on popery and advocacy of indiscriminate violence proved demoralizing and destabilizing, and led to defections into rebellion.[39] In turn, as Old English Catholics embraced the rising, Dublin Castle could further justify the brutality of New English attacks in the Pale. Thus, by the late spring of 1642, the Ulster-centred and Irish-led rebellion had morphed into a nationwide and multi-ethnic revolution.

During the spring and summer of 1642, the conflict moved into a period of internationalization and stalemate. Although the Dublin administration seemed in danger of collapse in October and November 1641, by April 1642 things had turned around considerably. Troops based in Dublin had mostly pacified the Pale, albeit at the cost of alienating and driving away many loyal Catholics. Following a string of victories early in the war, Phelim O'Neill suffered a major defeat when New English troops raised the siege of Drogheda in March 1642, and with the coming of spring, reinforcements from England and Scotland could be expected. A force of 2500 Scots under General Robert Munro arrived in April, and proved immediately successful in rolling back the tide of rebellion in east Ulster.

Many of these developments occurred in spite of rather than as a result of actions in the English parliament. Although parliamentary business in late 1641 had been dominated by Irish affairs, a concrete response to the rising developed slowly. Through the end of December 1641, the Commons focused primarily on symbolic acts, such as the Grand Remonstrance and the celebration of fast days to reflect on the crisis in Ireland. Inaction in parliament provided traction for claims of a popish plot, with some critics asserting that the long delays revealed the sinister machinations of a popish fifth column comprised of the Laudian bishops, Catholic lords, members of the Queen's household, and English recusants.

After the king's flight from London in mid-January 1642, Irish affairs became a point of moderate cooperation between crown and parliament. In late January, Charles I authorized the Act for a Speedy Contribution and Loan, which created a mechanism for raising money to be used towards the relief of displaced Irish Protestants.[40] In March, the more ambitious Act for the Speedy and Effectual Reducing of the Rebels in His Majesty's Kingdom of Ireland, more commonly known as the Adventurers' Act, passed into law.[41] With the Adventurers' Act, the English parliament claimed authority to seize and redistribute property belonging to men who had taken up arms in Ireland. On a practical level, the Adventurers' Act funded the pacification of the rebellion with money contributed by English investors who would eventually be reimbursed with Irish land.[42]

Realignment: Charles I, the Catholic Confederation, and the Cessation

The Adventures' Act left little doubt that an English victory in Ireland would be followed by massive dispossession of Catholic property and a vigorous English parliamentary intrusion into Irish affairs. The Act formalized the constitutional revisions that the English parliament had been asserting since the trial of Thomas Wentworth. In what amounted to a heavy-handed intrusion on the king's prerogatives, the Act prohibited royal pardons for Irish rebels without parliamentary authorization, gave the English parliament the mandate to determine when the counter-offensive in Ireland was complete, and created a panel of commissioners who would report directly to parliament on the progress of the war. Charles I did try to rein in some of this transformative momentum, refusing, for example, to provide a royal warrant to the parliamentary commissioners sent to Dublin in the autumn of 1642. Even so, the language of the new statute clearly indicated that the English parliament and its investor allies would play a much-expanded role in post-conquest Ireland.

With the Adventurers' Act, the Long Parliament thus created a mechanism for waging a war of conquest framed around the extinction of Irish Catholic political and economic interests. For Irish Catholics, this development played a key role in the formation of the Catholic Confederation in June 1642. As early as March 1642, Catholic clergy meeting at Kells agreed to excommunicate any Catholic who took up arms for Dublin Castle. In May and June 1642, meetings of priests and the heads of key Irish and Old English families at Kilkenny formalized these measures by creating a structure for managing the political and military situation in rebel-controlled territory.[43] In the summer and autumn of 1642, Irish soldiers who had served Spain on the Continent began to return to Ireland. These professional soldiers helped improve the Confederate army, which in turn strengthened the bargaining position of the Catholic Confederation.

A constitutional argument lay at the heart of Confederate activism. The oath of association promulgated at Kilkenny in June 1642 included a pledge of allegiance to Charles I.

The Confederates, however, married this claim of allegiance to a call for substantial revisions to Ireland's constitutional position in the British Isles. Confederate leaders hoped to see major concessions from Charles I, including the repeal of Poyning's Law and the creation of an autonomous Irish parliament, official recognition of distinct Irish legal traditions, and guarantees of the free practice of the Roman Catholic religion. In the context of the British crisis of 1641–2, the proposed constitutional revisions were not entirely implausible. Indeed, many of the key principles floated by the Confederation paralleled the constitutional arguments of the Scottish Covenanters.[44]

The outbreak of civil war in England and the stalemate that developed after the battle of Newbury enhanced the potential for a negotiated settlement between Charles I and the Catholic Confederation. From the crown's perspective, forces tied up in Ireland represented wasted resources, which could be used to the royalists' advantage in the English theatre of war if a workable peace could be achieved in Ireland. Moreover, as the English conflict wore on, serious divisions emerged among the New English in Ireland. These tensions pitted those who identified themselves as primarily loyal to Charles I against those who saw themselves as primarily loyal to the anti-popish offensive and viewed the English parliament's advocacy of the Adventurers' Act as an important component of Ireland's future security.

The Confederate cause benefited from discord among New English and Protestant interests, but also showed signs of strain. As Micheál Ó Siochrú's essay in this volume argues, it is easy to overstate conflicts between the Old English and Irish within the Catholic Confederation. At the same time, however, tensions between those who had pre-rebellion properties and prestige to fall back on, including many of the prominent Old English families, and those who had already suffered dispossession as a result of the plantations could create very different outlooks on a negotiated settlement with the king.

Following several military setbacks in the spring of 1643, the Catholic Confederation entered into serious discussions with James Butler, first marquis of Ormond over a one-year ceasefire. When Ormond announced the Cessation on 15 September 1643, it reflected the hopes of both parties rather than any tangible agreement on the complicated political and constitutional issues. For the crown especially, the agreement had a great deal of dangerous potential. Further negotiations with the Confederation would likely require concessions on constitutional issues and the prosecution of men who had participated in the early months of the rebellion. The Adventurers' Act, however, rendered both requirements impossible. The potential for resumed hostilities when the Cessation expired also meant that Charles I would have to make a significant gamble if he intended to draw military resources out of Ireland to support the royalist cause in England.

The Cessation also had the immediate effect of devastating hopes for further accommodation between the royalist and anti-papist factions of the New English in Ireland.[45] A number of high-profile military commanders in service to Dublin Castle openly questioned or resisted the Cessation entirely. The Scots troops in Ulster also presented a major problem. The English parliament's cooperation with the Scots left a major military force in the field and beyond the reach of the ceasefire agreement. As the conflict in

Ireland evolved in the mid-1640s, these troops would become increasingly important in any political calculus.[46]

In a British context, the Cessation represented a major turning point. Predictably, the English parliament framed the Cessation as a major betrayal of the godly cause. Outrage over the Cessation in turn paved the way for formal cooperation between the English parliament and the Scottish Covenanters. On 25 September 1643, only ten days after publication of the ceasefire, parliament adopted the Solemn League and Covenant. This effectively completed the process of realignment that had begun in early 1643. Ormond and the Confederates had now entered into an uneasy and unpredictable ceasefire and began long-term negotiations for a peace favourable to English royalists. Tensions among the New English had exploded into open division. Opponents of the Cessation publicly connected themselves to the English parliamentary cause against the crown, and Ulster—seat of the 1641 rebellion and the region where the Irish rising had had its most important early successes—fell under occupation by Scottish forces allied with the English parliament.

In retrospect, Charles I lost the most as a result of this realignment. In 1641, hints of crown complicity in the rising had appeared on the fringes of political discourse and were presented as evidence of the rebels' treasonous disrespect for authority rather than as a criticism of the crown. With the Cessation, however, some Irish Protestant leaders now openly questioned the king. According to this view, Charles I, in an effort to expand his war against Protestants in England and Scotland, had allied himself with those Catholics who in 1641 had massacred scores of Protestant settlers. This was an important moment on the road to revolution in England. To his enemies, the crown's participation in the Cessation provided further evidence of an untrustworthy king who was willing to make war against his own Protestant subjects. The representation of Charles I as a 'man of blood' owed much to this development.

HISTORIOGRAPHY AND HISTORICAL MEMORY: THE LONG VIEW OF THE 1641 RISING

During the 1640s, published accounts of the rising often asserted authenticity by appealing to the authority of the Irish Lord Justices and by drawing on the 1641 depositions. Henry Jones's *Remonstrance of Diverse Remarkable Passages Concerning the Church and Kingdom of Ireland*, which appeared in the spring of 1642, represents an early example of this kind of account. Prefaced by letters from the Irish Lord Justices attesting to its veracity, the *Remonstrance* assembled heavily edited and excised versions of depositions taken during the first month of the rising into an assertion of rebel intentions to enact 'a general extirpation even to the last and least drop of English blood'.[47]

The same general structure appears in Sir John Temple's *The Irish Rebellion*, first published in London in 1646. Like Jones, Temple presented selectively edited information from the depositions and supporting material from Dublin Castle administrators. *The Irish Rebellion* also reflected the realignments of the mid-1640s, presenting the Cessation as a betrayal of those Protestants who had suffered through the dislocations of 1641. Temple's work had a unique longevity, appearing in at least ten editions over the next century and a half, with the last appearing in 1812.[48] Asserting a simple version of the rising as an indiscriminate and brutal massacre of Protestants, Temple's work fit comfortably with other early modern accounts of Protestant martyrdom, particularly John Foxe's *Acts and Monuments*.[49] It also asserted the grossly exaggerated claim of more than 100,000 Protestant deaths, a figure that became deeply entrenched in slanted accounts of the rising.[50]

During episodes of political stress in the British Isles, appeals to memories of the 1641 rising could serve the interests of Protestant polemicists. John Milton's *Eikonoklastes*, for example, justified the regicide in part by asserting that Charles I bore responsibility for more than half a million Protestant deaths in Ireland by having been 'ever friendly to the Irish papists'.[51] In the 1680s and 90s, a flurry of works drawing on memories of 1641 appeared in both England and Ireland, including a new edition of Temple and Edmund Borlase's similarly structured *History of the Execrable Irish Rebellion*.[52] Well into the nineteenth century, works of historical fiction such as William Godwin's *Mandeville* (1817) and James Meikle's *Killinchy* (1839), likewise asserted as fact a general and indiscriminate massacre of Protestants in 1641.[53]

Protestant commemorative culture sustained memories of the 1641 rising. From 1661 into the late eighteenth century, commemorations of the rising occurred in Dublin on 23 October.[54] Printed versions of 23 October sermons, often stressing the cruelty of Roman Catholics and the theme of providential deliverance, began to appear in the crisis years of the mid-1680s and intensified after the Glorious Revolution.[55] These fit into an arc of Protestant celebration that also incorporated commemorations of William III's birthday (4 November) and Gunpowder Plot (5 November).[56] Simplistic narrations of the rising stressing Catholic-on-Protestant violence survived in the service of sectarian agendas into the twenty-first century. References to mass drownings at Portadown, for example, appeared on Orange Order marching banners and public memorials.[57] Essays disseminated by the Ian Paisley-affiliated European Institute of Protestant Studies likewise continue to present the rising as a 'vicious, unprovoked bloodbath engineered by Rome against Protestants'.[58]

In part thanks to the dispossession of Irish Catholics in the aftermath of the Cromwellian conquest and the War of the Two Kings, few competing accounts of the rising appeared in the seventeenth and eighteenth centuries. Irish Catholics, however, did recognize the significant power of historical memory and the ways that commemorative culture in particular sustained interpretations of the rising that served anti-popish agendas. Thus, the short-lived Irish Patriot Parliament called by James II in 1689 abolished commemorations of 23 October.[59] Occasional printed pieces framed the Irish rising as a matter of Catholic self-defence, critiqued the massively inflated casualty figures found in Temple and similar works, and counterpoised evidence of Protestant atrocities, including massacres of non-combatants, during the war. Hugh Reily's *Ireland's Case Briefly Stated*, originally published in 1695 and reprinted at several points in the eighteenth century represents the most thorough of such retorts to the Protestant historiography.[60]

Some of the earliest syntheses of the rising, particularly Jones's *Remonstrance* and Temple's *Irish Rebellion*, drew upon the 1641 depositions as evidence. It should therefore come as no surprise that debates on the reliability of the archive played an important role in the early historiography of the rising.[61] Historians began to tentatively probe the depositions during the late nineteenth century. Much of this early work, however, misused the depositions and repeated assertions that would be familiar to seventeenth-century readers of John Temple. James Anthony Froude's *The English in Ireland in the Eighteenth Century*, for example, asserted that the depositions represented an 'eternal witness of blood, which the Irish Catholics have from that time to this been vainly trying to wash away'.[62] Mary Hickson's *Ireland in the Seventeenth Century* bore an imperious preface by Froude and printed heavily edited versions of selected depositions that asserted universal 'massacres . . . begun by the Roman Catholics on the 23rd of October at the instigation of the majority of their priests'.[63] On the other side, critics such as Robert Dunlop and John T. Gilbert countered that the self-interested motives of the Dublin Castle administrators, the commissioners responsible for compiling the depositions, and the deponents themselves rendered the entire archive suspect. The former concluded that virtually all evidence pertaining to violence in the depositions had been tainted by the biases of men and women 'maddened with recent losses and yearning for revenge', which 'rendered it impossible for us to discriminate between what was false and what was true in them'.[64]

Apart from an abortive attempt to calendar and publish the 1641 depositions under the auspices of the Irish Manuscripts Commission in the 1930s, the archive remained largely unutilized for much of the twentieth century.[65] Over the past three decades, however, historians have rediscovered the richness of the archive and significantly expanded scholarship on the rising. Work with the depositions necessitates engagement with the biases of the witnesses and those who recorded testimony. Despite these challenges, the archive contains a wealth of evidence on social, economic, and cultural issues. The online release of the depositions, including both facsimile and transcribed versions of the archive and full text search capacities, opens dramatic opportunities for many more studies of the social and cultural context of the rising.[66]

NOTES

1. Edward Hyde, First Earl of Clarendon, *The History of the Rebellion and Civil Wars in England*, ed. W. Dunn Macray (Oxford, 1888), I, 397.

2. John Nalson, *An Impartial Collection of the Great Affairs of State* (London, 1683), II, 514.

3. For historiographical surveys of literature on the rising, see in particular Toby Barnard, '1641: A Bibliographic Essay', in Brian Mac Cuarta (ed.), *Ulster 1641: Aspects of the Rising*

(Belfast, 1993), 173–86; Jane H. Ohlmeyer, 'Seventeenth Century Ireland and the New British Histories', *American Historical Review*, 104 (1999): 446–62.

4. Aidan Clarke, 'The 1641 Depositions', in Peter Fox (ed.), *Treasures of the Library: Trinity College Dublin* (Dublin, 1986), 111–22.

5. Aidan Clarke, 'Ireland and the General Crisis', *Past and Present [P&P]*, 48 (1970): 79–99; J. H. Elliott, 'A Europe of Composite Monarchies', *P&P*, 137 (1992): 58–9, 64–5; Geoffrey Parker, 'The Crisis of the Spanish and the Stuart Monarchies in the Mid-Seventeenth Century: Local Problems or Global Problems?', in Ciaran Brady and Jane H. Ohlmeyer (eds.), *British Interventions in Early Modern Ireland* (Cambridge, 2005), 252–79.

6. H. F. Kearney, *Strafford in Ireland, 1633–1641: A Study in Absolutism* (Manchester, 1959).

7. Nicholas Canny, *Making Ireland British, 1580–1650* (Oxford, 2001), 187–205.

8. Alan Ford, *The Protestant Reformation in Ireland, 1590–1641* (Dublin, 1997), 161–2.

9. John Rushworth, *Historical Collections of Private Passages of State* (London, 1721–), VIII, 11–14.

10. Maija Jansson (ed.), *Proceedings in the Opening Session of the Long Parliament* (Rochester, NY, 2000), I, pt. 1, 37.

11. Rushworth, *Historical Collections*, VIII, 73.

12. Rushworth, *Historical Collections*, VIII, 773.

13. M. Perceval-Maxwell, *The Outbreak of the Irish Rebellion of 1641* (Montreal, 1994), 166–176.

14. Canny, *Making Ireland British*, 353–6.

15. Perceval-Maxwell, *Outbreak of the Irish Rebellion*, 204–5, 219–20, 225–6; Canny, *Making Ireland British*, 493–4, 503–5.

16. Aidan Clarke, *The Old English in Ireland, 1625–1642* (Ithaca, NY, 1966), 165–8; Perceval-Maxwell, *Outbreak of the Irish Rebellion*, 218–19; Raymond Gillespie, 'Political Ideas and Their Social Contexts in Seventeenth-Century Ireland', in Jane H. Ohlmeyer (ed.), *Political Thought in Seventeenth-Century Ireland: Kingdom or Colony* (Cambridge, 2000), 113.

17. Trinity College Dublin Ms. 836, 18; R. Dunlop, 'The Forged Commission of 1641', *English Historical Review [EHR]*, 2 (1887): 530–3.

18. John T. Gilbert (ed.), *A Contemporary History of Affairs in Ireland from 1641 to 1652* (Dublin, 1879), I, pt. 1, 364.

19. Perceval-Maxwell, *Outbreak of the Irish Rebellion*, 234–5.

20. Micheál Ó Siochrú, 'Catholic Confederates and the Constitutional Relationship between Ireland and England, 1641–1649', in Brady and Ohlmeyer (eds.), *British Interventions in Early Modern Ireland*, 212–13.

21. Raymond Gillespie, 'The End of an Era: Ulster and the Outbreak of the 1641 Rising', in Ciaran Brady and Raymond Gillespie (eds.), *Natives and Newcomers: Essays on the Making of Irish Colonial Society* (Dublin, 1986), 205–7; Canny, *Making Ireland British*, 474–6; Perceval-Maxwell, *Outbreak of the Irish Rebellion*, 229–33.

22. Canny, *Making Ireland British*, 512.

23. Raymond Gillespie, 'The Murder of Arthur Champion and the 1641 Rising in Fermanagh', *Clogher Record*, 14 (1993): 52–66.

24. Joseph Cope, *England and the 1641 Irish Rebellion* (Woodbridge, 2009), 59–61.

25. Gilbert, *Contemporary History of Affairs in Ireland*, I, pt. 1, 494–7.

26. Kevin McKenny, *The Laggan Army in Ireland, 1640–1685: The Landed Interests, Political Ideologies and Military Campaigns of the North-West Ulster Settlers* (Dublin, 2005), 35–55; David Stevenson, *Scottish Covenanters and Irish Confederates: Scottish–Irish Relations in the Mid-Seventeenth Century* (Belfast, 1981), 93–6.

27. Canny, *Making Ireland British*, 482–3.

28. Perceval-Maxwell, *Outbreak of the Irish Rebellion*, 232–3; Canny, *Making Ireland British*, 497.

29. Keith J. Lindley, 'The Impact of the 1641 Irish Rebellion upon England and Wales, 1641–5', *Irish Historical Studies*, 18 (1972–3): 144–7; David O'Hara, *English Newsbooks and the Irish Rebellion, 1641–1649* (Dublin, 2006), 27–54.

30. Stephen Jerome, *Treason in Ireland* (London, 1641), 4–5.

31. Cope, *England and the 1641 Irish Rebellion*, 76–88.

32. Henry Jones, *Remonstrance of Diverse Remarkable Passages Concerning the Church and Kingdom of Ireland* (London, 1642), 2.

33. Hilary Simms, 'Violence in County Armagh', in Mac Cuarta (ed.), *Ulster 1641*, 123–38.

34. Mary O'Dowd, 'Women and War in Ireland in the 1640s', in Margaret MacCurtain and Mary O'Dowd (eds.), *Women in Early Modern Ireland* (Edinburgh, 1991), 91–111; Canny, *Making Ireland British*, 544–5.

35. Jones, *Remonstrance*, 5.

36. S. R. Gardiner (ed.), *Constitutional Documents of the Puritan Revolution, 1625–1660*, 3rd edn. (Oxford, 1906), 228.

37. Cope, *England and the 1641 Irish Rebellion*, 112–18; Robin Clifton, 'The Popular Fear of Catholics during the English Revolution', *P&P*, 52 (1971): 29–31.

38. Historical Manuscripts Commission, *Calendar of the Manuscripts of the Marquess of Ormonde*, new series (London, 1903), II, 1; Clarke, *Old English in Ireland*, 177; Jane H. Ohlmeyer, 'The Irish Peers, Political Power and Parliament, 1640–1', in Brady and Ohlmeyer (eds.), *British Interventions in Early Modern Ireland*, 174–5; Pádraig Lenihan, *Confederate Catholics at War, 1641–9* (Cork, 2001), 23.

39. Robert Armstrong, *Protestant War: The 'British' of Ireland and the Wars of the Three Kingdoms* (Manchester, 2005), 21–2, 33–6; Kenneth Nichols, 'The Other Massacres: English Killings of Irish, 1641–2', in David Edwards, Pádraig Lenihan, and Clodagh Tait (eds.), *Age of Atrocity: Violence and Political Conflict in Early Modern Ireland* (Dublin, 2007), 176–91.

40. John Raithby (ed.), *The Statutes that Passed into Law under Charles I and Charles II, Including the Legislation of the Long and Short Parliaments, before the Interregnum, and of the Restoration after* (London, 1819) [*SR*], V, 141–3.

41. *SR*, V, 168–72.

42. Karl S. Bottigheimer, *English Money and Irish Land: The 'Adventurers' in the Cromwellian Settlement of Ireland* (Oxford, 1971), 44–7; Patrick Little, 'The English Parliament and the Irish Constitution, 1641–9', in Micheál Ó Siochrú (ed.), *Kingdoms in Crisis: Ireland in the 1640s* (Dublin, 2001), 110–11.

43. Micheál Ó Siochrú, *Confederate Ireland 1642–1649: A Constitutional and Political Analysis* (Dublin, 1999), 43–53.

44. Michael Perceval-Maxwell, 'Ireland and the Monarchy in the Early Stuart Multiple Kingdom', *Historical Journal* [*HJ*] 34 (1991): 282–3.

45. Armstrong, *Protestant War*, 92–3.

46. Stevenson, *Scottish Covenanters and Irish Confederates*, 145–9.

47. Jones, *Remonstrance*, 7; Joseph Cope, 'Fashioning Victims: Dr. Henry Jones and the Plight of Irish Protestants', *Historical Research*, 74 (2001): 370–91.

48. Kathleen Noonan, ' "Martyrs in Flames": Sir John Temple and the Conception of the Irish in English Martyrologies', *Albion*, 36 (2004): 225; Kathleen Noonan, ' "The Cruel Pressure of an Enraged, Barbarous People": Irish and English Identity in Seventeenth-Century Policy and Propaganda', *HJ*, 41 (1998): 176.

49. Noonan, ' "Martyrs in Flames" ', 230–2.

50. John Temple, *The Irish Rebellion, Or an History of the Beginning and First Progress of the General Rebellion Raised within the Kingdom of Ireland* (London, 1646), 106.

51. John Milton, *The Prose Works of John Milton* (London, 1834), I, 306.

52. Toby Barnard, '"Parlour Entertainment in an Evening?" Histories of the 1640s', in Mac Cuarta (ed.), *Ulster 1641*, 28.

53. John Gibney, *The Shadow of a Year: The 1641 Rebellion in Irish History and Memory* (Madison, WI, 2013), 63–5, 97.

54. Toby Barnard, 'The Uses of 23 October 1641 and Irish Protestant Celebrations', *English Historical Review*, 106 (1991): 890; Toby Barnard, 'Crises of Identity among Irish Protestants, 1641–1685', *P&P*, 127 (1990): 56–7.

55. Barnard, 'The Uses of 23 October 1641', 894–5; Richard Anwell, 'The 1688 Revolution in Ireland and the Memory of 1641', in Mark Williams and Stephen Paul Forrest (eds.), *Constructing the Past: Writing Irish History, 1600–1800* (Woodbridge, 2010), 75–6, 84–5.

56. James Kelly, '"The Glorious and Immortal Memory": Commemoration and Protestant Identity in Ireland 1600–1800', *Proceedings of the Royal Irish Academy*, 94 (1994): 42–3.

57. Brian Mac Cuarta, 'Introduction', in Mac Cuarta (ed.), *Ulster 1641*, 187, n. 1.

58. Clive Gillis, *Caustic Comments in Brief: Days of Deliverance Part 7*, <http://www.ianpaisley.org/article.asp?ArtKey=deliverance7> (19 February 2013).

59. Kelly, '"The Glorious and Immortal Memory"', 29–30.

60. Gibney, *Shadow of a Year*, 79–81.

61. Barnard, '"Parlour Entertainment in an Evening"', 36.

62. James Anthony Froude, *The English in Ireland in the Eighteenth Century* (London, 1874), I, 101.

63. Mary Hickson, *Ireland in the Seventeenth Century, or the Irish Massacres of 1641–2* (London, 1884), I, 164.

64. R. Dunlop, 'The Depositions Relating to the Irish Massacres of 1641: A Response', *EHR*, 2 (1887): 339.

65. Gibney, *Shadow of a Year*, 138.

66. Trinity College Dublin Library, *The 1641 Depositions*, <http://1641.tcd.ie> (26 February 2013).

FURTHER READING

Armstrong, Robert, *Protestant War: the 'British' of Ireland and the Wars of the Three Kingdoms* (Manchester, 2005).

Bottigheimer, Karl S., *English Money and Irish Land: The 'Adventurers' in the Cromwellian Settlement of Ireland* (Oxford, 1971).

Canny, Nicholas, *Making Ireland British, 1580–1650* (Oxford, 2001).

Clarke, Aidan, *The Old English in Ireland, 1625–42* (Ithaca, NY, 1966).

Cope, Joseph, *England and the 1641 Irish Rebellion* (Woodbridge, 2009).

Gibney, John, *The Shadow of a Year: The 1641 Irish Rebellion in Irish History and Memory* (Madison, WI, 2013).

Lenihan, Pádraig, *Confederate Catholics at War, 1641–49* (Cork, 2001).

Mac Cuarta, Brian (ed.), *Ulster 1641: Aspects of the Rising* (Belfast, 1993).

Ó Siochrú, Micheál, *Confederate Ireland 1642–1649: A Constitutional and Political Analysis* (Dublin, 1999).

Ó Siochrú, Micheál (ed.), *Kingdoms in Crisis: Ireland in the 1640s* (Dublin, 2001).

O'Hara, David, *English Newsbooks and Irish Rebellion, 1641–1649* (Dublin, 2006).

Ohlmeyer, Jane H. (ed.), *Ireland from Independence to Occupation, 1641–1660* (Cambridge, 1990).

Perceval-Maxwell, Michael, *The Outbreak of the Irish Rebellion of 1641* (Montreal, 1994).

Russell, Conrad, 'The British Background to the Irish Rebellion of 1641', *Historical Research*, 61 (1988): 166–182.

Stevenson, David, *Scottish Covenanters and Irish Confederates: Scottish–Irish Relations in the Mid-Seventeenth Century* (Belfast, 1981).

CHAPTER 6

WAR AND POLITICS IN ENGLAND AND WALES, 1642–1646

MICHAEL J. BRADDICK

THERE are many histories of the war in England and many more histories of English politics of the 1640s, but attempts to link the two are more difficult to find. Political histories tend to track the fate of particular blocks of opinion, and their shifting fortunes at Westminster or at the heart of the royalist war effort in Oxford. Military histories, on the other hand, tend to narrate campaigns, having first described the ways in which armies were put together, supplied, and organized. In fact these processes continually intertwined, as politicians mobilized for war.[1] Military campaigns were an extension of the political process, part of an 'armed negotiation'. How the activists mobilized support varied over time, and an important element of the process was political persuasion. This produced a rapidly shifting terrain of political argument, amplified by the very public debates which the appeal for support encouraged. This chapter narrates these shifts, as England became the cockpit for a wider set of conflicts in all three kingdoms. I then reflect on the advantages of analysing political mobilization rather than allegiance as a way of understanding both the dynamism and creativity of civil war politics, and the relationship between this short-term crisis and the longer-term history of state formation.

THE OUTBREAK OF THE WAR IN ENGLAND

It is conventional to claim that during 1642 England slid into war. This familiar phrase is often difficult to comprehend, however—how can a war start accidentally, or at least without considerable and conscious will to start one? The explanation in this case is that activists tried to take control of armed resources pre-emptively, fearing attack by their enemies. Active opponents of royal policy sought to take control of the country's military resources in order to defend their political gains from what they feared would be a royalist reaction. Fundamentally, they were acting defensively—disarming first Catholics and then the malignant party that surrounded the king. The royalists, naturally, resisted this process, also seeking to take control of the military resources of the kingdom and in so doing fuelling fears for the future on the parliamentary side. Jostling became skirmishing and, in the autumn, open warfare.[2]

In the course of this process a paper war was fought, seeking to persuade a wider public about the fundamental principles at stake. Over the previous two years a print market had developed in England effectively free of pre-publication censorship; political issues were increasingly being discussed before an essentially unregulated audience. This went alongside escalating petitioning campaigns, and crowd actions. In London crowds had applied direct pressure on parliamentary proceedings, famously around the trial of the earl of Strafford, but also in the heated weeks leading to Charles's departure from the city. In the counties too, crowd actions had a decisive political and military influence, often drawing on the rhetoric of national politics as justification.[3] Many people saw these developments as a fundamental challenge to political decency. This process continued throughout the decade as political and military action was enabled, but also prompted by, the mobilization of constituencies that had previously been outside the reach of factional or partisan politics. Despite (or perhaps because of) the radicalization of the political process, this paper war was largely fought over the middle ground—both sides claimed to be acting to defend the constitution.

Following the king's departure from London in January 1642 parliament pursued strong measures to secure the kingdom for Protestantism. This involved both measures to exclude popish forces from political influence—such as excluding the bishops from the House of Lords—and measures of physical defence—disarming Catholics, preventing impressment by the king, and, in February, taking control of the command of the county militias.[4] Some of this was done by ordinance—that is legislation which passed the Houses of Parliament but which did not have the royal assent necessary to make it a statute. In itself, the use of ordinances in these circumstances was potentially revolutionary. The king, meanwhile, avoided confrontation, perhaps waiting until the queen, who was increasingly plainly identified as one of the chief sources of popish threat in the kingdom, had been safely dispatched to the continent.

By the time the Militia Ordinance had passed, on 5 March, Henrietta Maria was safe and Charles was in a more confrontational mood. There followed, during the spring of 1642, a series of public exchanges between king and parliament about the crisis, in a process that would have been unthinkable in normal times. Some of the most fundamental constitutional issues, and the most sensitive policy questions, were openly debated for an unregulated audience, and it included quite plain accusations about whose fault the crisis was. As the king moved northward the ideological claims escalated, and this was in close step with the radical political measures taken by parliament to 'secure the kingdom', leading to the articulation of a theory of parliamentary sovereignty and of a distinct view of the nature of political liberty. In May the Militia Ordinance was put into execution—that is, the county militias were ordered to muster and train under parliament's authority, by the power of ordinance.[5] To accept such a measure was not only to deliver the principal military resources of the kingdom to parliament, but also to accept fundamental constitutional claims about where political power really lay. Moreover, it was hard not to realize this latter implication, since partisans had been spelling it out in print throughout the spring.

Parliament therefore faced a considerable challenge in justifying its policies—taking political and military measures to secure the kingdom against the threat of popery—and the constitutional means being used to pursue them—ordinances. And the problem was made worse by the fact that attendance in both Houses was falling as those alarmed by these developments chose to stay away. Some of the key public arguments were framed 'conservatively'—that is, with reference to precedent. For example, it was claimed that parliament could act as the Great Council of the kingdom when the king was away or incapacitated, and that matched the current situation.[6]

As the confrontation escalated, however, some of the parliamentary arguments set out principles that were both fundamental and potentially revolutionary. In particular, the Nineteen Propositions—a list of demands issued in May in response to a royalist challenge—set out a number of specific measures which amounted to the subordination of royal authority in key areas to parliamentary approval. The royalist response very plausibly presented this as a change to the constitution and that prompted parliamentarian sympathizers to spell out a theory of parliamentary sovereignty—that the supreme authority in the land was the parliament because it was the body which preserved the *salus populi*, the good of the people.[7] This was populist in principle and practice, since the arguments were being rehearsed in print for an audience which could not be controlled, and there was a drift of support to the king by people alarmed by the implications of this, in the light of the street politics and rural discontents of the last two years.[8]

The practical royal response to the Militia Ordinance was to order musters by a different authority—Commissions of Array. Individuals were charged with mustering men by personal command of the king and out of personal loyalty to him. This forced a practical choice, whether to obey one or the other, as well as creating the basis for rival military powers.[9] Key military resources, such as the arsenals at Hull and Portsmouth, or Dover Castle, were contested, or taken over by sleight of hand, and over the summer command of local militias and strong points led to some tense military confrontations—in Manchester in July, for example, or at Sherbourne Castle in September.[10] Parliament won control of the navy, which was to help sustain beleaguered forces in the West Country in the early years of the war, although it was not a sufficient force to prevent the supply of the royalist armies.[11]

This struggle for control of local military resources for defensive reasons was entangled with the formation of field armies intended for active campaigning. It is conventional to date the latter development to August, when the king raised his standard at Nottingham and summoned his supporters to join him. In fact, the two processes had entwined for some time prior to that, and in early September parliament had created a field army under the earl of Essex recruited largely from the London musters. On the royalist side the musters under the Commission of Array provided the basis for the king's field army too.[12]

By the time open warfare came it was late in the campaign season—moving troops and equipment became much more difficult in winter and the most active fighting in the war took place in the summer months. The two armies manoeuvred in the midlands, leading to a skirmish at Powick Bridge, outside Worcester, which is usually seen as the first battle of the war. The two armies met in earnest a month later at Edgehill, near Banbury, as parliament sought to block the king's advance on London. The battle was bloody, and shocked most observers, but it was not decisive. Parliamentary forces withdrew northwards the next day, and battle was not rejoined. Following some delay the main royalist army continued its advance on London, an advance party storming Brentford and the main army drawing up to face the parliamentary defenders at Turnham Green. This time, however, there was to be no battle; after a day of confrontation the royalist army withdrew and the campaign season was over.[13]

The key political issues from late 1641 onwards were, on the one hand, the threat of popery and its influence within royalist counsels, and the measures necessary to defend against it, and on the other, the threat of populist parliamentarian Protestantism, and the challenge it posed to political decency and the constitution. These immediate issues led to the introduction of practical measures which required constitutional justification, and this ideological escalation had moved in step with military mobilization. This was to be a feature of the years of open warfare—the need to secure military security, or victory, prompted measures which in themselves required political justification. They were justified to public audiences in print, through rival mobilizations in the counties and on the streets of London. This created an increasingly chaotic political debate, out of which arose very radical political arguments.

ADMINISTRATIVE AND POLITICAL ESCALATION IN 1643

The end of the fighting in late 1642 allowed the resumption of direct negotiation. In January the royalists received parliamentary commissioners in Oxford for peace negotiations—the Oxford treaty—but there was little shift in position on either side and the arguments did not move very far. Part cause and part effect of this was the fact that while they negotiated, the two sides also sought to mobilize to win a war.[14] From the winter of 1642/3 onwards escalation brought political realignment within both camps: as war escalated so did tensions *within* each side.

This was something of a contrast with the winter and spring of the previous year: it was much more obviously an active, offensive, military action. On the parliamentary side in particular this shift to preparation for a war, as opposed to primarily defensive attempts to secure control of military resources, produced administrative innovations which dramatically shifted the political arguments about the nature of the parliamentary cause, and led to some changes of side. While much of the political argument continued to seek out consensual middle ground, it was more difficult to reconcile with what the two armed camps were actually doing. Charges of hypocrisy filled the air, while some more radical arguments were made in print.[15]

One symptom of the escalating military conflict was the reduced space in which to be neutral or non-combatant. Over the summer and autumn of 1642 a number of areas had seen formal agreements to avoid open war, but these proved increasingly difficult to sustain. Armed parties emerged for the first time in a number of places during the spring, and the official position on non-alignment hardened. In March, for example, parliament approved a Sequestration Ordinance, which gave powers to seize the property of 'malignants'. Not only did this subordinate property rights to the power of Ordinances, but the definition of malignant was also very broad—it included, for example, those who did not pay parliamentary taxes. In early May a penal tax, the 5th and 20th part, was imposed on those who failed to support the parliamentary cause.

As this suggests, one reason why the space for non-partisanship became narrower was the escalating scale of administrative and military mobilization: to fail actively to support the war effort was clearly to hinder it.[16] In late February, the Assessment Ordinance had established a new tax, primarily based on land, which hugely increased the burden of public taxation. Administrative districts had large sums allocated to them and were simply left to divide it up by whatever means seemed fair. The origins and fairness of the quota are difficult to evaluate. At the same time counties were associated together on a much larger scale, under new committees with extensive powers, replacing (or at least rivalling) the existing structure of county government. In March there was a proposal to introduce an excise tax on domestic consumption, something which before the war had been regarded with horror, and it was eventually imposed in August 1643. These novel taxes and administrative powers were coordinated by a new structure of national and local committees, again of questionable constitutional propriety.[17]

One difficulty arising from these new forms of mobilization was that they might make the cure look worse than the disease. The two sides were in fact coalitions, often held together by fear of what the other side was trying to do, rather than a shared view of the religious and political future. Those afraid of the king's constitutional innovations might now have pause for thought, given both these innovations and parliament's claims about sovereignty or its willingness to address political issues directly to the people. The core claim on the parliamentary side, stressed in the discussions of these administrative measures, was that parliament was in defensive arms to protect the kingdom's religion and liberties. During the spring this was interpreted as a call to further religious reformation: a parliamentary committee, the Harley Committee, set about purifying London of idolatrous images, the great Cross at Cheapside was pulled down, and, later, Charles's Book of Sports (which set out what diversions were acceptable on the Sabbath) was burned on the site.[18]

This pointed up tensions in the parliamentary alliance between those who, crudely stated, wanted to defend the church against Charles's popery, and those who saw the opportunity to complete the purification of an incompletely reformed church. In the press and public debate the dangers of religious pluralism and undisciplined zeal were increasingly stressed, creating tensions between different parts of the parliamentary alliance.[19]

As events shifted and new policies were introduced, the politics of the coalitions and individual allegiances had to be reconsidered. We know much more about this on the parliamentary side, but it seems to have been true among the royalists too. On the par-liamentary side there was a clear counter-pressure to fix definitive versions of the 'cause' around which the alliance could be secured. Two crucial measures here were to convene an Assembly at Westminster to debate and define the religious practice which parlia-ment would see established in place of the Caroline church, and the imposition of the Vow and Covenant (following the Waller plot to deliver London to the royalists), by which individuals swore to uphold a particular version of the parliamentary cause. Pym seems to have favoured this latter approach, seeking on a number of occasions to imitate the Scottish success in drafting a statement like the National Covenant behind which all the well-affected could line up. In England it failed. In the Eastern Association the initial desire had been to swear an oath and then mobilize voluntarily behind it, but in the event the war was supported by Ordinances enforced by committees. Nationally it failed as successive documents were produced, which were slightly at odds with one another—the Protestation, the Vow and Covenant, and, most notoriously and problem-atically, the Solemn League and Covenant later in the year.[20]

Royalist administrative innovation was, by contrast, less marked. The king's main army was formed on the basis of the Commissions of Array. These had been slow to get going and at Edgehill had resulted in some troops being poorly armed—Welsh contin-gents, for example, included men using pitchforks—but did eventually produce a sub-stantial army. This was probably the largest the infantry got, however, and thereafter numbers could be maintained only with difficulty. The 1643 recruitment drive concen-trated on filling the existing regiments, not reforming the structure. The numbers of horse, by contrast, were doubled in the subsequent eight months, and this remained the core of the cavalry in the main army into 1644. Although the regimental structure was retained there were attempts to regularize the supply of the army, but again they were much less radical than changes to the parliamentary mobilization. In January an assess-ment was agreed for Oxford which became a model for other counties, related to the number of troops to be quartered in any particular place. The system was decentralized, however: little of the money passed through royalist headquarters in Oxford, and there was a high degree of local negotiation, and some abuse. The pattern of royalist mobiliza-tion remained the raising of regional armies by individuals, which were loosely coordi-nated by the royal council of war, which was in any case politically divided.[21]

Nonetheless, the pressure of events was causing creative shifts in royalist thinking too. It has recently been suggested that between poles of opinion that sought, on the one hand, a clear military victory or, on the other, a speedy political accommodation were those who wanted to make enough concessions in order to cut the ground from under the feet of the 'fiery spirits' on the parliamentary side. The viability of this tactic was clearly affected by the military fortunes of the armies. It also intersected with the religious aims of the royalists. Rather than a dogged adherence to a pre-civil war church in the face of increasingly wide-ranging challenges, royalist religion has been interpreted as a much more dynamic phenomenon, in which defence of clerical authority, and a national church, took different forms according to circumstance. At the outbreak of the war, it could appear straightforwardly to be a defence of the established church (shorn of Laudian innovation) in the face of radical challenge. As war and negotiation developed, however, this clericalist position might lead royalist clergy into conflict with leading royalist politicians, and even to seek to protect their position from the king himself. These tensions gave rise to radical statements about episcopal and clerical authority, and even for religious toleration.[22]

By the late summer the increased tempo of military mobilization had not produced a decisive outcome, although the royalists had the better of the fighting. The parliamentary measures of reform in the spring and early summer had taken place against a backdrop of generally disheartening military news. Ralph Hopton fought a successful royalist campaign in the west through much of the year, culminating in the famous victory at Roundway Down on 13 July. The earl of Newcastle was similarly successful in the north of England, winning a famous victory at Adwalton Moor in June. Meanwhile Henrietta Maria had been able to land at Bridlington in the spring, bringing military supplies to the king, and Cholmley, the parliamentary commander at Scarborough, deserted the cause. Parliament had some success in Lancashire, leading the earl of Derby to flee into exile on the Isle of Man, and Charles Waller fought a successful campaign in the south of England. Campaigning in Cheshire was indecisive, despite the important royalist victory at Hopton Heath in March. The earl of Essex, who had been guarding western approaches to London, hampered by disease among his troops, finally advanced on Oxford in June, only to meet a decisive defeat at Chalgrove Field, where John Hampden, the parliamentary hero, received fatal injuries.[23]

These complicated regional campaigns, and the shifting picture they present, have sometimes been reduced to order by the claim that there was a royalist master plan—of a three-pronged advance on London from Oxford, and from the west (Hopton) and the north (Newcastle). It seems more likely that for contemporaries the picture was as it appears to us—a series of regional campaigns in which the armies moved in the directions they were best able to, and from which a mixed picture of victories and failures emerged.[24] The general consensus is clear, however: the royalists had the better of the fighting through the summer of 1643. However, the tide of royalist successes was stayed, if not turned, by relief of a siege of Gloucester by Essex's army in early September: it marched out from London and managed to get back there in time for winter quarters, having survived a major battle at Newbury on 19 September. More minor successes followed, notably in Lincolnshire where Oliver Cromwell was building a reputation as a cavalry commander, and the parliamentary military cause had survived.

Towards the end of the summer both sides had also secured outside help. Between 1640 and 1642 government in England had dissolved partly as a result of reactions to rebellions in Scotland and Ireland. Charles's reactions were feared to be revealing about the future direction of politics in England, and raised the stakes in discussion about how England should be governed. During 1643 military fortunes drove parliament to conclude a political deal with the Scots—the Solemn League and Covenant—which secured their help in winning the war in England, while the king was driven to negotiate a Cessation in Ireland, which would allow him to bring troops back to England.[25] This was, in effect, to unify political and military conflicts by creating a single war, the War of the Three Kingdoms. This added considerably to the complexity of negotiating a peace, of course, since the Scottish and Irish now had a stake in the English settlement. In particular, the terms agreed for Scottish involvement were irksome to a significant part of the parliamentary alliance, and caused much friction after the war. On the royalist side this represented a victory for the hawks, and led to fresh divisions over this foreign intervention in the English war.[26]

THE WAR OF THE THREE KINGDOMS

There had been no peace negotiations over the winter and the third year of the war opened at a new pitch of intensity. The Scots crossed into England in January, opening up a new front in the war in England. Troops arrived in England from Ireland throughout the year, although their numbers were probably exaggerated. This and the following year of the war were to see the largest numbers of deaths.[27] Military mobilization on both sides was now regularized, and involved the exercise of new powers. All this was hard to reconcile with the claims made by parliament in 1641 and 1642 about their defence of custom, property, and the established religion. Moreover, as a parliamentary victory began to seem more likely, tensions were evident over what kind of peace was required.

In another remarkable political escalation, Charles had called an alternative parliament, which assembled in Oxford on 22 January 1644. Under the direction of the Oxford parliament, following the defeat at Newbury, there were attempts to reform the royalist war effort. Auxiliary regiments were formed for defensive purposes, in order to free up regular soldiers for service in the field armies. Conscription, which had been used in the previous two years of the war, was stepped up in order to improve the strength of the infantry. There were also proposals to reform the cavalry by creating eight new regiments, partly though the amalgamation of existing units, which still bore the stamp of their origin in the response of individuals to the Commission of Array in 1642. The Oxford parliament was persuaded to imitate parliamentary sequestration and excise. Finally, there were attempts to regularize the royalist assessment in response to complaints from both soldiers and civilians. Nonetheless, infantry numbers remained below the level achieved in 1642 and early 1643, and the reform of the horse had achieved little by the time of a major muster at Aldbourne Chase, in the summer of 1644.[28] Neither did the Cessation add much to the effort—the numbers arriving back from Ireland were much lower than parliamentary propaganda suggested, and there was a high political cost in the (erroneous but much credited) accusation that they had effectively recruited Irish Catholics to suppress English religion and liberties.[29]

The principal development on the parliamentary side was the intervention of the Scots. They had not saved the day in late 1643—that had been achieved by the relief of Gloucester and relative success in the battle at Newbury—but there is no doubt that during 1644 the opening of a new front in the north of England considerably improved parliament's fortunes, and created the possibility of an outright military victory.[30]

In the spring the royalists were pushed back in the West Country by Waller in a campaign notable for the victory at Cheriton in March. The arrival of the Scots in the north of England put pressure on Newcastle's royalist army with the result that the royalists were now more stretched in protecting Oxford, and their strongholds in the north and west. By the late spring both Oxford and York, the most significant royalist city in the north, were under pressure, the latter under siege from April. The king's main army left Oxford, and drew Waller into an ultimately indecisive pursuit, which relieved pressure on the royalist cause in the West Country, and split the parliamentary effort in the south between Waller's manoeuvres and the earl of Essex's march to support parliamentary positions in the south.

By June, however, the position of York was desperate, and a royalist army was sent to relieve the city. Prince Rupert interpreted his orders as not just to lift the siege but to engage the parliamentary army in battle which he did, with disastrous consequences, at Marston Moor on 2 July. The parliamentary victory was complete: the north was lost, Newcastle went into exile, and while the cavalry escaped to regroup and fight again, the royalist infantry numbers never recovered.

The potential of this victorious battle to deliver victory in the war was lost, however. The earl of Essex, having carried out his orders to relieve parliamentary strong points in the south set off on a disastrous advance into the West Country, pursued by the king's army and was eventually cornered at Lostwithiel. The earl escaped but the parliamentary army was forced into humiliating surrender. Worse still, Manchester and the other northern commanders were slow to follow up the victory at Marston Moor, so that the king was able to regroup, relieve pressure on royalist garrisons in the south and west, and confront Manchester's army at the second, indecisive, battle of Newbury (28 October). These successful royalist campaigns, culminating at Lostwithiel and Newbury, did much to restore the overall position. Royalist recovery was further aided by the earl of Montrose who in August successfully raised a royalist army in Scotland.[31] His victory at Tippermuir on 1 September was the prelude to a series of military victories, which gave the Covenanting army in England reason not to stray too far south. On the parliamentary side, however, many people blamed the failure to build on the great victory at Marston Moor on the personal deficiencies of the earls of Essex and Manchester.

These disputes over military command were entwined with other issues too. The combined effects of administrative reform, political and constitutional innovation, and intensifying military conflict changed the nature of the debate, as did the widening of the English war (as it seems when viewed from this perspective) to embrace the wider War of the Three Kingdoms. The human and material costs were also rising, and the horrors witnessed by partisans and bystanders were multiplying.[32]

Parliament had clearly lost an opportunity for decisive victory and at Donnington Castle one element of the reason for this became clear. Cromwell, frustrated at the failure to capitalize on the victory at Newbury, argued with his commander, the earl of Manchester. Famously, Manchester remarked that 'If we beat the King ninety and nine times yet he is king still, and so will his posterity be after him; but if the King beat us once, we shall be all hanged, and our posterity be made slaves.' For Manchester, military victory could not achieve his ends, which remained defensive because the key issue was to avoid defeat while seeking a secure peace.[33]

This dispute reflected wider divisions over war aims but also over the nature of an acceptable peace settlement. Cracks were beginning to appear in the parliamentary coalition about how to bring an end to the conflict and about just what kind of peace would justify the suffering a victory would have entailed. Manchester was increasingly identified with the ambition to establish a presbyterian church in place of the existing church of England, and was a natural ally of the Scots in that respect. Cromwell not only wanted to prosecute the war more vigorously, but wanted to use military victory to establish a much wider liberty of conscience, which would be protected by preventing the establishment of a powerful national church with the capacity to police religious practice very closely. This dispute reflected an unresolved tension in the parliamentary alliance about whether the aim of reform was simply to roll back the religious innovations of Charles I's reign, or to take the opportunity to complete a reformation which had not been as thorough as it should have been; and if the latter, what kind of further reformation was necessary. In 1641 leading religious opponents of Charles's regime met at the house of Edmund Calamy and agreed to avoid public arguments over the future government of the church. But this pact began to break down in 1644, prompted in part by the publication of some influential independent pamphlets, which provoked presbyterian counter-blasts, partly by the military treaty with the Scots, and partly by the fate of the military cause.[34] Partisans in this argument took to print and, after the war, tried to take control of key institutions of government in order to secure the kind of peace that they thought necessary. It then gave rise to some of the most vicious polemics about religious belief, such as Thomas Edwards's *Gangraena*, launched by one wing of the parliamentary cause against the other.[35]

In 1644 these increasingly obvious tensions intersected with discontent over the command of the army, and gave rise to two dramatic measures—the Self-Denying Ordinance and the new modelling of the army.[36] The first measure barred members of parliament from military command, in part as a response to accusations that the war was creating vested interests (as indeed it was: the massive tax burden was a source of profit for some, of course). At a stroke this removed from military command all aristocrats, since they were members of the House of Lords. The suspicion that this was directed against particular commanders for more immediate political reasons was reinforced by the fact that Cromwell was exempted (he should have relinquished his command, being an MP). This was justified, initially, by the need for him to carry out immediate duties, but was subsequently renewed.[37]

This change of command, sometimes seen as symptomatic of a larger assault on aristocratic authority, went in tandem with the creation of a new national army, not beholden to any regional association and answering directly to parliament's military command, the Committee of Both Kingdoms. It would have direct claims on pay and supply and would respond more efficiently to the strategic direction of parliament. It was also said to have been particularly attractive to those keen to prosecute the war vigorously and to resist a presbyterian settlement. That is something of an exaggeration, but the campaigns of 1645 seemed to reflect the advantages of this reorganization, as well as the radical religious and military zeal of many of the men.[38]

The Rise of the New Model Army

Behind the Self-Denying Ordinance and the new modelling of the parliamentary army lay an argument about the peace that was to continue after the war, and which ultimately gave rise to the revolution. The reforms proved militarily decisive—the New Model won decisive victories in 1645, which effectively ended the war—but in the final stages of the war political tensions on both sides rose. As military reform promised to deliver an end to the war the stakes were raised in the argument about what kind of political settlement a military resolution would serve.

Reorganization took some time though: the Self-Denying Ordinance and the New Model Ordinance were not passed until the later part of February, and the new officer list was not ready until March.[39] In the meantime there had been a new round of peace negotiations, this time at Uxbridge, which opened on 30 January and lasted only three weeks. The issues presented, and the respective positions in relation to them, had not moved, and Charles's own correspondence reveals how little store he had set by them.[40]

It was only in April that all the measures were in place and the New Model Army ready to march, and it did so to some scepticism on the royalist side. On 14 June, however, it won a crushing and decisive victory over the main royal army at Naseby. One thousand royalists died, as opposed to around 150 parliamentarians, but more importantly 4,000 prisoners were taken, along with artillery and supplies for a very large force.[41] Worse, perhaps, the king's correspondence was captured and later published, in an attempt to demonstrate that he was duplicitous and insincere in his negotiations with parliament.[42] And this was clearly not a presbyterian victory.

In the following months the advance of the New Model Army proved unstoppable. Leicester was captured on 18 June, Taunton eleven days later, and at Langport on 10 July Goring's forces suffered a devastating defeat. Further major strongholds were captured: Bridgewater on 23 July and Bristol on 10 September. In the course of these campaigns local forces, autonomously organized, played a significant part. These 'clubmen' associations were mobilized by local communities and were formally speaking neutral, seeking to protect the localities from the depredations of the field armies. In practice they were not neutral, but on the whole were a help to parliament and a hindrance to the royalist troops.[43]

An element of this story was the way the royalist campaign had been organized, which explained their relative ineffectiveness and the attitude of the local population. There had been attempts to remodel the royalist forces, and something had been achieved by force of circumstance—the disaster at Marston Moor had forced a reorganization of the horse. Many of those who fought at Naseby had been in the king's service for less than a year. Infantry numbers had suffered continual attrition, and desertion had been more or less winked at over the winter 1644/5 in the hope that the troops would return in the spring. They did not, however, and infantry numbers were low throughout 1645. In part this reflected a failure of supply. Money and arms continued to reach the royalist forces at least until the fall of Bristol in 1645.[44] Goring's troops, however, had been particularly ruthless in living off the land over the winter 1644/5, and they paid a price for that when their military fortunes faltered the following year as local people took the opportunity to withdraw support, or take revenge. While access to better resources is not now regarded as a determining factor in parliament's ultimate victory, it is clear that during 1645 the superior supply and discipline of the New Model Army made it less of a burden to the civilian population, and that was an important factor in the campaigns in the West Country that year.[45]

By the winter of 1645/6 royalist prospects were bleak in England. In Scotland Montrose's campaign had also collapsed. There was no further large-scale campaign between field armies but instead battles for control of the remaining royalist strongholds and the war in England during 1646 fizzled out in a return to 1642. Goring left for France in November while Hopton's army was destroyed at Torrington in February and he surrendered in March. The ignominious end of the royalist war effort came in April, when Charles left Oxford in disguise and after a week of apparently rather aimless wandering surrendered to the Scottish army then camped at Southwell on 5 May. Oxford surrendered in June and Rupert and Maurice fled the country, and the final surrenders were those of Pendennis and Raglan castles in August 1646, and Harlech, which held out until March 1647.

Royalist tactics had in one way become simplified by military defeat—to hold on to as much as possible, or to try to reopen the conflict in some way—although this continued to prompt disagreements about the propriety of foreign intervention, and creative thought about how to secure religious order and decency.[46] Charles had opened this effort shrewdly by surrendering to the Scots which created tensions between the various elements of the parliamentary coalition. One strength of this strategy was that parliamentary politics, no longer simply defensive, had by contrast become more complex: the need to design a new settlement for the kingdom that would satisfy the parties to the war and the interests created by it.

MOBILIZATION AND THE RADICALIZATION OF ENGLISH POLITICS

The story of how that played out is the story of the post-war revolution, but it is important to note what those post-war politics owe to the process of fighting the war itself. The failure to negotiate a peace prompted renewed fighting in 1648, and that was to lead to a further radicalization of views about what was necessary in order to secure a peace. Throughout the decade political and military mobilization were closely con-nected: focusing on that process of mobilization helps us better to understand both the military and the political history of the period. It brings into focus the costs of the war, the politicization of administration, and the emergence of new political interests and players and provides a context for understanding the radicalization of politics, as people of increasingly diverse views articulated positions intended to justify or end the fight-ing, and garnered support for those positions.

One important fact, perhaps the overriding fact arising from the war, was that it had been fought at appalling cost. Statistics derived from seventeenth-century sources are to be treated with caution, but it has been estimated quite plausibly that the war in England cost the lives of a greater proportion of the population than did the First World War. As many as one in ten adult males may have been in arms at some point during the war, perhaps one-fifth of the country's urban housing was destroyed, and the financial burden of taxes and the many other more or less informal exactions was unimaginably high by pre-war standards. Many people, unaware of the statistics, would have been all too aware of the horrors of early modern warfare—the wounds, the suffering and dis-location. It should also be acknowledged, of course, that some people clearly did well out of the war, and resentments about those vested interests also affected the post-war negotiation (just as they had informed the Self-Denying Ordinance).[47] At the very least, the fighting introduced new players onto the political scene. The army and the Scots, for example, were now key partners to any peace settlement in England, as well as, to some extent, the navy. It was also now common for institutions of government such as quarter sessions, assizes, or borough corporations to take on a partisan complexion, or to be at the heart of partisan battles for control. Domination of London's government, for exam-ple, had become the key to the pursuit of partisan politics.

If the costs of the war, and the means by which it had been fought, raised the stakes for making peace, the political arguments made to persuade people to support this massive mobilization also created an important backdrop to the development of revo-lutionary politics. Firstly, mobilization had fostered radical institutional innovation, with some long-lasting effects and some short-term challenges to conventional politi-cal thinking. The administrative measures taken to win the war were of long-standing significance, particularly the fiscal transformation, which doubled the share of national income being taxed and created new forms of taxation and borrowing that were crucial to the later financial revolution.[48] The great increase in state power in this arena was underpinned by measures of dubious legality and strained political arguments. Many saw in this new leviathan a roundhead tyranny far worse than the royal abuses they had set out to curb in 1640.[49]

The process of political mobilization led to other kinds of political radicalization. In the summer of 1642 parliament and the king had taken arguments about policy and constitutional principle to large audiences, in print and in battles for control of local institutions which could deliver control of the militia—assize and quarter sessions, grand juries, and, of course, the militias themselves (which had previously been cele-brated as the harmonious expression of a county's civic duty, but which were now the focus of partisan political battles).[50] Before that fateful spring, petitioning had become common—rival partisan networks seeking to mobilize local opinion in order to intervene in national political debate. Agrarian and other disputes were inflected with party politics, or party politics were used as a reason to settle long-standing grievances one way or another.[51]

As the war escalated so too did the complexity of public argument about it. People 'changed sides' or repudiated causes they now saw as having taken a false turn, and in doing so fuelled the public debate about policy, the constitution, the nature of the true religion, and the means by which arguments about these things could possibly be resolved. Fundamentally different views about the limits of religious toleration and the nature and origins of sovereign power were thrashed out for an audience restricted only by access to the pamphlets. The possibility existed for new groups to seize the means of administrative and political mobilization in order to promote their own political ends—astrologers, clubmen, witch-hunters, and radicals of many stripes launched initiatives which sought to lend meaning, establish certainty, or pursue necessary reformation as a way out of the crisis. Lush political debate created many new opportunities for political speculation, and political action.[52]

One way of imposing order on this complex story is through taxonomies of political opinion. Much of the political history of the period has sought to define party positions and to follow their fortunes over time: royalist, neutral, and parliamentarian; peace and war party parliamentarian; presbyterian and independent; swordsmen and courtiers in royal counsels.

There is of course plenty to be gained from taxonomizing political positions, but this chapter has been constructed on another principle: rather than plot allegiances I have put the process of mobilization at the heart of the politics. This helps to address a number of questions: the dynamism of civil war politics, the instability of the political alliances of the 1640s, and the relationship between popular and radical or revolutionary politics. It was the appeal to public audiences for support for incompatible views of the true religion and the constitution that created the space in which radically new answers could be developed. Revolutionary ideas were prompted, sharpened, and articulated in a political argument which had deliberately been take outside the institutions of government—the attempt to mobilize opinion outside those institutions in order to influence their workings had created the environment in which completely different kinds of politics could emerge.[53]

Emphasizing the mobilization of opinion offers another way of considering engagement with national issues, and contextualizes some forms of neutralism as active positions in relation to national politics. For example, the clubmen movements were not purely localist (their manifestos were published for a national audience) and they were in some cases responding both to the languages of national politics (appropriating them to local circumstance) and to particular developments on the national scene (such as the failure of the Uxbridge negotiations). In that sense then, this was a creative response to national politics, mobilized publicly, rather than an expression of a pure country rejection of national politics. In all sorts of ways local politics were inflected by national politics—in disputes over forest bounds, enclosures, or fenland drainage, for example, or the politics of the depression in the cloth trade.[54] The process of mobilization made a connection between popular, local, and national politics. Nonetheless, the strong emphasis placed on anti-war sentiment and neutralism in revisionist histories of the 1970s was an important one and should not be lost.[55] Historians do well to remember that not everyone is necessarily interested in politics, or willing to go to war for their convictions.

One way of reconciling this emphasis on mobilization with the taxonomy of allegiance is by considering how the dynamic of mobilization was revelatory for individuals—how it demonstrated to them what was malleable and what was not. Individuals might start in agreement but find that this process of self-examination took them in quite different directions: not just side changers like Cholmley or Dering, but one-time fellow travellers like Lilburne and Burton, or Lilburne and Cromwell.[56] Abstracted from the complexity of these individual crises of conscience we can see clear lines of argument, but we might do better to think of them as developing political logics to which people might be drawn or repelled as they considered their own circumstances and in the light of their own experiences. And, of course, one such consideration might easily be self-interest: profit, love, advancement, or self-preservation.

For some individuals, however, this experience of mobilization had laid bare or forced them to articulate political principles with revolutionary potential. The question for most contemporaries in the late 1640s was not, on the whole, 'is the revolution worth it?'[57] Instead they were asking what was necessary to extract England from this horror, and what was necessary to prevent a descent into this abyss for the future. For an increasingly powerful group this implied the necessity of fundamental religious and political reform, and the political conditions of post-war England afforded them the opportunity to act on their new-found certainties.

Notes

1. Austin Woolrych, an expert in both fields, is the outstanding exception. See *Britain in Revolution, 1625–1660* (Oxford, 2002). For an account of how the military history of the period is taking fuller account of social and political history see Hopper's chapter in this volume.
2. These events are covered in more detail in Cust's chapter in this volume.
3. See the chapters by Peacey and Walter in this volume. For the feverish politics of these 'December days' see Brian Manning, *The English People and the English Revolution* (Harmondsworth, 1978), chap. 4.
4. Michael Braddick, *God's Fury, England's Fire: A New History of the English Civil Wars* (London, 2008), 186.
5. This process is narrated by Conrad Russell, *The Fall of the British Monarchies 1637–1642* (Oxford, 1995), 478–87. His account of the content of the paper war is contentious.
6. James S. Hart, Jr., 'Rhetoric and Reality: Images of Parliament as a Great Council', in Michael J. Braddick and David L. Smith (eds.), *The Experience of Revolution in Stuart Britain and Ireland: Essays for John Morrill* (Cambridge, 2011), 74–95.

7. Michael J. Mendle, 'Politics and Political Thought', in Conrad Russell (ed.), *The Origins of the English Civil War* (London, 1973), 219–45; Mendle, 'Parliamentary Sovereignty: A Very English Absolutism', in Nicholas T. Phillipson and Quentin Skinner (eds.), *Political Discourse in Early Modern Britain* (Cambridge, 1993), 97–119; Quentin Skinner, 'Rethinking Political Liberty', *History Workshop Journal*, 61.1 (2006): 156–70. See also Alan Cromartie, *The Constitutionalist Revolution: An Essay on the History of England, 1450–1642* (Cambridge, 2006), chap. 8.

8. John Walter, *Understanding Popular Violence in the English Revolution: The Colchester Plunderers* (Cambridge, 1999); Manning, *English People*, chap. 3; John Morrill, *Revolt in the Provinces: The People of England and the Tragedies of War, 1630–48* (Harlow, 1998), 53–4. Manning gives these political positions a class basis, an interpretation that is not widely accepted.

9. Anthony Fletcher, *The Outbreak of the English Civil War* (London, 1985), chap. 11; Morrill, *Revolt*, 59–62.

10. Peter Young and Richard Holmes, *The English Civil War: A Military History of the Three Civil Wars, 1642–1651* (London, 1974), chaps. 2, 4, 5.

11. Malcolm Wanklyn and Frank Jones, *A Military History of the English Civil War, 1642–1646: Strategy and Tactics* (Harlow, 2005), 12–13. For the navy see Bernard Capp, 'Naval Operations', in John Kenyon and Jane Ohlmeyer (eds.), *The Civil Wars: A Military History of England, Scotland and Ireland 1638–1660* (Oxford, 1998), 156–91.

12. Ian Roy, 'The Royalist Army in the First Civil War', unpublished D.Phil. (Oxford, 1963), chap. 1; Ronald Hutton, *The Royalist War Effort 1642–1646*, 2nd edition (London, 1999), chaps. 1–2.

13. Young and Holmes, *English Civil War*, chap. 4; Wanklyn and Jones, *Military History*, chaps. 4–5; Malcolm Wanklyn, *Decisive Battles of the English Civil War: Myth and Reality* (Barnsley, 2006), chaps. 4–5.

14. David L. Smith, *Constitutional Royalism and the Search for Settlement, c.1640–1649* (Cambridge, 1994), 113–17.

15. For this and the following four paragraphs see Michael J. Braddick, 'History, Reformation, Liberty and the Cause: Parliamentarian Military and Ideological Escalation in 1643', in Braddick and Smith (eds.), *Experience of Revolution*, 117–34.

16. For the origins and spread of partisan language, expressed in simple binaries, see Tom Leng, ' "Citizens at the door": Mobilising Against the Enemy in Civil War London', *Journal of Historical Sociology* (forthcoming, 2015).

17. Michael J. Braddick, *Parliamentary Taxation in Seventeenth-Century England: Local Administration and Response* (Woodbridge, 1994), chaps. 3–4; Morrill, *Revolt*, 77–101.

18. Braddick, *God's Fury*, 273–9.

19. Braddick, *God's Fury*, 282–5.

20. Clive Holmes, *The Eastern Association in the English Civil War* (Cambridge, 1974), chap. 3, esp. 63–7; Edward Vallance, *Revolutionary England and the National Covenant: State Oaths, Protestantism and the Political Nation, 1553–1682* (Woodbridge, 2005).

21. Roy, 'Royalist Army', chap. 1; Hutton, *Royalist War Effort*, chap. 8.

22. David Scott, 'Rethinking Royalist Politics, 1642–9', in John Adamson (ed.), *The English Civil War* (Basingstoke, 2009), 36–60; Anthony Milton, 'Anglicanism and Royalism in the 1640s', in Adamson (ed.), *English Civil War*, 61–81; Milton, 'Sacrilege and Compromise: Court Divines and the King's Conscience, 1642–1649', in Braddick and Smith (eds.), *Experience of Revolution*, 135–53. See, more generally, Jason McElligott and David L. Smith (eds.), *Royalists and Royalism during the English Civil War* (Cambridge, 2007).

23. Young and Holmes, *English Civil War*, chaps. 6–10; P. R. Newman, *Atlas of the English Civil War* (London, 1985), maps 6–13.

24. Wanklyn and Jones, *Military History*, 92–4.

25. Woolrych, *Britain in Revolution*, 268–73.

26. Scott, 'Royalist Politics', 47–50.

27. Wanklyn and Jones, *Military History*, 15–16; Mark Stoyle, *Soldiers and Strangers: An Ethnic History of the English Civil War* (London, 2005), 61–5; Charles Carlton, *Going to the Wars: The Experience of the English Civil Wars, 1638–1651* (London, 1992), 204–6.

28. Roy, 'Royalist Army', chap. 3; Hutton, *Royalist War Effort*, 92–4.

29. Wanklyn and Jones, *Military History*, 15.

30. For the following three paragraphs see Young and Holmes, *English Civil War*, chaps. 12–16; Newman, *Atlas*, maps 14–28; Wanklyn and Jones, *Military History*, chaps. 14–18.

31. For Montrose see Edward J. Cowan, *Montrose: For Covenant and King* (London, 1977).

32. Robert Ashton, 'From Cavalier to Roundhead Tyranny, 1642–9', in John Morrill (ed.), *Reactions to the English Civil War 1642–1649* (Basingstoke, 1982), 185–207; Morrill, *Revolt*, chap. 3.

33. Quoted in Braddick, *God's Fury*, 334. See also Woolrych, *Britain in Revolution*, 290–1.

34. Braddick, *God's Fury*, 337–47.

35. Ann Hughes, *Gangraena and the Struggle for the English Revolution* (Oxford, 2004); Elliot Vernon, 'A Ministry of the Gospel: The Presbyterians during the English Revolution', unpublished Ph.D. thesis (Cambridge, 1999).

36. Mark Kishlansky, *The Rise of the New Model Army* (Cambridge, 1979), chap. 2; Ian Gentles, *The New Model Army in England, Ireland and Scotland, 1645–1653* (Oxford, 1992), chap. 1; John Adamson, 'The Baronial Context of the English Civil War', *Transactions of the Royal Historical Society*, 5th series, 40 (1990): 93–120, at 105–19.

37. Woolrych, *Britain in Revolution*, 301–6.

38. Gentles, *New Model Army*, chap. 4.

39. Gentles, *New Model Army*, 31–2; Kishlansky, *New Model Army*, chap. 2.

40. Smith, *Constitutional Royalism*, 121–4.

41. Gentles, *New Model Army*, 55–60; Wanklyn, *Decisive Battles*, chaps. 14–15.

42. Joad Raymond, 'Popular Representations of Charles I', in Thomas N. Corns (ed.), *The Royal Image: Representations of Charles I* (Cambridge, 1999), 47–73, at 56–60.

43. Gentles, *New Model Army*, chap. 3; David Underdown, *Somerset in the Civil War and Interregnum* (Newton Abbot, 1973), chaps. 5–6. For the clubmen see Braddick, *God's Fury*, 413–21, and the works cited there.

44. Roy, 'Royalist Army', 134–43, 198–206.

45. Roy, 'Royalist Army', 138–9; Underdown, *Somerset*, 86–92. See, in general, Ann Hughes, 'The King, the Parliament and the Localities during the English Civil War', *Journal of British Studies*, 24 (1985): 236–63.

46. Scott, 'Royalist Politics', esp. 54–7; Milton, 'Anglicanism and Royalism', esp. 75–9.

47. Carlton, *Going to the Wars*; Stephen Porter, *Destruction in the English Civil Wars* (Gloucester, 1994); Braddick, *God's Fury*, chap. 14.

48. Michael J. Braddick, *The Nerves of State: Taxation and the Financing of the English State, c.1558–1714* (Manchester, 1996); James Scott Wheeler, *The Making of a World Power: War and the Military Revolution in Seventeenth-Century England* (Stroud, 1999); D'Maris Coffman, 'Towards a New Jerusalem: The Committee for Regulating the Excise, 1649–1653', *English Historical Review*, 128 (2013): 1418–1450.

49. Ashton, 'Cavalier to Roundhead Tyranny'.
50. Fletcher, *Outbreak*, chaps. 11–12; Michael J. Braddick, 'Prayer Book and Protestation: Anti-Popery, Anti-Puritanism and the Outbreak of the English Civil War', in Charles W. A. Prior and Glenn Burgess (eds.), *England's Wars of Religion, Revisited* (Farnham, 2011), 125–45.
51. David Zaret, *Origins of Democratic Culture: Printing, Petitions, and the Public Sphere in Early Modern England* (Princeton, 2000); Walter, *Understanding Popular Violence*; Walter chapter in this volume.
52. Braddick, *God's Fury*, chaps. 15–16.
53. Michael J. Braddick, 'Mobilisation, Anxiety and Creativity in England during the 1640s', in John Morrow and Jonathan Scott (eds.), *Liberty, Authority, Formality: Political Ideas and Culture, 1600–1900* (Exeter, 2008), 175–93.
54. For some examples see Braddick, *God's Fury*, 184–5, 230–6, 413–26.
55. See the comments by Hutton, *Royalist War Effort*, xv–xvii.
56. For the general phenomenon see Andrew Hopper, *Turncoats and Renegadoes: Changing Sides in the English Civil Wars* (Oxford, 2012).
57. Paraphrasing the question posed by Ian Gentles, *The English Revolution and the Wars in the Three Kingdoms, 1638–1652* (Harlow, 2007), 433.

FURTHER READING

Braddick, Michael, *God's Fury, England's Fire: A New History of the English Civil Wars* (London, 2008).

Braddick, Michael J., 'Mobilisation, Anxiety and Creativity in England during the 1640s', in John Morrow and Jonathan Scott (eds.), *Liberty, Authority, Formality: Political Ideas and Culture, 1600–1900* (Exeter, 2008), 175–193.

Gentles, Ian, *The New Model Army in England, Ireland and Scotland, 1645–1653* (Oxford, 1992).

Hutton, Ronald, *The Royalist War Effort 1642–1646*, 2nd edition (London, 1999).

Kishlansky, Mark A., *The Rise of the New Model Army* (Cambridge, 1979).

Milton, Anthony, 'Anglicanism and Royalism in the 1640s', in John Adamson (ed.), *The English Civil War* (Basingstoke, 2009), 61–81.

Roy, Ian, 'The Royalist Army in the First Civil War', unpublished D.Phil. thesis, Oxford (1963).

Scott, David, 'Rethinking Royalist Politics, 1642–9', in John Adamson (ed.), *The English Civil War* (Basingstoke, 2009), 36–60.

Wanklyn, Malcolm and Frank Jones, *A Military History of the English Civil War, 1642–1646: Strategy and Tactics* (Harlow, 2005).

Woolrych, Austin, *Britain in Revolution, 1625–1660* (Oxford, 2002).

Young, Peter and Richard Holmes, *The English Civil War: A Military History of the Three Civil Wars 1642–1651* (Ware, 2000).

CHAPTER 7

SCOTTISH POLITICS, 1644–1651

LAURA A. M. STEWART

SCOTLAND IN THE LATER 1640S: 'DOWN-HILL ALL THE WAY'?

IN January 1644, a Scottish army crossed the River Tweed and invaded England. What made this moment remarkable was that the Scots had been invited to do so by the English. A group of parliamentarians, led by John Pym, negotiated an alliance with the ostensibly neutral Scots in order to bring them into a war that King Charles I seemed to be winning. The treaty, known as the Solemn League and Covenant, provided the English parliament with over 20,000 Scottish troops. For as long as this army was active on English soil, its pay and expenses would be met by the English parliament. In addition, the Scots were promised 'the reformation of religion in the kingdoms of England and Ireland'. Making the English and Irish churches more like their own was, for the Scots, the obvious way to ensure the safety of the true reformed faith in its presbyterian incarnation. The advocacy of reform 'according to the Word of God' and by 'the example of the best reformed Churches', plus an explicit condemnation of episcopacy, implied that the English would seek to create a presbyterian church but avoided commitments (and disagreements) on specifics.[1] It was a good deal for the Scottish Covenanters. Now their army had to make sure that the English kept to its terms.

The army of the Solemn League probably represented the largest concentration of foreign nationals to be found in England at any time during the seventeenth century. Some of the most stimulating recent work on this period has been generated by those historians, notably Mark Stoyle and David Scott, who have considered the impact of the Scottish presence on England's society and culture as well as its politics. In general terms, however, British approaches have often told us more about what the Scots were doing (or failing to do) in England than what was happening back in Scotland. This is not surprising. As David Scott has rightly pointed out, England was the seat of the British king's government and the most powerful of his kingdoms. An Anglocentric narrative for the British civil wars may simply be unavoidable.[2] Allan Macinnes has attempted to counter this view by depicting the 'British revolution' from a Scottish perspective. Although Macinnes's work offers a valuable reinterpretation of the period, it could be argued that his thesis confirms Scott's point. If there was a 'Scottish moment' in British politics between 1638 and 1645, what happened after that date?[3] We return to a familiar story: the Scots found themselves relegated to the second division as the New Model Army powered up the archipelagic league table, besting all comers (plus the Dutch) in the process.

Important recent studies have nuanced our understanding of Anglo-Scottish relations, but there are questions about Scotland's wars that do not necessarily benefit from a 'British' approach and they cannot all be asked, let alone answered, here. This chapter reconsiders Scottish politics during the later 1640s. Its focus will be the governing and representative bodies through which decision-making processes were conducted and experienced. From 1639, the Scottish body politic was given voice by the three estates, which had been reconstituted after the expulsion of the clerical elite as the nobility, barons (or lairds), and burgesses. The estates met either in full parliament or in a smaller, theoretically less authoritative assembly, known as a convention. An executive council, called the committee of estates, made day-to-day decisions, effectively replacing the king's emasculated privy council. Although these bodies were unicameral, the estates also deliberated separately. A parallel set of structures, headed by the General Assembly, governed the remodelled presbyterian church, or kirk. Although the kirk played a key political role in Covenanted Scotland, there is currently no satisfactory modern study to which students and scholars can be referred. Likewise, the near-total absence of research into popular, crowd, community, local, gendered, or subaltern politics in seventeenth-century Scotland are major lacunae that cannot be filled here.[4]

In the early years of the Covenanting period, stools were thrown at the heads of bishops, people protested on the streets, and emotionally charged mass swearings of the Covenant were held across the country. An English army was seen off—twice—and a British king was humbled. The second half of the 1640s, by contrast, has been depicted as 'down-hill all the way' even by those who rightly refuse to see Oliver Cromwell's shadow lying across the Solemn League.[5] This chapter will suggest that the Covenanters should not simply be dismissed as a spent force after 1644. Intervention in England did not enable the Scottish political elite to engineer a lasting peace settlement on its own terms or keep war beyond Scotland's borders. Nonetheless, the Covenanters escaped both destruction at the hands of royalist insurgents within Scotland and defeat in England. They retained control over the army's exit strategy from England in 1647 and executed it with sufficient skill to ensure the survival of Covenanted government.

During 1647, Scotland's leading politicians struggled with the fact that, by bringing the army home, they had relinquished the obvious direct means of exerting pressure in England. When the king was unexpectedly seized by the New Model Army in June 1647, it seemed that everything the Covenanters had achieved, and at such a very high price, was now under threat. Subsequent attempts to regain control of the British diplomatic agenda have usually been described in terms of a struggle between conservatives and radicals.[6] This polarity implies that tensions within the Covenanted body politic were always irreconcilable. Despite bitter divisions among political elites, however, Covenanting government remained vigorous and viable. Covenanted Scotland was far from ready to fall on Oliver Cromwell's sword in 1650.

Politics and Politicians in the Civil War Era

Scottish government in the early seventeenth century was highly decentralized. Control over a patchwork of local structures was predominantly in the hands of a semi-autonomous landed elite, whose interest in them was, more often than not, hereditary. Royal government could do little in the localities except through the mediation of a largely unaccountable landed elite. Covenanter government sought, from the beginning, to bypass royal officials and create its own centrally directed network of agencies. At the centre, the committee of estates acted as the coordinator of these new structures. During the war years, the executive divided in two, with one half remaining in Edinburgh while the other followed the army into England. As its workload expanded, the committee farmed out particular tasks to a range of sub-committees with flexible remits. The entire network, all historians agree, demanded the participation of an unprecedented number of people from a wider cross-section of landed and mercantile society. 'Oligarchic centralism', according to Macinnes, allowed power to become concentrated in the hands of a dominant few. It did not deliver total control and the extent of local discretion, in particular, probably remained considerable.[7]

Although the British civil wars had a Scottish dimension, Scotland's royalists were never able to establish a powerbase to rival the Covenanter capital at Edinburgh. By the autumn of 1641, anyone who wanted to attend parliament, acquire a clerical living, or hold any government office, had to sign the Covenant. Retreat to the splendid isolation of the family seat offered few consolations as it became harder to avoid the attentions of local committees equipped with lists of the politically unsound. There were royalists, who did resist, but they lacked the ideological unity and coherence of the Covenanting elite. The association of some key figures with Catholicism—George Gordon, 2nd marquis of Huntly, led a family that had traditionally remained loyal to the Catholic faith, while others such as Robert Maxwell, 1st earl of Nithsdale, were active adherents—further tainted the royalist cause. The erstwhile Covenanter, James Graham, marquis of Montrose, and his Irish commander, Alasdair MacColla, launched a campaign in 1644 that sought to restore the Anglo-Britannic *status quo ante bellum*. This implied both the sacrifice of Scotland's hard-won semi-autonomous status within a reconfigured regal union and the overthrow of the Presbyterian church. Montrose's reliance on Irish Catholics and Gaelic-speaking clansmen further alienated potential supporters, but the fact that he had to call on them at all was symptomatic of the limited appeal of his agenda in much of the Lowlands.

The successful negotiation of a favourable treaty with England in 1643 confirmed the dominance of a parliamentary grouping centred on four noblemen, Archibald Campbell, 1st marquis of Argyll, his distant kinsman and chancellor of Scotland, John Campbell, 1st earl of Loudoun, John Elphinstone, 2nd Lord Balmerino, and John Kennedy, 6th earl of Cassillis. Key allies included the respected co-architects of the National Covenant, the lawyer Archibald Johnstone of Wariston, and the cleric Alexander Henderson. Supporters of the king who had been prepared to accept the Covenanted constitution affirmed by Charles in November 1641, notably James, 3rd marquis and 1st duke of Hamilton, and his brother, William, 1st earl of Lanark (later 2nd duke of Hamilton), baulked at the Solemn League and initially resisted signing it. Charles's imprudent decision to detain Hamilton in Pendennis Castle, Cornwall, on suspicion of fomenting war between king and subjects, drove Lanark back into the welcoming arms of his Covenanted countrymen. Argyll has been justifiably depicted as the dominant figure throughout these years. Yet Cassillis, Balmerino, and Loudoun, although lacking his vast personal resources, were influential men in their own right whose advocacy of the cause predated Argyll's. All of them had to contend with the presence of substantial politicians, notably Lanark, who believed that they could do the king best service through legitimate channels and from within government. Charles, unfortunately, often failed to recognize this. The inclusion of the likes of Lanark was actively sought by the Covenanting elite and reflects the extent to which principles of unity, consensus, and consultation were far from mere rhetorical devices. Scottish politics was not a one-man show.

Argyll's grouping was once regarded by historians as an increasingly isolated faction of extremists, whose repeated failures convinced them that hordes of 'malignants' and 'delinquents' were undermining the cause from within. Purgation of the political nation was required; the 1646 Act of Classes supposedly began a process that culminated in the rule of a theocratically inclined 'Kirk Party' after September 1648. Recent work has rightly rejected the anachronistic labelling of Argyll's grouping as a coherent 'party' led by religious fanatics. By contrast, the Act of Classes continues to be seen as a radical piece of socio-political engineering, which seriously threatened, perhaps for the first time, the pre-eminence of the titled nobility. Passed by parliament in January 1646, then reframed with more severe penalties in January 1649, the Act categorized political malefactors according to the severity of their fault against 'God and this kingdom'.[8] As will be discussed below, however, the terms of the 1646 Act suggest that its taxonomy was not solely designed with punishment in mind. Re-admittance to the body politic was explicitly compassed in the same way that any moral transgressor, having made public repentance in his or her parish church, rejoined the fellowship of the congregation. Historians have emphasized the punitive nature of the Act at the expense of its redemptive aspect and thereby missed the opportunities it gave for sinners to return to the Covenanted fold.

Displays of contrition, especially in public, do not come easily to the powerful. The kirk's predilection for pressing great men onto their knees has been seen as emblematic of the factors that made an alliance between church and nobility seem 'unnatural'.

Yet elites often embraced the role of godly magistrate during the reformation century, as both a virtuous ideal and a means of reinforcing their social power.[9] The potency of the Covenant was derived, at least in part, from its fusion of the godly nation with the traditional political ideals of the commonweal. The result was an alliance between a muscular centralizing government and a national church committed to a second reformation. It implied that the civil sword should be wielded in accord with, and never in contradiction to, the church's decrees. Consequently, support from the kirk came on a strictly conditional basis and woe betide secular governors if they failed to satisfy the guardians of Scotland's collective public conscience.[10] The Engagement, agreed between three Scottish noblemen and Charles I in December 1647, was lambasted as 'contrary to the Word of God' by clerics who now threatened to break that alliance. Thereafter, the Engagers took control of the secular organs of central government, while the clerical elite used a formidable organizational network of pulpits and local church courts to back the anti-Engagers. Nonetheless, we will see that the Engagement crisis should not be understood simply in terms of a struggle between 'church' and 'state'. Indeed, it was the possibilities offered by the Engagement for reconciling Covenanting principles with the king's interest that may have convinced parliamentarians to support an otherwise risky venture. The anti-Engagers, restored to power in the autumn of 1648, tried to achieve something similar when Charles I's execution presented them with an opportunity to establish a Covenanted British monarchy.

The Contours of the Political Landscape

The signing of the Solemn League forced Scottish politicians to think hard about where the balance lay between the defence of true religion and the maintenance of the king's authority. 'Kirk' and 'king' have tended to be presented as two fixed poles on the Scottish political spectrum, around which 'radicals' and 'conservatives' clustered. In 1643, it has been argued, 'radicals' won the argument, leaving the 'conservative' coalition in 'disarray'; radical control over the machinery of government remained unchallenged until the Engagement crisis of 1648.[11] A slightly different interpretation sees a 'radical mainstream' cohering around a revolutionary set of progressive political and constitutional principles, which drew on a religious 'language', rather than religious conviction, to secure support. These principles were consistently maintained by the mainstream, except for a brief period when 'conservative elements' mounted an aristocratic reaction and secured the Engagement with the king.[12]

While the idea of a 'radical mainstream' usefully emphasizes essential continuities of leadership, it has the less desirable effect of fixing and homogenizing political opinion. The Solemn Leaguers had to share space with people who sought, in some measure, to defend the king's interests. What does this tell us about how political alignments formed and were sustained? For Stevenson, no such analysis was required because 'the defer-ence of a hierarchical society' guaranteed the acquiescence of a largely passive people to the disastrous policies promoted by noble and clerical leaders. An important correc-tive to this interpretation has been put forward by John Young. In a painstaking decon-struction of voting patterns and attendance records, Young sought to demonstrate that Argyll's grouping prevailed because its superior management techniques were directed at harnessing the innate political radicalism of the burgesses and gentry. The Scottish parliament, as it was reconstituted after 1639, apparently shifted power away from the nobility towards the lairds and burgesses. Argyll's brilliance therefore lay in his ability to recognize this fact and manage the radical agenda in his own interests.[13]

Young's thought-provoking thesis draws on difficult evidence that can support more than one interpretation. Membership and attendance records (sederunts) are relatively plentiful, so we often know who was on which committee and attended which meet-ing. Voting records are rare. Decisions, not deliberations, were written up in the official record. Mushrooming government committees certainly required ever more people to staff them but, while nobles gravitated towards the major decision-making bodies, the more tedious, labour-intensive tasks were left to lesser beings. Financial and administra-tive sub-committees, with their limited powers and crippling workloads, seem unlikely springboards for a revolution. Moreover, with such limited information about how peo-ple behaved once the meeting room doors were closed, it is unclear what, exactly, lairds and burgesses were doing with their new-found influence. No major political decision was taken without endorsement from a leading noble. No significant parliamentary alignment formed around a laird or burgess. No military leader emerged to challenge the power of an Argyll or Hamilton: Lieutenant-General David Leslie's parallel was more Sir Thomas Fairfax than Oliver Cromwell.[14]

Closer study of Covenanting government may show that the hierarchies of the local-ity exerted as much influence on political alignments as horizontal affinities within each estate. Elites who stood aloof from government risked exposing themselves and their family, kin, and friends, to unsympathetic treatment from their Covenanted neighbours, while those who participated could protect their own. An example from Aberdeenshire is perhaps instructive. In the mid-1640s, the north-east saw intensive government activ-ity, as a revivified regime sought to reassert control over the region from whence hailed not only Montrose, but also the marquis of Huntly. The power of the Gordons continued to impose a ceiling on the ambitions of ancient titled families, such as the Forbeses and Frasers, who led extensive—and generally Protestant—kin groups. At the forefront of energetic efforts to levy fines on the regime's enemies and secure compensation for those who had suffered at their hands were two stalwart Covenanters, Andrew, Lord Fraser and Sir William Forbes of Craigievar. Their names headed a petition to parliament in 1644, which asked that 'malignantes in the north and ther adherentes' be the ones to pay for their neighbours' losses. Commissions for investigating losses and compensa-tion claims were duly granted to a plethora of Forbeses and Frasers. The government's assurances that 'no encouragements sall be wanting to any of such approvin fidelitie and affectioun' as Lord Fraser also held good. He was granted tax rebates, exemptions from quartering, and permission to compensate himself handsomely from the revenues belonging to his rebellious near-neighbour, Sir Alexander Irvine of Drum.[15]

The exact contours of the local political landscape must have varied greatly. Kin and clan loyalties added a distinctive element in the north and west, but may have been of less significance in the more fertile, commercialized, and urbanized regions of the south and east. Scotland's fifty-plus royal burghs (which were set apart from other towns by their extensive economic and political privileges), formed a parliamentary estate, but individual burghs had their own interests and there were disagreements, especially over the tax burden. The ways in which localized relationships and concerns fed into political alignments at the centre remains poorly understood. Argyll's power, for example, had much to do with the fact that he could command several thousand kinsmen, yet they were of limited use as he navigated his way around the crowded interior of Edinburgh's parliament house. To some extent, Argyll's pre-eminence became self-reinforcing when the many favours this placed in his gift attracted people to him. The Edinburgh merchant, Sir John Smith of Grothill, must have been involved in negotiating both the Solemn League in 1643 and the treaty with Charles II in 1650 because he was backed by Argyll. A nobleman's influence had its limitations, however, reminding us that relations between patrons, clients, and the communities they came from, were reciprocal. Argyll was not able to protect Smith from public humiliation when he was accused of collaborating with Montrose (by releasing some of his men from Edinburgh's gaol in 1645). Edinburgh's governing elite may also have delivered a very pointed rebuff when Argyll sought to have its provost de-selected in 1647: he was duly confirmed in post for another year.[16]

Direct evidence for Smith's allegiances mentions not nobles, but the clergy. The role of the pulpit in shaping the political culture of Covenanted Scotland was surely of immense importance, yet historians know little about a national church that, almost uniquely in early modern Europe, successfully rejected episcopacy and Erastianism. Although John Coffey's biography of Samuel Rutherford has begun the rehabilitation of the Covenanted clergy, little attention has been given to the social, cultural, and political significance of the church in which they served. The presbyterian kirk continues to be portrayed as a political tool, through which a dominant 'radical' minority exercised control over a majority of 'moderate' brethren and, by implication, their congregations. This framework has restricted our understanding of the Covenanted *mentalité*. David Dickson was a respected biblical scholar, who led mass open-air services during the 1630s, coordinated resistance to the Prayer Book, and defended the contentious practice of family exercises (bible study in private homes). Past form should have placed Dickson with the Protesters and Remonstrants who, from 1649, rejected compromise with Charles II and those who had supported his father. Although he joined the ranks of the Resolutioners, who acknowledged the king's temporal authority, he was no more willing to accept royal supremacy in the church than his putatively more 'radical' colleagues. If the mind of a prominent scholar like Dickson remains mysterious to us, what of the rest of Scotland's 900 or so, largely anonymous, parish ministers? How were their views influenced by both the lay elders who held formal positions in the kirk hierarchy and the congregation as a whole? The kirk, as it described itself, was emphatically not just the clergy. Our understanding of the relationship between church and political nation, and between ministers and their flocks, is clearly in need of considerable refinement.

RECONCILING KING AND COVENANT: SCOTTISH INVOLVEMENT IN THE ENGLISH CIVIL WARS

Between 1644 and 1647, Scotland endured the Montrose–MacColla rising, terrible outbreaks of plague, and the burden of supporting armies that seemed intractably bogged down in England and Ireland. Intervention in the wars of sister-kingdoms had been predicated on the assumption that, through the deployment of force, the Scottish government would secure a permanent archipelagic settlement largely on its own terms. This was not achieved. Exaggerated hopes that the Scottish army would deliver a knock-out blow against the royalists had dissipated by the end of 1644 and it was now the focus of growing, and increasingly well-organized, criticism by its paymasters. If any Scots were calling for the army to cut its losses and get out of England, the Covenanting leadership proved adept at suppressing such talk. Mistrust of the king's intentions and disgust at what his lieutenants were doing in his name undoubtedly undermined the royalist cause and, with this in mind, it is not surprising that approaches to the Covenanting high command came to nothing. Fearing, nonetheless, that divisions at the top would undermine their diplomatic efforts in London, the Scottish commissioners wrote in uncompromising terms to their colleagues to remind them what was at stake:

> For if wee shalbe divided and rent asunder by parties and factions amongst ourselves, what can be expected but desolation at home, disreputation abroad, losse of all confidence heere, and—which is most of all and more to be regarded then our lives, liberties, or what is dearest to us on earth—the hazard of the cause itself . . .

Meanwhile, the royalist rising in Scotland threatened to sweep the Covenanters from power. The commissioners in London looked on in horror as their 'disnatured' countrymen fomented an 'unnatural' war against the defenders of the Covenant. In the seventeenth century, 'natural' was sometimes used to mean 'native of', thereby stemming it from the same Latin root, *nasci* (meaning 'to be born') as 'nation'.[17] Without detracting from the dynamic leadership provided by Montrose and MacColla, the refusal of the Solemn Leaguers to pull troops out of England until it was almost too late goes some way to explaining why such a poorly resourced, unpopular army came so close to seizing control of the country. This was a particularly dangerous time for Argyll. Determined to defend his lands in person from the many enemies descending upon them, Argyll achieved little more than the exposure of his own shortcomings as a general. Fortunately, Argyll was able to call on a real soldier to mop up after him. David Leslie's disciplined, battle-hardened army roared over the border on 7 September 1645. Within the week, the enemy had been located at Philiphaugh, near Selkirk, where Leslie's men exacted a merciless revenge on both Montrose's men and their female camp followers.

With the royalists in retreat, Covenanting government vigorously reasserted itself through exhaustive investigations into collaborations with the enemy. Reams of paper were produced by the process of preparing cases, taking witness statements, identifying the guilty, classifying their level of culpability, fining them, and hearing appeals. With the exception of four individuals singled out by parliament to give their own blood in lieu of Montrose's—he was exiled instead—the regime expressed a preference for pecuniary rather than physical punishments. It was all very unpleasant, but the interminable investigations had an important rationale. By blaming the weakness of individuals, who were then given opportunities to repent and redeem themselves, the government preserved the integrity of the larger project and protected it from censure.

The royalist rising did not topple the Covenanters in Scotland, but it did undermine their military effectiveness in England. By the end of 1645, it was widely felt that the Scots had outstayed their welcome and were draining precious resources from England's parliamentary forces. When the king handed himself over to the Scots in May 1646, in the hope that he could divide the parliamentary allies and continue the war, calls for their eviction grew shrill. There were fears that, if the Scottish army did not leave voluntarily, Fairfax would be sent to hasten its departure.[18] Charles, meanwhile, showed little interest in compromise. This made it impossible for his allies to convince Scottish parliamentarians that the king should be brought home to conclude a treaty. The duke of Hamilton, now back in Scotland, had been persuaded, apparently by Argyll, to take the Covenants and give his backing to the peace proposals then being offered to the king. There were heated debates in committee but, without credible assurances from the king regarding 'the covenant and religion', the Hamilton brothers had very little room for manoeuvre. In January 1647, parliament finally recalled the army. Charles was not invited to travel with it back to Scotland. Instead, the Covenanters demanded that they be allowed to retain a diplomatic presence in England and have a say in any future peace settlement. In addition, the English should maintain the current line of succession and ensure the safety of the king's person. Although these 'desires' were, for the time being, unenforceable, the peaceful withdrawal of the army meant that Scotland retained a significant military capability. Several thousand Scottish troops were still active in Ireland. A future Scottish military intervention in England remained possible.[19]

The Covenants Tested: The Engagement Crisis and its Repercussions

Although a peace treaty had eluded them, Argyll's grouping could take comfort from the successful extrication of the Scottish army from a dangerous situation. The Anglo-Scottish alliance, although threadbare, had not been destroyed, while the withdrawal of the much-resented Scottish army helped to strengthen the position of the English parliamentary presbyterians. Among Scotland's clerical elite, there was inevitable disappointment that a full presbyterian settlement in England had not been realized. Historians are fond of quoting the cleric Robert Baillie's disdain for the 'lame Erastian Presbyterie' with which the English seemed willing to content themselves. These were Baillie's private sentiments, however, and contrast with his public pronouncements to the Scottish General Assembly. Much had been achieved, the erstwhile commissioner to the Westminster Assembly informed his colleagues in August 1647; the churches were 'weell near one'.[20] However, the British diplomatic scene had lately undergone an unsettling transformation that made England's 'Erastian Presbyterie' look rather less 'lame' than Baillie had once thought. In June, the king had been taken into the custody of the English New Model Army, which was dominated by religious independents. The *Heads of Proposals*, published in August, condemned the Covenant and posited the restoration of limited episcopacy in return for a measure of toleration. Such a settlement would have invalidated the justifications given for intervening, at great cost, in the English civil war, thereby destroying the credibility of the Solemn Leaguers. Yet any attempt by the Scots forcibly to thwart a settlement would be taken in England as a breach of the League. How was this intractable dilemma to be resolved?

During the middle months of 1647, the Scottish government continued to seek the restoration of the king to his 'throne dignitie and royall government' on terms compatible with the Covenants.[21] Mutual suspicions among all parties played to the king's advantage. Lanark, Loudoun, and the Solemn Leaguer, John Maitland, 2nd earl of Lauderdale, were sent to England to negotiate with the king. Fearing that some form of resolution inimical to Scottish interests was imminent, the three noblemen signed an Engagement with Charles on 26 December 1647. The king was offered military assistance in return for parliamentary confirmation of the Covenants in both kingdoms. Charles was not personally required to take the Covenants and none would be pressed to do so against their consciences. Such lenient conditions had not been sanctioned by the committee of estates, but the fevered political atmosphere arguably permitted no further delays. London was under the control of Fairfax's troops and presbyterians had been purged from its government. Elements in the army were now openly calling for the king to be put on trial.

The Engagement has customarily been depicted as an aristocratic and conservative 'counter-revolution'. By March 1648, the Hamilton interest had captured secular government, enabling it to begin raising an army. The radicals, led by Argyll and strongly supported by the kirk leadership, were forced out of government. A titanic struggle ensued between these two great magnates, who seemed to personify the division between 'church' and 'state' that historians once regarded as an axiom of Scottish early modern history.[22] It is an appealingly dramatic narrative, given corroboration by the protagonists themselves. Thanks to John Scally's discovery of a journal of the 1648 parliament, we know that Argyll and Hamilton met face-to-face to discuss whether the Engagement provided 'sufficient secooritie' for the Covenants. The positions of the two men proved irreconcilable.[23]

The cleavage was real, but the personalized nature of Scottish politics encouraged efforts to restore unity and consensus. Thomas Reade, secretary to the English commissioners who spent a fruitless spring in Edinburgh trying to block the Engagement, was baffled by the frequent comings and goings between men that 'in publicque are quite oppositt'.[24] Uncertainty, confusion, and the likely costs of finding oneself on the losing side also kept opinion and allegiances fluid. The dilemma for many may not have been whether the preservation of the king took precedence over that of the Covenants, but whether the preservation of the Covenants was more likely to be achieved by preserving this king. Even if the guarantees were flimsy, the Engagement seemed to offer a better chance of securing the Covenants than waiting for England's presbyterians to seize the initiative from an army that had advocated the twin evils of episcopacy with liberty of conscience. As the Engager parliament explained, it was not possible for the Scots to be passive bystanders. Should the independents prevail in England, the 'securitie' of its neighbour would be imperilled just as, 'in the prelaticall tymes', the 'gangreene' infecting England had 'spread throw the whole'. Anti-Engagers agreed. They, too, were convinced that independents like Oliver Cromwell posed a threat to 'reformatioune and defence of religion', and they had said so in the mid-1640s. To argue now for a rapprochement with independents in order to avoid war risked charges of hypocrisy. What, then, was the alternative? Baillie offered only this response: if the king would not sign the Covenants, the wisest Scots could do nothing except wait on God's judgement.[25]

Hamilton's advantage was that, regardless of its feasibility, the Engagement offered an active strategy for settling the archipelago on Scottish terms. It could never satisfy those politicians and clerics who had come to believe that the principal threat to 'reformatioune and defence of religion' was Charles I. Samuel Rutherford, elaborating beyond the National Covenant's terse rehearsal of acts of parliament and General Assembly, essentially argued that kings existed to preserve true religion. When a king failed in this most fundamental duty, it therefore fell to 'all the inferior judges and people' to 'care for their own souls' and 'defend in their way true religion'. Those who chose to recall that Charles had attempted, ten years previously, to 'press a false and idolatrous worship upon them' may have followed Rutherford's logic and 'presumed to have no king'. Did Argyll's personal appeal to the House of Commons in June 1646 express a similar conviction that the relationship between God, monarch, and people was contractual? Scorning the idea that the Scots were 'too much affected with the Kings Interest', Argyll stated that 'personal regard to him' would never make the Scots 'forget that common Rule, *The Safety of the People is the Supreme Law*'. Perhaps he was reassuring the Commons, in language it understood, that the Scottish people would not risk the destruction of their 'safety', the army, to save the king. He could also have been hinting that a king who refused to take the Covenant was himself a threat to the safety of the Scottish people.[26]

One king had consistently refused to accept the Covenant. The emergence of his heir, Prince Charles, as a political figure in his own right made possible the development of an alternative strategy. Gilbert Burnet, writing one generation's remove from events, claimed that a third political grouping emerged early in 1648, whose aim was to use the prince as the means to reconcile king's men with kirkmen. Such hopes coalesced around Lauderdale, who had opened dialogue with the prince in the hope that he would reunite the body politic behind the Engagement by giving assurances for the safety of the kirk. Lauderdale's initiative bore fruit, but events were running ahead of him.[27] While Lauderdale was on a ship somewhere in the Channel, cementing a relationship with the prince that would endure for thirty years, his fellow-Engagers were struggling to raise an army. Argyll and other anti-Engagers had walked out of government. They supported vocal, and sometimes violent, resistance to the levy by parish ministers and other elements within local communities. Raising the required forces was slow going; it was early July before Hamilton, with 20,000 under-resourced troops and their bickering commanders, crossed over the border.

After Hamilton's army was destroyed near Preston in August, the anti-Engagers moved out of their powerbase in the western shires to recapture central government. Civil war threatened. It was Oliver Cromwell who settled the affair by taking his forces into Scotland to reinstall the anti-Engagers in government. Open conflict had been averted, but Cromwell demanded stringent guarantees for English security that Argyll and his supporters were in no position to resist. On 5 October 1648, Cromwell complained to the committee of estates that England had been menaced by 'the failing of the kingdom of Scotland in not suppressing malignants and incendiaries'. All such persons must now be identified and removed from positions of trust. If 'the honest party' forgot its obligations, the 4,000 English soldiers camped in and around Edinburgh were on hand to remind them.[28]

The purges of 1648 were more extensive than either the electoral manipulation used to secure the Covenant in 1638–9 or the targeted removal of royalist sympathizers from government in 1646. As well as resenting the intrusion of central agencies into their affairs, local governors were profoundly unsettled when a retrospective revocation of lawful government orders was used as a justification for removing people from office. In Linlithgow, about twenty miles west of Edinburgh, the council had elected itself, as normal, around Michaelmas (29 September), but was subsequently asked to give 'an accompt' of its proceedings. A new council was duly selected in December. Lewis Monteith and Thomas Hart were promoted as provost and one of the bailies respectively. They refused, unusually, to take up office. Given that both men had served on the pre- and post-Engagement councils, we may surmise that their actions were due, not to ideological scruples, but the perceived illegitimacy of the proceedings. Ultimately, Monteith and Hart agreed to 'conforme to the electioun'. Linlithgow's return to favour was signalled by the subsequent appointment of the burgh's parliamentary commissioner, James Campbell, to the committee of estates. No doubt Linlithgow, like many other communities, felt it literally could not afford to find itself beyond the political pale. The order for the council to make 'accompt' of itself arrived around the same time as the burgh was preparing to petition parliament about 'the great loss' it had sustained when anti-Engager forces had been quartered there.[29]

Although the purging of parliamentary and committee members did not directly target the peerage, as the abolition of the English House of Lords would do in May 1649, the rallying of many nobles behind the Engagement made them the obvious casualties. Action against the 'lait unlaufull engagement' was instigated by the reformed committee of estates in late September and given formal sanction when parliament convened in January 1649. As a result, only eighteen members of the peerage attended the new parliament: down two-thirds on its predecessor.[30] Nobles with a personal place in parliament could send no other in their stead, but shires and burghs, as corporate entities, could adapt to the legislation by nominating politically acceptable people as their representatives. While the absence of so many nobles made the reformed regime more reliant on burgesses and lairds, Covenanting government had always been predicated on cooperation between men who, titled or not, were all 'lesser magistrates'. Noble leadership was a given even in 1649. Hence, the most vigorous proponents of purging were noblemen who had been prominent in Covenanting government throughout the past decade: Argyll, who set the tone with a 'verey long speiche' against Engagers and malignants, Cassillis, Lord Balfour of Burleigh, and a repentant and rehabilitated Chancellor Loudoun. These were the men who had most to lose if Hamilton's allies, and especially his brother, Lanark, regained the political initiative. Parliament's unprecedented exclusionary measures aimed to prevent Lanark from mounting a second operation—and provoking a full-scale English invasion—to save not only his king, but also his brother. Hamilton, who had been captured by the English army after Preston, was executed only once the king was dead.[31]

The sight of the 'lesser party' making a faction of the greater may have been an eye-opener for Cromwell, but it was not the Covenanted way of doing politics.[32] Unlike the English body purged by Colonel Thomas Pride, the 1649 Scottish parliament, although carefully managed, witnessed no slights to its authority at the hands of soldiers. Burgh and shire commissioners from all parts of the country attended, indicating the continued relevance of parliament as the representative of the body politic. And with issues of such enormous importance to debate, it is little wonder that attendance was high. While the fate of Charles I and negotiations with his son inevitably predominated, parliament did other things in 1649 that were arguably of more direct relevance to many members. Vindicated by events and with moral authority on its side, the presbyterian church leadership campaigned successfully for the long-desired statute abolishing lay patronage: a measure that affected every parish in the land. The legislative 'assault on sin', which covered drunkenness and sexual deviance as well as witchcraft, was not the exclusive work of churchmen and the role of local elites in pushing this agenda needs to be fully explored. Heavily taxed communities that had been devastated by war and plague, and were now coping with rocketing grain prices, faced a crisis in poor relief. They seized on the impending parliament to strengthen the largely toothless legislation enacted during James VI's reign. Demands for a redistribution of the tax burden were another manifestation of recent political realignments. This was the first parliamentary challenge to the fiscal regime established since 1639, spearheaded by communities that had supported the anti-Engager coup and were now calling in favours. This was a busy, vigorous, and well-attended parliament, not a tyrannizing rump locked into 'a terminal spiral of defeat'.[33]

REGICIDE: THE SCOTTISH RESPONSE

On 30 January 1649, the king of Britain was judicially executed by a clique of his English subjects. Whether the leaders of Scottish government did 'all they could' to preserve Charles's life is addressed elsewhere in this volume, but a few words on the political context are appropriate here. It was almost certainly a widely held belief in Scotland that the Covenants had bound Scots and English alike to maintain the king's authority, but many people were unsure what to do when the king himself refused to enter into the arrangement. Not only the Covenants, but also much of the language in which politics was expressed, implied that the relationship between king and subjects was contractual. What this meant, like the injunction to defend true religion, remained open to debate and subject to the tests of practical politics. When circumstances altered, as they did with breath-taking rapidity in the later 1640s, politicians had to remain flexible without compromising essential principles. As the king's trial approached, Scottish parliamentarians tried to do just that. The commissioners in London were told on 9 January to prepare for a forced abdication *and* the possibility that Charles, at the eleventh hour, would sign the Covenants. Scotland was not 'craving his majesty's restitution to his government, *he not having satisfied his kingdoms*' (my italics): the implication was that, should his majesty choose to give them satisfaction, they would crave his majesty's restitution. All was not lost even if Charles was, one way or the other, detached from his regal title. He had a son. The prince's responsivenes to the overtures made by Lauderdale the previous spring had encouraged even leading kirkmen to think that they might succeed with a future king where they had failed with the current one. The English parliament was duly warned not to take any action 'against the monarchical government of the kingdoms in the person of the prince or the king's posterity'.[34]

It was not the Rump of the Long Parliament's approval of Charles I's execution that broke the British composite monarchy, but its decision, over three months later, to declare itself a republic. The Scottish parliament opted to reject what amounted to a grant of independence imposed unilaterally upon it, without its consent, by a regime it considered illegitimate.[35] Monarchic authority was intrinsic to the Covenants. By acknowledging this principle, the Covenanters had carried the body politic with them for most of the decade. Whether the Covenants obligated or allowed the swearer to defend the authority of a king who was not himself Covenanted had later become a major cause of confusion and disagreement. Charles I's death opened a path out of this dilemma. The Scottish parliament asserted that 'all the subjects of this kingdome are bound humblie and faithfullie to obey, maintayne and defend' the prince as their 'only righteous soveraigne lord and king'. The sting was that Charles II would not be admitted to 'the exercise of his royall dignitie' until he had bound himself to God and the subjects of his kingdom by signing the Covenants.[36] The son would embrace what the father had rejected and, however reluctantly and disingenuously he did it, this is ultimately what the Covenanters achieved in June 1650.

For that large body of nobles who had been excluded from power after September 1648, not to mention the smaller body of royalists who had been pariahs from an earlier date, Charles I's death signposted a route back into government. Had the anti-Engagers *not* proclaimed Charles II, their opponents would certainly have sought to do so instead, and without conditions. Charles II, meanwhile, could not have rested content as king of Scots. If his subjects had mistakenly chosen to call him by anything other than the title he believed was his by right, this would not have stopped the king of Britain viewing his northern kingdom as a launch-pad to reclaim his southern one. The result would have been the Scottish civil war that all serious politicians had strived to avoid throughout the 1640s. Even if the anti-Engagers had prevailed, it would have been a pyrrhic victory: the defeat of a royal army containing friends, family, and neighbours, and possibly the king himself, would have destroyed whatever vestiges of legitimacy the Covenanting cause possessed. On 5 February 1649, the Scottish government made a sensible decision. It declared Charles as king of Britain. At that moment, England was not yet a 'free commonwealth'. A regicidal regime that did not even know what to call itself cannot have inspired confidence in its survival. Scottish government was formed of the same institutions, and staffed largely by the same people, as it had been ten years previously. Of all the possible futures God was thought to have in mind for the peoples of Scotland in the spring of 1649, the conquest of their country by the regicide, Oliver Cromwell, must have seemed among the least likely. The declaration of Charles II did not lead directly and inevitably to the conquest of Scotland by the New Model Army.

INVASION AND CONQUEST

The decision to declare the monarch made political sense but there was a problem: the second Charles was no more enthusiastic about life as a Covenanted king than the first had been. Initial negotiations, conducted at The Hague during the spring of 1649, did not go well for the Scottish commissioners. Among the factions politicking energetically around the new king, the commissioners found erstwhile allies such as Montrose, Lanark (2nd duke of Hamilton since his brother's execution), and Lauderdale. Montrose, in particular, was seen to be in good standing with the king, who later authorized him to mount another invasion of Scotland. There were also hopes that, if a royalist coalition headed by James Butler, 1st marquis of Ormond, could seize control of Dublin, Ireland would provide Charles with the resources he needed to regain his British throne. With these other, more attractive, suits still in play, Charles could afford to offer terms that were even less advantageous to the Covenanters than those contained in the 1647 Engagement. The Scottish commissioners returned home empty-handed.

While the English regime remained preoccupied with Ireland, the main threat to Covenanted Scotland came from royalists. Existing tensions in the far north formed the backdrop to a rising launched in February 1649 by Sir Thomas Mackenzie of Pluscardine (brother of the clan chief, George, 2nd earl of Seaforth), against which the Edinburgh government was taking precautions even before its eponymous protagonist seems to have known what he was doing. Montrose's enterprise commenced only in March 1650, to allow time to recruit soldiers in northern Europe. Although compromised from the beginning by the king's decision to reopen negotiations with the Covenanters, Montrose's campaign, like Pluscardine's, failed for largely the same reasons that had always beleaguered oppositional royalists: leaders fell out among themselves, they lacked clear strategic objectives, and their troops were badly resourced (although David Leslie also had troubles in this regard.) Montrose himself, given his former transgressions, cannot have expected leniency after his defeat and capture at Carbisdale (Ross-shire) in April. Within the month, he had been executed.

The manner of Montrose's death reflected something more than a pragmatic need to prevent the survival of such a dangerous person becoming one of Charles's negotiating terms. Montrose's unusually violent military style, characteristic of the hired mercenary rather than the nobleman, may have been regarded as a betrayal, not only of Covenant and country, but also of the values of aristocratic society. A year earlier, Montrose's unreliable ally, Huntly, had achieved the unenviable distinction of becoming the first peer to be judicially executed by the Covenanters. Huntly was offered the more dignified, less terrible death by beheading; Montrose was hanged like a common criminal and his body parts cut up for display in the leading burghs of the kingdom.[37]

By the time that a ship carrying the as-yet uncovenanted king appeared in the Moray Firth, Ireland had been decisively brought under English military control, the English parliament had resolved to send an army against Scotland, and there was little prospect of assistance from other war-weary monarchic states. William, prince of Orange, who was keen to say goodbye to an expensive guest, reputedly advised his brother-in-law to regard the Covenants as the price of Scotland, just as Charles's grandfather, Henri IV, had deemed France worthy of a Mass.[38] The regrets expressed by the men who, on 23 June 1650, witnessed Charles grudgingly put his signature to the Covenants, reflected their sense of having won 'a hollow victory'.[39] Charles I's principled refusal to take the Covenant had, somewhat ironically, reinforced the Covenant's unique status; his son, by conspicuously regarding it as he would any other set of terms presented from subjects to kings—binding only insofar as necessity dictated—dealt its credibility a heavy blow. Having taken the Covenants, Charles could not realistically be denied the exercise of government and this was duly declared by parliament on 4 July.

Yet a king who had demonstrated his insincerity was surely no more fit for a place of public trust than anyone else found guilty of breaching the Covenants. Back in January, the government had issued a *Declaration* (in response to one issued, through a London press, by Montrose), which had implicitly likened Charles to the biblical King Jehoshaphat of Judah. Having ignored the warnings of the Lord's prophet and supported a war of conquest, Jehoshaphat and his kingdom had been duly punished: 'Shouldst thou help the ungodly, and love them that hate the Lord, therefore is wrath upon thee from before the Lord.'[40] Some Scots now feared that Charles/Jehoshaphat would bring God's vengeance down upon all of them.

The appearance of a Covenanted king on Scottish soil did not, as the commissioners hoped, heal the fissures in the body politic. It cracked them open. Charles's behaviour generated a justifiable fear that he was bent on abandoning the Covenants at the first opportunity. As a precautionary measure, lest the king and his supporters attempt to use the army to overthrow the government, some politicians insisted that it be thoroughly purged. This deeply offended Leslie, who resented the insult to his personal authority as well as the slur it put upon hitherto unimpeachably loyal troops. Others had come to the conclusion that only a truly godly army could prevail against Scotland's many enemies. In response, an alternative force, known as the Western Association, was formed. The Association was no lover of the English or independency, but some of its representatives, including Archibald Johnstone of Wariston, almost certainly contemplated sacrificing Charles to save their Covenanted country from destruction. Meetings between the Association and English commanders, reported in English newsletters, probably served only to confirm, on one side, that the Scottish people were deeply divided and, on the other, that the English were dreading the prospect of fighting a protestant people on their home turf.[41]

The very public splits in the Scottish body politic were easily and adeptly exploited by Cromwell through the medium of print. The king that Covenanters sought to defend, even at the price of 'a perpetuall War' with England, continued to maintain all his 'Malignant and Popish hopes and confidences'. 'There may be a Covenant made with death and hell', suggested Cromwell, alluding to the doom-laden prophecies of Isaiah. '(I will not say yours was so). But judge if such things have a politick aime, to avoid the overflowing scourge, or to accomplish worldly interests.' The Scots gave as good as they got. England, not Scotland, had broken the Covenant. 'Wee take not upon us to judge yow in any thing otherwise then by your cariage and fruites. These we see and know to be bitter as wormewood and gall.'[42] Cromwell's words may have reinforced existing doubts, but they probably did not change many minds. There is little evidence that an English invader's lectures on godliness attracted much favourable attention amongst the Scottish people.

Cromwell's expedition very nearly failed. His defeat of the Scottish army at Dunbar was terrible, in part, because it was unexpected. Leslie possessed the larger force and he knew his territory. Once on Scottish soil, Cromwell's army was cut off from its supply lines and his troops quickly began to sicken and starve. By the early days of September, Leslie's patient refusal to give battle had forced the New Model Army to turn back towards the border. Having blocked in his enemy at Doon Hill, near Dunbar, Leslie simply needed to select the right ground and moment to attack. On the evening of 2 September, Leslie allowed his men to stand down and move off the advantageous high ground. Seeing what was happening, the English high command seized the opportunity and, in the early hours of 3 September, went on the offensive. By the end of the day, up to 4,000 Scots were dead and 10,000 captured. What remained of the army retreated to Edinburgh.

Leslie had made an error of judgement at a critical moment. Once battle was joined, the purges that contemporaries believed were the main cause of the disaster became significant, as untested recruits found themselves facing a more disciplined and experienced force.[43] England's superior resources probably did not matter very much until *after* Dunbar: once the English army controlled Scottish harbours it was able to access the supplies that, in the absence of a Scottish navy, could be shipped easily and securely up the east coast. This factor proved decisive, for it enabled Cromwell to sustain a large army over winter in hostile Scottish territory: a feat matched only by another master of logistics, King Edward I.

At Dunbar, the English won a battle—albeit an important one—not a war. Cromwell's worry was that his army's morale, and his own health, might break before the Scots could be winkled out from behind Leslie's near-impregnable line at Stirling.[44] Scotland's survival now depended on the committal of all the country's resources to the defensive effort. Achieving this demanded the unified sense of purpose that had galvanized the country behind the Covenant in 1639. It proved impossible to recapture. This was not because Scottish politicians and churchmen were somehow more predisposed to 'ideological schism' than their English counterparts. The presence in Scotland of *a* king, and *this* king, had made differences irreconcilable. The young man who was hectored relentlessly by Scottish clerics about the sins of his father and mother was also a monarch who had sanctioned the invasion of Scotland even as he negotiated with its commissioners. His actions were reminiscent of nothing so much as those of his father a decade earlier. [45]

In this respect, Charles's involvement in an abortive plot known as the 'Start', which sought to use a force raised in the north to force a change of government, confirmed existing impressions about the king's untrustworthiness. His actions further convinced the Western Association that Scotland was being punished, through the instrument of an English 'sectarian' army, for its sinfulness. In October, a group of gentlemen, ministers, and commanders of the Association issued a Remonstrance insisting that Charles should not be allowed to exercise his royal powers until there were 'evidences given' of 'reall change in him'. Although John Lambert's cavalry destroyed the Association as a military force in early December, the Remonstrance continued to provoke heated debate. It has been suggested that the Remonstrance's 'isolated' and numerically 'limited' supporters were only heeded because the structures of the presbyterian church gave minority groupings a platform for their unrepresentative opinions.[46] Further research may reveal, on the contrary, that the Remonstrance's appeal to notions of limited, godly monarchy garnered considerable popular support in the Covenanting heartlands. This may better explain why the Remonstrance continued to prove so divisive and so difficult to contain in the years ahead.

With the English army now in control of some of Scotland's most fertile lands in the south, the pressure to stop the purges had become overwhelming. On 14 December, parliament issued a 'resolution' stating that, with due acknowledgement of certain reservations expressed by the kirk, those who wished to fight should be allowed to assist in the prosecution of this 'just and necessarie defensive warr'. In defiance of the so-called 'Resolutioners', a group of twenty-two clerics, led by key supporters of the remonstrance, issued a 'protest' against the readmittance of erstwhile Engagers and malignants to places of public trust.[47] Majority opinion in parliament and General Assembly favoured the

Resolutioner position, and the counter-campaign orchestrated by the Remonstrants and Protesters, although deeply principled, resulted only in time-consuming and distracting arguments. The acts of classes were finally repealed in June, but it was probably too late. Within the month, a force commanded by John Lambert had broken the stalemate by winning an important battle at Inverkeithing, on the north side of the Forth. A desperate remnant of an army now faced three unpalatable choices: starvation, surrender, or an invasion of England. A year to the day since the disaster at Dunbar, what remained of the Scottish army was completely routed in the west Midlands town of Worcester. A few days later, many of Scotland's leading politicians and clerics were captured by English forces at Alyth in Perthshire. The Covenanted state, as a political and military entity, had ceased to exist.

Robert Baillie lived to see 'our poor countrey made ane English province',[48] although it happened more than twelve years later than he had anticipated. At the end of 1651, those Scottish men and women who had not succumbed either to epidemic disease or death by some other violent means found themselves living in a world of religious schism, political crisis, military occupation, and economic hardship. These facts make it easy to see why most historians regard 'the covenanting movement' as 'a failure'.[49] Yet the defeat of the Covenanted state did not result in the total destruction of Covenanted society. Although the Covenant could never again act as the bedrock of a national church, its brief ascendancy helped to entrench the religious culture that would give Scottish public life—for good or ill—much of its distinctive aspect well into the eighteenth century. Differing interpretations of the significance of the Covenant poisoned the politics of the Restoration era, with a minority prepared to resort to violence to defend their ideals, but it is undeniable that the document itself remained a potent source of spiritual inspiration. In terms of its legacy, the Covenanting era has always suffered from unfavourable comparisons with both England and Enlightenment. The fiscal, military, and administrative innovations pioneered by Covenanters failed to make Scotland the equal of other small states like Sweden and the United Provinces, but they did transform how state power was experienced by the Scottish people in the decades leading up to the 1707 Union. Seventeenth-century Scottish political thought, particularly on those questions of authority, liberty, and sovereignty brought so contentiously to the fore by the Covenanting experiment, remains to be fully explored.[50] Covenanting government did not survive. Its achievements, ideals, and failings would profoundly influence Scottish society for generations to come.

Notes

1. *English Historical Documents, 1603–1660: Volume V(B)*, ed. Barry Coward and Peter Gaunt (London and New York, 2010), 582–3.
2. David Scott, *Politics and War in the Three Stuart Kingdoms* (Basingstoke, 2004), xii.
3. Allan I. Macinnes, *The British Revolution, 1629–1660* (Basingstoke, 2005); Allan I. Macinnes, 'The "Scottish Moment", 1638–45', in John Adamson (ed.), *The English Civil War* (Basingstoke, 2009), 125–52.

4. For further reflections, see Laura A. M. Stewart, 'Power and Faith in Early Modern Scotland', *Scottish Historical Review*, 92, suppl. 234 (2013).

5. David Stevenson, *Revolution and Counter-Revolution, 1644–51* (new edn., Edinburgh, 2003), p. xvi.

6. For example, Macinnes, *Revolution*, 187.

7. Allan I. Macinnes, 'The Scottish Constitution, 1638–51: The Rise and Fall of Oligarchic Centralism', in John Morrill (ed.), *The Scottish National Covenant in its British Context, 1638–51* (Edinburgh, 1990), 124–5. David Stevenson's groundbreaking survey remains invaluable, *Government under the Covenanters, 1637–1651* (Scottish History Society, 4th ser., vol. 18, Edinburgh, 1982), pp. x, xix, xxvii, xl, xliv. For a new approach, see Laura A. M. Stewart, 'Fiscal Revolution and State Formation in Mid Seventeenth Century Scotland', *Historical Research*, 84 (2011): 443–69.

8. Stevenson, *Revolution and Counter-Revolution*, passim. *Records of the Parliaments of Scotland to 1707*, ed. Keith M. Brown et al. (St Andrews, 2007–12), 1645/11/110, 1649/1/44 (hereafter *RPS*). The Acts were applied *after* parliament had determined that the accused was not guilty of crimes punishable by death. Permanent exclusion for first-class delinquents was enacted only in 1649.

9. David Stevenson, *The Scottish Revolution, 1637–44: The Triumph of the Covenanters* (Newton Abbot, 1973), 300, 302; Keith M. Brown, *Noble Society in Scotland: Wealth, Family, and Culture from Reformation to Revolution* (Edinburgh, 2004), 235, with caveats at 237–9.

10. General Assembly of the Church of Scotland, *The Declaration of the Commission of the General Assembly, to this Whole Kirk and Kingdom of Scotland of the Fifth of May: Concerning the Present Publike Proceedings towards an Engagement in Warre, so Farre as Religion is Therein Concerned* ([Edinburgh,] 1648), 8.

11. John R. Young, *The Scottish Parliament, 1639–41: A Political and Constitutional Analysis* (Edinburgh, 1996), 65, following Stevenson, *Scottish Revolution*, 276–8.

12. Macinnes, ' "Scottish Moment" ', 139; 'The Scottish Constitution', 123.

13. Young, *Scottish Parliament*, 44–6, 64, 108; Macinnes, 'The Scottish Constitution', 122–3; Stevenson, *Scottish Revolution*, 276–7, 299–310.

14. The Western Association, which issued the Remonstrance of October 1650 (see p. 131), might be considered an exception. No noble openly supported it, although there were individuals, notably Cassillis, who may have agreed with its sentiments. Stevenson, *Scottish Revolution*, 159.

15. National Archives of Scotland [NAS], Register of the Committee for Moneys (North), 1646, PA14/4, 52, 53–4, 116–17, 122; Reports to the Committee on Losses, 1646–7; for example, PA16/4, Reports to the Committee of Losses, nos. 6–9 (earl of Erroll), no. 10 (Forbes of Culloden); *RPS*, 'Comission to the marquis of Argyle', 1644/1/125; 'Reference in favoures of Andro, lord Fraiser and otheres', 1644/6/85.

16. Laura A. M. Stewart, *Urban Politics and the British Civil Wars: Edinburgh, 1617–53* (Leiden, 2006), 271–7.

17. *Correspondence of the Scots Commissioners in London, 1644–46*, ed. H. W. Meikle (Edinburgh, 1917), 53 [quotation], 69, 83, 121.

18. *Scots Commissioners*, ed. Meikle, 178.

19. *RPS*, 'Desires of the kingdome of Scotland', 1646/11/155; Gilbert Burnet, *Memoires of the Lives and Actions of James and William Dukes of Hamilton and Castleherald* (London, 1677), 393, 396.

20. Robert Baillie, *Letters and Journals, 1637–1662*, 3 vols., ed. David Laing (Bannatyne Club, 1841–2), II, 362; III, 11–13.

21. NAS, Register of Minutes: Committee of Estates, Mar. 1647–Feb. 1648, PA11/5, n.p., 11 June 1647; 19, 20 Aug. 1647.

22. Stevenson, *Scottish Revolution*, 83, 179; Macinnes, *British Revolution*, 187.

23. John J. Scally, 'The Rise and Fall of the Covenanter Parliaments, 1639–51', in Keith M. Brown and Alastair J. Mann (eds.), *The History of the Scottish Parliament, Volume 2: Parliament and Politics in Scotland, 1567–1707* (Edinburgh, 2005), 155–6.

24. 'Mr Thomas Reade's relation' in *Miscellany of the Scottish History Society: Volume II* (1st ser., Edinburgh, 1904), 296.

25. *RPS*, 'Act anent the resolutiones of parliament concerning the breaches of the covenant', 1648/3/66; Baillie, *Letters and Journals*, III, 24–8.

26. Samuel Rutherford, *Lex, Rex, or, The Law and the Prince . . .* (London, 1644), 99; *The Lord Marques of Argyle his Speech to a Grand Committee of both Houses, June 25. 1646* (London, 1646), 3–5. 'The safety of the people' was a term used by Rutherford, *Lex, Rex*, Qu. XXV.

27. Burnet was given privileged access to the Hamilton archive to write his account, *Memoirs*, pp. viii, xiv; 425.

28. *Writings and Speeches of Oliver Cromwell* (Cambridge, Mass., 1937–1947), ed. W. C. Abbott, I, 657, 663, 669.

29. NAS, Linlithgow Town Council Minutes, 1640–59, B48/9/2, 275–6, 278–9; *RPS*, 'Comisioune to the committe of estates', 1649/1/293. For contentious elections in Edinburgh, see Stewart, *Urban Politics*, 89–91, 279–84.

30. NAS, Register of minutes: committee of estates, Sept. 1648–Jan. 1649, PA11/7, fos. 1v, 11v–15v; Committee of Estates, *Wheras, many within this kingdom have joyned in armes for prosecuting of an unlawfull engagement against our neighbour nation of England . . .* (Edinburgh, 1648); Committee of Estates, *A declaration of the Committee of Estates concerning their proceedings in opposition to the late unlawfull engagement against England* (Edinburgh, 1648). Sixteen nobles attended, plus two noble officers of state, *RPS*, Sederunt, 4 January 1649, 1649/1/2.

31. Cf. Young, *Scottish Parliament*, 217, 221, 336; Stevenson, *Revolution*, 114–15. My interpretation is closer to Macinnes, 'Scottish Constitution', 107.

32. Abbott, *Writings and Speeches*, 678.

33. The best account remains Stevenson, *Scottish Revolution*, 113–21, 129; Scally, 'Covenanter Parliaments', 139 [quotation].

34. Stevenson, *Scottish Revolution*, 108, 126; Sean Kelsey, 'The Kings' Book: *Eikon basilike* and the English Revolution of 1649', in Nicholas Tyacke (ed.), *The English Revolution, c.1590–1720: Politics, Religion and Communities* (Manchester, 2007), 160–3; *RPS*, 'Instructions from the parlement of Scotland to their commissioners at London', 1649/1/21.

35. Cf. John Morrill, 'Introduction: Cromwell Redivivus' in Jane Mills (ed.), *Cromwell's Legacy* (Manchester, 2012), 10.

36. *RPS*, 'Proclamation of Charles the second king of Great Britane, France and Ireland', 1649/1/71.

37. Sir John Hurry, Sir William Hay of Dalgety, Colonel William Sibbald, and Captain John Spottiswood (grandchild of John, archbishop of St Andrews), were also executed in 1650, Stevenson, *Scottish Revolution*, 137. Allan Macinnes has suggested that Charles II's sacrifice of Montrose ruined prospects for an 'inclusive patriotic accommodation between Covenanters and Royalists in Scotland': *British Revolution*, 191, 193. Given the visceral hatred of Montrose

amongst Covenanters, any such alliance was highly unlikely on their part. See Edward J. Cowan, *Montrose: For Covenant and King* (Edinburgh, pbk edn, 1995), 266–7.

38. 'Letter from Paris, 17/27 April 1650', *Letters and Papers Illustrating the Relations between Charles the Second and Scotland in 1650*, ed. S. R. Gardiner (Edinburgh, 1894), 69.

39. Stevenson, *Scottish Revolution*, 141–2.

40. *A Declaration of the Committee of Estates of the Parliament of Scotland, in vindication of their proceedings from the aspersions of a scandalous pamphlet, published by that excommunicate traytor James Grahame . . .* (Edinburgh, 1650), 18, 21. An incomplete version exists in NAS, Register of Minutes: Committee of Estates, 5 December 1649–26 February 1650, PA11/9, fos. 38r–45v. King James Version, 2 Chronicles 18–19.

41. Abbott, *Writings and Speeches*, II, 307–8, 309.

42. Oliver Cromwell, *A Letter Sent to the General Assembly of the Kirke of Scotland . . .* (London, 1650), 4–5. *A Declaration of the Army of England upon their March into Scotland . . .* (London and Edinburgh, 1650), 7–8. Abbott, *Writings and Speeches*, II, 304–5.

43. John Nicoll, *A Diary of Public Transactions and Other Occurrences, Chiefly in Scotland, from January 1650 to June 1667*, ed. David Laing (Edinburgh, 1836), 20, 28.

44. Austin Woolrych, 'Cromwell as a Soldier', in John Morrill (ed.), *Oliver Cromwell and the English Revolution* (Harlow, 1990), 112–14. There is no good scholarly account of the campaigns from a Scottish perspective. For a balanced analysis of strengths and weaknesses on both sides, see Ian Gentles, *The English Revolution and the Wars in the Three Kingdoms, 1638–1652* (Harlow, 2007), chap. 12. For Cromwell's problems following Dunbar, see Abbott, *Writings and Speeches*, II, 393–8, 419–20; Cromwell to Speaker Lenthall, 21 July 1651, 432–3.

45. Macinnes, *British Revolution*, 191 [quotation]. See also Scott, *Politics and War*, 201. Stevenson, *Revolution*, 146.

46. Alexander Peterkin, *Records of the Kirk of Scotland, containing the Acts and Proceedings of the General Assemblies from the year 1638 . . .* (Edinburgh, 1838), 604. Stevenson, *Scottish Revolution*, 158.

47. *RPS*, 'Answer to the remonstrance from the commissioners of the general assembly', 14 December 1650, A1650/11/8.

48. Baillie, *Letters and Journals*, I, 65.

49. Stevenson, *Revolution*, 181.

50. Laura A. M. Stewart, 'Cromwell and the Scots', in Mills, ed., *Cromwell's Legacy*. Clare Jackson, *Restoration Scotland, 1660–1690: Royalist Politics, Religion and Ideas* (Woodbridge, 2003); Colin Kidd, *Unions and Unionism: Political Thought in Scotland, 1500–2000* (London, 2003), esp. chap. 6.

FURTHER READING

Coffey, John, *Politics, Religion and the British Revolutions: Samuel Rutherford and the Scottish Covenanters* (Cambridge, 1997).

Cowan, Edward J., *Montrose: For Covenant and King* (Edinburgh, new edn, 1995).

Gentles, Ian, *The English Revolution and the Wars in the Three Kingdoms, 1638–1652* (Harlow, 2007).

Macinnes, Allan I., *The British Revolution, 1629–1660* (Basingstoke, 2005).

Morrill, John (ed.), *The Scottish National Covenant in its British Context, 1638–51* (Edinburgh, 1990).

Scott, David, *Politics and War in the Three Stuart Kingdoms* (Basingstoke, 2004).

Stewart, Laura A. M., 'English Funding of the Scottish Armies in England and Ireland, 1640–48', *Historical Journal*, 52 (2009): 573–593.

Stewart, Laura A. M., 'Fiscal Revolution and State Formation in Mid Seventeenth Century Scotland', *Historical Research*, 84 (2011): 443–469.

Stewart, Laura A. M., *Rethinking the Scottish Revolutions: Covenanted Scotland, 1637–1651* (Oxford, forthcoming, 2015).

Stevenson, David (ed.), *Government under the Covenanters, 1637–1651* (Scottish History Society, 4th ser., vol. 18, Edinburgh, 1982).

Stevenson, David, *Highland Warrior: Alasdair MacColla and the Highland Problem in the Seventeenth Century* (Edinburgh, 1980).

Stevenson, David, ' "The Letter on Sovereign Power" and the Influence of Jean Bodin on Political Thought in Scotland', *Scottish Historical Review*, 61 (1982): 25–43.

Stevenson, David, *Revolution and Counter-Revolution, 1644–51* (new edn., Edinburgh, 2003).

Stoyle, Mark, 'English "Nationalism", Celtic Particularism, and the English Civil War', *Historical Journal*, 43 (2000): 1113–1128.

Young, John R., *The Scottish Parliament, 1639–41: A Political and Constitutional Analysis* (Edinburgh, 1996).

CHAPTER 8

·····································

THE CENTRE CANNOT HOLD

Ireland 1643–1649

·····································

MICHEÁL Ó SIOCHRÚ

> Turning and turning in the widening gyre
> The falcon cannot hear the falconer;
> Things fall apart; the centre cannot hold;
> Mere anarchy is loosed upon the world,
> The blood-dimmed tide is loosed, and everywhere
> The ceremony of innocence is drowned;
> The best lack all conviction, while the worst
> Are full of passionate intensity.[1]

On 15 September 1643, the king's representative in Ireland, James Butler, earl of Ormond, signed a Cessation of arms, valid for twelve months, with representatives of the Catholic Confederate association, bringing an end to almost two years of bloody conflict. The agreement divided the country into separate spheres of influence and was intended to create political space for the two sides to reach a permanent peace settlement, thus enabling Irish Catholic resources, including manpower, to be diverted to England.[2] Ten days after the Cessation in Ireland, the English parliament signed the Solemn League and Covenant with the Scottish Covenanters. Within a few months, a large Scottish army crossed south over the border and helped turn the tide of the war in England. Ormond, elevated to the rank of marquis and appointed as lord lieutenant in recognition of his service to the king, did manage to transport some royalist regiments back to England in late 1643 and early 1644 but a peace treaty with the Confederates proved elusive. In fact, over the next five years royalists and Confederates engaged in tortuous negotiations that did not reach a definitive conclusion until mid-January 1649, two weeks before the execution of Charles I. This long delay proved fatal to the king's interests throughout the three Stuart kingdoms and left Ireland vulnerable to decisive military intervention from England by Oliver Cromwell and the New Model Army.

HISTORICAL OVERVIEW

Despite the importance of this conflict in shaping the course of Irish history, scholars of the early modern period frequently neglected the 1640s, being drawn instead to the Nine Years War (1594–1603) or the Jacobite Wars (1688–91) at either end of the seventeenth century. Compared to the voluminous literature on the English civil war, very little was written on a struggle in Ireland seemingly characterized by nothing more than sectarian bloodshed, internecine feuding, and tedious negotiations. In the late nineteenth century, the antiquarian J. T. Gilbert produced an invaluable seven-volume collection of Confederate documents, including a narrative of the period by the secretary of the Confederate Supreme Council, Richard Bellings, and selections from the Carte manuscripts in the Bodleian Library, Oxford.[3] In 1882, C. P. Meehan reissued after a gap of almost forty years a revised and enlarged edition of his narrative survey of the 1640s, which acknowledged the importance of Gilbert's contribution. Meehan's work remained the standard account of Confederate Ireland for almost another hundred years.[4] Gilbert continued to collect, transcribe, and publish material relating to mid-seventeenth-century Ireland but he died in 1898 before completing a number of projects. The subsequent destruction of many official records during the Irish civil war in 1922 discouraged further research. Thereafter, historians shied away from major institutional, political studies, focusing instead on biographies of some of the key players, mainly from the Catholic side.[5]

In 1932, Michael Hynes analysed the controversial mission to Ireland of the papal nuncio, Giovanni Battista Rinuccini.[6] His work coincided with the publication in the original Latin of the first of five volumes of *Commentarius Rinuccinianus*, a contemporary account by two Irish clerics. In addition to the authors' narrative, the work contains copies and translations of original Confederate documents.[7] Over the next forty years little of importance appeared apart from two very effective chapters by Patrick Corish for volume three of the *New History of Ireland*, summarizing existing knowledge and providing an impressively coherent narrative of events.[8] In the early 1980s, a Scottish scholar, David Stevenson, explored the military links between Ireland and Scotland in two monographs, one of which dealt with the dramatic career of Alasdair MacColla.[9] Shortly afterwards, Jerrold Casway produced an authoritative biography of Owen Roe O'Neill, the iconic leader of the Ulster Irish, who secured their only major battlefield victory at Benburb in June 1646.[10] Finally, Jane Ohlmeyer's seminal life of the influential if maverick figure of Randal MacDonnell, earl of Antrim, adopted a 'three-kingdoms' perspective, associated in many minds with the New British History, which emerged in the 1970s.[11] This model is still very much in vogue but as Peter Lake has argued, this 'is not so much a new subject (British history) as simply a more integrated reading of English, Scottish and Irish histories'.[12]

In 1999, my monograph, *Confederate Ireland 1642–1649: A Constitutional and Political Analysis*, became the first major dedicated study of the Confederate association to appear in print in over a hundred years.[13] *Confederate Ireland* sought to resurrect the association's considerable achievements, as the only example of sustained self-government by the Catholic Irish on a national level prior to the declaration of the Republic in January 1919. The book focused in particular on the emergence of an influential group of political moderates, who promoted a vision of strong, self-reliant Irish kingdom, tolerant of diversity, where loyalty to the Stuart monarchy rather than ethnicity or religious affiliation was the primary political consideration. *Confederate Ireland* argued that class ultimately determined political divisions within the Confederate association and blamed the collapse of Irish Catholic interests on the obstructive tactics of the marquis of Ormond and of his supporters within the association.

Since the appearance of *Confederate Ireland* four major studies have added greatly to our knowledge of the period, while at the same time challenging aspects of my interpretation. First out of the blocks was Pádraig Lenihan's *Confederate Catholics at War, 1641–49*, which evaluated the Confederate war effort on a number of different levels—logistical, technological, tactical, and strategic.[14] Lenihan contended that previous accounts of the 1640s, including *Confederate Ireland*, sought to attribute the Confederate defeat to political factionalism alone, neglecting obvious military shortcomings in the process, principally the inability to keep forces in the field. Tadhg Ó hAnnracháin's *Catholic Reformation in Ireland: The Mission of Rinuccini, 1645–1649* provided a nuanced analysis of papal intervention in Irish politics and religious life, placing developments in a broad European, Counter-Reformation context.[15] Ó hAnnracháin disputed the existence of a moderate middle ground in Confederate politics and placed ethno-religious considerations rather than class at the very heart of the conflict. Robert Armstrong's *Protestant War: The British of Ireland and the Wars of the Three Kingdoms* acted in many ways as a companion volume to *Confederate Ireland* by focusing exclusively on the Protestant community.[16] Armstrong argued that *Confederate Ireland* underestimated the difficulties faced by Ormond in pursuing a royalist agenda, which sought to obtain assistance from Irish Catholics without alienating the king's Protestant subjects. The political machinations of Ormond, according to Armstrong, reflected nothing more than the impossible nature of the task he faced. The latest contribution to the debate is by Jane Ohlmeyer, who in her recently published book, entitled *Making Ireland English: The Irish Aristocracy in the Seventeenth Century*, portrays the war in Ireland during the 1640s primarily as a baronial conflict.[17] While not disagreeing with the central thesis of *Confederate Ireland*, Ohlmeyer places a far greater emphasis on the role of leading aristocratic figures in shaping the Confederate agenda.

This essay will explore political developments between 1643 and 1649, in a country torn asunder by military intervention from England and Scotland, as well as ethno-religious violence between the Catholic Irish and Protestant newcomers, while at the same time re-evaluating the conclusions drawn in *Confederate Ireland* in light of observations and criticisms made by Lenihan, Ó hAnnracháin, Armstrong, and Ohlmeyer.

CONFEDERATE ASSOCIATION

The Ulster rebellion, which began on 22 October 1641, triggered a war in Ireland that would last almost twelve years and result in the death of over a quarter of the Irish population. The causes of the rebellion are still disputed by historians but it is abundantly clear that the conservative Catholic landowning elite, having planned and executed the initial revolt, quickly lost control of events.[18] Within days a nationwide rising targeted government strongholds and Protestant settler communities in an attempt to overturn successive plantation schemes in Ulster and elsewhere. The forces of the colonial government retaliated with brutal force, indiscriminately targeting the entire Catholic population, which further escalated the violence. Thousands probably died on both sides although the biased and imprecise nature of the surviving evidence precludes the possibility of a definitive statement on the number of casualties.[19] By early 1642, the Catholic elite, horrified by the complete collapse of social order, sought to regain the initiative through the establishment of governmental structures. With the assistance of the Catholic Church, these landowners, lawyers, and merchants formed the Confederate association. The association's primary function was to enforce law and order in its territory, to organize militarily, and then to negotiate a settlement with the king from a position of strength. The outbreak of the English civil war in August 1642 halted the flow of military supplies to colonial forces in Ireland, thus providing vital breathing space to the Confederates. Moreover, the king's breach with the Westminster parliament allowed him to develop an independent Irish policy for the first time since the Ulster rebellion began.

In Ireland, the support of the Catholic Church proved crucial in consolidating the authority of the fledgling Confederate regime. The bishops eagerly embraced the concept of aligning religious affiliation with national consciousness, and in May 1642 an Ecclesiastical Congregation declared the war, fought to defend the Catholic religion and the liberties of the kingdom, to be both 'lawful and just'.[20] Over the next six months, throughout rebel-controlled areas, priests administered an oath of association to the civilian population, which pledged its loyalty to the Roman Catholic Church, Charles I, and the kingdom of Ireland. The Confederate motto, 'Hiberni unanimes pro Deo Rege et Patria' ('Irishmen united for God, king and country'), neatly encapsulated this multi-layered allegiance. In October, following a number of lengthy meetings, the Confederates created elaborate power structures, based in Kilkenny, the heartland of rebel-controlled territory. A legislative General Assembly, similar in function to the Dublin parliament, debated the big issues of war and peace, while an executive Supreme Council assumed responsibility for the daily functions of government. Provincial and county councils extended Confederate authority throughout the localities, while provincial armies replaced those irregular levies badly mauled by government forces during the early months of the conflict. In effect, the Confederates established a parallel government to the colonial administration in Dublin, raising taxes and maintaining armies, as well other activities usually reserved to the crown, such as sending envoys to foreign courts.[21]

Traditional accounts focus on the existence of two distinct groups within the Confederate association, based primarily on ethnic grounds. Internal Confederate tensions throughout the 1640s are usually ascribed to the antipathy between the Old English, descendants of the original settlers from the twelfth and thirteenth centuries, and the indigenous Old Irish population.[22] Like all generalizations this interpretation contains an element of truth and many on both sides felt uncomfortable with the new alliance. Nonetheless, political and social interaction over four hundred years had increasingly blurred ethnic distinctions, while more recently both groups had suffered religious discrimination as a result of their adherence to the Catholic faith.

From the outset the Confederates made strenuous efforts to preserve ethnic harmony within their ranks. The first General Assembly in October 1642 ordered that no distinction or comparison be made between 'old Irish, and old and new English, or between septs or families, or between citizens and townsmen and countrymen, joining in union, upon pain of the highest punishment'.[23] As Catholics they joined together for mutual protection, but the Confederate leadership actively espoused a more inclusive form of national identity, insisting that the king treat all his Irish subjects, regardless of their ethnic background, equally before the law. Place of birth, rather than ancestral blood, now provided the essential criterion for membership of the Irish nation, potentially enabling Protestant newcomers to share a sense of community with their Catholic neighbours. As a Confederate delegation explained during subsequent peace talks with the royalists in 1644, 'for he that is born in Ireland, though his parents and all his ancestors were aliens [foreigners], nay if his parents are Indians or Turks, if converted to Christianity, is an Irishman as fully as if his ancestors were born here for thousands of years'.[24] This remarkable statement of inclusivity contrasted starkly with the bigoted utterances of many leading Irish Protestants and English parliamentarians, as well as the hysterical outpourings of the London newssheets. The Confederate leadership saw no contradiction between this emerging national identity in Ireland and loyalty to the Stuart monarchy. Indeed, from the very beginning all Confederates favoured a negotiated settlement with the royalist regime.

GOVERNMENT REACTION

Initially, the administration in Dublin, staffed for the most part by English parliamentary sympathizers, rejected any peace overtures. Unable to sustain a military offensive against the Catholic rebels, the Lords Justice sought instead to consolidate their control of enclaves around Dublin in the east, Cork in the south, and Derry in the north, launching occasional devastating raids in support of isolated outposts. In February 1643, Captain William Tucker described in glowing terms one such foray by Sir Richard Grenville, 'killing and destroying by fire and sword all that came in his way'.[25] At this time, however, startling news reached Dublin of the king's willingness to receive peace proposals from the Confederates, in the hope of obtaining supplies and manpower for use against the English parliament. The Lords Justice argued against any peace 'before the sword or famine' devastated the ranks of the rebels, making them more likely as a result to accept minimal concessions.[26] Despite these protestations, talks began shortly afterwards, while the commander of the colonial forces, the earl (and subsequently marquis) of Ormond, gradually seized control of Dublin for the royalist cause, removing the Lords Justice and their allies from office, and establishing tentative lines of communication with Kilkenny.

In addition to these important political developments, the impact of Continental veterans helped change the nature of the war in Ireland. With the eruption of hostilities in the three Stuart kingdoms, thousands of Irish and Scottish veterans returned from the continent. After prolonged exposure to the horrors of unrestrained warfare, they appreciated the advantages of military discipline, which had become increasingly evident in the latter stages of the Thirty Years War.[27] The principle of reciprocity gradually came to form the basis of the 'rules' of war in Ireland. From late 1642, the increased professionalism of the various armies, especially the Covenanting and Confederate forces, along with the threat of retaliation, acted as a moderating influence, as all sides acknowledged that the introduction of some general rules of engagement would be of mutual benefit.[28] The conflict continued to rage across the four provinces, with frequent raids and skirmishes, as well as sieges and the occasional set-piece battle. Yet, at least until 1647, no major massacres took place, terms of surrender were honoured, and prisoners were exchanged on a regular basis. The publication of strict codes of conduct also signalled efforts to regulate the behaviour of troops during large-scale military campaigns.[29] This is not to suggest that atrocities did not take place, but the reality in Ireland during much of the 1640s was far removed from the indiscriminate butchery of the early months of the conflict, as conventional armies on all sides operated largely according to accepted military standards.[30]

Increasing moderation on the battlefield gradually created the space for political dialogue, and following the Cessation of violence in September 1643, Ormond was able to ship thousands of troops back to assist the royalist cause in England, with mixed results.[31] The papal agent to Kilkenny, Pietro Francesco Scarampi, had opposed the truce, believing that the Confederate forces could achieve outright military victory. Such optimism was probably misplaced but the Cessation did create real difficulties for the Confederates about how best to pursue their military and political goals. They remained at war with the Scottish Covenanters in Ulster, while Munster Protestants switched their allegiance to the English parliament in 1644, establishing a hostile enclave in the southern province as a result. In the face of these threats, the Confederates equivocated between an insular and an external military strategy. An insular strategy involved defeating the various enemies of the Confederates, including the royalists, and then, with the entire kingdom under their control, negotiating a deal with Charles I from a position of strength, as the Scots had recently done. Those advocating an external strategy argued that the rights of Irish Catholics could only be protected by a royalist victory in England, which would curb the power of a hostile and predatory English parliament. After restoring his authority, so the argument went, a grateful king would happily bestow concessions on his loyal

Catholic subjects, who had provided crucial military aid. The Confederate leadership favoured an external strategy from 1643 to 1646, but in contrast to the intervention of the Scottish Covenanters on behalf of the English parliament, did not provide any direct military support to the king in England.[32] This failure to transport troops across the Irish Sea can be primarily attributed to the protracted nature of the negotiations between the Confederates and the king's representative in Ireland, the marquis of Ormond.

TREATY NEGOTIATIONS AND FACTIONAL POLITICS

Following the Cessation of violence in September 1643, intense negotiations, mainly in Dublin, dominated the political landscape for the next five years. Two main power blocs emerged at Kilkenny, namely the 'peace' and 'clerical' factions. The peace faction consisted primarily of existing landowners, aristocrats, and gentry, all with a considerable stake in society and most to lose in the event of military defeat. They favoured a limited settlement that would guarantee religious toleration, allowing Catholics to worship in private without hindrance, while preserving their estates and granting them access to public office. They provided an element of continuity in Irish political life. A significant number, both Old Irish and Old English, had sat in the Dublin parliament of 1640–1, men such as Richard Butler, Viscount Mountgarret, chairman of the Supreme Council, Richard Bellings, secretary of the Supreme Council, and Donough MacCarthy, Viscount Muskerry, another leading member of the Supreme Council. The close relationship of many in this group with the marquis of Ormond, primarily through marriage and business interests, led Confederate rivals to refer to them contemptuously as 'Ormondists', a term subsequently adopted by historians. The label is misleading, as a desire to preserve estates and social status, rather than any personal loyalty to Ormond, provided their primary motivation.

The clerical faction emerged as an increasingly vocal opposition in Kilkenny after 1644, particularly when peace talks with the royalists looked like reaching a conclusion. Convinced, with some justification, that the Confederate leadership would not insist on major religious or indeed political concessions, this group favoured a more radical settlement on the grounds that only the full restoration of the Roman Catholic Church, recognized by the state, could guarantee permanent religious security. The faction viewed with suspicion the more secular impulses of the Kilkenny leadership, which threatened to dilute the specifically Catholic elements of the Confederate association. The clerics received crucial support from returning exiles, most of them Old Irish in extraction, such as General Owen Roe O'Neill. Living for decades in Spanish territories, men like O'Neill never had to compromise on religious matters in the same manner as those who remained in Ireland. Many of these returnees, having lost out in successive plantation schemes, also demanded a more comprehensive land settlement, in the hope of recovering confiscated estates.

Ó hAnnracháin argues that ethnicity was the primary factor in deciding factional loyalty. The leadership of the 'peace' faction did indeed consist primarily of those of Old English descent, while the Old Irish predominated in the 'clerical' faction, but this traditional interpretation overlooks the centrality of landownership in determining the political outlook of any individual.[33] The possession of large estates, for example, enabled Donough MacCarthy, Viscount Muskerry, a man of Old Irish extraction, to be accepted as leader of the 'peace' faction, while his associates included those from the ranks of the so-called deserving Irish in the Ulster plantation settlement, such as Sir Phelim O'Neill and Alexander MacDonnell. Social status not ethnic background proved paramount, though Ó hAnnracháin is correct to point out that religious convictions did motivate a number of existing, if largely impoverished, landowners to support the clergy. Ohlmeyer, however, believes that social status effectively reflected ethnic divisions in Catholic Ireland, with the peace faction dominated by an Old English aristocracy, while the clerical faction represented the dispossessed Old Irish.[34] The aristocracy undoubtedly played a major role in political and military affairs during the 1640s. Nonetheless, the survival of the personal papers of many leading families, alongside the destruction of so many official records in successive fires, has distorted the picture to some extent, emphasizing the importance of the aristocracy in the Confederate association at the expense of key figures in the gentry, as well as in the legal and clerical professions.

PROTESTANT IRELAND

Tensions within the Confederate association increased dramatically with the arrival of a papal nuncio, Giovanni Battista Rinuccini, in late 1645. Appointed by Pope Innocent X to uphold the dignity of the Catholic Church in Ireland, Rinuccini refused to countenance any treaty with the royalists that did not contain significant religious concessions.[35] The demands of the clergy and their allies created enormous difficulties for the king, anxious to exploit the financial resources and manpower of Ireland, yet acutely conscious of the deep hostility felt by his English subjects towards the Catholic Irish. His strategy of reaching out to Kilkenny alienated many royalist supporters in Ireland and created enormous difficulties for the marquis of Ormond. After the initial shock of the insurrection, Irish Protestants eagerly joined those forces mobilized by the colonial administration to crush the rebellion, and advocated a purely military solution to the crisis. This made their loyalty to the king highly conditional. Many of them deeply resented the truce with the Confederates in 1643. According to Colonel Audley Mervin, a Protestant officer serving in Ulster,

> a peace with the Irish is generally a harsh sound to every ear and the reason of this is diverse. Some in conscience hold no toleration of their religion, some judge the blood of their friends yet unrevenged, some their personal lives not to be repaired, others that it is beyond the reach of state to provide for our security in the future, and not a few because the country is pleasant and held too good for them.[36]

In early 1644, representatives from the rump parliament still sitting in Dublin travelled to the royal court at Oxford to put the Protestant case. They demanded 'the establishment of the true Protestant religion in Ireland', the strict imposition of penal laws against Catholics, and an extension of the policy of plantation throughout the kingdom. After a short period of consultation, the king's advisers rejected these terms as too extreme.[37] Charles I urgently required a settlement with the Confederates before organized Protestant opposition completely undermined his Irish strategy. Typically, rather than take any tough decisions himself during talks at Oxford with a Confederate delegation headed by Muskerry, the king instructed Ormond to negotiate with the Kilkenny regime on his behalf.

Unfortunately for Charles, the marquis, fearful that any possible deal would result in further defections by Irish Protestant royalists to the English parliament, proved unequal to the task. The extent of the problems faced by Ormond became clear when in July 1644 the royalist commander in Cork, Lord Inchiquin, declared for parliament in protest at the continuing peace talks with the Confederates.[38] Similarly in Ulster, army officers loyal to the king watched helplessly as their subordinates eagerly embraced the Solemn League and Covenant, joining forces with the Scottish Covenanters.[39] Armstrong is correct to highlight the pressures on Ormond from within the Irish Protestant community, which undoubtedly limited his room for manoeuvre both politically and militarily. Nonetheless, an increasingly desperate king urgently required assistance from Ireland. As Armstrong readily concedes, 'to ingest [the Confederate association] back into the body politic was one route, but to disrupt and dismantle it through defections and defeats was another acceptable option'.[40] Acceptable to Ormond perhaps, and he ruthlessly pursued this latter strategy, even to the detriment of the king. What Armstrong perhaps does not fully appreciate is that Ormond's primary loyalty throughout the 1640s was to himself and to the Irish Protestant interest. He remained determined not to concede on key religious issues such as the redistribution of church property and revenue, a stance that threatened to derail the peace talks entirely. Charles I recognized the problem long before his military defeat in England and authorized the earl of Glamorgan to negotiate secret religious concessions with Kilkenny. Glamorgan signed a treaty with the Confederates in August 1645, but both the king and Ormond denounced the deal when the English parliament publicized the details in late 1645.[41] Despite this setback, the Confederate leadership, dominated by the peace faction, finally agreed terms with Ormond in late March 1646, ignoring clerical concerns about the absence of religious guarantees.

The lord lieutenant's intransigence, therefore, did succeed in destabilizing the Confederate association by further dividing the peace and clerical factions, but failed to produce any military aid for the king in England. Unable to assemble another field army after the disastrous defeat at Naseby, Charles I surrendered to the Scottish Covenanting army at Newark in Nottinghamshire in May 1646, effectively bringing the war in England to an end. The king spent the next two years negotiating a possible settlement with parliament, while at the same time attempting to form a new royalist alliance, incorporating supporters in England, Scotland, and Ireland.

CONFEDERATE CIVIL WAR

In Ireland, the war continued unabated, with Confederates, royalists, parliamentarians, and Covenanters engaged in a complex series of interlocking conflicts. In August 1646, the marquis of Ormond, on behalf of Charles I, finally proclaimed the peace with the Catholic Confederates agreed earlier in the year.[42] Although too late to intervene in the English civil war, Ormond still hoped to strengthen the king's hand in negotiations with parliament by threatening a royalist invasion from Ireland. The peace treaty granted many of the political and economic concessions sought by the Confederates, including guarantees for their existing estates, but did nothing for those who had lost out in the plantation process. It also carefully sidestepped the controversial issue of religion by postponing any decisions until the king regained his liberty. This compromise satisfied the conservative landowning leadership in Kilkenny, but outraged the Catholic clergy, led by Rinuccini. The nuncio condemned the treaty as contrary to the Confederate oath of association, and excommunicated all those who favoured peace with the royalists.[43] With the support of General Owen Roe O'Neill, fresh from his overwhelming victory over the Scots at Benburb, which removed the Covenanters as an active force in Irish political and military affairs for the remainder of the decade, Rinuccini staged a coup d'état and seized power in Kilkenny.[44] He ordered O'Neill, along with another leading returnee, General Thomas Preston, to move against Ormond in Dublin, but this potentially decisive offensive failed because of Confederate infighting and the onset of winter. Moreover, the diversion of resources to the Dublin campaign prevented the Confederates from pressing home major military gains in Ulster, Connacht, and Munster, undermining any prospect of seizing control of the entire kingdom.[45]

The setback before Dublin weakened the authority of the nuncio and his faction, allowing a group of moderates, led by Nicholas Plunkett, to dictate Confederate policy. A trained lawyer and major landowner from one of the most important Old English families of the Pale, Plunkett served as chairman of the General Assembly throughout the 1640s. He also sat on the Supreme Council and played a key role in the difficult negotiations with Ormond. Few, if any, Confederates matched his record of active involvement and political influence during this period. Plunkett's enduring ability to appeal to all sides enabled him to exploit dissatisfaction with the excesses of the two principal factions, and to move the Confederate association towards the political middle ground.[46] In August 1646, sent by the ruling junta in Kilkenny as an envoy to assuage clerical opposition to the Ormond treaty, he dramatically switched sides in a move that facilitated the nuncio's seizure of power. He soon developed his own agenda, however, ably assisted by Nicholas French, bishop of Ferns. Initially, an enthusiastic member of the clerical faction, French had adopted a hard line against Protestants in his hometown of Wexford during the early years of the war.[47] The failure of the Dublin offensive convinced the bishop to adopt a more pragmatic approach. Plunkett and French advocated a new deal with the royalists, albeit with significantly enhanced conditions, particularly on matters of religion, but Ormond proved intractable. The marquis felt betrayed by the Confederate rejection of the peace treaty, while the assault on Dublin convinced him of the futility of the king's cause in Ireland, despite the growing prominence of the moderates at Kilkenny.

Ó hAnnracháin disputes the existence of this moderate grouping, arguing with some justification that the somewhat fluid membership of the different factions makes it difficult to identify political allegiance with any degree of certainty.[48] Plunkett, as outlined above, switched between factions on several occasions but in so doing managed to create political space for himself and likeminded individuals. These factions were not, however, political parties in the modern sense, but rather a loose grouping of individuals, held together by a desire to influence policy in a certain direction. Indeed, the moderates did not necessarily identify themselves as a separate group. Nonetheless, Plunkett and his associates successfully steered a middle course at a crucial juncture in late 1646/early 1647 before ultimately succumbing to factional pressures in the face of successive military disasters, brought about by the decision of the English parliament to re-enter the Irish war.

With Ormond isolated in Dublin, and the Scottish Covenanters on the defensive following their disastrous defeat at Benburb, the English parliament sensed an opportunity to seize the military initiative in Ireland. The end of the war in England allowed it to consider diverting resources to Ireland for the first time since the summer of 1642. In February 1647, a parliamentary expedition landed in Munster, ostensibly to support the local Protestant commander, Lord Inchiquin. Tensions between Inchiquin and the expedition's leader, Philip Sidney, Lord Lisle, undermined the mission, which achieved nothing of consequence, apart from providing some desperately needed military supplies to local Protestant forces.[49] A second foray into Ireland that summer proved far more successful, when in June commissioners from Westminster convinced Ormond to surrender the city of Dublin to the English parliament. Ormond's actions directly contravened orders from Queen Henrietta Maria at the exiled royal court in France, who favoured an accommodation with the Confederates as the basis for a renewed alliance against parliament. Ormond, failing to recognize the significance of the shift of power in Kilkenny, away from the clerical faction and towards the moderates, refused to hand Dublin over to 'the tyranny of those that then ruled amongst the Irish'.[50] He left for England shortly afterwards to deliver a report on his actions to the king, before joining the other royalist exiles on the Continent. In a conspicuous display of his own prejudices, the marquis preferred English Protestants of whatever political persuasion to Irish Catholics, a decision that subsequently proved disastrous for both royalists and Confederates.[51] His actions, however, were entirely consistent with his political stance throughout the 1640s and should not have surprised anybody. Like all Irish Protestants, he was loyal to the king only to a point. Perhaps Charles I deserved no better from his subjects.

The new parliamentary governor of Dublin, Colonel Michael Jones, commanded an army comprising local Protestants and troops recently arrived from England. On 8 August 1647, he annihilated the best equipped and best trained Confederate army at Dungan's Hill near Dublin, while in Munster the rabidly anti-Catholic Lord Inchiquin, reinforced with fresh supplies of arms and men from England, launched a destructive raid deep into Confederate territory. Inchiquin's campaign culminated in the destruction of yet another Confederate army at the battle of Knocknanuss in November. The Confederate association faced total defeat but the outbreak of the second English civil war in 1648 prevented further military supplies reaching Ireland, and temporarily stalled the parliamentary offensive.

Nonetheless, the military and political situation remained extremely fluid and unpredictable. In April 1648, Lord Inchiquin declared for the king and agreed a controversial truce with Kilkenny, while the return of Ormond to Ireland in September raised the possibility of a renewed formal alliance between the royalists and Confederates.[52] Rinuccini and Owen Roe O'Neill, fearing an attempt to revive the discredited peace treaty, opposed these moves, plunging the Confederate association into an inconclusive civil war. Starved of supplies from England, Michael Jones in Dublin could do little to take advantage of the situation. A triumphant English parliament, however, shorn of all moderate members, and without the restraining influence of the king, was likely to commit significant resources to the 'pacification' of the Catholic Irish in the near future. Indeed, news of the king's impending trial generated a greater sense of urgency in the talks between Ormond and the Confederates, and on 17 January 1649 the two sides signed a second peace treaty in Kilkenny.[53] Concern for the fate of the king temporarily papered over many of the cracks. Ormond graciously promised further concessions, but Catholic Ireland remained deeply divided, while Rinuccini departed for Rome shortly afterwards.[54] Moreover, within two weeks the execution of Charles I removed with the stroke of an axe the final obstacle to major English military intervention in Ireland. The time to avenge the massacre of Protestant settlers in 1641, and reassert English dominance, was close at hand. In August, Oliver Cromwell landed on the outskirts of Dublin with an army of 12,000 men and the largest train of artillery yet seen in Ireland. Over the next four years parliamentary forces crushed all resistance and re-established English colonial rule, dealing a fatal blow to the Irish Catholic landowning class in the process. The Cromwellians spent over £1,000,000 a year in subjugating Ireland, demonstrating the economic dominance of the English state over the Confederates, who throughout the 1640s had struggled to raise £70,000 annually.[55] These major financial resources, combined with a well-established military machine and a deep-seated hatred of the Catholic Irish, drove the English on to a bloody and costly victory.[56]

CONCLUSION

The horrors of the Cromwellian conquest in many ways continue to overshadow the events of the mid-seventeenth century in Ireland. The period was dominated by extreme violence, sectarian hatreds, and indiscriminate bloodshed and yet the 1640s also witnessed a remarkable flowering of Irish national sentiment through the Confederate association, anticipating by almost two centuries the reforming nationalist tradition of Daniel O'Connell and Charles Stewart Parnell. *Confederate Ireland* focused on these positive aspects as well as the negative and the central tenets of its thesis retain their validity, albeit that our understanding of Catholic Ireland's great experiment in self-government has been greatly enhanced by the works of Lenihan and Ó hAnnracháin, while Armstrong and Ohlmeyer, in different ways, provide an invaluable counter-balance. The experiment ended in failure and for historians there is no ignoring the harsh military realities of the situation. In the absence of significant outside intervention by the Catholic powers of Europe, the Confederate association proved incapable of withstanding the full might of the English state.[57] This fact, however, as Lenihan succinctly explains, 'is not to overstate the importance of military factors at the expense of political factionalism; the two are inextricably linked'.[58] The Confederates did not control sufficient resources to compete militarily with the English Commonwealth over a prolonged period but internecine feuding further undermined the war effort and hastened the process of defeat. The English civil war delayed the reconquest by seven years but ultimately Irish Catholics, bitterly divided and chronically under-resourced, had no answer to Oliver Cromwell and the New Model Army.

Notes

1. 'The Second Coming', in W. B. Yeats, *Michael Robartes and the Dancer* (Dublin, 1920).
2. *A collection of all the papers which passed upon the late treaty touching the cessation of armes in Ireland . . .* Dublin, 1643 (RIA vol. 38, box 34, tract 1).
3. See J. T. Gilbert (ed.), *History of the Irish Confederation and the War in Ireland*, 7 vols. (Dublin, 1882–91). He had already published three volumes of documents dealing mainly with the Cromwellian period, including the anonymous memoirs entitled 'Aphorismical discovery of treasonable faction', a savage critique of the earl/marquis of Ormond. J. T. Gilbert (ed.), *A Contemporary History of Affairs in Ireland from 1641 to 1652*, 3 vols. (Dublin, 1879–80). The 272 volumes of the Carte collection in the Bodleian Library, Oxford, manuscripts originally held by the Butler family in Kilkenny, remain the major source on seventeenth-century Irish history.
4. See the dedication in C. P. Meehan, *The Confederation of Kilkenny* (Dublin, 1882). The first edition appeared in 1846.
5. Irish history still awaits a major biography of Ormond, who dominated the political landscape for almost fifty years. J. C. Beckett, *The Cavalier Duke: A Life of James Butler, First Duke of Ormond, 1610–1688* (Belfast, 1990) provides an uncritical overview. Perhaps the sheer scale of the surviving sources acts as a disincentive.
6. Michael Hynes, *The Mission of Rinuccini, Nuncio Extraordinary to Ireland, 1645–1649* (Louvain, 1932).
7. Richard O'Ferrall and Robert O'Connell, *Commentarius Rinuccinianus, de sedis apostolicae legatione ad foederatos Hiberniae catholicos per annos 1645–9*, 6 vols. (Dublin, 1932–49). The sixth volume consists of an English language summary and an extensive index. The Irish Manuscript Commission is currently preparing a five-volume English translation for publication.
8. See Patrick J. Corish, 'The Rising of 1641 and the Catholic Confederacy, 1641–5' and 'Ormond, Rinuccini, and the Confederates, 1645–9', both in T. W. Moody, F. X. Martin, and F. J. Byrne (eds.), *A New History of Ireland*, vol. III: *Early Modern Ireland, 1534–1691* (Oxford, 1976), 289–316, 316–35. While publications remained thin on the ground, three

significant doctoral theses covered unchartered territory—Hugh Hazlett, 'A History of the Military Forces Operating in Ireland, 1641–1649', 2 vols. (unpublished Ph.D. thesis, Queen's University, Belfast, 1938); Dónal Cregan, 'The Confederation of Kilkenny: Its Organisation, Personnel and History' (unpublished Ph.D. thesis, University College Dublin, 1947); John Lowe, 'The Negotiations between Charles I and the Confederation of Kilkenny, 1642–9' (unpublished Ph.D. thesis, University of London, 1960).

9. David Stevenson, *Alasdair MacColla and the Highland Problem in the Seventeenth Century* (Edinburgh, 1981). The other book, *Scottish Covenanters and Irish Confederates: Scottish–Irish Relations in the Mid-Seventeenth Century* (Belfast, 1981), concentrated on the impact of the Scottish Covananting army in Ulster during the 1640s.

10. Jerrold I. Casway, *Owen Roe O'Neill and the Struggle for Catholic Ireland* (Philadelphia, 1984).

11. Jane Ohlmeyer, *Civil War and Restoration in the Three Stuart Kingdoms: The Career of Randal MacDonnell, Marquis of Antrim, 1609–1683* (Cambridge, 1993).

12. Peter Lake is quoted in Jane Ohlmeyer, 'Seventeenth-Century Ireland and the New British and Atlantic Histories', *American Historical Review*, 104 (1999): 446–62, at 448. Irish historians for the most part have responded negatively to the New British History, levelling charges against it of Anglo-centrism and anti-Europeanism. See for example, Nicholas Canny, *Making Ireland British, 1580–1650* (Oxford, 2001), p. vii.

13. Micheál Ó Siochrú, *Confederate Ireland, 1642–1649: A Constitutional and Political Analysis* (Dublin, 1999; 2nd edition 2008). In 1954, T. L. Coonan wrote a confused and deeply flawed narrative of the period, entitled *The Irish Catholic Confederacy and the Puritan Revolution* (Dublin, 1954), from a traditional and totally uncritical Irish nationalist perspective.

14. Pádraig Lenihan, *Confederate Catholics at War, 1641–49* (Cork, 2001).

15. Tadhg Ó hAnnracháin, *Catholic Reformation in Ireland: The Mission of Rinuccini, 1645–1649* (Oxford, 2002).

16. Robert Armstrong, *Protestant War: The British of Ireland and the Wars of the Three Kingdoms* (Manchester, 2005).

17. Jane Ohlmeyer, *Making Ireland English: The Irish Aristocracy in the Seventeenth Century* (New Haven, 2012).

18. The extremes of the argument are probably best represented by on the one side Raymond Gillespie, who agrees with many contemporaries that the uprising came as a complete surprise to a society largely adapting to the new colonial system, and on the other by David Edwards, who stresses the endemic nature of violence in early modern Irish society. See Raymond Gillespie, *Seventeenth Century Ireland* (Dublin, 2006), 143–51, and David Edwards, 'Out of the Blue? Provincial Unrest in Ireland before 1641', in Jane Ohlmeyer and Micheál Ó Siochrú (eds.), *Ireland 1641: Contexts and Reactions* (Manchester, 2013).

19. Aidan Clarke makes this point very forcibly. See 'The 1641 Massacres', in Ohlmeyer and Ó Siochrú (eds.), *Ireland 1641*. Between 2007 and 2010 an AHRC and IRCHSS-funded project transcribed, digitized, and published online (<http://1641.tcd.ie>) the 1641 depositions, 8,000 witness statements by Protestant refugees fleeing rebel forces, which had been lodged in the Trinity College Dublin Library in 1741. The accessibility of this source to scholars throughout the world will help transform our understanding of this crucial period in Irish history.

20. 'Acts of the Ecclesiastical Congregation, 10–13 May 1642' in British Library [BL] Stowe Ms 82, fos. 271–4.

21. The workings of Confederate government are discussed in detail in Ó Siochrú, *Confederate Ireland*, 205–36.

22. Corish reinforced this interpretation in his own analysis of the period. See Corish, 'The Rising of 1641', 320–2.

23. 'Acts of General Assembly of Confederation, October 1642', in Gilbert (ed.), *History of Irish Confederation*, II, 73–84.

24. 'Confederate explanation of propositions, 1644', in Gilbert (ed.), *History of Irish Confederation*, II, 298–305.

25. 'Journal of Captain William Tucker, 1642–3', in Gilbert (ed.), *History of Irish Confederation*, II, 199.

26. Lords Justices and others to the King, 16 March 1643, in Historical Manuscripts Commission [HMC], *Ormond MSS*, new series, II, 251–2.

27. Peter Wilson, *Europe's Tragedy: A History of the Thirty Years War* (London, 2009) is a superb account of this formative conflict. Wilson is one of the few historians to give equal coverage to the latter stages of the war and in so doing charts this gradual moderation in conduct.

28. One critic later accused Ormond of 'a slack and unfaithful prosecution of the war', and reported incredulously how he refused to retaliate for an alleged breach of quarter by the Catholic Irish. [Adam Meredith,] *Ormond's curtain drawn: in a short discourse concerning Ireland* (London, 1646), 13, 29.

29. This argument is discussed in detail in Micheál Ó Siochrú, 'Atrocity, Codes of Conduct and the Irish in the British Civil Wars 1641–1653', *Past and Present*, 195 (2007): 55–86.

30. The belief persists among most historians that the conflict in Ireland somehow operated outside the acceptable laws of war as understood in the seventeenth century. Robin Clifton stated that unlike England and Scotland it was only in Ireland 'that civil war unleashed humanity's full capacity for wholesale and pitiless slaughter', while Nicholas Canny argues that despite the efforts of some professional soldiers, 'it quickly became apparent that warfare in Ireland was constrained by no moral economies'. See Robin Clifton, 'An Indiscriminate Blackness? Massacre, Counter-massacre and Ethnic Cleansing in Ireland', in Mark Levene and Penny Roberts (eds.), *The Massacre in History* (Oxford, 1999), 107; Nicholas Canny, *Making Ireland British, 1580–1650* (Oxford, 2001), 568. Similarly, according to John Morrill, massacres perpetrated by Oliver Cromwell merely reflected the codes of military conflict in the Irish theatre. See John Morrill, 'Historical Introduction and Overview: The Un-English Civil War', in J. R. Young (ed.), *Celtic Dimensions of the British Civil Wars* (Edinburgh, 1997), 6.

31. Estimates of the number of troops transported to England by Ormond have gradually declined. According to Pádraig Lenihan, 2,000 troops were transported from Munster to Bristol in November 1643. Five under-strength regiments travelled from Dublin to Chester, in addition to two further regiments and four cavalry troops, totalling perhaps 3,000 men: Lenihan, *Confederate Catholics at War*, 76. See also Keith Lindley, 'The Impact of the 1641 Rebellion upon England and Wales, 1641–5', *Irish Historical Studies*, 18 (1972): 143–76; Mark Stoyle, *Soldiers and Strangers: An Ethnic History of the English Civil War* (New Haven, 2005).

32. In 1644, the Confederate leadership sanctioned a campaign in Scotland led by Alasdair MacColla with 2,000 troops. His small force, in association with the marquis of Montrose, achieved a remarkable string of victories before being defeated and dispersed in late 1645. See Stevenson, *Alasdair MacColla*.

33. Ó hAnnracháin, *Catholic Reformation in Ireland*, 80–1.

34. Ohlmeyer, *Making Ireland English*, 274–6.

35. Instructions from Innocent X to Rinuccini, in G. Aiazza (ed.), *The Embassy in Ireland of Monsignor G. B. Rinuccini, Archbishop of Fermo, in the years 1645–49*, translated into English by Annie Hutton (Dublin, 1873), pp. xxvii–xlix.

36. Colonel Audley Mervin to Ormond, 4 February 1645, in HMC, *Manuscripts of the Marquess of Ormond*, vol. I, 14th report, appendix part 7 (London, 1895), 93.

37. John Rushworth, *Historical Collections of Private Passages of State* (London, 1721–), V, 953–71.

38. *A letter from the Right Honourable Lord Inchiquin and other commanders in Munster to his Majestie* (London, 1644). The letter book of Roger Boyle, Lord Broghill (later earl of Orrery) contains a number of the declarations on behalf of 'all his Majesty's Protestant subjects in the province of Munster'. See BL Add. MSS 25287, fos. 4v–12. Inchiquin may also have been piqued by his failure to obtain the position of Lord President of Munster.

39. These developments are discussed in detail in Armstrong, *Protestant War*, 95–118.

40. Armstrong, *Protestant War*, 125.

41. 'Articles of agreement between Glamorgan and the confederates, 25 August 1645', BL, Add. MSS 25277, fo. 62.

42. The treaty articles are in Gilbert (ed.), *Irish Confederation*, V, 286–310.

43. The decree of excommunication was published on 1 September 1646. See Bodleian, Carte MS 18, fo. 414.

44. For the decline in the power of the Covananters in Ulster post 1646, see Stevenson, *Scottish Covenanters and Irish Confederates*, 237–52.

45. In addition to the victory at Benburb, the Confederates had seized the strategically vital castle at Bunratty at the mouth of the Shannon, which the parliamentarians had hoped to use as a potential launching pad for further incursion into Munster. Preston had also made major inroads into Connacht, including the capture of Roscommon. See Lenihan, *Confederate Catholics at War*, 90–5.

46. The rise of a 'Middle Group' group in Confederate politics, following the rejection of the first Ormond peace treaty, is discussed in detail in Ó Siochrú, *Confederate Ireland*, 118–42.

47. For the outbreak of the rebellion in Wexford see Jason McHugh, 'For Our Own Defence: Catholic Insurrection in Wexford', in Brian MacCuarta (ed.), *Reshaping Ireland, 1550–1700: Colonization and its Consequences* (Dublin, 2011), 214–40.

48. Ó hAnnracháin, *Catholic Reformation in Ireland*, 171–5.

49. The war in Munster has received relatively little attention from historians. For Lisle's expedition see Patrick Little 'The Irish Independents and Viscount Lisle's Lieutenancy of Ireland', *Historical Journal [HJ]*, 44 (2001): 941–61; John Adamson, 'Strafford's Ghost: The British Context of Viscount Lisle's Lieutenancy of Ireland', in Jane Ohlmeyer (ed.), *Ireland from Independence to Occupation, 1641–1660* (Cambridge, 1995), 128–59.

50. 'Ormond's report to the king at Hampton Court', BL Egerton MS 2541, fos. 377–81.

51. On 2 August 1649, while attempting to regain Dublin from the forces of the English parliament, Ormond's royalist/Confederate alliance suffered a catastrophic defeat at Rathmines. Less than two weeks later, Oliver Cromwell landed unopposed in Dublin and used the city as the base from which to launch his devastating conquest of Ireland. Ormond's prestige and authority never really recovered from this disaster.

52. The articles of agreement between Inchiquin and the Confederate Supreme Council, 20 May 1648, Bodleian, Carte MS 22, fo. 99.

53. The second Ormond Peace is published in Gilbert (ed.), *Irish Confederation*, vol. 7, 184–211.

54. *The Marquesse of Ormond's proclamation concerning the peace concluded with the Irish rebels . . . with a speech delivered by Sir Richard Blake . . . also a speech delivered by the marquesse of Ormond* (London, 1649).
55. Lenihan, *Confederate Catholics at War*, 222–3.
56. For a detailed account of the Cromwellian conquest, see Micheál Ó Siochrú, *God's Executioner: Oliver Cromwell and the Conquest of Ireland* (London, 2009).
57. For Confederate relations with the Catholic powers of Europe, see Jane Ohlmeyer, 'Ireland Independent: Confederate Foreign Policy and International Relations during the Mid-Seventeenth Century', in Jane Ohlmeyer (ed.), *Ireland from Independence to Occupation, 1641–1660* (Cambridge, 1995), 89–111. See also Micheál Ó Siochrú, 'The Duke of Lorraine and the International Struggle for Ireland, 1649–1653', *HJ*, 48 (2005): 905–32.
58. Lenihan, *Confederate Catholics at War*, 224.

FURTHER READING

Armstrong, Robert, *Protestant War: The British of Ireland and the Wars of the Three Kingdoms* (Manchester, 2005).
Brady, Ciaran and Jane Ohlmeyer (eds.), *British Interventions in Early Modern Ireland* (Cambridge, 2005).
Edwards, David, Pádraig Lenihan and Clodagh Tait (eds.), *Age of Atrocity: Violence and Political Conflict in Early Modern Ireland* (Dublin, 2007).
Lenihan, Pádraig, *Confederate Catholics at War, 1641–49* (Cork, 2001).
Murphy, Elaine, *Ireland and the War at Sea, 1641–1653* (Woodbridge, 2012).
Ó hAnnracháin, Tadhg, *Catholic Reformation in Ireland: The Mission of Rinuccini, 1645–1649* (Oxford, 2002).
O'Hara, David, *English Newsbooks and the Irish Rebellion, 1641–1649* (Dublin, 2006).
Ohlmeyer, Jane, *Civil War and Restoration in the Three Stuart Kingdoms: The Career of Randal MacDonnell, Marquis of Antrim* (2nd edition, Dublin, 2001).
Ohlmeyer, Jane, *Making Ireland English: The Irish Aristocracy in the Seventeenth Century* (New Haven, 2012).
Ó Siochrú, Micheál, *Confederate Ireland, 1642–1649: A Constitutional and Political Analysis* (2nd edition, Dublin, 2008).
Ó Siochrú, Micheál (ed.), *Kingdoms in Crisis: Ireland in the 1640s* (Dublin, 2001).
Stoyle, Mark, *Soldiers and Strangers: An Ethnic History of the English Civil War* (New Haven, 2005).
Wheeler, James Scott, *The Irish and British Wars, 1637–54: Triumph, Tragedy and Failure* (London, 2002).

CHAPTER 9

....

THE REGICIDE

....

PHILIP BAKER

THE execution of Charles I by his English subjects on 30 January 1649 is arguably the single most dramatic and iconic event in English history.[1] Having been publicly tried and convicted in the grandeur of Westminster Hall, the king was beheaded, once again in public, on a scaffold erected before his own neo-classical Banqueting House in Whitehall. The symbolic and bloody act of regicide provides the cornerstone of popular memories of the English revolution, and it is unsurprising that professional historians attach comparable significance to the event, albeit for a variety of reasons. For some, it represented the climax of a revolution that began earlier in the decade, perhaps as early as November 1640, with the convening of the Long Parliament, or as recently as December 1648, with the army's purge of that institution. For others, it heralded the arrival of a distinctive and revolutionary period in English history that endured until the collapse of the republican regime and the restoration of the Stuart monarchy in 1660. For others still, it marked the beginning of what proved to be an abortive revolution that failed to radically transform the political, social, and economic axioms of early modern society.[2] These contrasting readings are attributable, at a general level, to divergent views of the entire 1640–60 period and of whether it encompassed any recognizable form of revolution at all. But they are also the result of heated scholarly debate over specific issues concerning the regicide and its immediate consequences. These include the motivations and objectives of those who brought the king to trial; the rationale behind the formal charge that was levied against him; and the justifications for his execution, the abolition of the monarchy, and the establishment of a republic.

Such issues lie at the heart of this chapter and a review of them now may be considered timely. For much of the twentieth century, the standard reading of the regicide was as the act of a small, committed body of men in the army and House of Commons, who became thoroughly convinced of the king's guilt for the civil wars and of the need to destroy him, along with the monarchy, in order to bring peace and settlement to England. The twenty-first century has seen a fundamental challenge to this interpretation. It has been argued that the trial, verdict against, and death of Charles I were all far from foregone conclusions; that the king contributed to his own downfall by overplaying the relative strength of his position during the trial; and that the whole episode of the regicide needs to be viewed within a multiple kingdoms context and not simply through the prism of events at Westminster. Aspects of this thesis have been accepted by many scholars and have found their way into recent general writing on the period, but dissenting voices have provided a vigorous critique of this apparent new orthodoxy, seeking to rejuvenate the more traditional view. As a result, the subject of the regicide has become something of an historiographical minefield for scholars and students alike. This chapter aims to steer a path through these recent controversies, highlighting the crucial points of disagreement and suggesting a possible means for their resolution. But it also considers how different approaches could move the debate on the regicide beyond its current parameters and open up future avenues of research.

TREASONABLE WORDS AND THEORIES OF REGICIDE, 1640–6

It is extremely unlikely that any of the men who took up arms in Scotland in 1639, in Ireland in 1641, or in England in 1642, did so with the intent of bringing Charles I to the executioner's block, or ever imagined that that would be the king's fate within a matter of years. However, when so much of the recent literature on the regicide has taken the form of a forensic investigation of the events surrounding the final weeks and days of the king's life, it may be worthwhile standing back momentarily and adopting a longer-term perspective. This is, of course, not to argue that the immediate causes of the regicide need to be traced back to events in the late 1630s, or still earlier. Rather, it is to suggest that the combined constitutional, political, and cultural experiences of England, Ireland, and Scotland during the long decade of the 1640s created a climate of opinion in which it became possible for people within all three kingdoms to publicly debate the future of Charles I and the Stuart monarchy, and in which the end of both was no longer regarded as unthinkable. This public discourse—which involved commoners and soldiers as well as the political elite—was the result of a variety of factors, and the chapter begins by considering how a number of them contributed in some way to the final act of regicide.

If those who initially assumed arms against Charles I did not directly seek his death, his demise was nonetheless spoken of by small numbers of his subjects from the very outset of the civil wars. This, in itself, was nothing new. Evidence of treasonable and seditious utterances against early modern English monarchs, including openly discussing their death, has recently been traced back to the time of Henry VI. But during a protracted civil war, for which some increasingly held Charles personally responsible, such talk gradually increased, and this demeaning and dishonouring of the king can be seen as an implicit challenge to his authority to rule and as a deconsecration of his majesty.[3] Moreover, it was not simply idle countrymen, fuelled by drink, who spoke out against their king. As early as 1641, the MP Henry Marten—one of the few genuine contemporary republicans—is said to have declared, 'I do not think one man wise enough to govern us all.' Two years later, he allegedly opined that 'it was better one family should be destroyed then [sic] many'.⁴ By 1646, meanwhile, and in the aftermath of the parliamentarian victory over Charles I, the earl of Northumberland argued that, 'he being conquered, they might dispose of the kingdome and affaires as they pleased'.⁵

If such statements were not entirely without precedent historically, what was more novel about the situation in the 1640s is that they often now appeared in print. Whereas previously, treasonable language had largely been restricted to oral and scribal circulation, the outbreak of unlicensed printing in the early 1640s increased its potential to reach a much larger audience and to influence people's thinking, and thus to create a wider public debate. Once again, both the incidence of such language and the audaciousness of the views expressed escalated over time, something that can be attributed to the increasing boldness of authors and printers and a gradual hardening of attitudes towards the king. For example, the decade began, somewhat ominously for Charles, with a notable pamphlet interest in the reign of that most tyrannical of English monarchs, the deposed and murdered Richard II. By 1643, a tract by the minister John Saltmarsh intimated that strict adherence to the religious clauses of parliament's oath of allegiance of that year, the Vow and Covenant, could, under certain circumstances, compel the lawful killing of the king.⁶ Four years later, an anonymous Leveller publication, *Regall tyrannie discovered*, was somewhat more forthright: 'C.[harles] R.[ex] ought to be executed.'⁷

These expressions, of course, represented the opinions of only a tiny minority and were equally shocking to royalists and mainstream parliamentarians alike. For their appearance, however, the political elite in all three Stuart kingdoms bore at least some responsibility. It was they, after all, who between 1638 and 1642 unceremoniously stripped Charles I of many of his most important prerogative powers and led their peoples into civil war, thereby raising fundamental questions about the nature of monarchy, the right of resistance, and the position of the king in a future settlement. And once such issues became part of a larger public debate, the political elite were simply unable to prevent other groups from airing increasingly radical opinions and may, in fact, have inadvertently encouraged them. For example, one consequence of the propaganda war in England between leading royalists and parliamentarians during the early 1640s was the open discussion in print of a number of the ideas that were later used in justification of the king's trial and execution. These included the association of Charles's monarchy with tyranny, the contractual nature of government, the sovereignty of the people, and the right of subjects to resist an unjust ruler. Moreover, the onus on parliamentarian writers to publicly assert and validate such theories could have unintended consequences. Thus in 1643, a pamphlet by the presbyterian lawyer William Prynne—later a vehement opponent of the trial and execution of Charles I—included translated passages from the *Vindiciae contra tyrannos*, a work that justified the right to resist a monarch but which also contained arguments for their censure, deposition, and the act of tyrannicide.⁸ Thus, and as observed wryly by David Wootton, for all that mainstream parliamentarians abhorred the wielding of the axe in 1649, a number of them had contributed to its sharpening.⁹

But despite the fact that both the idea of executing Charles I and theories supporting regicide circulated from relatively early in the 1640s, it was universally expected that a constitutional settlement with the king would follow the parliamentarian victory in the first civil war in England in 1646. That it did not was largely down to Charles himself, and it is that failure to reach a settlement, and its consequences, to which we now turn.

THE NEW MODEL ARMY AND
'THAT MAN OF BLOOD'

Although defeated on the battlefield, Charles of course remained King of England, Scotland, and Ireland, and, as such, essentially refused to accept that his position had in any way been weakened. Moreover, he fully expected his opponents to fall out among themselves, given ample time and opportunity, and thus purposely stalled negotiations at every possible turn. Hence in 1646, it proved impossible for the English parliament and the Covenanter Scots to reach a settlement with a king who believed that the increasing desperation of his enemies for a deal would guarantee that the next set of terms offered to him would always be more generous than the last. And this strategy reaped obvious rewards in July 1647, when the New Model Army, which had recently entered the political sphere as a result of its conflict with the presbyterian faction in parliament, presented Charles with its own, relatively moderate terms for settlement, the *Heads of the Proposals*.

The New Model has long been regarded as the driving force behind the regicide, and its ill-fated negotiations with the king in 1647 are seen as one of a number of factors that irrevocably turned its men against him after the first civil war. During the army's famous debates at Putney that autumn, by when a settlement based on the *Heads* seemed increasingly unlikely, trooper Edward Sexby spoke out against monarchy itself and two officers referred to Charles as 'a man of blood'—one who shed innocent blood and with whom God would have no peace. Oliver Cromwell, too, acknowledged that the king remained a threat but urged caution, arguing that God had yet to make it plain that either Charles or monarchy were to be destroyed, or that the army would be the instrument of divine judgement. By contrast, and at a time when some regiments were displaying royalist sympathies, trooper William Allen openly expressed his desire to see the king restored to his throne, if upon the right terms.[10] These conflicting attitudes, which, as we shall see, were clearly in evidence up until the time of the regicide itself, demonstrate that the entirety of the army was never committed indubitably to the destruction of Charles I. Indeed, Cromwell's words at Putney emphasize that regicide was only one of a number of possible outcomes, with deposition or an enforced abdication obvious alternatives, and from none of these did the abolition of the monarchy inevitably follow; the future of Charles Stuart and the future of the Stuart regime were not intrinsically linked. Given the events of the following year, most obviously the king's culpability for a second civil war in England, it seems safe to assume that many more of the army supported the notion of regicide by 1649. But, as noted below, evidence of both the division and indecision revealed at Putney was still apparent during the course of the king's trial.

On the final day of the debates, 11 November, Charles escaped the army's custody, in which he had remained since June, in a further effort to obtain more generous terms. Within a matter of weeks, he had rejected another set of propositions from the English parliament and, through the Engagement, secured military support in Scotland for an invasion of England on his behalf. Leading members of the army and their allies at Westminster were suitably enraged at this attempt (as Cromwell later put it) to vassalize them to a foreign nation that in January 1648 they pushed through parliament a Vote of No Addresses, which brought negotiation with the king to an abrupt end. Charles's revival of the 'British problem' in this manner had significant repercussions. A year later, the act setting up the court for the king's trial explicitly referred to the need to prevent further invasions of England, and the intermittent presence of foreign troops in its northern counties over most of the previous decade has been seen as an explanation for the relatively high proportion of regicides from that region.[11]

By April 1648, with war clouds once again gathering over England, a prayer-meeting of army officers took place at which, it is alleged, Charles Stuart was once again branded 'a man of blood', and those present agreed to bring him to account for his crimes against God and the nation. Two points are worthy of note here. First, that far too much is often made of this incident as evidence of a definitive commitment by the army to undertake the trial and execution of the king. There are only two extant accounts of the meeting and both were published some years later, the main one in 1659, which raises obvious questions about their accuracy and reliability. Moreover, while the stated pledge to bring the king 'to an account' may (or may not) be read as a reference to a trial, neither pamphlet makes any form of reference to regicide.[12] The second point refers to the notion of 'blood guilt', which, as Patricia Crawford has emphasized, could have a number of meanings. The idea of blood for blood, that only Charles's death could cleanse a defiled land, might certainly be derived from a strict reading of Scripture (Genesis 9:6; Numbers 35:33). But the concept could also imply moral guilt that did not necessarily warrant punishment, as in those instances when presbyterian and Scot ministers—hardly would-be regicides—applied it to the king in the 1640s. Arguments about blood guilt could be used to justify or reinforce the need for action that fell well short of Charles's execution. This is not to ignore evidence that the idea, or at least the rhetoric, of blood for blood was in some minds in January 1649; for example, John Bradshaw, president of the High Court of Justice, referred to both of the biblical passages cited above before declaring the king guilty. But it seems significant that it was not until a declaration of August 1650 that the army itself sought to explain the regicide on the basis of the expiation of blood guilt alone.[13]

The renewal of bloodshed in England and Wales during the second civil war, the invasion of a foreign army from Scotland, and the prospect (if never realized) of a second one from Ireland, only further hardened attitudes towards the king and his allies among sections of the army and its supporters in parliament. Some historians also detect an increasing brutality to the conflict, indicative of the vengeful mood of the New Model and thus of the likely fate of Charles Stuart. In August, for example, at the end of the protracted and bitter siege of Colchester, the army's commander, Thomas, Lord Fairfax, denied mercy to two of the surrendering royalists—Sir George Lisle and Sir Charles Lucas—who were summarily shot to death. But this action was not without justification under the existing laws of war, and Fairfax's later decision to exempt himself from the proceedings of the king's trial indicates that he regarded sanctioning the execution of knights of the realm as altogether different to that of the nation's anointed sovereign.

Much to the utter disgust of the army, over the spring the majority of the English parliament revealed the full extent of their desperation for a personal treaty by voting to reopen negotiations with Charles—an obvious prerequisite for any settlement that would involve all three Stuart kingdoms—at the very time that the New Model was still fighting the forces that had risen in his name. By August, after the army's defeat of the Engagers at Preston, the Vote of No Addresses was formally repealed, and the king, with no other options, prepared himself for another round of peace talks. With no royalist forces to speak of in England and the military and political demise of the Engagers in Scotland, his hopes now rested on a peace in Ireland allowing him to launch a third civil war in England. By contrast, it was precisely on the basis of their desire to bring a permanent end to military conflict in England that the presbyterian majority in parliament sought a personal treaty with Charles. Meanwhile, the realization of either of these scenarios represented an obvious threat to the army. On the one hand, an invasion from Ireland would once more force them to make the supreme sacrifice and defend the nation from a foreign army. On the other hand, a presbyterian-backed personal treaty was likely to betray all for which they had fought by restoring the king to the throne with much of his previous power intact and, consequently, leaving its men vulnerable to future reprisals. In this sense, the New Model's actions in the aftermath of the second civil war were driven as much by self-preservation and the need to secure an alternative form of settlement as by any overt hostility towards the person of Charles Stuart.

THE ARMY REMONSTRANCE

The army was not alone in opposing any form of personal treaty with the king. News of Charles's impending negotiations with the English parliament saw a notable shift of opinion in the majority of provincial petitions, with those against a deal now outweighing those for. Doubtless, members of the army and its allies were heavily involved in mobilizing anti-treaty literature, but there was genuine wider support for the view that further discussion with the king was now futile.[14] In London, for example, the Levellers' 'Large Petition' of 11 September criticized parliament for continuing to negotiate with Charles, and demanded an end to the negative voices of both the king and the Lords, if not their outright destruction. But pointedly, it also called for the equality of all—including kings—before the law and for 'Justice upon the Capitall Authors and

Promoters of the former or late Wars', though exactly what was meant by this was not spelt out. Alleged to have attracted 40,000 signatories, the petition marked something of a high mark of Leveller agitation and was explicitly endorsed by a number of New Model officers and regiments over the following two months. Indeed, its impact on the main direction of army thinking over that period may have been considerable, and one historian has referred to the petition as 'the first salvo in the political battle whose culmination was the trial and execution of the king'.[15]

Against this backdrop, discussions between Charles and parliament opened at Newport in September. The king's policy, as ever, was to string along his opponents until a more attractive option materialized—on this occasion, in the form of an army from Ireland. Nevertheless, the outward appearance was that the two sides were moving towards a settlement, thereby heightening tensions in the army, where the key figure during this period was not Fairfax or Cromwell but the latter's son-in-law, Commissary-General Henry Ireton. At the Putney debates, Ireton had strongly opposed any talk of destroying monarchy or stripping the king of all power, but had acknowledged a willingness to submit to such designs if ever he believed them to be God's will. A year on, Providence had evidently caused him to revise his beliefs, as revealed by the arguments of the army *Remonstrance* of November, of which he is considered the major author.

What the *Remonstrance* does, or does not, say about the army's intentions towards the king is one of the key issues that has prompted recent, heated scholarly debate over the regicide, and the document as a whole is worthy of some discussion.[16] On one level, its arguments are clear enough. The *Remonstrance* states that the army's intervention in politics is grounded upon the maxim *salus populi suprema lex* (the welfare of the people is the supreme law) and questions how a personal treaty with the king can be compatible with the public good. As a result, the 'evil' negotiations at Newport should cease immediately. Charles is accused of having broken his covenant with the people by his pursuit of private over public interest, with constitutional reform being the only means of guaranteeing against this situation in the future. On the basis that political authority originates in the people themselves, parliament must be reformed to become a true representative of the nation, one that meets regularly and to which the executive must be fully accountable. Finally, a form of elective monarchy would be retained, with a figurehead king lacking any power of legislative veto.

But what of Charles himself?[17] The traditional view of the *Remonstrance* as a clarion call for his execution has been challenged by Sean Kelsey, who maintains that its calls for 'justice' against the king do not equate to demands for regicide and betray a more ambivalent attitude towards him. The document may have charged him with treason, tyranny, and murder, and asserted that, as a result, he should stand trial. But the verdict in any trial was not presented as a fait accompli, and a capital sentence was not openly demanded. Although this interpretation has been strongly refuted by Clive Holmes, it is grounded on an accurate, if literal, reading of the *Remonstrance*. One will struggle to find an *explicit* call for the execution of Charles I in either the *Remonstrance* itself, a document of some 25,000 words, or its shorter contemporary abridgements. Arguments certainly abound for 'justice' or for the 'execution of justice' against the king, and these may have been coded allusions to his death. But, at the same time, they are hardly clear-cut demands for regicide. Similarly, calls for 'capital punishment upon the principal author . . . of our late wars' or for justice 'without regard to persons', left the identity of the potential victims open to interpretation. It is tempting, of course, to see all this as a rather feeble act of subterfuge and to deduce that readers must have known what the army was really saying. But if contemporaries were well aware that the *Remonstrance* presented an obvious threat to the king and to the Newport treaty, it was not universally interpreted as a blatant demand for Charles's head. The document was a bald statement of the army's intent to kill the Newport negotiations rather than Charles Stuart.

The *Remonstrance*, then, falls short as a definitive blueprint for regicide, and a degree of ambiguity, leaving open at least the possibility of an alternate path to a settlement, can be detected. In fact, few, if indeed any, of the calls for 'justice' during the autumn and winter of 1648/9 went so far as to call irrefutably for the king's death.[18] Given we have seen that some contemporaries did so willingly from relatively early in the 1640s, this is curious, to say the least, and is a subject worthy of further research. The obvious starting point would be a detailed textual analysis and study of the authorship and composition of the *Remonstrance* itself. We know, for example, that when someone—presumably, though not certainly, Ireton—presented an early draft of what was to become the *Remonstrance* to a council of officers on 10 November, it was put aside. Five days later, and seemingly with many more officers in attendance, the council is reported to have approved it unanimously. Whether or not its content was altered during this interval, in what ways, and by whom, remain as unanswered questions. Moreover, according to the Leveller leader John Lilburne, this approved draft underwent subsequent revision when he and a number of allies successfully lobbied to have passages that were critical of the Levellers removed.[19] Indeed, in its published form, the *Remonstrance* openly commended the Levellers' 'Large Petition' on more than one occasion, and the nature of the relationship between the two documents might also be usefully explored. Finally, the convoluted history of the *Remonstrance* presumably had a considerable impact on its content and construction, and a close textual analysis may prove revealing with regard to the issues of its authorship and the presentation of its arguments concerning the king.[20]

The final version of the *Remonstrance* was presented to the House of Commons on 20 November, taking some four hours to read, but was never formally discussed or answered over the following days. As an obvious threat to both the king and the members of the Commons themselves, in proposing a settlement grounded in the dismantling of the existing constitution and its replacement by a form of 'Agreement of the People', it probably made most MPs only more eager to secure a personal treaty with Charles, the principal cause of the army's anger in the first place. On 5 December, the Commons voted to continue negotiations with the king based on his most recent answer to their propositions. The army, which had already once more taken custody of the king and moved its headquarters to Whitehall in an attempt to pressurize the Commons into discussing the *Remonstrance*, acted swiftly in response. On 6 and 7 December, troops led by Colonel Thomas Pride turned away or arrested those MPs with a history of hostility towards the New Model or who had supported the Newport treaty, while others simply kept away from Westminster through fear. In reducing parliament to a mere 'rump' of the army's supporters, Pride's purge killed off any further prospects of a personal treaty between its members and the king. Whether it also spelt the death knell for Charles himself is the question to which we now turn.

Final Negotiations?

Since the late nineteenth century, historians of the regicide have placed varying degrees of emphasis on the period in the weeks following Pride's purge as one in which the army and its parliamentary allies attempted to negotiate with the king. For some, it was the failure of these attempts that ultimately sealed Charles's fate. A long historiographical tradition, for example, sets great store by the purported 'Denbigh mission' of late December, the 'final' effort to strike a deal with the king. This refers to the rumoured attempt by the earl of Denbigh, with Cromwell's backing, to present Charles with settlement terms, a design that faltered when the earl was not even admitted to the royal presence. As a result, Cromwell is often regarded as having turned against the king irrevocably.[21] However, there is speculation concerning a later attempt at an accommodation, via an approach made by the earl of Richmond in mid-January, and even after that rumours continued to circulate of a design to depose the king and replace him with his youngest son, the duke of Gloucester.[22] Much of the evidence of these plans is entirely typical of a great deal of the surviving material that details the events surrounding the final weeks of the king's life. It is of doubtful or at least questionable provenance, opaque, based on rumour and wishful thinking, self-interested. Mark Kishlansky's recent deconstruction of the Denbigh mission has demonstrated vividly how scholars erected an elaborate narrative of an attempted settlement on the flimsiest of evidence.[23] That lesson is an important one. The reinstatement of the Vote of No Addresses on 13 December, the strict conditions of the king's confinement, all this would have made negotiation extremely difficult. But we cannot say with certainty that it made it impossible. The obvious need for absolute secrecy means that the historical record is unlikely to contain more than the faintest trace of any such discussions, most likely in the form of rumours or allegations. And this is precisely the nature of the evidence that describes the final attempts to negotiate with Charles but also numerous other incidents over the winter of 1648/9, and there is an extremely thin line between the acceptance and rejection of this type of material as reliable among scholars of the regicide.

That final overtures to Charles were made after Pride's purge in order to avoid his trial cannot be proven unequivocally, but they were rumoured to have taken place and remain at least as a possibility. Why they would have occurred at all is a question that also needs to be addressed. Recent literature has identified the imminent threat of an invasion from Ireland and of a third civil war in England as an obvious motivating factor.[24] In Ireland, the royalist lord lieutenant, the marquis of Ormond, had been working for some months to secure an alliance between royalist forces and the Confederate Catholic government that would result in an invasion of England in the name of the king. Moreover, by mid-December it was known that the Confederates had signed a commercial treaty with the Dutch, raising the threat of a naval alliance between royalist, Irish, and Dutch forces. Thus a treaty with Charles, in which he ordered Ormond to desist with his invasion plans, would immediately remove a pressing external threat to the army and its political allies. A number of historians have dismissed the seriousness of this threat, emphasizing that royalist commentators deliberately exaggerated the strength of the forces in Ireland and that, for all his bluster, Ormond turned out to be a paper tiger. But not until the summer of 1649 did the weakness of Ormond's coalition became fully apparent, and the weight of the evidence suggests that its potential threat was taken exceedingly seriously over the winter of 1648/9. This seems emphatic from the formal charge against the king at his trial, which accused Charles explicitly of continuing his commission to Ormond and the rebels in Ireland with the aim of invasion. It was during the trial that news reached London of the conclusion of Ormond's treaty with the Confederates, and this final evidence of the king's commitment to another war is seen as having convinced at least some of his judges of the need for his death, on the grounds that personal loyalty to Charles I was the strongest force holding Ormond's coalition together.

Thus the problem of reaching a stable form of settlement within a multiple kingdoms context was an obvious reason for keeping channels of communication open with Charles. Another was that his opponents were seemingly undecided on exactly what to do with him. From 18 December, Cromwell held a series of meetings with two of the Commons' leading lawyers, in which he invited them to draw up proposals for a constitutional settlement by parliament, rather than the sword. Nothing came of this and on 23 December the New Model published an indictment of Charles and called for his trial. However, three days later, during a Commons debate on whether the king would stand trial for his life, Cromwell declared his inability to yet offer his advice on that point.[25] Intriguing evidence of wider indecision within the army comes in the form of the willingness of the council of officers, on two occasions in late December and early January, to consult a prophetess, Elizabeth Poole, with regard to how the Lord wished them to proceed. On the second of these, she informed the officers that she had received a command from God that they might try and depose but should not kill the king. Questioned as to whether her arguments were based on revelation, she confirmed it to be so.[26] For men ever intent on seeking the will of the Lord, this cannot but have made a powerful impression at a time when preparations for the trial of the king were already underway.

THE TRIAL OF THE KING

Traditionally, the verdict and outcome of the trial of Charles I, which was staged between 20 and 27 January 1649, has been regarded as a foregone conclusion. Even those historians who maintained that further overtures to the king were made after Pride's

purge have assumed that his judges were fully intent on his destruction by the opening of the proceedings. This scholarly consensus has recently been challenged by Sean
Kelsey, who has presented the trial as a process of 'extended negotiation' with the king in
which his judges sought a final settlement, one that would have preserved both Charles
himself and the substance of the ancient constitution. On this basis, Kelsey asserts that
the destruction of the king was not the purpose of the trial at all and that his judges
were 'reluctant regicides', forced to condemn him only when he refused to acknowledge
the authority of the court and thus to negotiate at all.[27] This thesis has been criticized
robustly by Clive Holmes, who supports the more traditional reading of the trial,[28] and
this section reviews a number of the crucial points of disagreement between these interpretations while also highlighting some of the most significant aspects of the trial.

It seems clear, for example, that the trial was not only about the fate of Charles Stuart;
it was also an attempt to establish the origins of legitimate political power. When in early
January, the House of Lords rejected an ordinance establishing a high court of justice
for the king's trial, the Commons responded with a declaration of popular sovereignty
and of its own supremacy. On this basis, an act establishing the court was subsequently
passed by the Commons alone on 6 January, and the repeated efforts (some seven in
all) to get Charles to plead during the trial and thus to acknowledge the authority of the
court, can be read as an attempt to get him to at least tacitly acknowledge the supremacy
of the Commons. Elements of the staging of the trial—its location in Westminster Hall,
home of the central courts of English justice; the replacement of the royal coat of arms
that originally hung over the proceedings by a shield bearing the cross of St George;
the decision to allow the trial to be publicly reported, presumably on the basis that the
king was expected to plead—seem deliberately engineered to emphasize that it was
undertaken in the name of the people of England. All this seemingly had little impact on
Charles himself, however, who was consistent throughout the trial in refusing to recognize the jurisdiction and legitimacy of the court.[29]

Had the king pleaded not guilty, it can be assumed that his reintegration into the constitutional structure as a figurehead monarch, stripped of all power, would only have followed his formal acquittal. The ease with which this could have been achieved, based on
the nature of the charge levelled against him, is heavily disputed. On the one hand, the
charge is regarded as having been deliberately enfeebled in order to give Charles ample
opportunity to clear his name; on the other, it is seen as leading incontrovertibly to a finding of the king's guilt. The argument that the charge—which accused Charles of attempting
to tyrannize England by overriding the law and destroying parliament—was inherently
weak can certainly be disputed, but neither, somewhat curiously, did it contain an explicit
allegation of treason. Moreover, if the sole purpose of any charge was to guarantee the
king's guilt, why did the trial commissioners, after much protracted discussion, reject the
notion of a far more extensive charge, listing the purported ills of his entire reign, that
some of them had clearly wanted?[30] Much more remains to be said on these points.

The indecision over the king's charge can be related to the palpable uneasiness of
many of those involved of the proceedings in general. There were clearly no precedents
in English law for the formal trial of a monarch, and the legal basis of the proceedings

remains somewhat unclear, with the use of a charge, rather than an indictment, and of commissioners serving as both judge and jury being reminiscent of a trial by martial law.[31] The act establishing the high court of justice named 156 civilians and soldiers as commissioners: forty-seven of these never attended the court at all, only 101 attended sessions of the trial, and only fifty-nine signed the king's death warrant. The most conspicuous absentee was Fairfax, who, after attending the court's initial meeting on 8 January, never did so again and thereafter did all he could to distance himself from its proceedings. His behaviour may well be of significance for interpretations of the army's conduct hitherto. Was it only at that first meeting that the commander-in-chief of the New Model Army himself, the man in whose name its numerous political manifestos had been issued, became aware that some were actually committed to going through with the trial of the king and even the act of regicide, as a last resort?[32]

Unquestionably, the spectacle of the trial of the King of England provoked major anxieties among many of his judges. Even C. V. Wedgwood's classic account of the proceedings, in which the road to regicide is ineluctable, acknowledges the sheer extent of their apprehension, particularly in the face of the commanding performance given by Charles himself.[33] Whether that performance, which revolved around the king's refusal to plead, led to the deliberate extension of the trial in the hope he would eventually submit to the court, is another point of controversy. There may be something in the view that the apparent delays in the proceedings can be attributed simply to the need to secure as broad a consensus as possible behind their outcome. But if that outcome was predestined to be regicide, it is difficult to see how any such consensus was going to be formed. It seems far more likely that the long period between Pride's purge and the trial; the repeated opportunities given to Charles to plead; the two full days given over to the consideration of evidence against him; and the delays between his condemnation in the court (25 January), sentencing at trial (27), and execution (30), all suggest a more deliberate policy to threaten him, eventually on pain of death, to at least plead before his judges.[34]

Nevertheless, it is hard to accept the view that Charles overplayed his hand during the trial and threw away his life and the Stuart monarchy with it (at least temporarily).[35] Quite regardless of the intentions of his judges, it is difficult to imagine a scenario in which the king had formally acknowledged the authority of the court and entered a plea. His actions over the past decade, the very actions for which he then stood trial, were, in many respects, a continual demonstration of his absolute commitment to the notion of the sanctity and divinely ordained nature of monarchy and thus to the belief that he could never allow himself to relinquish his political power. Indeed, by reaffirming during the trial that he had a commitment to God to uphold the ancient laws of the land, he was able to argue effectively that, in refusing to plead before an illegitimate court, it was he, and not his judges, who stood for the rights and liberties of the people of England. Charles does not genuinely appear to have feared death on the basis of upholding these principles, and the *Eikon Basilike*, the work of martyrology available from the day of his execution, would ensure his immediate resurrection (and rescue of his historical reputation) as King Charles the Martyr.

Conclusion: The Impact of the Regicide

The act of regicide can be interpreted as marking the ultimate failure of the attempt to find a settlement in all three Stuart kingdoms following the parliamentarian victory in the first civil war. Indeed, its most obvious repercussion was to ensure that military conflict continued to scar those kingdoms for more than another two years. A tiny minority in England had overseen the execution of Charles I with the merest fig leaf of parliamentary respectability and against the wishes of the overwhelming majority of the English nation. With the exception of a handful of committed republicans, there had been little genuine desire for the king's death and thus the institutional revolution that followed was driven by pragmatism rather than idealism. In February 1649, the House of Lords and the monarchy were abolished on the grounds that they were a danger to the public interest, and a council of state was established to function as the country's new executive. Not until May was England declared a 'free commonwealth'. But in certain respects, there remained a great deal of continuity between this new regime and the old. For example, those still attending the House of Lords at its abolition found their way immediately into the new government, and the powers of the crown were essentially assumed by the council of state. The most obvious difference was the absence of an actual monarch.[36]

In a similar fashion, the judiciary was substantially remodelled in 1649 as a result of the prominent opposition to the regicide of many leading judges. But the main structures of the legal system remained unaltered. Cosmetic, but necessary, changes were the alteration of the name of the court of King's Bench to Upper Bench and the omission of the customary references to the king in judges' oaths. Finally, there was also continuity in the religious sphere, with the new regime continuing to support the at least nominal presbyterian national church structure alongside a *de facto* toleration of most other Protestant religious groups.

In this sense, for all the immediate shock value of the act of regicide itself, its structural impact on the English state was surprisingly minimal. On one level, this is because the trial of the king, while it had a clear constitutional objective in establishing the location of political power, addressed the issue of what to do with the person of Charles Stuart, not what to do with the state. The latter question was only really confronted as an *ex post facto* response to regicide, and future research needs to be sensitized as to how it is possible to approach what are clearly two connected issues nonetheless separately. But it may be possible to go still further and to offer a more fundamental challenge to both, on the one hand, the older idea of an interdependent relationship between monarchy and state and, on the other, the more recent notion of the centrality of the proceedings against the king to the development of a depersonalized understanding of the state.[37] This would entail arguing that the execution of Charles I and the abolition of the monarchy merely ratified formally a situation that already existed. The sheer range of powers assumed by the Long Parliament's executive committees, which played a key role in the parliamentarian government of England during the 1640s, certainly raise the issue of the extent to which the process of civil war state-formation had created a non-regal state *before* the regicide and whether the prerogatives of the crown were already in commission elsewhere long before the foundation of the council of state.[38] Thus in this, and in a number of other respects, too, while this chapter has sought to provide an overview of the current thinking on the subject, it hopefully has also demonstrated that much more still remains to be said about the place of the regicide in the overall history of the English revolution.

Notes

1. My thanks to the editor, Sean Kelsey, Mark Kishlansky, John Morrill, David Scott, and Elliot Vernon for discussion of the subject of this chapter.
2. Brian Manning, *1649: The Crisis of the English Revolution* (London, 1992), 13–24.
3. David Cressy, *Dangerous Talk: Scandalous, Seditious, and Treasonable Speech in Pre-Modern England* (Oxford, 2010).
4. Both quotations in Philip Baker, 'Rhetoric, Reality, and the Varieties of Civil War Radicalism', in John Adamson (ed.), *The English Civil War: Conflicts and Contexts* (Basingstoke, 2009), 212.
5. Quoted in David Scott, *Politics and War in the Three Stuart Kingdoms, 1637–49* (Basingstoke, 2003), 127.
6. Baker, 'Civil War Radicalism', 212.
7. *Regall tyrannie discovered* (London, 1647), sig. A2v.
8. The first complete English translation of the *Vindiciae* did not appear until 1648.
9. David Wootton, 'From Rebellion to Revolution: The Crisis of the Winter of 1642/3 and the Origins of Civil War Radicalism', *English Historical Review*, 105 (1990): 654–69.
10. John Morrill and Philip Baker, 'Oliver Cromwell, the Regicide, and the Sons of Zeruiah', in Jason Peacey (ed.), *The Regicides and the Execution of Charles I* (Basingstoke, 2001), 19–22; Austin Woolrych, *Soldiers and Statesmen: The General Council of the Army and its Debates, 1647–48* (Oxford, 1987), 263, 264.
11. David Scott, 'Motives for King-killing', in Peacey (ed.), *Regicides*, 138–60.
12. *The none-such Charles his character* (1651), 173–5; William Allen, *A faithful memorial* (1659), 3–5.
13. Patricia Crawford, 'Charles Stuart, that Man of Blood', *Journal of British Studies*, 16 (1977): 41–61.
14. Michael Braddick, *God's Fury, England's Fire: A New History of the English Civil Wars* (London, 2008), 553, 554.
15. Don M. Wolfe (ed.), *Leveller Manifestoes of the Puritan Revolution* (New York, 1967), 279–90; Ian Gentles, *The New Model Army in England, Ireland, and Scotland, 1645–53* (Oxford, 1992), 267–8, 269.
16. [Henry Ireton?,] *A remonstrance of his Excellency Thomas Lord Fairfax* (London, 1648).
17. This discussion is based on my own reading of the *Remonstrance* and the arguments and evidence presented in Sean Kelsey, 'The Death of Charles I', *Historical Journal* [*HJ*], 45 (2002): 729–31; Sean Kelsey, 'Politics and Procedure in the Trial of Charles I', *Law and History Review*, 22 (2004): 4–5, 15; Clive Holmes, 'The Trial and Execution of Charles I', *HJ*, 53 (2010): 304–9.

18. Kelsey, 'Death of Charles I', 729.
19. Gentles, *New Model Army*, 272–4.
20. A number of these points will no doubt be explored in forthcoming work by Sean Kelsey.
21. S. R. Gardiner, *History of the Great Civil War, 1642–49*, 4 vols. (London, 1893), IV, 287; David Underdown, *Pride's Purge: Politics in the Puritan Revolution* (Oxford, 1971), 171; Morrill and Baker, 'Oliver Cromwell', 31.
22. Kelsey, 'Death of Charles I', 740–2; Underdown, *Pride's Purge*, 170, 183, 292.
23. Mark Kishlansky, 'Mission Impossible: Charles I, Oliver Cromwell, and the Regicide', *English Historical Review [EHR]*, 125 (2010): 844–74.
24. See especially John Adamson, 'The Frighted Junto: Perceptions of Ireland, and the Last Attempts at Settlement with Charles I', in Peacey (ed.), *Regicides*, 36–70.
25. C. V. Wedgwood, *The Trial of Charles I* (London, 1966), 78–80.
26. C. H. Firth (ed.), *The Clarke Papers*, 5 vols. (London and Cambridge, 1891–2005), II, 150–4, 163–70.
27. See especially Kelsey, 'Death of Charles I'; Kelsey, 'Politics and Procedure'; Sean Kelsey, 'The Trial of Charles I', *EHR*, 118 (2003): 583–616.
28. Holmes, 'Trial and Execution'.
29. Sean Kelsey, 'The Ordinance for the Trial of Charles I', *Historical Research*, 76 (2003): 310–31; Sean Kelsey, 'Staging the Trial of Charles I', in Peacey (ed.), *Regicides*, 71–93; Kelsey, 'Death of Charles I', 733–4, 743–4; Kelsey, 'Trial of Charles I', 588–9, 594–8.
30. Kesley, 'Trial of Charles I', 598–601; Kelsey, 'Death of Charles I', 734–5; Holmes, 'Trial and Execution', 298–303.
31. The comparison with martial law proceedings has been made in work by John Collins of the University of Virginia.
32. Wedgwood, *Trial of Charles I*, 98, 105–7.
33. Wedgwood, *Trial of Charles I*, 134–6, 146–7.
34. Holmes, 'Trial and Execution', 314, 315; Kelsey, 'Death of Charles I', 734, 745–9.
35. Kelsey, 'Death of Charles I', 744–5.
36. Sean Kelsey, *Inventing a Republic: The Political Culture of the English Commonwealth, 1649–53* (Manchester, 1997).
37. On the latter point, see especially, Robert von Friedeburg, 'Introduction', in Robert von Friedeburg (ed.), *Murder and Monarchy: Regicide in European History, 1300–1800* (Basingstoke, 2004), 33–6.
38. These points will doubtless be explored in the forthcoming volumes of the *History of Parliament* covering the period 1640–60.

FURTHER READING

Burgess, Glenn, 'Regicide: The Execution of Charles I and English Political Thought', in Robert von Friedeburg (ed.), *Murder and Monarchy: Regicide in European History, 1300–1800* (Basingstoke, 2004), 212–236.

Crawford, Patricia, 'Charles Stuart, that Man of Blood', *Journal of British Studies*, 16 (1977): 41–61.

Gardiner, S. R., *History of the Great Civil War, 1642–49*, 4 vols. (London, 1893), IV.

Gentles, Ian, *The New Model Army in England, Ireland, and Scotland, 1645–53* (Oxford, 1992).

Holmes, Clive, 'The Trial and Execution of Charles I', *Historical Journal*, 53 (2010): 289–316.

Kelsey, Sean, 'The Death of Charles I', *Historical Journal*, 45 (2002): 727–754.

Kelsey, Sean, 'The Trial of Charles I', *English Historical Review*, 118 (2003): 583–616.

Kishlansky, Mark, 'Mission Impossible: Charles I, Oliver Cromwell, and the Regicide', *English Historical Review*, 125 (2010): 844–874.

Lagomarsino, David and Charles T. Wood (eds.), *The Trial of Charles I: A Documentary History* (Hanover, 1989).

Nenner, Howard, 'The Trial of Charles I and the Failed Search for a Bounded Monarchy', in Gordon J. Schochet, P. E. Tatspaugh, and Carol Brobeck (eds.), *Restoration, Ideology, and Revolution* (Washington, DC, 1990), 1–21.

Peacey, Jason (ed.), *The Regicides and the Execution of Charles I* (Basingstoke, 2001).

Underdown, David, *Pride's Purge: Politics in the Puritan Revolution* (Oxford, 1971).

Walzer, Michael, 'Regicide and Revolution', *Social Research*, 40 (1973): 617–642.

Wedgwood, C. V., *The Trial of Charles I* (London, 1964).

Wootton, David, 'From Rebellion to Revolution: The Crisis of the Winter of 1642/3 and the Origins of Civil War Radicalism', *English Historical Review*, 105 (1990): 654–669.

CHAPTER 10

SECURITY AND REFORM IN ENGLAND'S OTHER NATIONS, 1649–1658

DEREK HIRST

FROM its inception, the English Commonwealth had to pay heed to its closest neighbours. It had more than enough problems to wrestle with at home in the anxious and economically ruinous conditions of 1649, but the auguries abroad were even more threatening. French, Spanish, and Dutch rulers, though they had their own domestic difficulties, sought to make trouble among the republic's enemies, and there were plenty of these. Assorted royalist forces—Irish Catholics, Church of Ireland and Church of England Protestants, Scots presbyterians—still held most of Ireland, and were unlikely to rest content with what they had; in Scotland, the Covenanters now in power hurried to proclaim the young Charles Stuart as king not of Scotland but of Great Britain and Ireland, thus promising to replicate the recent aggressions of the Engager regime of 1648. The infant republic recognized that blood and treasure must flow outwards, but on what grounds? Since Scotland was an ancient and independent kingdom—few now could credit the old legend of the English crown's feudal superiority—only national security could justify counter-measures there, but parliament's insistence throughout the 1640s on the defensiveness of its war-aims must call any pre-emptive strike into question: indeed, in 1650 Lord General Fairfax's conscience drove him to resign on just this score. And what of Ireland? Action here ought to be straightforward enough. English identity was involved: the great seal of the Commonwealth featured Ireland on its outline map of England and so declared England and Ireland inseparable. Justice reinforced the case for action: the thousands—or was it hundreds of thousands?—of victims of the 1641 Rebellion must be avenged, and investments redeemed for the thousand and more English Adventurers (including one Oliver Cromwell, Esquire) who even before war broke out in England in 1642 had subscribed loans to vindicate the Protestant cause in Ireland. Were there other pressures as well? It may have been 'cruel necessity' that brought Charles I to the block on 30 January 1649, but many—surely most—of those who helped place him there looked for further reformation. Could this be the moment not merely to make England's world safe, but to spread true godliness and freedom? If so, Scotland too might be swept up. Indeed, when the English army did cross the border into Scotland in the summer of 1650, it issued a declaration at Musselburgh taking Jesus to be its 'king by profession'.

CONQUEST AND SETTLEMENT IN IRELAND

Security in the present took priority over advancing the millennium. The history of the republic, a pariah regime to most of Europe, could be written around the problem of security, and never more urgently than in 1649 when massive unpopularity at home offered so many opportunities to the Rump parliament's enemies abroad. Hostile neighbours could only be confronted piecemeal and sequentially since the regime's resources were stretched thin, and the Rump was lucky that presbyterian Scots and Catholic Irish had no interest in making common cause. The initial target readily declared itself: from his exile the young Charles II saw few attractive possibilities in Scotland, for there the radical Covenanters whose position Cromwell's army had secured in late 1648 were entrenching themselves in presbyterian intransigence; however distasteful the configurations in Ireland might seem, the dominant figure there, at least in name, was the marquis of Ormond, the reassuringly Anglican and august lord lieutenant. The first royalist challenge would come from the west, where England anyway claimed good title to act. The regime made its calculations accordingly.

The disentangling of threats can seem something of an academic exercise, since crises overlapped. Cromwell is often praised for delaying his departure for Ireland until August—uncomfortably late in the campaigning season—in order to equip his expeditionary force with transport and supplies. But he had other reasons for delay, not least since it was only in May that at Burford in Oxfordshire Fairfax crushed army discontent. In turn, domestic mutiny rippled outwards, for it had been in face of unrewarded deployment to Ireland that the New Model soldiery had radicalized in the spring of 1647; two years later, the generals surely worried when Leveller calls for sympathy for Ireland's hard-pressed Roman Catholics circulated among soldiers who had their own bleak prospects as well as their own hopes of religious toleration.[1] Cross-currents appeared too in John Milton's decision to put off writing *Eikonoklastes*, his answer to the alarmingly popular *Eikon Basilike* of Charles I, until he had finished *Observations on the Articles of Peace*, his diatribe against Ulster presbyterians who had allied with Ormond. But the Ulster alliance possessed its own dangers in an Ireland that was almost wholly lost to England by early 1649; probably even more important, domestic enemies (the English presbyterians) might be blackened if they could be linked to co-religionists in Ireland.

Milton was not alone in trying to drive a wedge into the opposition, for as England's Irish campaign made uneven progress in 1649–50, hard-pressed commanders like

George Monck in Ulster did what they could to exploit the deep divisions among the foe. Others were tempted to lump rather than to split, and not surprisingly given the deluge of Irish atrocity stories that had swept England following the 1641 Rebellion. As he urged the Council of State to decisive action against its enemies in the spring of 1649, Cromwell declared the 'Irish interest'—which he left undifferentiated—'the most dangerous . . . for all the world knows their barbarism'. As if to implement that judgement, when in early September the English royalist commander of Drogheda refused his summons to surrender, Cromwell consigned the garrison to the sword, stretching blood-guilt for the massacres of 1641 over all of them as he did so—though Drogheda in 1641 had held out against the rebels, and many of its 1649 garrison were English. But once the fury of the assault had left him, Cromwell did discriminate. The severed heads he sent from Drogheda to Dublin for display on the gates were those of English officers, condemned now for joining with the Irish when God had already and emphatically pronounced that England's destiny lay not with the royalist cause. If we can measure intensity of feeling by the indignities inflicted, we may judge that Cromwell deemed some of the English more blameworthy than even the Catholic Irish.[2] More broadly, Cromwell—though often not his men, and least of all at the storming of Wexford in October—tried to spare civilians in Ireland. But he did execute out of hand priests taken in places of storm, and when he confronted an assembly of Catholic bishops at Clonmacnoise in December 1649, he berated them for their 'covenant . . . with Death and Hell'—all the while insisting that he made none suffer for belief.[3] Some of his followers were more single-minded: the baptist and regicide Colonel Daniel Axtell, court-martialled for executing captives after they had surrendered on promise of quarter, justified himself with the claim that he was God's agent against the Irish.[4] Cromwell's own responsibility direct or indirect for Drogheda and Wexford, and the behaviour of men such as Axtell under his command, turn our attention to surely the most indelible legacy of the English revolution, the conquest and settlement of Ireland.

Most scholars estimate the demographic cost of the wars in Ireland in the decade from 1642 at the appalling level of around or even above one-third of the pre-war Irish population—a far higher casualty rate than in England or Scotland, and on a par with that of Germany in the Thirty Years War. Irish nationalists have sometimes pinned the blame on Cromwell, but such claims seem implausible. Other commanders committed their own massacres. Ulster Scots had cause to remember with anger Owen Roe O'Neill after so many of their number drowned at Benburb in 1646; Lord Inchiquin, a Gaelic Protestant, was with reason known locally as 'Murrough of the Burnings'; and the blood-bath at Scarrifholis in Ulster in June 1650—just after Cromwell himself had returned to England—was the work of the New English Protestant Charles Coote, a name (father and son) freighted with a history of atrocities. Furthermore, the once-fertile hinterlands of Dublin and Cork had repeatedly been devastated, while typhus was endemic. And despite the shock value of Drogheda and Wexford, Cromwell knew the laws of war; indeed, those awful examples ensured that most strong points surrendered to him fairly quickly, and he carefully upheld the terms of agreements, even when in the disaster at Clonmel in May 1650 he had been tricked. Cromwell's receptiveness as Protector in the mid-1650s to petitions from individual Irish Catholics for protection underscores the complexity of his record.[5] Nevertheless, there is no mistaking the epochal significance if not of Cromwell himself then of what we might with all its horrors call the Cromwellian moment. The English polymath and surveyor William Petty estimated that around 50,000 fighting men left Ireland permanently in the aftermath of defeat, whether to serve as mercenaries in Europe or for servitude in Barbados and other plantations, while Scarrifholis destroyed the last remaining Gaelic Irish officer corps. Most of all, the settlement of Ireland, ushered in by statute in 1652, transformed the landholding structure, reducing the percentage of land in Catholic hands from 61% in 1641 to 8% in the mid-1650s, before it climbed back to about 20% at the Restoration.[6]

That sweeping settlement was at first justified by the concern for security. Even before the act passed, Cromwell's short-lived successor in the Irish command, his son-in-law Henry Ireton, had ordered the entire Catholic populations of Limerick and Waterford expelled as security risks from those strategic ports. The settlement commissioners went further as they set about 'transplanting' the remaining Catholic landed elite to Connacht, the westernmost, and therefore safest, province, and then decreed a cordon of Protestant settlement around its perimeter. And they extended Ireton's urban strictures by expelling Catholics from all walled towns (though not the suburbs). But there were other considerations, most obviously a vengeful justice. Anybody involved in the 1641 Rebellion before the Catholic forces were regularized in 1642 was to be executed; Protestants who had opposed the English parliamentarians were to lose one-third of their lands, Catholic landowners two-thirds and face transplantation to Connacht for the remainder; even those Catholics who had stayed neutral would lose one-third to transplantation. The executions were in fact relatively few—hundreds at most rather than the 80,000 or so who might have been liable—as were the transplantations to Connacht in that inadequately administered and labour-short time; most Catholic former landowners remained as tenants in their old neighbourhoods, but overwhelmingly they were dispossessed. Their lands proved more desirable than their lives, and the Rump—hard-pressed by its creditors among the thousands of unpaid soldiers and the unrepaid Adventurers from 1642 just as its parliamentary predecessors had been in 1647—saw to the taking. Indeed, it was the creditors' needs, rather than justice or fear, that from the outset explained the scale of the confiscations. Although the exercise is often called the 'Cromwellian settlement', Cromwell himself once away from the walls of Drogheda found the principle of collective guilt less persuasive, and he genuinely (and not just politically) had no wish to make martyrs; it was probably because of their suspicion of his sympathies that the Rumpers passed the Act of Settlement for Ireland in 1652 when he was not in the House.[7] Later, as Lord Protector, he continued to facilitate the Protestant settlement of Ireland, most obviously at the end of 1654 by allowing Petty's commission to draw up the great 'down survey' of the Irish land that was to be settled; nevertheless, he exasperated some of his servants in Ireland by his readiness to listen to individual Catholic appeals. And his son Henry, with the Protector's manifest consent, wound up the practice of transplantation, and the execution of priests, after he took command in Ireland in 1655.[8] Presumably with the Protector's consent too, Henry

Cromwell in 1656 began to restore the municipal charters that had been confiscated by an army suspicious in the early days of conquest of all sectors of Irish life.

It was not just Cromwellian clemency that made the settlement of Ireland less sweeping, and perhaps therefore less secure, than its makers had hoped. English Protestants willing to settle Irish land were fewer than had been expected. Not all the Catholic defeated left Ireland, and the continuing resistance of 'tory' marauders in a ruined landscape deterred many Englishmen who could find some prospects elsewhere as the economy in England began to improve and the Americas beckoned too. Meanwhile, delays, confusions, conflicting claims in the apportionment process, and the dawning realization that there was not enough land to go around gave the soldiers incentive to sell out at a massive discount to their officers those debentures—promissory certificates—they had received for grants of land in lieu of arrears of pay. The Adventurers, who had been waiting long for their reckoning, were subject to similar pressures. Only about 12,000 of the 35,000 soldiers entitled to land actually settled, and by 1660 probably only about 7,500 of these remained; of just over 1,500 original Adventurers around 1,000 remained to draw lots in 1653–4, and about 500 of these were still in place at the Restoration.[9] The big winners were those well-placed locally to gain information, to gain access to the corridors of power, and to buy out other claimants: in other words, the New English, the Protestant settlers of an earlier generation who soon—to distinguish them from the New Protestant settlers of this generation—became known as the Old Protestants. Many were the existing estates that grew larger.

The failure to establish a Protestant yeomanry in Ireland was both a symptom and a cause of the wider failure of reform. Cromwell joined John Cook—the government's solicitor at the trial of Charles I and its choice as chief justice of Munster—in imagining conquered Ireland as a 'white paper' capable of taking whatever impression reformers chose to write on it. Both of them had hopes of cheap and speedy justice in the localities, and of freeing the poor from subservience to their superiors—of freeing the poor too, educated and evangelized at last, from domination by their clergy. To the Catholic bishops at Clonmacnoise, Cromwell had insisted that his army came 'to hold forth and maintain the luster and glory of English liberty in a nation where we have an undoubted right to do it—wherein the people of Ireland (if they listen not to such seducers as you are) may equally participate in all benefits, to use liberty and fortune equally with Englishmen, if they keep out of arms'. Others would have taken such efforts further than law reform. For the cosmopolitan circle of reformers around the German exile Samuel Hartlib in England, this could be a transformative moment of improvement: the greatest achievement of the group was surely the publication in 1652 of *Ireland's Naturall History*, by the émigré Dutch brothers, Gerard and Arnold Boate. But the energy that might have gone into the mining and manufactures that they advocated was soon focused on land-measurement and confiscation. And while Cook certainly laboured to provide equitable and summary justice in Munster, anxious local lawyers and landowners hemmed him in when they prevailed on the Protector's son Henry in 1655 to revive Dublin's traditional courts and procedures. Cook found the judgeship in the central courts that Henry Cromwell offered him easy to refuse, and his resignation left the cause of law reform and social reform with little to show after the high hopes born of conquest.[10]

The New English recovery not only guaranteed the slow process of the lawyers; it also lessened the chances that the landscape of Irish Protestantism would be significantly reshaped. The officers and soldiers of the New Model, many of them baptists or independents, included numbers of lay preachers, and to the dismay of surviving Protestant churchmen—and the curiosity of not a few Roman Catholic bystanders—these exercised their talents in the garrison towns and even beyond. When General Charles Fleetwood, Ireton's successor as commander and as Cromwell's son-in-law too, took over the government in 1652, he was happy to encourage them, for he saw himself as the patron of radical good causes. He and still more Henry Cromwell encouraged others as well: at the latter's arrival in Ireland there were 110 preachers who received government salaries, and by 1658 the number had risen to 250 as the state attempted to make good on its promises to spread the Word and free the churches of the stigma of tithe support. A few of these salaried preachers were existing presbyterian ministers in Ulster who were persuaded to come into the establishment as the government made its peace with the presbyterian majority in Scotland after 1655, but the majority were independents enticed over from England. Nevertheless, if the Word was being spread, it was being spread thinly: by the end of the 1660s, the number of Church of Ireland clergy was probably double the 1658 total of salaried preachers. On the other hand, the salaries granted in the 1650s were considerably higher than most clergy in Ireland could aspire to after the Restoration.[11]

There were other disappointments beyond the paucity of bodies in pulpits. As separatist congregations gathered, controversies broke out locally and in print, particularly over the nature of baptism and over access to the pulpit, just as they did in England. Even had the theology of the sects, often fiercely Calvinist and exclusive, disposed them to evangelize among the Irish, internal disputes left them ill-placed to exploit an ecclesiastical field largely cleared for them by the banishment or even execution of so many Catholic priests.[12] When the spread of peace allowed under-employed soldiers to vent their energies in politicking as well as preaching, the noise of dispute proved counter-productive. Baptists and other sectaries who refashioned themselves as republican critics of an increasingly conservative Protectorate attracted the suspicion of Henry Cromwell when he arrived in 1655 to supplement and then replace Fleetwood and to check army discontent. Although he looked for allies first among some of the more mainstream independents around Dublin, he grew wearied by waves of appeals and counter-appeals to Whitehall; he soon turned for mutual support to the Old Protestants in matters ecclesiastical as well as political, and the increasing visibility in Ireland of the yet more radical Quakers gave him some political cover in this. He then came out conclusively in favour of the conservative option, tithe maintenance for the clergy and the patronage rights of landowners. Conservatism did not mean inaction: the younger Cromwell took plans for a second university at Dublin to a fairly advanced stage, and to this end he acquired the massive library of James Ussher, the Anglo-Irish and Protestant archbishop of Armagh, who died in 1656 (though after reform was defeated in 1659 the collection eventually found its way to Trinity College Dublin). Nevertheless, the young chief governor did little to foster outreach to the Gaelic Irish beyond sending orphans to be Anglicized in the Caribbean plantations.

The differences between Fleetwood and Henry Cromwell went to the heart of the failure of the republic to live up to its reformist aspirations, and they did so because they expressed the hesitancy of the Lord Protector himself. Oliver Protector it was who sent out his son Henry to check on Fleetwood and the army radicals, and who appointed him commander in Ireland in 1655; but it was Oliver as well who left Fleetwood with the title of lord deputy until 1657 and the respect and influence that went with it, even when he had been recalled to England; and it was Oliver who continued to listen to Fleetwood on Irish matters up to the end, even after Henry Cromwell had succeeded to the deputyship. The division of authority left appointments, particularly to judgeships, unmade, it left the Irish council often inquorate, and it left radical critics unchecked. Since Henry in Ireland, even as lord deputy, needed the council's approval for much of his business, Oliver's inability to decide between his own increasingly conservative instincts and his continuing respect for army colleagues hamstrung the Irish government in many key areas—personnel, ecclesiastical, even fiscal. Some modest peacetime economic recovery did occur in the 1650s, particularly after Henry Cromwell started to restore town charters and lifted the wartime English restrictions on crucial Irish exports such as cattle, hides, and butter; and in its later years the regime increasingly earned goodwill from the Old Protestants. How far these should be credited among the Protectorate's positive achievements may be questioned.

CONQUEST AND UNION WITH SCOTLAND

Despite massive differences in political and military context—Scotland, a unitary state in a way that Ireland was not, retained the luxury of building national armies that went down to disaster in style—the English record in Scotland curiously mirrors aspects of English performance in Ireland. Shortly after his army crossed the Scottish border, Cromwell wrote to the presbyterian clergy of Edinburgh sounding some of the same anticlerical notes as those heard by the Catholic bishops at Clonmacnoise less than a year earlier. The rhetoric now was conditional: the Scots—surely godly Protestants—*may* be mistaken, they *may* be asserting claims similar to the pope's, but the rhetoric was strong nevertheless.[13] And any concession was spiritual, not political. Cromwell and his soldiers and indeed most newsbook-reading Englishmen were as certain of the tyranny of Scottish ecclesiastical and political forms, and the unacceptability of the Scottish desire to coerce England, as they were of the blasphemies of the Irish Catholic hierarchy. They were as certain too of the incivility of both peoples.[14]

The style of campaigning in Scotland was very different from that in Ireland, with the result determined by major battles (Dunbar, Hamilton, Worcester) rather than a series of minor sieges; but the final outcome—thousands of English troops in each of the two countries throughout the Protectorate, scattered in garrisons large and small—showed a common and continuing reliance on force and a recognition of the absence anywhere of local support. The objectives at the beginning were diverse. The English authorities thought they knew more or less what they wanted to do with Ireland. Its dependency on England and English law had long been declared (Poynings' Law in 1495, the Act for a Kingly Title in 1541, the Treaty of London in 1641). Accordingly, lords lieutenant and lords deputy—traditional titles both—exercised power there intermittently in the 1650s. All that was needed was to bring the country back to due obedience and to impose (at last) the Protestantism and civility to which generations of English would-be conquerors had aspired. Scotland was another matter. The journalists' derision for Scots' barbarities and indecencies made clear their conviction that the work of cultivation was needed as much there as in Ireland, but the godly in the army and the capital knew that Scotland was a Protestant country in which the strenuous work of repression and/or evangelization that must be Ireland's lot was not needed. Cromwell and his allies hoped at first to find Scots who would persuade their countrymen to be content with their own borders, perhaps guaranteed by England's occupation of a southern zone.

Any prospect of such a partial outcome was soon lost, not so much with the 'crowning mercy' that God conferred on Cromwell (and England) at Worcester on 3 September 1651 as with George Monck's capture a week earlier of the Scottish government at Alyth near Dundee. The scale of the victories had some of the Rump's excited supporters urging that England should make of this 'a conquest' and (presumably) absorb Scotland forcibly as England had long ago tried to absorb Ireland. But Cromwell for one wanted to treat the former ally with respect. Under his prompting, the Rump quickly opted to 'incorporate' Scotland into the Commonwealth, somewhat on the model of the 'incorporation' of Wales into Henry VIII's England; after at least a show of consultation with commissioners the Rump had sent north as an interim government, the Scottish shires and royal burghs 'voted' in April 1652 on a Tender of Union. Although the riven parliaments of the Protectorate did not manage to enact until 1657 the union with Scotland that the Tender had promised, the Protector and his council did unilaterally pass an ordinance of union in the spring of 1654. There were implications here for England's other new conquest: perhaps something more could be achieved as a frame of rule for the island nations as a whole than the deputized government to which Ireland had been consigned since the Tudor conquest. What that would be was never fully and formally articulated—and certainly Ireland was not offered any consultation—but in practice the two conquered nations received parallel treatment.[15] A handful of members with connections (usually official) to Ireland and Scotland sat in the Barebones assembly in 1653, and each country was allocated thirty parliamentary seats under the Instrument of Government at the end of the year.

Despite the diverse beginnings of the English republic's rule in Scotland and in Ireland, and despite the very different political and religious cultures of those nations, their histories at England's hands in the 1650s reveal a surprising symmetry, and even something of an imperial framework. It was not that the republic or its apologists marked out the two neighbours as England's empire, or even part of it: the official title, 'The Commonwealth of England, Scotland, and Ireland', was scarcely categorical, and Cromwell himself habitually and vaguely referred to 'the nations' or 'these nations'. But in both countries, more or less military rule gave place in 1655 to more courtly forms: in Ireland Henry Cromwell, a temperamental civilian albeit in title a major general, replaced Fleetwood, while in Edinburgh Lord Broghill, Old Protestant and congenital courtier, arrived from Ireland to become president of the Scottish council. The symmetry was not complete, for local aspirations in the two neighbours were so very different and differently entrenched. Nor was it neat, for local interests in both countries had to contend with the strenuous efforts of the army interest at Whitehall to contain the civilian drift. But it was there.[16]

There were parallels too in the republic's reform plans and the obstacles they encountered. The Rump's diagnosis of Scotland's ills rested on similar assumptions to those that shaped its attempt to reform Ireland. The goals in both cases were the spread of a Protestantism—preferably Independency—that did not repress other Protestants, and of a sturdy Protestant yeomanry, freed from an overweening clergy and freed too from the influence of local landowners. No more in Scotland than in Ireland was that goal attainable with the resources to hand. The handful of independent divines that the Rump sent north with inflated salaries to spread non-presbyterian ways among a laity presumed to be yearning for freedom had some initial success with the curious in garrison towns and among some of the gentry ready enough to be rid of the kirk's iron hand, but their energies were soon distracted by baptist preachers, most of them members of the army. The baptists certainly mounted a more dramatic challenge to a presbyterian clericalism weakened by defeat and division, and they at first benefited largely from their access to military sanction and protection—Colonel Robert Lilburne, commanding in Scotland in the early 1650s, was himself a baptist. But by late 1654 they were undercut—as in Ireland—by the Protector's sense that religious sectarianism kept dangerously close company with political dissent. The recall of Lilburne from Scotland amid intensified royalist guerrilla activity allowed his successor in command, Monck, to put restraints on baptists and their preachings. The corollary was the survival at the local level of presbyteries and even kirk sessions. The appearance of small numbers of Quakers by the mid-1650s—as in Ireland, largely although not entirely following in the soldiers' wake—did open small fissures in the kirk's dominion, but there is no question that the Rump's commissioners for Scotland, just as Cromwell himself, would have thought these scant return on the hopes of 1652. On the other hand, the blows inflicted at Dunbar and Worcester had shattered the kirk's long-held hopes of a presbyterian international: the dream of exporting John Knox's truths to London, which had shaped so much British history since the 1550s, was no more. In his more prosaic moments, Cromwell—who had in 1649 indicated his reluctance to intervene in Scotland—might have thought that enough of a success.[17]

Experience in the 1650s of the divisions and resentments within presbyterianism probably confirmed Cromwell in such an unadventurous assessment. The Scots' Engagement of December 1647 with Charles I continued to reverberate within the kirk. For years afterwards, Resolutioners, who had finally been willing to imagine Charles and then in 1650–1 his son the young Charles II as a Covenanted king, confronted the minority Protesters, Covenanting fundamentalists, who had insisted on the ungodliness of Charles I and insisted still that Charles II must show genuine repentance. The feuding was bitter—it was surely partly responsible for the massive Scottish witch-hunt of 1649–50—and in 1652 the kirk's General Assembly ceased to meet under the strain. More alarmingly, the politics of the split appeared as, in the aftermath of the disaster at Worcester, Resolutioners steadfastly prayed for their king and his family. But a few Protesters, eager to outflank and purge their enemies, were ready to collaborate with the English regime. Patrick Gillespie, who became rector of Glasgow University, convinced the Protector of his loyalty sufficiently to earn from him what became known as 'Gillespie's charter', allowing the Protester leaders the prospect of control over appointments in the kirk quite independent of the Presbyterian institutions that they did not dominate. The outcry from the Resolutioners, whose greater moderation on the question of the binding nature of the Covenant was damagingly offset by their public prayers for Charles Stuart, took up far too much of the time of Lord Broghill after his arrival in Edinburgh, and even of the Protector himself. The atmosphere was so poisonous that Broghill's eventual success in persuading the majority Resolutioners to abandon their public devotions to the absent king—allowing them to regain influence within the kirk and thus to restore some political stability—is justly taken as one of the republic's significant achievements in Scotland.[18] But it was a purely defensive one.

The English design for Scotland was only marginally more successful in the field of law. The Rump's commissioners recognized that the invasion of England in 1648 had been more the work of the nobility than of the churchmen; though they left intact the feudal tenures that shaped so much of Scots law, they moved speedily (though how successfully is not clear) to eliminate the feudal jurisdictions that underwrote a society of subordination. The Rump's replacement for the local feudal courts was the English device of assize circuits, on the assumption that judges from the central courts would make impartial justice available to all out in the counties. To this end, in the autumn of 1652 the English majority among the seven commissioners for the administration of justice whom the Rump had appointed began riding circuit. Meanwhile, the sheriffs' authority in the counties was divided between Scots and English officials, in the hope of securing impartiality and performance. Although one Scottish observer wrote pityingly of the entry of 'kinless loons' into a feuding society—several English officials were murdered—approving comments were soon heard about the less partial and speedier justice handed down by the new judges, outsiders all. Most of the applause came from English observers, but there is no doubt that Scots in the localities did appreciate the resumption of justice after so many years of war and revolution. The success of Monck and Broghill and the soldiers after 1655 in securing the justices of the peace—officers whom James VI had tried to promote long ago—helped spread justice further into the grass roots. But compromise was unavoidable: in parts of the Highlands, Monck allowed clan chiefs to enforce justice against cattle thieves, and in some of the Lowlands by the end of the decade English officials were turning to presbyterian kirk sessions to provide a measure of petty justice just as kirk sessions had in earlier generations.[19] This was at best pragmatic reform and not the remodelling that the journalists had forecast in 1650–1.

The smallness of the return on reformist hopes owed more to pressure of business—not surprising, when debt and adultery formed the largest classes of legal business—than to the opposition of the Scottish nobility.[20] At first, it had seemed that the opposite would be the case. The Act of Classes that in January 1649 followed the destruction of the Engagers at the battle of Preston brought political proscription for Engager notables. Noblemen whose finances were already wrecked—by the wars and fines of the 1640s, by Scottish law's refusal to let them compound for debts incurred while raising troops—and who now faced at the Rump's hands heavy fines for their Engaging along with the elimination of their feudal superiorities soon concluded they had little to lose. The English authorities faced less of a threat than they might have done since the greatest Scottish noble, the marquis of Argyll, concluded that a royalist triumph would threaten him more than the English did; nevertheless, in 1653 and 1654 endemic resistance in the Highlands flared into Glencairn's Revolt, named after its not very effective figurehead. And though Lilburne correctly identified the political steps—reduction of the pressure on the nobility—needed to limit the violence, he lacked the stomach for an anti-guerrilla campaign. This his replacement, George Monck, emphatically possessed. Monck's devastation of the central Highlands in 1654–5 proved as effective as his implementation of Lilburne's recommendation that the fines on the Engager notables be reduced or remitted. Thereafter, most of the nobles concentrated on rebuilding their ruined estates and shattered finances.

English rule in Scotland may not have had the same major consequence, social, political, ecclesiastical, as the land settlement had in Ireland, but there were a few material gains. The presence of garrisons in distant places such as Inverness did something to stimulate local economies and even to suppress petty brigandage. And while the slow and partial incorporation of Scotland within the framework of the 1651 Navigation Act and England's trading world did not outlast the republic, it did introduce the merchants of Glasgow to the rewards of a tobacco trade that they continued to exploit illicitly and to considerable profit under the restored monarchy. Less positive was the experience of the thousands of Scots soldiers who were captured at Dunbar and sent—by a hard-pressed English regime lacking prison facilities and caught in an economic and political crisis—to labour in the Caribbean plantations.[21] Those who survived the appalling journey learned a bleaker reality of the nascent empire that so many Scots were to administer in the following centuries.

AN IMPERIAL REPUBLIC AND ITS COSTS

The English too were learning about empire, and the conquests of 1649–54 proved a crucial moment. The respect of European powers for a regime that had almost simultaneously crushed resistance in Ireland and Scotland and built a navy was temporary—under the supine Charles II in the 1670s, respect was to give way to mild contempt. Nevertheless, the English suddenly came to think of themselves as considerable, worthy of consideration, in a way they had not done before the wars. The change can be tracked in the panegyrics of the 1650s: for example, in the work of Edmund Waller, Andrew Marvell, and John Dryden, and in the way the high notes sounded there continued to swell in the Restoration. More systematically, James Harrington predicated the republican empire he imagined in *Oceana* (1656) on English energies combined with Irish material and Scottish human resources. But not for the last time, acquiring an empire proved a little easier than knowing quite what to do with it.

Cromwell's strategic uncertainty is legendary. Was the new state to be driven by Protestant imperatives or by *realpolitik*? Was Spain or France the enemy? That uncertainty was matched in concerns closer to home yet just far enough away to unnerve. The generals and colonels at Whitehall found the freedom of movement of the Protector's representatives, Henry Cromwell and Lord Broghill, in Dublin and Edinburgh increasingly disconcerting: particularly their civilian leanings, their appreciation of the trappings of rule, and their lapses from the sternest policies in religion. The classic instance of the generals' machinations is the way Fleetwood in 1655 encouraged the Baptist officer and settler, Colonel Richard Lawrence, to answer in print (*The Interest of England in the Irish Transplantation Stated*) the printed protest of Vincent Gookin, an Old Protestant and soon Henry Cromwell's friend, against the transplantation to Connacht of such a valuable resource as the native Irish (*The Great Case of Transplantation in Ireland Discussed*).[22] Such suspicions and countervailing urgings—the cause of religion and security against the cause of economy and rationality—reduced Whitehall to paralysis at times, and brought officials in those secondary capitals to despair as instructions and answers failed to come through.

The generals and their contemporaries faced problems constitutional as well as political in their attempts to make sense of Scotland and Ireland. Matters seemed clear enough at the beginning: Ireland was manifestly a dependency and, as the design of the great seal asserted, in important respects part of England; Scotland was offered union by the 1652 Tender of Union and protagonists doubtless hoped that it would be folded in to English parliamentary ways as Wales had been integrated generations earlier. Such was the unpopularity of both Scots and Irish in England that to bring their representatives into the Westminster system would have been provocative at any time; extending England's political boundaries during the protectorate, when so much else was in flux, was doomed. The Protectorate's kingship crisis in 1657 gave republican opponents of the regime a provocative reminder of the voting implications of Scottish and Irish representation in parliament. The Humble Petition and Advice, with its confirmation of the 'single person', was passed by fewer than the sixty votes that Scotland and Ireland combined carried; and since Broghill had come down from Edinburgh to manage the parliamentary campaign for kingship, and since he had electioneered heavily in both Ireland and Scotland, republicans had every reason to wish the members for Scotland and Ireland gone.[23] The Humble Petition and Advice, with its emphasis on the traditional constitution, replaced the Instrument of Government, but it was the Instrument that had contained parliamentary provision for Scotland and Ireland. Republicans in the last session of Oliver's second parliament and in the parliament of his son Richard were therefore able to spend vast amounts of time debating the general issue of whether members for Scotland and Ireland were rightfully present in an English parliament chamber constituted on ancient lines. The Protectorate had fallen before the issue could be resolved. And in the meantime, 'old English' republican animosity against Scottish and Irish members had been displayed in an attempt in 1658 to send to the Tower members for Ireland who protested in parliament against the burden of taxation on a nation whose economy had suffered greater devastation than either England's or Scotland's.[24] Here was a case of familiarity breeding contempt.

The mid-century decades were of critical significance for the mutual relations of the three island nations. Rebellion, massacre, expropriation, and emigration set in progress the formation of the 'Protestant Ascendancy' that was to dominate Ireland for over a century and a half, and generated too the powerful narrative of the scheming, murderous, and (most visibly in the form of the papal nuncio of 1645–9, Rinuccini) priest-ridden Catholic that was to be used to justify that ascendancy. Those years also provided incontrovertible evidence of the inability of the Protestants of Ireland to sustain themselves, and their dependence too on massive support from England. Indeed, despite sustained efforts during the 1650s to reduce the size of the garrison—by the middle of the Protectorate the army in Ireland had been cut to about 16,000—the island's government, military and civil combined, still ran a deficit of about £96,000 p.a. at the time of Oliver's death.[25] It was perhaps no wonder that those resentful voices were raised at Westminster in 1658 against the tax burden on England that Ireland represented. Neither perhaps was it any wonder that, even though Ireland was deemed an incorporated part of the three-nation Commonwealth, it was consigned very much to subordinate status. Imports from the colonies had to enter by way of English ports, and Ireland (like London, also suspect to non-presbyterians) remained woefully under-represented in parliament.

Scotland may for these few years have received more privileged access than Ireland to England's trading world, but otherwise its experience was only marginally less harsh. The great witch-hunts of 1649–50 and 1661–2 that bracket Scotland's conquered decade must be taken at least in part as marks of social and cultural stress; the roots of such stress may be surmised not just in prolonged economic suffering and heavy taxation but in the challenge that the Cromwellian conquest represented to Scotland's shaping myths of pure kirk and unconquered kingdom. Nor were the English inclined to think better of Scots at the end of the day than they were of the Irish. True, the Scots had not perpetrated massacres but they had invaded England repeatedly in the 1640s; further, at the end of 1646 they had—the cardinal sin in royalist eyes—sold their king into parliamentarian captivity and ultimately sold him to execution. The resentment that slight inspired is palpable in Thomas Hobbes's likening of it in his *Leviathan* (1651) to Judas Iscariot's sale of Christ; he was, in his language and his contempt, far less outspoken than many of his contemporaries.[26] English politicians and pamphleteers in the Restoration period derisively took the Scots for granted, and the reports that filtered back from English soldiers in Scotland of the extreme poverty they found there help explain why. General Monck confirmed these in 1658 when he persuaded the Council of State not to raise Scotland's tax burden further though Scottish revenues consistently covered less than half of expenditures: on the eve of the Protectorate's fall in 1659 the Edinburgh administration was running a massive finan-cial deficit of £164,000.[27] Scotland was manifestly too poor a country to support a sizeable garrison, though by 1659 that garrison had been reduced to about half the strength of 20,000 or so that had been concentrated in Scotland during Glencairn's Rising.

The inability of an impoverished Scotland and a devastated Ireland to support the troops that holding them seemed to require raised a larger question: the troops could be maintained there if England would bear the burden. England manifestly could bear the burden—it had after all paid much higher taxes in the 1640s when the purposes had been sufficiently clear and urgent to persuade enough people of the need. But would it bear such a burden now? There was no tax-payers' strike during the Protectorate and the taxes demanded came in right to the end: in that most basic sense, England could have continued to impose its will forcibly on the neighbour nations. But to speak of 'the taxes demanded' is to conceal what would in the early modern period have been called an *arcanum imperii*, a mystery of rule—or, here, of misrule. The republic's gov-ernment consistently failed to demand enough taxes. It was too nervous of politi-cal opinion in England to provide itself with the resources that would have allowed it to reform Scotland and Ireland as it had hoped to do. Meanwhile, the costs and taxes incurred in holding operations in Scotland and Ireland, a huge factor in the state's budget—throughout the Protectorate, close to two-thirds of the entire army establish-ment was serving in Scotland and Ireland—were quite sufficient to justify the govern-ment's nervousness about English opinion.[28] Far more than the navy, whose purposes were generally accepted and which vied with the army in cost, it was the fiscal bur-den of the army, and thus in effect the cost of Scotland and Ireland, that destabilized the Protector's relations with his parliaments and that frustrated the prospects of a Cromwellian settlement in England.

The cycle that began with the Covenanters' revolt in 1638 and the protests against Strafford's rule in Ireland two years later was a vicious one indeed. Scottish and Irish resentments at the imposition from England of alien priorities brought down the Stuart regime in the early 1640s; continuing Scottish and Irish restiveness gave Charles I the false hopes that plunged England in 1648–9 into its revolutionary moment. Although the republic's rulers built a military machine that could hold Scotland and Ireland with ease, they found the price of that was the steady alienation of an English public that had in the aftermath of Worcester seemed briefly to be with them. Like his royal predeces-sor, Cromwell occasionally believed that he might bind the three nations together; like Charles, he learned that what they chiefly shared was a mutual repugnance.

Notes

1. Norah Carlin, 'The Levellers and the Conquest of Ireland in 1649', *Historical Journal [HJ]*, 30 (1987): 269–88.
2. John Morrill, 'The Drogheda Massacre in Cromwellian Context', in David Edwards, Pádraig Lenihan, and Clodagh Tait (eds.), *Age of Atrocity: Violence and Political Conflict in Early Modern Ireland* (Dublin, 2007), 242–65.

3. Thomas Carlyle and S. C. Lomas (eds.), *The Letters and Speeches of Oliver Cromwell*, 3 vols. (London, 1904), II, 5–23.

4. 'Axtell, Daniel (bap. 1622, d. 1660)', *Oxford Dictionary of National Biography*.

5. John Cunningham, 'Oliver Cromwell and the "Cromwellian" Settlement of Ireland', *HJ*, 53 (2010): 919–37.

6. Kevin McKenny, 'The Restoration Land Settlement in Ireland: A Statistical Interpretation', in Coleman A. Dennehy (ed.), *Restoration Ireland: Always Settling and Never Settled* (Aldershot, 2008), 35–52.

7. John Morrill, 'Cromwell, Parliament, Ireland and a Commonwealth in Crisis: 1652 Revisited', *Parliamentary History*, 30 (2011): 193–214.

8. Austin Woolrych, *Britain in Revolution 1625–1660* (Oxford, 2002), 676.

9. Karl R. Bottigheimer, *English Money and Irish Land: The Adventurers in the Cromwellian Settlement of Ireland* (Oxford, 1971); Ian Gentles, *The English Revolution and the Wars in the Three Kingdoms 1638–1652* (Harlow, 2007), 410–11.

10. For all matters of reform in Ireland, see Toby Barnard, *Cromwellian Ireland: English Government and Reform in Ireland 1649–1660* (Oxford, 1975).

11. Barnard, *Cromwellian Ireland*, 153–68.

12. Crawford Gribben, *God's Irishmen: Theological Debates in Cromwellian Ireland* (Oxford, 2007).

13. Carlyle and Lomas (eds.), *Letters and Speeches of Oliver Cromwell*, II, 125–33.

14. Derek Hirst, 'The English Republic and the Meaning of Britain', *Journal of Modern History*, 66 (1994), 474.

15. For a broad comparison, see David Stevenson, 'Cromwell, Scotland and Ireland', in John Morrill (ed.), *Oliver Cromwell and the English Revolution* (London, 1990), 149–80.

16. Patrick Little, 'The Irish and Scottish Councils and the Dislocation of the Protectoral Union', in Patrick Little (ed.), *The Cromwellian Protectorate* (Woodbridge, 2007), 117–43.

17. R. Scott Spurlock, *Cromwell and Scotland: Conquest and Religion, 1650–1660* (Edinburgh, 2007).

18. Julia Buckroyd, 'Lord Broghill and the Scottish Church, 1655–1656', *Journal of Ecclesiastical History*, 27 (1976): 359–68.

19. Leslie M. Smith, 'Scotland and Cromwell: A Study in Early Modern Government' (unpublished D.Phil. dissertation, University of Oxford, 1987), 72, 202; Leslie M. Smith, 'Sackcloth for the Sinner or Punishment for the Crime: Church and Secular Courts in Cromwellian Scotland', in John Dwyer, Roger A. Mason, and Alexander Murdoch (eds.), *New Perspectives on the Politics and Culture of Early Modern Scotland* (Edinburgh, 1982), 116–32.

20. Smith, 'Scotland and Cromwell', 120, 163.

21. Hirst, 'English Republic', 481.

22. Toby Barnard, 'Planters and Policies in Cromwellian Ireland', *Past and Present*, 61 (1973): 31–69.

23. Patrick Little, *Lord Broghill and the Cromwellian Union with Ireland and Scotland* (Woodbridge, 2004).

24. Woolrych, *Britain in Revolution*, 672; Gentles, *English Revolution and the Wars in the Three Kingdoms*, 433–56.

25. Barnard, *Cromwellian Ireland*, 27.

26. Hobbes, *Leviathan*, chap. 3.

27. Dow, *Cromwellian Scotland*, 219.

28. For the distribution of troops (more broadly than its title suggests), see Henry Reece, *The Army in Cromwellian England, 1649–1660* (Oxford, 2013).

FURTHER READING

Barnard, Toby, *Cromwellian Ireland: English Government and Reform in Ireland 1649–1660* (Oxford, 1975).

Barnard, Toby, *The Kingdom of Ireland, 1641–1760* (Basingstoke, 2004).

Bottigheimer, Karl R., *English Money and Irish Land: The Adventurers in the Cromwellian Settlement of Ireland* (Oxford, 1971).

Coffey, John, *Politics, Religion and the British Revolutions: The Mind of Samuel Rutherford* (Cambridge, 1997).

Dow, Frances D., *Cromwellian Scotland 1651–1660* (Edinburgh, 1979).

Gribben, Crawford, *God's Irishmen: Theological Debates in Cromwellian Ireland* (Oxford, 2007).

Little, Patrick, *Lord Broghill and the Cromwellian Union with Ireland and Scotland* (Woodbridge, 2004).

Macinnes, Allan I., *The British Confederate: Archibald Campbell, Marquess of Argyll, c.1607–1661* (Edinburgh, 2010).

Macinnes, Allan I., *The British Revolution, 1629–1660* (Basingstoke, 2005).

Moody, T. W., F. X. Martin, and T. J. Byrne (eds.), *A New History of Ireland. Vol. 3. Early Modern Ireland, 1534–1691* (Oxford, 1976).

Ohlmeyer, Jane H. (ed.), *Ireland from Independence to Occupation 1641–1660* (Cambridge, 1995).

Siochrú, Micheál Ó, *God's Executioner: Oliver Cromwell and the Conquest of Ireland* (London, 2008).

Spurlock, R. Scott, *Cromwell and Scotland: Conquest and Religion, 1650–1660* (Edinburgh, 2007).

Wheeler, Scott, *The Irish and British Wars, 1637–1654* (London, 2002).

Woolrych, Austin, *Britain in Revolution 1625–1660* (Oxford, 2002).

CHAPTER 11

···

ENGLISH POLITICS
IN THE 1650S

···

DAVID L. SMITH

INTRODUCTION

··

As Philip Baker argued in his chapter in this volume,[1] the regicide was brought about by a determined minority who could see no other way of achieving a lasting settlement than to remove Charles I and abolish the monarchy. The New Model Army played a pivotal role in this process, and the army remained crucially important throughout the 1650s. In a sense, the republic was never able to escape the circumstances of its birth, and English politics during that decade were characterized by constant tension between army leaders and civilian politicians. These two elements needed each other but found it extremely difficult to work together. Only Oliver Cromwell had sufficient stature within each camp to hold them in some sort of equilibrium, and this ability to bridge the two worlds is the key to his remarkable political dominance during the Interregnum.

This chapter will explore the political consequences of this troubled relationship between the army leadership and the civilians. Christopher Hill once wrote that 'the Protectorate was sitting on bayonets, and not much else', and his comment holds good for the Commonwealth as well.[2] Conscious that those who had actively sought Charles I's trial and execution were never more than a minority of the population, the leading civilians of the republic needed the army's protection. It was the army that had brought the republic into being and that safeguarded it throughout the 1650s. In the end, only Oliver Cromwell proved equal to the task of balancing the competing political pressures of civilians and officers, and following his death in September 1658, the disparate elements of the republic fell apart within less than two years. The final irony was that it was a section of the army leadership that was responsible for the destruction of the republic and the restoration of the monarchy in 1660. What the army had created, the army ultimately destroyed.

THE CREATION OF THE COMMONWEALTH

The Commonwealth took some months to establish. Following the king's execution, the Rump parliament voted on 7 February to abolish the monarchy in England and Ireland as 'unnecessary, burdensome and dangerous to the liberty, safety and public interest of the people'. The previous day, it had voted to abolish the House of Lords as 'useless and dangerous'. These two votes were translated into Acts of Parliament on 17 and 19 March respectively. On 13 February the executive functions of monarchy were vested in a Council of State to be elected annually by—and predominantly from among—members of parliament. It was not, however, until 19 May that an Act was passed declaring that England and 'all the dominions and territories thereunto belonging' were 'a Commonwealth and Free State' to be governed 'by the supreme authority of this nation, the representatives of the people in Parliament, . . . and that without any King or House of Lords'. On 2 January 1650, all adult males were required to take an Engagement declaring that they would be 'true and faithful to the Commonwealth of England, as it is now established, without a King or House of Lords', and on 17 July a further Act rounded off the creation of the Commonwealth by making it treason to deny the 'supreme authority' of the Commons.[3]

The Rump now faced the challenge of what to do with this 'supreme authority'. Although roughly 210 members sat at some stage between January 1649 and the Rump's dissolution in April 1653, only about sixty or seventy were at all active and average attendances were usually between fifty and sixty.[4] Members could readily agree on issues of immediate concern, such as security and defence. They were able to make common cause in supporting the conquests of Ireland (1649–50) and Scotland (1650–1) and on measures against continental enemies, such as the Navigation Act of October 1651 which was targeted against the Dutch Republic.[5] Where the Rumpers became seriously divided was over how far to promote positive domestic reforms, especially in the areas of religion and the law. On religion, the most significant reform was the Toleration Act of September 1650, which abolished compulsory attendance at parish churches. But conservative opinion was reluctant to abandon the parish system or to grant further concessions to religious radicals, and stern measures were passed against blasphemy and adultery.[6] As for the law, a special Commission on Law Reform, chaired by Sir Matthew Hale, proposed far-reaching reforms of the legal system in 1652, but these were strongly opposed by the professional lawyers among the Rumpers.[7]

In general, the Rump gave priority to urgent matters, such as finance, taxation, and defence, rather than to more fundamental reforms. A representative sample of 131 Acts passed in the periods January–May 1649, January–May 1651, and 1 January–20 April 1653 reveals that seventy-four dealt with matters of security, finance, or taxation, forty-three with local government or the army, and fourteen with social problems. Only six were concerned with economic and social reform, five with religious issues, and three with law reform.[8] The Rump's energies gradually waned. The number of Acts passed steadily fell, from 124 in 1649 to seventy-eight in 1650, fifty-four in 1651, forty-four in 1652, and ten between 1 January and 20 April 1653. The corresponding figures for the number of committees appointed to draft new legislation showed a similar decline: 152, ninety-eight, sixty-one, fifty-one, twelve.[9] The Rump was, in John Morrill's words, 'a body that lived from hand to mouth' and 'fended off its problems'.[10]

THE DOWNFALL OF THE RUMP PARLIAMENT

For the army leaders, the Rump's performance was profoundly disappointing. Cromwell's conquests of Ireland and Scotland in 1649–51 made him ever more conscious of parliament's responsibilities, and he became increasingly preoccupied with three questions: was the Rump discharging its duties to God's cause and people; when would it dissolve itself; and how would it make provision for a successor parliament that would be sympathetic to the godly cause? On all three issues, Cromwell's frustration with the Rump steadily mounted. On 4 September 1651, the day after his victory at Worcester, Cromwell wrote to the Speaker of the Rump, William Lenthall, expressing the hope that this 'crowning mercy' would 'provoke those that are concerned in it to thankfulness, and the Parliament to do the will of Him who hath done His will for it, and for the nation'. Cromwell urged 'that the fear of the Lord, even for His mercies, may keep an authority and a people so prospered, and blessed, and witnessed unto, humble and faithful, and that justice and righteousness, mercy and truth may flow from you, as a thankful return to our gracious God'.[11] In Cromwell's view, however, the Rumpers conspicuously failed to make such a 'thankful return', and he pressed them to set a date by which they would end their sitting.

After much dragging of feet, in November 1651 the Rumpers agreed that the parliament would dissolve itself no later than 3 November 1654. This then raised the question of what body would succeed it, and in August 1652 the army petitioned the Rump 'that for public satisfaction of the good people of this nation, speedy consideration may be had of such qualifications for future and successive Parliaments as tend to the election only of such as are pious and faithful to the interest of the Commonwealth, to sit and serve as members in the said Parliament'.[12] To that end, from the following October Cromwell convened a series of meetings between leading Rumpers and army officers to discuss a bill for a 'new representative'.[13] Eventually, on 19 April 1653, Cromwell believed that he had secured an agreement whereby the Rump would dissolve itself and transfer authority to an interim council of officers and MPs which would then organize fresh elections in which former royalists and 'Presbyters and neuters' would be disqualified.

The following day, however, the Rump rejected this plan for a temporary council and decided instead to hold immediate elections. Concerned that these elections might take place without adequate safeguards to exclude the ungodly, Cromwell rushed to Westminster with a body of troops, berated the members, telling them that 'you have sat too long here for any good you have been doing lately', and then dissolved the Rump.[14] Two days later, he published a declaration[15] in which he argued that 'the Parliament had opportunity . . . to settle a due liberty both in reference to civil and spiritual things', and 'to proceed vigorously in reforming what was amiss in government, and to the settling of the Commonwealth upon a foundation of justice and righteousness'. Instead of doing these things, Cromwell complained, the Rumpers had acted 'with much bitterness and opposition to the people of God, and his spirit acting in them', and he also claimed (probably wrongly)[16] that they had a desire 'of perpetuating themselves in the supreme government'. Cromwell asserted that the Rump would 'never answer those ends which God, his people, and the whole nation expected from them', and that 'the interest of all honest men and of this glorious cause had been in danger to be laid in the dust'. He insisted that it was his duty 'to call to the government persons of approved fidelity and honesty' in the belief 'that if persons so qualified be chosen, the fruits of a just and right-eous reformation, so long prayed and wished for, will, by the blessing of God, be in due time obtained'. As he later argued, the Rump had committed 'an high breach of trust' and to dissolve it was therefore 'as necessary to be done as the preservation of this cause'.[17]

Barebone's Parliament

Cromwell's dramatic dissolution of the Rump left him arguably more powerful than at any other time in his career, either before or afterwards.[18] He and the Army Council chose to adopt a scheme proposed by one of the officers, the Fifth Monarchist Major-General Thomas Harrison, for a nominated assembly, often known as Barebone's Parliament.[19] Cromwell apparently envisaged this as an interim assembly that would sit no later than 3 November 1654, by which time he hoped the nation would be sufficiently settled to resume electing regular parliaments.[20] He opened it on 4 July 1653 with an exhilarated speech in which he told members that 'God hath called you to this work by, I think, as wonder-ful providences as ever passed upon the sons of men in so short a time. . . . It's come, therefore, to you by the way of necessity; by the wise Providence of God . . . Therefore, own your call!'[21] Over the weeks that followed, however, Barebone's became more and more divided, especially over how far to pursue reform of religion and the law. The mem-bers could agree on a range of social, administrative, and financial issues and they passed in all nearly thirty Acts on these matters. However, members were quite diverse in their religious and political views, and they differed over which reforms to prioritize and how rapidly to proceed.[22] The forty members with some legal training were alarmed when a majority voted to abolish the Court of Chancery and to codify the English common law into a pocket-sized digest. More moderate members deplored a vote to suppress lay rights to nominate the ministers of parishes, seeing it as a threat to property. The final straw came on 10 December, when members voted by the narrowest of margins (fifty-six votes to fifty-four) to abolish tithes, many of which were paid to the laity. Two days later, nearly eighty moderate members exploited the absence of many of their more radical colleagues at a prayer meeting and voted 'to deliver up unto the Lord General Cromwell the powers which they had received from him'.[23]

Cromwell professed surprise at this outcome, but he appears to have had few regrets. Later he described Barebone's as 'a story of my own weakness and folly'.[24] He and his fellow officers had become increasingly concerned that Barebone's was hostile towards the army. In an effort to reduce the tax burden on England, members voted not to renew the excise, and they then turned to review the monthly assessment, which was the main source of financial support for the army. Some radicals even suggested that senior officers should serve for a year without pay.[25] It was against this background of growing antagonism between the army and Barebone's that Major-General John Lambert began, from mid-October 1653, to draft a new paper constitution, the Instrument of Government.[26] This drew on earlier army terms, especially the Heads of the Proposals (1647) and the Officers' Agreement of the People (1649).[27] Lambert initially hoped that Cromwell would accept the title of King, but he steadfastly refused and so instead the Instrument made him Lord Protector for life. Following the demise of Barebone's, the Army Council adopted the Instrument on 15 December and the following day, wearing a plain black suit and cloak, Cromwell was installed as Lord Protector in Westminster Hall.[28]

THE ESTABLISHMENT OF
THE PROTECTORATE

The terms of the Instrument reflected its army origins, and Barry Coward has written that 'running through the new constitution is an intense distrust of Parliaments'.[29] Conversely, many of the former Rumpers who had strongly supported the Commonwealth—figures like Sir Arthur Hesilrige, Sir Henry Vane, Thomas Scott, and John Bradshaw—were appalled at the establishment of the Protectorate, and at what they saw as Cromwell's betrayal of the causes of godliness and liberty for the sake of his own ambition.[30] In May 1654, John Milton published *The Second Defence of the People of England* in which he warned Cromwell: 'if that man than whom no one has been considered more just, more holy, more excellent, shall afterwards attack that liberty which he himself has defended, such an act must necessarily be dangerous and well-nigh fatal not only to liberty itself but also to the cause of all virtue and piety'.[31] Cromwell and his fellow officers had imposed a new written constitution, but at the cost of alienating significant numbers of civilian Commonwealthsmen.

The Instrument's provisions for the election and composition of parliaments are discussed more fully below.[32] Here it is worth emphasising how much the new constitution reflected the army's priorities, especially concerning religious liberty of conscience and the maintenance of a standing army. On the first of these issues, the Instrument stipulated that 'such as profess faith in God by Jesus Christ (though differing in judgement from the doctrine, worship or discipline publicly held forth) shall not be restrained from, but shall be protected in, the profession of the faith and exercise of their religion', provided that 'they abuse not this liberty to the civil injury of others and to the actual disturbance of the public peace on their parts', and that 'this liberty' would not be 'extended to Popery or Prelacy, nor to such as, under the profession of Christ, hold forth and practise licentiousness'. On the second issue, 'a constant yearly revenue' was to be raised to support '10,000 horse and dragoons, and 20,000 foot, in England, Scotland and Ireland', plus £200,000 per annum for defraying the other necessary charges of administration of justice, and other expenses of the Government', terms that could not be altered 'but by the consent of the Lord Protector and the Parliament'.[33] These religious and military arrangements would later cause friction in the Protectorate parliaments, as would the extent of the powers vested in the Lord Protector and the Council of State.[34]

The Instrument scheduled the first Protectorate parliament to meet in September 1654 and until then the Lord Protector and Council of State could issue ordinances with the force of law but subject to parliamentary ratification. They used this power to produce about a hundred and eighty ordinances addressing a wide range of financial and administrative issues.[35] Among the most notable were those uniting England and Scotland, reforming Chancery, and establishing a High Court of Justice. Perhaps even closer to Cromwell's heart were the ordinances relating to the settlement of religion, especially the creation of a national body of 'triers' to examine all new ministers before allowing them to preach, and county commissions of 'ejectors' to remove 'scandalous, ignorant and insufficient ministers and schoolmasters'.[36] Cromwell hoped that the first Protectorate parliament would confirm and build on these measures, but he was to be bitterly disappointed.

THE FIRST PROTECTORATE PARLIAMENT

Cromwell opened the parliament on 4 September with a speech full of optimism. He told members that they had upon their shoulders 'the interest of all the Christian people in the world': the parliament offered 'a door of hope', and that one of its 'great ends' was 'that this ship of the Commonwealth may be brought into a safe harbour'.[37] Instead of adopting the Instrument as he had hoped, however, the parliament began to debate a series of amendments that would strengthen its own powers, and also established an Assembly of Divines to give advice on religious reforms and measures against radical religious sects. On 11 September, they voted that government should be 'in a Parliament and single person limited and restrained as the Parliament should think fit'. The following day, Cromwell ordered the House to be locked and guarded by soldiers, and gave a lengthy speech outlining four 'fundamentals' of government that he regarded as non-negotiable: that parliaments should not sit perpetually and should be elected frequently; 'government by a single person and a Parliament'; 'liberty of conscience' in religion; and shared control of the militia between parliament and the Lord Protector. He then insisted that before they could resume their seats members had to subscribe a Recognition affirming their loyalty to the Lord Protector and to the principle of 'government by a single person and a Parliament'. At this point, between fifty and eighty members, including prominent Commonwealthsmen such as Hesilrige, Scott, and Bradshaw, withdrew in protest.[38]

The depleted House nevertheless pressed ahead with drafting a Parliamentary Constitution intended to strengthen parliament's powers and reduce those of the Lord Protector and the Council of State. This took the form of a 'constitutional bill' which included the provision that parliaments could not be adjourned, prorogued, or dissolved without their own consent, and the assertion of greater parliamentary control over the militia.[39] Many of the powers of the Council of State were to be transferred to parliament, and demands for a considerable reduction in the armed forces were only narrowly defeated. In particular, the Parliamentary Constitution sought to reduce the legislative powers of the Lord Protector by limiting his veto over parliamentary bills.[40] The majority of members were of presbyterian sympathies: they wanted to strengthen the provision and maintenance of a national ministry and were deeply fearful of extending liberty of conscience any further. As a result, the Parliamentary Constitution contained a clause that 'such bills as shall be agreed upon by the Parliament, for the restraining of atheism, blasphemy, damnable heresies, to be particularly enumerated by this Parliament, popery, prelacy, licentiousness, or profaneness' were to become law 'within twenty days after their presentation to the Lord Protector, although he shall not give his consent thereunto.'[41] The parliament prepared about forty bills in addition to the Parliamentary Constitution, on subjects as diverse as probate of wills and the management of saltpetre.[42] However, members' energies were primarily devoted to the 'constitutional bill' and it was this, above all, that made Cromwell determined to be rid of the parliament at the earliest possible moment.

The Instrument of Government had specified that parliaments should sit for a minimum of five months.[43] Cromwell chose to interpret this not as five *calendar* months but as five *lunar* months, lasting until 22 January, and on that date he dissolved the parliament. His lengthy speech on that occasion denounced members for having missed opportunities to 'have given a just liberty to godly men of different judgments' and 'to have settled peace and quietness amongst all professing godliness'. Instead, he complained, 'dissettlement and division, discontent and dissatisfaction, together with real dangers to the whole, has been more multiplied within these five months of your sitting, than in some years before'. He concluded: 'I think it my duty to tell you that it is not for the profit of these nations, nor fit for the common and public good, for you to continue here any longer.'[44]

THE MAJOR-GENERALS

Cromwell's angry dissolution of the first Protectorate parliament got 1655 off to a bad start, and there was worse news to come. In March an abortive royalist rising in Wiltshire, led by Sir John Penruddock, unnerved the government and showed that royalism, though defeated, was not dead. Then, in July, came news that the Western Design—Cromwell's campaign against Spanish power in the West Indies—had suffered a serious defeat.[45] The combination of all these developments convinced Cromwell and the Council of State that a major new policy was necessary. In August it was decided that England and Wales should be divided into ten (later eleven) regions, each ruled by a Major-General. Impatient with parliaments, the army was to take direct control of government.

The first duty of the Major-Generals was to preserve security. They were instructed to suppress 'all tumults, insurrections, rebellions or other unlawful assemblies', to disarm 'all papists and others who have been in arms against the Parliament', and to arrest all 'thieves, robbers, highwaymen and other dangerous persons'. To achieve these goals, they were authorized to raise new regional militias totalling 6,000 horse paid for by a Decimation Tax, a 10 per cent income tax on all former royalists. The Major-Generals had a second purpose as well, which was to promote what Cromwell called a 'reformation of manners' in the localities. They were to 'encourage and promote godliness and virtue, and discourage and discountenance all profaneness and ungodliness', and to enforce 'the laws against drunkenness, blaspheming, and taking of the name of God in vain, by swearing and cursing, plays and interludes, and profaning the Lord's Day, and such like wickedness and abominations'. Horse-races, cock-fighting, bear-baiting, stage-plays and 'any unlawful assemblies' were banned, as were alehouses 'except such as are necessary and convenient to travellers'.[46] This was military rule with a strong moral dimension.

Cromwell later praised the Major-Generals as 'justifiable as to necessity, and honest in every respect', and he claimed that they were 'more effectual towards the discountenancing of vice and settling religion than anything done these fifty years'.[47] Historians have generally been less positive and have suggested that their impact was at best patchy. In the most detailed account of this episode, Christopher Durston argued that the Major-Generals achieved some success in improving security but that in terms of 'creating a more godly society' they 'failed unequivocally'.[48] Their remit was too extensive, and they were not given enough time or support, for them to make more than very slow progress towards godly reformation. In those regions where they found sympathetic local commissioners, for example in Staffordshire, they had some success, but in much of England popular enthusiasm for Cromwell's vision was distinctly limited.[49] What was common to virtually all areas, however, was an intense dislike of military rule. When Cromwell's plans for further campaigns against Spain together with the continuing costs of military rule forced him to call another parliament to meet in September 1656, the elections were dominated by cries of 'no swordsmen, no decimators' and they produced a parliament strongly opposed to the Major-Generals.[50]

THE SECOND PROTECTORATE PARLIAMENT

In an effort to counteract this outcome, the Council of State, acting on advice from the Major-Generals, excluded just over a hundred members before the parliament assembled, whereupon a further sixty or so immediately withdrew in protest.[51] Among those excluded were significant numbers of Commonwealthsmen, such as Hesilrige and Scott, as well as presbyterians, like John Birch and John Bulkeley, who had obstructed the extension of liberty of conscience in 1654–5. Yet these exclusions and withdrawals did not make the new parliament any more malleable. In his opening speech on 17 September 1656, Cromwell hoped that members would unite against what he called the 'natural enemy' of Spain, and that they would 'knit together in one bond' to 'suppress everything that is evil and encourage whatsoever is of godliness'.[52] Instead, however, they soon began to address two particular areas of concern—liberty of conscience and the powers of the Major-Generals—both of which put them on collision course with Cromwell and his fellow officers.

The first of these issues came to a head in a remarkable way with the case of a Quaker, James Nayler, who in October 1656 re-enacted Christ's entry into Jerusalem on Palm Sunday by riding into Bristol on a horse, with his supporters shouting hosannas and throwing garments in his path. Members were deeply divided over how to proceed against him—whether by legislation or by judicial procedure—and over how severe a sentence to impose. During December there were lengthy debates about Nayler's fate, in which the more lenient speakers included army officers such as Lambert, Desborough, and Sydenham. By contrast, prominent civilian presbyterians like Sir William Strickland, Thomas Bampfield, and Thomas Beake, were among those who urged that Nayler be put to death. The case revealed widespread fears of 'errors, heresies and blasphemies' in general, and particularly of Quakers, who Sir William Strickland described as 'a growing evil, and the greatest that ever was'. Eventually, the House voted to impose savage corporal punishments on Nayler but to spare his life. Cromwell did not interfere in these debates, but he did query the 'grounds and reasons whereupon they have proceeded', and he increasingly wondered whether another chamber might be needed to act as 'a check or balancing power' on the Commons.[53]

Parliament's second major concern was the influence of the army. On 25 December 1656, Major-General Desborough introduced a Militia Bill that would have perpetuated the Major-Generals and the Decimation Tax. This provoked howls of protest from civilian members. Many argued that the Decimation Tax violated the Rump's Act of Oblivion (1652) which had granted a general pardon to former royalists. John Trevor spoke for many when he complained that the Militia Bill would 'cantonize the nation' by sanctioning 'a power that was never set up in any nation without dangerous consequences'. In parliament, and even within the Council of State, officers and civilians found themselves bitterly at odds over the Bill. The House refused to vote £400,000 towards further campaigns against Spain until after the Bill was defeated, to the intense annoyance of the Major-Generals and other officers, on 29 January 1657.[54]

These divisions became even worse over the weeks that followed. In a bid to curtail the Lord Protector's powers and reduce the army's influence, on 23 February a group of civilians led by Lord Broghill, the Secretary of State John Thurloe, Bulstrode Whitelocke, and Nathaniel Fiennes presented a new written constitution to Cromwell in the form of a Remonstrance. This urged him 'to assume the name, style, title, dignity and office of King of England, Scotland and Ireland'. By assuming the ancient office of

King, Cromwell's powers would have been more clearly defined and less open-ended than those he wielded as Lord Protector. The Remonstrance further requested that 'the ancient and undoubted liberties and privileges of Parliament . . . be preserved and maintained'. Parliament's powers were to be strengthened at the expense of those of the Council of State, for example in relation to the exclusion of members. A second chamber would be established, known as the Other House, containing between forty and seventy members, and any who died or were 'legally removed' were to be replaced 'by consent of the House itself'. Liberty of conscience was not to be extended to 'such who publish horrible blasphemies or practise or hold forth licentiousness or profaneness under the profession of Christ'.[55] This Remonstrance, and specifically its offer of the kingship, presented Cromwell with the most difficult dilemma of his career, and he agonized for over two months before reaching a decision.

THE KINGSHIP CRISIS

The Remonstrance was a civilian attempt to curb the powers of Cromwell and the army, and it provoked a major political battle between the civilian and military interests. This battle was focused on the question of whether or not Cromwell would become king, and as he struggled to make up his mind he was lobbied by competing groups. The supporters of the Remonstrance argued that it would establish a constitutional monarchy—with powers similar to those of Charles I in 1641–2—that would safeguard the people's liberties and secure the long-term stability of the regime.[56] They were conscious that Miles Sindercombe's recent attempts to assassinate Cromwell had provided a stark reminder of how much the Protectorate depended on one man's life.[57] Aware of Cromwell's aversion to the hereditary principle, the authors of the Remonstrance had sweetened the pill with a clause allowing him to nominate his own successor.[58] By contrast, the most concerted resistance to the Remonstrance came from senior army officers, especially Lambert, Desborough, Sydenham, and Fleetwood, who insisted that it would be a betrayal of all that they had fought for in the civil wars. They correctly saw it as a serious threat to the army's influence in government and threatened to resign their commissions if Cromwell accepted the kingship.[59]

It was testimony to how successfully Cromwell had thus far managed to straddle the worlds of the officers and the civilians that he found it so desperately difficult to adjudicate between these conflicting lines of advice. In a series of speeches to parliamentary representatives between late March and early May, he pondered the pros and cons of the offer, probing whether it was 'necessary' or merely 'convenient' for him to become king, and if it would be offensive to God and to 'good men' for him to take a title that he felt had been providentially 'laid aside'.[60] On 13 April, he memorably declared that 'God hath seemed providentially . . . not only to strike at the family but at the name . . . I will not seek to set up that that providence hath destroyed and laid in the dust, and I would not build Jericho again'.[61] Finally, on 8 May he gave his definitive answer: he was 'not to be convinced of the necessity of that thing that hath been so often insisted on by you, to wit, the title of king', and therefore 'I cannot undertake this government with that title of king'.[62] In reaching this decision, the army leaders' opposition probably weighed very heavily with him. It is also likely, as Blair Worden has argued, that he was extremely sensitive to possible accusations of greed and ambition, and that he was haunted by the wounding charge of committing the 'sin of Achan' that Vane had levelled against him the previous year in *A Healing Question Propounded*.[63]

With the question of the kingship settled, the other sections of the Remonstrance were adopted in slightly revised form in a new written constitution, the Humble Petition and Advice, the central principle of which remained the strengthening of parliament at the expense of both Protector and Council.[64] The quasi-monarchical character of this new constitution was reinforced by the renaming of the Council of State as the Privy Council.[65] When Cromwell was reinstalled as Lord Protector in Westminster Hall on 26 June, he was invested with 'a robe of purple velvet, lined with ermine, being the habit anciently used at the solemn investiture of princes', together with a bible, a sword and 'a scepter, being of massie gold'. After taking his oath of office, he was proclaimed Lord Protector, whereupon 'the trumpets sounded, and the people made several great acclamations with loud shouts, God save the Lord Protector'. Then, 'in his princely habit', he departed in 'his coach of state'.[66] Cromwell now had all the trappings of a king, except the title and the crown.

OLIVER CROMWELL'S FINAL MONTHS

The underlying tensions within the regime persisted through the remaining fourteen months of Cromwell's life. The end of military rule brought a degree of stability, but at the cost of alienating the army leaders who resented the Humble Petition and Advice as a civilian constitution which reduced their influence and curtailed liberty of conscience. The Commonwealthsmen remained implacably hostile to the Protectorate. These issues came to a head in the brief second session of the second Protectorate parliament which lasted just two weeks in January–February 1658. The Humble Petition had not continued the Council's power to exclude members of parliament of whom it disapproved. As a result, about twenty of the members excluded in 1656 returned to the House, including Hesilrige and Scott. Cromwell had also nominated to the Other House some of his most senior army colleagues, such as Fleetwood, Desborough, and Sydenham. These two developments made the Commons much more difficult to manage and there was soon a major revolt, led by the Commonwealthsmen, against recognizing the Other House.[67]

In an attempt to quell this, Cromwell delivered a lengthy speech on 25 January in which he warned of the dangers that faced the country both at home and abroad. He deplored the 'calamities and divisions among' the nation and asked members: 'What is the general spirit of this nation? . . . What is it that possesseth every sect? What is it? That every sect may be uppermost!' He complained that 'it were a happy thing if the nation would be content with rule', for 'misrule is better than no rule; and an ill government, a bad one, better than none'. Then, in an extraordinary image, he lamented that so many people were 'not only making wounds, but widening those already made, as if we should see one making wounds in a man's side, and would desire nothing more than to be grop-ing and groveling with his fingers in those wounds'.[68] His rhetoric was to no avail. The House became entangled in a fractious debate over the Other House and on 4 February, convinced that the parliament was 'not to be satisfied', Cromwell dissolved it.[69]

This was the last time that Cromwell addressed a parliament. Over the weeks that fol-lowed his health and morale deteriorated, and he died on 3 September 1658. In death, he was treated as a king in all but name. For his lying in state at Somerset House, an effigy of Cromwell was made, wearing 'a kirtle robe of purple velvet, laced with a rich gold lace, and furr'd with ermins'. The effigy held a sceptre in one hand and an orb in the other and behind its head was 'a rich chair of estate of cloth of gold tissued' on which stood 'the imperial crown set with stones'.[70] Cromwell's funeral in Westminster Abbey was mod-elled on that of James VI and I in 1625, and for this his effigy was 'vested with royal robes, a scepter in one hand, a globe in the other, and a crown on the head'.[71] The regality of the lying in state and funeral prompted criticism from Commonwealthsmen such as Edmund Ludlow who castigated 'this folly and profusion'.[72]

Behind the monarchical ceremonial there lurked a familiar power struggle. It was announced that on his deathbed Cromwell had nominated his eldest son as his successor, and Richard Cromwell was duly proclaimed Lord Protector on 4 September. Jonathan Fitzgibbons has recently argued that Cromwell may not in fact have nominated Richard and that instead the Privy Council may have chosen Richard as the most suitable and least contentious candidate and then claimed that he was his father's choice.[73] This is a plausible reading of the surviving evidence, and it would certainly make sense in terms of the continuing tensions between the civilian and military interests. A candidate from among the army officers, such as Fleetwood, would have been wholly unacceptable to the civilians. Richard, by contrast, was attractive to civilians while also being acceptable to officers who thought they could control him. To a Council that was deeply divided and finely balanced between officers and civilians, he seemed an appealing compromise candidate. Once again, however, the cracks in the regime had only been papered over, not removed.

RICHARD CROMWELL AND THE FALL
OF THE PROTECTORATE

In recent years, historians have tended to take a more positive view of Richard Cromwell's viability as Lord Protector, and to argue that his downfall was not inevitable. Although aged only thirty-one when he took office, he demonstrated energy and politi-cal ability, and his presbyterian sympathies enabled him to win the support of some who had viewed his father with suspicion. He was more cautious than Oliver about extending liberty of conscience, and had even advocated the death sentence for Nayler. This helped him to build bridges with the presbyterians who were much more supportive of Richard than they had been of his father. Richard's greatest problems were with the army (which had reservations about his civilian background) and the Commonwealthsmen (who had always disliked the Protectorate), and it was an alliance between these two elements that ultimately brought down first Richard and then the Protectorate itself in April–May 1659.[74]

Although the army officers had acquiesced in Richard's appointment as Lord Protector they remained sceptical about his lack of military experience and never regarded him as one of their own as they had his father. Considerable tensions persisted within the Privy Council between the civilian and military interests. Richard's strongest supporters were the civilians, led by Thurloe, Nathaniel Fiennes, and the Lord President Henry Lawrence. By contrast, the military element, including Fleetwood and Desborough, while pledging loyalty to Richard, obstructed his attempt to strengthen the civilian presence on the Council by the appointments of Lords Broghill and Fauconberg.

These tensions came to a head when Richard—facing a total state debt of nearly £2.5 million and army arrears of £890,000—summoned a parliament to meet in late January 1659.[75] With the Council powerless to exclude any of those who were elected, a significant number of Commonwealthsmen were returned, including Hesilrige and Scott, and Richard also preserved his father's composition of the Other House, which kept some of his ablest allies out of the Commons.[76] Nevertheless, this parliament was by no means doomed to failure. Members of all complexions expressed their loyalty to Richard, and the support of presbyterian members enabled him to defeat the resistance of the Commonwealthsmen on several key issues, including the recognition of him as Lord Protector, the legitimacy of the Other House, and the presence of Irish and Scottish members in the Commons. By March 1659 it seemed that events were steadily moving in Richard's favour. Behind the scenes, however, an alliance against Richard was developing between army leaders, especially Fleetwood and Desborough, and Commonwealthsmen like Hesilrige and Scott, who remained entrenched in their antipathy towards the Protectorate. The officers felt that Richard, a civilian of presbyterian attitudes, was far less sympathetic to their interests than his father had been. In particular, they deplored his reluctance either to guarantee payment of their arrears or to discuss their grievances with any degree of urgency. When, in early April, the officers submitted a representation of their case to Richard, he initially ordered Fleetwood to suppress it and only forwarded it to the Houses with great reluctance. Instead of discussing it, the Commons resolved that the Army Council should not meet while the parliament was sitting and they then began to debate settling the armed forces as a militia, possibly under parliamentary control, which was precisely what the officers most feared. At this point, the power struggle between the military and civilian interests came dramatically into the open. On 21 April, Fleetwood and Desborough demanded the parliament's immediate dissolution and the recall of the Rump. The army ordered a rendezvous at St James's, whereupon Richard tried to organize a counter-rendezvous which proved a disastrous failure. The next day the parliament was dispersed under threat of military force and on 24 May Richard resigned as Lord Protector.[77]

The fall of the Protectorate was not inevitable. The army coup that broke it came about for essentially short-term reasons, and if Richard had been granted longer to build up a base of civilian support centred on the presbyterians he might have been in a stronger position to face down the alliance of army officers and Commonwealthsmen that confronted him. That said, the coup of April–May 1659 marked the latest dramatic episode in a struggle between civilian and military interests whose origins can be traced back to the very beginning of the Interregnum and the circumstances of the republic's birth.

The Collapse of the Republic

Tim Harris examines the complex series of events that led from the fall of the Protectorate to the restoration of the Stuart monarchy in May 1660 below.[78] The theme I want to highlight in this section is the continuing, and eventually fatal, instability that lay at the heart of the relationship between civilian politicians and army officers. With the end of the Protectorate, the army officers held the political initiative, and during the last twelve months of the Interregnum they tried to establish a civilian regime that would safeguard both their own interests and the 'good old cause' for which they had fought. These attempts proved vain, and ultimately the only solution they could find was to restore Charles II.[79]

Initially, the army officers tried to work with their Commonwealthsmen allies in the restored Rump, but they soon tired of the latter's failure to provide for army arrears and their reluctance to extend liberty of conscience. In early October, Desborough presented a Humble Representation and Petition of the Officers of the Army urging the Rump to safeguard the army's interests. Instead the Rump pressed ahead with an Act nullifying all legislation passed since April 1653. At this point the officers' patience ran out and they dissolved the Rump on 13 October. General George Monck, leader of the army in Scotland, demanded the recall of the Rump, but instead the Army Council established a Committee of Safety, chaired by Fleetwood, to 'secure the people's liberties as men and Christians, reform the law, provide for a godly preaching ministry, and settle the constitution without a single person or a House of Lords'. This Committee proved quite unequal to the situation it faced—with growing economic depression, tax strikes, declining public order, and the threat of army mutiny in the North—and it dispersed on 17 December. Monck now made his decisive intervention. Marching south, he brushed Lambert's forces aside, while three regiments in London followed Monck's example and reinstated the Rump. After his arrival in London in early February, Monck secured the return of the Long Parliament: this organized fresh elections and then dissolved itself. These elections produced a strongly pro-royalist Convention which agreed to recognize Charles II as already king since 30 January 1649. So it was that a final army coup brought about the restoration of the monarchy. This irony was not lost on contemporaries. When

Charles II entered London on 29 May, the royalist diarist John Evelyn 'stood in the Strand, and beheld it, and blessed God: And all this without one drop of blood, and by that very army, which rebelled against him'.[80]

Conclusion

No more than any other historical developments were these events inevitable. Had Oliver Cromwell lived longer, or accepted the kingship, or had Richard been given longer to develop his own bases of support in different ways from his father, it is not impossible that the Protectorate might have survived for longer. But both Lord Protectors had to contend with the fundamental divide between army leaders and civilian politicians that dogged the republic from its very creation. Oliver handled this by performing a very adroit balancing act between the two interests. Further light on the political skills that enabled him to do this is likely to be shed by the forthcoming publication, probably in 2016, of a new critical edition of his writings and speeches, under the general editorship of John Morrill. Oliver naturally remains the dominant figure in any account of English politics in the 1650s, for he proved to be unique in his capacity to hold the disparate elements of the regime together for any length of time. That task was not impossible, but it was extremely challenging, and in the end this was a challenge that defeated Richard. In a way, the officer/civilian divide reflected a duality within Oliver's own complex character. He epitomized in his own person the conflicting values of the gentry and the army officers, and to that extent he embodied the dilemmas that lay at the heart of the English revolution. The 1650s were not an inevitable trek back towards monarchy, but the Restoration did grow out of a fault-line that had existed since 1649 and that stemmed from the very creation of the republic. In that sense, the dilemmas of the revolution—as Cromwell knew perhaps better than anybody—were ultimately insoluble.

Notes

1. Chapter 9, above.
2. Christopher Hill, *The Century of Revolution, 1603–1714* (London, 1961), 135.
3. S. R. Gardiner (ed.), *The Constitutional Documents of the Puritan Revolution, 1625–1660* (3rd edition, Oxford, 1906), 381–91.
4. Blair Worden, *The Rump Parliament, 1648–1653* (Cambridge, 1974), chap. 1.
5. C. H. Firth and R. S. Rait (eds.), *Acts and Ordinances of the Interregnum, 1642–1660*, 3 vols. (London, 1911), II, 559–62.
6. Firth and Rait (eds.), *Acts and Ordinances*, II, 387–9, 409–12, 423–5; Worden, *Rump Parliament*, chap. 7.
7. Worden, *Rump Parliament*, chap. 6; Mary Cotterell, 'Interregnum Law Reform: The Hale Commission of 1652', *English Historical Review*, 83 (1968): 689–704.
8. Firth and Rait (eds.), *Acts and Ordinances*, III, lxvi–lxxi, lxxxii–lxxxiv, xc–xci.

9. Worden, *Rump Parliament*, 92.

10. John Morrill, *Stuart Britain: A Very Short Introduction* (Oxford, 2000), 54.

11. S. C. Lomas (ed.), *The Letters and Speeches of Oliver Cromwell, with elucidations by Thomas Carlyle*, 3 vols. (London, 1904) [hereafter cited as Carlyle-Lomas], II, 226.

12. Austin Woolrych, *Commonwealth to Protectorate* (Oxford, 1982), 41.

13. Worden, *Rump Parliament*, chaps. 14–16.

14. Carlyle-Lomas, II, 264–5.

15. Gardiner (ed.), *Constitutional Documents*, 400–4.

16. Worden, *Rump Parliament*, chaps. 15–17; Carlyle-Lomas, II, 284.

17. Carlyle-Lomas, II, 284, 288.

18. Cf. J. C. Davis's discussion of the options facing Cromwell, in chap. 13, below.

19. For the composition of Barebone's Parliament, see chap. 14, below.

20. Austin Woolrych, *Britain in Revolution, 1625–1660* (Oxford, 2002), chap. 17; Woolrych, *Commonwealth to Protectorate*, 144–53.

21. Carlyle-Lomas, II, 290, 296.

22. Woolrych, *Commonwealth to Protectorate*, chaps. 6–7.

23. Woolrych, *Commonwealth to Protectorate*, chaps. 8–10.

24. Carlyle-Lomas, III, 98.

25. Woolrych, *Commonwealth to Protectorate*, 306–10.

26. David Farr, *John Lambert, Parliamentary Soldier and Cromwellian Major-General, 1619–1684* (Woodbridge, 2003), 124–129; Gardiner (ed.), *Constitutional Documents*, 405–17.

27. Gardiner (ed.), *Constitutional Documents*, 316–26, 359–71.

28. Woolrych, *Commonwealth to Protectorate*, chap. 9.

29. Barry Coward, *Oliver Cromwell* (London, 1991), 104.

30. Jonathan Scott, *Commonwealth Principles: Republican Writing of the English Revolution* (Cambridge, 2004), chaps. 12–13.

31. Don M. Wolfe (ed.), *Complete Prose Works of John Milton, Volume 5: 1650–1655, Part 1* (New Haven, 1966), 673; Blair Worden, *Literature and Politics in Cromwellian England: John Milton, Andrew Marvell, Marchamont Nedham* (Oxford, 2007), chap. 12.

32. Smith, chap. 14, below.

33. Gardiner (ed.), *Constitutional Documents*, 414, 416.

34. See chap. 14, below.

35. Peter Gaunt, '"To create a little world out of chaos": The Protectoral Ordinances of 1653–1654 Reconsidered', in Patrick Little (ed.), *The Cromwellian Protectorate* (Woodbridge, 2007), 105–26; Ivan Roots, 'Cromwell's Ordinances: The Early Legislation of the Protectorate', in G. E. Aylmer (ed.), *The Interregnum: The Quest for Settlement, 1646–1660* (London, 1972), 143–64.

36. Firth and Rait (eds.), *Acts and Ordinances*, II, 855–8, 871–5, 917–18, 949–67, 968–90.

37. Carlyle-Lomas, II, 339, 358.

38. Patrick Little and David L. Smith, *Parliaments and Politics during the Cromwellian Protectorate* (Cambridge, 2007), 84–6.

39. Gardiner (ed.), *Constitutional Documents*, 427–47.

40. Little and Smith, *Parliaments and Politics*, chap. 2.

41. Little and Smith, *Parliaments and Politics*, 200–1; Gardiner (ed.), *Constitutional Documents*, 443.

42. Peter Gaunt, 'Law-making in the First Protectorate Parliament', in Colin Jones, Malyn Newitt, and Stephen Roberts (eds.), *Politics and People in Revolutionary England* (Oxford, 1986), 163–86.

43. Gardiner (ed.), *Constitutional Documents*, 406.

44. Carlyle-Lomas, II, 409, 416–17, 430.

45. Woolrych, *Britain in Revolution*, 620–2, 630–4.

46. J. P. Kenyon, *The Stuart Constitution: Documents and Commentary* (2nd edition, Cambridge, 1986), 322–324; Christopher Durston, *Cromwell's Major-Generals: Godly Government during the English Revolution* (Manchester, 2001).

47. Carlyle-Lomas, II, 531, 543.

48. Durston, *Cromwell's Major-Generals*, 228.

49. Henry Reece, *The Army in Cromwellian England, 1649–1660* (Oxford, 2013), chaps. 7–8; John Sutton, 'Cromwell's Commissioners for Preserving the Peace of the Commonwealth: A Staffordshire Case Study', in Ian Gentles, John Morrill, and Blair Worden (eds.), *Soldiers, Writers and Statesmen of the English Revolution* (Cambridge, 1998), 151–82.

50. Little and Smith, *Parliaments and Politics*, 59–71; Durston, *Cromwell's Major-Generals*, chap. 9.

51. Little and Smith, *Parliaments and Politics*, 87–93, 302–5.

52. Carlyle-Lomas, II, 511, 549.

53. Little and Smith, *Parliaments and Politics*, 138, 183–6, 211–14.

54. Little and Smith, *Parliaments and Politics*, 109–10, 115–16, 252–4; Durston, *Cromwell's Major-Generals*, chap. 10; Christopher Durston, 'The Fall of Cromwell's Major-Generals', *English Historical Review*, 113 (1998): 18–37.

55. Little and Smith, *Parliaments and Politics*, 12–48, 306–12.

56. Patrick Little, *Lord Broghill and the Cromwellian Union with Ireland and Scotland* (Woodbridge, 2004), chap. 5.

57. Patrick Little, 'John Thurloe and the Offer of the Crown to Oliver Cromwell', in Little (ed.), *Oliver Cromwell*, 216–40.

58. Jonathan Fitzgibbons, 'Hereditary Succession and the Cromwellian Protectorate: The Offer of the Crown Reconsidered', *English Historical Review*, 128 (2013): 1095–128.

59. Farr, *John Lambert*, 143–7; Little and Smith, *Parliaments and Politics*, 110–11.

60. Benjamin Woodford, *Perceptions of a Monarchy without a King: Reactions to Oliver Cromwell's Power* (Montreal and Kingston, 2013), chap. 1.

61. Carlyle-Lomas, III, 70–1.

62. Carlyle-Lomas, III, 127–9.

63. Blair Worden, *God's Instruments: Political Conduct in the England of Oliver Cromwell* (Oxford, 2012), chap. 1.

64. For an analysis of the Humble Petition and Advice, see chap. 14, below; the text is printed in Gardiner (ed.), *Constitutional Documents*, 447–59.

65. Blair Worden, 'Oliver Cromwell and the Council', in Little (ed.), *Cromwellian Protectorate*, 82–104.

66. *Mercurius Publicus*, 369 (25 June–2 July 1657): 7881–4 (British Library [BL], Thomason E 505/1).

67. Little and Smith, *Parliaments and Politics*, 97–8, 111–12, 120, 139–40; see also chapter 14, below.

68. Carlyle-Lomas, III, 173–5.

69. Carlyle-Lomas, III, 187–92; Little and Smith, *Parliaments and Politics*, 97–8, 139–40, 189–91.

70. *Mercurius Politicus*, 438 (14–21 October 1658): 927–8 (BL, Thomason E 760/6).

71. *Mercurius Politicus*, 443 (18–25 November 1658): 30 (BL, Thomason E 760/16); Laura Lunger Knoppers, *Constructing Cromwell: Ceremony, Portrait, and Print, 1645–1661* (Cambridge, 2000), 133–6.

72. Knoppers, *Constructing Cromwell*, 145–6.

73. Jonathan Fitzgibbons, '"Not in any doubtfull dispute"? Reassessing the nomination of Richard Cromwell', *Historical Research*, 83 (2010): 281–300.

74. Jason Peacey, '"Fit for Public Services": The Upbringing of Richard Cromwell', in Little (ed.), *Oliver Cromwell*, 241–64; Jason Peacey, 'The Protector Humbled: Richard Cromwell and the Constitution', in Little (ed.), *Cromwellian Protectorate*, 32–52; Little and Smith, *Parliaments and Politics*, chap. 7.

75. See chap. 14, below.

76. Little and Smith, *Parliaments and Politics*, 72–9.

77. Little and Smith, *Parliaments and Politics*, 112, 120–2, 153–70.

78. Chap. 12, below.

79. Reece, *Army in Cromwellian England*, chaps. 9–10; Scott, *Commonwealth Principles*, chap. 14; Woolrych, *Britain in Revolution*, chap. 26; Farr, *John Lambert*, chap. 10.

80. John Bowle (ed.), *The Diary of John Evelyn* (Oxford, 1985), 182.

FURTHER READING

Coward, Barry, *The Cromwellian Protectorate* (Manchester, 2002).

Davis, J. C., *Oliver Cromwell* (London, 2001).

Durston, Christopher, *Cromwell's Major-Generals: Godly Government during the English Revolution* (Manchester, 2001).

Holmes, Clive, *Why was Charles I Executed?* (London, 2006).

Kenyon, J. P., *The Stuart Constitution: Documents and Commentary* (2nd edition, Cambridge, 1986).

Little, Patrick (ed.), *The Cromwellian Protectorate* (Woodbridge, 2007).

Little, Patrick (ed.), *Oliver Cromwell: New Perspectives* (Basingstoke, 2009).

Little, Patrick and David L. Smith, *Parliaments and Politics during the Cromwellian Protectorate* (Cambridge, 2007).

Morrill, John, *Oliver Cromwell* (Oxford, 2007).

Smith, David L. (ed.), *Cromwell and the Interregnum: The Essential Readings* (Oxford, 2003).

Smith, David L., *The Stuart Parliaments, 1603–1689* (London, 1999).

Woolrych, Austin, *Britain in Revolution, 1625–1660* (Oxford, 2002).

Woolrych, Austin, *Commonwealth to Protectorate* (Oxford, 1982).

Worden, Blair, *The English Civil Wars, 1640–1660* (London, 2009).

Worden, Blair, *God's Instruments: Political Conduct in the England of Oliver Cromwell* (Oxford, 2012).

Worden, Blair, *The Rump Parliament, 1648–1653* (Cambridge, 1974).

CHAPTER 12

....

THE RESTORATION IN
BRITAIN AND IRELAND

....

TIM HARRIS

'WE cannot but with all humility and thankfulness admire and adore the infinite mercy
and immediate goodness of Almighty God, when wee seriously consider how beyond
all humane expectations and endeavours he has by the gratious interposition only of
his owne power, and wisdom, thus miraculously, and without effusion of blood restored
your most excellent Majesty in honor and safety to your Thrones and people.' So wrote
the 'most humble and most dutifull Subjects' of Dorset in their address to Charles II
congratulating him on his restoration to the thrones of his three kingdoms in May
1660.[1] Charles's restoration did indeed seem miraculous. After years of failed attempts
to restore the Stuart monarchy by force[2]—even as late as August 1659 a conspiracy led
by General George Booth in Cheshire had been easily put down—Charles was eventually to reclaim his inheritance without a drop of blood being shed: he was simply invited
to return to his kingdoms by the English Convention parliament which opened on 25
April. As the loyal address from the ministers of Devon and Exeter put it, 'that which the
lord denyed to your sword he hath given you without the expence of treasure or blood'.[3]

The decision to recall Charles II was greeted with widespread rejoicing throughout
England, Scotland, and Ireland. The Convention's resolution on 1 May 1660 that 'the
Government . . . ought to be, by King, Lords and Commons' prompted bonfire celebrations across the whole kingdom, while there were similar displays when Charles was
publicly proclaimed king in London on 8 May and in the provinces a week later. When
Charles was proclaimed in Boston, Lincolnshire, the 'yonge men' of the town took down
the republic's coat of arms and 'pissed and sh[itted] on them' before committing them to
a bonfire they had made 'for joy' at the recalling of the king.[4] Charles's eventual return
to the capital on 29 May, his thirtieth birthday, prompted 'three days and three nights'
of rejoicing, as conduits ran with wine and huge crowds toasted the restored monarch
and burned effigies of Oliver Cromwell 'and other rebels'.[5] Nor was it just England that
rejoiced. When Charles was proclaimed in Dublin, 'the streets ran with Wine', there were
fireworks and 'almost a Bonfire at every house', and an elaborate mock funeral of the Rump

parliament. In Edinburgh magistrates and citizens celebrated 'this great deliverance' with bells, fireworks, and bonfires, while on 19 June, the official day of thanksgiving in Scotland for the king's restoration, an effigy of Oliver Cromwell, with the Devil pursuing him, was 'blown up' on Castle Hill.[6]

The hope was that the return of monarchy would restore unity and stability. In his Declaration issued from Breda in the Low Countries on 4 April, Charles had represented himself as the only person who could heal the bleeding wounds in church and state, promising 'a free and general Pardon' to all supporters of the republic (save those who might subsequently be excepted by parliament) and 'a Liberty to tender Consciences'.[7] The editor of a collection of songs and ballads composed to celebrate the demise of the republic rejoiced in June 1660 that 'we have lived to that day, that there is no Cavalier, because there is nothing else'.[8] One song celebrating George Monck, the man who had engineered the Restoration by forcing the dissolution of the republican Rump parliament in February 1660, stressed how all the inhabitants of Britain and Ireland had cause to rejoice: 'Then of[f] with your Pots, English, Irish and Scots, / And loyal Cambro-Brittains', opened the chorus, while a final verse urged 'Now Jockey, Teag, and Shenkin, / Pray no more to St. Andrew / To Patrick or Davie, / But St. George, who, to sav'ee, / 'Gainst Dragon Rump like a man drew'.[9]

Yet unity did not materialize. The longed-for stability proved elusive. England, Scotland, and Ireland were to see further plots and conspiracies against the state under both Charles II and his successor James VII and II, and in the end all three kingdoms were to succumb once more to revolution in 1688–9. How, then, to understand the Restoration? How was it brought about—and what were those who helped bring it about hoping to achieve? What was the nature of the Restoration settlement, and why, ultimately, did it fail to heal the three kingdoms' wounds?

THE ROAD TO RESTORATION

As with the crisis that developed in the late 1630s and triggered the descent into civil war, the restoration of the monarchy needs to be set in a Britannic context. This is not simply because Charles II would end up being restored to the thrones of England, Scotland, and Ireland. It was because the Cromwellian Protectorate had forged a British state, giving the Scots and Irish representation in the Protectorate parliaments, and the unravelling of this state could not be otherwise than a British affair. The fall of the Protectorate in the spring of 1659 and the resumption of political power by the Rump of the Long Parliament that had been forcibly dissolved in 1653 had the effect of voiding the legislation that had forged the Cromwellian union. In Ireland, a power struggle developed between different factions of the army, and as the radicals under Edmund Ludlow gained the ascendancy, Protestant landowners began to fear for the security of their newly acquired estates. When the army in England under Major-General Lambert seized power from the Rump in October 1659, the more conservative army leaders in Ireland decided to take action.

In December a group of officers led by Sir Theophilus Jones and backed by gentry of Old Protestant stock seized Dublin Castle, while Sir Charles Coote and Lord Broghill, two ex-royalists turned Cromwellian collaborators, secured various garrisons in Connacht and Munster. Now in possession of the key military strongholds in the kingdom, the instigators of this coup called for an Irish Convention, elected by the pre-war constituencies, to meet in Dublin in February—an assembly which under the skilful management of Broghill and Coote would go on to call for the restoration of monarchy.[10] As the 2nd earl of Clarendon was later to recall, it was the English in Ireland who 'made the Earliest advances towards his Majesties Restoration'.[11] In England, following the army's expulsion of the Rump, Anthony Ashley Cooper (the future 1st earl of Shaftesbury) and other former members of the Cromwellian council approached General George Monck, the commander of the army in Scotland, about the possibility of his marching into England to secure 'the restoration of the Parliament'. Although the Rump was restored to share power with the army on 26 December, this proved too little too late; Monck marched south on 1 January, thereby setting in motion the train of events that was to lead to restoration. On 11 February Monck forced the Rump to readmit the secluded members, paving the way for the Rump to vote its own dissolution a week later and to call elections for the meeting of a free parliament. According to Ashley Cooper, Monck would never have done what he did without knowing that he had the support of Coote and the army in Ireland.[12]

It is not quite that prior revolts in Ireland and Scotland—external and contingent events—triggered the collapse of the regime in England. Here we have a Britannic conspiracy by agents of the British state, involving a certain degree of coordination between the key actors in Ireland, Scotland, and England, all of whom were either English (Ashley Cooper, Monck) or of Protestant Anglo-Irish stock (Broghill, Coote, and Jones). Moreover, as in 1638–41, the only reason why developments in Ireland and Scotland could have the effect they did on England in 1659–60 was because the regime in England was already beginning to collapse from within. By late 1659 the war with Spain, begun by Cromwell in 1655, had caused a severe economic downtown: trade was disrupted, bullion was in short supply, and there was a rise in unemployment. The war could only be sustained by high taxation, which an already heavily taxed population could ill afford, while grain prices also rose dramatically in the late 1650s. With people having less money to spend on consumables, urban shopkeepers were doing badly. London was particularly badly hit, with its population of merchants, shopkeepers, and apprentices. And these economic woes came at a time when there was a revival of sectarian radicalism in the army following the fall of the Protectorate, a cause of alarm not only to Anglican royalists but also to many old-style puritans (presbyterians, congregationalists) who had championed the parliamentarian cause in the 1640s. When the army expelled the Rump, Londoners responded by threatening a tax strike and petitioning the City authorities for an end to army rule. There were violent clashes with troops on 5 December as apprentices went to deliver a petition to the Lord Mayor calling either for the return of the secluded members (a full parliament) or free elections for a new parliament: the soldiers opened fire, killing half a dozen, which caused a public outcry.[13] It was this seeming drift into anarchy in the nation's capital which prompted Monck to march south to restore order, while the people of England were now firmly convinced that the only solution to their woes would be a full or free parliament.

Those who campaigned against army rule did not call explicitly for a return of monarchy. What they wanted was a restoration of parliamentary government and the rule of law; they embraced the language of popular liberties and the people's birth-rights, not of Stuart legitimism. The apprentice petition of 5 December claimed 'the freedome and priviledges of our Parliaments' as 'our undoubted birth right', 'the great Charter of the people of England', and 'the most probable means' to 'establish the true Protestant Religion, reform the Lawes, secure our Liberties' and to restore 'Trading'.[14] Similarly, *The Free-Mens Petition* of late 1659 argued that the only way to heal 'these distracted and divided Nations and City' was through the summoning of 'a free English Parliament', 'according to the Laws of this Nation' and the Triennial Act of 1641.[15] A petition from the 'Well-Affected Householders and Freemen' of London of 8 February 1660 claimed that without 'A Free Parliament' the 'undoubted Birthright of the English Nation' and 'all Liberties, both Religious and Civil' could 'never be preserved', since legitimate authority could only be derived from 'the rightfull Representatives of the people, by whom every individual doth consent'; the petitioners wanted 'lawfull Government and Protection, According to Magna Charta and the Petition of Right'.[16] Similar sentiments were reflected in addresses sent to Monck from the provinces. The gentry of Lincolnshire in February identified their grievances as being 'The Violent Alterations of Government; the Heavy Impositions of Unheard-of Taxes', which had 'Ruined our Trade, and Impoverished the whole Nation', and 'the many Violations and Breaches made upon our Known Established Laws, and Fundamental Liberties'. 'The onely Remedy' was 'a Free Full Parliament . . . wherein the Votes of all the Free People of this Nation may be included', since only such could 'have a Legal Capacity to Enact Laws and Statutes, that may equally bind all the Free People of England'.[17] The nobility and gentry of York insisted that without either a full or free parliament, they could not be 'obliged to pay . . . Taxes', since they did not enjoy 'the Fundamentall Rights of this Nation to consent to [their] own Laws by equall Representatives'.[18]

Was the demand for a full or free parliament nevertheless an implicit call for the restoration of monarchy? After all, the original Long Parliament had had to be dramatically purged in the first place before it proceeded to try Charles I and set up a republic, and the free parliament that was to be elected in the spring of 1660 did go on to restore Charles II. It would have been risky, in the latter months of 1659, to have called explicitly for the return of monarchy, since this would have been treason—although it should be pointed out that calling for a full and free parliament at this time was also treason and petitioning for such a parliament could be a life-threatening activity. Undoubtedly there was a certain amount of tactical positioning, as those who petitioned against the army and the Rump chose to express themselves in ways which they deemed likely to be most effective. The London apprentices, in reply to the charge by the army that they were threatening the peace of the Commonwealth, insisted that they were not asking for anything which the army itself had not 'all along, even to this very day, declared to assert, procure, and maintain', namely 'our Birth-right . . . as due unto us by the Laws'.[19] Roger L'Estrange, the future government licenser of the press and crown propagandist under Charles II, published a number of anonymous pieces in 1659–60, many in the form of remonstrances and engagements purporting to have some degree of public endorsement, which he subsequently claimed testified to his royalist credentials on the eve of the Restoration; yet revealingly L'Estrange restricted himself to calling for a full parliament and in one piece even explicitly stated that a return to monarchy was 'not . . . the thing we contend for'.[20]

Support for Monck was not necessarily closet support for Charles II. Monck did not march south with the intent of restoring monarchy, and for several weeks it seemed unclear what course of action he might take. The uncertainty over which way Monck might turn meant that those who wanted Monck to get rid of the Rump had strong reasons for not wishing to appear overtly royalist, although it is clear that by early 1660 a solution to the crisis which would involve Charles II being restored to his thrones was a perceived possibility. Thus a published letter from a 'citizen' of London to Monck of 3 February 1660—possibly one of L'Estrange's 'impersonations', although not included by L'Estrange in his later published anthology of such works—stated that he was 'neither for a Commonwealth, nor Kingship, neither for Charles Stuart, nor for your self [Monck]', but for whatever could secure 'the Good, Safety, Peace, and Tranquility of the whole Nation'. 'The Poor want bread, the rich live not secure . . . the generality . . . have spent their Blood and Treasure to beggar themselves, and enrich a few', and only 'A Free Parliament', 'the Nation's undoubted Right', this writer believed, could retrieve 'our Liberties from the Grave' and redeem 'a poor Nation from Bondage'.[21]

Monck was bowing to public pressure when he forced the Rump to readmit the secluded members on 11 February and then subsequently to vote its own dissolution, initiatives that were celebrated with the roasting of rumps of 'oxen, poultry or other animals' around huge bonfires. Only now did it become safe openly to voice support for Charles Stuart: according to the Venetian resident in England, 'the citizens and soldiers spent the whole night drinking together and shouting about the streets' not only 'for a free parliament' but also 'for King Charles, whose name came openly from all lips without any fear'.[22]

Poems and songs composed at this time condemning the Rump were often explicitly pro-Charles II. 'The Devil's Arse a Peake', for example, chastised 'Foolish Britannicks' for having 'Cutt off your own Head' and urged '*Vive le Roy* let's merrily Sing / Can any Man well in his Wits, / Think worser of Charles our Noble good King, / Than those who do Govern by Fits?'[23] Yet instead of being the authentic voice of popular culture, most of these songs were Cavalier propaganda, journalistic creations that probably were never sung—an attempt to claim anti-Rump sentiment for the royalist cause, thereby hinting, perhaps, that there was doubt in Cavalier minds as to whether the mood of the people really was for the restoration of monarchy.[24] Tellingly, even the most explicitly royalist anti-Rump balladry saw the need to appeal to popular grievances or to embrace the libertarian rhetoric of the anti-army and anti-Rump petitions. Thus songs lamented how 'three Kingdoms' had been 'enslav'd and plunder'd', the Rump had ruled 'against

Customs and Laws', and soldiers 'wrack[ed] the poor out of dores', and celebrated the dissolution of the Rump as the day 'Old Magna Charta was confirm'd'.[25]

It is dangerous, then, to read history backwards and assume that because the outcome of the campaign against the army and the Rump was the restoration of monarchy, this must have been what the actors intended all along. Nevertheless, a movement which started out as being pro-parliament nevertheless came to be explicitly pro-Charles. As the monarchical solution came to appear increasingly inevitable, even those who had initially been less attracted to the idea came to support the return of Charles II. Yet among those who celebrated the downfall of the Rump, there were fundamental differences of opinion over the desired settlement that should ensue (even assuming that the vast majority did come to favour a restoration). Much of the anti-Rump balladry looked for the restoration of the old church of bishops and prayer book. One recalled how 'It was that Parliament that took / Out of our Churches our Service book'; another rhymed 'All sober Men know that 'tis a mischeivous Fate, / A Kingdome to turn into a popular State, / And Episcopacy into a Presbyterate'.[26] The London petitions of late 1659, by contrast, while somewhat vague on the desired religious settlement, did not explicitly declare for bishops and prayer book. One of 15 November, for example, called for the restoration of the religion established by 'our three last Princes, with some amendment in Discipline'.[27] That of early December emphasized the importance of encouraging and countenancing a learned ministry and 'the faithfull preaching and dispensing of Gods holy Word and Sacraments'.[28] There was certainly a violent backlash against the sects in late 1659, early 1660, and even riotous attacks on Quakers and baptists.[29] Yet mainstream English puritans, and English presbyterians and congregationalists, could be just as hostile to the sects as any Anglican. *The Humble Petition and Address of the Sea-men and Watermen* of London of late 1659, for example—which was drawn up by the famous anti-Laudian campaigner William Prynne—lamented 'the Extraordinary decay of Merchandize, Trade, Religion, Justice, Piety, and all sorts of Oppressions, Miseries, Rapines, Wars, Tumults, Sects, Heresies, Blasphemies, Alterations of Government, and destructive Confusions'.[30]

Not all welcomed the Restoration. There are abundant examples of people who got into trouble for speaking out against the return of monarchy, some going so far as to wish Charles dead and even threatening to kill him themselves. What has come down to us is doubtless just the tip of the iceberg. The survival of provincial quarter sessions records is patchy, and there are very few sessions records for the City of London prior to 1666 due to the Great Fire. Not everyone who spoke out against the restoration of monarchy ended up in court, raising the question of the relationship between reported and unreported crime, while of course it was not a criminal offence to speak out against the monarchy until the monarchy had actually been restored. Yet the fact that such speech would not have left a trace in the historical record unless it had been prosecuted also tells us something. Often the only reason why we know of cases of alleged seditious speech is because those who heard the words spoken reported them to the authorities, opening the intriguing possibility that the examples of anti-monarchical sentiment at the time of the Restoration that have left a trace in the historical record also tell us something about popular monarchism.

The only reason why we know that Thomas Blacklocke, speaking in a Southwark pub on May Day 1660, thought that 'if ever the Kinge come into England . . . he shold be hanged at the said Blacklocke's Dore' and that 'he wold helpe to hange him there himselfe' is because a sawyer, a watermen, two watermen's wives, and the wife of an oarmaker came forward to testify against him.[31]

What this type of evidence clearly does tell us is that this was a society with scores to settle, where bitter rivalries and resentments remained. In May 1660 two Kentishmen came forward to give information against George Keddell of Rolvenden, Kent, a former JP, alleging that he had been active in soliciting 'hands for the Tryall of the late King Charles' back in early 1649, had 'very much oppressed the Country where he Lives both poore and rich', and had said shortly before the proclamation of Charles II 'That hee had as leave see his owne heart Blood on the earth and his Neighbors dead at their doores As to heare a King proclaymed'.[32] In July 1660 Lincolnshire gentleman William Shepley came forward to denounce a local minister for trying to extinguish bonfires made to celebrate the proclaiming of Charles II and a local yeoman for having said back in 1650 'That it was the blessedst day that ever came to England when the Kinge was beheaded, and that hee hoped none of the whore's [i.e. Henrietta Maria's] posterity should ever reigne'.[33] Such was the climate of recrimination at this time that on 30 May Charles II found it necessary to issue a proclamation against 'Debauch'd and Prophane Persons', who, on pretence of affection for the king, spent their time in taverns drinking the king's health 'and Inveighing against all others . . . not of their own dissolute temper'.[34]

It was the sects who were most opposed to the restoration of monarchy. Shortly after Charles was proclaimed in London, the Venetian resident observed how 'Among the sectaries, i.e. the Anabaptists, Quakers and others . . . many are disconsolate and some are abusive so that arrests take place daily'.[35] Some remained die-hard republicans and were to engage in conspiracies against the government in the early 1660s.[36] Most of the separatists, however, well aware of which way the tide was turning, hastened to make their peace with the Restoration, putting their faith in the promise Charles II had made from Breda that he would guarantee liberty for tender consciences.[37]

THE RESTORATION SETTLEMENT IN ENGLAND

Ultimately, then, the vast majority of people in England came to acquiesce in the restoration of monarchy, most enthusiastically welcomed it, and large numbers were actively involved in helping to bring it about. Nevertheless, people expected different things from the restored monarch.

Constitutionally, the Restoration put the clock back to 1641, keeping on the books the reforming legislation of the early months of the Long Parliament which had abolished the prerogative courts of Star Chamber and High Commission, feudal dues such as wardship and knighthood fines, and extra-parliamentary levies such as ship money, and had tied the crown to meeting parliament at last every three years. Yet it would be wrong to infer that there was a consensus over returning to the position of 1641. A group of presbyterian peers and MPs known as 'the Knot' pressed for a conditional restoration, along the lines of the proposed Newport Treaty of 1648, which would have given parliament control over the militia and the right of appointment to all major offices of state. Others favoured a return to the monarchy of the Personal Rule. In 1660 the decision was taken that any legislation enacted that had received the royal assent, freely given, should remain on the statute books, while any that had not should be declared null and void. Since in a monarchy legislation required the royal assent, any conditions imposed on Charles II prior to his return would be vulnerable to being deemed legally invalid; on the same logic, restoring to the monarchy powers that had been legislated against in 1641 would in turn require fresh legislation. The full working out of the settlement in church and state would have to await the meeting of a parliament called by the king—and this was to be the Cavalier parliament that met in May 1661—since the Convention itself was an irregular assembly summoned before there was a king. For this reason, it was inevitable the Restoration would be a process.

Some ultra-royalists did campaign for the restoration of Star Chamber in the early 1660s, though without success. However, the Triennial Act was modified in 1664, removing the enforcement mechanism that allowed election writs to be sent out in the king's name if the king failed to call a parliament within three years (hence how Charles II was able to get by without calling a parliament in England between March 1681 and his death in February 1685). Lest there was any doubt over who controlled the power of the sword, two Militia Acts of 1661 and 1662 affirmed the sole control of the militia to be in the crown, in rejection of parliament's Militia Ordinance of March 1642. This was therefore a monarchy that retained considerable power. The king had the sole right to choose his own ministers, he determined all questions of policy, both foreign and domestic, and he could veto legislation. The major constraint was financial. Although in compensation for the loss of feudal dues Charles received the excise tax and a new tax on fireplaces set up on 1662, the revenues of the monarchy initially fell far short of those needed to meet the expenses of government, making the crown heavily dependent upon grants of parliamentary taxation.[38] It was not until the 1680s, that the more efficient collection of the excise and hearth tax and an increase in revenue from customs dues, thanks to an expansion of trade, afforded the crown the possibility of being financially independent of parliament.

Yet there was room for debate as to what type of monarchy had been restored. There could be no escaping the fact that the English had restored their parliament before they had restored their king and that Charles had been called back by an elected representative assembly. Contemporaries—even those who were eager to prove their loyalty to the new regime by denouncing those they suspected of harbouring republican sympathies—spoke of Charles II having been 'voted Kinge'.[39] The official line, however, was that Charles had been restored as a result of divine agency. In his speech to the king and members of the Convention at the Banqueting House on 29 May 1660, the speaker of the Commons Sir Harbottle Grimston (himself one of the presbyterian Knot) noted that 'the restitution' of the king to his 'most indubitable Native Right of

Soveraignty' had been 'brought to pass by a miraculous way of Divine Providence'; "'Tis God and God alone', Grimston insisted, 'to whom be that Glory'.[40] A providentialist view of the Restoration opened the door for the revival of divine-right theory, the view that kings were 'God's Vice-gerents' and 'accountable to none but God'.[41] Yet Anglicans and Cavaliers concurred that above all else the restoration of monarchy marked a return of 'our Laws, Liberties, Properties'.[42] In his coronation sermon of 23 April 1661 the bishop of Worcester George Morley insisted that the English monarchy was 'Political', 'not Despotical', that the king did not govern his subjects 'arbitrarily' but 'by Equal and Just Lawes, made with their own consent to them'.[43] The 1st earl of Clarendon, speaking in the Lords on 10 May 1661, rejoiced that 'we have our King again, and our Laws again, and Parliaments again'.[44]

The most divisive aspect of the Restoration settlement concerned the church, with the sects hoping for liberty of conscience, the presbyterians and old puritans for the return of the old pre-war church 'with some amendment in discipline', and the Anglicans for the return of bishops and prayer book. Charles II was probably sincere in professing that he wanted liberty of conscience. However, the Anglican-Cavalier gentry who dominated the parliament elected in 1661 re-established an intolerant episcopalian church. Not only was there no toleration for the sects, there were no concessions with regard to the liturgy that might have enabled presbyterians to be comprehended within a broader national church. Under the terms of the Act of Uniformity of 1662 all ministers and teachers had to testify their 'unfeigned assent and consent' to everything in the Book of Common Prayer by 24 August (St Bartholomew's Day) or face deprivation. Nearly 1,000 clergymen (about 10% of the ministry) found themselves unable to comply, and were forced to give up their livings as a result.[45] A fierce penal code was established in an attempt to keep nonconformists out of town government and away from major urban centres—the Corporation Act (1661), the Five Mile Act (1665)—and to criminalize nonconformist worship—the Quaker Act (1662), the Conventicle Acts (1664, 1670). There was considerable support for the revival of episcopacy in England, not just among the landed elite but also among more humble parish Anglicans; even the presbyterians came to acknowledge the inevitability that bishops would be restored and hoped instead for limited episcopacy (though to no avail). Measures against the sects also had widespread support. But the legislation against mainstream puritans and presbyterians proved much more controversial, and achieved only narrow majorities in the Cavalier parliament.[46]

Those who found themselves unable to conform to the established church risked heavy fines, distraint of goods, periods of imprisonment, transportation (under the 1664 Conventicle Act), even death (since large numbers were to die in jail). England became a persecuting society, although persecution tended to come in waves, depending on the threat to state security that various nonconformist groups were perceived to pose at any given time. Yet intolerance was not justified on religious grounds, as punishment for adhering to a false religion. The rationale was political. Nonconformist ministers were thought to preach resistance to divinely ordained monarchs; conventicles were feared as places where people plotted against the state.[47] The campaign against Protestant dissent, to its supporters, therefore, was no persecution, since one could only suffer persecution for doing something which God commanded; the nonconformists were being 'justly prosecuted' for disobeying the law.[48]

The church that was re-established after 1660 was not that of 1641, which by then was a church of bishops and prayer book purged of its Laudian excesses. Although the religious fault-line that emerged as England descended into civil war in 1641–2 is normally seen as being between puritans and non-Laudian Anglicans (with everyone eager to distance themselves from Archbishop Laud's reform agenda of the 1630s), the Restoration church was to contain distinctly Laudian elements. There was not a complete Laudian revival. Charles's desire for an inclusive church led him to appoint a new bench of bishops in 1660–1 that reflected a broad range of churchmanship: the diocese of Coventry and Lichfield went to the critic of Laudianism John Hacket, that of Lincoln to the conformist Calvinist Robert Sanderson, and that of Norwich to the former presbyterian Edward Reynolds. Charles even tried to persuade the famous puritan divine Richard Baxter to accept a bishopric, though Baxter declined. Yet not only were Laudians also elevated to bishoprics, they came to dominate the key positions in the church: William Juxon was elevated to Canterbury, Gilbert Sheldon to London and subsequently to Canterbury, Brian Duppa to Winchester, John Cosin to Durham. Sheldon's successor as archbishop was William Sancroft, one of a younger generation of Restoration divines who identified with a nexus of ideas that had come to influence churchmanship in the 1630s under Laud: an attachment to Arminian views on grace, strict adherence to the formularies and canons of the church, the creation of a richly ceremonial setting for divine worship, and marked hostility to puritan nonconformity. Charles was a Laudian in his devotions, and at his restoration had the chapel royal at Whitehall refitted with organs, tapestries, and a railed-in altar. The cathedrals and many college chapels followed suit in embracing Laudian-style ceremonialism and furnishings. Railed-in altars also began to be restored in local churches, with some communities even calling for those responsible for despoiling the local church 'in the late unhappy times' to be named and held accountable, although this proved a more contentious issue, and initially only a handful of parishes were prepared to back the change. The rebuilding of the London churches by Christopher Wren following the Great Fire, however, popularized railed-in altars, and by the end of the century they were both widespread and widely accepted.[49]

Yet although the presbyterians and separatists lost out, it would be wrong to see the Restoration as a clear-cut victory for the Cavalier-Anglicans. Many Cavaliers were alarmed at the moderation shown to those who had been associated with the republican regimes. The Act of Indemnity and Oblivion of August 1660, for instance, exempted a mere thirty-three individuals from the pardon, of whom only a third were executed. Particularly galling was to see many parliamentarians and former Cromwellians receive honours and office under the restored monarchy. Moreover, although many Cavaliers were able to regain lands that had been confiscated during the 1640s and 1650s (much to the resentment of their Cromwellian purchasers), nothing was done to help those who had 'voluntarily' sold their land to help the royalist cause. Disappointed

Cavaliers came to complain that the king had passed 'an act of oblivion for his friends and of indemnity for his enemies'.[50]

THE RESTORATION SETTLEMENTS IN SCOTLAND AND IRELAND

The Restoration gave Scotland and Ireland back their political independence and restored Charles as king of three separate kingdoms. Yet the respective settlements were asymmetrical. In Scotland parliament passed a sweeping Rescissory Act in March 1661, rescinding all legislation enacted from 1640, thereby putting the constitutional clock back to 1633. The logic, as with England, was that any legislation that had not received the royal assent was null and void. In contrast to the English, however, the Scots had rebelled prior to the enactment of any reforming legislation. In Scotland, therefore, the monarchy was restored to the height of its powers during the personal rule, the legislation of the Covenanter revolution undone, and presbyterianism disestablished.

Very few in Scotland had supported the regicide. The Scots had declared Charles II king immediately following the execution of his father, and they had crowned him king at Scone in January 1651. Their ideal had been a Covenanted king and they had made Charles II sign the National Covenant of 1638 and the Solemn League and Covenant of 1643 before crowning him. However, Charles II disliked presbyterianism and resented the way he had been treated by the Scots in 1651. Years of presbyterian rule had also generated an anticlerical reaction among the traditional ruling classes in Scotland, who were eager to diminish the influence of the clerical estate and to do what they could to please their restored monarch in the hope of reviving their own political and economic fortunes. In March 1661 the Scottish parliament approved legislation giving the king the right to settle a frame of church government that was 'most agreeable to the word of God, most suteable to monarchicall Government, and most complying with the publict peace and quyet of the kingdome', and in mid-August Charles II simply announced that he had decided to restore 'government by bishops, as it was by law before the late troubles'. A legislative package formally re-establishing episcopacy was enacted during the parliamentary session of 1662, and this was followed by the enactment of a fierce penal code against presbyterian dissent. Approximately one-third of the established ministry of about 952 were driven out of the church, with the south-western shires being the worst hit: in the synod of Galloway alone, thirty-four ministers were deprived in a total of just thirty-seven parishes. There was also no generalized indemnity in Scotland; when a Scottish Act of Indemnity was eventually passed in September 1662, some 700 were excluded from its provisions.[51]

In Ireland, the constitutional and ecclesiastical situation that had existed prior to the outbreak of the civil war was in essence restored. The crucial difference in Ireland, however, was the vital role played in bringing about the Restoration by those who had benefited from the Cromwellian regime. These proved willing to make compromises on the political and religious front, so long as they could keep what they had come to Ireland for in the first place, namely land. Hence in Ireland the clock was certainly not put back to 1641.[52]

Those who sat in the Irish Convention of 1660 saw the need for a state church, although there was some disagreement over whether or not an episcopalian or presbyterian settlement was preferable. When the commissioners sent to London to treat with the king learned of Charles's own preference for episcopacy, the Convention agreed that the church in Ireland should be 'resettled in Doctrine, Discipline and Worship' according to the laws in force in Ireland in Charles I's time, though 'with such Liberty to tender Consciences' as Charles II had promised in his Declaration of Breda. Charles immediately began making appointments to the vacant bishoprics and by the beginning of 1661 episcopalianism had been fully restored. Yet there was to be no formal toleration. On 22 January 1661 the king issued a proclamation declaring all meetings by papists, presbyterians, independents, and separatists illegal, while in May the newly assembled Irish parliament issued a proclamation requiring 'all persons whatsoever' to obey the laws establishing the government of the church by bishops and to conform to the prayer book. For the time being, the legal basis of the restored church remained the old Elizabethan Acts of Supremacy and Uniformity of 1560, together with the articles and canons of 1634. It was not until 1666 that the Irish parliament passed its own Act of Uniformity, based on the English Act of 1662. Yet although both Catholics and Protestant dissenters were to be excluded from full political and economic rights, in practice there was a considerable degree of *de facto* toleration.

The most contentious issue proved to be the land settlement. Those—both Protestant and Catholic—who had lost their lands in the 1640s and 1650s for supporting Charles I expected to be recompensed for their loyalty. Yet although their lands had been given in the first place to those who had supported the war effort against Charles I, many of these had in turn sold them on in the 1650s, and the new purchasers wanted to protect what they believed they had legally acquired. In an attempt to appease these competing interests, Charles issued a declaration on 30 November 1660 promising that Catholics innocent of involvement in the Irish Rebellion of 1641 would be restored to their estates and that Protestant soldiers and adventurers should be compensated ('reprised') for any of the land they had to restore to innocents, and offering land to Protestants who had served in the royal forces in Ireland before June 1649. Charles's declaration was given statutory force by the Act of Settlement of May 1662, which added further clauses in favour of particular individuals and groups. The problem was that there was simply not enough land in Ireland to satisfy all legitimate claimants, while Charles himself did not help matters by giving land taken from the regicides and Cromwellians to his brother the duke of York and courtiers like the duke of Ormonde. A court of claims set up to administer the Act's provisions heard some 800 cases, issuing 566 decrees of innocence to Catholics, 141 to Protestants, and declaring 113 Catholics 'nocent', but several thousand claims remained unheard. Finally in 1665 the Act of Explanation determined that soldiers and adventurers should hand over one-third of their land to meet the requirements of restoration and reprisal, confirmed existing decrees of innocence, but decided that no more claims would be heard, instead simply naming certain individuals who were to have full or partial restoration of their estates. Large numbers of Catholics were denied an opportunity even to have their day in court. The result was that whereas on the eve of the Irish Rebellion, Catholics had held some 66% of the land of Ireland in 1641—a figure which was reduced to less than 10% as a result of the Cromwellian confiscations—by the mid-1670s Catholics held a mere 29%. Moreover, land was concentrated in fewer hands. Thus whereas there had been 6756 Catholic landowners in 1641, there were only 1353 by the late 1660s. In short, the Restoration settlement left Catholics in possession of less than half the amount of land they had owned prior to the Irish Rebellion and reduced the number of Catholic landowners to a mere one-fifth of the pre-Rebellion total.[53] One Old English author styled the Restoration land settlement 'the greatest injustice' ever seen, with 'an innocent nation' being 'excluded from their birth-rights'. The Gaelic Irish poet David Ó Bruadair lamented how the settlement had left the Irish nobility 'all cloakless and shirtless in poverty'. Protestants, on the other hand, thought they had given up too much of their land, insisting they had invested a lot of money improving the land they had obtained and that it was therefore worth more.

CONCLUSION

Consensus was not restored after 1660 because the Restoration was not born of consensus. The longed-for stability proved elusive not because significant numbers of people never wanted the return of monarchy in the first place (though some did not), but rather because people expected different things from the restored monarch. In all three kingdoms, the Restoration ended up bequeathing a politics of resentment, as many of those who had initially rejoiced at Charles II's return came to feel betrayed by the respective settlements worked out in the separate kingdoms. Yet it was not simply that there were various groups who obviously lost out: the Protestant nonconformists (in England and Ireland), the Scottish presbyterians, the vast majority of Irish Catholics. It is not clear who the winners were. Cavalier-Anglicans in England had cause to feel frustrated that their sufferings on behalf of the royalist cause had not been sufficiently recompensed. Protestants of the established church in Ireland resented having to give back as much land as they did and felt themselves a beleaguered minority (just 10% of the population) in a country where the crown was too soft on both Protestant and Catholic dissent. Even the episcopalian interest, in both England and Scotland, came to feel undermined by Charles II's various attempts in the 1660s and 1670s to secure toleration by dint of the royal prerogative. The story of Restoration politics was to become one not only of the efforts by disappointed or disenfranchised groups, in all three kingdoms, to remedy their grievances (or, for the more extreme, to overthrow the regime that had betrayed them). It was one also of the struggles by the Cavaliers and Anglicans (and episcopalian interest north of the border) to keep the man who was supposed to be *their* king in line. It was a struggle which they did not really come to win until the years of the Tory Reaction in the 1680s, in the aftermath of the Exclusion Crisis. The victory was to be short-lived, since their vision of Cavalier-Anglican kingship was to be betrayed once more by Charles II's brother and successor, James II. It would prove to be the beginning of the end for the Stuart dynasty.

Notes

1. The National Archives [TNA], PRO SP 29/1, fos. 55, 56. I am grateful to the Andrew W. Mellon Foundation for funding a period of extended leave at the Institute for Advanced Study in Princeton, during which time I undertook the research and writing of this chapter.

2. David Underdown, *Royalist Conspiracy in England, 1649–1660* (New Haven, 1960); Geoffrey Smith, *Royalist Agents, Conspirators and Spies: Their Role in the British Civil Wars, 1640–1660* (Farnham, 2011).

3. TNA, PRO SP 29/1, fos. 54.

4. *Diurnal of Thomas Rugg*, ed. William L. Sachse, Camden Soc., third series, 91 (1961), 84.

5. *Calendar of State Papers, Venetian* [*CSPVen*], *1659–61*, 155–6.

6. Tim Harris, *Restoration: Charles II and His Kingdoms, 1660–1685* (London, 2005), 89, 105.

7. *Journals of the House of Lords* [*LJ*], XI, 7.

8. Alexander Brome (ed.), *The Rump; Or, A Collection of Songs and Ballads made upon those who would be a Parliament* (London, 1660), sig. A2.

9. *The Cock-Crowing at the Approach of a Free-Parliament* (London, 1660).

10. J. I. McGuire, 'The Dublin Convention, the Protestant Community and the Emergence of an Ecclesiastical Settlement in 1660', in Art Cosgrove and J. I. McGuire (eds.), *Parliament and Community* (Belfast, 1983), 121–46; Aidan Clarke, *Prelude to Restoration in Ireland: The End of the Commonwealth, 1659–1660* (Cambridge, 1999); Patrick Little, *Lord Broghill and the Cromwellian Union with Ireland and Scotland* (Woodbridge, 2004), 170–9.

11. British Library [BL], Add. MS 28,085, fo. 217.

12. W. D. Christie, *A Life of Anthony Ashley Cooper, First Earl of Shaftesbury. 1621–1683*, 2 vols. (1871), I, 210.

13. Tim Harris, *London Crowds in the Reign of Charles II* (Cambridge, 1987), 43–4.

14. *To the Right Honourable . . . the Lord Mayor . . . The Most Humble Petition and Address of Divers Young Men, on the Behalf of Themselves and the Apprentices in and about this Honourable City* (London, 1659).

15. *The Free-Mens Petition: To the Right Honourable, The Lord Mayor* [London, 1659].

16. *To the Right Honourable the Lord Maior . . . The Humble Petition of divers Well-affected Householders and Freemen of the said City* [London, 1660].

17. *A Letter from Divers of the Gentry of the County of Lincolne: To His Excellency the Lord General Monck* (London, 1659[/60]).

18. *A Letter and Declaration of the Nobility and Gentry of the County of York, To His Excellency the Lord Generall Monck* [London, 1660].

19. *A Vindication of the London Apprentices Petition and The Legality of their Subscriptions Asserted* (London, 1659), 4.

20. *L'Estrange His Apology* (London, 1660), 60; Mark Knights, 'Roger L'Estrange, Printed Petitions and the Problem of Intentionality', in John Morrow and John Scott (eds.), *Liberty, Authority, Formality: Political Ideas and Culture, 1600–1900* (Exeter, 2008), 125.

21. J. B., *A Letter Presented to His Excellency General Monck, By A Citizen at His Coming to London, Feb. 3 1659* [London, 1660]; Knights, 'Roger L'Estrange, Printed Petitions', 125–6, note 50.

22. *CSPVen, 1659–61*, 119.

23. 'The Devil's Arse a Peake', in Brome, ed., *Rump*, sigs. E6v, E7v.

24. Angela McShane, 'Debate: The Roasting of the Rump: Scatology and the Body Politic in Restoration England', *Past and Present [P&P]*, 196 (2007): 253–72, a corrective to Mark S. R. Jenner, 'The Roasting of the Rump: Scatology and the Body Politic in Restoration England', *P&P*, 177 (2002): 84–120.

25. 'The Rump', 'The City of London's New Letany', and 'Sir Eglamor and the Dragon', all in Brome, ed., *Rump*, 27, sigs. F7, M8v.

26. 'A Christmas Song, When the Rump was First Dissolved', in Brome (ed.), *Rump*, sig. D8; *The Rump Serv'd in with a Grand Sallet* (London, 1660).

27. *The Remonstrance of the Apprentices in and about London* (London, 1659).

28. *To the Right Honourable . . . Lord Mayor . . . The Most Humble Petition and Address of Divers Young Men.*

29. Barry Reay, 'The Quakers, 1659, and the Restoration of the Monarchy', *History*, 63 (1978): 193–213; Barry Reay, 'Popular Hostility to the Quakers in Mid-Seventeenth-Century England', *Social History*, 5 (1980): 387–407.

30. [William Prynne], *To the Right Honourable, the Lord Mayor . . . The Humble Petition and Address of the Sea-men, and Waterman, in and about the said City of London* [London, 1659].

31. House of Lords Record Office, Main Papers, 28 May 1660. For further examples of seditious words against the restored monarchy, see David Cressy, *Dangerous Talk: Scandalous, Seditious and Treasonable Speech in Pre-Modern England* (Oxford, 2010), chap. 9.

32. TNA, PRO SP 29/1, fo. 109.

33. TNA, PRO SP 29/7, fo. 27.

34. Charles II, *A Proclamation against Vicious, Debauch'd, and Prophane Persons* (London, 1660); Robert Steele, *A Bibliography of Royal Proclamations of the Tudor and Stuart Sovereigns*, 3 vols. in 2 (New York, 1967), I, 3212.

35. *CSPVen, 1659–61*, 146.

36. Richard L. Greaves, *Deliver Us from Evil: The Radical Underground in Britain, 1660–1663* (Oxford, 1986).

37. Harris, *London Crowds*, 60.

38. Paul Seaward, *The Cavalier Parliament and the Reconstruction of the Old Regime, 1661–1667* (Cambridge, 1989).

39. TNA, PRO SP 29/7, fo. 53.

40. *The Speech of Sir Harbottle Grimston . . . 29 May 1660* (London, 1660), 3–5.

41. Francis Gregory, *David's Returne from His Punishment* (Oxford, 1660), 12.

42. Gilbert Sheldon, *David's Deliverance and Thanksgiving* (London, 1660), 32.

43. George Morley, *A Sermon Preached at the Magnificent Coronation of . . . Charles the 2d* (London, 1661), 36.

44. *LJ*, XI, 248.

45. David J. Appleby, *Black Bartholomew's Day: Preaching, Polemic and Restoration Nonconformity* (Manchester, 2007).

46. Seaward, *Cavalier Parliament*, 193.

47. John Marshall, *John Locke, Toleration and Early Enlightenment Culture* (Cambridge, 2006), chaps. 3, 5; George Southcombe and Grant Tapsell, *Restoration Politics, Religion, and Culture: Britain and Ireland, 1660–1714* (Basingstoke, 2010), chap. 2.

48. George Hickes, *The True Notion of Persecution* (London, 1681), 6; Mark Goldie, 'The Huguenot Experience and the Problem of Toleration in Restoration England', in C. E. J. Caldicott, H. Gough, and J.-P. Pittion (eds.), *The Huguenots and Ireland: Anatomy of an Emigration* (Dublin, 1987), 175–203.

49. Kenneth Fincham and Nicholas Tyacke, *Altars Restored: The Changing Face of English Religious Worship, 1547–c.1700* (Oxford, 2007), chap. 8; Kenneth Fincham, ' "According to Ancient Custom": The Return of Altars in the Restoration Church of England', *Transactions of the Royal Historical Society*, 13 (2003): 29–54; Julie Spraggon, *Puritan Iconoclasm during the English Civil War* (Woodbridge, 2003), 130–1.

50. Gilbert Burnet, *The History of My Own Time*, ed. Osmund Airy, 2 vols. (Oxford, 1897–1900), I, 289. For 'the frustrations of the Cavaliers', see John Miller, *After the English Civil Wars: English Politics and Government in the Reign of Charles II* (Harlow, 2000), chap. 9.

51. Harris, *Restoration*, 106–14.

52. For the following two paragraphs, see Harris, *Restoration*, 89–94.

53. The latest figures can be found in Kevin McKenny, 'The Restoration Land Settlement in Ireland: A Statistical Interpretation', in Coleman A. Dennehy (ed.), *Restoration Ireland: Always Settling and Never Settled* (Aldershot, 2008), 39–40. See also Jane Ohlmeyer, *Making Ireland English: The Irish Aristocracy in the Seventeenth Century* (New Haven, 2012), chap. 11.

FURTHER READING

Buckroyd, Julia, *Church and State in Scotland, 1660–1681* (Edinburgh, 1980).

Clarke, Aidan, *Prelude to Restoration in Ireland: The End of the Commonwealth, 1659–1660* (Cambridge, 1999).

Dennehy, Coleman A. (ed.), *Restoration Ireland: Always Settling and Never Settled* (Aldershot, 2008).

Fincham, Kenneth and Nicholas Tyacke, *Altars Restored: The Changing Face of English Religious Worship, 1547–c.1700* (Oxford, 2007).

Greaves, Richard L., *Deliver Us from Evil: The Radical Underground in Britain, 1660–1663* (Oxford, 1986).

Harris, Tim, *London Crowds in the Reign of Charles II* (Cambridge, 1987).

Harris, Tim, *Restoration: Charles II and His Kingdoms, 1660–1685* (London, 2005).

Hutton, Ronald, *The Restoration: A Political and Religious History of England and Wales, 1658–1667* (Oxford, 1987).

Jackson, Clare, *Restoration Scotland, 1660–1690: Royalist Politics, Religion and Ideas* (Woodbridge, 2003).

Keeble, Neil H., *The Restoration: England in the 1660s* (Oxford, 2002).

Miller, John, *After the English Civil Wars: English Politics and Government in the Reign of Charles II* (Harlow, 2000).

Ohlmeyer, Jane, *Making Ireland English: The Irish Aristocracy in the Seventeenth Century* (New Haven, 2012),

Seaward, Paul, *The Cavalier Parliament and the Reconstruction of the Old Regime, 1661–1667* (Cambridge, 1989).

Southcombe, George and Grant Tapsell, *Restoration Politics, Religion, and Culture: Britain and Ireland, 1660–1714* (Basingstoke, 2010).

PART III

INSTITUTIONS AND ACTORS

CHAPTER 13

OLIVER CROMWELL

J.C. DAVIS

THE PROBLEM

WE barely know Oliver Cromwell. For all his fame and for all the ruminating on his steadfast integrity or his moral deviousness, we have insufficient reliable, unambiguous, first-hand evidence to escape the clutches of rumour and speculation. This is not to deny or undervalue the important contribution that has been made by scholars working on him in the last twenty or so years but even the most rigorous attempts to pin an incontestable understanding of 'our chief of men' to the evidence find themselves, at more or less critical moments, flirting with 'if', 'perhaps', 'it is reasonable to assume', and 'it may be that'. The 'would have' school of biography has had a long run in Cromwell studies.

The problem has a number of dimensions. The archival record is patchy. Before he reaches the age of forty we feed off scraps and even for critical phases such as that determining the fate of the English republic and the emergence of the Protectorate (September 1651 to December 1653) there is no personal correspondence. Then again, perceptions of Cromwell in his own time and since have been highly contested. His deeds, achievements, and failures ensure that he remains a controversial figure. The editions of his 'own' words—letters and speeches (often recorded by others and, in the case of more official correspondence, most likely penned by others)—have, until the present, been unsatisfactory.[1] Those words that we can take as authentic are often opaque, presenting different facets of a complex personality to different audiences or to the same audience in different situations. Among his words are a number of highly quotable and almost instantly recognizable phrases, fertile with the sense that they convey something of the real man. But those brilliant moments of illumination lurch out of the shadows at us leaving the nagging suspicion that the darkness may still contain some key we have not only not grasped but of whose existence we remain—and possibly will remain—uneasily unaware.

The new critical edition of Cromwell's letters and speeches, which is currently in progress, offers the prospect of having at last a bedrock of his authenticated words and their contexts. But it would be too much to expect the problems of understanding Cromwell to be thereby eliminated. Compared, for example, with an ancient letter writer and orator like Cicero, the Cromwellian harvest of first-person documentation looks sparse and bitty.[2] For all their limitations, these pathways into Cromwell's mind have been assiduously explored and, in the last two decades, the results have been some impressive biographical essays. But they remain essays. Accordingly, a sense has grown in recent years that the biographical approach, based on close reading of Cromwell's own words, insofar as we have them, is exhausted.[3]

In response we have seen a renewed resort to less direct evidence, sources other than Cromwell's own words. Given that a considerable part of what we might credibly wish to say about any major historical figure has to be expressed with reservations, we can still point to areas where the balance of probability has been productive of a new consensus or has moved the debate in new directions. John Morrill's penetrating and influential re-examination of the early life[4] gave us a real sense of the fragility of Cromwell's social status down to at least 1636. His political humiliation on the small stage of his home town, Huntingdon, in 1630 led him in his early thirties to sell up what was a relatively mean estate for a gentleman and become a tenant farmer in St Ives.[5] We can agree with Morrill that by the end of 1639, and entering his forties, he had become 'a radicalized puritan'[6] but certainty evaporates when we try to date his conversion or spiritual rebirth. Was it a decade earlier in 1628–9[7] or did his apparent attempt in 1635 to have his wealthy, maternal uncle declared a lunatic, in order to secure his own inheritance from him, precipitate a spiritual crisis resulting in conversion (or perhaps even a second conversion)? Here agreement runs out and sceptics doubt that he ever acted against his uncle.[8] The probability of his extempore preaching among the East Anglian godly, voiced over seventy years ago by Abbott, now seems to be generally accepted.[9] We now know, with a fair degree of certainty, that he became MP for Cambridge in 1640 as the result of smart, quick-footed action by a godly clique of otherwise obscure individuals rather than as a result of aristocratic patronage.[10] Interesting work has also been done on Cromwell's relationship with money. The greed that may have been reflected in his 1635 action against his uncle (if that took place) seems anything but typical.[11] For a man with considerable family responsibilities, he showed a surprisingly casual, open-handed, even restless, attitude to personal finance which might have typified a gambler were it not more likely a reflection of his reliance on providence.[12] Rather than an inept blunderer in the pre-war Long Parliament, Cromwell is now to be seen as an effective and resolute front man for godly petitioners, an emerging presence in committees, relations between the two Houses, and in the Commons itself.[13] Recent work on his military career has stressed his outstanding capacity as a recruiter of men and, in some cases and not so convincingly, called into question the extent of his military reputation.[14] As a mature politician, we have been advised to take his radicalism more seriously and a considerable case has been made for his having a more collaborative relationship with the Levellers, at least until 1649, than had been thought to be the case.[15] Equally, the whole notion of a 'Cromwellian settlement' in Ireland has been called into question. Rather, the Protector has been shown to be a mitigator of the harshness and rigour of that settlement.[16] The character of the Protectorate itself has become another controversial area as a result of new work and revised assessments. On the one hand, it has been suggested that Cromwell manipulated the system virtually at will, surrounding himself with effective but malleable and dependent councillors.[17] An extreme version of this is the argument that the offer of the crown to Cromwell in 1657 was an elaborate confidence trick orchestrated by John Thurloe, his secretary, and in the promotion of which he and Cromwell acted as one.[18] On the other hand, the constitutionality of his behaviour, limited by both Council and parliament, during the Protectorate, whether under the Instrument of Government or the Humble Petition and Advice, has been emphasized. In this view, it is rather compliance, verging on passivity, and frustration which typify Cromwell's experience as the 'single person'.[19]

It remains, nevertheless, the case that attempts to read Cromwell's life using words other than his own have so far had mixed results, hedged with conditionality. For example, the claim that the progressive development of a 'monarchical' culture was a feature of the Protectorate from which we might read some aspects of Cromwell's political thinking and that of his opponents[20] has been met with some scepticism[21] and the provisional nature of the findings of even the most skilful of its advocates has been revealing. Reliance on words other than Cromwell's own often leads to increased recourse to 'likelihood', 'may', 'probably', 'must have', and 'seems rather less improbable'.[22] At the end of one of the most impressive recent investigations of the sources around Cromwell, rather than directly by him, Andrew Barclay concluded that none of the arguments based on one of his key sources could 'be presented with any certainty'.[23]

Despite the advances recently made, we still know frustratingly little about his childhood, youth, marriage, and domestic life; about the extra-scriptural furnishing of his mind; as we know agonizingly little about his involvement in the army's seizure of the king or the events leading up to Pride's Purge, the precise motivation for his dramatic expulsion of the Rump, or the precise way in which his mind worked over the issue of kingship and his refusal of it. Accordingly, in too many cases we become reliant on supposition or context. We may not know much about his childhood but we know something about childhood in the period—and so on. In too many accounts the general has to do business for the particular—even though it is a particular and, in key respects, an unusual individual in whom we are interested.

ASSESSMENT AND ITS CHALLENGES

Assessment is then a slippery business but we exacerbate the problem either by resorting to anachronistic standards or by judging him in terms of moral standards rendered inappropriate by being those of his enemies/friends. But moral judgement is not only hostage to partisanship or the imposition of our own moral standards. It is also prey to the assumption such assessments require that Cromwell was a free agent, with unimpeded choice between the 'right' and the 'wrong' options. Indeed, he has frequently been pictured as someone so free that his moments of apparent 'hesitation' require immediate explanation and may not be taken as moments when a politician faces limited options, often not of his own choosing, options which, with their possible consequences, have to be weighed carefully in the balance before an irrevocable decision is reached. Finally, there is the problem that when we have made our moral assessments our understanding of Cromwell has barely been advanced if at all. As we shall see shortly, Cromwell's own self-assessment could be more devastatingly critical than almost anything written since.

The focus of assessment has commonly been on the observance or breach of rules, be they moral, military, legal, or constitutional, to the neglect of the political figure for whom negotiation, compromise, and circumscribed room for manoeuvre were inescapable essentials. In that sense, Cromwell the warrior and regicide gets in the way of Cromwell the politician. He seldom justified himself in terms of his scrupulosity with regard to the rules whatever they might have been. His justifications came most commonly by way of his instrumentality in the hands of a God who was himself a breaker of rules, apparently indifferent to human laws and constitutions.[24] In one of his own, most dramatic self-assessments, bemoaning his lack of freedom of action, he depicted himself as a front man for others and a 'drudge upon all occasions', someone who had negotiated away his own agency (A, IV, 417). It would be hard to find a more devastating assessment of his record but it is also one which implies that much of his politics involved collaborating with and accommodating others. Elsewhere, Cromwell identified himself as consistently struggling for religious and civil liberty (A, IV, 705). The more we look at those causes in his life the more we see that they were intertwined and repeatedly subjects both for negotiation and of frequent frustration for Cromwell. In other words, forceful as he was capable of being, Cromwell also had to engage with others through processes of negotiation and not infrequently the results appear less than congenial to him. Polarizing the man of principle and the sinuous politician, or the God-driven saint versus the calculating operator[25] is to miss this essence of Cromwell the politician.

If it is time to put aside, as too partisan or too simplistic and anachronistic, the moral assessment of Cromwell, we may still be left with two Cromwells in tension one with another. On the one hand, he may be the tough-minded hardliner who engaged in an all-out attack on his military commander, the earl of Manchester, or who ruthlessly crushed the Levellers, who, in the end almost by force of personality, engineered the death of the king, who forcefully and energetically suppressed the Irish and subdued the Scots, and who had the capacity (putting it delicately) to be brusque with parliaments and judges. On the other hand, we are also dealing with a man of firm religious convictions in an intolerant age who, nevertheless, sought some sort of accommodation with presbyterians (A, I, 509), Quakers (A, I, 309, 440; III, 638–9), Fifth Monarchists (A, III, 606), even with Anglicans (A, I, 501; III, 714; IV, 69, 102, 122) and, on a *de facto* basis with Catholics;[26] or with the regicide who sought to reconcile those who had no stomach for king-killing; with the man who could show some measure of generosity towards ex-royalists; the general who, while insistent on military discipline, engaged in debate with his troops, listened to their criticism and even attended to their prayerful leading. Are these two Cromwells—the hardliner and the accommodator—reconcilable?

To redress the balance, bringing the political to the fore, context is, as usual, all important. There are three contextual dimensions to be stressed here. The first is that of the aspiration to a godly society which inevitably involved the virtually inextricable mix of religion and politics. Second, the dispersed nature of the distribution of authority, responsibility, and decision-taking in the early modern state meant that authority was always mediated, brokered, and subject to the complicity (or its absence) of unpaid office-holders and high rates of participation by heads of households in office-holding.[27] The third dimension is an extension of this. In the substantial absence of a full-time paid bureaucracy, of party machines and of coercive capacity on a sustained basis, early modern politics, administration, and even war were to a large extent matters of negotiation and the creation, maintenance, and reconfiguration of loose coalitions.[28]

NEGOTIATION, COALITION, AND POLITICAL CONTEXT

It may be true that all politics is coalition politics, but, in a world without, and indeed with an abhorrence of, party and party discipline, such coalitions become both more necessary and more unstable. In other words, the necessity of negotiation, persuasion, and compromise become all the more pressing.[29] Early Stuart England lacked a bureaucracy or effective coercive power, and so the legitimate sovereign had to wait upon the unpaid office-holders of the counties, hundreds, parishes, and boroughs who made up the effective fabric and authority of the early modern state. A live-and-let-live attitude, punctuated by occasional flashes of coercive bullying and outright violence on either side, plus the subversion of central authority by lethargy of response, silent non-compliance, or wilful ignorance as modes of 'resistance' was by no means untypical of the monarchy's exercise of sovereignty. The attempt to use the King's Council as a goading, quasi-coercive overseer of the local implementation of policy was hard to sustain for any length of time.[30] Nevertheless, the use of prerogative instruments in a systematic and sustained way to monitor, cajole, and rebuke by Charles I in the 1630s was sufficiently threatening as to be regarded as 'tyrannical'. Given the opportunity, an essentially conservative parliament embraced a revolution bringing the system underpinning the personal rule down,[31] precipitating a civil war which was both about the terms on which 'normal' politics could be restored and the engine productive of military, fiscal, and religious forces which would exacerbate the difficulties of doing precisely that. At the same time, the royal establishment had to abandon its 'normal' terms of negotiation both because its fiscal base and credit worthiness were now dependent on parliament and because these and its military incapacity had been laid bare in the Bishops' Wars. Here was the 'dissolution of government' which James Harrington saw as the cause of the Britannic civil wars. But the wartime absence of a 'normal' centre of power/authority underwrote the already pervasive sense that these things were all about negotiation and coalitions of the willing or the persuaded.[32] That perspective was further developed and enhanced by the quest for peace. So that, within as well as between the warring coalitions, negotiation was a continuing multiplicity of processes. The dimensions of those processes were further complicated as the victorious found their wartime coalitions falling apart over the vexed question of what to do with their victory. In the absence of formal party discipline, oaths might be used to engender some sort of subscriptional cohesion but their limited success threw serious politicians back on the negotiation, renegotiation, generation, maintenance, and salvaging of fragile alliances or coalitions.

The politics of the 1640s and 1650s were then essentially premised on negotiation either between sides or within sides, negotiations whose foci and fronts shifted with alarming rapidity as circumstances changed. The price of any kind of political leverage was the successful and sustained negotiation of groups of supporters. Those who ceased to negotiate came to an abrupt end as political actors, as did Essex, Holles, Fairfax, and Charles I. Civil war engendered competing minority governments, competing for access to resources, men, and money, the sinews of war, which others controlled. Stopping the cycle of violence in an international and domestic context required negotiation, as did the management of violence itself, of armies and their grievances, and of volatility, of sieges and terms of surrender, of suppliers and civilian authorities, of the treatment of disabled soldiers, widows, and orphans, of indemnity for one's own soldiers and fair treatment of the enemy's. New to the 1640s was the use of the press to influence leverage in, and the terms of, negotiation.[33] Negotiation was so central to the politics of the period, from the XIX Propositions to the Newport Treaty and beyond, that it is tempting to see the civil wars as negotiation by other means.

Cromwell's Early Political Career in Context

The most basic survey of Cromwell's political career can be used to illustrate the growing importance of this dimension of seventeenth-century politics to him. A standard image of him before the age of forty has been that of a rather blundering, black-versus-white, holy warrior whose ineptitude and unwillingness to compromise cost him his standing in Huntingdon, for which he had been MP in 1628, and led to his exile and reduced social status in St Ives. Even so, there are examples in his early correspondence of the negotiator (A, I, 80–1). In the later 1630s, the inheritance of his almost estranged uncle's estate brought him into some sort of working relationship with the episcopal authorities of Ely despite his aversion to the religious policies of the bishop, Matthew Wren, and this must have involved some delicate, if undocumented, negotiation. On the other hand, his election as MP for Cambridge to both the Short and Long Parliaments in 1640 was an investment in him as an uncompromising spokesman against the Laudian establishment and the likes of Matthew Wren. In the Long Parliament he began to collaborate with a coalition engineered by men senior to himself among whom were several of his kinsmen and godly contacts. He may have been a junior member of that coalition but as an active committee man, manager of the presentation of petitions to the House, and go-between in relations between the two Houses negotiation was his milieu. He was even more active in what was essentially work of coalition building and maintenance after the 1641 recess.[34] The importance of cohesion and its fragility in relation to, for example, the Grand Remonstrance, mounting disorder outside of parliament and the Irish insurrection was manifest. While he may have been one of a small group of men who welcomed civil war, 1642–3 saw him negotiating with local office-holders and local committees for a war effort[35] and his dependence on their responses often left him in a state of near panic.[36] Cromwell's ability to recruit tended to outstrip the logistical and financial support which was in the hands of others (for examples see A, I, 211, 212, 213, 217, 218, 221, 228–9, 247, 249, 253). Backing the Protestation, a formulation of subscriptional coalition, he argued that 'combination carries strength with it; its dreadful to adversaries'.[37] But if civil war was a shattering of his political innocence,[38] it was also, in a sense, a shattering of religious innocence. If the price of a quality fighting force was a conscientious army with an ecumenical approach to recruitment and promotion, it was soon apparent that one cost of this would be ceaseless negotiation between the fractious godly and prayerful attempts at reconciliation which would not always be successful (A, I, 258, 277–8, 377).[39]

When a Scots Covenanting army of 21,000 men entered England in 1644 it was the largest single force of the 1640s and for a while it threatened to make the Scots dominant in their alliance with the English. As a member of the newly formed Committee of Both Kingdoms, Cromwell was soon aware of this. Debates ensued over war aims, over the price for the Scots alliance, and over what form of religious settlement would satisfy the conditions of the Solemn League and Covenant. The ecumenical approach to recruitment and promotion was under pressure and signs of a Scots/presbyterian will to impose a settlement raised the question of which elements in the coalition would triumph in the event of a parliamentary victory. Inevitably, this had consequences for the prosecution of the war by, among others, both Manchester and Cromwell.[40] The resultant breakdown of negotiations internal to the parliamentary coalition, which we know as the Manchester quarrel,[41] was resolved by a negotiated compromise,[42] the Self Denying Ordinance, the formation of the New Model Army, and a defining moment in Cromwell's political maturation.[43]

The growing ascendancy of the New Model Army in 1645 and 1646 did not end these tensions as the Commons' censoring of Cromwell's reports after the battle of Naseby and the fall of Bristol bear witness. Cromwell clearly saw the army itself as a coalition offering an example to the parliamentary alliance in general (A, I, 377–8, 677).[44] A successful army proved politically and financially costly, generating a deeply fissured coalition held together only by the necessity to achieve outright victory. That outcome brought fragmentation. It was the presbyterians, led by Holles, who at that victorious moment, turned their backs on the wartime coalition. They sought to break the political influence and reduce the costs of the army while seeking a settlement with the defeated king.

Significantly, Cromwell's first response was to take on the role of mediator. To maintain the wartime coalition, the army must obey parliament but its reasonable grievances must also be met. In March 1647 at Saffron Walden he was urging the army to compliance with parliament. Still in November at Putney his line was that 'the considering of what is fitt for the Kingedom does belonge to the Parliament'.[45] Across this period and under considerable duress and a dawning awareness that there were serious limits to army obedience, Cromwell was 'working to prevent the parliamentarian movement from disintegrating'.[46] His main political goal remained coalition maintenance. Indeed his involvement in and support of the Heads of Proposals can be seen as an attempt at national settlement by broadening that coalition and offering something to the army, parliament, the king and his supporters and even to radicals like the Levellers.[47] The king's intransigence, his final preference for a deal with the Scots and the fear of army indiscipline put paid to that prospect.

Faced with insurrection in Wales and the threat of a Scots invasion in favour of a Covenanted Charles I, Cromwell's immediate task, in 1648, was to hold together any usable coalition and to regenerate army unity. After the officers' prayer meeting at Windsor in late March and early April,[48] that looked likely to be at the price of serving justice on Charles I, 'that man of blood'. Nevertheless, Cromwell found time amidst his military efforts to attempt to bring independents and presbyterians together in a common ecclesiastical policy.[49] Despite his victory at Preston, efforts were renewed to find a negotiated settlement and to preserve or renew a broader coalition but to no avail.[50] While he lamented the failure of 'union and right understanding' (A, I, 677), he recognized that 'If we cannot bring the army to our sense, we must go to theirs.'[51] The last-ditch effort to save the king's life and the House of Lords, and thereby preserve something of the wider coalition, was always compromised by the king's intransigence and growing distrust of his reliability. Most critically these two factors had pushed the army to the limits of subordination and a prospect which haunted Cromwell from 1647 and even more strongly from 1648–9 was of a purely political army, liberated to impose its own settlement by force with the attendant risk of renewed civil war and anarchy.

After the politically costly purge of parliament, the emergence of the Rump and the regicide, it was Cromwell who led the attempt to reconcile as many as possible to the new regime, to rebuild a broader coalition. 'His instincts were to do everything possible to broaden the basis of support for the embattled regime, opening the doors to anyone willing to walk through them.'[52] The ideal of limited reform, not revolution, was reflected in the eventual composition of the Rump and the Council of State and owed much to Cromwell's influence. The threat from Ireland and Scotland was dealt with by the forceful establishment of English control and, in both theatres, Cromwell played a leading part. What is striking, however, is the degree to which he sought to maintain control on the basis of a broader coalition in both countries throughout the 1650s.[53] Meanwhile, the Rump responded to the successes of Cromwell and the army in what was an increasingly frustrating manner. Dilatory on reform, obstructive of Cromwell's attempts to reconcile moderate former royalists,[54] at times the frustration verged on personal humiliation.[55] Even so, he continued to hold meetings in quest of a consensual approach to the republic's problems.[56] However inexplicable the expulsion of the Rump in April 1653, it remains the case that the day before that dramatic explosion of frustration Cromwell had still been attempting a negotiated way forward.[57] In conversation with Bulstrode Whitelocke in November 1652, his aim, he said, had been 'to unite our Counsels, and Hands and hearts, to make good what we have so dearly bought'. Instead they had 'Jarrings and Animosities one against another'; the triumph of 'private Janglings'. How, he wondered, could parliament be restrained? (A, II, 588–9). These are the words of a seeker of consensus, a coalition builder, and Cromwell was to continue down that path in the years ahead. The alternatives to negotiation, as he had realized some years before, were bleak and violent, with the potential for further civil conflict and anarchy (A, I, 599).

From the coup of April 1653, through the experiment of the Nominated Assembly and on to the emergence of the Protectorate, Cromwell sought an institutional framework which would facilitate stable government by a broader coalition than merely that of the military and/or the religious zealots. A case in point is the quest for an inclusive religious settlement.[58] More generally, negotiation went on to avoid a situation in which the army would be called upon to impose ever more unpopular policies at even greater fiscal and political cost. Both before and after 1653 there is a consistency and continuity in Cromwell's stubborn persistence in seeking to resolve differences and negotiate a broader coalition than the one he was operating with.[59]

NEGOTIATION AND PROTECTORAL CHOICE

The choice facing Cromwell after the ousting of the Rump in April 1653 and the surrender of authority to him by the Nominated Assembly in December 1653 was whether to impose peace by force of arms or to make peace by building a civilian coalition to which government might be entrusted. The problem has been unacknowledged by many of his critics past and present.[60] John Milton and Marchamont Nedham, for instance, supported the expulsion of the Rump but were dismayed at Cromwell's apparently waning interest in the kind of radical reform which because of its minority support would have to be imposed by force. The dilemma was that, on the one hand and in the most difficult of circumstances, Cromwell chose to negotiate a new coalition rather than rely on military force,[61] the *sine qua non* of imposing reform on a war weary and essentially conservative nation. On the other hand, could such a 'conservative' coalition be engineered while allowing some scope for liberty of conscience and some aspects of civil and legal reform?

The narrower the coalition, the more imposing it would have to be.[62] The broader the coalition, the more healing and settling could be made a real prospect but the harder it would be to sustain, since the more diverse the elements which had to be contained and kept on board. At its most intransigent, after 1647 there were no guarantees that an aggrieved army would not turn on its political masters. Cromwell devoted considerable energy to managing this problem, from his weekly meetings with officers in London, to tolerating Fleetwood's and Lambert's disruption of the work of his deputies in Scotland and Ireland.[63] As we have seen, he was prepared to go to considerable lengths to win back the allegiance of former allies, like Ludlow (A, IV, 45–7, 220–2), or by talking to malcontents and those among the disgruntled saints who might stir them to action.[64] When his son, Henry, was wearied by the constant sniping of the discontented, Oliver responded with the enduring faith of the coalition builder: 'Time and patience may work them to a better frame of spirit, and see that which, for the present, is hid from them... ' (A, IV, 26; see A, IV, 740 for him still trying to conciliate army officers in early 1658).

So Cromwell blenched at the narrow coalition option and its implications and consistently tried for the broadest, sustainable alternative. But the dilemma remained: while winning new supporters, how could he keep the old ones on board as they saw their rivals achieve positions of inclusion and influence?[65] For Cromwell then, the mid-1650s were arguably not a period of quasi-monarchical triumph so much as a period of endlessly frustrating and often bruising negotiation with old allies (including Ludlow, Hutchinson, Lilburne, Fifth Monarchists, Quakers, army colonels, and councillors like Lambert and Fleetwood) and enemies alike (examples at A, III, 119, 125, 225, 373, 504, 546, 606–10, 639; IV, 45–6, 221–2, 230, 309). The task was made even more daunting by the aspiration to a Britannic coalition which could stabilize the archipelago, prepare it for godliness and a form of wider Protestant imperialism while preserving some of the moderate achievements of the 'English revolution'. To some extent this meant offsetting the attempts, or perceived attempts, of others to form counter-coalitions opposed to the Protectorate.[66] In other respects, it meant repeated appeals for reconciliation and union.

To the Nominated Assembly that appeal was in the call for 'respect unto all, though of different judgements' (A, III, 62). The Instrument of Government, with its roots in the Heads of Proposals, was intended to provide an institutional framework with wide appeal (A, III, 435–8). Its 'fundamentals' were few and, for the rest, it was open to debate.[67] Even the Major Generals can be read as a misguided attempt to appeal to the godly minorities of the counties while reducing the cost and tax burden of the military establishment. Their abandonment was a reversion to the quest for a wider basis of potential support.[68] To his second protectoral parliament he appealed for 'a common head' against the dangers besetting them (A, IV, 270). This was indeed a coalition speech in which he described his desired relationship with the members as 'an union, really it is an union, between you and me, and both of us united in faith and love to Jesus Christ, and to his peculiar interest in the world, that must ground this work' (A, IV, 277). Part of the appeal of the Humble Petition and Advice was that it came with a ready-made civilian coalition. Lord Broghill, its principal patron, was, like Cromwell, a broker of political alliances.[69] Oliver's justification for rejecting the offer of the crown was, in part, that it threatened the hard-won unity of honest, godly men. He begged the committee waiting on him to 'have a tenderness, even if possibly it be to their weakness'. A better path to unity was 'complying, indulging and being patient unto the weaknesses and infirmities of men that have been faithful' (A, IV, 472). This was the straining point of the old coalition, just as much as accepting the crown might be a defiance of providence. 'I would not that you should lose a friend for it' (A, IV, 474).

In retrospect we can see that this was a naive hope. Friends were lost by Oliver's refusal. In his speech to MPs on 25 January 1658 we hear the hand-wringing over lost hopes but also the last hurrah of the coalition ideal. The country was 'full of calamities and divisions'. That 'consistency and agreement' that had been required of parliament had not been forthcoming. Without their agreement, growing military arrears faced England, Scotland, and Ireland with the prospect of free-quarter in all three countries. 'I pray God… give you one heart and mind… ' 'Let us have one heart and soul, one mind to maintain the honest and just rights of this nation… ' Without such consensual politics the future was dismal. 'Dissension, division, destruction… if we return again to folly let every man consider if it be not like to our destruction' (A, IV, 716, 718, 719–20). It was too late.

Of course, the Protectorate's failure can be read as Cromwell's; his lack of political skill or finesse, his choice of the wrong allies. But that case has yet to be convincingly made. Like every negotiator Cromwell had his red lines, the points beyond which there was no compromise. There could be no defying of, or consorting with those who defied providence (for example, A, I, 621). There must be liberty for tender consciences and this must extend to the weakest of God's saints and even to passive and loyalist Anglicans and Catholics (A, II, 104; III, 590; IV, 472). On the other hand, liberty of conscience was not to be stretched to the denial of the divinity of Christ or blasphemy (A, III, 834). And there could be no public celebration of the mass, nor proselytizing by Roman Catholics (A, II, 146, 202). Clerical dominance in religious and civil life was to be ended, along with the distinction between clerical and lay (A, II, 325, 335, 340). There should be successive parliaments, not sitting permanently. Reform of the law should be a priority (A, III, 6). Cromwell was explicit and remarkably consistent about each of these so that the question arises as to whether he was too inflexible, not pliable enough about them. There is a balance then in Cromwell's politics which may not simply be reduced to ambition versus principle. He never saw himself as a stickler for fine detail; not one glued and wedded to forms. In August 1650 he wrote to the General Assembly of the Kirk of Scotland urging them to read Isaiah 28 verses five to fifteen with its scorn for the clerically minded for whom religion was a matter of 'precept upon precept; line upon line, line upon line; here a little, and there a little' (A, II, 307). But the escape from formality[70] was never an abandonment of principle. The red lines remained.

In this reading the singular importance of Cromwell, and indeed his status as a major political player in the English revolution, does not rest on his military accomplishments. Plenty of others—Fairfax, Lambert—were arguably as accomplished. Military standing gave him 'weight' but it was what he did with it which distinguishes him from the ruck of New Model warriors and indeed from the majority of scattered and divided, single-focus politicians. The importance of Cromwell is as a coalition builder, an early modern politician caught up in a bitterly divisive civil war who yet sought reconciliation, 'healing and settling', to make rather than to impose peace. For a poet like Edmund

Waller, he was a bridge builder, moderator, mediator, promoting union over faction, consolidation after conquest.[71] A major consequence of Cromwell's coalition building activities was that they provided material not only for admirers but also for those hostile to him. The negotiator was all too easy to identify as the Machiavellian schemer bent on personal aggrandizement. The problem which persists[72] with the latter approach is that of explaining the opportunities to increase his personal power and influence which Cromwell shunned or neglected—for instance on his triumphant return from the battle of Worcester, after the expulsion of the Rump, or when offered the crown by parliament. For contemporaries committed to their version of the cause (Lilburne, Ludlow) or lacking his interest in a solution which would reconcile all, friends and, to some extent, foes (Vane, Milton, Nedham, Baxter) Cromwell could be seen, as coalitions and their terms shifted, as frustrating or betraying their hopes. Their appraisals should be treated with caution as either failing to grasp what he was about or unwilling to acknowledge the consequences of the abandonment of his project.

Reputational Consequences

The two Cromwells are then, not the man of integrity versus the manipulative and deceitful politician but, on the one hand, the negotiator, conciliator, reconciler, and coalition builder, and on the other, the man whose 'red lines' as a negotiator obliged him, in extremis, to resort to coercive and disciplinary means. But those red lines are what give him the appearance of an honourable integrity and prompt the admiration of 'principled' commentators. They may, nevertheless, be what ultimately cost him his best hope of achieving a broader settlement. We should not, however, be too ready to assume the inevitability of this in either an English or a Britannic context. Had he, for example, been willing to abandon the cause of liberty of conscience might a firm coalition with presbyterians and moderate episcopalians, such as that achieved by his successor, have proved more sustainable? Recent work on Cromwell's parliaments has stressed the willingness of English, Scots, and Irish communities to engage with them. His persistence, despite the frustrations, with representative government can be seen as the maintenance of a forum for national and Britannic negotiation. The endorsement of conciliar ordinances for union of the three kingdoms by parliamentary legislation was vigorously promoted by Irish and Scots members and frustrated only by parliamentary timetables and the priority given by English members to debates on other constitutional matters. The current consensus is that Cromwell's parliaments came closer to uniting the three kingdoms and engaging communities throughout them than has hitherto been acknowledged. It may have been the prospect of Richard Cromwell's building on that partial success, rather than his weakness, which precipitated the army coup against him which brought the Protectorate down.[73]

Recent work has again laid emphasis on honour as a key value for those on either side in the civil wars and, indeed, even for turncoats.[74] Thomas Hobbes, so often identified as the expounder of a politics driven by fear, saw the three great determinants of a political culture as honour, fear, and profit and in that order.[75] But Cromwell's political lexicon is almost devoid of the language of honour. The exception (and it is a narrow one) is military honour involving the observance of the articles of war and surrender.[76] For the writers of the new vogue of prose romances all characters, except Cromwell, were struggling to maintain or regain their personal honour.[77] In his post-Restoration critique of the Protectorate, Slingsby Bethel, pointed scorn at the Protector not only for his misconceived foreign policy but for his willingness to ignore the demands of honour.[78] But honour, as those who negotiated with the devious Charles I came to realize, induced inflexibility and brought negotiation to an end. The potential violence of early modern political culture and social life, from the duel to aristocratic rebellion, had much to do with honour. The ideal of modern liberal politics has been depicted as a 'reasonable pluralism', the establishment of which is dependent on negotiation to establish overlapping consensus.[79] In that sense, did Cromwell, with his lack of interest in honorific codes and pursuit of the broader coalition, represent a new politics; one which appealed not to honour but to the negotiation of common ground and the pursuit of common interests?

It has been suggested that the reconciliation which Cromwell sought to achieve in the 1650s was an impossible reconciliation of incompatible elements, a coalition too far.[80] Certainly, collaborative rapprochement between parliament, the army, and the godly was difficult to achieve. Maintaining the army was expensive and unpopular with parliament; the majority of MPs wanted a return to religious discipline and conformity, while key players in the military were implacably opposed to the forcing of tender consciences. Cromwell's persistence in attempting to bridge these gaps worried both his secretary, John Thurloe, and his son, Henry.[81] But the costs of abandoning the attempt were also potentially substantial. Any imposed, or non-consensual, settlement meant a military settlement. Could this be achieved without further expansion and professionalization of the New Model Army, increasing fiscal and logistical demands, and the new modelling of the state to meet those demands; in other words, the sweeping away of the old regime's monarchical (or unacknowledged) republic and its replacement by something more approximate to a modern centralized, bureaucratic, and militarized state?

In this context, Cromwell looks more like a tragic than a tyrannical figure. Revolution was impossible without tyranny as understood in the seventeenth century and Cromwell proved not to have the stomach for that kind of revolution. Reconciliation—healing and settling—depended on the good will and ability to compromise of others as well as of himself. In his political maturity, he was a non-revolutionary in the sense that he wanted to negotiate with the establishment rather than destroy it. In the end that establishment's key representative made that impossible. But, disrupted as it might be, for Cromwell the negotiation went on.[82] He was radical in the sense that he always wanted to negotiate with the establishment on his terms not theirs although in his support for the Heads of Proposals terms were stretched in the direction of the establishment as far as they were ever likely to go.

CONCLUSION

Twenty years ago, Conrad Russell identified three long-term causes of instability underpinning the dissolution of Stuart government: managing multiple kingdoms, maintaining confessional unity in the face of plurality of religions, and the generation of a military/fiscal state.[83] Under the Protectorate only the first of these had been brought under what was beginning to look like stable management through a combination of military force and negotiated coalitions. Religion may have looked as if it were settling but remained unstable. Cromwell approached the military/fiscal problem by cutting taxation and reducing the armed forces but he could not achieve the latter fast enough to keep up with the former.[84] Consequently, he bequeathed a debt crisis to his son but it is worth noting George Monck's advice to Richard: essentially, broaden your coalition base by identifying your rule with 'those of power and interest among the people'.[85] Ironically Oliver may, in his last years, have been seeking to unwind what elements of a military fiscal state had been achieved since 1642, thus anticipating the military and foreign policy weaknesses of the restored Stuarts. In religious terms, the Restoration alternative to Cromwellian 'license' was repression and persecution sponsored by the parliamentary classes with whom Cromwell had found it so difficult to negotiate.

Whatever we make of his achievements and failures, it is clear that Cromwell did not engineer a coalition wide and stable enough to make 'healing and settling' a sustainable reality.[86] After him, British politics came to be dominated by division and adversarial antagonism such that opposition had finally to be institutionalized. In making and sustaining such alliances honour has to be at a discount. In this world, the sticklers for their honour, like Charles I, come to a more or less sticky end.[87] Cromwell the soldier was sensitive to the observance of terms negotiated, of military honour. Equally, divine providence would always determine outcomes. But God's chosen instruments had to recognize His freedom of choice. His instruments were diverse as were their commissions and the saint had to respect this. So politics for Cromwell was, under God's overall determining, not about honour so much as closing the deal, winning over others, and forging or renewing alliances, above all in appealing to the interests of potential partners.[88] And this was the direction in which politics was to go and has gone ever since. With his sensitivity to the politically negotiable rather than to honour, Cromwell may then be the first of the new politicians.

NOTES

1. Carlyle's editions are forceful but careless while the 'standard' edition, *Writings and Speeches of Oliver Cromwell* (Cambridge, Mass., 1937–1947), ed. W. C. Abbott, is fatally flawed. See John Morrill, 'Textualizing and Contextualizing Cromwell', *Historical Journal* [*HJ*], 33 (1990): 629–39.

2. Peter White, *Cicero in Letters* (Oxford, 2010).

3. See, for example, Patrick Little, 'Introduction', in Little (ed.), *Oliver Cromwell: New Perspectives* (Basingstoke, 2009), 2–3 (and the review of this book by Ronald Hutton at Reviews in History: <http://www.history.ac.uk/reviews/paper/hutton2.html>). Andrew Barclay, *Electing Cromwell: The Making of a Politician* (London, 2011), 3–4.

4. John Morrill, 'The Making of Oliver Cromwell', in Morrill (ed.), *Cromwell and the English Revolution* (London, 1990), 19–48.

5. See also Barclay, *Electing Cromwell*, 9–10.

6. John Morrill, *Oliver Cromwell* (Oxford, 2007), 9.

7. Morrill, *Oliver Cromwell*, 5–6.

8. See Patrick Little, 'Introduction', in Little (ed.), *New Perspectives*, 13; Simon Healy, '1636: The Unmaking of Oliver Cromwell', in Little (ed.), *New Perspectives*, 28–9; Barclay, *Electing Cromwell*, 11.

9. See Abbott, *Writings and Speeches*, II, 51. References to this work will henceforward be in parentheses in the text in the form of A followed by volume and page(s) number(s).

10. Barclay, *Electing Cromwell*, chaps. 2–8. Compare Morrill, 'Making', 44–5.

11. David Farr, 'Oliver Cromwell and a 1647 Case in Chancery', *Historical Research* 71 (1998): 314–17.

12. Healy, 'Unmaking', 28–31; Ian Gentles, *Oliver Cromwell: God's Warrior and the English Revolution* (Basingstoke, 2011), chap. 10.

13. Stephen K. Roberts, ' "One that Would Sit Well at the Mark": The Early Parliamentary Career of Oliver Cromwell, 1640–1642', in Little (ed.), *New Perspectives*, 38–63. The view of Cromwell as a rather more serious player in the early years of the Long Parliament had been anticipated in Sir Charles Firth, *Oliver Cromwell and the Rule of the Puritans in England* (Oxford, 1953, 1966), 53–5.

14. Gentles, *Cromwell*, 24; Peter Young, 'Cromwell as a Military Leader', *Cromwelliana* (1975): 21; Alan Marshall, *Oliver Cromwell, Soldier: The Military Life of a Revolutionary at War* (London, 2004), 273.

15. Philip Baker, ' "A Despicable Contemtible Generation of Men"? Cromwell and the Levellers', in Little (ed.), *New Perspectives*, 90–113.

16. See, for example, John Cunningham, 'Oliver Cromwell and the "Cromwellian" Settlement of Ireland', *HJ*, 53 (2010): 919–37.

17. Blair Worden, 'Oliver Cromwell and the Council', in Patrick Little (ed.), *The Cromwellian Protectorate* (Woodbridge, 2007), 82–104; Blair Worden, *The English Civil Wars, 1640–1660* (London, 2009), 130, 135; Blair Worden, 'Oliver Cromwell and the Protectorate', *Transactions of the Royal Historical Society*, 6th series, 20 (2010): 57–83.

18. Patrick Little, 'John Thurloe and the Offer of the Crown to Oliver Cromwell', in Little (ed.), *New Perspectives*, 216–40, especially 232–3, 235–6.

19. Peter Gaunt, ' "The Single Person's Confidants and Dependents"? Oliver Cromwell and his Protectoral Cou/ncillors', *HJ*, 32 (1989): 537–60; Gaunt, 'The Protectoral Ordinances of 1653–4 Reconsidered', in Little (ed.), *Cromwellian Protectorate*, 105–26; Derek Hirst, 'The Lord Protector', in Morrill (ed.), *Cromwell and the English Revolution*, chap. 5; Morrill, *Cromwell*, 83, 87.

20. The pioneering work here was Roy Sherwood, *Oliver Cromwell: King in All But Name, 1653–1658* (Stroud, 1997). See also Kevin Sharpe, *Remapping Early Modern England: The Culture of Seventeenth Century Politics* (Cambridge, 2000), 22, 214–17. Paul M. Hunneyball, 'Cromwellian Style: The Architectural Trappings of the Protectoral Regime', in Little (ed.),

The Cromwellian Protectorate, 53–81. Andrew Barclay, 'The Lord Protector and his Court', in Little (ed.), *New Perspectives*, 195–215.

21. Tim Wilks, 'Art, Architecture and Politics', in Barry Coward (ed.), *A Companion to Stuart Britain* (Oxford, 2009), 199; Sean Kelsey, *Inventing a Republic: The Political Culture of the English Commonwealth, 1649–53* (Manchester, 1997), 105; Laura Lunger Knoppers, *Constructing Cromwell: Ceremony, Portrait and Print, 1645–1661* (Cambridge, 2000), 3, 8, 108–9, 123; Laura Lunger Knoppers, 'The Politics of Portraiture: Oliver Cromwell and the Plain Style', *Renaissance Quarterly*, 51 (1998): 1282–1319; Joad Raymond, 'An Eye-Witness to King Cromwell', *History Today*, 47 (1997), 38, 39: Simon Thurley, 'The Stuart Kings, Oliver Cromwell and the Chapel Royal 1618–1685', *Architectural History*, 45 (2002): 238–74.

22. Barclay, 'Lord Protector', 198–9; Morrill, *Cromwell*, 8, 70, 73–4; Barclay, *Electing Cromwell*, 75, 100.

23. Barclay, *Electing Cromwell*, 177.

24. J. C. Davis, 'Living with the Living God: Radical Religion and the English Revolution', in Christopher Durston and Judith Maltby (eds.), *Religion in Revolutionary England* (Manchester, 2006), 19–41.

25. Compare Gentles, *Cromwell*, xvii.

26. Albert J. Loomis, 'Oliver Cromwell's Policy Toward the English Catholics: The Appraisal by Diplomats, 1654–1658', *Catholic Historical Review*, 90 (2004): 29–44: Morrill, *Cromwell*, 94; Bernard Capp, 'Cromwell and Religion in a Multi-Faith Society', in Jane A. Mills (ed.), *Cromwell's Legacy* (Manchester, 2012), 93–112.

27. Michael Braddick, *God's Fury, England's Fire: A New History of the English Civil Wars* (London, 2008), 61, 63, 67 (emphasizing the dependence of local government 'on a degree of consensus-building and informal negotiations') and the references there.

28. Compare Blair Worden, *The Rump Parliament, 1648–53* (Cambridge, 1974), 27. For Cromwell as a coalition builder as well as a follower of providence see Worden, 'Providence and Politics in Cromwellian England', *Past and Present*, 109 (1985): 95. For an important alternative approach to the issue of negotiating power in early modern England see Michael J. Braddick and John Walter (eds.), *Negotiating Power in Early Modern Society: Order, Hierarchy and Subordination in Britain and Ireland* (Cambridge, 2001).

29. Barbara Taft, 'The Humble Petition of Several Colonels of the Army: Causes, Character, and Results of Military Opposition to Cromwell's Protectorate', *Huntington Library Quarterly*, 42 (1978–9): 39 for Cromwell's mixture of firmness, conciliation, and clemency (the tools of the negotiator).

30. See, for example, Derek Hirst, 'The Privy Council and the Problems of Enforcement in the 1620s', *Journal of British Studies [JBS]*, 18 (1978): 46–66.

31. David Cressy, *England on Edge: Crisis and Revolution, 1640–1642* (Oxford, 2006).

32. Michael J. Braddick, 'History, Liberty, Reformation and the Cause: Parliamentary, Military and Ideological Escalation in 1643', in Michael J. Braddick and David L. Smith (eds.), *The Experience of Revolution in Stuart Britain and Ireland: Essays for John Morrill* (Cambridge, 2011), 124; David Scott, 'Rethinking Royalist Politics, 1642–9', in John Adamson (ed.), *The English Civil War: Conflicts and Contexts, 1640–49* (London, 2009), 38, 46, 51, 59–60.

33. This may be an aspect of Cromwell's early grasp of the importance of print. S. L. Sadler, ' "Lord of the Fens": Oliver Cromwell's Reputation and the First Civil War', in Little (ed.), *New Perspectives*, 77–8.

34. Roberts, 'Early Parliamentary Career'.

35. Gentles, *Cromwell*, 18, 40.

36. Clive Holmes, *The Eastern Association in the English Civil War* (Cambridge, 1974), 81, 92.

37. Roger Howell, Jr., *Cromwell* (London, 1977), 31–2.

38. Barry Coward, *Oliver Cromwell* (London, 1992), 24.

39. For the importance of reconciliation in godly communities, see Roger Thompson, *From Deference to Defiance: Charlestown, Massachusetts, 1629–1692* (Boston, MA, 2012), 435.

40. Malcolm Wanklyn, 'Oliver Cromwell and the Performance of Parliament's Armies in the Newbury Campaign 20 October–21 November 1644', *History*, 96 (2011): 3–25.

41. For an important sidelight on this and the emergent alliance between the Fairfaxes and Cromwell (among others) see Andrew Hopper (ed.), *The Papers of the Hothams, Governors of Hull During the Civil War*, Camden Fifth Series, 39 (Cambridge, 2011), 29. For the background see David Scott, 'The "Northern Gentlemen", the Parliamentary Independents, and Anglo-Scottish Relations in the Long Parliament', *HJ*, 42 (1999): 347–75.

42. Keith Lindley and David Scott (eds.), *The Journal of Thomas Juxon, 1644–1661*, Camden Fifth Series, 13 (Cambridge, 1999), 36; Bennett, *Cromwell*, 95.

43. John Bruce and David Masson (eds.), *The Quarrel Between the Earl of Manchester and Oliver Cromwell*, Camden Society, New Series XII (1875).

44. See also the insightful comments of M. A. Barg, *The English Revolution of the Seventeenth Century Through Portraits of the Leading Figures* (Moscow, 1990), 144.

45. C. H. Firth (ed.), *The Clarke Papers*, 2 vols. (London, 1992), I, 370.

46. Morrill, *Cromwell*, 31–2, also 34, 37.

47. For the Heads of Proposals see John Adamson, 'The English Nobility and the Projected Settlement of 1647', *HJ*, 30 (1987): 567–603. For Cromwell's relationship with the Levellers see Baker, 'Cromwell and the Levellers'. For Cromwell as the negotiator at Putney see A, I, 519, 534, 540, 544.

48. William Allen, *A Faithful Memorial* (London, 1659).

49. Robert S. Paul, *The Lord Protector: Religion and Politics in the Life of Oliver Cromwell* (London, 1955), 161.

50. John Morrill and Philip Baker, 'Oliver Cromwell, the Regicide and the Sons of Zeruiah', in David L. Smith (ed.), *Cromwell and the Interregnum* (Oxford, 2003), 15–36.

51. Howell, *Cromwell*, 105.

52. Morrill, *Cromwell*, 51, 55, 56; Worden, *The Rump*, 64–7; Gentles, *Cromwell*, 77–8, 146.

53. For Ireland see A, II, 146, 202–5, 241–3, 257, 264, 283–8; James Scott Wheeler, *Cromwell in Ireland* (Dublin, 1999); John Morrill, 'The Drogheda Massacre in Cromwellian Context', in David Edwards, Pádraig Lenihan, and Clodagh Tait (eds.), *Age of Atrocity: Violence and Political Conflict in Early Modern Ireland* (Dublin, 2010), 242–65; Toby Barnard, 'Cromwell's Irish Reputation', in Mills (ed.), *Cromwell's Legacy*, 191–218; Morrill, *Cromwell*, 70; Cunningham, ' "Cromwellian" Settlement'. For the attempt to build as wide as possible a coalition in relation to his activities in Scotland see A, II, 277, 283–8, 328–9, 335–46; Firth, *Cromwell and the Rule of the Puritans*, 278; Gentles, *Cromwell*, 122, 126; John D. Grainger, *Cromwell Against the Scots: The Last Anglo-Scottish Wars, 1650–52* (East Lothian, 1997), 36, 51; Laura M. Stewart, 'Cromwell and the Scots', in Mills (ed.), *Cromwell's Legacy*, 173, 177–9. But see also Derek Hirst, 'The English Republic and the Meaning of Britain', *Journal of Modern History*, 66 (1994): 451–86.

54. David L. Smith, *Constitutional Royalism and the Search for Settlement, c.1640–1649* (Cambridge, 1994), 271; George F. Warner (ed.), *The Nicholas Papers*, 2 vols., Camden Society, New Series, 40, 50 (1886, 1892), I, 268.

55. John Morrill, 'Cromwell, Parliament, Ireland and a Commonwealth in Crisis: 1652 Revisited', *Parliamentary History*, 30 (2011): 194–9, 210–13.

56. For example, A, II, 505–7; Bennett, *Cromwell*, 197–8, 206.

57. Ivan Roots (ed.), *Cromwell: A Profile* (London, 1973), 75; Worden, *The Rump*, 1.

58. Ann Hughes, 'Religion 1640–1660', in Coward (ed.), *Companion*, 359.

59. There is abundant evidence of this. See, for instances, A, III, 434–43, 451–2, 510–11, 579–93.

60. See, for example, Blair Worden, 'Marchamont Nedham and the Beginnings of English Republicanism', in David Wootton (ed.), *Republicanism, Liberty, and Commercial Society* (Stanford, 1994), 75.

61. Austin Woolrych, 'The Cromwellian Protectorate: A Military Dictatorship?' *History*, 75 (1990): 207–31. For Henry Cromwell's defence of his father as eschewing the maintenance of government by force of arms see Robert W. Ramsey, *Henry Cromwell* (London, 1933), 39–40. The difference, in his view, was between using the sword to restore people to their rights and privileges or in order to rob and despoil them.

62. Addressing the republican exclusivity of Vane, Milton, Nedham, Baxter, and Stubbe, James Harrington proposed a radical inclusivity, significantly choosing Cromwell as his would-be patron. Ruth E. Mayer, 'Real and Practicable, not Imaginary and Notional: Sir Henry Vane's *A Healing Question* and the Problems of the Protectorate', *Albion*, 27 (1995): 37–72; Jonathan Scott, 'James Harrington's Prescription for Healing and Settling', in Braddick and Smith (eds.), *Experience of Revolution*, 190–209.

63. Patrick Little, 'The Irish and Scottish Councils and the Dislocation of the Protectoral Union', in Little (ed.), *Cromwellian Protectorate*, 127–42; Patrick Little, *Lord Broghill and the Cromwellian Union with Ireland and Scotland* (Woodbridge, 2004), 106–7.

64. This is where I take issue with the judgement of Clive Holmes that Cromwell by 1657 was washing his hands of the saints. Compare Clive Holmes, *Why was Charles I Executed?* (London, 2006), 155–7.

65. See, for example, the accusation that he was too ingratiating of the old Presbyterians. Robert Pitilloh, *The Hammer of Persecution* (1659), 11. For the complex interaction and competition between such coalitions at both local and national levels see Derek Hirst, 'The Fracturing of the Cromwellian Allaince: Leeds and Adam Baynes', *English Historical Review*, 108 (1993): 868–94.

66. For example, Charles Harding Firth, The *Last Years of the Protectorate*, 2 vols. (London, 1909 edn), I, 5–6.

67. Patrick Little and David L. Smith, *Parliaments and Politics during the Cromwellian Protectorate* (Cambridge, 2007), 294–5.

68. Christopher Durston, *Cromwell's Major-Generals: Godly Government During the English Revolution* (Manchester, 2001).

69. Little, *Broghill*.

70. J. C. Davis, 'Cromwell's Religion', in Morrill (ed.), *Cromwell and the English Revolution*, 181–208.

71. Edward Holberton, *Poetry and the Cromwellian Protectorate: Culture, Politics and Institutions* (Oxford, 2008), 88–92, 109.

72. Worden, *Civil Wars*, 128, 130, 135, 145–6.

73. Little and Smith, *Parliaments and Politics*, 232–8, chap. 12.

74. Kelsey, *Inventing a Republic*, chap. 4; Barbara Donagan, 'The Web of Honour: Soldiers, Christians and Gentlemen in the English Civil War', *HJ*, 44 (2001): 365–89; Monica Patterson-Tutschka, 'Honour Thy King: Honouring as a Royalist Theory of Praxis in Civil

War England 1640–1660', *History of Political Thought*, 32 (2011): 465–98; Andrew James Hopper, 'The Self-Fashioning of Gentry Turncoats during the English Civil Wars', *JBS*, 49 (2010): 1–22. For the aspiration to honour in early modern England and the modern literature on it see Keith Thomas, *The Ends of Life: Roads to Fulfilment in Early Modern England* (Oxford, 2010), chap. 5.

75. Thomas Hobbes, *Eight Books of the Peloponnesian War, Written by Thucydides The Son of Olorus*, in Sir William Molesworth (ed.), *The English Works of Thomas Hobbes of Malmesbury*, vols. 8 and 9 (London, 1843), I, 82.

76. Even so, see Marshall, *Cromwell: Soldier*, 274 for the view that Cromwell's military aims were not glory and honour but 'a just peace and a righteous religious settlement'.

77. See, for example, [Richard Braithwaite,] *Panthalia* (1659), 114–18; [Percy Herbert,] *The Princess Cloria… Written by a Person of Honour* (1661), 529; [Roger Boyle,] *Parthenissa* (1669), 60–90. The last of these was by the onetime Lord Broghill and laid great stress on honour as essential to civil life.

78. [Slingsby Bethel,] *The World's Mistake in Oliver Cromwell* (1668), 2, 15, 16.

79. John Rawls, *Political Liberalism: Expanded Edition* (New York, 2005), 147, see also 441.

80. Holmes, *Why was Charles I Executed?*, 152; Gentles, *Cromwell*, 153, 177, 198–203.

81. Ramsey, *Henry Cromwell*, 244. His son-in-law, Charles Fleetwood, was also worried by Cromwell's conciliatory attitudes towards Irish Catholics and English royalists. Patrick Little, 'Cromwell and Sons: Oliver Cromwell's Intended Legacy', in Mills (ed.), *Cromwell's Legacy*, 22.

82. Compare Roger Howell, Jr., 'Cromwell and English Liberty', in R. C. Richardson (ed.), *Images of Oliver Cromwell: Essays for and by Roger Howell, Jr.* (Manchester, 1993), 164 for Cromwell's continuing faith in the resolution of problems by discussion and mutual understanding.

83. Conrad Russell, *The Causes of the English Civil War* (Oxford, 1990), chap. 9.

84. James Scott Wheeler, *The Making of a World Power: War and the Military Revolution in Seventeenth Century England* (Stroud, 1999), 83, 192.

85. Holmes, *Why was Charles I Executed?*, 181. For the attempt to rehabilitate Richard see Jason Peacey, 'The Protector Humbled: Richard Cromwell and the Constitution', in Little (ed.), *Cromwellian Protectorate*, 32–52.

86. For the case that it was always a matter of a minority agenda searching for majority support see David L. Smith, 'Oliver Cromwell, the First Protectorate Parliament and Religious Reform', *Parliamentary History*, 19 (2000): 38–48.

87. For honour as a key preoccupation for Charles I see Richard Cust, *Charles I* (London, 2007).

88. Austin Woolrych, *Commonwealth to Protectorate* (Oxford, 1982), 397. C. V. Wedgwood's 'unbending' Cromwell probably owed something to Carlyle: Wedgwood, *Oliver Cromwell* (London, 1939). Ivan Roots was one of the first to depict Cromwell's political persona as 'inconsistent and ambivalent, diffuse and contradictory': Roots (ed.), *Profile*, p. viii. See also Worden, *Civil Wars*, 130 for an emphasis on less principled flexibility.

FURTHER READING

Barclay, Andrew, *Electing Cromwell: The Making of a Politician* (London, 2011).

Coward, Barry, *The Cromwellian Protectorate* (Manchester, 2002).

Coward, Barry, *Oliver Cromwell* (Harlow, 1991).

Davis, J. C., *Oliver Cromwell* (London, 2001).

Durston, Christopher, *Cromwell's Major-Generals: Godly Government During the English Revolution* (Manchester, 2001).

Gaunt, Peter, *Oliver Cromwell* (London, 1997).

Gentles, Ian, *Oliver Cromwell: God's Warrior and the English Revolution* (Basingstoke, 2011).

Little, Patrick (ed.), *The Cromwellian Protectorate* (Woodbridge, 2007).

Little, Patrick (ed.), *Oliver Cromwell: New Perspectives* (Basingstoke, 2009).

Little, Patrick and David L. Smith, *Parliaments and Politics during the Cromwellian Protectorate* (Cambridge, 2007).

Morrill, John (ed.), *Cromwell and the English Revolution* (London, 1990).

Morrill, John, *Oliver Cromwell* (Oxford, 2007).

Smith, David L. (ed.), *Cromwell and the Interregnum* (Oxford, 2003).

CHAPTER 14

....

PARLIAMENTS AND
CONSTITUTIONS

....

DAVID L. SMITH

INTRODUCTION

....

THE recent turn towards three kingdoms perspectives on political developments, when applied to representative institutions, has shed much new light on the formation of such institutions in each of the three kingdoms while also raising interesting questions about the interrelations between them. From dissimilar starting points they found themselves facing similar pressures, and these in turn produced contrastive results. To understand them alongside each other has proved immensely illuminating, and has opened up important new research questions. New resources, and novel ways of accessing familiar primary sources, will make this subject much easier to study in the future. Beyond this lies the still larger question of how these institutions served to create and represent political elites, and thus of how these societies worked politically.

In 1640, at the beginning of the English revolution, and again in 1660, at the Restoration, the three kingdoms of England, Scotland, and Ireland each had their own separate parliament with its own distinctive structures and traditions. The thrust of much recent research on all three parliaments has been to stress that these were royal institutions: they formed part of the machinery of monarchical government rather than a counterweight to it, and they were useful (if at times problematic) institutions that provided the monarch with advice, legislation, and taxation. They remained royal courts and councils, and they were summoned and dismissed entirely at the monarch's discretion. The operation of these parliaments was shaped largely by custom and precedent, and there were no written constitutions.

During the revolutionary period of the 1640s and 1650s, this picture changed radically. All three kingdoms saw determined and highly effective attempts to curtail the monarch's authority over parliament and to guarantee the existence of regular parliaments independently of the monarch's will. New structures were created—especially in the form of committees—to give parliaments a more continuous institutional existence and to reinforce the authority of their members even during the intervals between sessions. Although these innovations were to some extent variations on a theme, the exact form that they took was different in each kingdom. Then, most dramatically of all, in 1649–51 the English Commonwealth conquered Scotland and Ireland, and in 1653 the Protectorate was established with a British parliament containing representatives from all three kingdoms. This was regulated for the first time by a written constitution, the Instrument of Government, and a second, modified constitution, the Humble Petition and Advice, followed in 1657. These developments thus marked a complete reversal of the situation that obtained before 1640 and after 1660: instead of an unwritten constitution in which three separate parliaments existed within a multiple monarchy, there was a written constitution that defined the workings of a single parliament within a unitary republican state.

This chapter will try to explain how and why these remarkable changes came about. It will analyse the aims of the members of parliament in each kingdom, the challenges they faced, and how they sought to overcome them. We will trace the relationship between parliaments and constitutions, and the modifications that were made to parliaments as institutions. We will follow parliaments on a journey that came to an end with the Restoration of the Stuarts, and assess whether or not the arrangements after 1660 represented a complete return to those that had existed before the revolution. First, therefore, we need to start by examining the nature of the parliaments in each kingdom at the beginning of the revolutionary period.

Parliaments in 1640

In 1640, the three parliaments of the Stuart monarchy presented a picture of diversity. The most obvious common denominator was that they were all ruled by Charles I and therefore had to find ways of coping with his often authoritarian style of kingship. Beyond that, each of the parliaments could be regarded as the odd one out in the group depending on what criteria are applied.

The parliament of England (and Wales) was the largest of the three, the most powerful, and also the one with the longest interval since its last meeting in 1629. It was bicameral, and consisted of the House of Lords and the House of Commons. In the Lords sat the twenty-six bishops (including the archbishops of Canterbury and York) together with the lay peerage, which in 1640 numbered 123, and certain senior officers of state and legal 'assistants'. The members of the Commons comprised ninety knights of the shire (two for each English county and one for each Welsh), and 417 burgesses who represented the towns and cities. The knights of the shire were chosen by those inhabitants who owned freehold land worth at least forty shillings a year. In the towns and cities the franchise was defined by the borough's charter, and here the qualification varied immensely: freedom of the borough, membership of the corporation, ownership of certain levels of wealth or types of property were all used in different places, and could produce an electorate of anywhere between over two thousand and less than ten.[1] In practice, in both shire and borough elections, most members were selected by informal processes of consultation and negotiation, and only where these time-honoured mechanisms broke down did an election take place.[2] The English parliament met twice in 1640: first in the Short Parliament which Charles I dissolved after three weeks (13 April–5 May), and then in the Long Parliament, which assembled on 3 November and whose existence did not definitively end until March 1660. Members were in a very touchy mood, conscious that the previous parliament in 1628–9 had seen a breakdown in relations with the king, and resentful that Charles had avoided calling another for eleven years. As a result, as soon as parliament met there was a bitter outpouring of religious, political, and legal grievances that had accumulated during Charles's personal rule.

The king's decision to recall parliament in England arose from his failure to quell the Covenanter rebellion in his northern kingdom. The Scottish parliament was the only one in the Stuart monarchies that consisted of a single chamber in which all three estates were represented. The General Assembly had abolished the clerical estate in 1638: as a result, when the parliament next met on 31 August 1639 the three estates were redefined as the nobility, the commissioners of the shires (in effect the gentry), and the commissioners of the burghs. This reform was confirmed by the act 'anent the constitution of the present and all future Parliaments' of 2 June 1640, a measure which also granted the two commissioners from each shire one vote each, rather than one per shire, thereby doubling at a stroke the voting power of the parliamentary gentry who lay at the heart of the Covenanting movement. The parliament which assembled in August 1639 consisted of fifty nobles, forty-seven gentry representing twenty-five shires, and fifty-two burgesses representing fifty-one burghs.[3] Historically, the Scottish parliament had been managed through the Lords of the Articles, a committee in which the crown nominated representatives of the nobles (and hitherto the bishops) who then chose representatives of the shires and burghs. This had previously given the monarch considerable control over parliamentary proceedings, as in the Jacobean parliaments or Charles I's coronation parliament of 1633, but by 1639 the Covenanters were demanding that the Lords of the Articles be abolished, or at least reformed.

If the Scottish parliament was unusual in being unicameral, the Irish parliament was modelled very closely on the English structure of a House of Lords and a House of Commons. In 1640, the Lords contained the twenty-four Irish bishops together with ninety-nine lay peers, roughly two-thirds of whom were Protestant New English, and about a third non-resident. The Commons contained 235 members representing eighty-eight borough and thirty-two county constituencies, and chosen on an English-style franchise. Among these members, Protestants outnumbered Catholics by 161 to seventy-four, figures which reflected Strafford's attempt to weaken the Catholic presence by reducing the number of borough constituencies from ninety-five in the previous parliament of 1634–5. The distinctiveness of the Irish parliament lay in the fact that it was the parliament most directly controlled from outside its own kingdom, through Poynings' Law (1494) which stated that no Irish parliament could meet without a licence from the English monarch, and that no bill could be introduced into it unless it had the approval of the king and privy council in England. In 1541, the Act of Kingly Title stipulated that Ireland was 'united and knit to the imperial crown of the realm of England', thus making Ireland a dependency of the English crown.[4] The Irish parliament was nevertheless very careful to defend its independence from the parliament of England. With the king's approval, Strafford summoned it to meet on 16 March 1640, principally in order to raise money and men against the Scots, but it soon became clear that his policies as Lord Deputy since 1633 had alienated many of the New English as well as the Old Irish and the Old English. Despite his attempts to secure a pliable assembly with a Protestant majority in both Houses, the parliament was determined to put an end to Strafford's rule. Prominent among its immediate goals were the creation of direct channels of communication with the monarch, and the repeal, or at least suspension, of Poynings Law.[5]

The crisis of the late 1630s in Scotland thus led to the recall of parliament not only there but in England and Ireland as well. These parliaments rapidly became the institutional foci for resistance to Charles I's regime. Their assembly provided an opportunity for members to demand redress of grievances and to promote reforms that involved fundamental constitutional changes in each kingdom.

Parliaments and the Constitutional Settlements of 1640–2

A central aim of these reforms was to strengthen the position of parliaments in relation to royal authority. The Scottish parliament led the way in this process.[6] The Triennial Act (6 June 1640) established that a 'full and frie' parliament was to be held at least every three years, while a further Act of 10 June asserted that parliament was the highest court of the realm, and had the right to assemble at regular intervals and on its own authority. The monarch thus lost the discretionary power to choose when to summon parliament. The Lords of the Articles were reconstituted as an optional body, and instead a Committee of Estates was to sit in the intervals between parliamentary sessions. This Committee comprised twelve nobles, sixteen gentry, and twelve burgesses, each chosen by the relevant Estate, and it wielded extensive fiscal and military powers. In September 1641, further legislation gave parliament the right to approve the monarch's choice of officers of state, privy councillors, and lords of session, again giving parliamentary control over decisions that had hitherto been at the royal discretion. The significance of these reforms was not lost on contemporaries, and the antiquary Sir James Balfour wrote that the Scottish constitutional settlement of 1640–1 in effect 'ouerturned not onlie the ancient state gouernment, bot fettered monarchie with chynes and sett new limits and marckes to the same, beyond wich it was not legally to proceed'.[7]

This Scottish settlement provided a constitutional model for the English parliament in a way that reveals how much the parliaments of the three kingdoms could learn from each other in this period.[8] One of the Long Parliament's earliest priorities was to emulate the Scottish Triennial Act, and an English version was passed on 15 February 1641. Charles's control over the sitting of parliament was further curtailed by an Act of 11 May 1641 which forbade the adjournment, prorogation, or dissolution of the Long Parliament 'unless it be by themselves or by their own order'.[9] Parliament also set about impeaching those advisers most closely associated with Charles's personal rule. In close cooperation with members of the Irish parliament, they attempted to impeach Strafford, and when this failed he was attainted and executed on 12 May 1641. The following month, in the Ten Propositions, parliament requested that the King appoint to his Council 'such officers and counsellors as his people and parliament have just cause to confide in', thereby seeking to imitate the Scots in curtailing Charles's freedom to choose his own advisers.[10]

The Irish parliament, meanwhile, was pursuing its own programme of constitutional reform. Having secured Strafford's execution, and determined to restrict the powers of the executive, the parliament insisted that the Irish judges answer the twenty-one 'Queries' exploring the legality of Strafford's rule in Ireland. Then, in July 1641, the Irish House of Commons asserted that 'the subjects of this His Majesty's kingdom are a free people... to be governed only according to the common law of England, and statutes made and established by the parliament in this kingdom of Ireland, and according to the lawful customs used in the same'.[11] The Irish parliament also sought the repeal, or at least the suspension, of Poynings' Law. All these measures commanded a high level of support among both Catholic and Protestant members. In late October, however, the Irish parliament was overtaken by events: a Catholic rebellion broke out in the north of the country, and to make matters even worse, the rebel leaders claimed to be acting on a commission (almost certainly forged) from Charles I himself.

News of the Irish rebellion and the alleged royal commission prompted the Long Parliament to draw up far-reaching constitutional demands in the form of the Grand Remonstrance of 22 November 1641. These included parliamentary approval of the king's choice of advisers, a demand that Charles blankly refused on the grounds that it was 'the undoubted right of the Crown of England to call such persons to our secret counsels... as we shall think fit'.[12] Instead, on 4 January 1642, in a flagrant breach of parliamentary privilege, he attempted to arrest five of his leading critics in the Commons and one in the Lords. The two Houses responded by developing a radical new doctrine of parliamentary sovereignty. They asserted that in such an emergency they could legislate by passing ordinances which had the force of law even though they had not received the royal assent. This idea, first expressed in the Militia Ordinance of 5 March 1642, was based on the revolutionary claim that 'the King's supreme and royal pleasure is exercised and declared in this High Court of law and council, after a more eminent and obligatory manner than it can be by personal act or resolution of his own'.[13] Once parliament adopted this position, the outbreak of civil war in England was only a matter of time, and Charles raised his standard against the parliamentary 'rebels' at Nottingham on 22 August 1642.

THE CONSTITUTIONAL IMPACT OF WAR ON PARLIAMENTS, 1642–9

The interlocking conflicts of the 1640s, sometimes called the wars of the three kingdoms, had a profound constitutional impact on all three parliaments. This impact was complex and reflected not only the distinctive traditions of each parliament but also the fast-moving events of the war in each theatre. The strongest resemblances were between the Scottish and the English parliaments, especially in their creation of an elaborate committee structure, and here again the Long Parliament learnt from and drew on models that had already been pioneered north of the border.

The Scottish parliament of 1639–41 made provision for two main categories of parliamentary committees: session committees, which met while the parliament was in session, and interval committees, which met during the intervals between sessions. The most important of the interval committees were the Committee of Estates, the Commission for the Conservators of the Peace, the Committee for the Common Burdens, and the Committee for Brotherly Assistance. These bodies, which included some gentry and burgesses who were not members of parliament, increasingly bypassed the privy council and in effect governed Scotland until the next parliament assembled under the terms of the Triennial Act. This first Triennial Parliament met for six sessions between June 1644 and March 1647. Further interval committees were created as deemed necessary, such as the Committee for Monies, set up in February 1646 to handle the fining of royalist 'malignants'. The first Triennial Parliament also established a large number of session committees to deal with a wide range of financial, executive, diplomatic, and military matters. Among the most significant of these session committees were the Committee for Irish Affairs (April 1644), the Committee for the Levy (June 1644), and the Committee for the Provision of the Army (July 1645). To give added flexibility, certain committees operated as both session committees and interval committees: these included the Committee for Managing the War (January 1645), the Committee for Selling Forfeited Lands (February 1645), and the Committee for the Losses (December 1645). The Scottish parliament also created a network of shire committees, and various local committees, such as the Committee for the Burned Lands in Perthshire, or the Committee anent the Losses of the Sheriffdom of Aberdeen. These regional committees bore some resemblance to the county committees that parliament set up in England.[14]

Nomination to the various committees, and influence within them, became a crucial ingredient of political power in Scotland during the 1640s. Radical peers such as Argyll and Balmerino were able to ally with the representatives of the shires and boroughs to ensure that the Covenanters dominated many of the committees and eclipsed the influence of the royalist peers led by Hamilton and Lanark. Despite attempts to reassert conservative influence during the Scottish civil war of 1644–5, and again when the second Triennial Parliament met in March 1648, the radicals' success in securing membership of many committees ensured their dominance, especially after the defeat of the royalist

('Engager') invasion of England in the summer of 1648. These political trends reflected the increasing assertiveness of the gentry and burgesses against the nobility, a marked feature of Scottish parliaments during this period which John Young has called 'the emergence of a Scottish Commons'.[15]

In England, meanwhile, the Long Parliament sat continuously throughout the 1640s. To handle the vast amount of wartime business, it created a series of joint committees, containing members from both the Lords and the Commons, with extensive powers conferred by ordinance. As with the Scottish interval committees, membership of these joint committees was not confined exclusively to those who sat in the Houses. The Committee of Safety, modelled on the Scottish Committee of Estates, was set up in July 1642 to direct parliament's war effort. Following Scotland's entry into the war under the Solemn League and Covenant of September 1643, this body was replaced in February 1644 by the Committee of Both Kingdoms, known from 1647 as the Derby House Committee. This was parliament's main executive committee, and it gained considerable independence from the Houses. It was assisted by various other committees with more specialized functions. The Committee for the Advance of Money was created in November 1642 to raise loans and impose assessments on those of substance who refused to lend voluntarily to parliament in 1642–3. The Committee for the Sequestration of Delinquents' Estates (March 1643) was empowered to confiscate and administer the estates of Catholics and royalists. This committee was later merged with the Committee for Compounding with Delinquents (August 1645), which allowed the less active royalists ('delinquents') to compound for their estates by paying a composition fine and taking an oath of loyalty (the more hardline royalists ['malignants'] were debarred from regaining their property). As the war progressed, further committees were added by ordinance as the need arose. The Committee for Plundered Ministers was established in August 1643 to assist in finding livings for, and raising the stipends of, ministers loyal to parliament. In May 1647 the Committee for Indemnity was created to grant protection to civilian officials for things done under parliamentary ordinances, and to soldiers for actions committed in time and place of war.[16]

The powers conferred on these committees were sweeping and often allowed them to operate outside the common law. As the parliamentarian peer Lord Wharton observed in the summer of 1643, 'they were not tied to a law for these were times of necessity and imminent danger'.[17] Much the same was true of the network of county committees which the Houses established in the areas that they controlled. In each county there was an overarching committee and then a number of more specialized committees (for sequestrations, plundered ministers, and so on) which mirrored the structure of the central committees in London. This administrative apparatus and the parliamentarian armies were funded by two ruthlessly efficient taxes introduced by ordinance. The weekly (later monthly) assessment (February 1643) was a land tax, while the excise (July 1643) was a sales tax on certain vital commodities; subsequent ordinances extended the list of items on which it was chargeable. The burden of these taxes was extremely heavy: Kent, for example, was paying more per month in assessments by 1645–6 than it had for a whole year of ship money.

This financial load contributed to a growing perception that parliament was acting unconstitutionally; by the mid-1640s, the Houses also seemed less and less representative. The bishops had been excluded in February 1642, and two-thirds of the lay peers sided with the king, with the result that by the second half of 1647 average attendance in the Lords had fallen to between eight and twelve. In the Commons large numbers left to join the king—over a hundred attended the Oxford parliament which he summoned in January 1644—or withdrew to their localities. Between 1645 and 1648, the Commons therefore held 'recruiter elections' to fill the 250 or so seats vacated by those who had departed or been debarred ('disabled') from sitting because of their royalism. These elections were often keenly contested by the two main groupings which by then dominated Westminster politics, the presbyterians and the independents.[18]

The story of the Irish parliament during these years was rather different from either the Scottish or the English parliament. After the outbreak of rebellion in October 1641, the Catholic members of both Houses were either expelled or withdrew voluntarily, leaving a small Protestant remnant that continued to sit until June 1648. Instead, the bulk of the Catholic peers and 104 former members of the Commons took their seats in a series of Confederate General Assemblies which met at Kilkenny between October 1642 and January 1649. The General Assembly was a unicameral legislative body, with an executive (the Supreme Council) subordinate to it. In effect, it was an alternative parliament: the lords temporal and spiritual were summoned by writs; the counties returned members on a forty-shilling franchise, the boroughs on the basis of their own voting systems. Interestingly, Confederate government also included a network of provincial and county councils that bore a slight resemblance to the Scottish shire committees and the English county committees.[19]

The Confederates consistently proclaimed their loyalty to Charles I. Their principal goals were the immediate suspension—and in the longer term the repeal—of Poynings' Law, and the passing of legislation to ensure the independence of the Irish parliament from the English parliament. They called for an act specifying that 'the parliament of Ireland is a free parliament of itself, independent of and not subordinate to the parliament of England, and that the subjects of Ireland are immediately subject to your Majesty as in right of your crown'.[20] These remained key Confederate demands throughout their prolonged negotiations with the king and the royalists. Charles's defeat in the English civil war, and his surrender to the Scots in May 1646, only heightened Confederate fears that the parliament at Westminster would try to legislate for Ireland. When eventually a compromise agreement was reached in January 1649, however, it was soon rendered obsolete by the regicide and the Cromwellian conquest of Ireland.

Those events grew out of the New Model Army's increasingly aggressive interventions against the English parliament in 1647 and 1648. During the summer of 1647, following attempts by leading presbyterians to disband the army, the long-standing links between many of the officers and the independents in both Houses became ever closer. When, in late July, London rioters, probably encouraged by the presbyterians, burst into the Commons, about fifty independents fled to the army, which reinstated them ten days later. The following year, as a second civil war broke out, many of the army officers came to believe that Charles was a 'man of blood' whose guilt in shedding the blood of his subjects was an obstacle to any lasting peace settlement. By the autumn of 1648, having quashed royalist revolts in parts of England and Wales, and defeated an invading army of Scottish royalists, the officers joined with the independent minority in parliament in calling for the king to be brought to justice. The presbyterian majority, however, could still see no alternative but to negotiate with Charles, and when they persisted with the Treaty of Newport the army launched a military coup against the Commons. On 6 December 1648, Colonel Thomas Pride stood at the entrance to the House with a detachment of troops. He arrested forty-five members and secluded 186, while a further eighty-six withdrew in protest. He thus removed those members who opposed bringing Charles to trial, and left behind a radical minority of barely a hundred, which came to be known as the Rump.[21]

Less than a month later, on 4 January 1649, the Rump took a dramatic new constitutional step by passing three resolutions: 'That the people are, under God, the original of all just power;... that the Commons of England in parliament assembled, being chosen by and representing the people, have the supreme power in this nation; and... that whatsoever is enacted and declared for law by the Commons in parliament assembled has the force of law... although the consent and concurrence of the King and House of Lords be not had thereunto'.[22] The claim of 1642 that the two Houses could legislate without the monarch's assent thus gave way to the idea of a sovereign Commons that could rule without either the king or the Lords. This truly revolutionary principle opened the way to the trial and execution of Charles I in January 1649 and then shortly afterwards to the abolition of the monarchy and the Lords. All this was done on the authority of a small section of the English House of Commons without consulting either the Scottish or Irish parliaments. Hitherto, all three parliaments had formed part of a system of monarchical government; it remained to be seen how they would now fare in the context of a republic.

PARLIAMENTS AND THE WRITTEN CONSTITUTIONS OF THE 1650S

The short answer is that initially they fared very badly. One by one, the parliaments of the three kingdoms ceased to exist. In Ireland, no parliament had sat in Dublin since June 1648 and it was automatically dissolved by the king's execution; the final General Assembly at Kilkenny likewise dissolved itself in January 1649. Thereafter, the whole Irish landscape was changed irrevocably by the Cromwellian conquest of 1649–50 and the settlement imposed on Ireland by the Rump's Act for the Settlement of Ireland (12 August 1652). The Irish parliament's worst fear of an English parliament legislating for Ireland was thus realized. In Scotland, the second Triennial Parliament met for seven sessions between March 1648 and June 1651.[23] Appalled at the regicide, it proclaimed

Charles II King of Great Britain, France, and Ireland in February 1649 provided he took the Covenants. Once Cromwell returned from Ireland, he invaded Scotland in July 1650 and defeated royalist forces at Dunbar on 3 September. Charles II, having taken the Covenants, was crowned at Scone on 1 January 1651, but his invasion of England the following summer was crushed by Cromwell at Worcester (3 September 1651). These events overtook the Scottish parliament, which had adjourned itself until 3 November, and on 28 October the Rump issued a declaration incorporating Scotland into a single Commonwealth with England. Parliament lasted longest in England, where the Rump survived until the spring of 1653.[24] Gradually, its relationship with the army leaders deteriorated as they tried to secure a date for its dissolution, until on 20 April 1653, convinced that it was no longer 'a Parliament for God's people' and that it 'would never answer those ends which God, His people, and the whole nation expected from them',[25] Cromwell stormed down to Westminster and expelled it. In these various ways, the parliaments of all three kingdoms were thus victims of Cromwell and the New Model Army. It seemed at first as if they could not survive for long without a monarch. Soon, however, new and different parliaments were created by the very army which had destroyed the previous ones, first with Major-General Harrison's short-lived idea of the Nominated Assembly, and then more robustly in the parliamentary constitutions of the Protectorate.

The Nominated Assembly—often called Barebone's Parliament after one of its members, Praise-God Barebone—was a unique episode in British constitutional history. More like a constituent assembly than a parliament, it was modelled on the ancient Jewish Sanhedrin and contained 140 'persons fearing God, and of approved fidelity and honesty', nominated by the radical religious congregations of London, and added to by the Army Council. These 140 included six Irish representatives and five Scottish. Radical though many of the members were in their religious beliefs, the social composition of Barebone's did not differ greatly from that of other seventeenth-century parliaments: four-fifths were gentry, forty-four had some legal training, and 119 had served as justices of the peace. It was no wonder, therefore, that the Assembly soon became bitterly divided over certain reforms, especially the abolition of tithes and of Chancery: on 12 December 1653 it voted to dissolve itself and surrendered power back to Cromwell.[26]

Within days of the collapse of Barebone's, the Army Council introduced a new written constitution, the Instrument of Government, which established Cromwell as Lord Protector (16 December 1653).[27] The Instrument, prepared by Major-General Lambert, was Britain's first written constitution and it drew on earlier army terms, especially the Heads of the Proposals (1647). It was a parliamentary constitution, based on the principle that 'supreme legislative authority' should reside 'in one person, and the people assembled in Parliament'. There were to be triennial parliaments which would sit for a minimum of five months. These were genuinely British parliaments, indeed the only three-kingdom parliaments in British history other than those between 1801 and 1922. They comprised 375 English members, thirty each from Scotland and Ireland, and twenty-five from Wales. The English seats were redistributed to give the counties far more representation: there were now 236 seats for the counties, 137 for boroughs, and one each for the Universities of Oxford and Cambridge. The county franchise was broadened to include all those who possessed 'any estate, real or personal' to the capital value of £200 or more, but there was no attempt to reform the very varied borough franchises for those towns and cities which still retained parliamentary seats. Members were to be 'persons of known integrity, fearing God, and of good conversation'; Roman Catholics, royalists, and any who had 'advised, assisted or abetted the rebellion in Ireland' or 'any war against the Parliament' since 1 January 1642 were banned from being either electors or elected. These requirements would be enforced by a Council of State, containing between thirteen and twenty-one members, chosen by parliament (and when parliament was not sitting by co-option). Cromwell was to be Lord Protector for life: future Lord Protectors would be elected by the Council of State and confirmed by parliament. In the intervals between parliaments, the Lord Protector could issue ordinances which had the force of law but which were subject to ratification by the next parliament.

This constitution placed a considerable load on the relationship between the Lord Protector and parliament, a relationship that turned out to be frequently strained.[28] The first Protectorate parliament met on 4 September 1654 and insisted on drawing up a parliamentary constitution which tried to specify the Protector's powers in more detail and to enhance those of parliament. On 12 September Cromwell required members to sign a Recognition promising that they would not seek 'to alter the Government, as it is settled in one person and a Parliament', whereupon between fifty and eighty withdrew in protest. Those who remained pressed ahead with the parliamentary constitution, strengthening parliament's executive as well as legislative powers at the expense of both the Council and the Lord Protector.[29] Cromwell grew so frustrated that he dissolved the parliament at the first possible constitutional opportunity, after five *lunar* rather than five *calendar* months, on 22 January 1655.

The second Protectorate parliament, which assembled on 17 September 1656, was more productive but still far from harmonious, even after the Council's exclusion of around a hundred members before it opened. Many who sat in the parliament feared that Cromwell's powers remained too open-ended; they also disliked the rule of the Major Generals, established in the summer of 1655, and ended this by defeating the militia bill in January 1657. Members then drafted another parliamentary constitution in the form of a Remonstrance which later formed the basis of the second written constitution of the Interregnum, the Humble Petition and Advice.[30] In its final version (June 1657), the Humble Petition asserted the constitutional position of parliament in relation to both the Lord Protector and the Council. The Protector was to govern 'according to the laws of these nations', and parliament's 'ancient and undoubted liberties and privileges' were to be 'preserved and maintained'. The power to exclude members of the Commons was to rest solely with commissioners chosen by the House and not with the Council. Several features of the Humble Petition marked a step back towards more traditional patterns. The Council was once again styled the 'Privy Council': it was to contain up to twenty-one members, chosen by the Lord Protector and 'approved' by parliament. Parliament would again be bicameral: a second chamber called the 'Other House' was to be created, comprising between forty and seventy members nominated by the Lord Protector, and Cromwell welcomed this as 'a check or balancing power' on the Commons. In response to presbyterian fears, especially following the case of the Quaker James Nayler, greater limitations were placed on 'liberty of conscience' than in the Instrument. The Remonstrance had initially offered Cromwell the kingship as a further way of limiting his powers, but after agonizing for over two months he declined and decided to remain Lord Protector, with the right to choose his own successor.

The Humble Petition was in many ways a much vaguer document than the Instrument of Government. Nothing was said, for example, about the franchise or the redistribution of seats, or about the status of the Scottish and Irish members. By superseding the Instrument without making any explicit provisions on these matters, the Humble Petition created areas of considerable constitutional uncertainty. When the second Protectorate parliament met for a second session on 20 January 1658, the Other House proved to be a bitter disappointment: only forty-two of the sixty-three individuals whom Cromwell summoned (and only two of the seven peers) actually attended, although that was still enough to take some of his staunchest supporters out of the Commons. The Council no longer had the power to exclude from the Commons; as a result, over twenty of those excluded in 1656 returned, among them prominent Commonwealthsmen such as Sir Arthur Hesilrige and Thomas Scott. They had always been hostile to the Protectorate and now they bitterly attacked the Other House as far too reminiscent of the old House of Lords. Exasperated, Cromwell dissolved the parliament after just two weeks, on 4 February, with the concluding words 'let God judge between you and me'.

The third and last of the Protectorate parliaments was called by Richard Cromwell and met on 27 January 1659. In the absence of any stipulations in the Humble Petition, the English and Welsh members were chosen on the same franchise and distribution of seats as in 1640, together with thirty each for Ireland and Scotland. With the Council unable to intervene, many enemies of the Protectorate, including Commonwealthsmen and crypto-royalists, were returned. When the parliament met, the Commonwealthsmen immediately challenged whether the Irish and Scottish members could legitimately attend. They also opposed recognizing Richard Cromwell as Lord Protector, and refused to acknowledge the Other House. Although Richard eventually secured the Commons' support on all these issues, he failed to win the confidence of the army officers. Led by Fleetwood and Desborough, the officers allied with the Commonwealthsmen to force Richard to dissolve the parliament (22 April) and then resign as Lord Protector (24 May). The army, having created the Protectorate in 1653, had now destroyed it.

This was the latest in a series of army interventions against parliament, following those of August 1647, December 1648, April 1653, and September 1654. It marked the end of the written constitutions of the Interregnum, and instead over the next twelve months army leaders orchestrated a series of short-lived regimes: first the Rump was restored (May–October 1659), then the Committee of Safety was established (October–December 1659), and then finally, from February 1660, there was a return to the Long Parliament, including those members whom Pride had purged in December 1648. It was as though the regimes of the 1640s and early 1650s were being rewound at dizzying speed and in reverse order. It was the commander of the army in Scotland,

General Monck, who secured the return of the Long Parliament, and his intervention proved decisive. The Long Parliament voted to call free elections and then dissolved itself on 16 March 1660. These elections produced a pro-royalist Convention, which on 8 May declared that Charles II had been king since the moment of his father's execution on 30 January 1649.

PARLIAMENTS AND THE RESTORATION

The restoration of the king was accompanied by the return of separate parliaments in all three of his kingdoms. Each recognized Charles II as already king since January 1649: there was no sense in which he was restored to the throne or created monarch on parliamentary authority. The nature of the parliaments was once again different in each kingdom, and it is worth examining them to assess how similar they were to the parliaments that had existed in 1640.

In England, the Convention which assembled on 25 April 1660 comprised a Commons elected on the same franchise and distribution of seats as in 1640, and a Lords that was complete except for the bishops. The latter returned in November 1661, following the repeal of the act that had excluded them in February 1642. Otherwise, the guiding principle of the Restoration settlement in England was that all acts that had received Charles I's assent continued in force, while the 1200 or so ordinances passed since March 1642 on the authority of the Houses were declared null and void. This meant that the reforms of 1640–1, including the abolition of the Courts of Star Chamber and High Commission and prerogative revenues such as ship money, remained in place. The only measure to be significantly modified was the Triennial Act, which was replaced in 1664 by a watered-down Act that did not require fresh elections to be held every three years but merely a session of parliament at least every third year. To compensate the king for the loss of prerogative revenues, he was granted an ordinary income estimated at £1.2 million (though it actually yielded much less than this for most of his reign) based on the customs and excise.[31]

If the aim in England was to return to the situation of 1641, in Scotland the clock was turned back to 1633, the year of Charles I's coronation parliament. When parliament assembled on 1 January 1661, it consisted of seventy-five nobles, fifty-nine gentry representing thirty-one shires, and sixty-one burgesses representing sixty burghs. In March, the parliament passed a General Act of Rescissory repealing all legislation since 1633, thereby annulling not only the constitutional reforms of the 1640s but also the hated religious innovations of 1633–7. Royal prerogative powers were restored in full, including the right to appoint all officers of state and privy councillors. The clerical estate was re-established, as were the Lords of the Articles which once again enabled firm royal management of parliament. The crown was granted revenues of £480,000 Scots a year derived from customs duties and the excise on ale and beer. In marked contrast to England, nothing of the radical constitutional changes of 1640–1 survived in Scotland.[32]

Ironically, England, which had learnt much from the northern kingdom in framing those reforms in the early 1640s, managed to preserve them at the Restoration in a way that Scotland did not.

Ireland was the last of the three kingdoms to see parliament's return, on 8 May 1661, and this was also the parliament whose composition was most dramatically changed since 1640. The native Irish and the Old English found themselves excluded from the Commons, which was henceforth a purely Protestant body, although Catholic peers continued to attend the Lords. The Protestant dominance of parliament ensured that no attempt was made to overturn the Cromwellian land settlement by which the proportion of Irish land owned by Catholics had fallen from 59% in 1641 to just 22% in 1660. Instead, in July 1662, the Irish parliament passed a strongly anti-Catholic Act of Settlement. The parliament continued to be controlled from London—Poynings' Law remained in force—and it became part of the institutional machinery of the Protestant ascendancy which endured through the eighteenth and nineteenth centuries.[33]

Each parliament thus reached its own settlement with the restored monarchy, each with its own particular blend of change and continuity. As in 1640, the parliaments of the three kingdoms presented a picture of diversity, but the events of the intervening two decades had left their mark on the nature of that diversity. In England the return to 1641 preserved those royal concessions that had received Charles I's assent; in Scotland the return to 1633 restored the crown's prerogative powers in full and cancelled the reforms of 1640–1; and in Ireland the parliament was transformed by the sweeping land transfers of the 1640s and 1650s and the marginalization of the Catholic community. Overall, the Restoration saw a return to separate parliaments in each kingdom, based on unwritten constitutions and controlled by royal discretionary powers. The nature and extent of those powers varied from kingdom to kingdom but they remained considerable even in England, and in restoring them the architects of the Restoration settlement inadvertently restored many of the constitutional grey areas that had helped to cause the revolution in the first place. It would take another revolution in 1688–9 and the years that followed for these issues to be addressed once again and for royal discretionary powers to be decisively checked.

Conclusions

Finally, it is worth closing with two observations about possible directions for future research on this subject. Firstly, the amount of relevant primary sources now electronically available is vastly greater than even a decade ago. These include the *Journals* of both Houses of the English parliament as well as their acts and ordinances,[34] and the magnificent new edition of *The Records of the Parliament of Scotland to 1707*.[35] Although the records of the Irish parliament have survived more patchily, another excellent new website, the *1641 Depositions*, offers a huge amount of evidence for the history of Ireland in this period.[36] These resources make researching the parliamentary history of each kingdom much more convenient than ever before, and the rich material they contain will take scholars some time to absorb. We also eagerly await the *History of Parliament* volumes covering the period 1640–60, due to be published in 2018. With their articles on every member of the English Commons during these years, including the British parliaments of the Protectorate, and their accounts of each constituency, these will offer a wealth of further information. All these developments will make it much easier to pursue the comparative and shared history of these various institutions.

Secondly, the next big question for historians to explore in this area may well concern the relationship between the parliaments and the social, political, religious, and local elites in each kingdom. Much research has rightly concentrated on how parliaments managed their relationships with successive monarchs. Their ongoing relationships with the various elites from which they were drawn, and which they represented, have—with some notable exceptions[37] —generally received rather less attention. Gillian H. MacIntosh and Roland J. Tanner have recently made a perceptive point about the Scottish parliament: 'In many respects a well-attended parliament did not *represent* the country, it *was* the country. Anybody with significant power was there—no modern institution comes close to that concentration of wealth and power in one room.'[38] This is an insight that can usefully be tested for the English and Irish parliaments as well. Much research remains to be done on the relationship between these institutions and political elites: how they represented them, how their existence influenced the development of elites as a parliamentary class, and how the parliaments shaped political developments. This in turn opens up new ways of thinking about the interactions between elite politics and the life of these institutions as they faced massive political crisis. To ask such questions is to take a further step away from measuring seventeenth-century parliaments by anachronistically modern criteria of representation and towards understanding them in terms of the highly personal, often face-to-face world of early modern politics and government to which they belonged. It is a world in which there is still much to explore.

Notes

1. David L. Smith, *The Stuart Parliaments, 1603–1689* (London, 1999), chap. 1.
2. Mark A. Kishlansky, *Parliamentary Selection: Social and Political Choice in Early Modern England* (Cambridge, 1986), especially chaps. 1–4.
3. John R. Young, *The Scottish Parliament, 1639–1661: A Political and Constitutional Analysis* (Edinburgh, 1996), chap. 1.
4. Maija Jansson (ed.), *Realities of Representation: State Building in Early Modern Europe and European America* (Basingstoke, 2007), 117.
5. Jansson (ed.), *Realities of Representation*, 116–21; Ciaran Brady and Jane Ohlmeyer (eds.), *British Interventions in Early Modern Ireland* (Cambridge, 2005), chaps. 8–10.
6. Young, *Scottish Parliament*, chap. 2.
7. Young, *Scottish Parliament*, 24.

8. Cf. John Morrill, 'Historical Introduction and Overview: The Un-English Civil War', in John R. Young (ed.), *Celtic Dimensions of the British Civil Wars* (Edinburgh, 1997), 1–17, at 12.

9. S. R. Gardiner (ed.), *Constitutional Documents of the Puritan Revolution, 1625–1660*, 3rd edn. (Oxford, 1906), 158–9.

10. Gardiner, *Constitutional Documents*, 164.

11. Jansson (ed.), *Realities of Representation*, 121.

12. Gardiner, *Constitutional Documents*, 235.

13. J. P. Kenyon, *The Stuart Constitution: Documents and Commentary* (2nd edition, Cambridge, 1986), 227.

14. Young, *Scottish Parliament*, chaps. 3–8.

15. Young, *Scottish Parliament*, 327–8; John R. Young, 'The Scottish Parliament and the Covenanting Revolution: The Emergence of a Scottish Commons', in Young (ed.), *Celtic Dimensions*, 164–84.

16. Smith, *Stuart Parliaments*, 57, 74.

17. John Morrill, *Revolt in the Provinces: The People of England and the Tragedies of War, 1630–1648* (2nd edition, Harlow, 1999), 75, 197.

18. David Underdown, 'Party Management in the Recruiter Elections, 1645–1648', *English Historical Review*, 83 (1968): 235–64.

19. Micheál Ó Siochrú, *Confederate Ireland, 1642–1649: A Constitutional and Political Analysis* (2nd edition, Dublin, 2008).

20. Brady and Ohlmeyer (eds.), *British Interventions*, 217.

21. David Underdown, *Pride's Purge: Politics in the Puritan Revolution* (Oxford, 1971), chaps. 6–8.

22. Kenyon, *Stuart Constitution*, 292.

23. Young, *Scottish Parliament*, chaps. 8–11.

24. Blair Worden, *The Rump Parliament, 1648–1653* (Cambridge, 1974).

25. Gardiner, *Constitutional Documents*, 401.

26. Austin Woolrych, *Commonwealth to Protectorate* (Oxford, 1982).

27. Gardiner, *Constitutional Documents*, 405–17.

28. Patrick Little and David L. Smith, *Parliaments and Politics during the Cromwellian Protectorate* (Cambridge, 2007).

29. Gardiner, *Constitutional Documents*, 427–47.

30. Little and Smith, *Parliaments and Politics*, 306–12; Gardiner, *Constitutional Documents*, 447–64.

31. Smith, *Stuart Parliaments*, 147–50; Andrew Swatland, *The House of Lords in the Reign of Charles II* (Cambridge, 1996), chaps. 2–3.

32. Young, *Scottish Parliament*, chap. 13; Gillian H. MacIntosh, *The Scottish Parliament under Charles II* (Edinburgh, 2007), chap. 1.

33. Coleman A. Dennehy (ed.), *Restoration Ireland: Always Settling and Never Settled* (Aldershot, 2008), chap. 4.

34. <http://www.british-history.ac.uk>. On the sources for the Westminster parliament, see Maurice F. Bond, *Guide to the Records of Parliament* (London, 1971).

35. <http://www.rps.ac.uk>.

36. <http://1641.tcd.ie>. On the sources for the Irish parliament, see Dermot Englefield, *The Printed Records of the Parliament of Ireland, 1613–1800* (London, 1978); and Coleman A.

Dennehy, 'Some Manuscript Alternatives to the Printed Irish Parliamentary Journals', *Parliaments, Estates and Representation*, 30 (2010): 129–43.

37. For two recent examples, see Jansson (ed.), *Realities of Representation*; Keith M. Brown and Alan R. MacDonald (eds.), *The History of the Scottish Parliament, Volume 3: Parliament in Context, 1235–1707* (Edinburgh, 2010), chaps. 2–4.

38. Brown and MacDonald (eds.), *History of the Scottish Parliament, Volume 3*, 8.

FURTHER READING

Brady, Ciaran and Jane Ohlmeyer (eds.), *British Interventions in Early Modern Ireland* (Cambridge, 2005).

Brown, Keith M. et al. (eds.), *The History of the Scottish Parliament*, 3 vols. (Edinburgh, 2004–10).

Hart, James S., *Justice upon Petition: The House of Lords and the Reformation of Justice, 1621–1675* (London, 1991).

Jansson, Maija (ed.), *Realities of Representation: State Building in Early Modern Europe and European America* (Basingstoke, 2007).

Jones, Clyve (ed.), *A Short History of Parliament: England, Great Britain, the United Kingdom, Ireland and Scotland* (Woodbridge, 2009).

Kenyon, J. P., *The Stuart Constitution: Documents and Commentary* (2nd edition, Cambridge, 1986).

Kyle, Chris R. and Jason Peacey (eds.), *Parliament at Work: Parliamentary Committees, Political Power and Public Access in Early Modern England* (Woodbridge, 2002).

Little, Patrick and David L. Smith, *Parliaments and Politics during the Cromwellian Protectorate* (Cambridge, 2007).

MacDonald, Alan R., *The Burghs and Parliament in Scotland, c.1550–1651* (Aldershot, 2007).

Moody, T. W., F. X. Martin, and F. J. Byrne (eds.), *A New History of Ireland, III, 1534–1691* (Oxford, 1976).

Ó Siochrú, Micheál, *Confederate Ireland, 1642–1649: A Constitutional and Political Analysis* (2nd edition, Dublin, 2008).

Ó Siochrú, Micheál (ed.), *Kingdoms in Crisis: Ireland, 1642–1649* (Dublin, 2001).

Smith, David L., *The Stuart Parliaments, 1603–1689* (London, 1999).

Woolrych, Austin, *Commonwealth to Protectorate* (Oxford, 1982).

Worden, Blair, *The Rump Parliament, 1648–1653* (Cambridge, 1974).

Young, John R. (ed.), *Celtic Dimensions of the British Civil Wars* (Edinburgh, 1997).

Young, John R., *The Scottish Parliament, 1639–1661: A Political and Constitutional Analysis* (Edinburgh, 1996).

CHAPTER 15

···

THE ARMIES

···

ANDREW HOPPER

THE military history of the civil wars has long attracted a wide public audience, despite languishing as an unfashionable, marginalized sub-discipline in universities. Many academics unhelpfully stereotype the campaign and battlefield aspects of civil war history to be sterile, peripheral, and the narrow preserve of enthusiasts intent on assessing the competence of rival commanders. Despite such condescension, civil war military history has been popularized over the last forty years by historical re-enactment. This has increased knowledge about soldiers' clothing, equipment, drill, and ranks, but has tended to avoid the wider questions of army organization, funding, and maintenance, as well as the processes by which armies engaged in politics. Army histories need to develop broader conceptual appeal and significance. The sub-discipline of military history has yielded many new findings, but the time is now ripe for military history to be reconnected to wider debates about the causes, course, consequences, and experience of the mid-century crisis and, indeed, to the wider history of early modern England. In recent years there are encouraging signs that such a process is already underway. For example, battlefield studies are increasingly informed by topographical reconstruction, field-walking, and landscape archaeology.[1] There have also been advances in studies of the funding, supply, and care of the soldiery, while the politicization of the military, in particular, the New Model Army continues to produce vibrant debate.

MILITARY MOBILIZATION AND POPULAR POLITICS

···

One means of widening military history is to examine the social composition and organization of armies from the bottom up. Determining the soldiers' origins and recruitment leads us to the interaction between elite and popular allegiance. Numerous problems remain in reconstructing popular allegiance based upon patterns of military support. Analysis of contemporary reactions to events does not necessarily uncover their motives. Outward behaviour might not accurately reflect an individual's mindset and standpoint. Many in arms were reluctant or coerced, so historians ought to be wary of deducing political allegiance merely from military service. Rachel Weil has advanced such views further by arguing that contemporaries 'did not adhere to a uniform or coherent understanding of allegiance'. Instead, allegiance was more about outward and visible actions, and how individuals presented themselves to those in authority. In 2008 Michael Braddick's *God's Fury, England's Fire* developed these arguments conceptually to suggest that it 'might be better to think in terms of the responses to particular mobilizations rather than a fixed allegiance to one of two sides'. These 'mobilizations' required an ongoing process of attracting support, or 'continuous coalition-building' against a backdrop of changing political circumstances.[2] In short, maintaining armed support was just as critical as attracting it in the first place because military personnel frequently deserted or changed sides. Inspired by these developments, the process by which parliament maintained support in south-east England has recently been subjected to closer scrutiny, with stronger emphasis upon studying the external actions of individuals in contributing resources rather than attempting to unpick internal beliefs and motives.[3]

Yet more might still be learned about the identity of the soldiers themselves. They are worthy of closer study because they risked their lives, whether as volunteers or conscripts, to decide the civil wars' outcome. Angela McShane has recently quipped that: 'Historiographically, the position of the ordinary rank and file soldier has not progressed much further than the 1644 report which listed ordinary military casualties (other than those of officers and colors) after the horses.' Indeed, Ian Gentles once maintained that knowing much less about soldiers than their officers was 'not a serious drawback since it was the officers who stamped the armies with their distinctive character'.[4] Yet the rank and file influenced army identities too, and historians ignore them at their peril. Soldiers' mounts, equipment, training, diet, medical care, pay, discipline, and social background influenced their fighting capacity, as well as the strategic and tactical choices available to their commanders. For example, during 1643 the strategies of both the earl of Essex and the Fairfaxes revolved around avoiding champion landscapes where the royalists could unleash their superior cavalry. Essex did so by keeping his army close to enclosed country during the Newbury campaign, while the Fairfaxes gave battle on urban landscapes at Tadcaster, Leeds, and Wakefield, where their musketry could be deployed most lethally. Short of cavalry, the Fairfaxes' reliance upon clothworkers armed with muskets and clubs meant their success ended once they were compelled to give battle outside their urban strongholds.

Closer attention to the processes of recruitment should enhance our understanding of soldier identities. Soldiers might volunteer for religious, political, adventurous, or deferential reasons. They might volunteer out of desperation and necessity, or from hopes of maintenance and survival; as Micheál Ó Siochrú has recently indicated, from 1649 even native Catholics were recruited into Cromwell's army in Ireland, thereby participating in their own conquest.[5] Recruits might be inspired, bribed, coerced, or impressed. Bonds of deference might remain an influence. In dealing with royalist recruitment, historians used to rely upon Clarendon's emphasis on magnate influence. While historians now suspect there might be more to royalist recruitment than this, Gerald Aylmer remained sceptical about the possibilities of investigating popular royalism. Nevertheless, Malcolm Wanklyn suggested the bulk of rank and file royalists in the west were artisans, while Ronald Hutton cited Ian Roy's doctoral thesis to argue that the 'horse regiments were always an assembly of troopers from all over the kingdom and the foot regiments were never the homogenous local units of the sort Clarendon describes'. While the processes of social mobility and promotion on merit are more usually associated with the New Model Army, P. R. Newman considered that as the war lengthened 'lesser men entrenched themselves even more firmly as first-rate active royalists'. More recently, Lloyd Bowen has investigated the nature of such popular royalism through utilizing legal records generated in cases of seditious speech.[6]

The old 'deference model' of English and Welsh landowners raising regiments from their tenants and dependants in 1642, while remaining true in some instances, is now acknowledged to be far from universally applicable. For instance, the marquis of Hertford, the earl of Bath, and Sir William Savile failed to enforce the Commission of Array in Marlborough, South Molton, and Halifax respectively, despite the location of these towns in a countryside dominated by their family estates.[7] In Yorkshire, contrary to the unsubstantiated claims of Sir Clements Markham and C. V. Wedgwood, the Fairfax family did not raise an army from their tenants. Rather, they recruited most heavily among the populous clothing towns in the centre of the West Riding which had demonstrated a conspicuous popular parliamentarian politics by spring 1643. One of their officers, the ironmaster Christopher Copley of Wadworth, recruited his troop from these clothing districts despite them being thirty miles distant from his seat. By 1646 only one of his troopers was from Wadworth. In places such as the Warwickshire Arden, north Devon, and parts of the West Riding, the recruitment of parliamentarian forces ran counter to the inclination of the majority of gentry, pushing these landowners towards a more authoritarian position.[8]

While major landowners shaped initial mobilizations in many places in 1642, once it became clear the war would last longer important structural changes in the nature of recruitment followed. For landowners who derived most of their income from rents, recruiting their tenants would deprive them of income. Two-way processes of negotiation emerged as leaders appealed to vested interests to attract recruits. For instance in 1642 the king raised hundreds of volunteers among Derbyshire's lead miners by offering them exemption from lead tithe. Mark Stoyle has argued royalists continued to recruit volunteers in Cornwall en masse late into 1645 by harnessing the cause of Cornish particularism to that of preventing parliamentarian victory.[9]

The link between the clergy and military mobilization also merits further attention. Preaching and sermons inspired men to take up arms, while clergymen retained important roles thereafter in the moral instruction of the soldiery. Most garrisons and regiments employed a chaplain in an official capacity, but more comparative research is needed, not just on clerical allegiance, but on the specific role and functions of clergymen in the British and Irish armies of the period. There were even some occasions where ministers were commissioned as captains of horse, such as the Warwickshire rector, Benjamin Lovell. Preaching, psalm singing, catechizing, and fasting might all strengthen a unit's cohesion, morale, and fighting capacity.[10] During 1642 the Protestation was usually tendered after the delivery of godly sermons, which were eventually intended to stimulate military recruitment. That spring at Otley in Yorkshire, parishioners were prepared for armed resistance by sermons that did not espouse rebellion but nevertheless clearly blamed the king and his advisers for the nation's troubles. In York and Hull, John Shaw's sermons encouraged his hearers to intervene politically to carry out God's will, while Shaw's preaching to Fairfax's army at Selby encouraged the soldiers to see themselves as persecuted saints. In some places, entire congregations were directly exhorted to rise in arms and resist the king, such as those contacted through the written notes placed in Calderdale's chapels in October 1643. Soldiers were exposed to sermons to remind them of the justice of their cause, while fiery preaching appears to have sparked some into iconoclasm.[11]

The Scots clergy also played a prominent role in recruitment, urging many to volunteer. At Burntisland in 1640, the minister drew up a list of recruits based on the communion roll. Likewise, in rural parishes ministers listed those eligible for service, and each Covenanter regiment contained a beneficed minister drawn from the locality of its recruitment, along with a kirk session of elders selected from the officers. In 1648, many of the kirk's ministers hampered royalist recruitment by attacking the Engagement in their sermons, while after 1649 the clergy were again prominent in the army purges and the drive to eradicate sinfulness in the military.[12]

Considering that much of the royalist infantry were recruited in Wales, the treatment of the principality in the fashionable 'three kingdoms' historiography has been surprisingly muted. In military topics, Wales is either lumped in with England, or largely ignored. Yet historians such as Mark Stoyle and Lloyd Bowen have explained Welsh royalism as a reaction to the hostility of London's press towards the principality. Godly parliamentarians considered Wales full of idolatry and superstition. A series of pamphlets scorned the Welsh as being motivated by a dangerous politics of subsistence. Welshness, religious backwardness, and royalism were linked in parliamentarian mentalities. Welsh royalism therefore had an ethnic dimension, seeking to preserve its cultural distinctiveness from the hostile Englishness represented by puritan Westminster and the New Model Army. However, in explaining the royalist mobilization in south Wales, Stephen Roberts has downplayed ethnicity and instead stressed the aristocratic dominance of the royalist peers the marquis of Worcester and earl of Carbery, as well as the largely unchallenged implementation of the Commission of Array. Whatever ethnic pressures may have come into play in recruitment during 1642–4, they faded thereafter as the complicated politics within south Wales made allegiance in the region especially fluid and prone to side-changing.[13]

Mark Stoyle has argued for similar ethnic influences in Cornwall, where the forces of 'Cornish particularism' ranged themselves against an Anglicizing and aggressively puritan Westminster bent on the destruction of Cornish separateness, in what he terms 'the war of the five peoples'. For a time, the king permitted Cornish-only regiments. The

Cornish royalist army originated with a popular uprising that ejected the parliamentarian gentry from the county. These insurgents were later recruited into royalist regiments in substantial numbers, on multiple occasions, and as late as December 1645. Stoyle has also stressed the ethnic diversity of the armies employed within the English theatre, and that they included English, Scottish, Irish, Welsh, Cornish, French, Dutch, Walloons, and other Europeans. He argues that while both royalists and parliamentarians procured foreign military assistance, the king grew more dependent upon ethnic diversity in his armies, just as parliament's armies became more exclusively English.[14] In parts of the three kingdoms, ethnicity clearly became at least an additional factor in shaping the recruitment and identity of armies.

In Ireland, the nobility played a greater role in recruitment. Initially, most Catholic peers were reluctant to join the rebels in 1641, but were compelled to take action by the government's backlash and in an attempt both to save their estates and exercise control over the insurgency. Their familial networks enabled them to call on personal armies as many Catholic commanders were heads of Gaelic septs, with their company officers often being their kinsmen and followers. While the marquis of Antrim recruited heavily from native Irish in Ulster, the capacity of his Protestant counterparts was equally impressive; Jane Ohlmeyer estimates that Protestant baronial networks in Ulster raised over 10,000 men by 1643. Irish peers such as Antrim and Viscount Inchiquin were able to mobilize considerable resources, embed themselves into coalitions and change sides while carrying considerable support with them as and when necessity required. The Confederates established an administrative structure to support the war effort: county and provincial councils were established as well as a national General Assembly, in order to maintain four armies, one for each province, together with one smaller 'running' army. As with parliament's regional associations in England, this structure led to rivalry between commanders and hampered strategic coordination. Another similarity with England was that impressment was utilized for recruitment, with each county required to produce quotas of men aged between eighteen and sixty. From 1643, the return of Continental veterans such as Owen Roe O'Neill did much to ensure Confederate armies became more disciplined, trained, and regularly equipped with pike and musket. Garret Barry wrote a military manual and introduced Swedish tactics to the Army of Munster, yet Confederate armies seem to have preferred sieges to battlefield engagements, while their commanders were rarely comfortable leading their ill-mounted cavalry on the field. After the defeat of the regular Confederate armies, guerrilla bands emerged, living off the land and striking from hideouts in woods and bogs. Often led by former Confederate officers, they became known to the English as Tories and continued the struggle against the Cromwellian conquest.[15]

This proposed blending of social and military history by giving due attention to an army's regional origins and the identity of its soldiery will broaden our understanding of the factors influencing campaign narratives. In turn, huge networks of support, transport, and mobilization were required for an army to even reach the battlefield. This process invites historians to build upon recent advances in the understanding of how armies were funded, supplied, and maintained.

Financing the Armies

All protagonists throughout the three kingdoms experienced tremendous difficulties in funding their armed forces. Despite these problems, the Scots Covenanters enjoyed remarkable success in funding their military during the 1640s, considering that for much of 1644–8 they were simultaneously maintaining armies in England, Scotland, and Ireland. From 1639, the Scots were the first to succeed in raising a national army based upon conscription. Its officers, sergeants, engineers, gunners, and muster masters were largely Scots veterans returning from Swedish service.[16] Initially, local communities bore the burden of supplying and equipping the Covenanter units as the Edinburgh government lacked the resources. For example, many towns offered volunteers the freedom of the burgh and supplied their contingents with coat and conduct money to convey them to the borders. Yet gradually the government increased control in order to field a modernized, national army. The Covenanters quartered troops on their own civilians, raised forced loans and expected civilian communities to provision the soldiery. Assessments, customs duties, and excise were collected with some efficiency, with shire war committees supervising the local war effort, and the Scottish mercantile community raising loans in Zeeland. Between 1644 and 1647, the £816 089 that the earl of Leven's Covenanter army received from Westminster enabled the Scots to intervene in England on favourable terms, and on a scale that would otherwise have proved impossible. The Scots produced a national, conscripted, standing army sustained by central government that anticipated the formation of the New Model Army by several years. The Scots in Ulster also enjoyed a measure of financial support from Westminster. Meanwhile the Scots themselves became more adept at extracting national wealth towards paying for their armies, and introduced new taxes such as the tenth penny and the twentieth penny. Laura Stewart has argued that this amounted to a fiscal revolution, which survived into the later seventeenth century despite the chaotic financing and supply of Hamilton's Army of the Engagement in 1648.[17]

In Ireland, the Confederates were unable to emulate these successes. At its height, the Confederation might have gathered taxation from most of Ireland, save for the localities around Dublin, the Munster towns, and those districts of East Ulster and Derry occupied by the Scots. The Confederates ordered that every man grant a quarter of his estate towards the war effort, while they developed a financial system based on county contributions, and tried to implement an excise. Their funding also partly depended upon large sums received from the papacy, France, and Spain. Having failed to capture the arms magazine in Dublin Castle, the insurgents became heavily reliant upon munitions imported from Continental Europe. Peter Edwards has argued that their victory at Benburb in 1646 owed as much to advancements in their pay and supply as to Owen Roe O'Neill's generalship. Despite the Confederates' shortcomings, until 1649 the pay and supply of Protestant forces were scarcely superior. From summer 1642, Ormond's royalists in Dublin received very little munitions from England. In Ulster, Robert Monro's campaigns were poorly supplied and this alienated the civilian population, provoking Alaisdair MacColla into joining the marquis of Montrose's campaign in Scotland against the Covenanters. Not until Cromwell's arrival with the New Model in August 1649 was there a decisive logistical breakthrough. Cromwell's success was underpinned by sound financial preparation and seaborne supply which freed his men from reliance upon local resources. This conquest has been calculated at costing the English government about £3,800,000 from May 1649 to November 1656, an average of about £37,000 per month.[18]

In England, it has long been recognized that parliament enjoyed a critical advantage in the funding and supply of its armies because of its control of the navy and the city of London. By contrast, the royalists are depicted as having struggled, with many of their infantry armed with cudgels and pitchforks at Edgehill. Thereafter, periodic deficiencies in the supply of the king's Oxford army were strategically decisive and do much to explain the royalist failure during the first Newbury campaign. As the war lengthened the funding of royalist armies grew more difficult because the territories under their control tended to be more war-torn and exhausted than those which supplied parliament.[19]

However, it does not follow that all royalist military finance was feeble or haphazard. From April 1643 the earl of Newcastle imposed upon Yorkshire what became known as the 'Great Sesse'. It was designed to raise £30,000 per month to support his army. Subdivided into the county's Ridings and wapentakes, it was collected by parish constables. Its surviving documentation is fragmented, but its collection continued until Newcastle's flight into York in April 1644. This was supplemented by the raising of loans, formalized by the Yorkshire Engagement, a document popularly known as the Yorkshire Magna Charta. Lenders were promised reimbursement from the Engagement's signatories, who pledged to repay loans according to their estates' size. By this means £19 445 was raised very quickly. Many were forced to make contributions or sign the Engagement against their will, under threat of plundering, or to procure their release from imprisonment. So rather than maintaining his forces merely by plunder and free quarter as suggested by parliamentarian propaganda, Newcastle developed effective financial mechanisms to support his forces on a long-term basis. Furthermore, Ian Atherton's study of the Lichfield garrison accounts has questioned the old notion that as the territory controlled by the king contracted, royalist military administration crumbled. Instead, Atherton demonstrates that in late 1645 the Lichfield royalists were better maintained and more disciplined than they had been two years earlier.[20]

There have also been advances in understanding the mounting, funding, and supply of the main parliamentary armies by subjecting the Commonwealth Exchequer Papers to ever closer scrutiny. Recent studies of pay warrants have done much to illuminate how the earl of Essex's army was raised in summer 1642. It has been suggested that during the Edgehill campaign a funding crisis emerged because the localities had no representation in its constituent units. This has provoked a counter-argument relocating the crisis to after Edgehill, with the claim that parliament initially developed an effective system for paying Essex's army. Yet with the realization that the war might prove lengthy, parliamentarian activists from November 1642 did much to diversify their efforts into raising separate armies and organizing regional military defence.[21]

Here, the process of funding the armies fed directly into factional politics and infighting. Disputes, inflamed by unclear command structures, often escalated between allied commanders in conflict over honour, money, and provisions. This was aggravated by the tendency of governors of towns, castles, and fortified houses to jealously guard their commands and territorial jurisdictions, and be quick to suspect plotting and treachery among their comrades. In this way the internal politics of the regional military associations established on both sides would merit further attention, along with how they maintained support in the localities and built interests at Oxford or Westminster.

For instance David Scott has demonstrated how the supply and funding of the Scots army in northern England in 1645–6 invited resentment, first among parliament's notoriously ill-funded Yorkshire forces and then the Northern Association. As the Scots lacked an English network of civilian administrators, committees, and sequestrators, their forces were compelled into taking free quarter and raising illegal assessments to supplement what they received from Westminster. The resulting antipathy towards the Scots' presence weakened the Northern Association forces and made them prone to mutiny, but bolstered the anti-Scots Independents at Westminster and developed for them a northern powerbase.[22] This in turn translated into much-needed political support for the New Model Army from within the parliamentarian coalition.

The civil wars increased the recognition that armies needed to be professional in order to succeed, with higher standards of drill, organization, equipment, discipline, funding, and supply. Whether or not the New Model was particularly novel and distinctive at its creation in 1645, it must be conceded that it was the army that eventually came closest to consistently meeting these higher standards. Its superior finances and maintenance, together with the strategic freedom enjoyed by its commanders marked it out as different. These improvements were reflected by its record of extraordinary successes not just on the battlefields at Naseby, Langport, Preston, Dunbar, and Worcester, but also in its largely prosperous conduct of siege operations throughout the three kingdoms. In addition, it developed a clout unparalleled by armies elsewhere in its ability to accelerate political change. Even before the second civil war was settled, perceptive contemporaries recognized that the New Model had been distinctively successful. Bulstrode Whitelocke cautioned the earl of Holland in June 1648 that 'the Parlements Army was in a formed body of old soldiers prosperous in their actions, & well provided of armes & ammunition, & that it would be a desperate and rash attempt for any to imagine to make a head against them with a new body'. These advances were part of a wider, European 'military revolution' in which the ability of a regime to pay and supply its soldiers became more critical than ever. For example, in December 1659 George Monck's prime advantage over John Lambert's force marching north against him was that Monck had up to £50,000 available to pay his men, while Lambert had very little, obliging his troops to live off free quarter.[23] This advantage contributed not a little to the restoration of the monarchy, and it brings us to our third key theme of military interventions in politics.

Armies and Politics

Merely by their existence, armies influenced politics. They constrained the terms under which peace negotiations could be made and they contributed to the factional infighting to which both sides were prone. Despite their victory in the first civil war, by 1647 parliament's armies had grown odious to the people because of the crushing burdens imposed for their maintenance. John Morrill has suggested the cost of billeting the troops probably exceeded the cost of direct taxation. By 1647 parliament owed approximately £2,800,000 to the New Model Army, as well as its garrison forces and provincial armies under Edward Massey and Sydenham Poyntz. Faced with increasing civilian hostility and little prospect of receiving their arrears, many soldiers questioned why they remained unpaid. Some perceived a conspiracy among those MPs seeking to disband the army before arrears were settled. Despite the usual focus on the New Model, soldiers from parliament's provincial forces were equally capable of organized political activity in response to issues of pay and indemnity. County committee men, excise officers, and sequestrators were seized and ransomed, while General Poyntz was arrested by his own soldiers.[24]

Yet the political intervention of parliament's soldiers stretched far beyond their personal and professional grievances to embrace wider issues such as liberty, the franchise, and the king's fate. As Ian Gentles has reminded us, the purge of parliament, the trial and execution of the king, and the establishment of a republic would have been unthinkable without the political interventions of the New Model Army. The exhilaration of continued victories gave them confidence to organize politically and demand outcomes from the war that recognized their sacrifices. The soldiers did not need John Lilburne to teach them political principles, as the election of representatives by mutinous soldiers was a common enough military practice elsewhere in Europe. The General Council of the Army, the Declaration of 14 June 1647, and the Vote of No Addresses all represent occasions where the New Model intervened in politics, while the strength of the soldiers' challenge to their generals at Putney may have been underplayed. Indeed, Philip Baker and Elliot Vernon have recently argued that the first *Agreement of the People* presented to the General Council of the Army at Putney on 28 October 1647 was not drafted by Leveller leaders such as John Lilburne, Richard Overton, or William Walwyn, but was rather collated by John Wildman in consultation with the army's new agents and its civilian counsellors such as Maximilian Petty. Of these, even Wildman himself was likely to have been a former trooper in the Eastern Association. So rather than seeing the Levellers as 'infiltrating' the army, there are now powerful arguments to envision 'a thoroughly politicized army that was capable of thinking for itself'.[25]

The concerns of parliament's soldiers were also a crucial factor in driving the regicide, despite the hesitancy of many of the trial commissioners. Sean Kelsey has postulated that a capital sentence against Charles was far from a foregone conclusion, even once the trial was underway. He has stressed reluctance to impose the death penalty, as well as divisions among the trial commissioners and army officers over the nature of the charges. Yet his claim that the decision to execute the king was only taken at the eleventh hour has been criticized for downplaying the implacable hostility of the army. Despite only eighteen out of fifty-nine regicides being army officers, the military played the leading role in forcing the king's execution. Military pressure for 'justice' against Charles I came from petitioning units dispersed all across England, not just the New Model regiments in and around London.[26] Consequently, the generals must have feared a collapse in discipline if the king was spared.

The army's political interventions thereafter remained no less critical in accelerating regime change, so much so that Austin Woolrych highlighted 'climacterics' around each time the army intervened against parliament in his structuring of the period. The legacy of these military interventions in 1647, 1653, and 1659 was the speed with which the army that restored Charles II was disbanded, to prevent it from meddling in politics again. Thereafter, during the later seventeenth century, standing armies were frequently equated with military tyranny and oppressive regimes. It was dark memories of the New Model, not the Army of the Covenant, or the Irish Confederacy, that were conjured when discussing the advisability of a standing army.[27] This reflects that no Scottish or Irish force achieved the same degree of influence within the state that the New Model achieved in England during the 1650s. Considering the internal divisions within the Covenanting and Confederate movements, as well as the provincial-based organization of the latter's military this is scarcely surprising.

Nevertheless, despite the New Model's retrospective pre-eminence, the soldiers of other civil war armies frequently intervened politically in ways that their masters would not have approved, suggesting that an overview of army mutinies in the war of the three kingdoms needs to be written. Political interventions from soldiers shaped the shifting coalitions and at times dictated events. For instance, Alasdair MacColla's invasion of Argyll in 1645 and Cornish attempts to separate themselves from mainstream royalism were overtly political acts that proved highly damaging to the royalist cause. Other examples include the deployment of Roman Catholic Irish soldiers in England, an outcome that proved to be very difficult even for some bellicose royalists to stomach. Finally, the prospect of further Irish landings in 1649 had important political consequences in England. When Charles I refused to order Ormond to desist from his preparations, he narrowed the political options available to his enemies, making regicide far more likely.[28]

Future Research

There have been several other recent developments in the study of civil war armies. Firstly, greater attention has been paid to the historical terrain over which armies moved and fought. This has sparked a major rethinking of the traditional battlefield narratives that were once fashioned largely from textual primary sources alone.

Historians are now rightly more wary of speaking about a battle without having closely studied its historical terrain. There is increased recognition that walking battlefield landscapes is as important as documentary study, and that it often opens up interrogation of traditional sources from new perspectives. This approach was pioneered by P. R. Newman in his walking of Marston Moor from 1978, and advanced further by Glenn Foard's study of Naseby in 1995. The application of written sources to landscapes and the understanding of how human land use has altered the terrain are now integral to reinterpreting civil war battlefields. Battlefield archaeology, artefact recovery projects, and shot-fall analysis have enabled major new reinterpretations of documentary sources, in particular for the decisive civil war battles of Marston Moor and Naseby. This kind of archaeology does not involve excavating trenches, but rather a disciplined use of metal detectors for mapping finds close to the surface. By mapping the recovery of battlefield debris, especially that of lead shot, historians can with more confidence link particular locations to flashpoints within a battle. Following in the footsteps of Newman and Foard, David Johnson has reconstructed the historical terrain at Adwalton Moor, built from references in the primary source accounts, antiquarian maps, battlefield visits, archaeological evidence, and landscape studies.[29] This kind of collaboration between disciplines is now being advanced by the Battlefields Trust. Founded in 1991, it is pledged to 'the presentation, interpretation and conservation of battlefield sites as educational and heritage resources'. The trust campaigns to prevent development of battlefields and improve public access. It provides interpretational panels and visitor facilities. Its website includes maps, archaeological plans, pictures, and aerial photographs of many civil war battlefield sites.

Another recent development has been the increased attention paid to military care. Only the day after Edgehill, parliament recognized a duty of care to its maimed soldiers, their wives, and children. This was the first time such recognition had been made by the English state and led to considerable improvements in military hospitals, nursing, and care. The Long Parliament, Rump, and Lord Protector were bombarded with petitions for pensions and relief by their maimed soldiery, war widows, and orphans during the 1640s and 1650s, while similar petitions were made to Charles II in the 1660s by former royalists. In the provinces, justices of the peace distributed military pensions to claimants at meetings of the quarter sessions.[30] Another related issue is the afterlives of the New Model's soldiery following their disbandment at the Restoration, a topic currently being investigated by David Appleby. These issues of aftercare have begun to be explored but much further research is needed as they retain massive contemporary resonance with Western governments continuing to indulge in costly warfare during economic recession.

Much more is now known about how the civil wars were fought, thanks to Barbara Donagan's well-researched publications, which have inspired a flurry of works dedicated to explaining atrocities and the infringement of codes of conduct. There have also been advances in more specialized fields such as a recent study of how parliament developed superior structures for the gathering and dissemination of military intelligence.[31] Greater attention has been paid to the practice of military side-changing, its representations in print, and the self-fashioning of the side-changers themselves, either on paper, in the courtroom, or upon the scaffold. This cultural turn in military history raises exciting possibilities in studying how martial culture was depicted in literature, on the stage, and in the cult of honour among officers and soldiers. Iconography, banners, portraits, medals, engravings of commanders, ballads, broadsides, and propaganda woodcuts in newsbooks all offer ways in which art history, print, and material culture might contribute to developing a new, much broader military history.[32]

The military history of the civil wars needs to be reconnected to the fields of social, political, and cultural history, and recent works provide the means to do so. Future research might focus on the social profile, geographical origins, and recruitment of civil war armies. With advances in computer software and genealogical techniques it might become possible to document soldier identities, and kinship networks within military units in greater depth, particularly for garrison forces where both muster rolls and local parish records survive. A thorough analysis of the certificates for the sale of crown lands, which list details of soldiers' debentures, would also illuminate the lives of those soldiers who rose through the ranks in parliament's armies.[33] The operation of provincial armies and regional military associations on both sides requires further scrutiny. How effective these associations were at mobilizing men and resources merits more attention, especially once it is considered that the personnel of the main field armies under Charles I, Rupert, Essex, and Fairfax, which have received the most attention from historians, represent only a minority of the men under arms. Such research would inform ongoing debates about the complex relationship between the centre and localities, and uncover how local rivalries impacted upon policy at Oxford and Westminster. Army histories might explain how the process of arming the people impacted upon political developments. They should also explore in what ways the social composition of armies influenced their commanders' strategies and their soldiers' battlefield behaviour. After all, the civil wars were decided by a combination of the mobilization of resources and the battlefield achievements of the armies. It should be remembered more often that these two factors were closely connected.

Notes

1. Malcolm Wanklyn and Frank Jones, *A Military History of the English Civil War, 1642–1646* (Harlow, 2005), 24, 279.
2. G. E. Aylmer, 'Collective Mentalities in Mid-Seventeenth-Century England: 4 Cross Currents: Neutrals, Trimmers and Others', *Transactions of the Royal Historical Society* [*TRHS*], 5th series, 39 (1989): 22; David Underdown, *Revel, Riot and Rebellion: Popular Politics and Culture in England, 1603–1660* (Oxford, 1985), 186; Rachel Weil, 'Thinking about Allegiance in the English Civil War', *History Workshop Journal*, 61 (2006): 190; Michael Braddick, *God's Fury, England's Fire: A New History of the English Civil Wars* (London, 2008), 233, 236.
3. Gavin Robinson, *Horses, People and Parliament in the English Civil War: Extracting Resources and Constructing Allegiance* (Farnham, 2012).

4. Angela McShane, 'Recruiting Citizens for Soldiers in Seventeenth-Century English Ballads', *Journal of Early Modern History*, 15 (2011): 107; Ian Gentles, 'The Civil Wars in England', in John Kenyon and Jane Ohlmeyer (eds.), *The Civil Wars: A Military History of England, Scotland and Ireland, 1638–1660* (Oxford, 1998), 110.

5. Micheál Ó Siochrú, *God's Executioner: Oliver Cromwell and the Conquest of Ireland* (London, 2008), 206–9.

6. G. E. Aylmer, 'Collective Mentalities in Mid-Seventeenth-Century England: 2 Royalist Attitudes', *TRHS*, 5th series, 37 (1987): 29; Ronald Hutton, 'Clarendon's History of the Rebellion', *English Historical Review*, 97, 382 (1982): 71, 74; P. R. Newman, 'The Royalist Officer Corps, 1642–1660: Army Command as a Reflexion of the Social Structure', *Historical Journal* [*HJ*] 26 (1983): 956; Lloyd Bowen, 'Seditious Speech and Popular Royalism, 1649–60', in Jason McElligott and David L. Smith (eds.), *Royalists and Royalism during the Interregnum* (Manchester, 2010), 44–66.

7. David Underdown, *Somerset in the Civil War and Interregnum* (Newton Abbot, 1973), 31; Mark Stoyle, *Loyalty and Locality: Popular Allegiance in Devon during the English Civil War* (Exeter, 1994), 143; British Library [BL], Thomason Tract E116(9), *The Last True Newes from Yorke, Nottingham, Coventry and Warwicke*, 24 August–4 September (London, 1642), sig. A3r.

8. Clements R. Markham, *A Life of the Great Lord Fairfax* (London, 1870), 51; C. V. Wedgwood, *The King's War, 1641–1647* (London, 1958), 196; Andrew Hopper, '*Black Tom': Sir Thomas Fairfax and the English Revolution* (Manchester, 2007), chaps. 2 and 7; Andrew Hopper, 'A Directory of Parliamentarian Allegiance in Yorkshire during the British Civil Wars', *Yorkshire Archaeological Journal*, 73 (2001): 120–2; Ann Hughes, *The Causes of the English Civil War* (2nd edition, Basingstoke, 1998), 140.

9. Andy Wood, 'Beyond Post Revisionism? The Civil War Allegiances of the Miners of the Derbyshire Peak Country', *HJ*, 40 (1997): 23–40; Mark Stoyle, *West Britons: Cornish Identities and the Early Modern British State* (Exeter, 2002), 91–112.

10. Anne Laurence, *Parliamentary Army Chaplains, 1642–1651* (Woodbridge, 1991); Margaret Griffin, *Regulating Religion and Morality in the King's Armies, 1639–1646* (Leiden, 2004); Ann Hughes, *Politics, Society and Civil War in Warwickshire, 1620–1660* (Cambridge, 1987), 197.

11. William Sheils, 'Provincial Preaching on the Eve of the Civil War: Some West Riding Fast Sermons', in Anthony Fletcher and Peter Roberts (eds.), *Religion, Culture and Society in Early Modern Britain* (Cambridge, 1994), 309–10; William Sheils, 'John Shawe and Edward Bowles: Civic Preachers at Peace and War', in Peter Lake and Kenneth Fincham (eds.), *Religious Politics in Post-Reformation England: Essays Presented to Nicholas Tyacke* (Woodbridge, 2006), 213–14; Andrew Hopper, 'The Clubmen of the West Riding of Yorkshire during the First Civil War: "Bradford Club-Law"', *Northern History*, 36 (2000): 68; Jacqueline Eales, 'Provincial Preaching and Allegiance in the First English Civil War', in Thomas Cogswell, Richard Cust, and Peter Lake (eds.), *Politics, Religion and Popularity in Early Stuart Britain* (Cambridge, 2002), 190, 196, 201, 207.

12. Edward Furgol, 'The Civil Wars in Scotland', in Kenyon and Ohlmeyer (eds.), *The Civil Wars*, 42, 46, 63, 65; Laura Stewart, 'Military Power and the Scottish Burghs, 1625–1651', *Journal of Early Modern History*, 15 (2011): 74.

13. Lloyd Bowen, 'Representations of Wales and the Welsh during the Civil Wars and Interregnum', *Historical Research* [*Hist. Res.*], 77 (2004): 362–4, 366; Mark Stoyle, 'Caricaturing Cymru: Images of the Welsh in the London Press 1642–46', in Diana Dunn

(ed.), *War and Society in Medieval and Early Modern Britain* (Liverpool, 2000), 162–3, 165; Stephen K. Roberts, 'How the West was Won: Parliamentary Politics, Religion and the Military in South Wales, 1642–9', *Welsh History Review*, 21 (2003): 648–9, 654.

14. Stoyle, *West Britons*, 59, 70–1, 75, 84, 87, 112; Mark Stoyle, 'Sir Richard Grenville's Creatures: The New Cornish Tertia, 1644–46', *Cornish Studies*, 4 (1996): 26–44; Mark Stoyle, 'Afterlife of an Army: The Old Cornish Regiments, 1643–44', *Cornish Studies*, 16 (2008): 26–47; Mark Stoyle, *Soldiers and Strangers: An Ethnic History of the English Civil War* (New Haven, 2005), 105–6, 109.

15. Jane Ohlmeyer, 'The Baronial Context of the Irish Civil Wars', in John Adamson (ed.), *The English Civil War: Conflict and Contexts, 1640–1649* (Basingstoke, 2009), 117, 119; Jane Ohlmeyer, 'The Marquis of Antrim: A Stuart Turn-Kilt?', *History Today*, 43 (1993): 13–18; Jane Ohlmeyer, 'The Civil Wars in Ireland', in Kenyon and Ohlmeyer (eds.), *The Civil Wars*, 77, 80–2, 86; Micheál Ó Siochrú, 'Atrocity, Codes of Conduct and the Irish in the British Civil Wars, 1641–1653', *Past and Present* [P&P], 195 (2007): 64–7; Martyn Bennett, *The Civil Wars in Britain and Ireland, 1638–1651* (Oxford, 1997), 346.

16. Stewart, 'Military Power and the Scottish Burghs', 62; Allan I. Macinnes, 'The "Scottish Moment", 1638–45', in Adamson (ed.), *The English Civil War*, 131.

17. Laura Stewart, 'Fiscal Revolution and State Formation in Mid-Seventeenth-Century Scotland', *Hist. Res.*, 84 (2011): 443–69; Laura Stewart, 'English Funding of the Scottish Armies in England and Ireland, 1640–1648', *HJ*, 52 (2009): 583, 586; Stewart, 'Military Power and the Scottish Burghs'; Macinnes, 'The "Scottish Moment", 1638–45', 152.

18. Peter Edwards, 'Logistics and Supply', in Kenyon and Ohlmeyer (eds.), *The Civil Wars*, 239, 251–2, 255, 257–8, 264–5, 269, 271; Peter Edwards, *Dealing in Death: The Arms Trade and the British Civil Wars, 1638–52* (Stroud, 2000), 40; Stewart, 'English Funding of the Scottish Armies', 585.

19. Gentles, 'The Civil Wars in England', 137; Edwards, *Dealing in Death*, 65, 210.

20. Bennett, *The Civil Wars in Britain and Ireland*, 179–84, 208; Martyn Bennett, *The Civil Wars Experienced: Britain and Ireland, 1638–1661* (London, 2000), 25–8, 31–6; The National Archives [TNA], State Papers 19/8/248–52, 353–4; SP 19/120/72, 76, 84, 111, 120; SP 19/10/308; Ian Atherton, 'Royalist Finances in the English Civil War: The Case of Lichfield Garrison, 1643–5', *Midland History*, 33 (2008): 43–67.

21. Gavin Robinson, 'Horse Supply and the Development of the New Model Army, 1642–1646', *War in History*, 15 (2008): 121–40; Aaron Graham, 'Finance, Localism and Military Representation in the Army of the Earl of Essex (June–December 1642)', *HJ*, 52 (2009): 879–98; Tom Crawshaw, 'Military Finance and the Earl of Essex's Infantry in 1642: A Reinterpretation', *HJ*, 53 (2010): 1037–48; Aaron Graham, 'The Earl of Essex and Parliament's Army at the Battle of Edgehill: A Reassessment', *War in History*, 17 (2010): 293.

22. David Scott, '"The Northern Gentlemen", the Parliamentary Independents, and Anglo-Scottish Relations in the Long Parliament', *HJ*, 42 (1999): 354–6; David Scott, 'The Barwis Affair: Political Allegiance and the Scots during the British Civil Wars', *English Historical Review*, 115 (2000): 849–50, 853, 855, 858–60; John Morrill, 'Mutiny and Discontent in English Provincial Armies, 1645–1647', *P&P*, 56 (1972): 69. For complaints of the Scots' ill-behaviour, including the use of bagpipe-related tortures to extort money from Yorkshire civilians, see TNA, State Papers 16/513/141.

23. Ruth Spalding (ed.), *The Diary of Bulstrode Whitelocke, 1605–1675* (Records of Social and Economic History, New Series, 13, Oxford, 1990), 217; James Scott Wheeler, *The Making of a World Power: War and the Military Revolution in Seventeenth-Century England*

(Stroud, 1999); F. M. S. McDonald, 'The Timing of General George Monck's March into England, 1 January 1660', *English Historical Review*, 105 (1990): 367.

24. Morrill, 'Mutiny and Discontent', 52, 62, 66; Gentles, 'The Civil Wars in England', 147.

25. Ian Gentles, 'The Politics of Fairfax's Army, 1645–9', in Adamson (ed.), *English Civil War*, 175–6, 188, 191, 200; Elliot Vernon and Philip Baker, 'What was the First Agreement of the People?', *HJ*, 53 (2010): 46, 58.

26. Sean Kelsey, 'The Death of Charles I', *HJ*, 45 (2002): 727–54; Sean Kelsey, 'The Trial of Charles I', *English Historical Review*, 118 (2003): 583–616; Sean Kelsey, 'Politics and Procedure in the Trial of Charles I', *Law and History Review*, 22 (2004); Gentles, 'The Civil Wars in England', 154; Gentles, 'The Politics of Fairfax's Army, 1645–9', 194–5; Bennett, *Civil Wars in Britain and Ireland*, 318.

27. Austin Woolrych, *Britain in Revolution, 1625–1660* (Oxford, 2002), 721; Alan Marshall, '"Pax Quaeritur Bello": The Cromwellian Military Legacy', in Jane Mills (ed.), *Cromwell's Legacy* (Manchester, 2012), 116.

28. David Scott, 'Rethinking Royalist Politics 1642–9', in Adamson (ed.), *English Civil War*, 48; John Adamson, 'The Frighted Junto: Perceptions of Ireland and the Last Attempts at Settlement with Charles I', in Jason Peacey (ed.), *The Regicides and the Execution of Charles I* (Basingstoke, 2001), 36–70.

29. P. R. Newman and P. R. Roberts, *Marston Moor, 1644: The Battle of the Five Armies* (Pickering, 2003), xiv–xviii; Glenn Foard, *Naseby: The Decisive Campaign* (Whitstable, 1995); David Johnson, *Adwalton Moor, 1643: The Battle that Changed a War* (Pickering, 2003).

30. Eric Gruber von Arni, *Justice to the Maimed Soldier: Nursing, Medical Care and Welfare for Sick and Wounded Soldiers and their Families during the English Civil Wars and Interregnum, 1642–1660* (Aldershot, 2001); Geoffrey L. Hudson, 'Negotiating for Blood Money: War Widows and the Courts in Seventeenth-Century England', in Jennifer Kermode and Garthine Walker (eds.), *Women, Crime and the Courts in Early Modern England* (London, 1994), 146–69; David Appleby, 'Unnecessary Persons? Maimed Soldiers and War Widows in Essex 1642–1662', *Essex Archaeology and History*, 32 (2001): 209–21; Mark Stoyle, 'Memories of the Maimed: The Testimony of Charles I's Former Soldiers, 1660–1730', *History*, 88 (2003): 204–26.

31. Barbara Donagan, *War in England, 1642–1649* (Oxford, 2008); Barbara Donagan, 'Codes and Conduct in the English Civil War', *P&P*, 118 (1988): 65–95; Barbara Donagan, 'Atrocity, War Crime, and Treason in the English Civil War', *American Historical Review*, 99 (1994): 1137–66; Ó Siochrú, 'Atrocity, Codes of Conduct and the Irish', 55–86; Mark Stoyle, 'The Road to Farndon Field: Explaining the Massacre of the Royalist Women at Naseby', *English Historical Review*, 123 (2008): 895–923; John Ellis, *'To Walk in the Dark': Military Intelligence during the English Civil War, 1642–1646* (Stroud, 2011), 53, 165, 197.

32. For examples of the possibilities here, see Andrew Hopper, *Turncoats and Renegadoes: Changing Sides in the English Civil Wars* (Oxford, 2012); Alan R. Young (ed.), *The English Emblem Tradition: 3. Emblematic Flag Devices of the English Civil Wars, 1642–1660* (Toronto, 1995); Ian Gentles, 'The Iconography of Revolution: England 1642–1649', in Ian Gentles, John Morrill, and Blair Worden (eds.), *Soldiers, Writers and Statesmen of the English Revolution: Essays Presented to Austin Woolrych* (Cambridge, 1998), 91–113; McShane, 'Recruiting Citizens for Soldiers in Seventeenth-Century English Ballads', 105–37.

33. Ian Gentles argues that by January 1648 more than 15% of the New Model Army's officers ranked captain and above had risen from the ranks: TNA, E121, Certificates for the Sale of

Crown Lands; Ian Gentles, 'The New Model Officer Corps in 1647: A Collective Portrait', *Social History*, 22 (1997): 137, 141.

FURTHER READING

Adamson, John (ed.), *The English Civil War: Conflict and Contexts, 1640–1649* (Basingstoke, 2009).

Carpenter, Stanley D. M. (ed.), *The English Civil War* (Aldershot, 2007).

Donagan, Barbara, *War in England 1642–1649* (Oxford, 2008).

Edwards, Peter, *Dealing in Death: The Arms Trade and the British Civil Wars, 1638–52* (Stroud, 2000).

Foard, Glenn, *Naseby: The Decisive Campaign* (Whitstable, 1995).

Gentles, Ian, *The New Model Army in England, Ireland and Scotland, 1645–1653* (Oxford, 1992).

Hopper, Andrew, *Turncoats and Renegadoes: Changing Sides in the English Civil Wars* (Oxford, 2012).

Kenyon, John and Jane Ohlmeyer (eds.), *The Civil Wars: A Military History of England, Scotland and Ireland, 1638–1660* (Oxford, 1998).

Ó Siochrú, Micheál, 'Atrocity, Codes of Conduct and the Irish in the British Civil Wars 1641–1653', *Past and Present*, 195 (2007): 55–86.

Ó Siochrú, Micheál, *God's Executioner: Oliver Cromwell and the Conquest of Ireland* (London, 2008).

Robinson, Gavin, *Horses, People and Parliament in the English Civil War: Extracting Resources and Constructing Allegiance* (Farnham, 2012).

Stoyle, Mark, *Soldiers and Strangers: An Ethnic History of the English Civil War* (New Haven, 2005).

Wanklyn, Malcolm, *Decisive Battles of the English Civil Wars: Myth and Reality* (Barnsley, 2006).

Wanklyn, Malcolm, *Warrior Generals: Winning the British Civil Wars* (New Haven, 2010).

Wanklyn, Malcolm and Frank Jones, *A Military History of the English Civil War, 1642–1646: Strategy and Tactics* (Harlow, 2005).

CHAPTER 16

THE REVOLUTION IN PRINT

JASON PEACEY

In January 1657, the governors of Bedlam took extraordinary precautions to isolate their most high-profile inmate from the outside world. The prisoner was ordered to be removed from 'the society of all people' and was searched for 'pen, ink and paper'. The windows of his chamber were glazed and covered with 'a close grate of wire', boards, and bars. And the series of doors that led to his cell were given new locks and keys, which were never to be allowed in the hands of any one individual at a time. This was despite the fact that the man was desperately sick, and recovering from having been pilloried and whipped through the streets of London, from being branded with a letter B (for blasphemer), and from having had his tongue pierced with a hot poker. As it happens, such measures did not work—his nurse was reprimanded for letting him have 'conference' with various visitors—but they are nevertheless telling. The prisoner was James Nayler, a notorious Quaker who had narrowly avoided being sentenced to death by parliament, and these draconian measures represented a desperate attempt to prevent him from waging war against the Cromwellian regime, by means of the kinds of inflammatory pamphlets for which he had become famous.[1] As such, he provides an apt way of introducing the issue with which this chapter is concerned: the print revolution. Indeed, he highlights three key dimensions of this much-discussed phenomenon, each of which needs to be considered in turn: the 'explosion' of cheap print after 1640; the transformation of political life that print facilitated; and the attempts to restore order and control over the print trade.

This is territory that is historiographically contested, and there is little scholarly consensus regarding the impact of print and its value to scholars of the revolutionary era, but the aims of this chapter are twofold. First, it will suggest that print culture sheds light on every aspect of the civil war: on its causes, its course, and its consequences; on the issues that were at stake and the people that were involved; and on the ways by which the wars were waged and in which they were experienced. Secondly, it will argue that while there is certainly a risk of overstating the impact of print upon contemporary political culture, it nevertheless makes sense to recognize that the 'public sphere' was a meaningful spectre which haunted the age. Indeed, while the liberating potential of the print revolution is apt to be exaggerated, it can also be demonstrated that the contested and complex history of this particularly intense phase of the print revolution left clear and indelible marks on both the political nation and public life, in ways that constitute a clear legacy of the revolutionary era.[2]

A Print Revolution: The Collapse of Censorship and the 'Explosion' of Print

The most common use of the term 'revolution' in relation to post-1640 print culture involves the attempt to characterize extraordinary *quantitative* change. Put simply, historians frequently refer to an 'explosion' of print, something that tends to be expressed with dramatic graphs depicting the output of London's presses across the early modern period. Such graphs are certainly striking, and they appear to be readily explicable in terms of the spikes in printing that coincided with moments of acute political tension, and with periods when authority was contested and weakened (e.g. 1641, 1647, 1659). Indeed, the most dramatic of these spikes is the one that seems the easiest to contextualize, and much has obviously been made of the link between the dramatic developments in both print culture and political affairs on the eve of the civil war. In other words, it is hard not to associate the period from the spring of 1641 to the outbreak of conflict with dramatic increases in both the willingness to publish and the freedom to do so. After all, the early reforms of the Long Parliament swept away the mechanisms associated with pre-publication censorship—with the abolition of Star Chamber and High Commission, and the removal of the licensers who were attached to Archbishop William Laud—amid fiery rhetoric about the threat to godliness and truth that had been posed by the Laudian *imprimatur*. More generally, of course, the return of parliament after the Personal Rule led to the outpouring of grievances and demands that had been difficult to express during the 1630s, while the religious and constitutional issues that emerged naturally led to discussion, debate, and division.[3] In sum, it appears plausible to link an apparent 'explosion' of print with the extraordinary circumstances of the early 1640s, not least because of contemporary complaints about living in a 'talkative' and 'scribbling' age, when people were rather too quick to give vent to their opinions, no matter how inflammatory and dangerous they might be.[4]

The problem with this picture is not that it is wrong, but rather that it is only half-right, and the obvious problem is that it fails to acknowledge that the total output of London's presses almost certainly did not (and could not) increase during these apparent bursts of activity. Whatever was represented by the spikes in the historian's graph, in other words, it was not an increase in the *volume* of printed material that was available to consumers. As such, the 'revolution' of 1641 involved not so much an explosion of print as a *qualitative* shift in what was being produced. Given the structures of England's print trade, in other words, it is vital to recognize that the descent into civil war was marked by something both more than and less than an increase in press freedom. By doing so it is possible to focus in more detail on three interrelated changes that were much more interesting and much more important: the rise of 'cheap print'; the development of new genres; and the emergence of new kinds of author.

First, therefore, the print revolution of the early 1640s was inextricably linked to the enhanced visibility of 'cheap' print, in terms of pamphlets and broadsides that were short and affordable, and that tended to be fairly accessible in terms of their content, and perhaps also in terms of their availability across the country. This is not to say that cheap print was an invention of the civil wars, of course, and considerable scholarly attention has been devoted to unearthing and analysing the many 'popular' genres that emerged during the Tudor and early Stuart period, from educational and instructional litera-ture to murder pamphlets, and from harmless ballads and chapbooks to primitive news reports, seditious libels and inflammatory religious and political polemics, not least those that emerged from the pens of men like Thomas Scot on issues like the 'Spanish match'.[5] However, it is to suggest that printed texts of this kind became a much more prominent feature of public discourse after the summoning of the Long Parliament, and it makes sense to characterize the 'explosion' of print of 1641 as involving a shift away from works of a substantial nature towards those that were relatively insubstantial, and an increase in the number of titles that appeared, rather than of the volume of print in circulation. This is certainly how many contemporaries saw it, and the period is replete with grumbling about the usurpation of scholarship by a 'riot' of 'unprofitable books pamphlets, playbooks, and ballads'.[6]

One striking example of this phenomenon involves the balladeer, Martin Parker, who had been active since the 1620s, but whose output increased markedly in 1640 and 1641. But what is striking about Parker's output is not just the quantity of texts that appeared but also their nature. Indeed, with texts like *A True Subjects Wish* (1640) Parker also symbolized another key aspect of the rise of cheap print: the topical and polemical turn within popular literature, and the domestication of political and religious debate. This particular work—a ballad to be sung to the tune of 'O how now, Mars'—offered sup-port for the king's forces in their campaign against the Scottish Covenanters, and it pro-vides evidence of the way in which the Covenanter rebellion and its apologists helped to inspire English authors and printers to produce works that addressed the most press-ing issues of the day: constitutional revolution and church reform.[7] Although it would be too simplistic to suggest that 1640 marked a watershed in cheap print—between a world of innocent popular piety and merry tales and one dominated by controversy and polemic—there is certainly mileage in suggesting that political and religious tracts loomed considerably larger on the print horizon as war approached. Indeed, it is also true that it became considerably less risky to publish what James I would have consid-ered 'lavish and licentious' discourse on topics that had previously been thought unfit for popular consumption. And it became much easier to produce such material on presses based in England, rather than to engage in surreptitious printing in the Low Countries, or clandestine publishing from a few underground presses in the capital. For polemicists like William Prynne and Henry Parker, in other words, the times demanded new kinds of text, on issues like episcopacy and the royal prerogative, and the political circumstances made such interventions much more feasible.[8]

A second and intimately related dimension to the qualitative print revolution of the early 1640s involved new kinds of text that undermined the *arcana imperii* in rather different ways. This involved varieties of political 'news', and yet another sense in which the revolutionary decades witnessed the domestication of political discourse. News, of course, had been a staple of cheap print since the sixteenth century, and more obviously since the 1620s. Indeed, the outbreak of the Thirty Years War had encouraged the widespread importation of European gazettes and 'corantos' for an educated and elite clientele—such as the Coke and Harley families—and then the development of a native news industry, led by characters like Nathaniel Butter and Nicholas Bourne. However, while contemporaries undoubtedly became more or less familiar with news pamphlets (occasional) and primitive newsbooks (serial) by 1640, successive governments ensured that people had little opportunity to read about domestic affairs rather than Continental conflicts. Home-grown news stories, in other words, remained confined to scribal newsletters, and more or less the preserve of wealthy members of the gentry, barring occasional coverage of episodes like the assassination of the duke of Buckingham or the murder of Doctor Lambe.[9] This changed rapidly and dramatically in the early 1640s, as a result of the return of parliament and of events in Scotland and Ireland. In part this involved stationers feeding (and perhaps fuelling) demand for news regarding the Bishops' Wars and the Irish Rebellion, the latter of which involved literally hundreds of short, lurid, and populist texts regarding the atrocities committed against English Protestant settlers, as well as reports on the progress of the English military campaign to restore royal authority.[10] When England became a theatre of war, of course, reporters and their publishers turned their attention to skirmishes and battles on English soil, but a much more important phenomenon involved the development of English 'diurnalls'— such as *Diurnall Occurrences* and the *Perfect Diurnall*—that fed English readers with regular and affordable doses of domestic news. This was a development of huge significance, the popularity of which is evident from the fact that the *Perfect Diurnall* spawned numerous imitators, many of which were little more than pirated editions. In the last week of July 1642, for example, no less than five different newspapers were available that bore this particular title. These represent a bewildering maze for the modern historian, but they attest to the contemporary appetite for 'current affairs'. Indeed, the number of different newspaper titles quickly ballooned—with as many as twenty different titles being available each week by the mid-1640s—in order to cater for every conceivable taste. Some supported the royalists (*Mercurius Aulicus*), while others favoured the parliamentarians (*Mercurius Civicus*), and some were extremely radical (*The Moderate*), and while some were dry and serious (*Kingdomes Weekly Intelligencer*), others were jocular and even semi-pornographic (*Mercurius Melancholicus*).

The 'news revolution' of the early 1640s thus offers striking evidence about how cultural resources were transferred from other areas and other genres, as private news 'agents' like Daniel Border and John Dillingham turned their hand to printed journalism, and as the publishers of ballads diversified into newsbooks.[11] But it also provides important clues regarding a third qualitative shift in print culture: the emergence of new kinds of author and new publishing practices. Here the key changes involved a much greater prominence for 'professional' authors who lived by their pens—a hitherto rare phenomenon, although one that was not entirely unknown—and for writers whose backgrounds were somewhat humble. The civil wars, in other words, witnessed the rise, if not necessarily the invention, of 'Grub Street', a real place that became associated with the seedier side of print culture, and a term that increasingly conjured images of impecunious hacks and uncouth publishing practices. From 1641 onwards, therefore, stories abounded about 'pettyfogging scribes' and 'pot-poets', who composed scandalous texts and invented fanciful news stories, and who then sold them for a few shillings to ruthless stationers. The latter tried to pass off such 'bum fodder' as 'true' relations, and they were accused of undermining the credibility of the print medium, and any number of individuals were arrested, hauled before the authorities, and imprisoned.[12]

This is not to say that such characters and practices predominated. There was almost certainly an element of scaremongering in contemporary rhetoric, and it was certainly the case that many of the most prominent polemicists and journalists of the age—from Parker to Prynne and from Peter Heylyn to Griffith Williams—hailed from gentry stock and had other sources of income, whether as clerics and lawyers or as 'privados' and 'civil servants'. Nevertheless, some well-bred authors began to make a good living from print—the most obvious case being Marchamont Nedham—and there are also fascinating cases of humble individuals rising to prominence through populist prose and professional guile. Here scholars have rightly dwelt on characters like John Taylor the Thames bargeman and Henry Walker the London ironmonger. This is not just because their many abusive pamphlets represented some of the earliest signs of the cheap print revolution, but also because Walker went on to become one of the pre-eminent journalists of the age.[13] However, the transformation of authorship also involved the way in which the circumstances of civil war and revolution—contested authority and intellectual creativity—led to the emergence of men and women who seized the opportunity to express radical ideas of all kinds, whether as hardline royalists, political radicals, or religious sectarians. Many of these are now entirely familiar to scholars and students alike. They included future Levellers, whose polemical careers began with membership of dissident congregations and involvement with underground presses, and they also included a plethora of soldiers and merchants from across the land, as well as London radicals like Katherine and Samuel Chidley. And of course they also included the troublesome Quaker, James Nayler, as well as any number of his associates.[14]

Levellers like Lilburne and Quakers like Nayler, not to mention 'Ranters' like Thomas Tany, sent shivers through sizeable sections of the political elite, because of both their ideas and their humble status. Indeed, for conservatives like Thomas Edwards they offered living proof of what happened when order, hierarchy, and deference were challenged by upstart men and women who had no legitimate role in public life.[15] However, what also caused concern was the blatant way in which they addressed humble citizens—the 'clubs and clouted shoes'—and the danger that they might 'stir up sedition' among the 'witless multitude'. To contemporaries, in other words, the 'print revolution' was thought to be intimately connected to novel political practices, and to an entirely new political 'style'.[16]

A REVOLUTION BY PRINT: FROM THE PROTESTATION TO THE REGICIDE

Much less common than the idea of a print revolution involving new freedoms, new genres, and new kinds of author is analysis of the link between print culture and the political revolution of the 1640s. Nevertheless, as scholars are beginning to recognize, print culture was intimately linked to new kinds of political behaviour, and to new kinds of relationship between political regimes and members of the wider public. The aim of this section, therefore, is to examine new practices, new ways of engaging with the people, and new kinds of interaction between citizens and their rulers in the conditions of civil war, from the Protestation of 1641 to the trial of the king in 1649. Central here will be the idea that the revolution was achieved in no small part by printed means. Political machinations, in other words, came to involve every branch of an expanded political nation—from 'hedgers at the hedges' to 'plowmen at the plough' and 'threshers in the barns', and from Nehemiah Wallington the woodturner to Thomas Rugg the barber—as public opinion and the 'public sphere' became conjurable spectres, if not necessarily demonstrable phenomena.[17]

The most obvious way in which historians have thought about the novel political style of the 1640s involves the idea of enhanced and intensified public debate. Previously, debates had either been restrained—as with the deliberate attempts to ensure that religious disputations were restricted to private and oral exchanges—or else contained, not least through William Laud's efforts to discourage printed exchanges which might cause controversies to be 'further stirred'. By the early 1640s, however, debates were much more obviously taking place in public, in print, and in a much less restrained fashion, and in relation to both the religious and political debates of the age. One way in which this became evident involved the tendency for formal religious disputations to spill over into print, but a more common pattern involved controversial pamphlets provoking printed responses which rapidly escalated into prolonged exchanges that drew in a wider group of authors.[18] This pattern emerged fairly quickly—as with the debate between Joseph Hall and 'Smectymnuus' or between Henry Ferne and Charles Herle—and it was one that became a firmly entrenched feature of civil war culture. This was true not just in terms of debates between spokesmen for royalism and parliamentarianism, but also in terms of arguments between different parliamentarian factions, on contentious issues like church reform or the merits and demerits of the republic's Engagement. However, this sense that political culture became notably *dialogic* was evident at the scurrilous as well as the serious end of the print spectrum—as with the exchanges between Walker and Taylor—and it became absolutely central to civil war journalism. This was certainly evident in terms of news pamphlets, where readers were frequently confronted with contradictory accounts of particular battles—all of which were described as 'true'—and it was also a central feature of early newsbooks, some of which were designed with the more or less express purpose of providing rapid rebuttals to the claims made by political rivals (e.g. *Mercurius Britanicus*). The danger, and one that was apparent to contemporaries as well as recent historians, was that debates would become increasingly acrimonious, and that readers would despair about the possibility of discerning the truth.[19]

Increasingly, however, historians have become fascinated by the ways in which print became centrally important not just to the dynamics of public debate but also to the processes by which elites engaged with the public in a much more direct and purposeful fashion. It was central, in other words, to new ways of mobilizing, enlisting popular support, and expressing public opinion, all of which became central to the political culture of the revolutionary era, and none of which could be done very readily without varieties of print media. Of course, it had long been common for regimes to address their citizens, and for individual politicians to engage in the dark arts of 'popularity', by courting and demonstrating public support, but this is another area where the early 1640s witnessed considerable change.[20] Indeed, as with so many other aspects of the print revolution this became dramatically apparent long before war broke out, and can be demonstrated with three of the most important phenomena of 1641: the Protestation, mass petitioning, and the Grand Remonstrance. The Protestation (May 1641), which was issued in the context of mounting political unrest and the fear of armed conflict, involved an oath of loyalty—nominally to the king and the established church, but effectively a proto-parliamentarian test of allegiance—and print technology permitted it to be circulated aggressively in print in order to reach into every corner of the political nation, both literally and metaphorically, and in order to enlist support and provide documentary evidence about the loyalty of even the most humble citizens. It offered a remarkable demonstration of inclusivity, and it can be shown to have been used as a totemic device in street politics. It was also treated as an empowering text that sanctioned the expression of popular opinions, and indeed fairly dramatic forms of popular political action, including religious iconoclasm.[21]

This sense that citizens were being mobilized in novel ways also became evident from the emergence of mass petitioning, and if the Protestation involved *creating* and *testing* popular allegiance then the petitioning campaigns undertaken both locally and nationally in the early 1640s revealed a determination to *invoke* mass support. What is striking about the kind of petitioning that became common in 1641, therefore, was that print provided a valuable means of demonstrating popular views, and that this was done in ways which tended to prioritize and validate numerical strength rather than social status. In other words, it was deemed to be more important to show that petitions had secured thousands of signatures—even if these came from humble citizens—than to prove that they were representative of the views of local elites.[22] The novelty of such tactics is evident from the controversy that they generated, and it was fairly common to find conservatives expressing disdain for tactics that sought to 'fill paper with names', and that sought to valorize the opinions of 'mean men'.[23]

Finally, with the Grand Remonstrance (November 1641) parliament made an equally blatant and controversial appeal for popular support. The novelty here was that a text which offered a detailed indictment of Caroline policies, as well as a detailed list of political and religious demands, was ordered to be printed for public consumption rather than merely presented to the king, and Sir Edward Dering complained that 'I did not dream that we should remonstrate downward, tell stories to the people, and talk of the king as of a third person.'[24] These three episodes not only set the tone for civil war political culture—from the 'paper war' between king and parliament in 1642, to the political campaigning over the Solemn League and Covenant and religious reform later in the decade—but also demonstrated clear political awareness that popular support could not be taken for granted, and that persuasion was a political necessity. They also reveal awareness not just that the views of ordinary citizens needed be moulded, but also that popular sentiment mattered to the political elite, and that it needed to be taken into account much more obviously than had been true in the past.

What is implicit in these three episodes is that print facilitated the enlargement of the political nation, both socially and geographically. This is an idea that has traditionally met with unwarranted scepticism from historians, and there is plentiful evidence that the transformation of political culture which accompanied the print revolution and the civil wars was experienced far beyond the capital, and in both urban and rural settings. In part this reflected a quiet revolution in the structures of the book trade—involving dramatic increases in the number of retail outlets that made print available, and a demonstrable shift in their stock from scholarly and educational texts to works containing news and topical debate—but it also involved novel habits and practices of consumption. Thus, in addition to the fact that cheap political texts became much more readily available in bookshops across the land, as well as from countless mercers and cobblers in provincial towns, they also started to fill the pedlar's pack, and any number of provincial citizens struck deals with local carriers in order to ensure regular supplies of up-to-the-minute information. Thus, while pamphlets and newsbooks continued to be circulated through gentry networks, and to the elite through the services of London stationers, they also became accessible to much more humble citizens, effectively by subscription. As such, stories abound of printed texts provoking conversations and debates on street corners and in shop doorways, and of the latest news being read to artisans and tradesmen in provincial inns and alehouses, and then being transmitted orally among friends and acquaintances, quite literally on the street. Indeed, it would not be an exaggeration to say that printed texts—from proclamations and declarations to newsbooks and pamphlets—became a ubiquitous feature of daily life even in the most remote corners of the land. And it seems clear that this also meant Scotland, Ireland, and Wales, where the impact of the print revolution has received much less attention. Quite apart from the innovative techniques for exploiting print that were developed by the Covenanters in the late 1630s, and the role of English troops as 'carriers' of both texts and ideas, contemporary correspondence clearly reveals prevalent *assumptions* that local residents—in both town and country—had ready access to the product of London's presses. Thus, while it would be wrong to suggest that the print revolution made exactly the same impact on the masses as it did on the elite, on rural areas as it did on towns, and on the provinces as it did on London, it would be equally unwise to deny that printed texts had considerable social and geographical reach, and that such material helped to foster a genuinely national culture of news and comment.

However, if the emergence of a political culture that was dialogic and politically integrative has begun to generate scholarly interest, and can be shown to have transformed the lives of people across the three kingdoms, then other changes to conventional political practice have received much less attention. Not the least of these is a dramatic increase in political transparency, a somewhat neglected aspect of the *arcana imperii*, and one that was profoundly affected by the print revolution. Indeed, the period after 1641 witnessed an unsteady but discernible process whereby political secrecy was undermined, either willingly or by means of aggressive tactics on the part of politicians and the press, or more commonly as a result of a complex mixture of factors and actors. One fairly obvious way in which this occurred involved parliamentary news, including detailed evidence about proceedings and processes at Westminster. This was indicative of a trend whereby information that had traditionally been regarded as secret, or at least 'privileged', became readily available, and one of its most dramatic manifestations involved the publication of speeches by many of the most prominent MPs and peers. Between 1640 and 1642, for example, more than fifty different pamphlets purported to contain speeches by John Pym, and although many of these were duplicate texts, and even forgeries, they are indicative of the enthusiasm with which parliamentary news was consumed, and the regularity with which it was supplied by entrepreneurial stationers. This was both winked at and frowned upon by MPs, depending on the circumstances in which it was done, and it can be shown to have made a fairly remarkable impact on the ways in which contemporaries followed parliamentary affairs, and indeed monitored the activities of their MPs.[25]

Such material represented merely a fraction of the evidence that pamphleteers and journalists made available about parliamentary affairs, and it was also representative of the way in which the print revolution facilitated the *individualization* of political life. This meant providing details not just about political processes and proceedings, but also about specific individuals within the ruling elite, in terms of their characters, their ideas, and their performance. On many occasions this was done consciously and willingly by public figures, not least in order to defend or boost their reputations, and to draw attention to their opinions and their service, but it could also be done in a more intrusive fashion. Perhaps the most famous example of this phenomenon involved the king himself, who became subject to unprecedented public scrutiny as a result of the capture of his private letters, most famously with the publication of the *King's Cabinet Opened* (1645). Although not everyone believed that these letters were genuine, the overwhelming impression was that the revelations which they contained proved highly damaging to Charles's reputation and political credibility.[26] However, this episode represented merely the most prominent example of a much broader trend, and it is legitimate to talk about the emergence of muckraking journalism in the 1640s, and about the origins of the political blacklist. In 1648, for example, royalists provided readers with detailed evidence about the perquisites and offices that were received and held by a group of prominent MPs, while aggressive journalists like Marchamont Nedham more than amply fulfilled their promises to use papers like *Britanicus* and *Pragmaticus* to expose 'the virtues and deserts of the best, the treachery, malignity, cavalierism of the worst'.[27]

The fourth and perhaps least understood transformation in political practice that can be associated with the print revolution involves the potential that was created for public participation in political life. Here the central idea is that the print media proved susceptible to being *appropriated* by members of the public, not just in order to express their views as actors in a 'public sphere' of discussion and debate, but also as contributors to political deliberations. This could be done individually as well as collectively, and it could involve the use of print as a tool for petitioning and lobbying, or as a means of organizing support, and it could also involve placing pressure on specific MPs. One particularly striking instance involved presbyterian activists in London creating hundreds of copies of printed petitions for distribution across the city, in the hope of encouraging supporters to 'get hands', and some of these even left spaces for the addition of signatures and for the insertion of the name of the parish from which they came. In 1647, meanwhile, activists within the army used printed texts in an aggressive fashion to heap obloquy on presbyterian MPs in the House of Commons, ahead of the impeachment of the eleven members. Indeed, during the tumultuous events of the 1640s it even proved possible to use print as a tool in street politics, in order to organize protesting crowds, as supporters of peace attempted to do with notices aimed at London apprentices in January 1643. Ultimately, where this led was to the innovative and imaginative use of print by more or less radical political and religious movements. London baptists used printed notices in order to encourage mass petitioning in every parish of London as early as 1643, and the Levellers famously employed similar tactics in the late 1640s, by producing literally thousands of incendiary texts for distribution across the south of England, and by using printed texts as an essential ingredient in the campaign to enlist support for the *Agreement of the People*.[28] The latter was literally intended to be signed by ordinary citizens, as part of the process of placing pressure on parliament and reforming the political system. In these cases, in other words, printed texts were absolutely central to the process by which radical movements not only operated but also came into being, something that has been made palpably clear for the Quakers, a movement whose missionary zeal may have come to nothing without the creation and distribution of vast quantities of printed material.[29]

What such examples provide is evidence with which to substantiate the fears expressed by any number of conservative contemporaries, namely that print was integral to the process by which ordinary citizens had 'invaded the sacred reins of government', that they had become 'statesmen', and that the period witnessed the 'king-ing of the multitude' and 'a sea of democracy'.[30] Indeed, this sense that print facilitated new ideas and practices regarding political participation, representation, and accounta-bility emerges extremely clearly during the trial of Charles I in 1649, which reveals much more than merely the existence of an intense debate about the legitimacy of the proceed-ings. The idea of putting the king on trial was promoted heavily in print, not least by the army, whose famous *Remonstrance* was supplemented by a vigorous lobbying cam-paign, in which printed petitions not only reflected sentiments within the ranks but also became devices for inspiring further agitation. Other texts, meanwhile, provided read-ers with detailed accounts of parliamentary politics in the weeks before the trial, includ-ing details about the MPs who were removed at Pride's Purge, and the texts of speeches like those of William Prynne, the latter of which was read communally by at least one group of interested onlookers in Essex. More particularly, the thorough—effectively verbatim—accounts of the trial that appeared in both pamphlets and newspapers as events unfolded provided readers with an unprecedentedly detailed account of the per-formance of the prosecutors, the defendant, and the judges. There are grounds, in other words, for arguing that the events surrounding the king's trial represented the acme of the print revolution.[31]

A Restorative Revolution: Censorship, Propaganda, and the Search for Order

However, the period surrounding the regicide also reveals other things about con-temporary print culture, from the imprisonment of seditious pamphleteers like John Lilburne to the hiring of salaried writers like John Milton and John Hall, and the passage of a new Act for regulating the press, which resulted in the silencing of a range of royal-ist, radical, and more or less unreliable journalists (September 1649).[32] Such evidence is indicative of determination to tame the press, and of a rather different kind of revolu-tion. For many contemporaries in the seventeenth century, of course, the term revolu-tion had *restorative* rather than *transformative* connotations, and as such there are also grounds for exploring a revolution in print which brought about political control rather than merely political liberation. This sense of the need to impose order on the print trade was most famously expressed after 1660 by Sir Roger L'Estrange, who argued that the press had made people 'too familiar with the actions and counsels of their superiors, too pragmatical and censorious', and that it had given them 'not only an itch but a kind of colourable right and license to be meddling with the government'. Indeed, he insisted that 'the people neither have had, nor ever can have, nor ought to have, any right, power of faculty of government'; that 'the subject's part is resignation and obedience'; and that it was necessary to instil 'dutiful and honest principles into the common people'. Indeed, he became notorious for arguing that ''tis the press that has made 'em mad, and the press that must set 'em right again'.[33] However, L'Estrange's tactics for controlling the press can only be understood in the context of policies that emerged from 1641 onwards, and most obviously during the republic and Protectorate. The punishment of Nayler, in other words, needs to be contextualized in terms of a protracted and complex process for regaining control over print culture.

First, as Henry Walker found to his cost on more than one occasion in the early 1640s, the Long Parliament was perfectly willing to punish authors and printers who were thought to have stepped out of line, and he repeatedly found himself in trouble for his printed antics, not least for throwing an inflammatory tract into the king's coach in January 1642. Indeed, the 1640s provide plentiful evidence that parliamentarians were determined to make an example of malefactors 'for a terror to the rest', and as such public book burnings quickly became a fairly common sight in London. In the spring of 1643, indeed, the Committee of Examinations ordered searches to be made for illicit presses, which were to be destroyed and their owners imprisoned, and it was also ordered that seditious books ought to be seized from bookshops and bookstalls. In addition, powers were granted to the Committee for Sequestrations to confiscate the estates of delinquent printers, and the authorities were also able to rely upon the zeal of the Stationers' Company, whose beadle, Joseph Hunscott, proved to be particularly active in the pursuit of offenders. Thus, the fact that the 1640s witnessed pleas for freedom of the press—from men like Henry Robinson, John Bachilor, and Gilbert Mabbott—ought to be seen as evidence that the collapse of press control, about which so much has been said, was never more than partial. Indeed, rather too much has probably been made of the tolerance of commentators like John Milton, whose *Areopagitica*—'a speech... for the liberty of unlicensed printing'—may not only have been ignored by most readers at the time, but also recognized clear limitations to the kinds of freedom that were thought to be desirable.[34]

Mention of Milton and his famous pamphlet, of course, raises another important issue relating to the revolution that occurred in relation to press freedom: licensing and pre-publication censorship. Here it is rather too easy for historians to dwell on the removal of the Laudian system in 1641, and to associate this with the end of censorship, and what needs to be recognized is that the principal aim of many MPs was to challenge the *substance* of Caroline licensing rather than its form. The problem, as Sir Edward Dering explained, was that it led to a situation in which 'truth is suppressed', while 'Popish pamphlets fly abroad, *cum privilegio*'. Indeed, a somewhat neglected aspect of print culture in the 1640s—beginning as early as 1641—was fairly determined experimentation with new methods for controlling the output of London's presses. In part this meant the establishment of a parliamentary licensing committee, under Dering's chairmanship, in order to approve books and pamphlets for publication, not least by authors who had been victimized by the Laudian regime. More obviously, however, it meant the appointment of new licensers, mostly from within the ranks of the (puritan) clergy, and the implementation of a new ordinance relating to press control (June 1643), as well as further similar measures in subsequent years, both during the late 1640s and the Rump parliament.[35]

With both of these aspects of censorship, however, it is important to recognize that the dynamic of press control during the 1640s was highly complex, and that the trajectory was far from smooth. This is partly because the press became a political battleground that was contested between rival groups *within* the parliamentarian cause, with licensing as a powerful weapon in factional tussles. There were, therefore, presbyterian licensers as well as independent licensers—who approved very different kinds of text, and who sometimes tussled for control of particular newspapers—as well as a few licensers who appear not to have believed in licensing at all. These included one John Milton, who served briefly as a licenser of republican newspapers in the early 1650s. This all suggests that pre-publication censorship was about more than merely press control, and among the factors that underpinned the new press regime in the 1640s and 1650s was the attempt to protect the guild of stationers as well as the interests of politicians. Indeed, the Stationers' Company remained an active partner in the enforcement of press control for most of the 1640s. That the company was eventually side-lined after 1649 is indicative not just of the fact that their presbyterian bias troubled the independents and the army, but also of a second crucial dimension of official policy during the revolutionary era: the growing power of the centralized state. After 1649, therefore, every aspect of press control, including the bulk of licensing, was undertaken by men who were civil servants, or else clerics who held official positions within the Council of State or Cromwellian regime.[36]

Thirdly, it makes sense to recognize not just that press policy was sometimes reactive rather than systematic, but also that one of the government's central aims was to 'police' the press rather than to silence critics entirely. It has recently been argued that this may also have been the goal of the early Stuart regimes, and that a policy of regulating the boundaries of acceptable discourse might make more sense of their decisions than the possibility that the government was either repressive or ineffective, but it much more clearly influenced the thinking of MPs in the 1640s.[37] The result was that concerted efforts were made to monitor London's presses, and to keep them under surveillance, but not necessarily to take action against every seditious pamphlet about which they became aware, even when they knew exactly who was responsible. The results *appeared* to involve inconsistent enforcement, but this almost certainly represented an attempt to gather information in order to be able to take decisive action when circumstances required that this should be done. Fourthly, and related, it also makes sense to argue that part of the strategy of successive regimes during the civil wars and Interregnum involved the attempt to *formalize* what was and was not acceptable in terms of printing and publishing. This meant ensuring that blasphemy and sedition were punished much more consistently than mere radicalism and royalism, and it also meant navigating a middle-way between the Scylla of oppressive official secrecy and the Charybdis of complete political transparency.

In other words, it is important neither to deny that attempts were made to tame the press after 1641 nor to characterize this as involving a simple return to an earlier model of regulation and control. Indeed, this is particularly clear from the fact that the period witnessed fairly innovative attempts to combine censorship and licensing with the subtle arts of 'spin' and 'propaganda'. Such terms are obviously anachronistic, and yet the concepts were clearly understood by contemporaries, and one of the hallmarks of the period was the emergence of fairly subtle methods for exerting a positive influence over the content of the press, and for deploying print in a tactical fashion. Here the devices that were used ranged from the traditional—such as official proclamations and declarations, which were produced in vast quantities and circulated zealously—to the novel and the experimental. Any number of authors and stationers worked with the political authorities in more or less clandestine ways, and print was regularly used not just to rally support and secure allegiance but also to convey official messages to diverse audiences, and to fly kites for controversial policies. Indeed, this is another area where enhanced subtlety and sophistication was accompanied by the intensification of state power, and the Interregnum witnessed an increasingly professionalized, bureaucratized, and well-funded machinery for the production of various kinds of propaganda.[38]

In other words, the 1640s and 1650s witnessed what might be thought of as a restorative revolution, in the sense that it is possible to reconstruct a concerted if complex and piecemeal campaign to ensure that some kind of order was restored to the print trade after the turmoil of 1641. However, close scrutiny reveals that this involved something other than a straightforward turning back of the political clocks, in order to reinvent a system with which Laud and Charles I would have been familiar. Press restraint after 1641 was qualitatively different to the policies of earlier regimes, and it was combined much more obviously with a determination to engage with the people through persuasion and the black arts of propaganda. Indeed, the result was an integrated and highly centralized system, in which surveillance, censorship, and punishment, as well as intelligence gathering, were overseen by the Council of State, and by men like John Thurloe. The most obvious symbol of this new approach to the press and print culture involved the measures taken in the summer of 1655, which ensured that the government effectively secured a press monopoly, at least in terms of the news industry, with two more or less closely controlled official newspapers under the editorship of a salaried journalist, Marchamont Nedham.[39] That this system did not survive the collapse of the Protectorate in 1659—when the return of the Rump was accompanied by new kinds of freedom and particularly intense public debates—is less important than the fact that it provided a very clear and attractive model for successive generations, and for men like Sir Roger L'Estrange. To the extent that the mid-seventeenth century witnessed a story of renewed official control over the print trades, therefore, it was one which began much earlier than 1660, and which occurred in an incomplete and highly complex fashion.

CONCLUSION: THE LEGACY OF REVOLUTION

That the story of print culture after the Restoration is one of both continuity and change provides a suitable way of thinking about the legacy of the print revolution. What has become clear is that the term 'revolution' must here be used in more than one way. In part the revolution involved a qualitative shift in the output of the press, an explosion of cheap print that brought news and comment to a much wider audience, and a transformation of the conditions in which authors and stationers worked, and in the processes by which their texts were produced. This print revolution had a profound impact on *who* was affected by the civil wars and *how* the revolution was experienced by ordinary citizens. But the revolution also had a fairly profound impact on the practice of politics, and was deeply implicated in the political upheavals and revolutions of the period. It played a part in the collapse of royal authority and the constitutional experimentation of the civil wars and Interregnum, and it was also integral to new kinds of relationship between governors and governed, and to new kinds of interaction between the political elite and the people. And while it would be naive to suggest that print *caused* these revolutionary changes, it would also be foolish to overlook the fact that such changes would not have happened without the print revolution. In this sense the print revolution both reflected, facilitated, and helped to shape the political revolution. And integral to this political revolution were impulses which ensured that print became a political tool for the elite as a well as a weapon of the weak, and there was no clearer indication of the potency of print culture than that successive regimes sought to tame and exploit a range of popular genres—most especially the newspapers—and to restore order to the print trade. The upshot was that the revolutionary decades witnessed novel manifestations of a perennial truth about the media: that there was a complex interplay between the forces of 'liberation' and the forces of 'authority'. Contemporaries, in other words, encountered different kinds of print revolution during the civil wars and Interregnum, which had different effects, and which occurred simultaneously. As such, the legacy of the revolution in print is far from straightforward. Nevertheless, what seems clear is that civil war print culture helped to ensure that the period witnessed more or less permanent changes in terms of the expansion of the political nation, the vulgarization of politics and information, and the emergence of something resembling a shared culture of news and comment. This meant that contemporaries both inside and outwith the political elite began to question accepted ideas and practices relating to participation, transparency, representation, and accountability, and although the debates that emerged did not produce consensus, or even very clear thinking, the intellectual goalposts and fault lines almost certainly changed irrevocably. And whether print was used as a means of liberation or oppression, its central impact was integrative, and it served to create an inclusive if not exactly equal political system.

Notes

1. Bethlem Royal Hospital Archives, BCB 9, pp. 784–6, 791–2, 794, 796–7, 815, 879–80.
2. Peter Lake and Steven Pincus (eds.), *The Politics of the Public Sphere in Early Modern England* (Manchester, 2007); David Zaret, *Origins of Democratic Culture* (Princeton, 2000).
3. Joad Raymond, *Pamphlets and Pamphleteering in Early Modern England* (Cambridge, 2003).
4. Folger Shakespeare Library, V.a.454, p. 69; British Library, Add. MS 20065, fo. 123v.

5. Peter Lake and Michael Questier, *The Antichrist's Lewd Hat* (Princeton, 2002); Tessa Watt, *Cheap Print and Popular Piety, 1550-1640* (Cambridge, 1991); Peter Lake, 'Constitutional Consensus and Puritan Opposition in the 1620s: Thomas Scott and the Spanish Match', *Historical Journal [HJ]*, 25 (1982): 805–25.

6. Henry E. Huntington Library, San Marino, HM 22039; BL, Harleian MS 4931, fo. 87v.

7. Martin Parker, *A True Subjects Wish* (London, 1640).

8. James F. Larkin and Paul L. Hughes, *Stuart Royal Proclamations* (Oxford, 1973), 495–6; David Como, 'Secret Printing, the Crisis of 1640 and the Origins of Civil War Radicalism', *Past and Present [P&P]*, 196 (2007): 37–82.

9. Joad Raymond, *The Invention of the Newspaper* (Oxford, 1996); Thomas Cogswell, 'John Felton, Popular Political Culture and the Assassination of the Duke of Buckingham', *HJ*, 49 (2006): 357–85; Alastair Bellany, 'The Murder of John Lambe: Crowd Violence, Court Scandal and Popular Politics in Early Seventeenth-Century England', *P&P*, 200 (2008): 37–76.

10. Ethan Shagan, 'Constructing Discord: Ideology, Propaganda, and English Responses to the Irish Rebellion of 1641', *Journal of British Studies*, 36 (1997): 4–34.

11. A. N. B. Cotton, 'John Dillingham, Journalist of the Middle Group', *English Historical Review*, 93 (1978): 817–34.

12. Michael Mendle, 'De Facto Freedom, de Facto Authority: Press and Parliament, 1640–1643', *HJ*, 38 (1995): 307–32.

13. Bernard Capp, *The World of John Taylor, the Water Poet, 1578–1653* (Oxford, 1994); Jason Peacey, *Politicians and Pamphleteers* (Aldershot, 2004), 64–131, 153–8, 192.

14. Ian Gentles, 'London Levellers in the English Revolution: The Chidleys and their Circle', *Journal of Ecclesiastical History*, 29 (1978): 281–309.

15. Ann Hughes, *Gangraena and the Struggle for the English Revolution* (Oxford, 2004).

16. Henry Cary, *Memorials of the Great Civil War* (London, 1842), 293; *A Scourge for Paper-Persecutors* (London, 1625), 2.

17. Antony House, Cornwall, BC/24/2, fo. 65; Paul Seaver, *Wallington's World* (London, 1985); *The Diurnal of Thomas Rugg, 1659-1661*, ed. William Lewis Sachse, Camden Society, 3rd series, 91 (London, 1961).

18. Peter Lake, *The Boxmaker's Revenge* (Manchester, 2001); *The Works of the Most Reverend Father in God, William Laud*, 7 vols. (Oxford, 1847–60), VI, 292.

19. Michael Braddick, *God's Fury, England's Fire: A New History of the English Civil Wars* (London, 2008), 303, 369, 459.

20. Thomas Cogswell, Richard Cust, and Peter Lake (eds.), *Politics, Religion and Popularity in Early Stuart Britain* (Cambridge, 2002); Peter Lake, 'The Politics of Popularity and the Public Sphere: The Monarchical Republic of Elizabeth I Defends Itself', in Lake and Pincus (eds.), *Public Sphere*, 59–94; Michael Braddick, 'Mobilisation, Anxiety and Creativity in England during the 1640s', in John Morrow and Jonathan Scott (eds.), *Liberty, Authority, Formality* (Exeter, 2008), 175–94.

21. David Cressy, 'The Protestation Protested, 1641 and 1642', *HJ*, 45 (2002): 251–79.

22. Zaret, *Origins*, 217–65.

23. Shropshire Archives, 212/364/72a; Antony House, BC/24/2, fo. 63.

24. Edward Dering, *A Collection of Speeches* (London, 1642), 109.

25. Jason Peacey, 'Print Culture and Political Lobbying during the English Civil Wars', *Parliamentary History*, 26 (2007): 30–48; Jason Peacey, 'Royalist News, Parliamentary Debates and Political Accountability, 1640-60', *Parliamentary History*, 26 (2007): 328–45;

Alan Cromartie, 'The Printing of Parliamentary Speeches, November 1640–July 1642', *HJ*, 33 (1990): 23–44; Jason Peacey, 'Sir Edward Dering, Popularity and the Public, 1640–1644', *HJ*, 54 (2011): 955–83; Jason Peacey, *Print and Public Politics in the English Revolution* (Cambridge, 2013), chaps. 5–6.

26. Jason Peacey, 'The Exploitation of Captured Royal Correspondence and Anglo-Scottish Relations in the British Civil Wars, 1645–6', *Scottish Historical Review*, 79 (2000): 213–32.

27. *A List of the Names* (London, 1648); *Mercurius Britanicus*, 28 (18–25 March 1644), 215.

28. Zaret, *Origins*, 240–50; Peacey, *Common Politics*, chaps. 7–11; Jason Peacey, 'The People of the Agreements', in Philip Baker and Elliot Vernon (eds.), *The Agreements of the People, the Levellers and the Constitutional Crisis of the English Revolution* (Basingstoke, 2012), 50–75.

29. Kate Peters, *Print Culture and the Early Quakers* (Cambridge, 2005).

30. Geoff Kemp, 'L'Estrange and the Publishing Sphere', in Jason McElligott (ed.), *Fear, Exclusion and Revolution* (Aldershot, 2006), 67–90; Northamptonshire RO, IC 353.

31. Essex RO, D/DQs18, fo. 70v; Jason Peacey, 'Reporting a Revolution: A Failed Propaganda Campaign', in Jason Peacey (ed.), *The Regicides and the Execution of Charles I* (Basingstoke, 2001), 161–80.

32. Peacey, *Politicians*, 158, 194–200.

33. *Intelligencer*, 1 (31 August 1663); Kemp, 'L'Estrange', 67–90; *Observator*, 1 (13 April 1681).

34. Peacey, *Politicians*, 143–5, 152, 157–8, 296.

35. Peacey, *Politicians*, 132–62.

36. Peacey, *Politicians*, 145–61.

37. Anthony Milton, 'Licensing, Censorship, and Religious Orthodoxy in Early Stuart England', *HJ*, 41 (1998): 625–51.

38. Peacey, *Politicians*, 95–131, 163–302.

39. Peacey, *Politicians*, 161, 193, 227–30, 269–70.

FURTHER READING

Como, David, 'Secret Printing, the Crisis of 1640 and the Origins of Civil War Radicalism', *Past and Present*, 196 (2007): 37–82.

Cressy, David, 'The Protestation Protested, 1641 and 1642', *Historical Journal*, 45 (2002): 251–279.

Cromartie, Alan, 'The Printing of Parliamentary Speeches, November 1640–July 1642', *Historical Journal*, 33 (1990): 23–44.

Hughes, Ann, *Gangraena and the Struggle for the English Revolution* (Oxford, 2004).

Lake, Peter and Steven Pincus (eds.), *The Politics of the Public Sphere in Early Modern England* (Manchester, 2007).

Peacey, Jason, *Politicians and Pamphleteers* (Aldershot, 2004).

Peacey, Jason, *Print and Public Politics in the English Revolution* (Cambridge, 2013).

Peacey, Jason, 'Print Culture and Political Lobbying during the English Civil Wars', *Parliamentary History*, 26 (2007): 30–48.

Peacey, Jason, 'Reporting a Revolution: A Failed Propaganda Campaign', in Jason Peacey (ed.), *The Regicides and the Execution of Charles I* (Basingstoke, 2001), 161–180.

Peacey, Jason, 'Royalist News, Parliamentary Debates and Political Accountability, 1640–60', *Parliamentary History*, 26 (2007): 328–345.

Peacey, Jason, 'Sir Edward Dering, Popularity and the Public, 1640–1644', *Historical Journal*, 54 (2011): 955–983.

Peters, Kate, *Print Culture and the Early Quakers* (Cambridge, 2005).

Raymond, Joad, *The Invention of the Newspaper* (Oxford, 1996).

Raymond, Joad, *Pamphlets and Pamphleteering in Early Modern England* (Cambridge, 2003).

Zaret, David, *Origins of Democratic Culture* (Princeton, 2000).

CHAPTER 17

STATE AND SOCIETY IN THE ENGLISH REVOLUTION

STEPHEN K. ROBERTS

HISTORICAL accounts of local government in England and Wales during the English revolution were most prolific in a twenty-year period after 1966, a year which saw the publication of a highly influential book by Alan Everitt on Kent. The context of these local studies was almost invariably the county, which offered to each researcher in a generation of Ph.D. students a focus, a manageable corpus of records, and a sense of personal proprietorship. Many of these studies sought to test the idea of 'localism', the idea that local society was characterized by a dominant aversion to, or lack of interest in, events unfolding in London or the royal court. Many also sought to refine or to test the notion of the county as a focus of primary cultural and governmental loyalty for the politically active, an idea summarized in the phrase 'county community' and associated strongly with Everitt and his work on Kent. By the 1980s both these concepts had been tested to destruction, as historians became convinced that neither localism nor the county community held a general validity.[1] For all the conceptual shortcomings and ruptures, however, this was a most productive period of scholarly research. Those studies of the period with an explicit focus on local government tended to be preoccupied with structures, concerned with how the system worked. There was also interest in exploring the relationship between the government of the localities and the directive bodies in Whitehall or the palace of Westminster, in which idioms appropriate to the state in the modern, developed world were deployed. There was thus some debate as to whether or not changes in governing local communities should be described as 'centralizing', in which the Major Generals of the Cromwellian Protectorate were seen as the most interventionist of superintendents.[2] Underlying these dominant questions of structures and systems lay a tacit assumption that government was something imposed on the people, in the interests of control, either control by those in power in London, or by those in the most important and authoritative local offices. Since the 1980s, historians have adopted concepts that are more subtle and more sensitive to local initiative and self-determination. Power in this period is now seen less as something imposed, government less as something done to people, and more as something negotiated between those governed and those in authority. This corrective to the purely structural approach restores the experience of the people in local communities to the narrative, and is a reminder of the investment of time, energy, and loyalty by a substantial swathe of citizens, townspeople, and countryfolk in attempts to sustain effective and tolerable local governance.

In December 1641, the House of Commons presented to the king a lengthy and detailed petition of grievances and proposed remedies, the Grand Remonstrance.[3] It was a comprehensive review of the ills of the kingdom, and conformed to contemporary perceptions in making no distinction between local affairs and national ones. Even so, many grievances strike us as essentially local in their impact. The levying of ship money and other non-parliamentary taxes and levies, the disarming of county trained bands, the exactions by a range of agents (including those minor figures such as clerks of the market, saltpetre-men, and monopolists, whose only significance as irritants was local) acting on the authority of the privy council and a number of 'new judicatories [law courts] erected without law' were declared to be among the most oppressive. The parliament-men were able to include in the Remonstrance a review of how prerogative courts had already been thrown down by legislation, and looked forward to the suppression of 'illegal grievances and exactions' in the courts of quarter sessions and assizes by juries, magistrates, and sheriffs. The problem was seen as one of innovation; the remedy the conservative one of restoration to wonted courses of government.

In the years that followed, civil war notwithstanding, progress was made in a number of the areas identified for remedy in the Remonstrance. But even more than the call for speedy and cheap justice enshrined in its paragraph 140, the return of local government to traditional ways proved an impossible course to follow, and the following years saw extensive innovation and heavier demands on the people by the state, in the name of parliament but also in that of the king. These demands and burdens, how they were mediated through local communities, and the variety of responses they provoked, can be discussed with reference to the concepts of participation, representativeness, and reaction: political, administrative, and cultural.

The Burden of the State

Any discussion of the quality and experience of local government must be set against the background of the massively increased financial demands of the state on the propertied. The creation of field armies and the management of the war effort on land against the king were complemented by parliament's success in winning over the navy from the king's party and pledging itself to satisfy the persistent demands by mercantile interests for the commercial fleet to be effectively protected at sea by a force funded from parliamentary taxation. Efforts to fund this demanding programme began with appeals by parliament for voluntary contributions, among them the 'weekly pay' and subscriptions on the 'Propositions' of July 1642. Such genuine voluntarism which had marked these early expedients quickly gave way to an urgency which made them ineluctable taxes in all but name. From February 1643 the principle of the weekly assessment, a direct tax, was established, and with various modifications became the mainstay of direct parliamentary taxation thereafter. The amount to be raised was enshrined in each ordinance, with a sum allocated to each county. Tax commissioners would then parcel up the county total according to the sub-divisions of the shire, the hundreds, lathes, or wapentakes, and set the amount on each parish. Below that, in a variety of practices across the country, parishioners would either allocate among themselves the sum expected from them, in a process which necessarily demanded local negotiation and placed a heavy burden of responsibility on hundredal and parish constables; or be visited by agents of the county committees. The proceeds of two mainstays of parliamentarian taxation, both established by legislation in 1643, added to the flow of revenue from the localities. Between 1643 and 1659, the sequestration of the estates of parliament's enemies, whereby the state enjoyed the rents and other revenues arising from property, raised £1.8 million, and the excise, a regressive tax on consumption, raised just over £5 million. Dwarfing these was the assessment, which brought in nearly £12.2 million, and was thus easily the most burdensome tax on local communities.[4]

The heavy weight of the assessment is well recorded in every county, and was a constant theme in petitions and complaints from local communities towards the seat of government in London. The plight of Thomas Warde, a yeoman of Allesley, near Coventry, who complained in 1644 to the earl of Denbigh, a parliamentarian general, can be taken as speaking for thousands of small proprietors: 'I have not received any rent this three quarters of this yeare, and I am not able to subsist. I have allowed fifty pounds a yeare out of a hundred for the weekly tax, and now my land is throne up into my owne hand, and noe body will take it of me.'[5] There were many corporate complaints as well as individual ones. Local political leaders petitioned against not only the burden, but also against the perceived inequality of one county's share as against another's, as when the standing committee of Devon complained that their weekly assessment in 1647 'was above three times more than all the dominion of Wales or more than of eight counties of this kingdom'.[6] The heavier weight of the state was felt in maritime communities. The merchants and shipowners were faced with fresh parliamentary customs duties, for example on coal and a new levy to combat piracy, while the principle established in 1640, that customs duties were granted by parliament and used only to finance the navy was quickly blurred, as certain customs revenues were deployed to fund port town garrisons. Those without property were liable to impressment in the expanding naval fleet.

Assessment, excise, and sequestration all brought with them the need for collections and collectors in town and country. But what appear as the dictates of central government, if judged on the texts of the uncompromising acts, ordinances, and proclamations of parliaments and councils of state, come across to us as a never-ending process of local negotiation if considered on the narrative records of collectors and local agents. Nowhere is this better illustrated than in the counties of Wales, where the management of church lands added to the local administrative burden throughout the 1650s. A sample of over fifty individual collectors, committee-men, and other agents of the state in Pembrokeshire reveals how every year there was a shake of the kaleidoscope of local government personnel and a constant return to local negotiations. Among the activities subject to these processes were the farming and letting of parish tithes and glebe, both to individuals and to parishioners collectively; the collection of rents of sequestered manors and livings; the paying of salaries to clergy and 'fifths' to clergy wives and widows; the settling of artisans' bills for church repairs; the collection of excise and the management of estates acquired by absentee politicians, not to mention the collection of the ever-demanding weekly or monthly assessment. As one of them put it to his later interlocutors, much local business depended on 'care, trust and well manadgment'.[7]

PARTICIPATION

It is a matter of continuing debate whether the English revolution widened or narrowed local participation in government. One of the difficulties in reaching a judgement on the question arises from the distorting impact of new or revived institutions called into being by both sides in the conflict of the first civil war as a way of establishing rival and parallel structures to those controlled by the enemy. On the parliamentary side, the defining institution of the English revolution was the committee. A well-known and often imitated contemporary parodic litany associated the committees of the countryside with sectarian religion and the parliamentarian dominance of London:

> From an extempore prayer and a godly ditty,
> From the churlish government of a city,
> From the power of a country committee,
>
> > Libera nos, Domine.[8]

The word 'committee' was applied to both the collective group and to the individual member who attended its meetings, and was a familiar, time-honoured device at Westminster for progressing parliamentary business. In naval administration, parliament's navy committee, dealing with a large but just about manageable number of agents in port towns, kept control of matters of supply, personnel, and shipping movements. Away from the seaports, more complex structures developed. Committees in the provinces, formed of local partisans, were the logical extension of the gatherings of MPs in London locations outside the palace of Westminster, an expedient forced on them by the king's botched attempt at arresting five parliament-men and one peer in January 1642. Parliament's militia ordinance, which aimed to transfer authority over county trained bands from king to parliament, was the earliest legislative attempt at establishing a rival structure, using the well-recognized terminology of lords lieutenant and deputies to describe the managers of the county forces it authorized. Thereafter, successive parliamentary ordinances subjected the local committees, the most protean of expedients, to a process of continuous revision, expansion, and adaptation.

The fragmentary quality of surviving source material has rather tended to influence the framing of studies of local committees in terms of the legislation which shaped them and the records of nominations to serve on them.[9] The pioneer study of committees in Wales, first published in 1954, looked at not a single shire but all the counties, in a bold synthesis based primarily on the ordinances and the names of committee-men they contained.[10] But official nominations to a committee bore little relationship to community activism. Almost invariably, the committee of a given county was formed of a core, a bedrock of local support, often visible even before the summer of 1642, at assizes and quarter sessions in county towns. Here, when the influential in local society flocked to transact business, hear sermons, serve on juries, present local grievances, and see justice dispensed, the courts provided a theatrical backdrop for public demonstrations, as at Hereford assizes in August 1642, when a crowd believed by parliamentarians to have been urged on by the leading royalist gentry known, in an echo of medieval chivalric symbolism, as the 'Nine Worthies', forced the summer assizes.[11] The core of support often remained essentially the same in size and composition regardless of legislation that established separate committees to wrest control of the county militia, to supervise the assessment, and to direct sequestrations. A similar pattern was visible in counties under the control of the king, where commissioners (citing their authority as the king's Commission of Array, a typically Caroline use of medieval precedent), imposed taxation on parishes on a monthly basis, arrested refusers and defaulters, and heard appeals on rating disputes judged by assessors. The royalist local administration was a curious fusion of military hierarchy and the traditional civilian county and parish structure, just as novel in practice as the rival committees appointed by parliamentary ordinance.[12] On both sides there was resort to the most readily available instruments of governance.

The lists of county committee-men nominated in successive waves of parliamentary ordinances are an eloquent testimony to the apparent expansion of local rule during the revolution. Yet to be set against this impression of added dimensions are a number of contrary indications suggesting elements of continuity with the past. Most of those MPs in the Long Parliament from minor gentry, mercantile, or legal backgrounds had been named to local commissions out of chancery or exchequer before 1640, so had served as sheriffs, subsidy-men, commissioners for charitable uses, commissioners of sewers, and the like, indicating how ubiquitous experience in local governance was. During the 1640s, there was a near collapse in some regions of the pre-civil institutions of governance, so that committee-men and sequestrators supplanted head constables and treasurers of the county rate rather than joined them in a functioning, complementary structure. Furthermore, it is amply clear from a mass of surviving narratives of those called to account at the court of exchequer after 1660 for their handling of wartime revenues that the same individuals held multiple and often diverse offices. Richard Clapp of Devon, for example, between 1643 and 1653, held the posts of deputy treasurer, deputy mustermaster, commissary of provisions, head collector of the monthly assessment in several hundredal divisions of his county, sub-commissioner for managing the estates of delinquents, steward of sequestered manors, and surveyor of the estates of Catholic recusants. In Hampshire during the Commonwealth the justices of the peace, commissioners of the militia, of assessments, and of sewers were 'virtually identical', and in Kent, Charles Bowles was receiver-general, treasurer, and commissary.[13] Flexibility became a dominant characteristic of local office-holding, affecting terms and conditions of service, including in the expanding para-naval administration. Of 204 customs posts in the Thames ports in 1649, only 37 were still held by the pre-1640 tenure of enrolled patent, while the rest were salaried. It may well be that the true significance of the revolution in terms of the pattern of participation lies in a sharper division between the 'middling sort' types who had in more peaceful times shouldered the burden of the drudgery of local office, and who now found themselves worked harder than ever before, but with marginally more security, and those who were either victims of war or, indeed, the state.

The world of the jury, the committee, and the town hall was largely a man's world. Women served on no juries, committees, or councils, and even where property-holding brought a woman in a parish the theoretical duty of constableship, she would provide a deputy. It is tempting therefore to consign women of the 1640s and 1650s to a world of passive citizenship or imagine them confined to the sphere of the private, that of household and family, as against that of the public. Recent writing on gender issues has shown how these distinctions are easily over-drawn and how readily the worlds of private and public were blurred. Women made frequent appearances in law courts, not just as victims or defendants, but as witnesses and as instigators of prosecutions. They had an official, institutional role as jurors of matrons, called upon to provide an opinion on contested cases which turned on pregnancy or maternity. Women paid taxes and lent money, as the accounts of Joyce Jeffreys, a spinster and one of the wealthiest residents of Hereford, amply reveal. Propertied women were taxable, and therefore were likely to be participants in the processes of negotiation over tax collection, as was Anna Trapnel, who 'paid taxes towards maintaining of the army then in the field; and this I did not grudgingly, but freely and willingly'.[14] In 1650, the London custom house, which received collections from all the provincial ports, was 'kept' by a woman, whose duties were partly managerial as well as domestic. More generally, women commonly witnessed legal documents including bonds, the principal instruments in financial transactions, and sued and were sued at law.

MOTIVATIONS

During the French revolution, the distinction between active and passive citizens was self-consciously and deliberately drawn, by those who promoted it, as a general tool by which supporters and opponents of the struggle for liberty could be identified.[15] Notwithstanding the importance of towns in the making and shaping of the revolution in England and Wales, and despite the advocacy of a degree of egalitarianism in print by Levellers and others, the concept of citizenship remained obstinately urban during the 1640s and 1650s, as it was tightly defined and conceptualized against the mass of the rural population. We have to look elsewhere for over-arching principles which identified friends and enemies of the military and political campaigns led by parliament, as they evolved both in countryside and in towns. Many who first explicitly and deliberately entered the service of parliament in the early 1640s were motivated by fear of popery or by a wish to help secure further reform of the church. Others were drawn in by obligations of tenancy to great landowners or by ties of extended family, and in this sense the motives of local office-holders paralleled the political behaviour of voters in parliamentary elections. There are few records of how committee-men or their agents articulated their loyalty to the state. Narratives of service have survived as incidental to the process of accounting, a forensic exercise which left no room for expansive declarations during the 1640s and 1650s, still less as part of the defensive statements made after 1660.

During the later 1640 and the 1650s, the nearest equivalent of the later French notion of active citizenship, and the immediate binary distinction it implied, was the concept of godliness, in this context meaning devotion to reformed Protestant principles, and to social reformation driven through in their name. Here was an organizing principle of the English revolution. Yet even under the auspices of the Commonwealth and the subsequent Cromwellian Protectorate, both governments which declared themselves dedicated to advancing the kingdom of Christ, the godly were never more than a minority in local communities. At the height of their confidence, after the execution of the king, the godly were inclined to rejoice in the triumph of the 'saints'. More usually, however, the self-image of godly local governors was inclined to be defensive, their petitions to parliament or the Council of State commonly resorting to biblical allusions which portrayed them as labourers who had 'borne the burden and heat of the day'. Another, even more general, trope of self-fashioning was the idea of honesty. David Underdown showed how the adjective 'honest' exerted a greater hold on contemporary discourse in the provinces than any appeal to tightly defined, secular political rights.[16] 'Honest' was a term which subsumed other adjectives such as loyal, faithful, godly, and reliable, was a word used between members of a group based on loyalty between themselves, and by definition was always likely to appear in verbal or written discourse constructing a contrast between the 'honest' party and their opponents. For this reason, while the word can doubtless be found used in this binary context from 1643, its use intensified from the time of the struggle in parliament between presbyterians and independents, a conflict which quickly spread into matters of government in the localities. The 'honest' were not necessarily all who had fought the king, and 'dishonesty' was less likely to mean the technically corrupt as it was to denote those who for some reason were thought not fully to share principles of Protestant godliness or sufficient dedication to the cause. A typical 'honest radical' in 1646 denounced Colonel John Birch, a garrison governor for parliament, as one who had 'neither the desire of setting up Christ's kingdom nor advancement of the public good (both which he hath much talked on and but talked only), but rather his own private interest'.[17] When the customs collector of south-east Wales in the 1650s recommended men for service in the navy or customs, 'honest' frequently appeared in his testimonials.

ACCOUNTABILITY

In a trenchant and highly influential critique of the Cromwellian Protectorate, the younger Sir Henry Vane argued that political sovereignty lay in the 'honest party', the 'whole body of adherents' to the cause, and that 'publique welfare' was threatened when the advantages of a godly commonwealth were 'wrested and misimproved to the enriching and greatning of ourselves'.[18] It might be imagined that as the volume of revenue raised in the localities expanded so dramatically during the 1640s and 1650s, so opportunities for the collectors of it to enrich themselves increased. In fact, the overwhelming conclusion from contemporary accounting records was that when it came to handling public revenue, the 'honest radicals' were indeed scrupulously honest. Nicholas Field was typical. In twelve weeks during 1646, as a divisional county treasurer, he collected £2353 from seventy-six parishes on behalf of the Devon county committee. After he had disbursed the sums he collected, on the committee's instructions, and had deducted his own salary of £29, he was left with £1 8s. over. Seventeen years later, he was able to produce his accounts and the surplus, attributing his employers' indifference to the fact that 'the said ballance was soe little or small'.[19] Such punctiliousness is commonly encountered in the records of post-Restoration scrutiny, which to the disappointment of cavaliers demonstrated only a culture of high financial rectitude by tax collectors, which had been sustained at least in part by accounting procedures that were reasonably robust despite the circumstances of administrative innovation and expedient. The keenly felt sense of accountability to God, a mark of Protestant sensibility, informed this culture. An assize sermon preached in Essex in 1655 explicitly compared the parish officer who 'set down every week what he receaves to a farthing, because he knowes he must give up account for all at the yeares end' to the sinner confessing before God.[20] From this sprang the sense that local governors had of themselves as acting out the parable of the talents, as servants either good and faithful, or unprofitable. In this spirit of conscientiousness, local officials often went literally to great lengths to fulfil public duties, especially in the difficult terrain of Wales. In the early 1650s, the collector of sequestered rents in Pembrokeshire lived forty miles from his territory, Thomas Michael travelled sixty miles in North Wales to make his accounts, and in South Wales John Byrd thought nothing of 140-mile round trips on customs business.[21] In the context of a discussion of local government in Warwickshire, it has been shown how calls for officials to be brought to account 'united… "popular" notions of equity and fair dealing and more "elite" ideas of legal procedure and correct administrative practice'.[22]

REGIONAL CORRUPTION

It is, however, obvious that no one with a past to hide would be likely to allow traces of it to emerge during parliamentary enquiry or the later scrutiny of the exchequer commissioners. Those whose reputations had already been tarnished by allegations of profiteering or self-enrichment at public expense provided no useful narratives of the shadier aspects of their careers for their enemies to pick over. Invariably, the characters from the regions whose power and wealth had become associated with abuse of office because of denunciations of them in public print went to ground or offered anodyne responses to interrogators from any quarter. Among the most notorious of these cases were Philip Jones, the most powerful politician in Glamorgan, Sir Arthur Hesilrige, a parallel figure in County Durham, and Edmund Prideaux, who conducted turf wars against competitors in the postal service. A number of preliminary or provisional remarks can be made about the phenomenon of political corruption in the provincial context while it awaits an enterprising historian. In each of these three typical cases, the allegations were laid at the door of an MP, and the complaints against them drew attention to their behaviour away from Westminster. Furthermore, it is likely that the critique of MPs as self-interested and acquisitive began at Westminster and spread out into country, rather than, as has been assumed, emerging first as a 'Country' analysis of political behaviour in the metropolis. Heightened perceptions of self-interested political behaviour emerged at Westminster and Whitehall during the crisis of 'self-denying' and 'new-modelling' in 1644–5, and from that period emerged the perception, given traction by pamphlet publication, that parliament-men and government place-men were acquiring offices for base personal advantage.

Inseparably linked to allegations of corruption, defined as financially acquisitive abuse of public office, were protests against local tyranny, and here the committees in the counties provided a focus for hostile reaction against heavy taxation and government outside normal due process of the common law. In Somerset, the chairman of the county committee, John Pyne, attracted a great deal of opprobrium, and came to personify the oppressiveness of committees in that region. Invariably, the committee-men were portrayed as social upstarts, 'a spawn sprung from a dunghill birth', a classic trope in early modern perceptions of oppressive and corrupt government.[23] This was a conservative, time-worn response to a social change that many contemporaries found disturbing, but as has been already suggested, the evidence points to a devolving of heavier responsibility on to the shoulders of those of the middling sort already active in government, not to a social revolution.

The use of print was crucial in the widening out into provincial culture of perceptions of corruption in government. Historians have been rather too quick to ignore the motives and self-interest of authors and distributors of the large volume of squibs, satires, catalogues, and *ad hominem* assaults in print that provide us with most of what we know about Interregnum corruption, but there is no doubt that the London presses, in a complex relationship with the often very distant provinces, exported narratives of corruption from the centre and imported different ones from, for example, places as diverse as Newcastle-upon-Tyne, Hereford, and Carmarthen. Publication in print in the 1640s and 1650s provides us with the first coherent and witting testimony in quantity that we have of detailed corruption narratives in provincial society, and in every case parliamentary executive authority is a common theme, but with the authors and distributors of these narratives more often than not part of the same narrative, as competitors for office or as victims, not as disinterested reporters. Print was the most effective medium for an author to bring to public notice the wickedness and folly of specific individuals, but there is a body of material in manuscript, often in verse, composed for private audiences or for circulation in areas remote from the London presses, in which critiques of parliamentary or republican rule were just as hostile but more general in content. As an example of scribal publication, there could hardly be a more stark, binary expression of hatred of new ways than that of the Welsh poet from a Catholic district who sang of

> *Y Cafalirs mwynion sydd ffyddlon a phur,*
> *A'u h'wyllys yn ddilys i ddelio fel gwŷr;*
> *A hwythau'r traeturiaid a dorrodd eu gair,*
> *Cwcwaldiaid, bastardiaid, gelyniaid Mab Mair.*[24]

[The gentle Cavaliers, faithful and pure, / whose wish is to conduct themselves as gentlemen; / and those who are traitors who broke their word, / cuckolds, bastards and enemies of the Son of Mary.]

REPRESENTATIVENESS

At the focal point of delivery of participatory government in local communities was the jury, the archetype of government by participation but without democracy. The jury lay at the heart of both the judicial and the administrative processes of government. In a court of quarter sessions or of assizes, juries were empanelled to consider whether an individual had a case to answer on allegations laid before the court. If the grand jury concluded that evidence against a defendant man or woman was sufficiently compelling to warrant a trial, the 'true bill' they brought in would proceed to trial before magistrates or judges and a trial jury. Grand juries and trial juries were generally drawn from distinctive and separate social groupings, the grand jurors generally of superior social rank to those who tried the cases. This distinction lay less in an imagined hierarchy of responsibility and more in the wider tasks that fell to the grand jury. The institution of the jury, highly participative though it was, did not originate in the middle ages in an impulse towards democracy, but as a practical solution to problems of local governance. The medieval jury had been self-informing, and the tasks that fell to it in seventeenth-century practice were a codification of initiatives it had once exercised with unrestricted investigative authority. Early modern juries made presentments to their courts of administrative and social ills brought to their attention by constables and other officials, by justices of the peace, and by themselves or by lay informants. That was usually the limit of their involvement in the administrative process, which by the end of the 1630s had come to lay a much heavier burden on magistrates and on specially appointed minor officials. This trend is visible during the personal rule of Charles I, when justices of the peace were responsible for reporting to the privy council on the enforcement of the Book of Orders and the regulation of harvests, and when county officials such as treasurers of hospitals and militia muster-masters were appointed from the ranks of the minor gentry and even the yeomanry.

It has been argued that the legislators of the Long Parliament were hostile to juries, since none of the ordinances that flowed from both Houses between 1642 and the end of the first civil war in 1646 found any place for a jury in their arrangements for local enforcement.[25] Ironically, it has been said, a parliament that came into being to curb arbitrary government by the sovereign and to protect the ancient liberties of the people soon found itself curtailing those liberties and setting up a government to outstrip the king's in authoritarian oppressiveness as well as in claims to authority itself. In respect of the role of the jury in local affairs this is only partially valid. The ordinances before 1647 did indeed expect little or nothing from juries, and they had little to say to the historic and recognized judicial system in general. Committees not juries, summary law not due process of common law, still less canon law, were more regularly factored into parliamentary ordinances. But it was emergency legislation, and was understood to be such, which was why parliamentary committees were set up from the mid-1640s to decide which if any of the ordinances would become adopted into the ordinary common law when the expected settlement with the king was finally reached. There was no talk in 1642 or 1646 of army control over parliament, or of regicide. Though the notion of the king having fallen into the clutches of evil counsellors was the idiom in which parliamentary discourse about the war was sustained, there is no evidence in any parliamentary speech or report that an assault on the common law and participatory government was anyone's perception or subliminal plan.

Furthermore, once the fighting of the first civil war came to an end, the jury began to emerge as part of the process of reconstruction. The texts of ordinances from 1645 began to acknowledge juries and the other components of the time-honoured common law processes. Juries came back with assizes and quarter sessions after the cessation of fighting allowed local reconstruction to take place, under the supervision of assize judges sent on circuit by parliament. The Devon assize jury in 1647 described itself pointedly to its superintendent judges as 'the representative body of the county'.[26] What made the case of Captain John Burley so shocking—he was tried and executed in 1648 for attempting to rouse the Isle of Wight to rescue Charles I from Carisbrooke Castle—was that a jury was ruthlessly steered towards a guilty verdict for political purposes. It was unusual for a jury to be so blatantly overborne in what was regarded as a show trial, and the episode was a gift to royalist propagandists. On the administrative side of the jury's functions, there was a parallel return to familiar practice, even if it was not so obvious. Juries presented offences and grievances in manorial and criminal courts as they had been wont to do. The surveyors of crown lands commissioned by the Commonwealth government depended for success on local knowledge in much the same way as those who two centuries later were to conducting the local surveys under the Tithe Commutation Act of 1836, which in seventeenth-century conditions meant consulting manorial jurors meeting formally or informally. The surviving surveys show that when Colonel William Webb and his officials travelled the country in the early 1650s to make their surveys, prior to the sale of crown property, they found not only juries active in the courts leet and courts baron of manors but also in county hundredal courts. In a manor in Hertfordshire they even allowed the jurors a dinner on expenses. The national surveys of church livings, conducted in 1649–50 with a view to rationalizing parish boundaries and resources, explicitly depended on empanelling juries to harness local knowledge, noting who held the advowson, the value of the tithes, and whether a parish had an incumbent 'painful preaching minister'. Not since *Valor Ecclesiasticus* under Henry VIII had such an exercise been undertaken. Much of this activity was so low-key it has been lost sight of by historians, but it suggests that jury-less local administration and justice were probably confined to limited periods of virtual anarchy during the worst of the civil war fighting, and that the jury, that most flexible and indispensable way of acquiring local information and sounding out local opinion, was resilient.

The Major Generals, often regarded as ruthlessly centralizing, intrusive, and directive in their approach to local government, worked to reform and improve juries. In the circumstances of 1655–6, improvement meant empanelling to juries men 'of cleerest integritte and prudence, of honest and blameless conversation'.[27] The brief to which the Major Generals worked was one in which godly reformation was a key goal, and they understood the importance of representative structures in harnessing the goodwill of people of property and local influence. It must be emphasized that despite the disruptions brought by competing armies and their supporting civilian committees, the common law courts stood up very well to the shock of civil war. The arguments in parliament in 1646–7 over which judges should ride the assize circuits evidenced the political sensitivity of local judicial appointments; the county committees subordinated themselves to due judicial process once the rule of law was deemed to have been secured, and by the time of the regicide and the establishment of the Commonwealth, it was the courts, and in towns and cities the chartered corporations, more than the committees, that came to represent the face of the new government in urban and rural England and Wales.

CHALLENGES TO REPRESENTATIVENESS

Even so, the emergencies of the civil war were enough to ensure that suspensions of due process occurred frequently enough, and at sufficient different social levels, to constitute serious disruption of due process. While episodes of genuine anarchy were probably very brief and confined to the desperate circumstances of battle or skirmish, the more frequently encountered suspensions of normality in the provinces were characterized as impositions of martial law. There was no separate legal code by this name, nor was martial law simply the imposition or enforcement of military regulations on those who served in the armies of king or parliament. It was rather 'a summary form of criminal justice', and as the jurist Sir Mathew Hale put it, 'not a law, but something rather indulged than allowed as a law... only in cases of necessity'.[28] The main interest among historians has been in the high-profile cases of gentry and aristocracy who were tried by martial law, among them (in 1643) Sir John Hotham and his son, John Hotham, turncoat governors of Hull.[29] There were also many cases of drumhead summary justice in the armies, as when in Shropshire thirteen parliamentarian soldiers were hanged by Prince Rupert in reprisal for an identical penalty meted to thirteen English and Irish royalist soldiers. But instances of martial law as applied to the mass of the civilian population probably constituted the most significant encroachment upon basic common law procedures during the 1640s and 1650s, certainly more so than the parliamentary ordinances per se. Not only soldiers but the populace as a whole was subject to martial law in areas where it was imposed, and the Commonwealth government after 1649 resorted to it in response to uprisings in places as far apart as Norfolk, Worcester, and Cardiganshire.

Given much more prominence by generations of historians than the local implications of suspensions of due common law procedure in favour of martial law has been the regime during 1655–7 of the Major Generals. Considered in the context of the civil wars and Interregnum as a whole, and with particular reference to their impact on local government, the so-called rule of the Major Generals was transient and ineffective, scarcely comparable with the *intendants* under Richelieu, still less with the deputies-on-mission of revolutionary France. Constitutionally, it can be argued that their 'cantonizing' of the provinces was unprecedented, and the high profile of the Major Generals in national politics meant that their doings were extensively scrutinized and commented on. As they were high-ranking army officers, they came to symbolize or personify two aspects of government in the 1650s anathematized in the writing of British history after the Restoration, namely the military presence in the localities, and intolerant and socially *dirigiste* forms of sectarian Protestantism. As practical reformers of local government, however, their effectiveness was very limited, as their territories were vast, their subordinates few in number, and their period of office fleeting, in terms of the period required to enforce sustained change in either systems or culture. Some aspects of their regime are of interest to students of local government, not least the efforts in establishing a central registry to record the bonds for good behaviour imposed on the Major Generals' 'suspects', most fruitfully in the case of the bonds from over 5,000 people in the west of England.

The faults and weaknesses of the Major Generals' tours of duty were common to those of other agencies in the period: poor communications, inconsistency, widely varying responses to administrative problems, and a varying degree of interest by politicians and senior public servants in London. While royalists and probably most of the MPs of the second Protectorate parliament were happy to see the Major Generals voted down in 1657, their departure was regretted by many of the 'honest' and 'godly' minor gentry, yeomanry, and modestly ranking professionals from whose ranks had not only the Major Generals' local commissioners been recruited, but who had formed the backbone of local government since 1642. In fact, the contemporary fuss over the Major Generals and the long political tradition of viewing them as symbols of unacceptable, intrusive military government has rather obscured a very solid growth of the government presence in the country. The increase in government revenue by over 120% between the 1630s and the 1650s, and the creation of England as a major international power by naval strength, had direct implications for the localities, seen in the creation of a 'naval interest' in maritime towns, with direct effects on regional economies and social discipline, strong enough to account for the election of a number of MPs to the parliaments of 1656 and 1659. In this way, the expansion of a government presence could feed into enduring representative institutions.

THE REFORMATION OF MANNERS

It was one thing to represent the godly commonwealth in scattered counties, each with challenges of transport and communications, and many dozens of parishes whose parishioners had to hand innumerable means of resisting or frustrating local agencies of government; quite another to impose godly rule on towns. Urban corporations were the jurisdictions where godly rule was more likely to take root. In towns like Dorchester, with a history before 1640 of puritan social action, the period between 1646 and 1660 saw the 'climax of the puritan attack on poverty and ignorance'. Not only was a free school revived, but instruction in spinning for young people was laid on by the town, payments were made for various socially approved causes, and, its modern historian remarks, 'for a brief moment in history Dorchester had something very like a municipal health service', the whole edifice underpinned by godly ideology and a municipal brewing scheme which provided the town fathers with healthy returns from their monopoly.[30] Despite this mechanism, the town's character as a godly commonwealth owed far less to local government systems than to local politico-religious will. Dorchester was the cynosure of west country reformers, but it was not typical. In many other west country towns and cities, there were to varying degrees the elements of the formula which made Dorchester so successful as a puritan mini-commonwealth, but in Sherborne, a town only twenty miles away from Dorchester, the reformation of manners made no headway. Because of the fitful, varying and unsustained pattern of godly reform, seen in the case of Great Yarmouth, where an intense drive against alehouses after 1649 had fizzled out by 1655, overall assessments of the reformation of manners in towns have been inclined rather to write it off. In fact, the later 1640s and 1650s saw an advance in civic consciousness which is partly attributable to puritan impulses, but partly to a recovered sense of civic pride following the recovery from the devastation of war, improved economic conditions, and the stimulus provided by opportunities for towns to acquire property confiscated by the state such as fee farm rents. The customized agendas that towns were able to pursue with some prospect of success during the 1650s vis-à-vis government in London, and the projects they were able to bring to fruition, fed back in turn into enhanced civic consciousness. Examples of such local projects in a survey by a twentieth-century historian of sixty-six towns were the municipalization of cathedrals, the development of libraries, and the acquisition of new charters.

Outside the towns, in the counties, the reformation of manners, like the rule of the Major Generals, was a patchy affair. Historians such as Derek Hirst and Christopher Durston have come to the view that both, if judged from the perspective of the godly magistrate, were unsuccessful. 'In the failure of constables to delate [to report an offence], of grand juries to present, and of trial juries to convict, we see the failure of the godly cause to put down adequate roots.'[31] To take just one topic pursued by reformers, that of sexual offences, it would seem that despite the long history of magisterial and civic concern about fornication, adultery, and bastardy before the revolution, local magistrates, officials, and jurors were reluctant fully to implement the act of May 1650 against sexual offences. This notorious legislation, with its ferocious penalty of death for adultery, was slow in coming (attempts to pass a bill on the topic earlier, in the Long Parliament, came to nothing) and when it did reach the statute book there was no rush to enforce it. Instead there was a pattern by which only certain magistrates took it upon themselves to pay special attention to this class of offence and in which juries were inclined to leniency, even if the response everywhere accepted the gendered assumptions of the act, which imposed heavier penalties on women than on men. A recent study of Middlesex suggests that a rather less dismissive assessment of the reformation of manners emerges when less attention is given to the formal court records of true bills and trials, and more to that most flexible instrument of the law, the recognizance. When the record of recognizances is examined, the impression of reluctant magistrates and unresponsive jurors gives way to one of allegations by 'resentful spouses' cooperating with puritan authorities in a pattern of official regulation of behaviour, by summonses to return to court for further binding over or discharge after consideration of cases: in other words by a further example of negotiation.

Conclusions

A convincing narrative of how state and society related to one another in the English revolution depends a great deal on how the enquiry is framed. Historians driven by whiggish traditions of locating their narratives in terms of what was or was not acceptable to the English and Welsh people conclude that social reformation failed, and that the failure was partly attributable to an absence of inclusivity. And when twentieth-century concepts of government effectiveness and efficiency were applied to the evidence, the councils of state, parliaments, and Major Generals failed to measure up. A different picture emerges when more attention is given to the experiences of the hard-pressed, hard-working middling sort who made government in the localities work. Problems of evidence surrounding multiple government functions by individuals make it hard to assess whether more people were active as agents of government, but it is probably the case that the thousands who were, became more conscious of their roles and more likely to define themselves against others. Representative institutions proved surprisingly durable in spite of the challenges by parliamentary ordinance and martial law, if only because such bodies as the jury were necessary instruments of government, not just hallowed 'liberties'. The culture of provincial government cultivated by successive parliamentary and republican regimes was notably honest and preoccupied with accounting and accountability: to the bench of magistrates, to the exchequer, to God. In the three areas of participation, representativeness, and accountability, which can embrace the effort at a reformation of manners and the role of women, in older narratives ignored as passive citizens, the notion of negotiation is a vital conceptual tool in encapsulating the provincial experience of government in these decades.

NOTES

1. A commentary on Alan Everitt, *The Community of Kent and the Great Rebellion 1640-60* (Leicester, 1966) is provided by Jacqueline Eales and Andrew Hopper (eds.), *The County Community in Seventeenth-Century England and Wales* (Hatfield, 2012).

2. For characteristic interventions in this debate see Andrew M. Coleby, *Central Government and the Localities: Hampshire 1649-1689* (Cambridge, 1987); Stephen K. Roberts, *Recovery and Restoration in an English County: Devon Local Administration, 1646-1670* (Exeter, 1985); Christopher Durston, *Cromwell's Major-Generals: Godly Government during the English Revolution* (Manchester, 2001); John Sutton, 'Cromwell's Commissioners for Preserving the Peace of the Commonwealth: A Staffordshire Case Study', in Ian Gentles, John Morrill, and Blair Worden (eds.), *Soldiers, Writers and Statesmen in the English Revolution* (Cambridge, 1996), 151–82.

3. S. R. Gardiner (ed.), *Constitutional Documents of the Puritan Revolution, 1625-1660* (3rd edition, Oxford, 1906), 202–32.

4. Ian Gentles, *The English Revolution and the Wars in the Three Kingdoms, 1638-1652* (Harlow, 2007), 108.

5. Quoted in Philip Tennant, *Edgehill and Beyond: The People's War in the South Midlands, 1642-1645* (Stroud, 1992), 140.

6. Devon Record Office, quarter sessions rolls, summer 1647.

7. The National Archives [TNA], E 113/1.

8. *Political Ballads of the Seventeenth and Eighteenth Centuries*, ed. William Walker Wilkins, 2 vols. (London, 1860), 23. Cf. the version of this stanza in J. S. Morrill, *Revolt in the Provinces: The People of England and the Tragedies of War, 1630-1648* (2nd edition, London, 1999), 107 where 'country' has become 'county', altering the significance.

9. For a still exemplary edition of committee records and commentary, see Donald H. Pennington and Ivan Roots (eds.), *The Committee at Stafford, 1643-1645* (Staffordshire Record Society, Collections for a History of Staffordshire, 4th ser. vol. I, Manchester, 1957).

10. A. H. Dodd, 'Nerth y Committee', in *Studies in Stuart Wales* (2nd edition, Cardiff, 1971), 110–76.

11. British Library [BL], Harl. 7189, ff. 241–2; Jacqueline Eales, *Puritans and Roundheads: The Harleys of Brampton Bryan and the Outbreak of the English Civil War* (Cambridge, 1990), chap. 6.

12. See, for example, the Worcestershire orders, in Bodleian Library, MS Rawl. D 924.

13. TNA, E113/6; Coleby, *Hampshire*, 20–1.

14. Quoted in Ann Hughes, *Gender and the English Revolution* (Abingdon, 2012), 5.

15. Peter McPhee, *Living the French Revolution, 1789-99* (Basingstoke, 2006), 56–7.

16. David Underdown, 'Honest Radicals in the Counties, 1642-1649', in Donald Pennington and Keith Thomas (eds.), *Puritans and Revolutionaries* (Oxford, 1978), 186–205.

17. BL, Add. 70,058, loose papers, John Flackett to Edward Harley, 6 January 1646.

18. Sir Henry Vane, *A Healing Question* (London, 1656), 310–12.

19. TNA, E 113/6.

20. John Warren, *The Unprofitable Servant. A Sermon Preached at the Assize Holden at Chelmesford* (London, 1655), 16.

21. TNA, E 113/1; E 112/566/691; *The Letter-Book of John Byrd, Customs Collector in South-East Wales 1648-80*, ed. Stephen K. Roberts (South Wales Record Society Publications, XIV, 1999).

22. Ann Hughes, *Politics, Society and Civil War in Warwickshire, 1620-1660* (Cambridge, 1987), 245.

23. Humphrey Willis, *Times Whirligig* (London, 1647), sig. B.

24. Anon., 'Hiraeth Merch am ei chariad a ymladde o blaid y Brenin', in *Hen Gerddi Gwleidyddol: 1588-1660*, Cymdeithas Llên Cymru II (Cardiff, 1901), 12.

25. J. S. Morrill, *Revolt in the Provinces* (2nd edition, London, 1999), 107.

26. *Journals of the House of Lords*, IX. 171.

27. BL, Add. 44058, ff. 40–2.

28. Quoted in J. V. Capua, 'The Early History of Martial Law in England from the Fourteenth Century to the Petition of Right', *Cambridge Law Journal*, 36 (1977): 152.

29. For the latest account of these trials, see *The Papers of the Hothams, Governors of Hull during the Civil War*, ed. Andrew Hopper (Camden 5th ser. XXXIX, Cambridge, 2011), 24–9.

30. David Underdown, *Fire from Heaven: The Life of an English Town in the Seventeenth Century* (London, 1992), 219–24.

31. D. Hirst, 'The Failure of Godly Rule in the English Republic', *Past and Present*, 132 (1991): 61.

Further Reading

Braddick, Michael J. and John Walter (eds.), *Negotiating Power in Early Modern Society: Order, Hierarchy and Subordination in Britain and Ireland* (Cambridge, 2001).

Capp, Bernard, *England's Culture Wars: Puritan Reformation and its Enemies in the Interregnum, 1649-1660* (Oxford, 2012).

Capp, Bernard, 'Republican Reformation: Family, Community and the State in Interregnum Middlesex, 1649-60', in Helen Berry and Elizabeth Foyster (eds.), *The Family in Early Modern England* (Cambridge, 2007), 40–66.

Coward, Barry, *The Cromwellian Protectorate* (Manchester, 2002).

Durston, Christopher, *Cromwell's Major-Generals: Godly Government during the English Revolution* (Manchester, 2001).

Eales, Jacqueline and Andrew Hopper (eds.), *The County Community in Seventeenth-Century England and Wales* (Hatfield, 2012).

Fletcher, Anthony, *Reform in the Provinces: The Government of Stuart England* (New Haven, 1986).

Goldie, Mark, 'The Unacknowledged Republic: Officeholding in Early Modern England', in Tim Harris (ed.), *The Politics of the Excluded, c.1500-1850* (Basingstoke, 2001), 153–194.

Halliday, Paul D., *Dismembering the Body Politic: Partisan Politics in England's Towns 1650-1730* (Cambridge, 1998).

Hughes, Ann, *Gender and the English Revolution* (Abingdon, 2012).

Little, Patrick (ed.), *The Cromwellian Protectorate* (Woodbridge, 2007).

Richardson, Roger C. (ed.), *Towns and Countryside during the English Revolution* (Manchester, 1992).

Roots, Ivan (ed.), *'Into Another Mould': Aspects of the Interregnum* (2nd edition, Exeter, 1998).

Roy, Ian, 'The English Republic: The View from the Town Hall', in Helmut G. Koenigsberger (ed.), *Schriften des Historischen Kollegs Kolloquien XI: Republiken und Republikanismus im Europa der Frühen Neuzeit* (Oldenburg, 1989), 213–237.

Underdown, David, *Fire from Heaven: The Life of an English Town in the Seventeenth Century* (London, 1992).

CHAPTER 18

URBAN CITIZENS AND ENGLAND'S CIVIL WARS

PHIL WITHINGTON

INTRODUCTION

SOMETIME during the 1650s the reformer Samuel Hartlib received a letter. Unsigned and undated, it attempted to answer the question, 'What course may be most proper for a Rich man to take, for the securing of his person or estate in these miserable times, from that extreme danger, or present ruin that impends?' The framing of the answer is intriguing. The correspondent divided 'rich man' into 'two sorts': those worth between £100 and £1,000, by which 'I do principally mean men of trade', and those 'possessed of some thousands, or maybe ten thousands and besides'. The relative size of particular 'estates' and 'stocks' was ultimately less important, however, than that both sorts had a 'surplus' of wealth to dispose. It was this surplus—or what today would be called capital—that qualified them as rich, and the ensuing discourse accordingly 'weighed in the balance of good Reason to find which of these is the best, likeliest fittest and safest course for such as rich man to take as... with the aforesaid surplus of his estate'. To this end Hartlib's correspondent delineated 'but three general ways whereby an Englishman in peace or war employ or secure his stock (if anything great), that is to say as a Merchant, as a Citizen, or as a Countryman and good husband[man]'.[1]

Another letter to Hartlib from around the same time cast English merchants and citizens in a different light. William Spencer presented them not as men of disposable 'surplus' so much as creatures of war and proposed that Hartlib support 'a Mathematical Lecture in the City of London, either in the Military Garden, or some other convenient place... for the teaching, and instructing such offices as shall take delight therein, in the Art of Fortification and other military exercises, with expedition, and delight'. One obvious reason for the initiative was 'that Civil and Intestine War [which] hath now so many years continued in the kingdoms of England, Scotland, and Ireland, and the Dominion of Wales'. Another was the precedent of 'our neighbour nations in cities far less opulent' than London. Most intriguingly, however, Spencer regarded the lectureship as the natural expression of urban citizenship itself. He pointed out that

> it would be no improvidence for the honourable Magistracy of the City of London (the Metropolis of this Kingdom) whose numerous Militia, hath been, and still is of so high concernment, for the preservation of the present Parliament itself, and the whole land, to erect at the publique charges a lecture mathematical, for the plain and easy and speedy training of the Art of Fortification with such other Military exercises as are belonging thereunto . . .

The move would have national as well as local ramifications: in only 'a few months space many hundreds of the city commanders, and officers employing but one hour a day therein, may be so fully instructed and enabled, as they may furnish all the land by their arts, and industry with fit and able engineers' and 'exceedingly conduce unto the safety of the said City, and of the whole Kingdom'. With rhetorical gusto he foresaw how the lectureship would 'add unto the Lustre, glory, and renown' which the citizenry 'already have most justly purchased, and be a means to propagate a nursery to all succeeding ages of able, active and sublimed spirits'.[2]

Hartlib's letters beg questions of historians of both the civil wars and English cities and towns. The former have not by and large taken English 'citizens' to be noteworthy participants in the mid-century troubles, let alone actors of 'high concernment'. There are important studies of individual cities and towns, in particular London and its constituent social groups, and the strategic significance of London is also recognized.[3] However, urban *citizens*, and the culture of *citizenship* which helped define them, are not generally invoked by historians to understand or explain the mid-century conflict. The wars do not have a 'citizen context' to sit alongside the 'baronial'; neither is citizenship taken to be a source of political imagination and mobilization in the manner of post-Reformation religion.[4] Even historians who have looked to cast Tudor and Stuart politics in expressly civic terms have ignored the one environment in which contemporaries actually described themselves as 'citizens'. For J. G. A. Pocock, urban citizens are not on the list of English people capable of developing 'a civic consciousness, an awareness of himself as a political actor in a public realm'.[5] More encompassing is Patrick Collinson's influential explication of the 'monarchical republic', which contends that following the death of Henry VIII the devolution of governance was such that England became 'a republic which also happened to be a monarchy: or vice versa'. Yet even for Collinson urban citizens did not initially spring to mind as 'citizens who were also subjects'.[6] This is in part because urban historians have not traditionally characterized their subjects as 'citizens', let alone as householders with 'surplus of estate' or 'active and sublimed spirits'. Rather, until recently it was usual to describe English towns in the hundred or so years after 1540 in terms of crisis and disorder: as places in which the communal certainties and comforts of the late medieval era degenerated into problematic demographics, economic dislocation, social stratification, and encroachments by the landed gentry.[7] According to this orthodoxy it was not citizens who dominated the English urban landscape before 1640 so much as the burgeoning ranks of the poor on the one hand and embattled and puritan oligarchic elites struggling to control them on the other.[8] Viewed in these terms, early modern citizenship was less an epithet of civic consciousness, more an archaism.[9]

Hartlib's letters suggest, then, something of a disjunction between the historical and the historiographical. This might simply reflect, of course, that they were written in a language which less educated contemporaries would have struggled to recognize; that their humanist rhetoric was far removed from the realities of everyday urban life. Yet if the 'cultural turn' has taught us anything, it must surely be that discursive dissonance between 'elite' and 'popular' needs to be demonstrated rather than presumed. Contrary to historiographical appearances, 'citizen' and its vernacular synonyms, 'freeman' and 'burgess', were still familiar terms of urban social description *circa* 1650; and Hartlib's anonymous correspondent used the language only slightly contentiously.[10] The correspondent explained that 'by Citizens or Trades men I mean the grand Trades as the Grocer, Mercer, Vintner etc. and not such handicrafts men as are capable of attaining to this degree [of citizen] by the following of that labour'. These 'grand Trades' were 'also so near of kin to the Merchants (though none themselves) that their trade depends on his'.[11] However, for other contemporaries the term citizen, along with freeman and burgess, denoted *all three* of these urban groups together: Hartlib's correspondent was particular in that he reserved the label for the 'grand Trades'. This is because citizen in the vernacular described, first and foremost, the act of belonging to, and participating in, incorporated urban communities: what contemporaries described as 'city commonwealths'.[12] And ever since their emergence in the medieval era, these commonwealths had been dominated by the civic trinity of craftsmen and manufacturers, tradesmen and retailers, and overseas merchants.

What follows builds on the insight that citizenship was a normative dimension of early modern English society and that the characterization of citizens as harbingers of capitalism and civic republicanism was entirely plausible. It argues that their role in the mid-century conflicts was as historically significant as it is historiographically unheralded. This is certainly true of the London citizenry, who were by far the most prominent and powerful civic body of freemen in early modern England. However, urban citizenship was not limited to the metropolis. Rather it was a national political culture which, in the hundred years after 1540, came to encompass provincial capitals, county towns, and most urban centres of England, Wales, and Ireland. This raises obvious questions about how provincial citizens participated in the civil wars. Far from being bastions of apolitical 'localism' or the simple extension of 'county communities', citizens, burgesses, and freemen could form highly politicized and well-informed bodies with a host of powers at their disposal and liberties and freedoms to protect. There was, of course, any number of factors which encouraged the allegiance of individuals. Likewise the impact of war on particular settlements was often determined by factors beyond communal control. Urban citizenship nevertheless delineated the institutions and discourses by which perhaps up to 10% of the English population experienced and engaged, directly and indirectly, with the unfolding conflagration.[13] For a significant minority of non-landed elites it demarcated, in effect, the very process of early modern politics itself.

While a chapter of this kind can never recreate in full the civic context of the civil wars, it hopefully reveals urban citizenship as a dimension of the revolutionary era worth pursuing. It divides into two sections. The first briefly traces the structures of urban citizenship and their role in disseminating civic attitudes and beliefs. The second section provides a model for recovering the importance of urban citizenship to the civil wars.

THE STRUCTURES OF URBAN CITIZENSHIP

Urban citizenship *circa* 1640 was based on charters of incorporation. These defined and governed the urban community in certain ways. The fundamental conceit was that groups of householders and their dependants (spouses, children, apprentices, and servants) formed an artificial body—the city commonwealth—which transcended the individual wills and interests of its constituent members. Recognized in law, this body was a fictional person with legal agency: it could sue in law, might be represented in parliament, and could hold extensive and exclusive governmental powers over its particular 'liberties'. The institutional expression of this body was the corporation, which was constituted as an interconnected system of self-selecting assemblies, common councils, and aldermanic courts. This system of conciliar government was responsible for the common 'weal', or prosperity, of the larger body. This weal was also organized corporately, with productive householders participating in those guilds and companies responsible for their crafts and trades. It was this participation which made householders freemen, 'freedom' denoting the right to practise an occupation within a particular city or town. Guilds and companies were accordingly represented in, and governed by, their corporation: indeed in London and most cities the acquisition of freedom was tantamount to citizenship, with freemen expected to hold civic office as and when required. However, as well as being an association of freemen the city commonwealth was also a composite of smaller territorial jurisdictions, most notably wards (city quarters) and parishes. This meant that corporations intersected not only with companies and guilds but also wardmotes and parochial offices such as constables and overseers of the poor. As a result, householders who were not necessarily freemen and citizens—that is, formally enfranchised to the city commonwealth—were nevertheless subject to corporate authority.[14]

In order to formalize these lines of authority, magisterial powers were increasingly transposed onto the corporate realm. From the later sixteenth century it was usual for mayors and one or more aldermen to be designated justices of the peace, Michael Dalton noting citizens formed a distinct kind of English magistrate.[15] The conflation of magistracy and corporatism was just one mechanism by which urban citizenship not only defined local communal relations but also positioned those communities within national political networks. As JPs, citizens were responsible for the 'stacks of statutes' which characterized the late Elizabethan and early Stuart polity: every time a proclamation or parliamentary act was addressed to county justices it was also directed to the mayor and aldermen of corporate towns. The larger cities were endowed with even greater judicial powers, convening their own city assizes, mustering their own militias, selecting their own sheriffs, and running courts of civil law. All of these functions established links with metropolitan institutions, and over the course of the period more towns became embroiled in ever busier networks. Corporations increasingly required legal professionals to advise them on the technical aspects of governance.[16] They appointed high stewards to represent them at court.[17] They endowed and governed city grammar schools and city lectureships. And most strikingly they were integral to the enlargement of the House of Commons, either by sending citizens directly to London or, increasingly, by electing lawyers, courtiers, and well-placed gentlemen to represent them.[18]

The corporate, judicial, legal, and representative dimensions of urban citizenship all had medieval antecedents. Yet far from declining after 1540, as is often assumed, they revivified dramatically. The sheer number of incorporated city commonwealths in England and Wales increased significantly.[19] Before 1540, 48 places had secured charters of incorporation. By 1560 this had risen to 92; by 1580 to 114; by 1600 to 140; by 1620 to 179; and by 1640 to 194. In Scotland over the same period the number of equivalent settlements rose from only 35 to 58.[20] The process was driven in part by cities and towns inscribing their customary privileges, liberties, and freedoms (whether practised or invented) into charters: London, for example, did not purchase its first charter of incorporation until 1614. More usually, however, incorporation involved townsmen securing corporate status for the first time, usually after decades of lobbying and campaigning: in Ludlow in Shropshire (1551), in Tewkesbury (1574), or Windsor (1604). Other places, such as Cirencester, never secured a charter despite intense lobbying. Either way, the developing standardization of charters to include judicial offices (JPs), conciliar government (common councils), legal counsel (town clerks and recorders), noble patronage (high stewards), militarism (militia musters), and parliamentary representation (MPs) meant the proliferation of concentrated and extensive civic activities and the emergence of an urban corporate system. The ramifications of this are most easily measured in terms of parliamentary representation. Between 1584 and November 1640 the proportion of all Commons' representation controlled by boroughs rose from 79% to 82%: this included both parliamentary boroughs (i.e. settlements customarily qualified to send MPs to London: the precursors of 'rotten boroughs') and incorporated parliamentary boroughs (i.e. city commonwealths with parliamentary representation). Over the same period, the proportion of borough representation in incorporated city commonwealths rose from 37% to 63%. As a result, the proportion of all parliamentary representation in the corporate system increased from 35% in 1584 to 52% by November 1640. In a very real sense, therefore, it was English citizens who were responsible for selecting the 'Long Parliament'.[21]

Three dynamics further distinguished early modern citizenship from its medieval precursor. The first of these—England's 'long reformation'—has been well studied by historians and need only be mentioned here. On the one hand, cities and boroughs were especially important to the spread of religious ideas and practices, of whatever stripe, and the organization of religious life.[22] On the other hand, Paul Slack and others have noted the apparent resonance between urban citizenship and Protestant evangelism

in many incorporated communities.[23] The other developments have been less appreciated historiographically, and take us back to the intimations of Hartlib's correspondents. Thus from the 1570s urban economies not only expanded but became 'more
capitalistically structured.'[24] The process was underpinned by a number of well-known
developments. The unprecedented expansion of overseas trade—with the traditional
European markets; in the Baltic, Iberia, and the Levant; in Asia; and eventually across
the Atlantic—created new cadres of wealthy merchants at the apex of civic society.[25]
These merchants supplied the goods for domestic traders and retailers profiting from
the doubling of national income between 1566 and 1641 and the consumer revolution
this precipitated.[26] These merchants and tradesmen formed Hartlib's 'rich men'; and a
vibrant urban property market and the promise of increased income from rents offered
further investment opportunities. Prosperity was not distributed evenly, however.
Overseas trade was monopolized by incorporated companies in Asia and the Levant
and more informal networks across the Atlantic: access to markets was accordingly circumscribed. Moreover, even as trading boundaries expanded and domestic commerce
intensified, prices rose and real wages fell. Craftsmen and manufacturers could prosper,
for sure, and apprenticeship numbers remained buoyant in all trades. It nevertheless
became much more difficult for journeymen to set up independent businesses and so
secure their freedom. Combined with the creep of suburban manufacturing, this significantly increased 'the numbers of unenfranchised wage-earners in the urban economy'.[27]
Further disparities were highlighted by the national poor relief system, which urban citizens were in the absolute vanguard of devising, legislating, and implementing from the
middle of the sixteenth century.[28] This transposed classes of rate payer and dole recipient
onto parish neighbourhoods. It also consolidated the authority of civic magistrates, who
took overall responsibility for urban assessment and collection and shifted income from
richer to poorer parishes on a weekly basis.[29]

The role of citizens in pioneering poor relief is a reminder, thirdly, that early modern citizenship became a palimpsest in which the values of Renaissance humanism were inscribed on, and extrapolated from, traditional civic practices. Jennifer
Bishop has shown, for example, how a network of London citizens was directly
responsible for translating Thomas More's *Utopia*—that quintessence of humanist learning—from Latin into English in the early 1550s. The same citizens were also
committed social reformers, driving through civic and parliamentary legislation and
establishing schools, hospitals, and houses of correction. For them as for their political ally, William Cecil, *Utopia* was less literary recreation and more a template for
good citizenship.[30] Depictions of city commonwealths as either classical or contemporary city states were increasingly frequent thereafter, most obviously for London and
the provincial capitals but also in smaller towns like Great Yarmouth, Tewkesbury,
and Truro.[31] This trend was part of the more general impact of educational reform
on the English political imagination. It also attracted degrees of ridicule from genteel
commentators who looked to monopolize such inferences for themselves.[32] However,
it is not difficult to see how some of the core characteristics of urban citizenship made
classical analogies especially resonant.

Like classical citizenship, urban citizenship was predicated on the principles of good counsel, with citizens expected to discourse and act for the public good in both their common councils and the House of Commons.[33] As a quintessentially corporate culture, citizenship was easily conceptualized in terms of *societas*, or 'societies civil': as voluntary associations of freemen inured in the rules of civility.[34] As participants in clearly delineated 'body politics', citizens and freemen could readily assimilate the Aristotelian political vocabulary that was vernacularized over the same period.[35] On these terms citizenship could constitute an *aristocracy*, or rule by the 'best' or 'better sort'; a *democracy*, in which all freemen had a voice; or a *mixed polity*, which involved elements of both. It could also denote the tyrannical alternatives of those types, in particular *oligarchy*, the self-interested rule of the few, and *populism*, the rule of the 'many-headed monster'.[36] Either way, the link between citizenship and *res publica*, or commonwealth, was palpable, so much so that by the 1620s citizens from across the corporate system were petitioning the crown to form autonomous citizen regiments along the lines of the Honourable Artillery Company in the name of the public good.[37] This trend coincided with fierce struggles between citizens and local gentry over the control of militias within urban jurisdictions: for example between the Slingsby family and the citizens of York during the 1630s.[38] Given this propensity for civic militarism it is hardly surprising that citizens not only countenanced the possibility of war in 1642 but were also deeply implicated in the three most significant military interventions in England before 1643: the seizure of London and Hull for parliament, and the parliamentary defence of London at Turnham Green.[39] This also explains, perhaps, why almost half of the 238 members of the New Model Army Officer Corps of 1647 hailed from London or other large cities and boroughs.[40]

Urban Citizenship and Civil War

Citizens selected more than half the representatives in the Long Parliament and were crucial in precipitating the shift from discursive combat to military violence in 1642. Quite as integral to early modern governance as 'county justices' and rural parish officers, they were accordingly vital in mobilizing partisan support and influencing local decision-making at the outbreak of war.[41] The prominence of urban citizenship in the 1640s was the outcome of a longer process of urbanization by which medieval institutions were revivified and reconfigured: the modern wines of 'surplus of estate' and 'sublime spirit' fermented, as it were, in familiar civic skins. This made for a complex culture which valorized both personal profit and public participation. It also points to a national polity that was more socially extensive and also urbanized than studies of 'county communities' suggest. It certainly casts doubt on Peter Laslett's old adage that in pre-industrial England only the gentry had the networks, permanency, and consciousness requisite of a 'class'.[42]

Of course the circumstances in each city commonwealth, not to mention the experiences of individual citizens and their dependants, were different. Despite the legal fiction on which they were predicated, incorporated communities were never homogeneous entities which acted according to a single will. Rather urban freedom encompassed a multiplicity of householders of different occupations and wealth, age and status, and education and religious conviction who took up different positions and participated in different social networks both within and outwith urban society. Corporate decision-making and collective action was accordingly the product of constant political process inflected by a range of interests and factors. Neither were city commonwealths the only, or even necessarily the most powerful claimants on urban space. Cathedral precincts and separate liberties, universities and colleges, law courts and Inns of Court, the palaces of monarchs and magnates, garrisons and shipyards: across the corporate system these urban institutions and their buildings loomed as alternative and often rival sources of power and authority. Likewise the urban neighbourhoods and networks they encouraged—of clerics, prelates, and booksellers; students, innsmen, and lawyers; liverymen, courtesans, and courtiers; gallants, soldiers, and sailors—were often distinct from and even contemptuous of enfranchised citizen bodies.

These complexities make it difficult to generalize about the practical impact of urban citizenship on the mid-century troubles. Indeed, in what is the most ambitious account of citizens and the revolutionary era—Robert Brenner's study of London overseas merchants and traders—citizenship is little more than a cypher for commercial motivations and interests. For Brenner 'the commercial classes' (as he terms citizens) were 'divided from, and in crucial ways set against, one another in consequence of their diverse relationships to production, property, and the state': 'their differing relationships to capitalist development and its effects' were paramount. Brenner accordingly describes 1640s London in terms of warring factions of 'overseas company traders' allied to 'patrimonial monarchy' (upon whom they depended for their trading monopolies); 'colonial interlopers' allied to 'leading sections of the parliamentary aristocracy' (who together had opened up the Atlantic trade); and 'retailers, ship captains, artisans, and small tradesmen' supportive, for whatever reasons, of the 'colonial interlopers'.[43] According to Brenner it was on the basis of these interests and alliances that allegiance to crown or parliament was forged: a pattern echoed in Bristol, where the great overseas merchants likewise formed a monopolistic clique at the expense of ordinary freemen. Yet what this fails to acknowledge is that, whatever the commercial basis of partisan allegiances (and the correlations drawn by Brenner are inevitably schematic), these different kinds of economic activity were all nevertheless predicated on urban citizenship, which remained a requisite for legitimate commerce, retail, and manufacture in London, and indeed Bristol, throughout the period. The warring 'commercial classes' of the revolutionary era were also citizens; it was as citizens that (among other things) they were able to pursue, contest, and protect their economic interests politically; and it was as citizens that they accordingly participated in the civil wars.

How, then, to account for the contingencies of urban citizenship while acknowledging its importance as a source of political identity and agency? The obvious method of comparing systematically the politics of each and every city and borough is clearly beyond a short chapter. A more practical approach, and perhaps more useful analytically, is to conceptualize urban citizenship in two interconnected ways. In the first instance, citizenship can be understood as the *field of conflict* in which individuals and groups moved and operated in order to achieve particular ends. This field was constituted by configurations of civic institutions, practices, vocabularies, and concepts which, as has been shown, were replicated across the corporate system by 1640. However, it was also shaped by the convergence of personalities, groupings, issues, circumstances, and other institutions which were particular to specific cities and towns and which altered (or remained the same) over time. In the process, the constitutive attributes of citizenship were also subject to contestation and alteration. This politics was conducted in the formal institutions of governance, such as common councils, quarter sessions, and guild halls, as well as innumerable and ephemeral interactions in parlour, alehouse, church, or street through rumour, gossip, news, subscriptions, petitions, assemblies, and riot. In the second place, urban citizenship can be understood as the *corporate decisions and actions* of incorporated bodies resulting from these ongoing conflicts. Such agency was usually governmental, in that it determined and implemented governance within cities; and representational, in that civic representatives were sanctioned to act on the part of citizens in different political settings (such as parliament, law courts, county committees). Either way, it was a capacity which transcended the power of individual citizens; which distinguished city commonwealths from other kinds of institutionally defined communities, such as parishes and manors; and which enabled relatively humble urban householders to match, collectively, the familial power of the nobility and greater gentry.

It was precisely this corporatism which made Hartlib's anonymous correspondent argue that, in time of civil war, 'the village' was much 'better and safer than any City, Town, etc. (saving only that City or Great Town whereof he is properly an inhabitant [i.e. a citizen])'. On the one hand, 'in any such City, Town, etc., it will be scarce possible [for the unenfranchised] to turn a penny, or drive any trade that good is… yet shall you pay much dearer for all necessaries'. On the other hand, even if you be 'a man of peace' the corporate pressures were such that 'you will yet be compelled to take up arms and pass upon such duty as may prove destructive to you'.[44] Such 'duty' and 'compulsion' were the outcomes of civic politics. In London in 1641, for example, the civic elections precipitated a purge of the aldermanic bench (pro-royalists were replaced by pro-parliamentarians), a shift in the balance of power between the common council and the court of alderman (towards the former), and confirmation that the six regiments of the city militia were now in the hands of citizens supportive of those MPs and Lords at loggerheads with Charles.[45] Brenner has noted that whereas privileged company merchants were disproportionately represented on the aldermanic bench before this civic 'revolution', a high percentage of their replacements were Atlantic and domestic traders possessed of a less benign view of the crown. However, a host of other factors ranging from Protestant militancy to Catholic rebellion in Ulster (where many London companies had investments) to deep suspicions of the king's 'evil counsellors' animated civic conflict. Positions were articulated through cheap print, through petitions, through demonstrations and riots. With city politics transformed, a powerful Levant trader like Sir Marmaduke Rawdon first plotted to capture the city for the king before quitting his citizenship, and his command in the militia, in order to fight and die in the royal army.[46] In the meantime Rawdon's fellow citizen, the recently enfranchised Thomas Juxon, progressed rapidly through the ranks of the city militia and became a significant player in civic politics.[47] By the mid-1640s Juxon's diary reveals a passionate and 'aristocratic' citizen (in the Aristotelian sense of the term) who was also an ardent parliamentarian, religious independent, and incipient republican; one embroiled in a civic politics which encompassed not only royalists but also presbyterians and emergent city 'democrats' like the Levellers.[48]

Across the corporate system the field of conflict and its political outcomes were different. In contrast to London, for example, the burgesses in early Stuart Cambridge were beleaguered and underpowered. The university rather than the corporation exercised magisterial authority, claimed urban precedence, employed a large number of urban householders, and sustained an itinerant population of wealthy students. Aside from their markets, their common lands, and Stourbridge Fair, the burgesses had little economic rationale. The majority were relatively humble townsmen and electoral procedures to the common council and other offices tended towards the democratic, combining sortition (selection by lot), co-option, and election.[49] In the 1620s the common council looked to cultivate royal patronage by making the courtier Thomas Coventry their High Steward; this led to unsettling levels of Carolinian interference rather than any enhancement in the state of Cambridge citizens.[50] What the burgesses did have, however, was parliamentary representation. This had previously been gifted to Coventry and his successor as High Steward, Sir John Finch, for their political patronage. However, in April 1640 a group of puritan burgesses engineered the freedom of a local gentleman, Oliver Cromwell. Although Cromwell did not meet the rule of inhabitancy his election to the Short Parliament, alongside Finch's client, followed.[51] It was a decisive act which, while procedurally dubious, had a transformative impact on the civic field of conflict and so the burgesses' voice in urban and national politics. In November Cromwell was returned again 'with the greatest part of the Burgesses of the Town being present'.[52] This time his fellow representative was John Lowry, a Cambridge chandler who subsequently served as a parliamentary colonel and who, as mayor, was conspicuous in facing down the authority of the university.[53] In the meantime another of Cromwell's allies, Robert Twells, was elected mayor after the burgesses replaced selection by seniority (an electoral system introduced by Coventry) with the customary practice of majority voice.[54] By procedural manipulation the habit of court dependency was broken; the civic ascendancy of godly burgesses secured; and the balance of power within Cambridge significantly altered in the burgesses' favour.

This outcome, if not the process behind it, was a common feature of civic politics in the early 1640s, certainly for city commonwealths sympathetic to the parliamentary cause. In Colchester a deeply divided and fractious urban populace of burgesses and clothworkers nevertheless coalesced in the name of puritanism, parliamentarianism, and anti-popery in the summer of 1642. The focus of their collective ire was the local royalist landlord, Sir John Lucas, whose attempts to muster his household for the king sparked a series of attacks and demonstrations against not only Lucas but also suspected Catholics, Laudian ministers, and other selected gentry targets.[55] The provincial capital of York proved, in contrast, to be a magnet for gentry, nobility, and royalist soldiers after 1640, so much so that in April 1642 the king, having escaped London, established his court in the cathedral liberty, Minster Yard. Yet the attitude of the citizenry was much more ambivalent. During the 1630s leading citizens like the merchant Thomas Hoyle suffered personal and sustained religious harassment.[56] They also presided over the alarming erosion of corporate authority by Archbishops Neale and Laud in Minster Yard, by Strafford in the Council of the North, and by the local deputy lieutenant, Sir Henry Slingsby. Despite or rather because of these pressures the citizens voted Hoyle and his fellow puritan, the draper William Allenson, as parliamentary representatives in November 1640. Even as York was fortified into the royalist northern headquarters, its MPs voted for the deaths of Strafford and Laud and the raising of parliamentary armies (Slingsby was executed for treason in 1658). Once Fairfax seized the city for parliament in 1644 royalist partisans were purged from the corporation and the remaining citizenry were entrusted with both military and religious authority.[57] According to Ian Roy this absorption by citizens of urban space and authority was frequent after 1645, as the leaders of city and national commonwealth recognized a symbiosis of interest.[58]

The Putney Debates of October 1647 revealed the ideology informing the reciprocity between city and national commonwealth. They also intimated perspectives which questioned the very principles upon which urban citizenship rested. On the one hand, Cromwell's son-in-law, the lawyer and soldier Henry Ireton, gave a succinct summary of the corporate/parliamentary 'interest':

> Every man that was born in the country, that is a denizen in it, that has a freedom, he was capable of trading to get money, to get estates by; and therefore this man, I think, had a great deal of reason to build up such a foundation of interest to himself: that is, that the will of one man should not be law… *Here* was a right that induced men to fight; and those men that had this interest, though this be not the utmost interest that other men have, yet they had some interest.[59]

The 'interest', 'freedom', and 'right' so invoked were not abstract or innate but rather particular and tangible. More, they constituted 'the whole permanent, local interest in the kingdom'. Ireton explained:

> I mean by 'permanent' and 'local', that it is not able to be removed anywhere else, as for instance he that has a freehold… and also there's a freeman of a corporation—a place which has the privilege of a market and trading—which if you would allow to all places equally, I do not see how you could preserve any peace in the kingdom.[60]

These freeholders and 'freemen of corporations' were looked upon by the former constitution to comprehend the 'permanent interest of the kingdom'. In the first instance, 'he that has his livelihood by his trade and by his freedom of trading in such a corporation—which he cannot exercise in another—he is tied to that place, and his livelihood depends on it'.[61] In the second place, 'that man has an interest—has a permanent interest there, upon which he may live, and live a freeman without dependence'. It was to protect this independency—an independency rooted, in the case of freemen, in their corporate collectivism—for which citizens had opposed the 'will' of their king in the later wars.[62]

On the other hand, the soldiers and Levellers arraigned against Ireton at Putney outlined what they took to be the inequities of the 'interest' so depicted. Their objections are well known. Edward Sexby conceived of 'liberty' (he avoided the term freedom) not so much as property as a birthright, arguing that:

> I see that though liberty [was] our end, there is a degeneration from it. We have engaged in this kingdom and ventured our lives, and it was all for this: to recover our birthrights and privileges as Englishmen; and by the arguments urged there are none… But it seems now, except a man has a fixed estate in this kingdom, he has no right in this kingdom.[63]

Thomas Rainborough regarded the corporate enclosure of parliamentary representation to be imprecise at best, tyrannous at worse. He expostulated that:

> As for this of corporations… it is contrary to freedom as may be. For, sir, what is it? The king he grants a patent under the Broad Seal of England to such a corporation to send burgesses. He grants to such a city to send burgesses. When a poor base corporation from the king's grant shall send two burgesses; when five hundred men of estate shall not send one; when those that are to make their laws are called by the king, or cannot act but by such a call; truly I think the people of England have little freedom.[64]

And John Wildman assumed that the time for defending the ancient constitution was over, famously observing:

> We are now engaged for our freedom. That's the end of parliaments: not to constitute what is already established but to act according to the just rules of government. Every person in England has as clear a right to elect his representative as the greatest person in England. I conceive that's the undeniable maxim of government: that all government is in the free consent of the people.

Here was an opportunity to return to first principles; to overcome the 'slavery' of laws that had been 'made by conquerors'.[65]

Such objections to urban citizenship have long outlived the political culture which inspired them. Ireton's investment in the corporate 'interest' and the conception of liberty it enshrined suggests that, insofar as understanding the English revolution is concerned, this is a mistake, not least because fifteen months later he signed the death warrant of his king. In appropriately symbiotic fashion, the court of aldermen in York ordered their sergeants to 'assist' in 'prohibiting the proclaiming of any person to be King'—an order that was subsequently scribbled over.[66] As importantly, the Putney objections to urban citizenship were in important respects immanent to the corporate system itself. This was true sociologically. All three opponents of Ireton had first-hand experience of the citizenship he espoused. Sexby had apprenticed to a London grocer, Edward Price, in 1632; Rainborough was the son of Levant merchant, traded with Turkey Company, and in 1647 became MP for the Worcestershire borough of Droitwich;

Wildman, along with John Lilburne, was deeply involved in the concurrent campaign by London freemen for democratic (rather than aristocratic) mayoral elections.[67] Lilburne himself was educated in Newcastle Grammar School, had apprenticed to the London clothier, Thomas Hewson, and married Elizabeth, daughter of a London merchant.[68] It was also true ideologically. First, the very fact that the normative culture of early modern citizenship was aristocratic meant that, as the Levellers most dramatically demonstrated, democracy became an imaginative and even practical possibility. Second, although the privileges and freedoms of citizenship were particularized and enclosed, their existence nonetheless demonstrated what such privileges and freedoms could be. The Putney critics of corporations sought to universalize (within limits) freedom and liberty rather than destroy them; to make them attributes of birthright or nature rather than place.[69]

Roy's contention that corporate communities successfully adjusted to post-regicide politics is borne out by local case studies.[70] Citizens recognized the continuities of 'commonwealth' even if they missed the legitimacy which monarchy gave them. They also made practical gains, in terms of powers and resources, especially in the absence of urban rivals. Ultimately, however, the revolution introduced into the civic field of conflict groups who were every bit as threatening to corporate liberties, freedom, independence, and commonweal as 'the will of one man'. The Leveller platform, with its democratic agenda and appeal to journeymen excluded from urban freedom, represented one set of dangers. Sects like the Quakers and Ranters—with their repudiation of church governance, espousal of 'liberty of conscience', and democratization of religious worship and discourse—embodied another. The midwife of both these disruptive elements, the New Model Army, constituted a third. Indeed one of the great ironies of the 1650s was that because liberty of conscience required military enforcement, and so garrisons, those corporate liberties for which citizens first supported parliament were now perceived to be threatened on a daily basis. And if democrats, sectarians, and soldiers became highly visible actors in 1650s urban culture, then common councils and guildhalls also politicized along confessional lines. Across the corporate system the 'honest party' not only enclosed power from 'malignant' royalists and Episcopalians after 1645. They also engaged in interminable and corrosive internecine politicking while struggling to orchestrate godly reformation. Citizens may well have been empowered by the revolution; but they were also disenchanted.

CONCLUSION

On his fateful march from Scotland to London in early 1660 George Monck met a lot of citizens. They greeted him in the numerous cities and boroughs where he quartered along the way; in Northampton, for example, 'where many gathered together in great companies, shouting as he came along the streets, [and] when he came to his Quarters, the Mayor of the Town with his Mace carried before him, attended him with his Brethren the Aldermen'.[71] They also met him repeatedly in London, so much so that by late February his diary was a whirl of 'entertainments', 'dinners', and 'banquets' with the lord mayor, aldermen, and trading companies.[72] Though Monck was a big man who clearly liked his food, this feasting was political rather than nutritional: at one especially important dinner in early March, 'the Lord Mayor and Officers showed so much respect, as did plainly demonstrate they were not only entertained with the purse, but the hearts of the city'.[73] Such enforced conviviality was an important dimension of the field of conflict which urban citizenship delineated. More, the sheer amount of time Monck spent with citizens indicates their collective power at this crucial political juncture; an importance only reinforced when Charles Stuart directed letters from Breda not only to parliament and the army but also 'the Lord Mayor, Aldermen, and Common Council of the City of London'.[74]

Their prominence should not be surprising. As integral to the outbreak of war in 1642 as Ireton's vision of 'the whole permanent local interest of the kingdom', citizens were equally participant in the Restoration. In the meantime, however, much had changed. Urban citizenship was now irreparably politicized: a field of conflict determined as much by partisanship as by claims to common weal.[75] Perhaps more fundamentally, the inference of the Corporation Act (1661) was that powerful groups now restored to power regarded the corporate system itself as culpable for the upheavals of the last eighteen years. Northampton, along with other towns, had its defensive walls demolished; and it is likely that Thomas Hobbes's view of corporations as 'many lesser Commonwealths in the bowels of a greater, like worms in the entrails of a natural man' was shared by his patrons at the Restoration court.[76] The conclusion of this chapter must be that there was no smoke without fire; that maybe Hartlib's correspondents had a point after all.

Notes

1. University of Sheffield [US], Hartlib Papers [HP], 26/79/1A-10B.
2. US, HP, 53127/1A-2B.
3. For London see, in addition to items listed in further reading, Gary de Krey, *London and the Restoration, 1659–1683* (Cambridge, 2005).
4. J. S. A. Adamson, 'The Baronial Context of the English Civil War', *Transactions of the Royal Historical Society*, 5th Series, 40 (1990): 93–120.
5. J. G. A. Pocock, *The Machiavellian Moment: Florentine Political Thought and the Atlantic Republican Tradition* (Princeton, 1974), 335.
6. Patrick Collinson, 'The Monarchical Republic of Queen Elizabeth I', in *Elizabethan Essays* (London, 1994), 43; Patrick Collinson, 'Afterword' in John F. McDiarmid (ed.), *The Monarchical Republic of Early Modern England: Essays in Response to Patrick Collinson* (Aldershot, 2007), 267–8.
7. Peter Clark and Paul Slack (eds.), *Crisis and Order in English Towns, 1500–1700* (London, 1972) and Peter Clark and Paul Slack, *English Towns in Transition, 1500–1700* (Oxford, 1976).
8. Peter Clark, 'The Ramoth-Gilead of the Good: Urban Change and Popular Radicalism at Gloucester 1540–1640', in Jonathan Barry (ed.), *The Tudor and Stuart Town: A Reader in English Urban History, 1530–1688* (Harlow, 1990), 244–73.

9. Keith Wrightson, 'Estates, Degrees and Sorts: Changing Perceptions of Society in Tudor and Stuart England', in Penelope Corfield (ed.), *Language, History and Class* (Oxford, 1991), 51.

10. Phil Withington, *The Politics of Commonwealth: Citizens and Freemen in Early Modern England* (Cambridge, 2005).

11. US, HP, 26/79/3B.

12. Thomas Wilson, *The State of England Anno. Dom. 1600*, ed. F. J. Fisher, Camden Society, 3rd series, Camden Misc. XVI (London, 1936), 20.

13. Jan De Vries, *European Urbanization 1500–1800* (London, 1984), 64.

14. Withington, *Politics of Commonwealth*, 8–12.

15. Michael Dalton, *The Country Justice* (1619), 10–11.

16. Robert Tittler, *The Reformation and the Towns in England: Politics and Political Culture, c.1540–1640* (Oxford, 1998), 223–34; Paul Slack, 'The Public Conscience of Henry Sherfield', in John Morrill, Paul Slack, and Daniel Woolf (eds.), *Public Duty and Private Conscience in Seventeenth-Century England* (Oxford, 1993), 151–71.

17. Catherine F. Patterson, *Urban Patronage in Early Modern England: Corporate Boroughs, the Landed Elite, and the Crown, 1580–1640* (Stanford, 1999).

18. Derek Hirst, *The Representative of the People? Voters and Voting in England Under the Early Stuarts* (Cambridge, 1992); Thomas Smith, *De Republica Anglorum*, ed. Mary Dewar (Cambridge, 1982), 73.

19. Tittler, *Reformation*, 87–96 and 'The Incorporation of the Boroughs, 1540–1558', *History*, 62 (1977): 24–42.

20. Withington, *Politics of Commonwealth*, 18–25.

21. Withington, *Politics of Commonwealth*, 38–44.

22. Patrick Collinson, *The Birthpangs of Protestant England: Religious and Cultural Change in the Sixteenth and Seventeenth Centuries* (Basingstoke, 1998), 28–59.

23. Paul Slack, *From Reformation to Improvement: Public Welfare in Early Modern England* (Oxford, 1999), 29–52.

24. Keith Wrightson, *Earthly Necessities: Economic Lives in Early Modern Britain, 1470–1750* (London, 2002), 194.

25. Robert Brenner, *Merchants and Revolution: Commercial Change, Political Conflict, and London's Overseas Traders, 1550–1653* (London, 2003), Part One.

26. Wrightson, *Earthly Necessities*, 181.

27. Wrightson, *Earthly Necessities*, 193; John Walter, *Understanding Popular Violence in the English Revolution: The Colchester Plunderers* (Cambridge, 1999), 243–56.

28. Slack, *From Reformation to Improvement*, 36–46.

29. Withington, *Politics of Commonwealth*, 181–2.

30. Jennifer Bishop, 'Utopia and Civic Politics in Mid-Sixteenth Century London', *Historical Journal [HJ]*, 54 (2011): 933–53.

31. Henry Manship, *The History of Great Yarmouth*, ed. Charles John Palmer (1854), 23; John Barston, *The Safeguard of Societies* (1576); Richard Carew, *The Survey of Cornwall*, ed. F. E. Halliday (London, 1954), 157–8.

32. Carew, *Survey*, 157–8.

33. Manship, *History*, 55.

34. Smith, *De Republica*, 57; Barston, *Safeguard*, passim.

35. Phil Withington, *Society in Early Modern England: The Vernacular Origins of Some Powerful Ideas* (Cambridge, 2010), 141–6, 156.

36. Tittler, *Reformation*, 141–8, 183–4; Withington, *Politics of Commonwealth*, 66–75.

37. William Hunt, 'Civic Chivalry and the English Civil War', in Anthony Grafton and Ann Blair (eds.), *The Transmission of Culture in Early Modern Europe* (Philadelphia, 1992).

38. Claire Cross, 'A Man of Conscience in Seventeenth-Century Urban Politics: Alderman Hoyle of York', in Morrill, Slack, and Wolf (eds.), *Public Duty*, 210.

39. Keith Roberts, 'Citizen Soldiers: The Military Power of the City of London', in Stephen Porter (ed.), *London and the Civil Wars* (Basingstoke, 1996), 89–111.

40. Ian Gentles, 'The New Model Officer Corps in 1647: A Collective Portrait', *Social History*, 22 (1997): 133.

41. Michael Braddick, *God's Fury, England's Fire: A New History of the English Civil Wars* (London, 2008), 209–38.

42. Peter Laslett, *The World We Have Lost: Further Explored* (Abingdon, 2005), 22–3, 48–9. Jonathan Barry, 'Bourgeois Collectivism? Urban Association and the Middling Sort', in Jonathan Barry and Christopher Brooks (eds.), *The Middling Sort of People: Culture, Society and Politics in England, 1550–1800* (Basingstoke, 1994), 84–112.

43. Brenner, *Merchants and Revolution*, 649–50.

44. US, HP, 26/79/8.

45. Lawson Nagel, ' "A Great Bouncing at Everyman's Door": The Struggle for London's Militia in 1642', in Porter (ed.), *London*, 65–88; Keith Lindley, 'London's Citizenry in the English Revolution', in R. C. Richardson (ed.), *Town and Countryside in the English Revolution* (Manchester, 1992), 19–34.

46. Phil Withington, 'Citizens and Soldiers: The Renaissance Context', *Journal of Early Modern History*, 15 (2011): 7–10.

47. Keith Lindley and David Scott (eds.), *The Diary of Thomas Juxon, 1644–1647*, Camden Society, Fifth Series, XIII (Cambridge, 1999), 1–3.

48. Lindley and Scott (eds.), *The Diary of Thomas Juxon*, 26–7, 29–32.

49. Withington, *Politics of Commonwealth*, 90–5.

50. Phil Withington, 'Agency, Custom, and the English Corporate System', in Henry French and Jonathan Barry (eds.), *Identity and Agency in England, 1500–1800* (Basingstoke, 2004), 216–17.

51. Withington, 'Agency', 216–17.

52. Cambridge City Record Office, City Shelf C, Book 7, f. 313.

53. 'The University of Cambridge: The Early Stuarts and the Civil War', in *A History of the County of Cambridge and the Isle of Ely, Vol. 3, The City and University of Cambridge* (1959), 191–210.

54. Withington, 'Agency', 217.

55. Walter, *Understanding Popular Violence*, 339–40, 31–52.

56. Cross, 'Man of Conscience', 216–18.

57. Withington, *Politics of Commonwealth*, 241–2; David Scott, 'Politics and Government in York, 1640–1662', in Richardson (ed.), *Town and Countryside*, 55–65.

58. Ian Roy, 'The English Republic, 1649–1660: The View from the Town Hall', in Helmut G. Koenigsberger (ed.), *Republiken und Republikanismus im Europa der Fruhen Neuzeit* (Munich, 1988), 236–7; Phil Withington, 'Views from the Bridge: Revolution and Restoration in Seventeenth-Century York', *Past and Present*, 170 (2001): 133–9.

59. Andrew Sharpe (ed.), *The English Levellers* (Cambridge, 1998), 123.

60. Sharpe (ed.), *The English Levellers*, 108.

61. Sharpe (ed.), *The English Levellers*, 108.

62. Jonathan Barry, 'Civility and Civic Culture in Early Modern England: The Meanings of Urban Freedom', in Peter Burke, Brian Harrison, and Paul Slack (eds.), *Civil Histories: Essays Presented to Sir Keith Thomas* (Oxford, 2000), 181–96.

63. Sharpe (ed.), *English Levellers*, 119–20.

64. Sharpe (ed.), *English Levellers*, 106–7.

65. Sharpe (ed.), *English Levellers*, 116.

66. York City Archives, B36, f. 222.

67. 'Rainborowe [Rainborow], Thomas (d. 1648)', 'Sexby, Edward (c.1616–1658)', 'Wildman, Sir John (1622/3–1693)', *Oxford Dictionary of National Biography* [*ODNB*]; Withington, *Politics of Commonwealth*, 80.

68. 'Lilburne, John (1615?–1657)', *ODNB*.

69. Patricia Crawford, 'The Poorest She: Women and Citizenship in Early Modern England', in Michael Mendle (ed.), *The Putney Debates of 1647: The Army, the Levellers, and the English State* (Cambridge, 2001), 216–17.

70. Bernard Capp, *England's Culture Wars: Puritan Reformation and its Enemies in the Interregnum, 1649–1660* (Oxford, 2012), 221–56.

71. *The Parliamentary Intelligencer* [*PI*], 6, 1659/60, 72.

72. See for example *PI*, 11, 153; *PI*, 12, 183, 188; *PI*, 16, 246, 256.

73. *PI*, 10, 143.

74. *PI*, 19, 289; De Krey, *London*, 19–69.

75. Paul D. Halliday, *Dismembering the Body Politic: Partisan Politics in England's Towns, 1650–1730* (Cambridge, 1998).

76. Ann Hughes, 'Coventry and the English Revolution', reprinted in Richardson (ed.), *Town and Countryside*, 69–99, at 9–10; Thomas Hobbes, *Leviathan*, ed. Richard Tuck (Cambridge, 1992), 230.

FURTHER READING

Ashton, Robert, *The City and the Court, 1603–1643* (Cambridge, 1979).

Barry, Jonathan, 'Civility and Civic Culture in Early Modern England: The Meanings of Urban Freedom', in Peter Burke, Brian Harrison, and Paul Slack (eds.), *Civil Histories: Essays Presented to Sir Keith Thomas* (Oxford, 2000), 181–196.

Brenner, Robert, *Merchants and Revolution: Commercial Change, Political Conflict, and London's Overseas Traders, 1550–1653* (London, 2003).

Capp, Bernard, *England's Culture Wars: Puritan Reformation and its Enemies in the Interregnum, 1649–1660* (Oxford, 2012).

Halliday, Paul D., *Dismembering the Body Politic: Partisan Politics in England's Towns, 1650–1730* (Cambridge, 1998).

Hunt, William, 'Civic Chivalry and the English Civil War', in Anthony Grafton and Ann Blair (eds.), *The Transmission of Culture in Early Modern Europe* (Philadelphia, 1992), 204–237.

Lindley, Keith, *Popular Politics and Religion in Civil War London* (Aldershot, 1997).

Pearl, Valerie, *London and the Outbreak of the Puritan Revolution: City Government and National Politics, 1625–1643* (Oxford, 1961).

Porter, Stephen (ed.), *London and the Civil Wars* (Basingstoke, 1996).

Richardson, R. C. (ed.), *The English Civil Wars: Local Aspects* (Manchester, 1997).

Richardson, R. C. (ed.), *Town and Countryside in the English Revolution* (Manchester, 1992).

Roy, Ian, 'The English Republic, 1649–1660: The View from the Town Hall', in Helmut G. Koenigsberger (ed.), *Republiken und Republikanismus im Europa der Fruhen Neuzeit* (Munich, 1988), 213–237.

Walter, John, *Understanding Popular Violence in the English Revolution: The Colchester Plunderers* (Cambridge, 1999).

Withington, Phil, 'Citizens and Soldiers: The Renaissance Context', *Journal of Early Modern History*, 15 (2011): 3–30.

Withington, Phil, *The Politics of Commonwealth: Citizens and Freemen in Early Modern England* (Cambridge, 2005).

Withington, Phil, 'Views from the Bridge: Revolution and Restoration in Seventeenth-Century York', *Past and Present*, 170 (2001): 121–151.

CHAPTER 19

··

CROWDS AND POPULAR POLITICS IN THE ENGLISH REVOLUTION

··

JOHN WALTER

A contemporary woodcut depicted the civil war being fought on a stage while the people gazed on as spectators. This image captures the then dominant elite view of the politics of the people. The people's role in the revolution was to provide the muscle and the money that allowed their 'betters'—parliament and the king—to fight a civil war that had its origins in a squabble *within* a landed elite. This was a view of the role of the people that continued to dominate historical accounts from the seventeenth century on, until it was challenged by radical populist histories (in the nineteenth century) and Marxist histories (in the twentieth century). This view of the people as having neither a voice nor a vote in early modern politics found its justification in large part in the then contemporary image of the people as 'the many-headed monster', illiterate, ill-informed, and irrational; in a critique of the dangers of 'democracy' buttressed by cautionary tales of popular violence in the classical world that, post-Renaissance, dominated the humanist education of the landed classes; and in a (mis-)reading of the violence of popular rebellions from 1381 on.

Recent work has challenged this view of the people and of popular politics. It has emphasized the shared ideas between elite and people that existed in early modern political culture and the depth of political knowledge and sophistication with which crowds protested.[1] In accounts of the civil war, attempts have been made to balance the earlier emphasis on the deference and localism that were thought to have characterized popular attitudes with analyses that recognize the existence of both an active popular parliamentarianism and royalism. Explanation for these patterns of popular allegiance, it has been suggested, are to be found structurally in differential regional patternings in settlement types, social relations, and political culture and contingently and chronologically in shifting political mobilizations which successfully aligned popular beliefs with political programmes.[2]

Much depended, of course, on who were the people. All those below the level of the gentry were known collectively as the people, the commons. But economic change had opened up significant differences within this top-down and indiscriminatory term. Mercantile and agrarian capitalism had seen the rise, remarkable by contemporary European standards, of a significant bloc of wealthy traders, merchants (with some successful artisans), and capitalist farmers. Growing ambition in the state and greater complexity in society had also seen significant growth among professional groups. Taken collectively, these groups were known to contemporaries as 'the middling sort'. It was primarily from these groups of local elites that the rulers of both town and village had long been drawn, dominating office-holding in both borough and manor. This was a development that long preceded the early modern period.[3] But the expansion of Tudor and early Stuart royal government had multiplied the responsibilities (and hence knowledge) of office-holders in local and county government. Below the level of gentry, it was the middling sort that largely staffed the expansion of royal administration into the local community, as churchwardens, high and petty constables, overseers of the poor, and jurors in the courts of assizes and quarter sessions. Significantly, this social depth to office-holding has led some historians of early modern England to talk of an 'unacknowledged republic' of participatory citizenship.[4]

The middling sort therefore had considerable experience and knowledge of the process of government. But popular participation might extend beyond this into the formal realm of politics (not least in elections for parliament where candidates who were enclosers or who had sought to profit from high prices on the grain market in conditions of dearth might face popular criticism). Not only did the middling sort hold office, they were also acquiring a vote in parliamentary elections. This was a process to be explained in part by their economic success allowing them to meet the financial qualifications needed for the franchise, qualifications that a prolonged period of inflation was anyway eroding. But this was also a process that was to be deliberately encouraged by a House of Commons anxious to emphasize its representative character in the face of perceived threats to parliament's continuing existence. In a series of decisions in disputed elections the Commons had sought to widen the franchise to include in boroughs even those below the level of the middling sort.[5]

Despite the argument that selection, rather than election, more accurately captures the process in early modern England whereby elites chose the candidates and presented them to the electorate for approval, elections could and did become occasions for the rehearsal of political and religious grievances with the government, as events from the 1620s on showed. The elections to both the Short and Long Parliaments in 1640 then saw some of the earliest episodes of popular politics in the revolution with contested elections and crowds appearing at the hustings.

Popular knowledge and involvement in government in early modern England extended beyond the middling sort. Early modern government needed to publicize its policies to the country. That much local government remained self-government at the king's command meant that royal government needed to pursue an active policy of publicizing the laws and policies it wanted enforced, for example through proclamations designed to be publicly posted and read from the pulpit or market cross. That the landed class acting as unpaid justices of the peace might on occasion have an agenda that promoted their own interests in ways that might conflict with that of the government in critical areas like enclosure or religion compounded the need to speak to the country. Moreover, the government, in the absence of a professional bureaucracy, used the law and its courts not only to police crime but also to administer the realm, making local and provincial courts another point of contact where policy in both secular and religious matters was publicly rehearsed.

Popular knowledge of politics and policy could also be derived from the experience of local society policing itself in the realm of religion. Post-Reformation, royal government had both to educate the people as to what was the true religion and to involve local communities in the policing of orthodoxy. Through the local detection and presentation of offenders in both the church and secular courts the people were actively involved in presenting and punishing heresy and heterodoxy.

All of this represented an education in government for the people more generally. But there was a further way, vital if less tangible, in which the people were necessarily involved in politics of the realm. Despite what was publicly said, the people did have an important political role in legitimating authority. Popular acclamation of the monarch was of course a formal part of rites of passage of monarchs from birth through marriage to coronation. But the realities of a political system that stressed the obligation of the monarch to the realm and which depended on popular participation in the enforcement of royal rule gave the people a potential agency that was never formally intended. In a state which lacked the defining institutions of the modern state—professional army, police force, and bureaucracy—and which therefore felt itself vulnerable to outbreaks of rebellion and riot, the monarch, and the magistrates under him, needed to secure acceptance of their power as legitimate authority by gaining the consent of their subjects to their rule. That in the 1640s king and parliament were in competition for popular support, and that in the 1650s novel parliamentary regimes struggled for acceptance, made public displays of popular consent to their rule yet more important. This is not to say that the state could not impose its authority by violence. The punishment of offenders employed the highly public symbols of the pillory and the gallows, with what have been called 'last dying speeches' of those condemned as traitors in the hope of royal mercy or divine pardon used to re-state policy and to re-assert—not always successfully—a culture of obedience. Co-opting crowds as witnesses, punishment too offered an education for the people. But the abrasive nature of coercion made this an advisedly selective policy. In the everyday, royal government sought to ground consent to its rule in a series of public transcripts that emphasized the benefits of obedience in the guarantee of social order and the protection of the common good in what was termed the commonwealth. Commonwealth was the highly charged (and increasingly contested) term which depicted both polity and society as a series of interlocking and reciprocal hierarchies, in which *inter alia* obedience to superiors was grounded on their fulfilment of their responsibilities to their inferiors. It therefore placed obligations on power-holders, including the monarch, and might afford agency in its defence to the people. Before the revolution, the people either covertly by the posting of libels in what has been called the 'crime of anonymity' or publicly by protesting crowds had demonstrated a popular belief in such obligations and an ability to use these 'weapons of the weak' to defend the commonwealth and in it their access to both land and food.

Kings (and lords) of course, should be obeyed. But the development of these public transcripts could, under the pressure of religious and political crisis, come to give obedience a conditional nature. Popular monarchism carried within it a potentially critical message. It was the *good* king (and the *good* lord) who had a right to obedience. Claims of misrule could thus undercut a culture of obedience. Despite the presence of what was effectively a standing army after the king's execution, the political instability of successive political regimes, all claiming to rule in the interests of the Commonwealth and the public good, enlarged this popular role.

All this helps to explain why for example popular protest both before and during the revolution might be conducted within the realm of body politics. Gestural dissidence—the refusal to acknowledge subordination to betters through the correct use of the gestural vocabulary of kneeling and hat honour—was a political weapon deliberately deployed by, among others, the radical groups that emerged in the course of the revolution. Within a tightly hierarchical society, the refusal to uncover in the presence of those accustomed to have their claims to social superiority thus publicly acknowledged or to use appropriate forms of address could be taken as further evidence of a world being turned upside down and threaten the popular consent on which much of the monarch's and elites' rule ultimately rested. Both foreign ambassadors and political opponents paid attention to the social grammar of gesture displayed in crowds' reactions to the parades, processions, and punishments in order to gauge the level of support for the regime.[6] Beyond the politics of the crowd there was then an intangible area, hard for the historian adequately to document or for contemporary governments accurately to measure, where either popular acclaim or its denial had a role to play.

Historians have yet to recover the full range of actions by which the people were able to voice their political beliefs or to express dissent. Inevitably, given their visibility in the historical record, attention has focused on rebellion and riot. Reifying protesters as *the crowd* and treating this as a surrogate for an otherwise unrecoverable popular opinion is not without its problems. Despite the prohibitions within a culture of obedience on political protest, the people demonstrated an often subtle ability to evade such prohibitions in actions that did not require assembling a crowd. Within the 'crime of anonymity', the texts of threatening letters and libels (popular doggerel verses) displayed an ability to manipulate the public transcript in defence of perceived rights and to criticize unpopular ministers or royal favourites like the detested duke of Buckingham in the 1620s.[7] Exuberant and extravagant celebrations in which bells were rung and bonfires lit, as in 1623 when Charles escaped marriage to the Catholic Spanish Infanta, were displays of loyalty that nevertheless expressed critical popular political values, in this case that the godly prince should not marry a Catholic.[8] As the religious policies pursued by Charles I and the Laudian bishops gave rise to a fear of the return of popery similarly enthusiastic celebrations within the Protestant month of November on Gunpowder

Treason Day and on the 17th, the accession day of Queen Elizabeth, England's saviour against the Spanish Armada, expressed political dissent. Again, the role assigned to the people at the sites of punishment, as vociferous and noisy witnesses to the fate of traitors and others, might allow them to subvert the intended political message by remaining silent or, by contrast, feting as heroes those whose beliefs they shared, for example from the 1630s the puritan victims of Laudian repression: Bastwick, Burton, and Prynne.

Thus, while governments and gentlemen might *publicly* insist that the people should have no role in or knowledge of the *arcanum imperii*, the affairs of state, they knew the reality to be very different. Before the 1640s there was therefore already a disjuncture between public pronouncements that denied the people a role in the politics of the state and a more complex reality in which sections of the people held local office, participated in the policing of church and state, and where the people more generally were encouraged to believe that concern for the common good should inform the exercise of power by monarchs and magistrates.

Something of the political potential of these arrangements was reflected in the character of rebellions of the sixteenth century. Complex in causation and social composition, these movements could contain minority war parties intent on challenging the royal ruler, particularly post-Reformation where religion was the primary cause of revolt. But as recent work has shown, for the majority these were movements that drew legitimation from the belief that they were seeking the redress of justice in the enforcement of policies approved by the monarch but prevented by corrupt government and evil counsels. Seeking to uphold a mirror to magistrates and to embarrass them by citing royal policy they should have been enforcing, these rebellions reflected the depth of political knowledge on which the people might draw. Similar political knowledge informed other forms of popular political action before 1640. Within what might be termed the politics of subsistence, crowds protesting against enclosure or perceived malpractices in the marketing of grain, the most common causes of pre-war protest, drew on detailed knowledge of relevant laws or on the public transcripts of monarchy and magistracy to justify and give shape to their actions.[9]

Popular politics, therefore, was not the creation of the English revolution. The structures that underpinned popular politics pre-1640 and the forms these gave rise to continued. But political developments in the revolution combined to create a new and enlarged space for the exercise of a popular agency. Popular politics in the 1640s and 1650s was characterized both by familiar continuities and by striking discontinuities.

CROWDS AND THE POLITICS OF SUBSISTENCE IN THE ENGLISH REVOLUTION

The earliest form of crowd action in the 1640s was agrarian protest, in which crowds destroyed enclosures.[10] Beginning in 1640 there were both large- and small-scale episodes in which crowds pulled down hedges to reclaim common rights over disputed land. This was a continuation of traditional forms of protest. But exploiting the dislocations in power that political division between king and parliament brought produced a level of protest perhaps not seen since either the popular rebellions of 1549 or even 1381. It was Charles I's large-scale enclosing activities, seeking to address royal financial problems by exploiting the crown's extensive holdings in the forests in the west and fens in the east of England, that prompted the most riots. That and the fact that the protesters' targets were predominantly those associated with the discredited regime of the Personal Rule—bishops, court nobility, and city financiers—gave crowd actions a potential political character. Elite commentators feared that these forms of protest (to be joined later by rent strikes) presaged what in modern terms we might call a class war. The widespread destruction of deer on royal and some aristocratic parklands compounded this.[11] This was a fear deliberately cultivated in the paper wars between supporters of the crown and parliament. The royalists tried to use the spectre of 'the many-headed monster', called into being they claimed by parliament's attack on the monarch, to persuade the gentry to support their king as the keystone of the social order.

But despite these fears, radical groups failed to lead or shape this wave of agrarian protest. The one exception was the Diggers who in the later 1640s sought to establish communities on the wastes and commons. Agrarian protesters might enjoy taunting magistrates who tried to suppress them with loud claims to support their political rivals or take advantage of the denunciation of Catholic landlords as enemies of the state to settle old scores, but for the most part their politics remained part of the politics of subsistence. And outside the areas of forest and fen, divisions *within* the people, between commoners and capitalist farmers, the latter increasingly in favour of enclosure, saw some regions largely immune to these forms of crowd action. By the later 1640s, large-scale agrarian protest had died down, only to flare up again in the 1650s when those associated with successive parliamentary and protectorate regimes attempted to re-enclose.[12]

Successive years of harvest failure in the later 1640s saw the reoccurrence of the other main form of crowd action within the politics of subsistence: protests over food. Again their appearance prompted concern. But despite the ability of some of the protesters to couch their demands in the new political vocabulary, in terms of their numbers and geographical spread there were in fact fewer riots than in earlier years of dearth. This undoubtedly reflects the impact of a set of complex social and economic changes reducing, if only temporarily, the vulnerability of some groups and regions. But it also points to one of the more important factors helping to explain popular quiescence and acquiescence in the revolution. Despite dislocations of government at the centre, there was already an entrenched tradition of administrative responses to economic crisis which saw local elites not only able in the absence of royal government to maintain policies for combating dearth but also to increase payments under the poor law to those fortunate to be on relief. Thus, despite a secular trend of increasing poverty and the impact of a significant increase in regressive taxation (by the later 1640s there were some tax riots against the new excise), popular politics in the English revolution were not to be characterized by a rising of the countryside that drove later revolutions.

CROWDS AND THE POLITICS OF THE ENGLISH REVOLUTION

Popular politics in the 1640s and 1650s were marked by change as well as by continuity. The collapse of personal rule changed in important ways the context within which popular politics operated. The fracturing of royal authority and political divisions among the elite led to the abolition or temporary collapse of courts, like the Star Chamber, hitherto important in prosecuting riot and libel. By contrast, the revolutionary regimes created a plethora of new committees whose offices needed staffing and whose proceedings opened up new opportunities for popular agency, for example in parishioners petitioning parliament or in testifying against their local minister before one of the county committees for 'scandalous ministers', a.k.a Laudian and Arminian clergymen. The (temporary) collapse of censorship made access to print easier for both authors and audiences. Both the civil wars and subsequent attempts at settlement in church and state were also fought as paper wars, conducted through the medium of print, and aimed *inter alia* at a popular audience who could either read or have read to them what was being produced. This explosion in print was, as Jason Peacey points out in his chapter, largely driven by the production of newsbooks and small pamphlets, cheap print aimed at a popular readership and reflecting an increasing access to education and a corresponding reduction in rates of popular illiteracy. Whatever the power of (a diminishing) respect for one's lord in a post-feudal society in mobilizing an army, both the king and parliament had to address the people directly and to justify their appeals in the ideologies of the post-Reformation state. Since—initially at least—both employed a common language of the defence of mixed monarchy and the true Protestant religion, this had the unintended consequence of making their audiences the adjudicators of allegiance. This would have been unheard of in the pre-1640 culture of obedience. After 1649, with the abolition of monarchy and episcopacy and the subsequent search for settlement in church and state, print saw both spirited defences of the old order of king and church (now made more attractive by the descent into parliamentary tyranny and religious schism) and the advancing of radically new ideas about the family, society, church, and state. One consequence of this was confirmation that there had never been a monolithic popular political culture: popular radical religious and political movements coexisted with a revived popular royalism.

As Charles I had observed, 'people are governed by the pulpit more than the sword in time of peace'.[13] But the central importance of salvation to early modern men and women in a period of confessional strife could make what was preached from the pulpit political and transform the parish church, particularly at moments of religious controversy or crisis both at home or abroad, into a site for local debates that had national or even international resonances. This was something borne out by reactions to Laudian reforms in the 1630s. These were heavily marked by the use of the language of anti-popery, a development that was to become even more prominent into the early

1640s when its use was extended publicly by parliament in its declarations to label and condemn those 'malignant' forces counselling and corrupting Charles I.

The recall of parliament in 1640 signalled the emergence of crowd actions that engaged with the post-Reformation politics of church and state. In the 1630s opponents of changes in local parish churches had had to employ symbolic forms of resistance. Those who resisted Laudian altar policy with its elevation, railing in and renaming of the communion table as altar, together with associated (and often elaborate) gestural protocols of repeated bowings and kneelings, attacked this as both idolatrous and popish. A, sometimes collective, refusal to bend the knee to receive communion at the altar rails or to remove their hats in church was designed to contest Laudian ideas of the nature of divine worship and its role in constituting sacred space. After 1640 gestural dissidence was to be accompanied by acts of popular iconoclasm.[14] In what were often deliberately ritualized and highly symbolic forms of crowd action, the hated symbols of Laudianism—altar rails, images, stained glass windows, and surplices—were attacked, removed from the church and often burnt, their purging by fire recalling Old Testament denunciations of idolatry. Less frequently, but more ominously, prayer books and, on occasion, Laudian ministers were attacked.

Iconoclasts saw themselves as reformers, defending the church against popish practices. Thus, their actions were, in their own eyes, 'acts of piety'. They found legitimation for their reformation in the tradition of anti-popery and Protestant iconophobia powerfully reiterated after 1640 by parliament, preachers, and press. Episodes of iconoclasm were, however, denounced as acts of profanation and vandalism by supporters of the king who again accused parliament of being responsible for popular violence. Royalist authors, for the most part, silently dropped defence of Laudian altar policy and, exaggerating the violence and destruction involved, sought with some success to reframe such episodes as sectarian attacks on prayer-book Protestantism.

Acts of popular iconoclasm clustered in the early 1640s. Into the civil war, cathedrals which had been the forcing houses of Laudian reform became the target for attacks by parliamentary troops. But they became less common in parish churches as the House of Commons began to issue orders for the removal of rails and images and, ultimately, to establish commissions to secure the removal of what were denounced as popish relics. But if by the end of the first civil war popular iconoclasm had largely ceased, religion remained an important area for popular protest. Divisions between puritans and what were beginning to be called Anglicans and the splintering of the godly into competing churches and sects intensified the politics of religion. They were debated in a popular press in which rumour and misrepresentation and name-calling were commonplace. Popish plots and Catholic cruelty, especially after the outbreak of the Irish rebellion in November 1641, had dominated what was reported in print in the early 1640s. But very quickly the lurid threat supposedly posed to the social and sexual order by the sects was given similar prominence.

Stereotyping in print was linked to scapegoating in popular attacks. In the early 1640s, crowds attacked Catholics in episodes like the Stour Valley riots where crowds numbered in some thousands systematically attacked the houses of local Catholic gentry families.[15] Elsewhere attempts by supporters of the king to raise troops under the Commission of Array led to similar acts of popular resistance. In areas where popular royalism was strong, for example rural Herefordshire, or where in the civil war royalist troops were in control it was supporters of parliament who were the victims of crowds. Later, street politics in cities like London or Bristol saw meetings of religious radicals attacked. In the 1650s, it was the Quakers, not yet the pacifists they would become, with their disruptions of church services and challenges to the social grammars of gesture and language, who bore the brunt of such attacks.[16]

What is noticeable about these religious conflicts is that, in striking contrast to what happened in wars of religion on the Continent, physical attacks by civilian crowds did not usually result in deaths and certainly not in massacres. The attacks on Protestant settlers in Ireland in the 1641 Rising and their subsequent retaliation were, however, an important exception to this.[17] (The descent into civil war meant that all armies were on occasion guilty of atrocities in which in the case of both England and Ireland confessional identities played a large part.[18]) The reasons for this contrast remain to be explored. But the contrast should not be overdrawn. The potential for religious differences to prompt popular violence in England was brought out as early as 1640 when troops assembled to fight in the unpopular so-called Bishops' Wars against the Scots mutinied. Reluctant to fight brother Protestants, troubled by rumours that the war was part of a larger Catholic plot, and anxious that they were being led by Catholic officers, troops forced their officers to take communion with them, on occasion reportedly tying them up and carrying them to church, in order to test their loyalty to the Protestant religion. In exceptional but widely reported episodes this led to troops ritualistically killing their Catholic officer.[19]

STREET POLITICS IN THE ENGLISH REVOLUTION

It shocked and alarmed the propertied classes that attacks by crowds supporting either king or parliament could cross class boundaries. Assaults on the houses that symbolized gentry rule in the countryside were not perhaps widespread, but they were believed to be so and reported as such. Transgressive physical attacks on their betters flouted the unwritten but powerful protocols of a tradition of riot in which violence was directed against property but not persons. Unpopular government ministers had in the past been the subjects of anonymous libels, but in May 1640 libels against Archbishop Laud, popularly believed to be a crypto-Catholic and widely blamed for the king's recent dissolution of the Short Parliament, were followed by an attack on Laud at his palace at Lambeth. Laud managed to escape across the river to Whitehall, but had he been caught the conclusion to this episode might well have been fatal. Here was a street politics with the ominous overtones of 1381 or 1450 when crowds had occupied London, seizing and slaying unpopular royal ministers. It was perhaps not by chance that an account of the revolt of 1381 appeared in print in 1642.[20] Nor that Charles I should remove himself, his French Catholic wife (the obvious target for both verbal and scribbled threats) and their family from the capital. In thus denying Charles control of his capital (and its wealth of resources), popular politics made a major contribution to the outcome of the civil wars.

In the recent past, London had seen occasional crowds on its streets: the attack by apprentices on the London brothels on Shrove Tuesday or May Day had become a near-annual event and there had been the occasional episode in which, for example, crowds of sailors or demobilized soldiers had demonstrated over arrears of pay. But the attack on Laud signalled a very different form of street politics in the capital. This would see the emergence of the London crowd as a semi-permanent feature of the revolution, always ready to be called into being and claiming a *political voice*. At moments of political crisis large crowds assembled around parliament, subjecting members of both Houses to noisy entreaties and even, as in 1647, invading parliament itself.[21] In what might be called the English spring, crowds assembled on successive days in May 1641 to defend parliament against the threat of a royalist coup and to demand justice against those responsible for the ills of the realm. In alliance with the leaders of the parliamentary opposition, the London crowds provided the necessary political pressure to persuade the king to agree to the execution of his leading minister the earl of Strafford, to dissuade Catholic peers from attending the Lords, and later in the year to secure the exclusion of the bishops from parliament. This alliance of the Commons and crowds was repeated in further street protests in late 1641/early 1642 when the king attempted to arrest his opponents in parliament.[22]

New faces within the crowds emphasized the novelty of this form of street politics. Apprentices, whose reputation for rowdy behaviour had seen this youth group used to police morality within the community, might have been expected to be a large part of any London crowd, and they were throughout the 1640s and 1650s. But in the crowds that assembled to defend parliament against feared royal coups in May 1641 and again in January 1642 commentators noted the presence of respectable citizens. And to the reported horror of some MPs and Lords women were also on the streets demonstrating. Women petitioning parliament in 1649 were told to 'looke after your owne businesse, an[d] meddle with your huswifery'.[23] Finding legitimation in their gendered role in the maintenance of the household and licence in their ambiguous status before the law, women had always been an important presence in protests within the politics of subsistence over access to common rights or grain. But now they reworked this gendered role to claim a voice in settling those grievances in church and state that they believed threatened their households.[24] The revolutionary potential of the period for (at least some) women's politics is brought out in the radical claim by women active in the street politics of the Levellers for a political voice, 'since we are assured of our creation in the image of God, and of an interest in Christ equal unto men, as also of a proportionable share in the freedoms of this commonwealth'.

Thus, the period of the revolution saw the emergence of what in a later period would come to be called 'the nation out of doors'. The presence of crowds on the streets of the capital demonstrating around parliament suggests, despite the recent emphasis in the historical literature on parliament as an event, an institution without a permanent presence in the constitution and summoned only at the whim of the monarch, that parliament had long been seen by the people as an institutional arena for the redress of popular grievances. This was something reflected in the demands of sixteenth-century rebels for remedy by the calling of a parliament. Over the period, demonstrations in London became more sophisticated: taverns were used as places to organize and proselytize, print to publicize future meetings, and the wearing of colours and parading of symbols to signal solidarities and to communicate the demonstrators' objectives.

At the level of the people, as of the elite, there were sharp political differences. Crowds in London in the early 1640s had demonstrated in support of the parliamentary opposition. But later, crowds demonstrated for peace, for and against the intervention of the New Model Army into politics and into London, and both for and against the sects and in support of radical groups like the Levellers. These differences certainly reflected a shifting response to the pressures (and financial costs) of war and to the seeming breakdown in order in church and state. But they also challenge the notion that there was ever a single London crowd and hint perhaps at a more complicated political geography in London and the suburbs that has yet to be adequately explored.

The Politics of Popular Protest: A 'Free-Born' Citizenry?

The new political space of the 1640s and 1650s sponsored an increasing sophistication in the forms and politics of popular protest. The presentation of petitions and the collection of subscriptions often provided the focus for these demonstrations. Collective popular petitioning represented another important development in popular politics. The level of petitioning was unprecedented, both in terms of the number of petitions and the numbers putting their hands to them. Petitioning went in waves that reflected particular episodes of political crisis or opportunity. The recall of parliament in 1640 saw over the next two years perhaps the single largest number of petitions, but similar waves recurred throughout the period, for example during the peace movement of early 1643 or the petitions calling for justice against Charles I at the end of the decade.

Petitioning now defied the earlier protocols governing this form of privileged communication.[25] Before 1640, petitions were meant to be initiated by local elites and delivered in the name of institutions like counties or corporations. They were meant to be scribal, deferential, and supplicatory, articulating grievances but neither criticizing authority nor prescribing solutions. Petitioning in the 1640s and 1650s challenged all these rules. Petitions began to be printed, to appeal to a secondary audience of readers, and to invoke public opinion to justify their demands. Groups hitherto denied a legitimate political voice—women, apprentices, seamen, porters, and labourers—presented *and* had printed their own petitions to king and parliament.

As their wave-like patterns and parroted content suggested, petitions were often responding to cues from those who sought to claim public opinion was on their side. Indeed, some petitions claiming to articulate the public voice were in reality attempts to construct and thus to invoke or appropriate public opinion. But even petitioning as a form of sponsored popular political activity had unintended consequences. That county petitions claimed to have been subscribed (or marked by those unable to write) in their thousands meant that those beyond the normal boundaries of formal political participation were pulled into the political process. Scribal and printed copies of petitions were circulated from hand to hand and read out from the pulpit or in the local alehouse, their dissemination or their subscription at places of public meeting like the provincial courts prompting further political discussion. The emergence of cross-petitioning, in which both parliamentarians and royalists attempted to produce petitions to combat that of their rivals, could force would-be subscribers to think for themselves, and in attempting to secure subscription to their version of events they provided a public with the materials to reason for themselves.

Printing petitions (and newsbooks), which happened in increasingly large numbers, in allowing readers to read what was apparently being said and thought from Cumberland to Cornwall, helped also to create a national political culture. This addressed one of the fundamental weaknesses of a pre-war popular political culture that had reflected the local and at best regional nature of early modern society. Before 1640, local communities might have been well aware of what was happening at the centre, but this ran well ahead of their ability to know what was going on in the nation. The potential for a new form of popular politics through petitioning was brought to its fullest expression in the later emergence of the radical groups. The Levellers, for example, had their organizational as well as ideological origins in the London-based petitioning campaign for greater religious freedom. Their use of petitions to recruit support and to organize demonstrations meant that like other radical groups they might be best seen as *textual communities*, able to use printed petitions to secure support and to organize demonstrations at their presentation and—potentially—to communicate beyond the otherwise serious limitations on their ability physically to organize across the nation in a society that remained local and regional.

The agency claimed by the people through innovations in petitioning was echoed in another new development—the introduction of state oaths. This too had important consequences for early modern popular political culture. Introduced initially by parliament, these oaths were an attempt to gather the public support it needed in its struggle with the king. Individual oaths taken individually had long been part of the legal and political culture of early modern England. But what was new about the state oaths introduced by parliament was the attempt, in effect, to swear the nation and to do so simultaneously. Parliament introduced a succession of oaths: in May 1641 the Protestation, the Vow and Covenant (June 1643), the Covenant (March 1644), and in 1649/50 the Engagement.[26] These were in effect loyalty oaths. They prompted the later introduction of similar oaths in royalist-controlled areas.

The consequences of oath-taking for popular politics can be illustrated from the example of the first oath introduced, the Protestation. Owing something to earlier English precedents and to the Scottish National Covenant which had signalled the rebellion there against Charles I, the Protestation was taken in parliament in the first week of May. It was introduced by the leaders of the parliamentary opposition in an attempt to counter recently discovered plots. These originated from courtiers around Charles's French queen, Henrietta Maria, and in which the king became implicated. They were designed to seize the Tower and rescue the imprisoned earl of Strafford and to use the army assembled to fight the Scots to overawe the parliamentary opposition. On the face of it, the Protestation required subscription to a series of political commonplaces: the taker vowed to protect the 'true reformed Protestant religion', the king, parliament, and individual liberties against popery and 'popish innovation', the latter a code word for Laudian and Arminian reforms. But the Protestation had radical intentions—and consequences. The day after its taking in the House of Commons crowds of Londoners, led by godly ministers, petitioned to be allowed to take it. This granted, the leaders of the parliamentary opposition sought to secure a bill that would impose taking the Protestation through the nation, while MPs were required to send copies of the Protestation to their constituencies with an encouragement that it should be taken locally. Copies of the Protestation rapidly appeared in various editions that must eventually have run into their thousands. These were followed by debates in the press over the meaning of the Protestation. Was it an oath and what obligations did it impose on those who took it? What was 'the true reformed Protestant religion'? Prevented from securing a bill by opposition in the Lords, the Commons subsequently issued the Protestation under their own authority in response to the king's attempted arrest of the Five Members in January 1642. Within three months it had been taken in every county.

When the Protestation was taken in the country, inhabitants gathered together in the local parish church, usually on a Sunday and, after a sermon setting out the grounds for taking it, subscribed or marked their names. A return listing the names of those who had taken it and of those—usually Catholics—who had refused was to be sent to the parliament. Taking the Protestation after taking communion together or on the day when contributions for the Protestant victims of the massacre in Ireland were to be collected heightened the significance of the occasion. Its taking often occasioned local debate, especially where the parish minister refused to administer it. Taking and subscribing the Protestation also gave an identity to those whose political identity was otherwise subsumed in that of the patriarchal head of household. Since all over 18 were expected to take it, it offered empowerment to young unmarried males and since parliament in its arrangements to take the oath used the non-gendered language of 'inhabitants' in some communities women also took and subscribed the Protestation.

Widely believed to be an oath sworn in the presence of God, the Protestation could be taken to provide legitimation for forms of popular political initiative. The example of one London church where taking the oath was immediately followed by the pulling down of the altar rails as marks of popery reflects the wider use made of the Protestation in providing legitimation for popular acts of iconoclasm or opposing ceremonialism in the church.[27] Parliament's subsequent use of the Protestation as a validating charter for the war against the king had important consequences for popular politics. For example, the originating attack on Sir John Lucas, a noted supporter of the king, in the Stour Valley riots in eastern England was prompted by a printed parliamentary declaration reminding the people of their obligations under the Protestation of opposing those, Catholics and others, thought to be corrupting the king.[28]

POPULAR POLITICAL CULTURE AND THE ENGLISH REVOLUTION

Taken together, events in the English revolution created a new space for popular politics. The collapse of censorship saw an unprecedented flow of newsbooks and cheap pamphlets challenging old certainties and offering radical new ideas about the ordering of state, church, and society. With a divided elite competing for popular support, both king and parliament had had to issue printed declarations, orders, and oaths that actively sought to advance and explain their cause. Dislocations in central authority and in the provinces the collapse of the church courts and temporary cessation of assizes and quarter sessions made it harder to prevent and punish episodes of rioting. Military mobilization institutionalized attacks by plebeians on their betters which saw crowds attacking gentlemen as enemies of (either the royalist or parliamentarian) state. The politicization of the New Model Army showed what the consequence might be of removing men from the local supervision of magistrate, master, or minister. The troops elected their own representatives—the 'agitators'—drew up petitions, and debated with the military leadership in the newly formed General Council of the Army a blueprint for political reform.[29]

As this response showed, one consequence of these developments might be the emergence of an active citizenry in place of the subject whose primary political role pre-1640 had been defined in terms of the obligations of obedience. And although citizenship was to be conceived in highly gendered terms of manhood (and for many republicans was meant to be restrictively coded by class), the period offered opportunities for at least some women to challenge and renegotiate their role, not least in the new religious groups where women dominated membership and might claim agency as preacher or prophetess.

In the past popular politics had been informed by the simple binary of xenophobia and anti-popery (the two often conflated). This had provided the main vocabulary within which the people understood politics. But after 1640 the politics of religion became far more complex and it played a far more radical role in the English revolution. The emergence of religious sects and, by the later 1640s, radical political groups like the Levellers, Diggers, and Fifth Monarchists, in whose precocious political programmes a radical re-reading of Christian texts played an important part, reflected one culmination of the creation of this new political space. These radical groups failed to achieve their programmes in part because the parliamentary regime had now acquired a standing army (which it was to use in the 1650s to put down a whole range of popular protests) but also because of their failure to mobilize mass popular support. At a time of dearth and distress, their political programmes failed to mesh with a preceding pattern of popular politics in which the politics of subsistence loomed large. While the Leveller leaders largely ignored agrarian grievances, the Diggers' visionary policy of common cultivation of the wastes and commons (allied to a labour strike that they hoped would force lords of the manor and yeomen ultimately to join them) fell foul of the hostility of local communities where opposition to enclosure had been driven by defence of common rights as a valuable adjunct to the shrinking individual holdings of husbandmen and cottagers. And the belief of many radicals in the power of the rightness of their ideas to win over men and women given by God at Creation the capacity to reason for themselves—in what would later come to be called moral force—was to be disappointed, not least since misrepresentation of their ideas and programmes in print frightened many.

If the late 1640s saw in the emergence of radical groups the culmination of one strand of popular politics in response to the new political space opened up by the civil war, they also saw a popular backlash. The emergence in the mid-1640s in many counties of south-western England and the Welsh borders of the Clubmen, semi-independent and largely uncoordinated popular movements that sought to protect the local communities against the depredations of either royalist or parliamentarian armies, represented a response to the costs of a civil war that was to become more common, if less organized, into the later 1640s and 1650s.[30] The combination of higher taxation, driven amongst other things by the needs to keep an army paid and in place, religious schism, and the unpopularity of the stillborn Presbyterian settlement, and the failure to secure a stable political regime all help to explain the growing popular support for the restoration of monarchy and prayer book Anglicanism, the latter the focus of popular risings and demonstrations in 1647. By the later 1650s, in a now even more divided popular political culture, London street politics would come to be dominated by crowds whose behaviour and demands would in a later period come to be labelled 'Church and King'.

In 1660 popular hostility to the restoration of the Stuart monarchy was forced back into the underworld of seditious utterances, while popular fiestas of bells and bonfires acclaimed the return of Charles II. Popular political culture was now divided and would become hereafter partisan. The potential for active citizenship had not been realized. But the revolution had seen the emergence of a political culture in which public opinion was to be something more than a discursive fiction and which was again to play an important role in the contested politics of the later seventeenth century.

NOTES

1. John Walter, *Crowds and Popular Politics in Early Modern England* (Manchester, 2006); David Underdown, *A Freeborn People: Politics and the Nation in Seventeenth-Century England* (Oxford, 1996).

2. David Underdown, *Revel, Riot and Rebellion: Popular Politics and Culture in England, 1603–1660* (Oxford, 1985); Michael J. Braddick, 'Prayer Book and Protestation: Anti-Popery, Anti-Puritanism and the Outbreak of the English Civil War', in Charles W. Prior and Glenn Burgess (eds.), *England's Wars of Religion Revisited* (Farnham, 2011), 125–45.

3. John Watts, 'The Pressure of the Public in Later Medieval Politics', in Linda Clarke and Christine Carpenter (eds.), *The Fifteenth Century, IV: Political Culture in Late Medieval Britain* (Woodbridge, 2004), 159–80.

4. Mark Goldie, 'The Unacknowledged Republic: Officeholding in Early Modern England', in Tim Harris (ed.), *The Politics of the Excluded, c.1500–1850* (Basingstoke, 2001), 153–94.

5. Derek Hirst, *The Representative of the People? Voters and Voting in England under the Early Stuarts* (Cambridge, 1975).

6. John Walter, 'Body Politics in the English Revolution', in Stephen Taylor and Grant Tapsell (eds.), *The Nature of the English Revolution Revisited: Essays in Honour of John Morrill* (Woodbridge, 2013).

7. *Early Stuart Libels: An Edition of Poetry from Manuscript Sources*, ed. Alastair Bellany and Andrew McRae, Early Modern Literary Studies Text Series I (2005) <http://purl.oclc.org/emls/texts/libels>.

8. David Cressy, *Bonfires and Bells: National Memory and the Protestant Calendar in Elizabethan and Stuart England* (London, 1989).

9. Walter, *Crowds and Popular Politics*, 1–26.

10. Brian Manning, *The English People and the English Revolution* (London, 1976), chaps. 6–7.

11. Daniel C. Beaver, *Hunting and the Politics of Violence before the English Civil War* (Cambridge, 2008).

12. John Walter, 'The English People and the English Revolution Revisited', *History Workshop Journal*, 61 (2006): 171–82.

13. Quoted in Christopher Hill, *The Century of Revolution, 1603–1714* (London, 1971), 76.

14. John Walter, ' "Abolishing Superstition with Sedition"? The Politics of Popular Iconoclasm in England 1640–1642', *Past and Present* [*P&P*], 183 (2004): 79–123.

15. John Walter, *Understanding Popular Violence in the English Revolution: The Colchester Plunderers* (Cambridge, 1999).

16. Barry Reay, 'Popular Hostility towards the Quakers in the Mid-Seventeenth-Century England', *Social History*, 5 (1980): 387–407.

17. John Walter, 'Performative Violence and the Politics of Violence in the 1641 Depositions', in Jane Ohlmeyer and Micheál Ó Siochrú (eds.), *Ireland 1641: Contexts and Reactions* (Manchester, 2013), 134–52.

18. Mark Stoyle, 'The Road to Farndon Field: Explaining the Massacre of the Royalist Women at Naseby', *English Historical Review*, 123 (2008): 895–923.

19. David Cressy, *England on Edge: Crisis and Revolution, 1640–1642* (Oxford, 2006), 86–90.

20. *The iust reward of rebels, or The life and death of Jack Straw and Wat Tyler…* (London, 1642).

21. Keith Lindley, *Popular Politics and Religion in Civil War London* (Aldershot, 1997).

22. Conrad Russell, *The Fall of the British Monarchies, 1637–1642* (Oxford, 1991), chaps. 7 and 11.

23. Patricia Higgins, 'The Reactions of Women, with Special Reference to Women Petitioners', in Brian Manning (ed.), *Politics, Religion and the English Civil War* (London, 1973), 179–222 (quotation at 203).

24. Ann Hughes, *Gender and the English Revolution* (London, 2012), 54–61.

25. David Zaret, *Origins of Democratic Culture: Printing, Petitions, and the Public Sphere in Early-Modern England* (Princeton, 2000).

26. Edward Vallance, *Revolutionary England and the National Covenant: State Oaths, Protestantism and the Political Nation, 1553–1682* (Woodbridge, 2005).

27. I. W., *Certaine Affirmations In defence of the pulling down of Communion Rails, by divers rash and misguided people, judiciously and religiously answered* (London, 1641); Parliamentary Archives, Main Papers, House of Lords 30 June 1641.

28. Walter, *Understanding Popular Violence*, 292–7.

29. Austin Woolrych, *Soldiers and Statesmen: The General Council of the Army and its Debates, 1647–1648* (Oxford, 1987).

30. David Underdown, 'The Chalk and the Cheese: Contrasts among the English Clubmen', *P&P*, 85 (1979): 25–48.

FURTHER READING

Baker, Philip and Elliot Vernon (eds.), *The Agreement of the People, the Levellers, and the Constitutional Crisis of the English Revolution* (Basingstoke, 2012).

Braddick, Michael J., *God's Fury, England's Fire: A New History of the English Civil Wars* (London, 2008).

Cressy, David, *England on Edge: Crisis and Revolution 1640–1642* (Oxford, 2006).

Gurney, John, *Brave Community: The Digger Movement in the English Revolution* (Manchester, 2007).

Hill, Christopher, *The World Turned Upside Down: Radical Ideas during the English Revolution* (London, 1972).

Hughes, Ann, *Gender and the English Revolution* (London, 2012).

Manning, Brian, *The English People and the English Revolution* (London, 1976).

Underdown, David, *A Freeborn People: Politics and the Nation in Seventeenth-Century England* (Oxford, 1996).

Underdown, David, *Revel, Riot and Rebellion: Popular Politics and Culture in England 1603–1660* (Oxford, 1985).

Vallance, Edward, *Revolutionary England and the National Covenant: State Oaths, Protestantism and the Political Nation, 1553–1682* (Woodbridge, 2005).

Walter, John, '"Abolishing Superstition with Sedition"? The Politics of Popular Iconoclasm in England 1640–1642', *Past and Present*, 183 (2004): 79–123.

Walter, John, 'Body Politics in the English Revolution', in Stephen Taylor and Grant Tapsell (eds.), *The Nature of the English Revolution Revisited: Essays in Honour of John Morrill* (Woodbridge, 2013), 81–102.

Walter, John, *Crowds and Popular Politics in Early Modern England* (Manchester, 2006).

Walter, John, *Understanding Popular Violence in the English Revolution: The Colchester Plunderers* (Cambridge, 1999).

Zaret, David, *Origins of Democratic Culture: Printing, Petitions, and the Public Sphere in Early-Modern England* (Princeton, 2000).

CHAPTER 20

'GENDER TROUBLE'

Women's Agency and Gender Relations in the English Revolution

ANN HUGHES

INTRODUCTION: GENDERING THE ENGLISH REVOLUTION

THE decisive parliamentarian victory at the battle of Naseby in June 1645 was crucial to the eclipse of royalism in England. Naseby, less predictably, serves well to introduce the themes of this chapter. For Charles I the battle was a propaganda as well as a military disaster. The king lost hundreds of soldiers killed and thousands taken prisoner, but lost as well were his coach and his private correspondence, including letters from Henrietta Maria, his cherished French Catholic wife. Parliament seized on the opportunity to discredit the king by publishing the letters along with a self-righteous commentary that stressed the queen's influence and the king's hypocrisy. *The King's Cabinet Opened* connected the king's failure as a ruler with his inadequacy as a husband and a man. As an analogy to fatherhood was a profoundly important way of understanding and legitimating monarchical authority, so a man in thrall to an imperious, papist woman could not be a good king. The parliamentarian editors of the correspondence stressed that the king's 'counsels were wholly managed by the Queen', one of 'the weaker sex, born an alien, and bred up in a contrary religion'. They insisted, in carefully chosen terms, that Charles was 'a prince seduced out of his proper sphere', behaving in a way 'unbeseeming' for a man who claimed to be 'the tender father of his country'. A newsbook made the point more emphatically: 'It were ridiculous in a private man, much more a king, to submit to his wife upon every trifle.'[1] The problem, of course, was that the queen's advice was not confined to trifles, but dealt with pressing matters of royalist policy including peace negotiations with parliament.

Naseby saw also the single worst atrocity of the English civil wars, when parliament's victorious army slaughtered at least one hundred royalist camp women followers and mutilated many more. This is stark evidence for the presence of women at the heart of the struggles of the 1640s, and a disturbing reminder of the vulnerability of women who were judged to have transgressed conventional female roles. The Naseby victims were assimilated to other troubling but more familiar stereotypes of unruly women—whores and witches—and their punishments (such as nose slitting) echoed legal and community sanctions against deviant women. Ethnic stereotypes contributed to the atrocity; the English parliamentary soldiers thought the women were Welsh or Irish, making the further assumption that these women were particularly likely to be whores and witches.[2]

This chapter will offer a brief review of the many ways in which women played active parts in the war effort itself, and still more in the political and religious upheavals of the revolution. Henrietta Maria, and the butchered camp followers, are extreme examples, but when we explore the many other women representing most opinions and most social groups who made their mark on the 1640s and 1650s, we can identify some common themes: women's enterprising and resilient capacity to appeal to traditional social roles and stereotypes as justifications for dramatic interventions; and the perennial risk they faced of ridicule, harassment, or worse, if not always from men in general, then certainly from men holding opposing positions. Female initiatives often unleashed troubling fears in men, founded on enduring stereotypes of dangerous or disruptive women. But a concern with gender is not identical with a focus on the experiences of women; as *The King's Cabinet Opened* reveals, what it meant to be a man was also at stake in a period of war, particularly civil war, and revolution. The upheavals of the 1640s and 1650s shook the commonplaces that connected political and familial authority. Political authority in early modern England was naturalized and legitimated through a series of familial or bodily analogies that were inextricably bound up with understandings of gendered hierarchies, of the proper natures, roles, and relationships of men and women. Monarchy was associated with the power of a husband or father in the household, or with the head of a properly constituted body. Consequently criticism of a king or broader political rivalries among men might provoke controversy about the nature of manhood. If a king was the father of his people, what might be the impact of challenging a monarch in battle, and then trying and executing him in the name of the people?

Gender matters to a full understanding of the English revolution as to any major historical transformation. The crisis brought many opportunities and many dilemmas for both women and men, and it disrupted comfortable assumptions about the foundations of political authority. Gender is a fundamental ordering category in all societies as well as a profoundly important imaginative or interpretive resource through which people understand, experience, and challenge their world.[3] The specific characteristics associated with male and female roles and identities, and with fundamental hierarchies of gender, both help to structure and are potentially transformed by war and political upheaval. Indeed it may be that civil wars, traumatic, intimate conflicts that divide those normally united as neighbours, friends, or kin, are particularly likely to arouse personal and familial anxieties, and particularly prone to encourage recourse to gendered imagery and comparisons as tools of interpretation.[4]

Consequently the disturbing traumas of political conflict and religious fragmentation might be expressed in extravagant fantasies of dominant females, monstrous births, and deviant sexuality. Such themes were the staple of cheap print from the alarming emergence of religious sects into plain sight in the early 1640s, through the unbridgeable cleavages within parliamentarianism in the later 1640s, to the downfall of the Rump parliament and the restoration of the monarchy in 1660. Sexually explicit ballads and pamphlets recounted the exotic misdeeds of the sectaries. A woodcut of cavorting naked men and women featuring a rare erect penis in early English printing history, was used in an unlikely account of the probably fictitious 'Adamites' in 1641; it was recycled a decade later to highlight the threats posed by 'Ranters'. Women who rejected infant baptism gave birth to headless babies, while vaguer monstrous births and grotesque female figures were associated with discredited regimes:

> 'Tis strange a Rump that roasted, boiled and broiled
> Should after death bring forth a child,
> Got by some pettifogging knight of the post
> Who in her womb did leave this horrid ghost
> To vex the honest people of this nation
> By her base brat, pretending Reformation

Political absurdities were highlighted in pamphlets describing parliaments of women, sitting together mocking men and telling dirty jokes. The mixture of laughter, voyeurism, and horror aroused by these tropes and genres was a ways of coping with a world and a gender hierarchy out of joint.[5]

It is equally striking how easy it was for both sides in the civil war to assert their own identities or to denounce their opponents through gendered insults or sexual stereotyping of both men and women. Gendered political debate was sometimes founded on the conventional assumption that in any binary opposition the female represents the subordinate or inferior pole; at others it was founded on routine understandings of exemplary male and female behaviour. Royalists presented themselves as brave, honourable men—the ideal Cavalier was 'a child of honour, a gentleman well born and bred; that loves his king for conscience sake, of a clearer countenance and bolder look than other men because of a more loyal heart'. Parliamentarians attacked these bold men through condemnations of 'a vaunting, bragging, boasting Cavalierism' in the words of one parliamentarian preacher. The 'swearing, roaring, whoring cavalier' was a complex male figure in parliamentarian presentations, combining hyper-masculine brutality and excess with an effeminate preoccupation with dress and deportment. [6] In contrast, parliamentarian men saw themselves as sober and restrained, godly, rational and authoritative figures who had risked all for true religion and the public good: 'If a man have a religion in him, then (say they) he is a Roundhead… he that is no swearer, curser, cheater, drunkard, whoremaster, quarreller, he is scandalized with the name of a Roundhead.' In some contexts this stance was developed into an overtly republican stress on independent manly citizenship, contrasted with a supine, effeminate royalism, as we shall suggest below.[7]

On the other hand, royalists characterized parliamentarian men as cowardly cuckolds, unmanned by formidable puritan women. Royalists had rich propaganda pickings in the real life marital misfortunes of parliament's first commander, the earl of Essex, and the well-earned ferocious reputation of Lady Anne Waller, wife to another parliamentarian general, Sir William. Essex's first marriage had been annulled on the grounds of his impotence so that his wife could marry Robert Carr, James I's Scottish favourite; his second wife was a notorious adulteress. Essex had been the butt of derisive verse and contemptuous gossip for some thirty years and his civil war enemies made the most of his unhappiness, in newsbooks, verse, and scurrilous alehouse talk. The banners of royalist regiments portrayed Essex, and by extension the parliamentary army, as cuckolds, with the slogan 'Cuckolds we come', only the most obvious royalist motto. Death offered him no release; Essex's tomb in Westminster Abbey was promptly vandalized, quite rightly in the view of one royalist poet who bemoaned the intrusion of 'his horned image' in the temple of 'our ancient kings'.[8]

Royalism and parliamentarianism might also be defined by their enemies through struggles over the reputations of women. Lady Anne Waller was a particular butt of *Mercurius Aulicus*, the royalist newsbook; it claimed, for example, that if Sir William Waller tried to discuss religion with his wife 'her ladyship would rebuke him, saying, peace Master William, you know your weaknesses in those things, since which time Sir William hath ever gone for the weaker vessel'. Parliamentarians came to Lady Anne's defence: 'She is not like your court-madams, *Aulicus*; uses no oil of talc, no false teeth, no wanton frisking gate, no caterwauling in Spring Gardens [a notorious site of London prostitution]. She bestows not all her time upon her body and leaves none for the soul... The fullness of the Gospel will not admit of carnality, masquings, close meetings, looseness and lasciviousness.'[9] Here the conscientious godliness of parliamentarian womanhood was contrasted with royalist women, denounced as indulgent, sexually promiscuous, and frivolous conspirators, and the court itself pictured as a haunt of political intrigue and immoral liaisons. The association of royalist women with intrigue was highlighted in the person of Katherine Stuart, Lady Aubigny, who played a parallel role in parliamentarian pamphlets to that occupied by Lady Anne Waller in the royalist press. Lady Aubigny was a real conspirator who had smuggled a commission from Charles I into the city of London in May 1643 to prompt a plot against the parliament, but as late as 1646 she featured in the parliamentarian imagination, with her portrait the centrepiece in a parliamentarian broadside identifying their most notorious royalist enemies.[10] If the royal court was a household where women, in parliament's eyes, had too great and too dishonourable an influence, the 'private' households of defeated royalists after 1646 became, for their adherents, beacons of quiet, domestic generosity, rebuking the repressive, socially inferior, and niggardly Puritan regime. Here a female culture was valorized, through the plentiful hospitality portrayed in aristocratic cookery books and through household entertainments, versifying, and music-making that celebrated friendship and loyalty in hard times. Such private activities turned retreat into a form of resilience and resistance.[11]

WOMEN'S AGENCY IN THE ENGLISH REVOLUTION

The household—as a social and political unit, and as imaginative resource—is crucial then to understandings of female agency and the workings of gender during the English revolution. Religious assumptions, philosophical and medical teaching, and political analogies, expressed in learned treatises and popular culture alike, united in stressing women's inferiority and the necessity of their subordination to the authority of fathers and husbands. The nature of women was, however, repeatedly debated and contested in cheap print and scholarly controversy, and the need to insist over and over again on the subordination of women suggests that relationships were more complex in both theory and practice. It was accepted that good order in community, church, and state rested on proper, male-headed authority within the 'little commonwealth' of the household, but it was also clear that in practice energetic and competent women were essential to the running of households at all social levels, so that men were both dominant and, more anxiously, dependent on women's cooperation. Furthermore, the achievement of solid, household status as a married man of some economic security was an aspiration rather than an automatic achievement for many men; about a fifth of men never married and so never achieved independent household status, while the rising numbers of wage labourers also lacked the autonomy crucial to full participation in their communities.[12] There were complex tensions here that were exacerbated by female activism among the upheavals of civil war. The household embodied male authority but left room for female agency, and it provided fertile ground for thinking about politics.

Many female initiatives during the revolution were founded on a sense of their household status and responsibilities, from the activities of the queen or Lady Aubigny within the royal court, to the efforts humble war widows made to preserve their homes and children. Elite women took decisive steps to defend their houses from siege and capture, or, less dramatically, lobbied the authorities to limit the impact of enemy exactions on family property. The Herefordshire parliamentarian Brilliana Harley defied royalist assault in domestic terms: 'my dear husband hath entrusted me with his house and children, and therefore I cannot dispose of his house but according to his pleasure', while the royalists Lady Mary Bankes and the countess of Derby led resolute defences of Corfe Castle in Dorset and Lathom House in Lancashire respectively, Derby, at least, acting more aggressively than her more conciliatory husband would have wished.[13] When defeated royalist landowners faced punitive fines and sometimes outright confiscation and sale of their property, women, less clearly implicated in political disgrace, were most useful intermediaries with the parliamentary authorities. Royalist author the countess of Newcastle summed up developments in scathing fashion:

> the customs of England being changed as well as the laws, where women become pleaders, attorneys, petitioners, and the like, running about with their several causes, complaining of their several grievances, exclaiming against their several enemies, bragging of their several favours they receive from the powerful.[14]

But Newcastle had conveniently forgotten that her own relatively comfortable exile owed a great deal to the efforts of her step-daughter Jane to preserve what she could of the family estates, and her remarks belittle the many ways in which women worked energetically in the most difficult circumstances on behalf of their families.

More ordinary women were prominent in building the defences of besieged cities, in royalist Chester, Hereford, and Worcester, and parliamentarian London, Hull, Coventry, and Bristol alike. In Bristol a leading role was taken by Dorothy Hazzard, the founder of a gathered congregation in the city, who mustered 200 women and girls to resist the royalist assault at Frome Gate in 1643.[15] When royalist clergymen were ejected by the parliament, they lost their homes as well as their employment, but many clergy wives mounted effective tactics to delay the implementation of parliamentarian measures. Poorer women petitioned for pensions when their husbands were killed or mutilated in the parliament's service, often revealing a canny knowledge of their rights under parliamentarian legislation, and a capacity for strategic self-presentation, that stressed the voluntary sacrifice of husbands, and the poignant sufferings of widows and orphans.[16]

Evocation of household responsibilities, combined with an acknowledgement of the inferiority or weakness of women, frequently justified direct female intervention in the political process. Petitioning, on an individual and, more rarely, on a communal basis, was a staple of early modern English political processes, broadly conceived. The revolution saw the dramatic development of collective petitioning by parliamentarian women on overtly political matters, in favour of peace or of more militant policies in the early 1640s, and by Leveller women in the late 1640s and early 1650s. A radical parliamentarian petition from women in early 1642 seems to have influenced later Leveller rhetoric. The petitioners insisted that 'Domestical dangers' in England were as threatening to 'gentlewomen and tradesmen's wives' as they were to their husbands; indeed their 'frail condition' meant that grievances 'do more nearly concern us, and do deeply terrify our souls'. The women feared to see their husbands 'murthered and mangled and cut in pieces before our eyes, to see our children dashed against the stones, and the mother's milk mingled with the infant's blood, running down the streets, to see our houses on flaming fire over our heads: oh how dreadful would this be?'[17] It was thus their concern for their homes and families that propelled these women into political action, and Leveller women made similar arguments when they mounted protests against the imprisonment of Leveller leaders in spring 1649. 'Would you have us keep at home in our houses, when men of such faithfulness and integrity as the four prisoners our friends in the Tower, are fetched out of their beds, and forced from their houses by soldiers to the affrighting of themselves, their wives, children and families?', they asked, presenting the invasion of honest households as a potent definition of parliament's tyranny.[18] Like the petitioners of 1642, they stressed that it was women, the 'weaker vessel', who were especially troubled by 'public calamity and distress'.[19]

These references to the household as grounds for action were not politically empty, or neutral; female interventions rested also on ideological claims. The loyal households and friendship networks of Interregnum royalists were thinly disguised critiques of a republican regime of hypocritical usurpers. Brilliana Harley, a mainstream parliamentarian whose husband and sons became mainstays of presbyterian parliamentarianism, insisted that she relied on 'the laws and liberties of this kingdom' and that 'It is the Lord's cause we have stood for'.[20] The radical women petitioners of 1642 declared that their 'hearts have joined cheerfully with all those petitions which have been exhibited unto you in the behalf of the purity of religion, and the liberty of our husband's persons and estates', regarding these as the 'common privileges' of women and men.[21] The Leveller women, similarly, used a language of common rights in spring 1649: 'have we not an equal interest with the men of this nation, in those liberties and securities contained in the Petition of Right, and other good laws of the land?'[22] Women, as much as men, were caught up with the potential for creative radicalization on parliament's side as the pressures of war led to contested interpretations of what parliament was fighting for.[23] Women's remarkable interventions into national, parliamentary politics were combined with conventional views on the place of women in the household. Women petitioners defended their rights to political agency in sometimes contradictory ways. They claimed 'an equal share and interest with men in the commonwealth' and therefore an undoubted right to petition, while also explaining that it was not their 'custom' to petition: they were acting in exceptional fashion, in a dire, national emergency. Politically active women were rarely defying men in general, but men of opposed political factions, and they were, in turn, treated with contempt or worse by male opponents. Women peace petitioners in 1643 were dismissed as 'the very scum of the suburbs' and then dispersed by force, while the Leveller women of 1649 were told to go home and do their housework.[24]

Parliamentarian women also claimed to be fighting the Lord's battles; this conviction, and, still more, the increasingly bitter struggles within parliamentarianism over the precise nature of true religion, offered many opportunities for female agency. Many parliamentarians came to feel they were living in the last days before Christ's second coming to rule with his Saints, and they knew that in these end times, God was likely to achieve his purposes through weak and unlikely instruments. The Leveller women of 1649 were heartened by 'knowing that for our encouragement and example, God hath wrought many deliverances for several nations from age to age, by the weak hand of women'. Like their forebears of 1642, they appealed to biblical exemplars: the supplicant Esther, the judge and prophetess Deborah, and, more disturbingly, the assassin Jael, and they evoked notions of spiritual equality: 'Christ hath purchased us at as dear a rate as he hath men' so that they were equally concerned with 'a flourishing estate of the church and commonwealth'.[25]

In extraordinary times, it was plausible to many that God would speak directly to his people through human instruments, and it was likely that female weakness and passivity made women particularly suitable conduits for divine messages. The prophet Joel had explained that God would 'pour out my spirit upon all flesh; and your sons and your daughters shall prophesy', his spirit alighting particularly on servants and handmaids (Joel 2:28–9). So when Elizabeth Poole, a 'servant of the most high God', interrupted the army council in the winter of 1648–9, with a divine warning against regicide, the officers broke off their deliberations to listen to her, although they ultimately rejected her unwelcome message. Some hundreds of women from the Quakers and other radical groups are known to have preached and prophesied during the revolution and to have attracted both followers and aggressive opposition. The implications were ambiguous; these women had a clear public impact, but as passive instruments of God's purposes, rather than through their own, acknowledged agency.[26] The career of Anna Trapnel, the most influential female prophet of the revolution, illustrates the ambiguities. The unmarried daughter of a London artisan, Trapnel became a prominent member of the politically engaged millenarian movement, the 'Fifth Monarchists', campaigning in the early 1650s for the rule of the Saints under King Jesus, in place of the earthly monarchies thrown down by God's judgements. Her denunciations of Cromwell, following his elevation to the Protectorate, attracted the alarmed attention of the authorities, as she recounted 'visions of God, relating to the governors, army, churches, ministry, universities, and the whole nation... by an inspiration extraordinary, and full of wonder'. Trapnel's influence spread through print and through a well-organized prophesying tour of the west country; she was denounced as a witch by the sceptical and the exasperated government eventually had her locked up in Bridewell, with vagrants, prostitutes, and other deviant women. Trapnel was, at the same time, merely a conduit for God's words, 'a weak worthless creature', who 'heard only the voice of God sounding forth unto me', and a defiant and independent woman who welcomed her real public influence. When the Cornish magistrates challenged her independent travelling, she retorted: 'I am a single person... why may not I go where I please, if the Lord so will', and she rejoiced in her 'public-spiritedness', promising that 'while I have tongue and breath I shall go forth for the Fifth monarchy-laws, teaching and practice'.[27]

Trapnel, as a convinced Calvinist, did not approve of Quakers, but Quaker women had a comparable public impact, as organizers, authors, itinerant preachers, and prophets denouncing the hireling clergy and the corruption of worldly authorities. They faced similarly hard treatment, punished as vagrants or scolds, but active preaching women became a defining characteristic of the early Quakers and male leaders almost consistently defended women's speaking in public, although the internal records of the movement suggest that men were privately more worried about their assertive sisters.[28]

Religious divisions in themselves offered women opportunities for independent decision-making and determined action, and complicated understandings of gender hierarchies. Radical or sectarian religion has attracted most scholarly attention, but women's defence of old ways might also mean evading or defying male authority. The correct administration of life-cycle rituals was of particular concern to women. Lady Mary Verney, alone in England during a strenuous campaign to lift the sequestration on her exiled husband's estates, planned to have her new baby baptized by 'a minister in the house that will do it the old way, for 'tis not the fashion here to have godfathers or godmothers'. But her husband was less enthusiastic for the Anglican rituals of the Common Prayer Book, urging Mary 'to give no offence to the state'.[29] Many women welcomed the gathered congregations emerging in the religious marketplace of the revolution, and indeed women often were the majority of the members. This was the case in the Broadmead independent/baptist congregation in Bristol, founded by Dorothy Hazzard, in a Canterbury independent congregation, and in many general baptist groups. There is no need to question the genuine commitment behind these specific religious choices, but it is also clear that religious pluralism offered opportunities to assertive and argumentative women, who were not easily cowed by the male ministers and elders, who retained formal authority even in these radical groups. Sarah Day of Canterbury 'followed seducers' who encouraged her 'corrupt opinions' on the Trinity, and remained 'pertinacious and obstinate', offering 'unfitting speeches' to the men who rebuked her.

Religious fragmentation and competition thus brought troubling dilemmas for men in the gathered and separatist churches. The scripturalism of most of these groups intensified conventional belief in the subordination of women, and in the Pauline injunction for women to keep silent in the church. But everyone also held that women should follow their consciences, that they should defend true religion against error, and obey God rather than man. Women who had made a conscious decision to separate from parochial worship were not always susceptible to marginalization or discipline within their new congregations. Thus most churches struggled over the proper role of women members. The Calvinist baptists insisted that women should not preach publicly although they could exercise a gift in private, and bear witness to their own faith. In Hazzard's Broadmead church there were no women preachers or elders although women participated in choosing the ministers. The Fifth Monarchist John Roger allowed women greater sway in his Dublin church, on the grounds that 'though there is a civil subjection to men in their oeconomical relations... there is not any servile subjection due to them, whereby poor souls are enslaved'. Here, controversially, women were able to speak and vote as full members of the congregation, but not allowed to preach. In many congregations women were members but their husbands were not, and in the last analysis, and with some reluctance, the men in authority insisted that loyalty to the church took precedence over wifely obedience. Thus the west country baptists advised that a woman whose husband was not a member of the church could 'dispose of outward substance' without his knowledge or consent and the general baptist churches of East Anglia, who were struggling to prevent defections to the Quakers, did not accept women's excuses that their husbands had encouraged them to read Quaker books or go to Quaker meetings. [30]

Manhood, Politics, and Revolution

Men were, of course, affected by new possibilities for religious expression or political agency. Attention to gender in history has been initiated by historians of women, but more recently, we have realized the importance of complicating ideas of manliness.

As already suggested, the dominant masculine ideal centred on the authoritative and independent head of household, an estate that was not automatically achieved, and one that always involved cooperation with women.[31] The common parallels drawn between household authority and the political realm, particularly the monarchical realm, might produce female rule through the anomalies of inheritance, as in sixteenth-century England, but there were equally influential, classically derived understandings of politics in which formal, public, political power was confined to men. But during a civil war it was not clear how or by whom legitimate political authority was to be exercised, and, hence, as we have seen, political disputes often became arguments about true manhood or involved insults against inadequate men, cuckolded generals, an effeminized monarch, and drunken cavaliers.

The challenges civil war and revolution posed to notions of manhood could be addressed in many ways; for reasons of space I will here focus on the rival, and not always coherent versions of male political agency found among radical parliamentarians. As in the contests between royalists and parliamentarians, radical denunciations of the tyranny, as they held it, of parliamentarians often involved accusations of invalid manhood. The Leveller Richard Overton figured tyranny as a struggle between the cruelty of parliament's officials, and the modest, supportive bravery of his wife Mary. Mary Overton was sent to Bridewell, the 'receptacle of bawds, whores and strumpets', for her support of Richard's unauthorized printing, but her 'modesty, civility and chastity' could not be obliterated by the brutality of a 'turkey-cock marshall' who 'struts towards her like a crow in a gutter, and with his valiant looks like a man of mettle... by violence attempted to pluck the tender babe out of her arms, but she forcibly defended it, and kept it in spite of his manhood'. The marshall's animalistic brutality in fact destroyed him as a man.[32] Overton, and other Levellers, presented themselves as honest householders, with loyal and active but clearly subordinate wives and servants. The civil war, however, challenged the connection between male household authority and political participation, for many reasons. In the first place, it became even more difficult than in settled times for men to achieve the ideal 'estate' of manhood, as heads of stable households. Men suffered from the economic dislocation that accompanied the war, from the terrible economic circumstances of the later 1640s, and, in many cases, from the physical consequences of wounds and disease. At the same time women perforce took on more responsibilities for the preservation of their families, and some took advantage of new religious and political opportunities.

More positively, many of the processes through which parliament sought to rally support took no notice of restrictions of marital and household status, age, or wealth that usually determined the right to vote or to hold office in parish, manor, or company. These processes owed much to habits of popular participation in 'normal' times, but they became more overtly political through the revolutionary changes of the 1640s.[33] Oaths are an obvious example: the Protestation Oath of May 1641 was to be taken by people (in practice usually men) over eighteen, 'both householders and others', while the 1643 Solemn League and Covenant was tendered to all men over eighteen, 'as well lodgers and inhabitants'. Apprentices and other younger and poorer men engaged in petitioning as well as male householders. Many prominent religious leaders, especially in the Quakers, were remarkably young men, and the sects in general welcomed young and single men alongside women and heads of households as well as householders; they recast patriarchal, biological families in spiritual terms, with members described in sibling language, as brothers and sisters. Above all, military service raised questions about claims to male political authority. In self-image and self-presentation if not always in reality, parliament's was an army of volunteer citizen soldiers, serving not for money but for the people's rights and a godly cause. The sacrifices and bravery of these men had won unparalleled victories that demanded some recompense in terms of political rights, as radical soldiers argued at the Putney debates in 1647 when the army's representatives debated the future of the kingdom.

At Putney, Thomas Rainborough, challenging the more traditional views of Henry Ireton that political rights should be confined to settled, independent men of some property, dismissed the legitimating comparison with the family:

> With respect to the divine law which says 'Honour thy father and thy mother'... for my part I look upon the people of England so, that wherein they have not voices in the choosing of their governors—their civil fathers and mothers—they are not bound to that commandment.

He further denied the economic foundations for political participation: 'many a man whose zeal and affection to God and this kingdom has carried him forth in this cause, has so spent his estate that, in the way the state and the army are going, he shall not hold up his head, if, when his estate is lost and not worth forty shillings a year, a man shall not have any interest' (the last reference is to the parliamentary franchise in the counties). Rather, Rainborough argued, all men had innate birthrights, centred on their rationality: 'This gift of reason without other property may seem a small thing, yet I think there is nothing God has given a man that anyone else can take from him.' Thus even when a man lost what he had for 'the maintenance of his family' he could not lose 'that which God and nature has given him', so that, in Rainborough's enduring phrase, 'the poorest he that is in England has a life to live as the greatest he' and should be able to give 'his own consent' to any government.

Rainborough's arguments were rejected by Ireton, but they are also at odds with the emphases of other radicals. Some Leveller manifestos worried about granting citizenship to men whose precarious economic and social status made them dependent on the wills of others, even as they supported the rights of women and apprentices to petition. Leveller pamphlets, as we have already seen with Overton, consistently presented their heroes as family men, householders with loyal wives and servants. A less familiar example can be added: much was made of the loyalty of the servants of the Leveller printer William Larner, who followed their master to prison in March 1646, rather than give evidence against him. Larner's pregnant wife emphasized that this was a family catastrophe, as Larner's aged father and mother 'past labour' languished in Gloucestershire for want of his support. Larner himself explained in a petition to the Lords that his family faced ruin if he could not 'have his liberty and be permitted to follow his calling for the maintenance of himself, wife and family'. Inability to provide for his family made Larner 'worse than an infidel, but woe be to them that are the causes thereof'. For Larner, as for Overton or Leveller women petitioners, the tyranny of parliament was exposed by the assault on honest households; Rainborough, in contrast, condemned those who refused political rights to men who could not support households.[34]

A different approach was taken by another revolutionary, the 'Digger' Gerrard Winstanley, whose vision of a just society involved the reconstitution of patriarchy. Winstanley embraced the paternal comparisons rejected by Rainborough: 'Adam was the first governor or officer in the earth, because as he was the first father', and so fatherhood was 'the first link of the chain magistracy'. More akin to Rainborough, Winstanley bemoaned the economic hardship brought by civil war: 'now my health and estate is decayed, and I grown in age, I must either beg or work for day wages, which I was never brought up to, for another; when as the Earth is as freely my inheritance, as his whom I must work for'. In Winstanley's ideal world, the land would be made free to all, but family structures remained under male authority: 'Though the earth and storehouses be common to every family, yet every family shall live apart as they do, and every man's house, wife, children, and furniture for ornament of his house... is all a propriety to that family, for the peace thereof.' In this world, in contrast with many implications of the revolution, authority was based on a 'natural' hierarchy of age as well as gender. A man had to be 'of age, and of rational carriage before he be a governor of a family'; all officers in Winstanley's commonwealth were men aged more than forty, and 'all ancient men, above sixty years of age' were to be general overseers. In this new society, patriarchy would be strengthened: if a father died before his children were grown, or if he was 'weak, sick, or naturally foolish, wanting the power of wisdom and government', then the children would be transferred to a family in the same trade. Mothers were not mentioned, yet in the real world of early modern England, perhaps a fifth of all households were headed by women, while civil war, as we have seen, increased the scope of women's responsibilities as wives and mothers.[35]

CONCLUSIONS: GENDER, REVOLUTION AND POLITICAL CHANGE

Radical men did not agree on how or even whether male political rights should be connected to their roles, real or ideal, in the household or family. No one, however, used the mobilizations of the 1640s to argue for formal political rights for women, despite their participation in many initiatives. Women, as we have seen, were active in the sects; they petitioned the authorities as individuals and in groups; they were readers, hawkers, and printers of cheap print and they occasionally took the parliament's oaths. At times men overtly rejected any suggestion that women might thus be empowered. The former soldier and lay preacher Edmund Chillenden argued that the scriptural prohibition against women preaching in itself meant that all gifted men could preach; while petitioning apprentices insisted that their dependence was temporary, in contrast to the permanent, natural subordination of women.[36]

Within parliamentarian discourse, there were contradictory tendencies, often involving the same people, both to resort to analogies between the family and the state, and to deny the validity of such parallels through a distinction between the public and the private realms.[37] For obvious reasons, parliamentarian men did not want their challenge to royal authority to have implications for fathers in families. The parliamentarian propagandist Henry Parker, writing in 1642, denied the parallel between kingship and fatherhood, and also challenged the comparison between the body politic and the human body:

> the head naturally doth not more depend upon the body, than that does upon the head, both head and members must live and die together; but it is otherwise with the head political, for that receives more subsistence from the body than it gives, and being subservient to that, it has no being when that is dissolved, and that may be preserved after its dissolution.

Thus the body supported the head, and a body politic might survive the destruction of the head.[38] The denial of familial parallels, and the insistence on a distinct, male political realm was especially characteristic of republican thinking after the regicide; as John Milton explained:[39]

> Fathers and kings are very different things: our fathers begot us, but our kings did not, and it is we, rather, who created the king. It is nature which gave the people fathers, and the people who gave themselves a king.

But familial discussions and metaphors were hard to resist, as when Milton insisted that it was authoritative rule of their households that fitted men for public service in the state, and contrasted manly republican citizenship with the effeminacy of supine royalists: 'For in vain does he prattle about liberty in assembly and market-place who at home endures the slavery most unworthy of man, slavery to an inferior.'[40] For republicans male rationality and commitment to the public interest was contrasted with a selfish, feminized, privacy. For the king's prosecutor, John Cook, monarchy was a 'foul mistress'. It was preposterous, and against the law of God and nature, for men to 'enslave themselves to the arbitrary and lawless lusts of one man and his posterity, whether they be idiots, children, knaves, thieves, murderers, fornicators, gluttons, drunkards, idolators or women'. Politics was for rational men: 'words are women, proofs are men; it is reason that must be the chariot to carry men to give their concurrence in this judgement [to condemn the king]'.[41] These deeply gendered distinctions return us to some important contrasts with a royalism that endorsed familial parallels, and, in the years of defeat and exile, valorized private pleasures and virtues.

The long-term effects of the gender troubles of the English revolution are difficult to assess. It may be that after 1649 it was impossible to make easy, taken-for-granted connections between familial and political authority; the arguments developed an artificiality or self-consciousness that revealed the difficulties of the enterprise. But the comparisons remained tempting as the recourse to Filmerian patriarchalism in the later Stuart crisis revealed.[42] Clear-cut patterns are equally elusive. A gendered analysis of the revolution defeats any simple narrative of progress to modernity: some historians and political theorists have argued that as men claimed more political rights, women were increasingly regarded as disqualified by their sex from political roles, as sharper distinctions were made between all men and all women.[43] We have shown above that women's visibility in religious and political affairs did prompt a reinforcement of distinctions or contrasts between male and female roles so this is a plausible conclusion. On the other hand, we know that women found ways of influencing political life after 1660, and they continued to play a major part in the *de facto* religious pluralism that survived the Restoration. Within the Quakers or more mainstream nonconformity, but also in many forms of Anglican piety, women followed the dictates of their consciences and found spiritual autonomy. Their place was, in theory at least, carefully circumscribed but female initiatives always had the potential to evade male control. We do not need neat conclusions to justify attempts at a comprehensive gendered approach to the English revolution. Attention to gender reminds us most obviously that we can only fully understand the revolution through careful attention to the social and cultural assumptions of the world in which it emerged. Allegiance in a traumatic civil war was not based straightforwardly on rational decisions about political programmes, but was also profoundly influenced by less easily defined matters of interest, imagination, and emotion. The revolution dislocated basic social structures, but it also challenged intimate aspects of personal identity; to all these issues gender is fundamental.

Notes

1. *The King's Cabinet Opened* (London, 1645), 38–9; *Mercurius Britanicus*, 14–21 July 1645. This chapter derives much of its evidence and arguments from Ann Hughes, *Gender and the English Revolution* (London, 2011), for the king's correspondence, see 66, 119. The title of the chapter is inspired by Mary Fissell, *Vernacular Bodies: The Politics of Reproduction in Early Modern England* (Oxford, 2004) and Judith Butler, *Gender Trouble: Feminism and the Subversion of Identity* (London, 1990).
2. Mark Stoyle, 'The Road to Farndon Field: Explaining the Massacre of the Royalist Women at Naseby', *English Historical Review*, 133 (2008): 895–923.
3. The classic statement is Joan Scott, 'Gender: A Useful Category of Historical Analysis', in her *Gender and the Politics of History* (New York, 1988), 28–52.
4. Compare Dror Wahrman, *The Making of the Modern Self* (New Haven, 2004), 238–42, on the impact of the American War of Independence (understood as a British civil war).
5. Hughes, *Gender*, 126–33; Fissell, *Vernacular Bodies*, 157–62; Sarah Toulalan, *Imagining Sex: Pornography and Bodies in Seventeenth-Century England* (Oxford, 2007); Mark Jenner, 'The Roasting of the Rump: Scatology and the Body Politic in Restoration England', *Past and Present*, 177 (2002): 84–120.

6. Edmund Symmons, quoted in Jerome de Groot, *Royalist Identities* (Basingstoke, 2004), 92; *A description of the Roundhead and Rattlehead* (London, 1642), 1; the minister William Bridge quoted in Hughes, *Gender*, 91.

7. *Twenty Lookes over all the Roundheads that ever lived in the world* (London, 1642).

8. Ian Gentles, 'The Iconography of Revolution, England 1642–49', in Ian Gentles, John Morrill, and Blair Worden (eds.), *Soldiers, Writers and Statesmen of the English Revolution* (Cambridge, 1998), 91–113; Mark Robson, 'Swansongs: Reading Voice in the Poetry of Lady Hester Pulter', *English Manuscript Studies*, 9 (2000): 238–56; Hughes, *Gender*.

9. *Mercurius Aulicus*, week ending 3 August 1644; *The Spie*, 26 April–1 May 1644.

10. *Englands Monuments of Mercies* (London, 1646).

11. Hero Chalmers, *Royalist Women Writers* (Oxford, 2004).

12. Alexandra Shephard, *Meanings of Manhood in Early Modern England* (Oxford, 2003).

13. Hughes, *Gender*, 38.

14. Margaret Cavendish, *Natures Pictures* (London, 1656), 379–80.

15. Hughes, *Gender*, 37, 75.

16. Hughes, *Gender*, 43.

17. *The Humble Petition of many hundreds of distressed women, tradesmen's wives and widdows* (London, 1642), Patricia Higgins, 'The Reactions of Women, with Special Reference to Women Petitioners', in Brian Manning (ed.), *Politics, Religion and the English Civil War* (London, 1973), 179–224; Hughes, *Gender*, 55–6.

18. *To the Supreme Authority of England* (London, 1649).

19. *To the Supreame Authority of this Nation* (London, 1649); Ann Hughes, 'Gender and Politics in Leveller Literature', in Susan D. Amussen and Mark A. Kishlansky (eds.), *Political Culture and Cultural Politics in Early Modern England* (Manchester, 1995), 162–88.

20. Hughes, *Gender*, 38.

21. *The Humble Petition of many hundreds of distressed women*.

22. *To the Supreame Authority of this Nation*.

23. Michael Braddick, *God's Fury, England's Fire: A New History of the English Civil Wars* (London, 2008), esp. chap. 16.

24. Hughes, *Gender*, 57, 60.

25. *The Humble Petition of many hundreds of distressed women; To the Supreme Authority of England*.

26. Phyllis Mack, *Visionary Women: Ecstatic Prophecy in Seventeenth-Century England* (Berkeley, 1994).

27. The account of Trapnel is based on Ann Hughes, '"Not Gideon of old": Anna Trapnel and Oliver Cromwell', *Cromwelliana*, Series II (2005): 77–96, and Hughes, *Gender*, 78–82.

28. Kate Peters, *Print Culture and the Early Quakers* (Cambridge, 2005).

29. Hughes, *Gender*, 72.

30. For gender relations in the sects see Hughes, *Gender*, 74–6, 84–8.

31. Shepard, *Meanings of Manhood*.

32. Richard Overton, *The Commoners' Complaint* (London, 1647), 17–20.

33. See John Walter, 'The English People and the English Revolution Revisited', *History Workshop*, 61 (2006): 170–82; and his chapter in this volume.

34. A fuller account of the varieties of radical manhood is in Hughes, *Gender*, 108–18; the material from the Putney Debates is taken from Andrew Sharp (ed.), *The English Levellers* (Cambridge, 1998), and for Larner see William Larner, *A Vindication of Every Free-mans*

Libertie (London, 1646); Larner, *A True Relation of all the remarkable passages and illegall proceedings… against William Larner, a freeman of England* (London, 1646).

35. Gerrard Winstanley, *The Law of Freedom in a Platform* (London, 1652) here taken from *The Complete Works of Gerrard Winstanley*, 2 vols., ed. Thomas Corns, Ann Hughes, and David Loewenstein (Oxford, 2009), II, 312–15, 352–3, 290, 378, 371.

36. Edmund Chillenden, *Preaching without Ordination* (London, 1647); Mihoko Suzuki, *Subordinate Subjects: Gender, the Political Nation and Literary Form in England 1588–1688* (Aldershot, 2003), 135–45.

37. Ann Hughes, 'Men, the "Public" and the "Private" in the English Revolution', in Peter Lake and Steve Pincus (eds.), *The Politics of the Public Sphere in Early Modern England* (Manchester, 2007), 191–212; Su Fang Ng, *Literature and the Politics of the Family in Seventeenth-Century England* (Cambridge, 2007).

38. Henry Parker, *Observations upon some of his Majesties Late Answers and Expresses* (1642), quoted in Hughes, *Gender*, 140.

39. John Milton's 'First Defence' (1651), quoted in Hughes, *Gender*, 107.

40. John Milton, *Defensio Secunda* (1654), quoted in Hughes, *Gender*, 98.

41. John Cook, *Monarchy no Creature of God's Making* (1651), quoted in Hughes, *Gender*, 121.

42. Michael McKeon, *The Secret History of Domesticity: Public, Private and the Division of Knowledge* (Baltimore, MD, 2005); Rachel Weil, 'The Family in the Exclusion Crisis: Locke versus Filmer Revisited', in Alan Houston and Steve Pincus (eds.), *A Nation Transformed: England after the Restoration* (Cambridge, 2001), 100–24.

43. Hilda Smith, *All Men and Both Sexes: Gender, Politics and the False Universal in England, 1640–1832* (University Park, PA, 2002); Carole Pateman, *The Disorder of Women: Democracy, Feminism and Political Theory* (Stanford, 1989).

Further Reading

de Groot, Jerome, *Royalist Identities* (Basingstoke, 2004).

Fissell, Mary, *Vernacular Bodies: The Politics of Reproduction in Early Modern England* (Oxford, 2004).

Higgins, Patricia, 'The Reactions of Women, with Special Reference to Women Petitioners', in Brian Manning (ed.), *Politics, Religion and the English Civil War* (London, 1973), 179–224.

Hinds, Hilary, *God's Englishwomen: Seventeenth-Century Radical Sectarian Writing and Feminist Criticism* (Manchester, 1996).

Hughes, Ann, *Gender and the English Revolution* (London, 2011).

Nevitt, Marcus, *Women and the Pamphlet Culture of Revolutionary England* (Aldershot, 2006).

Peters, Kate, *Print Culture and the Early Quakers* (Cambridge, 2005).

Purkiss, Diane, *Literature, Gender and Politics during the English Civil War* (Cambridge, 2005).

Scott, Joan, 'Gender: A Useful Category of Historical Analysis', in Joan Scott, *Gender and the Politics of History* (New York, 1988), 28–52.

Shepard, Alexandra, *Meanings of Manhood in Early Modern England* (Oxford, 2003).

Wiseman, Susan, *Conspiracy and Virtue: Women, Writing, and Politics in Seventeenth-Century England* (Oxford, 2006).

CHAPTER 21

STATE, POLITICS, AND SOCIETY IN SCOTLAND, 1637–1660

R. SCOTT SPURLOCK

THE role Scotland played in the broader political events of Britain and Ireland between 1637 and 1660 is well documented and has become an integral part of the historiography of the period. Yet what is much less developed is the impact the events of this period had upon Scotland itself. While the Covenanting experiment and its legacy have taken a prominent place in Scotland's national narrative, the actual social, political, and cultural impact continue to be little understood. Certainly nothing like the depth of scholarship focusing upon the impact of these years on the localities and the nation has been produced for Scotland as recent decades have for England and, to a lesser degree, Ireland. This may be, to some extent, a reflection of the relative limitations of the sources but has other explanations, no doubt, in the way that the period has been memorialized. The Covenanting achievement has been celebrated, particularly in histories of ecclesiastical and political development, but much less attention has been placed on the effect of these events on popular politics, local religious and political life, or of the effects of the experience of war on long-term changes in local and regional socio-political and economic dynamics. This chapter offers an introduction to some of these issues.

POPULAR POLITICS

Integral to the success of the Covenanting movement was the mobilization of popular support. But the degree to which there was an autonomous 'popular' engagement with this crisis remains questionable. From July 1637 popular protests broke out in Edinburgh at the introduction of a new Anglicized liturgy, yet in truth the stage had been set before the unveiling of the Prayer Book on 23 July. In the week prior 'discourses, declamations, pamphlets' primed the people for action.[1] While carefully presented to the authorities as a spontaneous eruption of popular dissatisfaction, scholars generally accept that it had been prudently organized by nobles, lairds, and clergy whose dissatisfaction stretched back even beyond the beginning of Charles I's reign. The seemingly sudden surge of widespread dissatisfaction and mobilization of popular support forced the authorities to take the crowds seriously, despite the instincts of the king (observing from the safe distance of London).

When a second round of riots broke out in October 1637 the 'spontaneous' public turmoil was carefully transformed into a more orderly and 'representative' format. Members of the privy council suggested that representatives should be elected, a suggestion that led to the formation of the Tables. By November four Tables representing the nobility, gentry, burghs, and clergy were formed from the separate informal meetings comprising members of the individual Estates. By December a Fifth Table made up of elected representatives from the other four had been established and served as an executive. While the Fifth Table may have been representative, Allan Macinnes has demonstrated the carefully controlled nature of these 'elections'—directed by the nobility, 'a few gentry', and the ministers Alexander Henderson and David Dickson—and it must be remembered that the franchise for electing them remained limited with the final result being domination by the nobility.[2] While there can be little doubt that a significant proportion of the Scottish population was anxious to respond to the call to take action, the result of the Covenanting ascendancy, in political terms, was a reassertion of the traditional rights of Scotland's traditional Estates—with the caveat that the clerical estate was redefined to exclude the bishops at the General Assembly of 1638.

While this popular mobilization was to some extent solicited by social elites, and was subsequently institutionalized in a way that limited its subversive potential, it is clear that opinion on the streets was very significant to the Covenanting crisis. It forced the government to take the complaints seriously. However, while widespread—though not uniform—dissatisfaction with absolutist royal policies provided fodder at the outset of the Covenanting movement, once this anxiety had been eased by the Bishops' Wars the protest subsequently proved heterogeneous and difficult to control. On two occasions, in particular, popular protest turned against the Covenanting regime to express dissatisfaction at policies. In January 1644, in response to a proposed excise tax being discussed by the Committee of Estates, demonstrators gathered in Edinburgh, threatening to tear the proponent of the levy, Lord Balmerino, apart.[3] The second incident of significant popular protest against the Covenanting regime took place at Mauchline Moor in June 1648 against the backdrop of the Engagement controversy. On that occasion an outdoor communion season attended by perhaps as many as 2,000 armed communicants of the more religiously-radical end of the Covenanting spectrum, turned on a military detachment serving the Covenanters' government headed by John Middleton, 1st earl of Middleton and a notorious royalist, and James Livingstone, earl of Callendar.[4] Despite the difficulties of harnessing popular protest, and occasional evidence of popular hostility to the leadership, control of the Covenanting movement was successfully retained by traditional social elites.[5]

The Covenanting movement, even in its popular forms, was not associated with social levelling, not least because the National Covenant set clear limits on the aims of the movement, including a commitment to the monarchy, a presbyterian model of church government and the existing social hierarchy. Moreover, the kirk's pulpits remained the most important conduit of relaying information to the population, as government declarations were regularly commanded to be read in churches throughout Scotland and sermons unpacked both the political and theological significance of contemporary events.[6] The leading role of the nobility persisted until the failed Engagement of 1648, which led to the Act of Classes (January 1649) barring the guilty from a place in government and also contributing to the abolishing of lay patronage over ministerial charges in 1649. Although tensions and struggles may have existed, the nobility and the clergy led the nation throughout the 1640s.

Further radicalism was also limited by the relative absence of a culture of open public discourse in Scotland. As in England, the pulpit was an important focus for political engagement: in the run-up to supplication riots, pro-presbyterian clergy preached enthusiastically about the special place Protestant Scotland had in God's plans. After the Covenanting revolution churches became the primary point of dissemination for proclamations and acts, although these official declarations were also published. But Scotland did not develop an open forum for public discourse like that in England. Manuscript pasquils, supplications, and petitions circulated but press control remained very effective. The Covenanters' own press output was overwhelmingly directed at an English audience, seeking to justify their invasion of England, not as a provocation against the English people, but as a matter to be settled between the Scottish people and their king.[7] In addition they published official acts and proclamations, but little to foster public discourse. From 1638 the publication of any work deemed to touch on religion—thus anything relating to the interpretation or legitimacy of the Covenant—required pre-approval by Archibald Johnston of Wariston, one of the framers of the National Covenant and the clerk of the General Assembly.[8] Hence, public discourse in Scotland was more restricted to manuscript and the lively press discussion so influential in the events unfolding in England during the 1640s did not exist in Scotland; although, of course, it is equally true that Scottish opinion was less divided—in part due to the strict control of the public sphere by the Covenanting regime—and so there were fewer opposition voices that could have found expression in print.

Instead, the Covenanting regime utilized the kirk as a highly effective means of shaping public opinion. While local war committees facilitated the practicalities of mobilizing funds and manpower, organizing military training, and managing elections, pulpits served as the primary platform for disseminating proclamations from both the committee of the General Assembly and the Committee of Estates, as well as interpreting and framing them in relation to the Covenanters' ideological aims. Cromwell complained on his approach to Scotland that his army had access to Scottish papers, circulating freely in his army, but that the Covenanting regime was much less open to the expression in print of alternative opinion.[9] Thus, as a matter of urgency after taking Edinburgh, Cromwell opened the capital's leading press to the publication of important public texts. During the 1650s Scotland's book trade witnessed a substantial expansion, with the establishment of booksellers in provincial burghs and towns.[10] The period from 1637 to 1660 therefore represents an important transitional period in public engagement with national politics, such that this became a primary political concern that Charles II had to take seriously at the Restoration. The Interregnum in Scotland, particularly in the early years, saw lively public debates prompted by English soldiers and popular, polemic tracts appearing at a prodigious pace, and that culture was to persist.[11]

THE LONG-TERM SIGNIFICANCE OF THE NATIONAL COVENANT

The signing of the National Covenant in 1638 left an indelible mark on Scotland. The Covenant was a binding agreement between God and the people of Scotland. Individuals who subscribed the document took on personal culpability for fulfilling their sworn obligations under the threat of divine punishment. The individual nature of this binding contract was further strengthened through personal covenanting, wherein individuals drew up their own pact with the divine, cementing even more emphatically the onus of individual responsibility. The significance of this activity is the profound personal implication of the commitments made by the individual. That is to say, the success or failure of attaining the aims of the National Covenant (and any ancillary conditions added in a personal covenant) did not rest simply upon the nation, but on each individual subscriber. This implied the possibility of individual dissent if the expected outcomes envisioned by the individual were not attained. While such personal accountability no doubt gave great strength to the Covenanting movement, it could also, in complicated political conditions, create deep divisions, such as those during the Engagement of 1648 or in the wake of Scotland's humiliation at Dunbar.

Louise Yeoman's ground-breaking doctoral work demonstrates that this personal commitment to the Covenant created a social framework in which the pursuit of godliness and its outward expression allowed 'groups like women and godly members of the lower classes… [to] command respect, whilst traditional sources of external authority, such as the king, were castigated for their ungodly behaviour and even rebelled against'. This served as a powerful motivator, not merely to command external respect, but to the development of an internal sense of authority (derived from God) that provided a profound sense of empowerment and worth.[12] Nonetheless, while such a sense of empowerment encouraged women to participate enthusiastically in the Covenanting movement, their roles were circumscribed and while they could espouse the National Covenant they very rarely were permitted to sign it.[13] In 1643 when Scotland entered into the Solemn League and Covenant, it was commanded that men and women 'of all understanding' swear it in every church in the country.

Some women, notably Margaret Michelson, who prophesied the success of the godly cause in Scotland, acquired significant public prominence. According to a disparaging Episcopalian report of her celebrity in 1638, an 'incredible concourse of sorts of people, Noblemen, Gentlemen, Ministers, Women of all ranks and qualities, who watched or stayed by her day and night, curing the times of her pretended fits, and did admire her raptures and inspirations, as coming from Heaven'.[14] More generally the Covenanting movement encouraged a deep personal religion that many women embraced, but it had significant limitations, especially when the Covenanters had established their authority. In some ways, it may have begun internal processes that facilitated the move to more radical options during the 1650s. The arrival of Commissioners of the English parliament in early 1652 sought to establish a religious open marketplace in Scotland. This proved especially attractive to women with a number of Scots joining baptist and independent congregations or Quaker meetings.[15] Some women participated in a number of movements, such as Margaret Anderson. The wife of an Aberdeen bailie, she originally supported the Covenanting movement before joining the Aberdeen independents sometime after they withdrew from the kirk in November 1652; subsequently she was baptized at the hands of an English baptist soldier and eventually joined the Quakers before her death in 1663. While the window remained open for less than a decade, the life of Margaret is instructive of how participation in alternative religious communities allowed women to assert themselves in new ways within their communities, especially among the Quakers who recognized no distinction by gender. The arrival of Quakerism early in the 1650s marked the beginning of a movement that survived the Restoration only to swell in numbers, with women playing a prominent part.

While lay men and women did find opportunities to assert their personal religion, in the Covenanting movement, authority rested with the clergy. Baillie remarks in his journals of occasions when the laity overstepped their bounds and strayed towards 'Brunism' (referring to Robert Brown).[16] Covenanting, either in theory or practice, did not offer a means for fundamentally altering one's station in life for either men or women.

Women are given most prominence in the histories, even in those written by contemporaries, for the role they played in public disturbances. Perhaps most well known is the popular legend of Jenny (Janet or Margaret) Geddes initiating the revolt against the Prayer Book in 1637, but other examples are plentiful. As William Annan entered the church as a visiting preacher also in 1637 Robert Baillie records that a group of 'honest women' 'in his ear assured him, that if he should twitch the Service Book in his sermon, he should be rent out of the pulpit; he took the advice, and let the matter alone'. The issue was not laid to rest, however, as Baillie goes on to note that 'some hundredths of inraged women, of all qualities' later harangued him 'with neaves [fists], and staves [sticks], and peats, [but] no stones'.[17] Women regularly took part in dramatic public protests or civil unrest, particularly in the early years before the Covenanting regime fully established itself.[18]

The prominence of women in protest derived partly from the fact that the authorities were less likely to use physical violence against women, although there were exceptions. This made groups of women more difficult to deal with in some ways.[19] There is some question, however, as to whether women acted autonomously. Baillie indicated that the instigator of the women's actions against Annan was in fact the minister of the college parish in Glasgow, John Bell.[20] Close links between Covenanting ministers and female adherents abound and suggest their devotion was significant.[21] Yet female public disorder was not limited to the early days of the Covenanters. A famous case in Dunning in 1652 became immortalized in print. When representatives of the synod arrived at the parish church to remove the deposed minister George Muschet, his wife and perhaps a hundred other women (and according to the victims, men dressed as women) armed themselves with wooden clubs and bagpipes and chased the unwelcome visitors away. According to a contemporary account published by the Commonwealth regime, when one of the visiting ministers attempted to enter the church 'those Amazons' beat him 'for his paines'.[22] After the Restoration accounts do exist of Covenanting women asserting more independent, disruptive behaviour, but they derive from their opponents' accounts rather than their own writings.[23]

GOVERNANCE

The campaign around the National Covenant, and subsequently the Solemn League and Covenant (which to some degree further radicalized the religious commitments of the Covenanters by demanding a religious settlement throughout the British dominions that they were sure could only be interpreted as presbyterian) was the relationship between church and state. While modern historians generally deny that the Covenanter dominance of Scotland equated to a theocracy, it is to some degree a moot point. Though the General Assembly did not rule in secular matters, the position of 'ruling elders' in the kirk and their ascendancy in parliament ensured that the movement dominated politics.[24] This was achieved through a revolution in governance driven by necessity.

   What started as a protest against unconstitutional royal absolutism transformed into an overt assertion of legislative governance that privileged the Estates over the crown. From 1640 the Covenanters made fundamental constitutional changes to the way Scotland was governed. James Balfour described the parliament of 1640 as 'the reall grattest change at ane blow that euer hapned to this churche and staite thesse 600 years baypast; for in effecte it ouerturned not onlie the ancient state gouernment, bot fettered monarchie with chynes and sett new limitts and marckes to the same, beyond wich it was not legally to proceed'.[25] The parliament, convened without the crown's permission, abolished the clerical estate—meaning bishops could not sit in parliament—and barred officers of state from sitting in parliament on the basis of their office, while each shire representative was given their own vote (rather than sharing it with another member representing the shire) thereby doubling shire voting power. Greater control over the legislation that parliament would debate was achieved by removing the obligation for it to originate from the Lords of Articles, traditionally appointed by the crown. But perhaps the most significant change came with the passing of a Triennial Act and the establishment of a Committee of Estates to govern when parliament was not in session, thus taking the place of the privy council. Three sessions of parliament sat in 1639–41, two sessions of the convention of Estates in 1643–4, six parliamentary sessions in 1644–7, and eight session of parliament during 1648–51.[26] The demands that such a model of governance had on its personnel are demonstrated by the significant reduction in attendance at parliament and attempts to avoid being elected,[27] yet the effectiveness of the Covenanters' rule by committee did produce some significant changes. Perhaps most dynamically it facilitated what Laura Stewart has called a fiscal revolution.[28]

Local organization under the Covenanters was achieved very rapidly by utilizing committees originally established as shire war committees for mustering troops and supplying them with provisions, a necessity driven by the immediate threat of war with the king. Committees were formed in January and February 1639 comprising shire committees and three or four members of each presbytery and these continued to operate throughout the 1640s, serving as a crucial 'novelty' of the 1640s providing a 'network... and personnel that circumvented the existing royal officials to link parish, burgh and shire to the organs of central government in Edinburgh'.[29] Their primary function was initially military preparation, but they made a smooth transition to financial administration, in particular collecting taxes. The fact that the majority of the nation had subscribed the Covenant and faced constant military risks fostered the ability, at least in the early decades of the 1640s, to work effectively in localities. More importantly, however, the integral role of presbytery representatives on these committees meant that church and state worked hand in hand. The government soon put this innovative structure to use facilitating an equally innovative fiscal programme including a monthly maintenance and an excise tax to be collected for supporting the army, quartering of troops, and forced loans.[30]

In order to maximize its financial resources, the Covenanting regime made revaluations of taxable wealth. Additionally, they enlarged the tax income by taxing annual rents on the basis of accurate valuations and introducing a national tax known as the 'Tenth Penny'. In July 1644 parliament established an excise tax justified explicitly by the financial commitments brought about by entering into the Solemn League and Covenant and further military engagements in England.[31] Besides taxation and forced loans, another prominent source of income came through sequestering 'malignant' or 'delinquents' estates, which probably generated in excess of £800,000 Scots during the 1640s,[32] although it was ultimately more politically attractive to demonstrate leniency and encourage cooperation than to exact maximum fines and foster dissatisfaction. The scope of taxation and the local structure for collecting it allowed the government to gather nearly twice the amount of money between 1638 and 1650 than the crown had during a similar span (1621–33).[33] This fiscal revolution was prompted by the need to support military spending, by far the greatest expenditure between 1639 and 1651. Despite these changes, the decade of conflict Scotland waged both internally and externally took its toll. While the traditional historiography depicting Scotland as being completely spent by 1649 may be overly pessimistic, a staggering amount of debt accrued. But military necessity clearly prompted fundamental change in Scotland's fiscal regime.

This was because, although Scotland greatly benefited in 1639 from the return of thousands of Scots serving in Continental armies during the Thirty Years War, putting an army in the field presented significant difficulties and challenged some long-held rights. Under the shire war committees, burghs often found their autonomy in relation to mustering, equipping, organizing, and leading their citizens subsumed within the shires.[34] How men were mustered remains unclear, although in some burghs skilled workers or those in essential trades could be exempt. Certainly mustering in the shires proved easier, as feudal superiorities still prevailed.

Despite efforts to improve the administrative and financial support of the armies, the pressures of quartering soldiers in towns and burghs also created significant challenges, though magistrates and commanders tended to work together to minimize the ill effects and maintain order. Things became inevitably more complicated when a Scottish army plundered or occupied a Scottish city. These difficulties increased when civil war broke out on Scottish soil in 1644–5. Montrose's adoption of the 'royalist' cause was followed by the arrival of Alasdair MacColla at the head of at least 1500 Irish soldiers, in addition to some women and children who followed their train. This further complicated the resultant conflict, which brought great suffering, particularly in the north-east and Argyll. MacColla, for example, came to be known among the Campbells as the 'Destroyer of Houses',[35] a reflection of his tactics in destroying shelter and removing supplies to ensure maximum suffering of all who inhabited the land. 'Fire and sword', or the destruction of crops, food stores, livestock, and houses weakened an enemy's capacity and resolve to resist, but in the case of the Clan Donald actions against the Campbells the policy sought to maximize hardship and misery.

However, the experience of brutality and suffering was not one-sided. At the battle of Philiphaugh the triumphant Covenanter army refused to honour the quarter promised to the Irish serving under the Montrose, slaughtering fifty men and some 300 of the women and children who accompanied them. A later tradition related that eighty of the women and children who escaped were thrown off a bridge near Linlithgow to drown, just as Protestants had done in Portadown four years earlier.[36] Beyond the death brought by conflict, the disruption of trade, and a lack of provisions in Scotland, the nation also experienced plague in 1644–5, and again in 1647–8.[37] The decade took an immense toll on Scotland—not least emotional—especially in light of the expectations that had been fostered through promises of the nation's privileged place and impending providential blessing. Scots experienced a similar period of 'fire and sword' during the Interregnum. The ill-fated Glencairn's Rising (1653–5) witnessed royalist reprisals inflicted on the lands of Scots who accepted the English Commonwealth's conquest of Scotland, while in the summer of 1655 General Monck laid waste to rebels' crops and possessions to effectively bring an end to the lingering rebellion. As in England, war brought administrative revolution, but also great suffering, and cast doubt on the arguments which had justified the taking up of arms.

ECONOMIC AND SOCIAL CHANGE

While the cost of sustaining war in the 1640s had a significant effect on the burghs of Scotland, and the occupation of the 1650s opened the door for cheap English goods to flood Scottish markets, the traditional tale of economic dearth during the Interregnum is misleading. The work of Tom Devine has shown that both Aberdeen and Glasgow demonstrated significant signs of growth in both trade and registration of craftsmen, as well as early forays into transatlantic trade.[38] One trade in particular that grew during the period was bookselling. Not only did a number of new sellers appear in major burghs, but provincial towns became new outlets for the increasing demand for printed material.[39]

Commonwealth/Protectoral policies towards printing facilitated this growth, but the economic policies of the Covenanting parliaments had already set the stage for encouraging growth in manufacturing by controlling exports of raw materials and exempting manufacturers from taxes, levies, and quartering.[40] Stevenson notes that the innovative thinking demonstrated in Covenanting economic policy bore little fruit, due to the general upheaval and fiscal demands of the period, but argues it foreshadowed future legislation.[41]

The period did perhaps see a more significant shift in legal and judicial trends in Scotland. Feuding and local vendettas had begun to give way to centralized courts and legal professionals under the reign of James VI.[42] Jenny Wormald has argued that Covenanting legislation, administrative developments and attitudes significantly contributed to this transition,[43] but these were in some ways furthered during the Interregnum. The English regime reintroduced justices of the peace and circuit courts. While English soldiers filled some of these roles, such as Colonel Richard Ashfield in Glasgow and Colonel William Daniel in Perth, most were Scots. In light of the abolition of heritable jurisdictions by the Commonwealth in 1652, this allowed for the local administration of justice more effectively than it had under the Jacobean and Caroline system—when feudal claims inhibited the system, a trend that continued under the Covenanters.[44] According to Frances Dow, it 'marked a concession to the men of influence in the localities; and in comparison with the predominantly coercive, centralising and military tone of government... signified a move towards conciliation and co-operation with the local communities'.[45] Intervention in the legal system had another important aspect. Despite initially intending to reform Scots law by bringing it in line with English practices, the complexity proved too great. Instead, English judges worked alongside Scottish ones. The English influence resulted in effectively forcing Scottish nobility and gentry to pay their debtors, who may have been socially inferior. This fostered the fears of the nobility and gentry and contributed to expatriation and Glencairn's Rising. However, English intervention also resulted in a dramatic reduction in the number of witchcraft prosecutions and the first public challenges in the legal system to the existence of witches in Scotland.[46] In general, the implementation of justice under the Commonwealth and Protectorate met with popular support and served to defuse local vendettas, something English judges were quick to recognize as a cause for many of the cases that came before them.[47] The impact brought about by Scots sitting alongside English judges in the central law courts has been largely overlooked, but as J. D. Ford has argued it played a significant role in the formation of Viscount Stair's thinking on Scots law and its subsequent development.[48]

Despite initial intentions to break the feudal dominance that, along with the presbyterian kirk, they perceived had brought about Scotland's invasions of England, the Interregnum government eventually changed tack. Though they informally abolished all heritable jurisdictions in 1652 (reiterated in the Ordinance of Union in 1654),[49] they found it necessary to pursue policies that placated and engendered cooperation from Scotland's regional power brokers. As a result, many of the nobility and gentry who faced crippling fines or sequestration of their estates either from the Covenanting regime or the new English regime for the parts they played in the Covenanters' interference in English politics (on top of the debts they had accrued in financially supporting Covenanter government) were treated generously and brought onside, even if cooperation by most landed Scots was purely pragmatic.[50] Fines were greatly reduced and clan chiefs who cooperated with the regime were allowed to retain arms for maintaining order in the Highlands. Though a calculated risk on the part of the English, it proved far less expensive a policy than maintaining the more than sixty garrisons that at one time were dotted across the country.[51] Even in remote areas where encounters between English soldiers and clansmen had initially been bloody, cooperation and trust could be developed as the relationship between the government and Clan Cameron demonstrates.[52] This was not the experience across the board, however, as Glencairn's Rising and the challenge of moss-troopers proved. In both the Lowlands and the Highlands fostering cooperation with the traditional power brokers and lessening financial pressure on landowners reduced the likelihood they might be seduced by rebellion.

INTERREGNUM AND RESTORATION

To the extent that Oliver Cromwell's conquest of Scotland allowed for innovation in Scottish government and public life, it marked the failure of the Covenanting 'revolution' and emergent political divisions among Scots. In the wake of Scotland's humiliation at Dunbar, the Covenanters became divided. The moderate majority moved to relax the Act of Classes through the passage of the 'first public resolution' by a commission of the General Assembly on 14 December 1650, before fully rescinding it in January. Opponents to this course of action submitted a remonstrance, thus becoming known as Remonstrants, which argued for the reinstatement of the Act of Classes and the rejection of Charles II on the grounds that he lacked any real fervour for the Covenants. When the moderate majority at the general assemblies of 1651 and 1652 rejected these claims (passing their own resolutions thus becoming known as the Resolutioners) the Remonstrants submitted formal protests and became known as Protesters. While the

Resolutioners held that the Covenants required the maintenance of religion, monarchy, and Scottish liberties, the Protesters argued that the inclusion of the ungodly in government broke Scotland's obligation to right religion and that the godlessness of Charles II meant he could not meet the strict criteria of a Covenanted king. The two groups' positions on the monarchy set the tone for their relationships with the English regime that dominated Scotland until 1660, while the populace of Scotland was left with trying to make sense of why God had forsaken them. By the end of 1652 the English exerted martial law over most of Scotland, requiring little collaboration due to their dominant military presence. Nonetheless, there were divergent political responses to the English occupation, rather than a unanimous desire to overturn the Cromwellian settlement in favour of its Covenanter predecessor. While Frances Dow's *Cromwellian Scotland* remains the seminal study of Interregnum Scotland's administrative mechanisms, the range of Scottish responses—from the traditional image of indignant subjection and revolt, to passive acceptance, laudatory praise for presbyterianism's demise, political involvement in Commonwealth/Protectoral governance, and even Scottish enlistment in military service within the Commonwealth army in Scotland—persists in being under-appreciated by historians; as does the overall legacy of the period.[53] By the end of the Interregnum even the once fanatical author of the National Covenant, Archibald Johnston of Wariston, had come to terms with the Interregnum government, serving in the 1659 parliament and as the only Scot on the Committee of Estates.

For some of the same reasons the Restoration did not bring a return to a lost Covenanting consensus. Popular support for the monarchy ran high in 1660, with even hard-line Covenanters admitting that the majority of Scotland had lost their taste for the type of presbyterianism the previous decades had produced. As in England the return of Charles II was met by genuine public exhortations although, again like England, that did not mean that the resultant political and ecclesiastical settlement would not leave many disappointed. Yet even those who advocated a strong monarchy (sometimes interpreted as absolutist), such as Sir George Mackenzie of Rosehaugh, still vigorously upheld the imperatives of Scots law, sometimes to the limitation of what might be seen as the prerogatives of the crown. When Charles II sought to act without consent of parliament Mackenzie, as Lord Advocate, ruled such absolutism to be unconstitutional.[54]

Charles II's government contained many of the same individuals or families who were not only prominent before 1637, but who had actually taken leading roles in the establishment of the Covenanting experiment, such as: John Maitland, earl of Lauderdale (secretary of state for Scotland 1660), John Lindsay, 1st earl of Crawford-Lindsay (made treasurer for life in 1660, a role he had fulfilled for the Covenanters); John Hay, 1st Marquis of Tweeddale (appointed to the privy council 1661); John Sinclair, 9th Lord Sinclair (privy council 1661); Robert Balfour, 2nd Lord Balfour of Burleigh (Member of Parliament 1661–3); James Douglas, 2nd earl of Queensbury (commissioner of excise 1661 and JP 1663); John Carnegie, 1st earl of Northesk (dempster of parliament and of the justice and circuit courts of Forfarshire 1661, JP 1663); James Home, 3rd earl of Home (appointed to Lords of Articles in 1661 and sat in parliament 1661–3); James Dalrymple, 1st Viscount Stair (judge); Sir James Lockhart of Lee (father of William, lord of session 1661); Charles Seton, 2nd earl of

Dunfermline (privy council 1661); and John Leslie, 7th earl of Rothes (chancellor 1661–4, lord high commissioner 1667), whose father had been at the forefront of the Covenanting movement from the outset. There were, of course, examples made in the execution of Argyll and Wariston, as well as the radical cleric James Guthrie, but the social hierarchy of Scotland was overwhelmingly restored. Some, however, like William Kerr, 3rd earl of Lothian, and John Kennedy, 6th earl of Cassillis, refused to abjure the Covenants, instead opting to retire from public life. Yet despite the risings of the Restoration period, it seems that the majority of the population conformed fairly easily to the Restoration regime. The survival of the landed elites of Scotland and the maintenance of their political predominance is a crucial aspect of the period. The fact that so many who had spearheaded the Covenanting experiment were accepted into the Restoration government attests to the continuity of social hierarchy and oligarchic tendencies in state politics. It also suggests the resiliency that Keith Brown has argued the nobility showed from the Reformation to 1638, persisted through to the Restoration and beyond.[55]

The long-term impact of the Covenanting revolution on the government of Scotland was felt less in a transformation in the composition of the political elite than in the fact that cooperation with a centralized state, rather than local or kin-based resistance, became the norm for political progress. In addition, Scotland had begun to become accustomed to being ruled by an executive power based in London. And yet, the opposite could also be witnessed in subsequent decades, with the defiance of extreme Covenanters, albeit in small numbers. What sustained Covenanting resistance was the re-emergence of royal absolutism and especially the Act of Recissory of 1661 that annulled all parliamentary legislation since 1633, including the Covenants. In the case of the Covenanters who continued to espouse their principles after the Restoration, this was compounded by a sense of pious indignation and divine obligation to the aims of the Covenants. However, rather than the assertion of the nobility or landed gentry which had harnessed popular support, Covenanter resistance in the 1670s and 1680s emanated primarily from the lower classes. The framework of loyalty and responsibility set out in the National Covenant, and to a degree reiterated in the Solemn League and Covenant, gave leave for the individual conscience to determine whether the balance of political, social, and religious demands set out in 1638 were being fulfilled. This is because, as noted above, the Covenants themselves bound the individual, not just the nation, to commit to their fulfilment, thereby giving licence for conscientious resistance. Moreover, it also gave leave for popular corporate resistance.

While Covenanting never dominated the cultural landscape of Scotland after 1649, save for some areas of the south-west, it presented a crucial ideological platform for resistance to the state during the 1670s and 1680s. Although this fuelled a significant subculture and left an indelible mark that later generations could look to, especially for secessionists in the eighteenth century and during the crisis of the Church of Scotland mid-nineteenth century (such as in the writings of Thomas M'Crie),[56] the rhetoric of covenants remained marginal until the eighteenth century.

The Covenanting movement did not, explicitly or in practice, foster a social revolution. Political crisis and mobilization created new opportunities for popular political participation and for women to assume public roles, but these opportunities were constrained by Covenanting thought and practice. The dominance of existing social elites proved resilient. Covenanting theology encouraged personal engagement with the fate of national reform, and there was a lively manuscript debate around these issues, although the development of the presses was more limited than in England. With the political defeat of the Covenanting movement, in Cromwellian occupation and Stuart restoration, the religious culture was changed—those who subsequently laid claim to Covenanting heritage did so, usually, in rather different terms. In this and other ways the experience of the mid-century crisis marked a break in Scottish history—in the development of a public sphere more engaged with national politics, a legislative revolution, and in the growing importance of the central institutions of the state as against local bodies and jurisdictions. While these issues have not been fully explored by modern historians, it seems reasonable to suggest that the 1640s and 1650s saw the working out of political, social, and religious tensions heightened by the Reformation (but stretching back even further), in ways that were to shape Scotland's long-term development.

NOTES

1. Robert Baillie, *Letters and Journals, 1637–1662*, 3 vols., ed. David Laing (Bannatyne Club, 1841–2), I, 18.
2. Allan Macinnes, *Charles I and the Making of the Covenanting Movement, 1626–41* (Edinburgh, 1991), 166–8.
3. Laura A. M. Stewart, *Urban Politics and the British Civil Wars: Edinburgh, 1617–53* (Leiden, 2006), 275.
4. David Stevenson, 'The Battle of Mauchline Moor, 1648', *Ayrshire Collections*, 11 (1974): 1–24.
5. Allan I. Macinnes, 'The Scottish Constitution, 1638–51: The Rise and Fall of Oligarchic Centralism', in John Morrill (ed.), *The Scottish National Covenant in its British Context, 1638–51* (Edinburgh, 1990), 106–33.
6. L. Charles Jackson, 'For Kirk and Kingdom: The Public Career of Alexander Henderson (1637–1646)' (unpublished Ph.D. dissertation, University of Leicester, 2012), 121–77.
7. Sarah Waurechen, 'Covenanter Propaganda and Conceptualizations of the Public during the Bishops' Wars, 1638–1640', *Historical Journal*, 52 (2009): 63–86; Arthur Williamson, 'Scotland: International Politics, International Press', in Sabrina Alcorn Baron, Eric N. Lindquist, and Eleanor F. Shevlin (eds.), *Agent of Change* (Amherst, 2007), 193–215; David Stevenson, 'A Revolutionary Regime and the Press: The Scottish Covenanters and their Printers, 1638–1651', *The Library*, 6th series, 7 (1985): 315–27.
8. Church of Scotland, General Assembly, *Acts of the General Assembly of the Church of Scotland, 1638–1842*, ed. T. Pitcairn (Edinburgh, 1843), 30; Alastair J. Mann, *The Scottish Book Trade, 1500–1720* (East Linton, 2000), 144–5.
9. Oliver Cromwell, *A Letter Sent to the Generall Assembly of the Kirke of Scotland* (London, 1650), 3–4; *Writings and Speeches of Oliver Cromwell* (Cambridge, Mass., 1937–1947), ed. W. C. Abbott, I, 302.
10. Mann, *The Scottish Book Trade*, 31, 232; R. Scott Spurlock, 'Cromwell's Edinburgh Press and the Development of Print Culture in Scotland', *Scottish Historical Review* [*Scot. Hist. Rev.*], 90 (2011): 179–203.

11. R. Scott Spurlock, *Cromwell and Scotland: Conquest and Religion* (Edinburgh, 2007), 39–41, 54–71, 72–99.

12. Louise A. Yeoman, 'Heart-Work: Emotion, Empowerment and Authority in Covenanting Times' (unpublished Ph.D. dissertation, University of St Andrews, 1991), 276; 41–94.

13. R. A. Houston, *Scottish Literacy and the Scottish Identity: Illiteracy and Society in Scotland and Northern England, 1600–1800* (Cambridge, 1985), 84–8. For a discussion of the lack of women's subscriptions, see James Anderson, *The Ladies of the Covenant* (Glasgow, 1852), p. xxii, n. 1.

14. Walter Balcanquhall, *A Large Declaration concerning the Late Tumults in Scotland* (London, 1639), 227.

15. Spurlock, *Cromwell and Scotland*, 122, 137, 155, 162, 165–6, 173, 184–5, 191.

16. Baillie, *Letters and Journals*, I, 239–41; II, 45.

17. Baillie, *Letters and Journals*, I, 21.

18. Baillie, *Letters and Journals*, I, 23, 37, 66, 76, 94, 109, 220.

19. For a discussion of the role women played in popular unrest in Holland, see Rudolf M. Dekker, 'Women in Revolt', *Theory and Society*, 16 (1987): 337–62.

20. Baillie, *Letters and Journals*, I, 21.

21. David G. Mullan (ed.), *Women's Life Writing in Early Modern Scotland* (Aldershot, 2003); Samuel Rutherford, *Letters of Samuel Rutherford with a Sketch of his Life and Biographical Notes of his Correspondents*, ed. Andrew Bonar (Edinburgh, 1984), passim.

22. A. B., *A Fight at Dunin in Scotland, Between the Scots Women and the Presbyterian Kirkmen* (Edinburgh, 1652); *Mercurius Politicus*, 17–24 June 1652, at 1682, 1686–7. For a Presbyterian account, see J. Wilson, *Dunning: Its Parochial History, with Notes, Antiquarian, Ecclesiastical, Baronial, and Miscellaneous* (2nd edition, Crieff, 1906), 40ff.

23. David G. Mullan, *Narratives of the Religious Self in Early Modern Scotland* (Aldershot, 2010), 371.

24. Rosalind Mitchison, *Lordship and Patronage: Scotland 1603–1745* (London, 1983), 44–5.

25. Sir James Balfour, *Historical Works*, ed. J. Haig, 4 vols. (Edinburgh, 1824–5), II, 379.

26. Keith M. Brown, Roland Tanner, and Alastair J. Mann, *Parliament and Politics in Scotland, 1567–1707* (Edinburgh, 2005), 35; David Stevenson, *The Government of Scotland under the Covenanters* (Edinburgh, 1982), p. xxxix.

27. David Stevenson, 'The Burghs and the Scottish Revolution', in Michael Lynch (ed.), *The Early Modern Town in Scotland* (London, 1987), 182–3.

28. Laura A. M. Stewart, 'Fiscal Revolution and State Formation in Mid Seventeenth-Century Scotland', *Historical Research*, 84 (2011): 443–69.

29. Stewart, 'Fiscal Revolution', 444; Mark C. Fissel, *The Bishops' Wars: Charles I's Campaigns against Scotland 1638–1640* (Cambridge, 1994), 74.

30. David Stevenson, 'The Financing of the Cause of the Covenants, 1638–51', *Scot. Hist. Rev.*, 51 (1972): 89–123; Stewart, 'Fiscal Revolution'.

31. *The Records of the Parliaments of Scotland to 1707*, ed. K. M. Brown et al. (St Andrews, 2007–12), 1644/6/282 [accessed 15 October 2012]; *Act of Parliament and Commission, anent the excise and the collecting thereof, 29. July 1644* (Edinburgh, 1644).

32. Stewart, 'Fiscal Revolution', 457.

33. Stewart, 'Fiscal Revolution', 459–60.

34. Laura A. M. Stewart, 'Military Power and the Scottish Burghs, 1625–1651', *Journal of Early Modern History*, 15 (2011): 59–82.

35. David Stevenson, *Alasdair MacColla and the Highland Problem in the Seventeenth Century* (Edinburgh, 1980), 145ff.; Allan I. Macinnes, *Clanship, Commerce and the House of Stuart, 1603–1788* (Edinburgh, 1996), 110.

36. Samuel R. Gardiner, *History of the Great Civil War 1642–49* (London, 1889), II, 337.

37. K. Jillings, 'Aberdeen's Plague Epidemic of 1647–48', *Scottish Medical Journal*, 55 (2010): 43–5.

38. T. M. Devine, 'The Cromwellian Union and the Scottish Burghs: The Case of Aberdeen and Glasgow, 1652–60', in J. Butt and J. T. Ward (eds.), *Scottish Themes* (Edinburgh, 1976), 1–16.

39. Spurlock, 'Cromwell's Edinburgh Press', 179–203.

40. Gordon Marshall, *Presbyteries and Profits: Calvinism and the Development of Capitalism in Scotland* (Oxford, 1980), 131–2.

41. Stevenson, 'The Effects of Revolution and Conquest', 55–6.

42. Julian Goodare, *The Government of Scotland, 1560–1625* (Oxford, 2004); Keith Brown, *Bloodfeud in Scotland, 1573–1625* (Edinburgh, 1986).

43. J. Wormald, 'Bloodfeud, Kindred and Government in Early Modern Scotland', *Past and Present*, 87 (1980): 92–7.

44. Brian Levack notes that the Interregnum represented the only period in the seventeenth century when circuit courts operated as intended. Brian P. Levack, 'Decline and End of Scottish Witch-Hunting', in Julian Goodare (ed.), *The Scottish Witch-Hunt in Context* (Manchester, 2002), 166–81 at 173.

45. Dow, *Cromwellian Scotland*, 179.

46. For a discussion of the scepticism of English judges in the wider Scottish context, see Brian P. Levack, 'The Great Scottish Witch Hunt of 1661–1662', *Journal of British Studies*, 20 (1980): 90–108 at 91–4.

47. John Nicoll, *A Diary of Public Transactions and Other Occurrences, Chiefly in Scotland, 1650–1667*, ed. David Laing (Edinburgh, 1836), 104, 188; *Mercurius Politicus*, 28 October–4 November 1652, at 1652; Bulstrode Whitelock, *Memorials of the English Affairs* (London, 1732; 1853 edition), III, 458. John Lamont also mentions the leniency shown to accused witches in Stirling in September 1652, *The Diary of Mr John Lamont of Newton, 1649–1671*, ed. G. R. Kinloch (Edinburgh, 1830), 47.

48. J. D. Ford, *Law and Opinion in Scotland During the 17th Century* (Oxford, 2007), 123–80; A. R. G. M'Millan, 'The Judicial System of the Commonwealth in Scotland', *Juridical Review*, 49 (1937): 232–55; Adelyn L. M. Wilson, 'Practicks in Scotland's Interregnum', *Juridical Review* (October 2012): 319–52.

49. John W. Cairns, 'Historical Introduction', in Kenneth Reid and Reinhard Zimmerman (eds.), *A History of Private Law in Scotland* (Oxford, 2000), I, 120.

50. David Menarry, 'Scottish and Irish Landed Society during the Cromwellian Occupation' (unpublished Ph.D. dissertation, University of Aberdeen, 2001), 356–61.

51. Spurlock, *Cromwell and Scotland*, 42.

52. Charles H. Firth (ed.), *Scotland and the Commonwealth* (Edinburgh, 1895), xlii–xliii, 149–50, 279.

53. Spurlock, *Cromwell and Scotland*, 43–4.

54. Gordon Donaldson, *James V to James VII* (Edinburgh, 1965), 376.

55. Keith M. Brown, *Noble Power in Scotland from the Reformation to the Revolution* (Edinburgh, 2011).

56. Graeme Neil Forsyth, 'The Presbyterian Interpretation of Scottish History, 1800–1914' (unpublished Ph.D. dissertation, Stirling University, 2003), chap. 3.

Further Reading

Cowan, Edward J., *Montrose: For Covenant and King* (London, 1977).

Donald, Peter, *An Uncounselled King: Charles I and the Scottish Troubles, 1637–1641* (Cambridge, 1990).

Donaldson, Gordon, *James V to James VII* (Edinburgh, 1965).

Dow, Frances, *Cromwellian Scotland* (Edinburgh, 1979, 1999).

Fissel, Mark C., *The Bishops' Wars: Charles I's Campaigns against Scotland 1638–1640* (Cambridge, 1994).

Macinnes, Allan I., *The British Confederate: Archibald Campbell, Marquess of Argyll, c.1607–1661* (Edinburgh, 2011).

Macinnes, Allan I., *Charles I and the Making of the Covenanting Movement* (Edinburgh, 1996).

Makey, Walter, *The Church of the Covenant 1637–1651: Revolution and Social Change in Scotland* (Edinburgh, 1979).

Morrill, John (ed.), *The Scottish National Covenant in its British Context, 1638–51* (Edinburgh, 1990).

Spurlock, R. Scott, *Cromwell and Scotland: Conquest and Religion, 1650–1660* (Edinburgh, 2007).

Stevenson, David, *Revolution and Counter-Revolution in Scotland, 1644–1651* (London, 1977, 2003).

Stevenson, David, *The Scottish Revolution, 1637–44* (Edinburgh, 1973, 2003).

Stewart, Laura A. M., *Urban Politics and the British Civil Wars: Edinburgh, 1617–53* (Leiden, 2006).

Young, J. R., *The Scottish Parliament 1639–1661: A Political and Constitutional Analysis* (Edinburgh, 1996).

CHAPTER 22

STATE, POLITICS, AND SOCIETY IN IRELAND, 1641–1662

TOBY BARNARD

PROLONGED warfare during the 1640s, invasion from Scotland and England followed by reconquest and resettlement, ended the quiet that Ireland was alleged to have enjoyed in the 1630s. Physical and institutional upheavals left ideological and psychological rifts. Neither the losers (the Catholic majority bound loosely into the Confederacy) nor the winners (the Protestant minority in Ireland and its allies from Britain) had been united throughout the conflict. Disunity continued. It affected responses to the immediate aftermath of the war and to its longer-term consequences. Among the defeated there were recriminations about who was to blame for military and political failures and how best to minimize or reverse the resulting damage. These animosities weakened any common approach to opportunities and challenges thereafter. Arguably they persisted throughout the eighteenth century. Members of the Irish Protestant minority had reacted variously to the British civil wars and their own local predicaments, and continued to do so. Faced with an intrusive and revolutionary regime in the 1650s, then the restored Stuart monarchy, the imposition of William and Mary in 1689, and a domineering British state during the next century, Irish Protestants veered between servility, collaboration, and muted or strident criticism. In each distinct confessional community, whether Catholic or Protestant, the emergence of an Irish patriotism, even of a proto-nationalism, has been discerned and traced back to the middle decades of the seventeenth century.

Accordingly, it is necessary to assess both the transient and durable developments of the Interregnum. Three topics have excited the greatest interest among previous writers. Two concern Oliver Cromwell: his conduct as military commander and his influence over the shaping of Irish policy. The third relates to evaluating how far events in Ireland between 1641 and 1660 conformed to, intensified, or deviated from customary English treatment of Ireland. This discussion, while not ignoring the traditional concerns, concentrates on the longer-term consequences for the inhabitants of Ireland.

CROMWELL IN IRELAND

Cromwell's campaign in Ireland was brief. He disembarked near Dublin on 15 August 1649 and sailed away on 29 May 1650, summoned to quell trouble in Scotland. Predecessors, notably Michael Jones, with his victory at Rathmines (close to Dublin) on 2 August 1649 over a royalist army, prepared the ground for Cromwell's triumphs, perhaps decisively. Subordinates, such as his son-in-law and legal deputy as governor of Ireland, Henry Ireton, and Edmund Ludlow, completed what he had begun. Yet, short as Cromwell's time in Ireland was, it left him indelibly associated with Catholic Ireland's ruin. His reports of the storming of Drogheda and Wexford, sent to the Westminster parliament and quickly printed, seemed to glory in the gore. Civilians, at best tangentially linked with the resistance, had been killed alongside soldiers and priests. Possible explanations—the conventions of warfare, a belief in the guilt of those put to the sword, the need to avenge the deaths of those Protestants killed in 1641 and thereafter—show an ingenuity that sometimes verges on special pleading. Even the argument that exemplary savagery was intended to shorten the war and save further bloodshed is contradicted by the fact of the stiff resistance faced by Cromwell himself at Clonmel in the spring of the following year. Formal surrender was delayed until 1653 and thereafter sporadic guerrilla resistance persisted. It could be that at Drogheda the soldiers ran amok, and, for once, the tight discipline associated with Cromwell's command was allowed to slip.[1] Whatever military advantages were secured through the brutal tactics were offset by the damage to Cromwell's historical reputation, turning him into a butcher of the Irish. However, much of the condemnation came from later writers, by the twentieth century writing in the shadow of more recent atrocities.[2] At the time, judgements diverged in accordance with affiliations during the protracted war. The vanquished struggled to circulate news of barbarism; Cromwell and his backers controlled the presses in Britain and Ireland.

Cromwell's personal responsibility for what happened in Ireland in the 1650s was often represented as extending beyond military matters. Of the Irish policies attributed to him, at once most disruptive and most durable, was the confiscation of land from the defeated and its transfer to new owners. This came to be known as 'the Cromwellian Settlement'.[3] Involving approximately 2,500,000 acres, the scale of the change cannot be gainsaid. However, the novelty of the approach can be; as also can Cromwell's role in formulating and implementing the resettlement.

The 'Cromwellian' land settlement had antecedents reaching back to the earliest English involvement with Ireland. Reliable immigrants had long been encouraged to settle. Indigenes, especially when rebellious, were displaced and driven into less fertile regions. These plantations had intensified during the sixteenth century as the Tudors strove to make their writ run throughout all Ireland and provoked resistance. In particular, large tracts in the north-east and more scattered ones in the southern province of Munster had been bestowed on new proprietors. These processes, indeed, formed one of the sharpest grievances of the rebels in 1641. The English parliament responded to the uprising by renewing and extending confiscation. Those subsequently found guilty of revolt would be expropriated; their property was assigned to investors prepared to advance money to recover Ireland (known as 'adventurers') and—in time—the soldiery who accomplished the recovery.

The colossal task of transferring the sequestered properties could begin only when the war was won. It imposed a complex administrative burden on the overstretched Cromwellian regime in Ireland throughout the 1650s. It stimulated the ingenious to devise and oversee methods, both technical and logistical, through which the work could be done. William Petty, recently arrived from England, took credit for organizing and overseeing the preliminary surveys of land and then its allocation to the new proprietors. Petty, boastful of his ingenuity, he profited handsomely and attracted the inevitable opprobrium.[4] More generally the protracted business generated resentments and disappointments. Both adventurers and soldiers felt that their rewards were not commensurate with their contributions. Many quickly sold what they had been allocated rather than establishing themselves on the new holdings. In consequence, the predicted additions to the British and Protestant land-owning population of Ireland dwindled from 37,000 to perhaps 12,000.[5] The process favoured those loyal Protestants already in Ireland, who could supplement their property on extremely advantageous terms. The policy also had the unwelcome result of adding to the number of those absent from Ireland who owned property there.

The transformation proved less dramatic than had been projected. Scarcely had the property been assigned to the newcomers than Charles II was restored and the entire settlement was in flux. In the event, the contours of the Cromwellian landscape were modified but not erased.[6] Limited modifications and continuing uncertainties, which intensified in the 1670s and 1680s, mortified both Protestant incumbents and dispossessed Catholics. So far as Catholics were concerned, although they could trace the policy to the Cromwellian era, they reserved their most savage denunciation not for Cromwell but for those who were alleged to have advised Charles II not to overturn the entire settlement. Thus, it was Clarendon, chief minister in England between 1660 and 1665, and Ormond, lord lieutenant from 1661 to 1669, who were the culprits: evil councillors who stopped the king from acting on his wish to recompense his loyal Irish Catholic followers.

With the Cromwellian regime so swiftly superseded by the Stuart monarchy, there was little point in blaming Cromwell for the policies of the 1660s and later. Only in the 1690s, following the victories in Ireland of William III, was the new land-owning order confirmed and indeed consolidated. And once again, it was believed by the victims that the original intention of generosity towards them on the part of the monarch had been frustrated. In the 1690s, it was not royal councillors but a malevolent Irish parliament, now monopolized by Protestants, that refused to ratify the terms on which the last stronghold—Limerick—had surrendered. Treachery over the articles of Limerick, traceable to the leaders of Protestant Ireland, like the obloquy for Clarendon and Ormond, shielded Cromwell from the most vicious denunciations by Irish Catholic activists.

For another reason, criticizing Cromwell for the harsh Cromwellian land settlement of the 1650s would be gratuitous. In 1649, Cromwell inherited a policy for Ireland that had been devised by the Westminster parliament in the early stages of the uprising. The parliament had followed familiar precedents for suppressing rebellion and dealing with its aftermath. In addition, English members of parliament were pressed by opportunistic Protestants from Ireland to adopt a punitive policy towards the alleged rebels.[7] Lobbyists from Ireland, well-placed to gain from any fresh confiscations, exaggerated the offences of the insurgents. A black legend of gratuitous violence and massacres was created and propagated. Print assisted in its diffusion. Graphic stories of torture and murder, sometimes illustrated with crude woodcuts, imprinted the minds of those, like Cromwell, entrusted with the subjugation of Ireland. The latest accounts were superimposed on traditions that associated the Irish with barbarism, backwardness, and popery. Also, they recycled images and ideas from the religious warfare of continental Europe and the recent Thirty Years War.

Cromwell, conditioned by these materials, did not dissent from the already-agreed English approach to Ireland. Arguably, the direct result of his conditioning showed in his and his soldiers' behaviour at Drogheda and Wexford. Once a semblance of normality had returned to Ireland after 1653, the process of implementing the decisions of 1642 began. Formal measures fell to the successive parliaments in London and to the Irish council sitting in Dublin; the detail, to special commissions. Insofar as Cromwell is known to have interested himself in aspects of the scheme it was to intervene on behalf of individuals. Cromwell's interference was to soften the harshness.[8] Of course, the occasional beneficiaries do not alter Cromwell's, usually silent, endorsement of the retributive principles underlying the land settlement. Cromwell can be seen as exhibiting the conventional prejudices of the seventeenth-century English towards the Irish and of militant Protestants towards active Catholics. As commander of the army in 1649, more than as ruler of Ireland along with Scotland and England between 1649 and 1658, he had unusual power to affect what happened in Ireland. As head of state from 1653, he may have presided over the implementation of the Irish land settlement, but he was not its author.

The Confederate War of the 1640s had seen heavy casualties and incidents that smacked of gratuitous violence. The Cromwellian campaign was accompanied by devastation and destruction when scorched-earth policies were implemented, and by outbreaks of plague and epidemic diseases. The resultant mortality was heavy and severely delayed the economic and physical recovery which peace ought to have inaugurated. It is thought that the population did not return to its pre-war level until the 1680s.

Cromwell died in 1658; the Stuart monarchy was restored in Ireland, as in Scotland and England, in 1660. The bleakness of the 1650s and the short duration of the political order that ruled then meant that scant attention was devoted to them. The bleakness can be over-done; signs of recovery and innovation are discernible by 1655. A more conventional and less military complexion was evident in government. Even so, it was necessary to maintain a large army of occupation, to which administrative and policing duties were entrusted. Paying the occupying forces added to the burden and unpopularity of the regime and obliged high levels of taxation which were resented by the local population and stalled economic revival. Notwithstanding the unprecedentedly heavy taxes, the regime in Ireland had to be subsidized from England. This was a familiar problem and one which deepened English animosity to Ireland, sometimes leading to thoughts that it might be better if Ireland were relinquished as an English possession. But any notion of cutting Ireland loose was checked by the allure of Irish resources. The dream of plundering Ireland lay behind the massive confiscations initiated in 1642 and implemented in the 1650s. Land was the principal asset that Ireland could offer: it was used to pay off the adventurers and soldiers serving in the island.

At the same time, although short-term calculations were uppermost, more distant objectives were not entirely overlooked. The belief regularly recurred: that Ireland had immense potential to be transformed into a prosperous possession. The Interregnum was no exception. Brochures and manifestos elaborated on the latent riches that awaited development. Systematic exploitation would bring improvements that would end the draining of English money and manpower and turn Ireland into an asset for England. Those newly endowed with the forfeited lands were expected to perform these transformations. Through industry and experimentation, the newcomers would set an example which, bit by bit, would pacify and civilize the unruly indigenes. The latter, it was predicted, would become industrious, skilled, and—ideally—Protestant.[9]

Programmes of this sort had featured in the English agenda for Ireland since the sixteenth century (and earlier). They justified the apparently retributive and punitive approach, but also allowed for a relaxation of severity. Arguably this was what was seen in the mid-1650s, as the heavily militarized regime of Charles Fleetwood, a son-in-law of Cromwell, who headed the government in Dublin between 1652 and 1655, was superseded by that of Henry Cromwell, the Protector's younger son. Yet whatever tentative moves were made towards civilian rule (for example, the restoration of the traditional law courts and municipal government), there was no escaping the need to station a large army in Ireland.[10] To the possibility of internal disorders, with guerrilla resistance, was added that of foreign invasion. The outbreak of war between England and Spain in 1655 meant that, once more, the long and secluded Irish coast was vulnerable to a Spanish descent. Given the Catholicism shared by the Spaniards and the defeated Confederates, it was feared that any such landing would provoke fresh uprisings. In the event, the Spanish, too preoccupied with their fight against France in continental Europe, did not invade Ireland.

The vulnerability of Ireland, separate and remote, obsessed the English. The suspect loyalties of the Catholic majority added to apprehensions that it might invite in England's enemies or, were the latter to disembark, rally to their flag. These fears, while sometimes exaggerated and manipulated to cause panics or to justify repression, were not baseless. Foreign armies arrived and fought on Irish soil between 1689 and 1691; smaller contingents came ashore in 1760 and 1798; others were prevented only by bad weather.

The apparent failure to assimilate Ireland to English ways—most obviously to the Protestant religion—meant that England remained physically insecure. Even more so, the Protestant inhabitants of Ireland, especially those who thought of themselves as the English of Ireland, were alarmed by rumours of wars and insurrections, and apprehensive about the local repercussions. Legends about the barbarism of the 1641 uprising entered into Irish Protestant mythology and occasioned watchfulness and suspicion among the distinct confessional communities. During the 1640s, exiles had returned to Ireland with experience of soldiering. The likelihood of more veterans coming back and putting their military prowess to use against those who now occupied what the exiles regarded as their hereditary possessions troubled Protestants. The latter, disliked as interlopers, had reasons to feel insecure: the titles to their holdings might be cancelled or disregarded by an unsympathetic regime; the aggrieved might try to seize what they had lost. Insecurity sometimes manifested itself in aggression: an almost manic urge to enjoy what they currently held because of uncertainty as to how long it would be theirs. Perhaps connected with this trait was a propensity to proclaim their incumbency with conspicuous and provocative display. The self-advertisement included building on a lavish scale, excess in food, drink, and behaviour, and a ready recourse to violence. However, to trace this conduct to the blemished circumstances of their origins and the precariousness of their ascendancy would be to ignore the similarities of fashion and demeanour among the prosperous elites across Britain, continental Europe, and colonial America. Attempts to understand the individual and collective mentalities of the Irish Protestants have had to balance the flawed origins and precarious nature of their ascendancy against their physical and artistic achievements.[11]

Long Memories

Combatants looked back to the 1640s and 1650s as a testing time. Both Catholics and Protestants framed the events in biblical terms: refined in the fires, they hoped to emerge purified and strengthened. Successive generations were reminded of what their forebears had endured; at the same time, they were admonished not to repeat past mistakes. Protestants were heartened that they had recovered, not only holding on to what had been endangered after 1641 but enlarging their shares of power and property. They were at pains when opportunities arose with fresh Catholic defeats in 1689–91 to adopt measures, justified variously as defensive and retributive, that would permanently disable their Catholic rivals. The intention, detail, and effectiveness of these measures, often lumped together as a 'Penal Code', have been investigated. In the main, any idea that it was designed and functioned as a coherent code has been modified, even abandoned. Nevertheless, as a result of a series of laws enacted by the Irish parliament, the bulk between 1695 and 1709, Catholics were subject to numerous restrictions: some merely demeaning, others profoundly serious in material consequences. Overall, the effect was to relegate Catholics (and Protestant dissenters) to the status of second-class citizens.[12]

The downfall of individual Catholic families might sometimes be traced to the dislocations of the mid-seventeenth century. Death on the battlefield or owing to the privations of exile was less common than simple genetic failure or reduced circumstances which in time depressed status within Ireland. Loss of property, more than of life, was the climacteric in the annals of a dynasty.[13] But, as has been stressed, the process was a jerky one: setbacks could be reversed. Definitive decline might well result from the cumulative damage of warfare, with the costs of maintaining troops, loss of rentals, and the wasting and confiscation of property. Hopes of better times fluctuated. Not until the 1690s was there widespread acknowledgement that the Catholics' lot would not improve for generations. How the bulk of the Irish responded to the gloomy outlook has become a topic increasingly attractive to researchers.

During the seventeenth century, the Catholics' share of land shrank dramatically. The redistributions of the 1650s, coinciding in time with Cromwell's rule, speeded and deepened the process. Exactly what proportion of the profitable land that the Catholics had owned in 1641 was retained in the later part of the century has yet to be agreed. Estimates of their holdings on the eve of war vary between 59% and 66%. By 1688 the figure had fallen to 22%. Fresh confiscations brought the total down to 14% by 1704.[14] Although the trend was dramatically downwards, it was interrupted and even reversed under Charles II and James VII and II. Separately Catholics expected and Protestants feared changes under a Catholic king. Only in the wake of William III's victories was the dispossession of Catholics renewed and rendered apparently definitive. Even when, in the early eighteenth century, the Catholics' holdings of freehold land had shrunk so greatly, it is unclear how successfully the effects were either evaded or neutralized. The lucky or ingenious—such as the Bellews in Counties Louth and Galway and the O'Conors in County Roscommon—kept fragments of their patrimonies, living in a style of recognizable if reticent gentility, albeit diminished from past glories.

Others compensated for losses of freehold land by leasing, although a law of 1704 banned them from enjoying terms of longer than thirty-one years. Another option, taken by many, including some already leasing land, was to trade. Here they were assisted by a network of kindred and co-religionists scattered through the ports and provinces of continental Europe and further afield in the Caribbean and America. Occasional individuals, such as Thomas Wyse in Waterford, dealing in goods that would not have been out of place in Birmingham or Sheffield, paraded their spectacular successes. Many within Ireland otherwise in precarious and penurious circumstances were helped—materially and psychologically—by connections outside the island. Some of the most glamorous refugees flourished in continental armies and governments; others like Hennessy and Barton established themselves in profitable trades such as wine, brandy, or sherry. Romanticizing, embodied in the generic description of the exiles as 'wild geese', can obscure the extremes of wealth and poverty. The displaced were more likely to end their days in hospitals for military veterans or begging in the streets than ennobled by foreign princes and luxuriating in splendour.[15]

Gradually coming into clearer focus is the ability of talented exiles to prosper in England. London, growing rapidly and sustaining a variety of professions, services, and trades, was a powerful magnet. Irish Catholics were to be found at all social and economic levels in the city. Distinct provision was made for their religious needs; specific quarters, especially around St Giles's in the Fields, became warrens in which the poor Irish roomed. More scattered and generally less visible were the quiet successes. Specialist lawyers, because Catholics were debarred in Ireland and England from pleading in open courts, delivered their advice in chambers and thrived.[16]

The geographical dispersal of so many Catholics may have aggravated their disunity. Exiles tended to retain links with relations and former neighbours back in Ireland. Remittances may have helped the latter to avoid acute penury. The suspicious supposed that along the same channels that money and goods travelled, so too did disturbing news and subversive ideas. Catholics within Ireland were quick to receive tidings of the battles and campaigns fought in Europe and European colonies. Nervy Protestants assumed that the Catholics were merely biding their time and, on a signal or intelligence of particular triumphs by Britain's enemies, they would rise as they had in 1641. In the most extreme predictions, massacres as grim and extensive as those reputed to have occurred in the 1640s were to be feared. Less sensational but equally alarming was the dread that locals, secretly drilled and armed, would flock to the ranks of invading armies. None of this happened, but the renewed warfare on Irish soil between 1689 and 1691 and the briefer incursions in 1760 and 1798 showed that the anxieties were not fantasies. In contrast, the perspectives of continental powers had altered little since the mid-seventeenth century. Those at war with England might fish in the turbulent Irish waters in the hope of distracting the English from the main theatres of engagement. But foreign rulers showed little inclination to annex Ireland permanently as a province or, indeed, to improve the lot of fellow Catholics there.

Strains within the Irish Catholic community resembled those which had weakened it in the mid-seventeenth century. By the eighteenth century, if members of the diaspora dreamt of a restoration of a Catholic Ireland, and they and their families as leading elements within its government and society, for the time being they concentrated on bettering themselves. Few gave priority to training themselves one day in the foreseeable future to lead troops in reclaiming ancestral rights. Inevitably differences in tactics and outlook opened between those who had remained in Ireland and those who had chosen or been forced into exile. With the latter scattered throughout Britain, continental Europe, and (increasingly) more distant continents, coordinated action was impracticable. For those who stayed in the Hanoverians' territories, whether Ireland itself or elsewhere, there was an almost craven wish to demonstrate good affection. It was calculated that if, during potential crises, such as the Jacobite risings of 1715 and 1745, Irish Catholics remained quiet, then the government might be persuaded that they were loyal subjects deserving of more generous treatment. This stance yielded few concrete concessions before the 1780s, when some of the legal machinery of Protestant Ascendancy in Ireland started to be dismantled. But well before that some chafing restrictions were silently relaxed. A palpable although haphazard improvement of conditions under which the majority in Ireland lived strengthened the conviction of gradualists that their acceptance of the Protestant ruling order was working. Furthermore, the expanding apparatus of the Hanoverian empire required soldiers, sailors, and administrators. Irish as well as Scots moved into these roles, with less and less scrutiny of their religious loyalties.[17]

The penal era during which Irish Catholics were legally restrained in public activities has become the focus of argument. In particular, similarities with which religious groups outside the state church were treated elsewhere, even in Britain, have been emphasized. So far as the Cromwellian decade is concerned, it may not have inaugurated the relegation of the Catholic majority in Ireland to a depressed status, but it intensified it, and set precedents with exclusions which would be renewed and extended after 1691. In that sense, the decade was a rehearsal for the Protestant monopoly introduced in the 1690s. Clearly the penalties and losses of the 1650s were reversible, but, although moderated between 1660 and 1691, they were not abandoned. The other source of continuing debate is whether or not defeat and oppression welded the hitherto disparate, even discordant elements of Catholic Ireland into a unified entity. Concerted action remained rare between 1649 and 1829. Episodes that might have displayed a new cohesiveness forged in adversity—the war of 1689–91 and the uprisings of 1798—failed. The failures have been traced back to the same causes which undermined the Confederates during the 1640s. But, others have discerned a positive legacy: a unifying ideology of Catholic nationalism in response to British (or Cromwellian) butchery. Argument is set to continue over which interpretation is the more convincing.

For Protestants, the years of war and the English republic left legacies which varied from family to family. Privations in and after 1641 were remembered. Individuals' sufferings were subsumed in a collective experience: of trials, endurance, deliverance, and triumph. Mutual antipathy and suspicion between Protestant and Catholic neighbours bequeathed edginess. Rumours of new massacres of the kind alleged in 1641 recurred. Sometimes they were maliciously promoted in order to cause panics. But the facts that they were believed and could induce terror suggest that—at least in some localities in which the Protestant minority was hugely outnumbered—there were feelings of insecurity, even of guilt, about the legal primacy accorded to the Protestants. Against these fears, and their public recapitulation through the liturgy of the church of Ireland, have to be set the accommodations and harmony.[18] Even in 1689–91, notwithstanding grim predictions, there were relatively few episodes of gratuitous or impromptu inter-confessional violence. Similarly, throughout the eighteenth century, if anti-Catholic feelings and sectarian strife occasionally led to assaults, they tended to be on property more than on persons: at least until 1798. Protestants might counsel one another to engage only Protestants as household servants. However, any such self-denying ordinance was impossible to observe other than in grand Dublin residences or in the north-east.

Gratitude to Cromwell and his army as the deliverer of established Protestants from being overrun by the Catholic majority was seldom voiced. Families that established themselves in Ireland as beneficiaries of the confiscations of the 1650s were reticent about advertising the fact. Those supposed to have arrived during the 1650s were liable to be ridiculed for their lowly antecedents—mechanics or shoe-makers—and blamed for the regicide, religious divisions, and social confusion.[19] Close association with or indebtedness to Cromwell and his auxiliaries embarrassed. Cromwell never received public acclaim as a deliverer in the way that William III would.[20]

Yet, with time, perspectives altered. The enthusiasm for the restored Stuarts which, between 1660 and 1688, silenced praise of Cromwell, evaporated after James's defeat and flight. Those who identified the Stuart regime with absolutist and maybe Catholic aspirations and subservience to France could detect those inclinations in Charles I and his agents. As Charles's reputation dipped, Cromwell increased in stature. By the early eighteenth century, calf's head clubs celebrated the beheading of the king.[21] Still it can be argued it was the negative connotations of Charles rather than the positive allure of Cromwell that animated Irish Protestants. Even among the tiny minority enamoured of the republicanism of the regicides, Cromwell was a flawed or lost hero. Whatever republican principles he may have professed, they were abandoned after he assumed the supreme magistracy in 1653. True Whigs, in Ireland personified in John Toland or Robert Molesworth, seeking a genealogy, might look back to Edmund Ludlow. As an army officer and parliamentary commissioner in Ireland after 1649, Ludlow emerged as an opponent of the Cromwellian protectorate. His *Memoirs*, heavily doctored by editors in the 1690s to introduce a more consistently secular tone, were read in Ireland. Another text important to the intellectual formation of theoretical republicans, Harrington's *Oceana*, was reprinted by subscription in Dublin in 1737 and reissued in 1758.

Among those who subscribed to the *Oceana* were several of the presbyterian persuasion. One of the permanent legacies of the war and upheaval of the mid-seventeenth century was the splitting of the Protestant community. Protestants, always a minority, were further weakened by these fractures. Most of the resulting sects had originated in the 1640s and 1650s. The presbyterians, although they built on foundations laid during the early seventeenth-century plantation of Ulster, were replenished thanks to the patronage of the Scottish soldiers serving in the province during the 1640s, then by the support of the Cromwellian authorities, and finally by fresh waves of Scottish immigrants between the 1660s and 1690s. In 1649, the Presbyterians disagreed in their responses to Charles's execution, many abhorring it and condemning the religious pluralism which flourished during the 1650s. Yet, notwithstanding a record of resistance and opposition to the usurping regime, presbyterians in Scotland and Ireland were held responsible for setting in train the events that brought civil war and Charles to the scaffold. Presbyterians in all three kingdoms, dissenting from the re-established episcopacy in 1660, were at variance with the regime over its religious policies. Opposition on these grounds did not mean the rejection of monarchy or indeed of the Stuart monarchy. Moreover, after William and Mary's accession, the Scottish presbyterians were installed as the state church in Scotland. However, this was not their status in Ireland (or England), where they were subjected to the same disabilities as Catholics. Again, the legal penalties put presbyterians in Ireland at odds with the government. Critics contended that the presbyterians' dissatisfaction extended to the institution of monarchy and connected it with a supposed willingness to overthrow Charles I and introduce a republic. Jonathan Swift gave fresh currency to such slurs in the early eighteenth century.[22]

The presbyterians, in public utterances and publications, insisted on their loyalty to the Hanoverians. Yet, especially within the more intellectually curious and adventurous wing of the Irish presbyterians, the presbytery of Antrim, adherents were prepared to engage in cerebral exploration and speculation. Accordingly, republicanism was not ruled out.[23]

Smaller sects that emerged in the 1650s survived. Most drew sustenance from the civilians and soldiers who came to Ireland in the Cromwellian train. Quakers, religious independents, and Baptists lacked the numbers or geographical concentration of the presbyterians. They, too, insisted on their good affection to the incumbent regime. But they also excited suspicions, largely because they appeared to be the spawn of the radicals and revolutionaries of the 1640s.[24] Furthermore, they were members of organizations that embraced all three kingdoms with channels of communication along which other than purely spiritual messages might be transmitted. Moreover, because of the social composition of the sectaries, supported by few gentry, but mostly by traders and the middling and laborious sorts, they suffered a measure of snobbish disdain. Paradoxically, the prominence, notably of Quakers and presbyterians as merchants and manufacturers, could also be envied. A friendly interpretation would praise the Protestant dissenters for introducing greater variegation into Protestant Ireland. Individuals from these communities were conspicuous in charitable and cultural activities, and more generally the groups attached high importance to education. The hostile accused the dissenters of weakening the puny Protestant interest, and keeping alive brands of religious and political radicalism redolent of the Cromwellian era.

CONSEQUENCES

The ideologies which underlay English policies towards Ireland, as well as the practice, alternated between repression and conciliation. Cromwellian rule can readily be fitted into this pattern: the ferocity and horror of war gradually gave way to more settled conditions.[25] Government and administration struggled to maintain the essentials of tax collection and security from external and internal dangers. Alongside these basics were the demands imposed by the confiscations, transplantation to Connacht, and the projected settlement of civilians and demobilized soldiers. A blueprint had certainly been elaborated, but progress towards achieving it on the ground was uneven and generally disappointing. The Cromwellian settlement had not been completed before it was superseded by the Restoration one. In turn, the latter would give way to the Williamite settlement. Flux, both political and cultural, beset the country, reducing the Cromwellian interlude to just that: indecisive rather than formative for centuries to come.

Themes that appeared strongly during the Interregnum were seldom new: the exact relationship—constitutional, fiscal and economic, political and routine—between

Ireland and England. The enforced incorporation of Ireland into the British state, with representation in the Westminster parliament, would not be repeated until 1801. Then, as in 1653, Irish unruliness obliged draconian subjection and the curtailing of Irish independence. However, in the interval between 1661 and 1800, a parliament survived and indeed after 1692 thrived in Dublin. Its membership was confined to Protestants. Its assertiveness was viewed askance in England, where measures were devised to restrict its capacity for independent initiatives. Those running the Protestant kingdom of Ireland chafed and railed against heavy-handed and non-comprehending English behaviour. A fluent rhetoric of Irish patriotism developed, akin to that in other seemingly neglected elements in composite monarchies across Europe.[26] Ironically, some of the stresses were created by the fulfilment (at least partially) of hopes among those charged with the reconstructions of the 1650s. By the mid-eighteenth century, the prediction that the majority in Ireland would abandon Catholicism had not come to pass. However, the island was prospering and relatively stable. Prosperity brought unexpected problems. By the 1740s, taxes, collected with increasing efficiency, exceeded the costs of governing Ireland. English ministers eyed the surplus greedily and schemed to apply it to English purposes. Irish members of parliament insisted that the moneys be retained in Ireland and used there. The Irish view prevailed, but only after bruising struggles.[27]

Similar aggravations arose over the practice, which turned into a habit, of stationing a sizeable part of the army in Ireland and expecting Irish tax-payers to maintain it. Irish Protestants, in the light of the events of the 1640s and 1689–91, recognized that they required an external force to protect them, so were not averse to the presence of British soldiers. What they did object to was the priority given to British and imperial needs, with regiments withdrawn in emergencies and Ireland left with scant defences.

Politics and public controversy centred on such issues. They spoke of more settled conditions but still betrayed both tensions present during the 1640s and 1650s, and the legacy of those decades. Yet the generally unpopular experiment of enforced union of Ireland with Britain was abandoned until 1801. Friction regularly, even routinely, arose over both the mechanics and the nature of Ireland's subordination to England. The erection of a legal Protestant monopoly over office and profitable property furthered during the Interregnum would be completed by the 1690s, and endured until the 1780s. For these reasons it was a formative decade. However, to attribute to Cromwell and his auxiliaries the shaping of a Protestant ascendancy and the degradation of the Catholic Irish is to ignore the numerous precedents and how much successors contributed to the processes. What was guaranteed by the grim events of 1649–53 was that Ireland did not break free of English control, at least not for more than two centuries.

NOTES

1. John Morrill, 'The Drogheda Massacre in Cromwellian Context', in David Edwards, Pádraig Lenihan, and Clodagh Tait (eds.), *Age of Atrocity: Violence and Political Conflict in Early Modern Ireland* (Dublin, 2007), 242–65; Micheál Ó Siochrú, 'Propaganda, Rumour

and Myth: Oliver Cromwell and the Massacre at Drogheda', in Edwards, Lenihan, and Tait (eds.), *Age of Atrocity*, 266–82; Tom Reilly, *Cromwell: An Honourable Enemy* (Dingle, 1999). See chapter by Hirst in this volume.

2. T. C. Barnard, 'Irish Images of Cromwell', in R. C. Richardson (ed.), *Images of Oliver Cromwell: Essays for and by Roger Howell, Jr.* (Manchester, 1993), 180–206; Toby Barnard, 'Cromwell's Irish Reputation', in Jane A. Mills (ed.), *Cromwell's Legacy* (Manchester, 2012), 191–217.

3. John P. Prendergast, *The Cromwellian Settlement of Ireland* (London, 1865); new editions in 1870, 1922, and 1996. See the chapter by Hirst in this volume.

4. Ted McCormick, *William Petty and the Ambitions of Political Arithmetic* (Oxford, 2009), 84–118; William J. Smyth, *Map-Making, Landscapes and Memory: A Geography of Colonial and Early-Modern Ireland, c.1530–1750* (Cork, 2006), 166–97.

5. Karl S. Bottigheimer, *English Money and Irish Land: The 'Adventurers' in the Cromwellian Settlement of Ireland* (Oxford, 1973), 140.

6. See the chapter by Harris in this volume.

7. Joseph Cope, *England and the 1641 Irish Rebellion* (Woodbridge, 2009); Cope, 'Fashioning Victims: Dr Henry Jones and the Plight of Irish Protestants, 1642', *Historical Research*, 74 (2001): 370–91; K. Noonan, '"The cruell pressure of an enraged barbarous people": Irish and English Identity in Seventeenth-Century Policy and Propaganda', *Historical Journal*, 41 (1998): 151–78; Ethan Shagan, 'Constructing Discord: Ideology, Propaganda and English Responses to the Irish Rebellion of 1641', *Journal of British Studies*, 36 (1997): 4–34.

8. John Cunningham, *Conquest and Land in Ireland: The Transplantation to Connacht, 1649–1680* (Woodbridge, 2011), 67–9, 72–3, 97, 104–6; Jane H. Ohlmeyer, *Civil War and Restoration in Three Stuart Kingdoms: The Career of Randall MacDonnell, Marquess of Antrim* (Cambridge, 1993), 240–57.

9. Toby Barnard, *Improving Ireland? Projectors, Prophets and Profiteers, 1641–1786* (Dublin, 2008), 13–40.

10. T. C. Barnard, *Cromwellian Ireland: English Government and Reform in Ireland, 1649–1660* (Oxford, 1975).

11. Toby Barnard, *Making the Grand Figure: Lives and Possessions in Ireland, 1641–1770* (New Haven, 2004).

12. S. J. Connolly, *Religion, Law and Power: The Making of Protestant Ireland, 1660–1760* (Oxford, 1992), 263–313; Ian McBride, *Eighteenth-Century Ireland: The Isle of Slaves* (Dublin, 2009), 194–245; T. P. Power and Kevin Whelan (eds.), *Endurance and Emergence: Catholics in Ireland in the Eighteenth Century* (Dublin, 1990).

13. Jane H. Ohlmeyer, *Making Ireland English: The Irish Aristocracy in the Seventeenth Century* (New Haven, 2012), 280–335.

14. Kevin McKenny, *The Laggan Army in Ireland, 1640–1685* (Dublin, 2005), 160–1; J. G. Simms, *The Williamite Confiscation in Ireland, 1690–1703* (London, 1956), 195.

15. L. M. Cullen, *The Irish Brandy Houses in Eighteenth-Century France* (Dublin, 2000); Nathalie Genet-Rouffiac, *Le grand exil: les Jacobites en France, 1688–1715* (Vincennes, 2007); Mary Ann Lyons and Thomas O'Connor (eds.), *Strangers to Citizens: The Irish in Europe, 1600–1800* (Dublin, 2008); Thomas O'Connor (ed.), *The Irish in Europe, 1580–1815* (Dublin, 2001); Thomas O'Connor and Mary Ann Lyons (eds.), *Irish Communities in Early Modern Europe* (Dublin, 2006); Thomas O'Connor and Mary Ann Lyons (eds.), *Irish Migrants in Europe after Kinsale, 1602–1820* (Dublin, 2003); R. A. Stradling, *The Spanish Monarch and the Irish Mercenaries: The Wild Geese in Spain, 1618–68* (Dublin, 1994).

16. John Bergin, 'The Irish Catholic Interest at the London Inns of Court, 1674–1800', *Eighteenth-Century Ireland*, 24 (2009): 36–61.

17. Toby Barnard, *A New Anatomy of Ireland: The Irish Protestants, 1649–1770* (New Haven, 2003), 177–207; Charles Ivar McGrath, *Ireland and Empire, 1692–1770* (London, 2012), 69–166.

18. T. C. Barnard, 'The Uses of 23 October 1641 and Irish Protestant Celebrations', *English Historical Review*, 106 (1991): 889–920, reprinted in Barnard, *Irish Protestant Ascents and Descents* (Dublin, 2004), 111–42; Thomas P. Power, 'Publishing and Sectarian Tension in South Munster in the 1760s', *Eighteenth-Century Ireland*, 19 (2004): 75–110.

19. Barnard, *A New Anatomy of Ireland*, 30; Elizabeth Bowen, *Bowen's Court* (London, New York, and Toronto, 1942), 52–65; Dorothea Townshend and Richard Townshend (eds.), *An Officer of the Long Parliament and his Descendants* (London, 1902), viii–ix.

20. J. R. Hill, 'National Festivals, the State and "Protestant Ascendancy" in Ireland', *Irish Historical Studies*, 24 (1984–5): 30–51; James Kelly, '"The glorious and immortal memory": Commemoration and Protestant Identity in Ireland', *Proceedings of the Royal Irish Academy*, 94, sect. C (1994): 25–52; J. G. Simms, 'Remembering 1690', *Studies*, 63 (1974): 231–42.

21. Jonah Barrington, *Recollections* (Dublin, Cork, and Belfast, n.d.), 8–9.

22. S. J. Connolly, 'Swift and History', in Hermann J. Real (ed.), *Reading Swift: Papers from the Fifth Münster Symposium on Jonathan Swift* (München, 2008), 187–202; Christopher Fox, 'Swift's Scotophobia', *Bullán*, 6.2 (2002): 43–65.

23. I. R. McBride, *Scripture Politics: Ulster Presbyterians and Irish Radicalism in the Late Eighteenth Century* (Oxford, 1998).

24. Richard L. Greaves, *God's Other Children: Nonconformists and the Emergence of Denominational Churches in Ireland, 1660–1700* (Stanford, 1997); Phil Kilroy, *Protestant Dissent and Controversy in Ireland, 1660–1714* (Cork, 1994).

25. See the chapter by Hirst in this volume.

26. D. W. Hayton, *The Anglo-Irish Experience, 1680–1730* (Woodbridge, 2012); Hayton, *Ruling Ireland, 1685–1742* (Woodbridge, 2004); Hayton (ed.), *The Irish Parliament in the Eighteenth Century: The Long Apprenticeship* (Edinburgh, 2001); J. R. Hill, *From Patriots to Unionists* (Oxford, 1997); Joep Theodoor Leerssen, 'Anglo-Irish Patriotism and its Irish Context', *Eighteenth-Century Ireland*, 3 (1988): 7–24.

27. Eoin Magennis, 'Coal, Corn and Canals: The Dispersal of Public Moneys, 1695–1772', in Hayton (ed.), *The Irish Parliament*, 71–86; Eoin Magennis, *The Irish Political System, 1740–1765* (Dublin, 2000); A. P. W. Malcomson, *Nathaniel Clements: Government and the Governing Elite in Ireland, 1725–75* (Dublin, 2005); McGrath, *Ireland and Empire*, 167–79.

FURTHER READING

Barnard, T. C., *Cromwellian Ireland: English Government and Reform in Ireland, 1649–1660* (Oxford, 1975, repr. 2000).

Barnard, Toby, 'Cromwell's Irish Reputation', in Jane A. Mills (ed.), *Cromwell's Legacy* (Manchester, 2012), 191–217.

Barnard, T. C., 'Irish Images of Cromwell', in R. C. Richardson (ed.), *Images of Oliver Cromwell: Essays for and by Roger Howell, Jr.* (Manchester, 1993), 180–206.

Bottigheimer, Karl S., *English Money and Irish Land: The 'Adventurers' in the Cromwellian Settlement of Ireland* (Oxford, 1973).

Cunningham, John, *Conquest and Land in Ireland: The Transplantation to Connacht, 1649–1680* (Woodbridge, 2011).

Darcy, Eamon, *The Irish Rebellion of 1641 and the Wars of the Three Kingdoms* (Woodbridge, 2013).

Little, Patrick, *Lord Broghill and the Cromwellian Union with Ireland and Scotland* (Woodbridge, 2004).

Morrill, John, 'The Drogheda Massacre in Cromwellian Context', in David Edwards, Pádraig Lenihan, and Clodagh Tait (eds.), *Age of Atrocity: Violence and Political Conflict in Early Modern Ireland* (Dublin, 2007), 242–265.

Ohlmeyer, Jane H. and Micheál Ó Siochrú (eds.), *Ireland 1641: Contexts and Reactions* (Manchester, 2013).

Ó Siochrú, Micheál, 'Propaganda, Rumour and Myth: Oliver Cromwell and the Massacre at Drogheda', in David Edwards, Pádraig Lenihan, and Clodagh Tait (eds.), *Age of Atrocity: Violence and Political Conflict in Early Modern Ireland* (Dublin, 2007), 266–282.

Prendergast, John P., *The Cromwellian Settlement of Ireland* (London, 1865); new editions in 1870, 1922, and 1996.

Reilly, Tom, *Cromwell: An Honourable Enemy* (Dingle, 1999).

Smyth, William J., *Map-Making, Landscapes and Memory: A Geography of Colonial and Early-Modern Ireland, c.1530–1750* (Cork, 2006).

PART IV

PARTIES, IDEAS,
AND PEOPLE

CHAPTER 23

....

THE PERSISTENCE OF
ROYALISM

....

ALAN CROMARTIE

THE royalists were a party that was called into existence by Charles I's decision to resort to violence. By going to war in England in 1642, he created a distinctive kind of person that friends called 'loyal' and enemies 'malignant', and that ultimately accepted the label 'cavalier'; in choosing to fight, he gave shape to new political alignments, and crystallized a party—and an identity—that proved remarkably resilient.

In the end, that party won. The supporters Charles attracted in 1642 had one or both of two specific objectives: in the secular sphere, they wished to preserve the king's constitutional status in the form that it existed in late 1641; in the religious sphere, they were defenders of the organizational structure, liturgy, and property of an episcopalian Church of England. In both spheres, their explicit starting point was a rejection of the 1630s. They welcomed limitations on English monarchy that Charles had only recently accepted: the statutory provision for regular parliaments; the Act pronouncing Ship Money illegal; the abolition of such institutions as the Court of Star Chamber, the Forest Courts, and the Councils of the North and of the Marches. In religion, they presented themselves as moderate and mildly old-fashioned; they wished to uphold the 'protestant' (that is, in this context, 'non-puritan') religion of the Elizabethan and Jacobean church. In consequence, they were careful to dissociate themselves from Laudian ceremonial innovations and Laudian misuse of clerical power. In the course of the next twenty years, they barely altered these objectives; by 1662, they had gained a total victory.

A freely elected parliament with natural cavalier majorities restored the bishops to the House of Lords, affirmed the basic principle of personal monarchical control of the militia, and forced the clergy of the Church of England to 'assent and consent' to the Book of Common Prayer. There was no attempt, however, to turn the clock back further than 1641; the status quo that was restored excluded Star Chamber, the Forest Courts, the Court of High Commission, and most of the pre-war powers of the Council of the Marches (the Council of the North, which did fully revive, appears to have done so in response to regional demand). An Act of Parliament reaffirmed the illegality of Ship Money. It might have been expected that all this would be portrayed as an inevitable development: a reassertion of traditional order that followed the delayed but still predictable collapse of an un-English kind of innovation. But the dominant tone of reactions was rather different: the cavaliers themselves chose to regard the Restoration as an unlooked-for providential mercy.

The text that best exemplified this picture of events, Clarendon's *History of the Rebellion*, set out (in a passage written in 1646) to preserve 'the memory of those few who, out of duty and conscience, have opposed and resisted that torrent which hath overwhelmed them'. Though the concatenation of disasters gave unmistakable signs of 'the immediate finger and wrath of God', a diligent observer would find 'all this bulk of misery to have proceeded . . . from the same natural causes and means that have usually attended kingdoms swollen with long plenty, pride, and excess towards some signal mortification and castigation of heaven'. In practice, this meant that Clarendon was principally concerned with moral characteristics of individuals 'like so many atoms contributing jointly to this mass of confusion'. As his revealing simile suggested, his *History* was the analogue of the Christian atomism that was soon to become attractive to English scientists: the finger of God was detected in the emergence of a pattern from myriad chaotic interactions. Under the circumstances of 1646, he found this view of history consoling: precisely because the course of events was too complex for their eventual outcome to be foreseeable, it was possible that 'we may not find the cure so desperate, but that, by God's mercy, the wounds may be again bound up, though no question many must first bleed to death'. In the end, of course, his pious hope was largely vindicated; the *History*'s final paragraph (written in 1670) deliberately echoes this passage.[1]

He had good political reasons for his edifying stance; as we shall see, his providentialism helped justify the strategy that he and his immediate allies favoured. But he had still identified an interesting puzzle. It is not hard to find reasons why monarchy survived; all parties took it for granted that the general population preferred some form of royal government. But few expected the return of the king's legitimate heir on terms that met the basic aspirations of his long-standing cavalier supporters. The royalism invented in 1642 was not, in the end, much eroded by military defeat; the identity it offered could reproduce itself among the gentry and the graduate clergy. In the absence of a social revolution, these groups continued to be influential. In consequence, the cavaliers were never marginal; as the more acute republicans detected, they had established a strong claim on certain powerful values—'honour', 'civility', 'learning', and even 'liberty'—that played an indispensable role in the self-understanding of those who remained the country's natural rulers. This chapter will sketch out some reasons for their resilience.

ROYALISM AND THE ENGLISH CONSTITUTION

The natural place to start is with the person of the king to whose unusual character all parties were reacting. Charles Stuart was a small man, with a small man's upright bearing and a speech impediment. Unlike his quick-witted, gregarious, hard-drinking father, he organized around himself a relatively staid court in which he was protected from informal interaction. In many respects, this worked well, not least in maximizing the emotional effect of his occasional acts of condescension. But the opaqueness of the royal persona created the false impression that he was malleable.

As late as 1648, those who dealt with Charles at Newport appear to have been surprised that he could handle the negotiations (as at his trial, he was forced to act as his own spokesman). In a revealing comment, the Earl of Salisbury remarked that 'the king is wonderfully improved' (the royalist Sir Philip Warwick loyally replied 'no, my Lord, he was always so, but your Lordship too late discerned it').[2] Salisbury's patronizing view was probably quite common. Throughout the early period of the Long Parliament, the natural diagnosis of what was going wrong was that a personally weak king of a familiar type was listening to the wrong kind of adviser. The opposition did not mean—and were not accused of meaning—to threaten the king with death or deposition; their low estimate of Charles's independence fitted easily into a pattern of political ideas that actually precluded such solutions. The Caroline regime's most dedicated enemies were certain that the country faced a *systematic* problem that could be summarized as 'popery'; the idea that the nation's troubles were a coherent whole was central to the narrative of recent history of which John Pym was such a persuasive exponent. But popery had been understood for several generations as being, in its essence, a threat to monarchy. In consequence, resistance to popish novelties was also a defence of English kingship.

The monarchist assumptions of most opposition thought are evident from the so-called Protestation (1641) through which the vast majority of Protestant adult males undertook to 'maintain and defend . . . the true reformed religion expressed in the doctrine of the Church of England, against all popery and popish innovation within this realm, contrary to the said doctrine, and according to the duty of my allegiance to his Majesty's royal person, honour and estate'; as the rather tortured wording seemed designed to emphasize, defence of true religion and the person of the king were virtually inextricably tangled. The apprentices who wore the Protestation in their hats when they were shouting for the death of Strafford were digging themselves into an ideological hole. In 1643, they were to dig themselves still deeper by their subscription to the Covenant 'to preserve and defend the king's Majesty's person and authority, in the preservation and defence of the true religion and liberties of the kingdoms, that the world may bear witness with our consciences of our loyalty'.[3] At the heart, then, of the moderate parliamentarian position was an entrenched commitment to English monarchy; resistance to Charles Stuart was empowered and constrained by the emotional potency of kingship.

In consequence, the main purpose of the Nineteen Propositions (June 1642), the Houses' most important summary of their demands, was to compel the king to act through a reconstituted privy council that would be answerable to parliament; the most appropriate remedy for an ill-counselled king was a renewed conciliar apparatus. They did not, strictly speaking, aspire to sovereignty: their claim was 'that in this case of extreme danger, and of his Majesty's refusal, the ordinance agreed on by both Houses for the Militia, doth oblige the people and ought to be obeyed by the fundamental laws';[4]

the authority of the Houses rested on their capacity, considered as a court, to interpret the existing law of England, blended with their capacity, considered as a council, to substitute their policies for his own. Thus parliamentarianism was not a dilute version of republicanism, but an ad hoc response to the extraordinary problems created by a plainly inadequate monarch. Even in 1646, when the Houses thought (quite wrongly) that they had Charles at their mercy, the utmost that they asked for was that they control the militia for the next twenty years (in other words, up to the end of his probable lifetime).

In other words, the case to which the royalists reacted was an interpretation of English monarchy that emphasized the role of courts and councils. At the rather abstract level we are concerned with here, it followed that the central task of royalist polemic was to reassert an ethic of *personal* loyalty, preferably in the context of a wider theory in which it was the royalists who stood for legal values. In the first half of 1642, the king's principal advisers—Sir Edward Hyde, Viscount Falkland, and Sir John Culpeper—profited from their own pasts as critics of the court to work out a position that appealed to the 'known laws' and redescribed the king as the essential guarantor of individual private liberties. Falkland and Culpeper composed the *Answer to the Nineteen Propositions*, which drew a detailed picture of the English constitution as an idealized mixed monarchy in which 'the balance hangs even between the three Estates'. Within this constitution, the House of Commons existed in order to secure the 'good of democracy', which is 'liberty, and the courage and industry which liberty begets', but was utterly excluded from actual 'government'.[5] The ideal they asserted was a dynamic tension between an irreducibly personal kingship and the influence of the other two estates: the point of the concession that the king was an 'estate' was to stop the Houses claiming that his personal contribution was in the last analysis an inessential part of fully parliamentary decisions.

It has often been held that the *Answer* was a serious mistake: that in making this concession the royalists laid themselves open to counter-arguments about the possibility of 'co-ordinate' monarchy: if the King and the Houses were partners, and the partners disagreed, the Houses were entitled to resort to violence. But though such arguments were made (most notably, perhaps, by Philip Hunton),[6] they represented a strategic error. The original parliamentarian position had as it were dissolved the king within the legal system: it pitted the king's impersonal will as-interpreted-by-courts against the whims of fallible Charles Stuart. Those who heeded the call of the latter were a gang of criminals who could indeed be characterized as traitors. The modified position was subtly different: it accepted that the Houses were waging war *against* their lawful monarch: it played into the hands of royalist writers who were engaged in altering the subject of discussion from the nature of the country's constitution (a matter for historians and lawyers) to the legitimacy of rebellion (a matter for divines).

The nub of this royalist case was adequately summarized in the title of an influential pamphlet by Henry Ferne, Vice-Chancellor of Cambridge: *The resolving of conscience upon this question, whether upon such a supposition or case as is now usually made (the king will not discharge his trust but is bent or seduced to subvert religion, laws and liberties) subjects may take arms and resist? And whether that case is now?* (Cambridge, 1642).

This artfully begged the question of whether the Houses were in fact 'resisting', and whether their motives for doing so were religious; it shifted the debate onto some intellectual ground with which the royalist spokesmen were familiar. As the historian Tom May complained, 'they make it the question, whether subjects, taken in a general notion, may make war against their king for religion's sake'.[7] It was of course particularly likely that self-consciously puritan writers would fall into the trap of reaching for the Calvinist defences of rebellion. In doing so, they reinforced the impression that parliamentarianism was the religious cause of a discrete minority tradition.

As the debate developed, then, its focus subtly changed in ways that had a tendency to favour royalists. But the focus on the casuistic problem of whether a rebellion could be permissible did not prevent them using other lines of argument. They treated violations of Charles's personal rights (his ownership, for instance, of the country's armaments) as a disturbing threat to legal order. They also pointed out the fairly obvious parallel between the alleged emergency that justified the crown's Ship Money levies and the alleged emergency that justified the Houses' Militia Ordinance. The great advantage of these arguments was that they were available to royalists of all stripes. Even those who took a high view of the king's prerogative could after all take relish in *ad hominem* attacks on the hypocrisies of their opponents, who had (to quote a typical formulation) 'transformed this free kingdom into a large gaol, to *keep the Liberty of the Subject*'.[8] Fluent manipulation of this kind of rhetoric was perfectly compatible with being 'absolutist' (in the sense of allowing the monarch a discretionary power to override the privileges of subjects). The king himself was fond of a tag from Claudian (which he may have picked up from Sir Robert Filmer) to the effect that liberty is best enjoyed under the rule of a good monarch.[9] His thorough internalization of this royalist commonplace made possible his brilliant self-presentation when he was ultimately put on trial, when his repeated claims to stand for 'the liberties of the subject' culminated in his devastating final accusation: 'I am not suffered for to speak, expect what justice other people will have.'[10]

ROYALISM AND RELIGION

Successful internalization of the secular ideal of the defence of English liberties was central to the royalist achievement. But it is unintelligible in isolation from the larger process by which conservative worries about godly radicalism became a self-fulfilling prophecy. The process was much hastened by the availability of rival caricatures that each side sought to pin on its opponents. The consistently worse behaviour of royalist soldiers made it quite easy to present their movement as no more than an outbreak of simple lawlessness to be expected of a 'cavalier' (a term with unattractive connotations deriving from the Spanish *caballero*). An influential pamphlet of 1643 bore the descriptive title *Anti-Cavalierisme*.[11] But the royalists had the resources with which they could develop a counter-caricature. Pamphlets purporting to describe the characteristics of the ultra-godly—already quite often identified as 'roundheads'—were also readily available. In other words, the images of cavalier and roundhead owed little to the civil war experience; in most essentials, they predated it.

In the course of time, however, the royalists proved better at exploiting this recognized contrast. Precisely because the cavalier was an inverted roundhead, the term could be made the vessel of every social value that puritanism was believed to threaten. A witty pre-war pamphlet—*The resolution of the Roundheads: being a zealous declaration of the grievances wherewith their little wits are consumed to destruction* (1642)—suggests the possibilities of this kind of polemical inversion. In an inventively amusing swipe at puritan contempt for the ungodly multitude, the 'Roundheads' were made to complain that 'the multitude, called true protestants, endeavour to . . . maintain good order, discipline, and orthodox preaching in the church, learning in the universities, and peace in the commonwealth'. A less high-minded but equally typical passage demanded 'that no man whatsoever, that bears the name of a cavalier may be capable of making any of the brethren a cuckold unless he cut his hair and alter his profession'.[12]

The evident existence of a market for such pamphlets suggests an important conclusion about English royalism. As this early example suggests, royalist propaganda was entirely capable of packaging 'good order, discipline, and orthodox preaching' with boasts about superior cavalier virility and swipes at the sexual hypocrisy imputed to the roundheads. The readership they presupposed combined a conservative preference for the Church of England's practice with prejudice against the obtrusively godly. It is probably significant that puritan piety was generally thought of as a feminine characteristic; it is obviously important that the cavalier possessed a certain degree of transgressive allure by contrast. Respectable royalists naturally deplored this, but royalist culture was coloured by a certain tolerance for various hyper-masculine excesses. In a sermon deploring the licence that reigned in the royalist camp (complaining, in particular, about the cult of swearing), the famous liberal theologian William Chillingworth referred to 'publicans and sinners on the one side, scribes and pharisees on the other'.[13] But Chillingworth was a fanatical royal supporter, and it was hard to venture any such comparison without some implicit indulgence of the publicans and sinners. By the end of 1644, his fellow clergyman Robert Herrick was acclaiming his virtuous monarch as 'brave prince of cavaliers'.[14]

There was plenty of scope, in other words, for royalism to be populist. The moderate puritan leader Richard Baxter recalled that 'the malignant hatred of seriousness in religion did work so violently in the rabble where I lived [overwhelmingly royalist Worcestershire], that I could not stay at home with any probable safety of my life'. The occasion of the threat was a 'false rumour' that the parish's church wardens intended to obey the House of Commons by taking down 'the images of the Trinity about the church'. This was why Baxter thought that it was not too much to say that 'the war was begun in our streets before the king or parliament had any armies'.[15] It cannot be doubted, however, that the defence of bishops had special appeal for those people who had the most to lose. The pious royalist Sir Henry Slingsby did not suppose that government by bishops was 'of absolute necessity', but was influenced by the reflection that the 'common people' venerate 'long usage' and 'would think themselves loose and absolved from all government when they should see that which they so much venerated so easily subverted'. The less pious Edmund Waller expressed the same idea in a speech about the Root and Branch petition:

> I look upon episcopacy as a counter-scarf or outwork, which if it be taken by this assault of the people, and withal this mystery once revealed, that we must deny them nothing when they ask it thus in troops, we may in the next place have as hard a task to defend our propriety as we have lately had to recover it from the prerogative.[16]

Defence of the church's hierarchy was thus an element of the defence of hierarchy in general; Slingsby and Waller's subsequent careers had rather different trajectories: Slingsby was executed by the Protectoral regime for which Waller was to write a panegyric. But both agreed in making the future of the church the focus of their worries about the gentry's place in what they believed was a fragile social order.

Two years later, Waller made another speech in parliament, this time as the penitent leader of the so-called 'Waller Plot' with other crypto-royalists in London. He cut an undignified figure, but his abject recantation took an interesting form; he had been influenced, he confessed, by 'impatience of the inconveniences of the present war, looking on things with a carnal eye, and not minding that which chiefly (if not only) ought to have been considered, the inestimable value of the cause you have in hand, the cause of God and of religion'.[17] Much depended, of course, on the meaning of 'religion', but Waller's chosen rhetoric revealed beyond reasonable doubt that he was grovelling to puritans (a sensitive listener might have thought that his use of the word 'carnal' came dangerously close to parody). He was tacitly endorsing a royalist account of the two Houses' central motivation.

When sides were being taken, the accuracy of this account had not been obvious; it was something that the royalists had chosen to believe about a fairly complex and ambiguous situation. It was not until September of 1642, as a *result* of the approach of military conflict, that the two Houses finally resolved to change 'the government of the church of England by archbishops, bishops, their chancellors and commissaries ... and other ecclesiastical officers'.[18] But this was in the context of their dealings with the Scots, and their emphasis was plainly on the malign effects of a bloated jurisdictional apparatus. They were equally committed to consulting with divines, and it was not unlikely that the latter would recommend some version of 'reduced' episcopacy.

The radicalizing dynamic that stopped this happening was a consequence of three converging factors. One was the departure from London of those conservatives who were the natural brake on innovation. A second, more unexpected, was the virtually unanimous royalism even of anti-Laudians among the leading clergy. As Sir Philip Warwick noted, both the 'church-puritans' (the group that modern historians call 'Calvinist conformists') and 'the more canonical churchmen ... disclaimed the Reformation projected by our long Lay-Parliament-men and Assembly of Divines ... and were involved without discrimination in the church's misery'.[19] A third was the pressure exerted by the necessity of seeking Scottish military assistance; historians have long noticed that impulses to move towards a presbyterian model were strongest in parliament's phases of military weakness.[20] Together, these encouraged a much more thorough puritanizing programme than moderate observers had expected, involving, amongst other things, the total abolition of any version of set liturgy.

The unprecedented nature of what was happening meant that conservative sentiment about religious questions was one of the royalist cause's greatest assets. But some royalists were Catholics with no particular grounds to favour particular versions of Protestant error. Even among the Protestants, a distinction can be drawn between those ready to sacrifice the church to save the king and those whose commitment to the church was in practice absolute. As his secular-minded advisers Jermyn and Culpeper explained to Charles in 1646, 'the denying or qualification of those [demands] concerning the militia, your honour, and party, is as absolutely necessary to the power and dignity of your majesty and crown as the seasonable granting presbytery is for your preservation'.[21] Royalists of this cast of mind were not necessarily hostile to the institutional church; they took the reasonable view that the bishops' long-term hopes required the survival of a strong monarchy. But the history of their movement has on the whole been written from the implacably opposed perspective of the then Sir Edward Hyde (the future Earl of Clarendon).

Hyde was a close friend of Archbishop Laud's (so much so that he took great risks to visit him in prison).[22] He was virtually alone among his lay contemporaries in having sympathy with the view that 'without bishops there could be no ordination of ministers, and consequently no administration of sacraments, or performance of the ministerial functions'.[23] Both he and his close associate Sir Edward Nicholas were noticeably free with the vague label 'atheist' for those who were indifferent to such considerations. In consequence, their invariable tactical advice was that a royal alliance with presbyterians was both unprincipled and counterproductive: agreements with the Scots would undermine the loyalty of the episcopalians in England. There was a great deal to be said for this analysis: while the Stuarts were committed to the interests of the church, they could rely on the substantial body of opinion that was religiously conservative. Whatever their view of the secular points at issue, such people had no other possible ally. This explains why willingness to compromise on matters that affected the king's prerogative was often found in company with strong religious feelings. It is a remarkable triumph of Hyde's literary art that people who were primarily episcopalian diehards are usually described as 'moderates'.

ROYALISM AND ELITE CULTURE

The royalists thus combined a legalistic rhetoric with an appeal to anyone who saw religious value in any of the practices the Prayer Book laid out. Both features of their case had wide appeal; the latter ensured that an influential body of opinion was trapped in royalist intransigence. They also had a third kind of advantage arising from more general cultural developments. The free parliamentary election of 1661 revealed that cavalier values were potentially attractive even to those unwilling to take any real risks to bring about the monarch's restoration. Such values were experienced as a coherent package that offered a comprehensive and adequate response to the emergence of disturbing forces from the middle of the 1640s onwards.

The problem to which they responded was conveniently summed up in one of Oliver Cromwell's best-known speeches: 'it pleased God, much about the midst of this war, to winnow (if I may so say), the forces of this nation; and to put them into the hands of other men of other principles than those that did engage at the first'. The purpose of this winnowing was that God 'might raise up a poor and contemptible company of men . . . even through the owning of a principle of godliness and of religion'.[24] What these outsiders wanted most was 'liberty of conscience' (that is, liberty for those deemed conscience-driven), but they were increasingly capable of finding common ground with anyone who favoured the quite different idea of general religious toleration, including some ex-royalists whose anti-puritanism was anticlerical in character. As Cromwell implied, their irruption into English politics was, if anything, most threatening to 'presbyterians', that is, to those old-fashioned moderates committed to a puritanized but intolerant national church in the political context of a shackled monarchy. It was difficult for such people to criticize 'enthusiasts' to their religious left without echoing the tropes of much royalist writing.

In the later 1640s, the works of William Prynne and Thomas Edwards provide well-known examples of the hysteria with which the presbyterians could view more radical spirits. But a more telling index of shifting attitudes is a sermon preached as early as 1647 to a largely presbyterian House of Commons, and subsequently published with its encouragement. The preacher, Ralph Cudworth, the Master of Christ's College, Cambridge, maintained that *we may safely draw conclusions concerning our state and condition from the conformity of our lives to the will of Christ*. He contrasted the person who built on this 'foundation' with one 'that builds all his comfort upon an ungrounded persuasion, that God from all eternity hath loved him, and absolutely decreed him for life and happiness'.[25] Cudworth's innovative position was to some extent concealed by a veneer of godly-sounding language, but it exactly inverted the usual emphasis of mainstream puritan divinity, in which predestination (when rightly understood) was seen as a legitimate source of comfort, contrasted with the lack of a reliable 'foundation' in anything connected with human agency. In the context of parliament's clash with the New Model Army, an otherwise godly assembly could welcome an attack on the spirit of traditional Calvinism.

This was an early symptom of a momentous shift in gentry values that was to have significant political implications. There had probably long been a certain tension between the modes of feeling and behaviour expected of a puritan 'professor' and those expected of a gentleman; as a glance at their portraits reveals, the aristocratic leaders of the parliamentarian cause were seldom in the narrowest sense roundheads (Lucy Hutchinson's biography of her godly republican husband is at pains to record his refusal to puritanize his hair).[26] But the political triumph of Oliver Cromwell's 'poor and contemptible company of men' coincided with, and arguably hastened, the further marginalization of traditional godliness among the landed and the educated. In the general population, the presbyterians were probably not diminishing in numbers (in London, they were strong enough to capture all four seats even in the elections of 1661), but their religious attitudes and practice were losing contact with elite assumptions, which were coming, to a large extent, to be defined against them. The cavaliers were burdened with no such handicap. They had established and sustained a clear identity that could appear the natural expression of certain kinds of socio-cultural status.

Some parts of this identity were probably counterproductive, at least if they were viewed in isolation. It goes without saying that the royalist gentry believed that their allegiance was the natural result of certain class-specific obligations; conversely, revolution had been the consequence of the reluctance of their fellow-gentry to act in ways appropriate to their station. As late as 1655, a royalist reporting a Cromwellian proclamation that banished known ex-royalists from London maintained, with optimism that verged on fantasy, that 'London is abandoned almost by all the gentry'.[27] Such attitudes had a corollary; if the landed class were at least disposed to be loyal, then they must surely have been overborne by an overwhelming weight of wealth and numbers. As the Marquis of Newcastle asked Charles II, 'what kept up your royal father so long but part of the nobility and gentry … maintaining themselves and his war, almost at their own charge, and held out beyond all expectation?'[28] Clarendon's whole conception of the conflict was dominated by a sense of 'universal apostasy' in which 'the poor people' were 'furiously hurried into actions introducing atheism'.[29] On this view, royalism was the cause of an upper-class remnant, displaying the gentleman's virtue of personal loyalty, in the face of mass political derangement.

Such royalists had what might be called a minoritarian mindset. When they were pessimistic, they simply ignored the existence of popular royalism; when they were optimistic, this was in part a function of an over-estimate of their own personal influence on their inferiors. As Clarendon himself recalled, 'the party in all places which wished well to the king, which consisted of most of the gentry in most counties … had so good an opinion of their own reputation and interest that they believed they were able, upon the assistance of few troops, to suppress their neighbours who were of the other party'.[30] Given these attitudes, there was scope for royalism to dwindle into a marginal phenomenon. The cavalier identity was at once too weak and too strong. It was too weak to mobilize a military force that posed a threat to the New Model Army; it was too strong for cavaliers to build a coalition combining the full strength of the original royalist party with Scots or English presbyterians. Clarendon's treatment of the fate of the London presbyterian Christopher Love (executed in 1651 for conspiring with the Scots) is notable for expressing a detached astonishment at the bizarreness of the latter's motives.[31] Much later in the decade, when the fall of Richard Cromwell unexpectedly revived the royalists' chances, it seems to have been cavalier rigidity and suspicion that doomed the prospect of collaboration. The government double-agent Sir Richard Willis was able to discourage a complicated scheme when he 'decried the undertaking as totally presbyterian'.[32] From the exiled Stuarts' perspective, it might have been no bad thing if such an allegation had been strictly accurate; the only royalist rising of 1659 that actually assembled a small army was Sir George Booth's presbyterian rebellion.

It was unlikely, then, that the cavalier party would ever have been able to fight its way back into power. But while they were enduring short-term military failure, they were laying the foundations of electoral success. The implicit claim of a wide range of royalist publications was that it was cavalier values that were most compatible with numerous established practices. In some spheres, and in some respects, their enemies made their task easy: the puritans had not only closed the theatres, but abdicated any claim on the associated literature. In the first civil war, when the journalist Marchamont Nedham was writing parliamentarian propaganda, he was scornful about 'Shakespeare's works and such prelatical trash'; when he became a royalist, his new affiliation involved him in reversing this opinion.[33] Both sides thus agreed that the reading of plays was a consciously royalist practice; parliament had created the opportunity of a new kind of cultural consumption involving the self-conscious cultivation of an implicitly political taste. But cavalier writers and printers took steps to help themselves: they sustained the idea of a package of cultural attitudes of which political action to help the exiled Stuarts was an entirely natural expression. When the royalist bookseller Humphrey Moseley, purveyor (to borrow a useful phrase) of 'subversion for the polite reader',[34] published Andrewes's *Private devotions* (1647) or Sir John Denham's royalist poem *Cooper's Hill* (1650) or *A censure of the presbyterian censures* (1658), he was obviously contributing to this package. But the same could be said of the cynically titillating stories of *Choice novels and amarous tales written by the most refined wits of Italy* (1652), whose only royalist feature was that they instructed their readers in the ways of 'cavaliers'.

The interest of someone like Moseley, for present purposes, is that he was a conscious cultural warrior who lost no opportunity for subtle politicization of the high-status products in which he specialized. When he published Waller's *Poems* (1645), for example, he took the opportunity to add the poet's ambiguous recantation, and gave some prominence on the title page to the boast that the poems had been set by 'Mr Henry Lawes, Gent, of the King's Chapel, and one of his Majesties Private Music' (and also, by this stage, a dedicated cavalier). Moseley did the same again (in the same words) on the main title pages of Sir John Suckling's *Fragmenta aurea* (1646), the first post-war edition of the *Poems* of Thomas Carew (1651), and even, astonishingly, *The poems of Mr John Milton, both Latin and English* (1645).

As Milton too was plainly a self-conscious operator, it is a sensitive index of the balance of cultural forces that he was ready to accept this treatment. In February next year (that is, before the fighting ended), he wrote the well-known sonnet ('Harry whose tuneful and well-measured song') that celebrates Lawes's complementary talent. Moreover, his poem was printed in yet another Moseley publication, *Choice Psalmes ... with divers elegies upon the death of William Lawes* (1648), in spite of the fact that the latter was a memorial volume for Henry's brother William, a cavalier who had been killed in battle. Nor was this the end of the story. Milton once again offered his sonnet as a prefatory poem to the next of the composer's publications: the first of the three sets of *Choice ayres and dialogues* (1653, 1655, 1658) put out by Moseley's analogue in music publishing, the printer and ex-cavalier John Playford. In a rather similar gesture, the republican James Harrington contributed two 'dialogues' to the second (1655).[35] But all three were plainly intended for a cavalier readership. The 'Catalogue of music books' with which the third concludes adds a list of 'other books sold at the same place worth buying'. It was headed by a volume of last speeches of royalist martyrs.[36] In asserting his credentials as an artist, even the author of *Eikonoklastes* was ready, on occasion, to enter a cavalier world on cavalier terms.

The extreme case of Milton and Lawes was the most striking symptom of an asymmetry that dogged most efforts at conciliation. It was conventional wisdom that the Republic needed to broaden its appeal. The people best placed to assist were men of anticlerical or heterodox views whose greatest political fear was presbyterian dominance. But people of this sort had very little interest in making puritans less marginal. The greatest of them, Harrington, was so far from believing that the cavaliers were wicked that his most important practical objective was their reintegration into structures so robust that their opinions would no longer matter; conversely, he maintained that 'they of all the rest are the most dangerous who, holding that the saints must govern, go about to reduce the commonwealth unto a party'.[37] The cavaliers were misguided, but the true political threat derived from ultra-puritan extremists.

Nowhere was this perception more widely held and practically important than in the field of academic 'learning'. As we have seen, those moderates who opposed Archbishop Laud—the group Sir Edward Walker had called 'church-puritans'—had plumped, in general, for royalism. As a parliamentarian noted in the first months of the war, the upshot was that 'scholars are not active on both sides alike' and that royalists had access to a somewhat richer pool of literary and intellectual talent: 'though too many papers are scattered of both sides, yet those of the king's are most of them serious, and done by able men'.[38] Whatever the truth of this judgement, it was certainly the case that both the universities were largely royalist. Cambridge's geographical location in parliamentarian East Anglia made its political sympathies particularly striking. Though many of its leaders had been church-puritans, the university made a real effort (frustrated, as it happens, by Oliver Cromwell) to send the colleges' plate to the king's army. The university printer was later to publish Ferne's *The resolving of conscience* (1642) and several wartime royal declarations.

Even after 1646, both institutions were recalcitrant. The Oxford Convocation produced a succinct restatement of its corporate attitude, *The reasons of the present judgement of the University of Oxford* (Oxford, 1647), that yielded no ground on any question. Cambridge had no equivalent (though something similar was at one stage mooted),[39] but royalist opinions continued to be usual. The group of younger Cambridge academics who produced the tract *Querela Cantabrigiensis* (1647) referred contemptuously to 'so senseless a rebellion cried up only by the illiterate herd'.[40] The republican John Hall of Durham, who attended St John's College, Cambridge and disliked it, paints an entertaining picture of named reactionaries compulsively consuming royalist newsbooks.[41]

Needless to say, this was a serious matter. If student numbers are a guide, the country's universities had never been more influential; despite the reduced attractions of a clerical career, recruitment in the 1650s was only a little below its pre-war levels.[42] Proposals for reform were a backhanded compliment to the importance of their social function. It was therefore quite alarming that Oxford had a thriving Prayer Book conventicle, which met in the house of the cleverest of a new generation of innovative medical researchers. At Cambridge, 'the general outcry was that the whole University was over-run with Arminianism, and was full of men of a prelatical spirit'.[43] Among those Oxford students who later became MPs, 'the products of the Laudian and of the Restoration university were more likely to be whig than tory: those of Cromwellian Oxford were more likely to be tory than whig'.[44] External intervention could weed out cavaliers by raising barriers to the conscientious, but only at a certain cost to 'learning'. Hall admitted that the imposition of the Covenant 'removed many persons of a more thriving and consistent growth in learning, than it either left there, or planted in their steads'.[45] Though Cromwell entertained the hope that 'God hath for the ministry a very great seed in the youth in the universities, who instead of studying books study their hearts',[46] his main academic supporters sought respectability by firm repudiation of this standpoint. When the learned Edward Pococke, Oxford Professor of Arabic, was threatened with losing his living for making use of elements of the old Prayer Book service, his congregationalist Vice-Chancellor set out to rescue him, describing his radical critics, in a revealing phrase, as 'some few men of mean quality and condition, rash, heady, enemies of tithes'.[47] At Cambridge, Antony Tuckney, who ended the period as Master of royalist St John's, was a figure of impeccably godly credentials, including personal links with Massachusetts. He nonetheless selected fellows for their 'scholarship', on the grounds that 'they may deceive me in their godliness; they cannot in their scholarship'.[48]

The result of commitment to 'learning' was that the universities were never puritanized. There were ways of being 'learned' without favouring the bishops, but episcopalianism continued to be seen as an intellectual option that an otherwise virtuous person might find defensible. Even before the king's return, Richard Baxter was producing polemical writings that presupposed that 'episcopal men' were ineradicable.[49] Between 1646 and 1660, around 2,500 of the clergy made the illegal gesture of seeking out episcopal ordination (in other words, episcopal ordination continued to run at more than half its usual pre-war level).[50] Such people necessarily preferred a kind of church that only Charles II could deliver. From a puritan perspective, Tuckney's enlightened policy of favouring 'scholarship' turned out to be disastrously counterproductive. With one possible exception, no fellow of St John's opposed the Restoration Church of England; twenty-four of them denounced him, in 1661, for absenting himself from Chapel to avoid the Prayer Book service.[51]

THE PERSISTENCE OF ROYALISM

The most remarkable feature of the Interregnum years is that the cavalier package was never marginalized; it was a continuing option within what continued to count as the cultural mainstream. The cavalier gentry as a class were never threatened with annihilation or even with protracted persecution. When they compounded to retrieve their forfeited estates, they were not asked to disavow their former principles, but only to swear the 'negative oath' that they would not rebel again in future. In February 1652, the Rump passed an Act of Oblivion that covered royalist activities down to the date of Charles's execution. Under this legislation, those royalists who had taken the Engagement (that is, who had 'declared and promised to be true and faithful to the commonwealth of England ... without a king and a House of Lords') were legally secure from any future punishment. The abortive royalist risings of 1655 led Cromwell to ignore the law by levying the discriminatory decimation tax, but the angry parliamentary reaction showed that even an assembly excluding royalists favoured conciliation at almost any cost. In the debates surrounding this unpopular policy, no one disputed that 'the cavaliers' continued to be a readily identifiable grouping and that their children generally shared their attitudes.

In the last months of Oliver's life, the regime was divided about the way ahead, but there was a consensus that a tax on cavaliers 'will [not] be swallowed by the parliament, who will not be persuaded to punish both nocent and innocent without distinction'. The Protector's shrewd son Henry shared this feeling, adding that it was foolish 'to provoke and necessitate to a perpetual enmity such in whose hand you leave power enough to destroy you'. He also remarked that 'I suppose the most considerable party of the late king's interest are the sons of such cavaliers as are now dead, or of such as have formerly been of your party; and by your narrowness not obliged, or thrust or kept out from a compliance with you'.[52] In other words, he diagnosed a form of 'narrowness' that sons of *parliamentarians* found off-putting.

In such a situation, the true threat to cavaliers was not so much a cultural or social transformation as an appropriation of their values. For a brief period, this seemed possible. From the moment at which Cromwell accepted power as a 'single person' (December 1653), his government could be seen as an effective restoration of basically monarchical arrangements. As Waller's *Panegyrick* (1655) was eager to explain, the 'only cure' for the nation's political troubles was 'so much power and clemency in one. / One, whose extraction from an ancient line / Gives hope again that well-born men may shine'.[53] This hope proved, in the end, to be well-founded: by the time of Oliver's death the Protectorate was delivering an ever-increasing proportion of the things that a conservative gentleman valued; conversely, it encouraged its more radical opponents in their own self-defeatingly minoritarian mindset, especially in a resentful self-description as the survivors of an 'honest party' that was committed to a 'good old cause'. Such opponents had good reason for suspicion: the Protector was creating peers, knights, and baronets, enforcing collection of tithes, and backing down from his attempts to change the legal system. A symbolic culmination of the process was the permission given to Sir William Davenant—poet, cavalier, close friend of Thomas Hobbes, and natural son (it was rumoured) of William Shakespeare—to re-open what amounted to a theatre. By the end of the Protectoral period, the Cromwells could even inspire a kind of monarchism that borrowed from its cavalier precursor. Andrew Marvell could grumble that 'commonwealthsmen' in the House of Commons were doing their best to cripple Richard Cromwell: 'they pretend that they are for a single person and this single person but without negative voice without militia'.[54] Only the Protector's surname distinguished this position from the political stance for which some cavaliers had long been fighting.

In the end, of course, the monarchist lurch proved unsustainable; the military republicans lost patience. But the Cromwellian episode was indirectly crucial to shaping the surprising political settlement whose features were described at the start of this chapter. In the dark days of the later 1650s, the royalists who kept the faith were the 'old cavaliers'—that is, the constitutionalist episcopalians: the Henry Slingsbys, not the Edmund Wallers. In the early Restoration, such people drew much strength from their consistency in loyalty: they were the hegemonic group within what had emerged as the politically dominant party. They could embarrass Charles II by pressing, with success, for a more rigid national church that had the effect of excluding most 'presbyterians'. In this and in other respects, their class-specific interests were frequently in tension with their sovereign's. As early as 1663, a promising proposal for additional revenue was defeated 'by the industry of those who have more earnestly put his Majesty upon the persecution of dissenters'. In the later 1660s, this persecution was itself experienced as a duty, enforced by a kind of reactionary political correctness: 'being suitable to the interest of the cavalier party (in which most of them, or their ancestors, have been engaged) and conformable to the former actings of the house, they knew not how in decency to appear against it if set afoot'.[55] Their history had equipped them with an ideology—libertarian, resentfully class-conscious, vindictive to 'fanatics', and protective of the church—that was to cause much trouble for the later Stuart kings to whom they fully intended to be loyal.

NOTES

1. Edward Hyde, Earl of Clarendon, *The History of the rebellion and civil wars in England*, ed. W. D. Macray, 6 vols. (Oxford, 1888), Book I, paragraphs 1–4; Book XVI, paragraph 247.
2. Sir Philip Warwick, *Memoires of the reign of King Charles I* (London, 1701), 324; for a similar but independent story, see Sir Edward Walker, *Historical discourses upon several occasions* (London, 1705), 319.
3. J. P. Kenyon, *The Stuart Constitution, 1603–1688: Documents and Commentary* (Cambridge, 1986), 200–1, 240–241.
4. Edward Husbands, *An exact collection* (London, 1643), 112.
5. Husbands, *An exact collection*, 320–1.
6. Philip Hunton, *A treatise of monarchie* (London, 1643).
7. Thomas May, *The history of the parliament of England* (London, 1647), 117–18.
8. *Querela Cantabrigiensis* (1647), 27.
9. Warwick, *Memoires*, 328; Sir Robert Filmer, *Patriarcha and Other Writings*, ed. Johann Sommerville (Cambridge, 1991), 69, 131.
10. *King Charls his tryal at the high court of justice* (London, 1649), 37–8, 46–7, 73.
11. John Goodwin, *Anticavalierisme* (London, 1643).
12. *The resolution of the roundheads* (1642), sig. A2, A3v.
13. William Chillingworth, *A sermon preached at the publike fast* (Oxford, 1644), 13.

14. Robert Herrick, *Hesperides* (London, 1648), 24.
15. Richard Baxter, *A holy commonwealth*, ed. William Lamont (Cambridge, 1994), 211.
16. *The Diary of Sir Henry Slingsby* (London, 1836), 68; Edmund Waller, *A speech made by Master Waller Esquire* (London, 1641), 4–5.
17. *Mr Waller's speech in the House of Commons* (London, 1643), 4.
18. *Journals of the House of Commons*, II, 747; *Journals of the House of Lords*, V, 350.
19. Warwick, *Memoires*, 88.
20. W. A. Shaw, *A History of the English Church During the Civil Wars and Under the Commonwealth*, 2 vols. (London, 1900), I, 139–41.
21. *State papers Collected by Edward Earl of Clarendon*, 3 vols. (Oxford, 1767), II, 264.
22. *The Works of the Most Reverend Father in God William Laud*, ed. William Scott and James Bliss, 7 vols. (London, 1847–60), III, 460.
23. Clarendon, *History*, VIII, 228.
24. W. C. Abbott (ed.), *The Writings and Speeches of Oliver Cromwell*, 4 vols. (Oxford, 1945), III, 53.
25. Italicization follows the first edition (Ralph Cudworth, *A sermon preached before the Honourable House of Commons* (Cambridge, 1647), 7–8).
26. Lucy Hutchinson, *Memoirs of the Life of Colonel Hutchinson*, ed. N. H. Keeble (London, 1995), 87.
27. *Correspondence of Sir Edward Nicholas*, ed. G. F. Warner, III, Camden Soc., new series 57 (1897), 25.
28. *Ideology and Politics on the Eve of Restoration: Newcastle's Advice to Charles II*, ed. T. P. Slaughter (Philadelphia, 1984), 46.
29. Clarendon, *History*, I, 1–2.
30. Clarendon, *History*, VIII, 2.
31. Clarendon, *History*, XIII, 118.
32. *The Letter-Book of John Viscount Mordaunt, 1658–1660*, ed. M. Coate, Camden Soc., third series, 69 (1945), 31.
33. Blair Worden, 'The Royalism of Andrew Marvell', in Jason McElligott and David L. Smith (eds.), *Royalists and Royalism During the English Civil Wars* (Cambridge, 2007), 216.
34. The phrase is Lois Potter's: *Secret Rites and Royalist Writing: Royalist Literature, 1641–1660* (Cambridge, 1989), 19: 'Subversion for the polite reader'. For references to the literature on Moseley, see Jason McElligott, *Royalism, Print, and Censorship in Revolutionary England* (Woodbridge, 2007), 217.
35. David Norbrook, *Writing the English Republic: Poetry, Rhetoric and Politics, 1627–1630* (Cambridge, 1999), 159–62, 362–3.
36. *Ayres and dialogues . . . the third book* (London, 1658), sig. Ov.
37. James Harrington, *The commonwealth of Oceana*, ed. J. G. A. Pocock (Cambridge, 1992), 62–3.
38. *Accommodation cordially desired and really intended* (London, 1642), 1, 3.
39. Peter Barwick, *The life of the reverend Dr John Barwick* (London, 1724), 40–1.
40. *Querela Cantabrigiensis*, 2.
41. *Mercurius Britanicus alive again*, no. 1 (16 May 1648) quoted in Norbrook, *Writing*, 176.
42. Victor Morgan and Christopher Brooke, *A History of the University of Cambridge*, II (Cambridge, 2004), 464.
43. S. P., *A brief account of the new sect of latitude-men* (London, 1662), 5.
44. Blair Worden, 'Cromwellian Oxford', in Nicholas Tyacke (ed.), *The History of the University of Oxford*, IV (Oxford, 1997), 762.

45. John Hall, *An humble petition to the parliament of England concerning the advancement of learning* (1649), 5.
46. Abbott, *Writings and Speeches*, IV, 273.
47. Worden, 'Cromwellian Oxford', 751-2.
48. *Eight letters of Dr Antony Tuckney and Dr Benjamin Whichcote*, ed. Samuel Salter (London, 1753), p. xv.
49. Richard Baxter, *Five disputations* (1659).
50. Kenneth Fincham and Stephen Taylor, 'Vital Statistics: Episcopal Ordination and Ordinands in England, 1646–60', *English Historical Review*, 196 (2011), 324.
51. Peter Linehan (ed.), *St John's College, Cambridge: A History* (Woodbridge, 2011), 149.
52. C. H. Firth, *The Last Years of the Protectorate: 1656–58*, 2 vols. (London, 1909), I, 275–6.
53. *A panegyrick to my Lord Protector, by a gentleman that loves the peace, union, and prosperity of the English nation* (London, 1655), 6.
54. *The Poems and Letters of Andrew Marvell*, ed. H. M. Margoliouth, 2 vols., 3rd edn. (Oxford, 1971), II, 307.
55. Paul Seaward, *The Cavalier Parliament and the Reconstruction of the Old Regime, 1661–67* (Cambridge, 198), 116, 67.

FURTHER READING

Clarendon, Edward Hyde, Earl of, *The History of the Rebellion and Civil Wars in England*, 6 vols. (Oxford, 1888).

Corns, Thomas N. (ed.), *The Royal Image: Representations of Charles I* (Cambridge, 1999).

Cromartie, Alan, *The Constitutionalist Revolution: An Essay on the History of England* (Cambridge, 2006).

Cust, Richard, *Charles I: A Political Life* (Harlow, 2007).

Hutton, Ronald, *The Royalist War Effort*, 2nd edn. (London, 1999).

Loxley, James, *Royalism and Poetry in the English Civil Wars: The Drawn Sword* (Basingstoke, 1997).

McElligott, Jason, *Royalism, Print, and Censorship in Revolutionary England* (Woodbridge, 2007).

McElligott, Jason and David L. Smith (eds.), *Royalists and Royalism During the English Civil Wars* (Cambridge, 2007).

McElligott, Jason and David L. Smith (eds.), *Royalists and Royalism During the Interregnum* (Manchester, 2010).

Norbrook, David, *Writing the English Republic: Poetry, Rhetoric and Politics, 1627–1660* (Cambridge, 1999).

Potter, Lois, *Secret Rites and Secret Writing: Royalist Literature, 1641–1661* (Cambridge, 1989).

Seaward, Paul, *The Cavalier Parliament and the Reconstruction of the Old Regime* (Cambridge, 1989).

Sharpe, Kevin, *Image Wars: Promoting Kings and Commonwealths in England, 1603–1660* (New Haven, 2010).

Smith, David L., *Constitutional Royalism and the Search for a Settlement, c.1640–1649* (Cambridge, 1994).

Wormald, B. H. G., *Clarendon: Politics, Historiography and Religion 1640–1660* (Cambridge, 1951).

CHAPTER 24

···

VARIETIES OF
PARLIAMENTARIANISM

···

RACHEL FOXLEY

AMID the bloodshed of the second civil war in 1648, a radical pamphleteer looked back to the mobilization of the opposing armies for war in the early 1640s, and asked his readers:

> was it sufficient thinke you now, that the Parliament invited you at first upon general terms, to fight for the maintenance of the true Protestant Religion, the Liberties of the People, and Privileges of Parliament; when neither themselves knew, for ought is yet seen, nor you, nor any body else, what they meant by the true Protestant Religion, or what the Liberties of the People were, or what those Privileges of Parliament were, for which yet nevertheless thousands of men have been slain, and thousands of Families destroyed?

The writer—probably the Leveller author William Walwyn—read, retrospectively, between the lines of the parliamentarian slogans. In spite of his protestations that nobody knew what these watchwords actually meant, he felt that he and his readers had reasonably interpreted them in particular ways: 'under the notion of religion' parliament must surely have intended the end to all compulsion or persecution in religion; by 'the Liberties of the People' they must have meant the sovereignty of the Commons in parliament, freed from the veto power of king or Lords. Walwyn's confident readings of these slogans are, of course, desperately tendentious; and even he attributed these understandings only to 'many of you that joined with the Parliament'.[1] The breadth and fragmentation of the parliamentarian coalition, its lack of ideological unity, was undeniable. Alongside the war against the king's forces, the parliamentarians were engaged, from 1642 onwards, in a second war: a war of interpretation, in which they struggled among themselves to define the cause for which they fought, and the terms on which they could settle.

The parliamentarian slogans which Walwyn outlined were not only unable to pin down parliament's concrete aims; they did not even serve to distinguish parliamentarians from royalists, who also invoked Protestantism, the liberty of the subject and the privileges of parliament. Indeed, the overlap between the rallying-cries of parliamentarians and royalists was even greater than Walwyn suggests, given that both the Protestation of May 1641 and the Solemn League and Covenant which bound the English parliamentarian cause together with that of the Scottish Covenanters required those who took them to defend the king as well as the true Protestant religion. Walwyn here was perhaps tendentiously referring to one of parliament's more partisan statements of principle, the Vow and Covenant of June 1643, which had controversially omitted the standard parliamentarian piety that parliament was fighting in defence of the king.[2] The parliamentarian party had evolved—in the two Houses, at least—through a process of gradual stages of differentiation within a political nation which had been largely united in opposition to many aspects of royal policy in 1640; a process which historians generally see as the creation of a royalist party from those who were, for various reasons, unwilling to travel further on the path of reform and potential resistance with their former allies. The parliamentarian residue naturally had much in common with the incipient royalists who peeled away from them. But just as political developments gradually sifted royalists from parliamentarians at the outbreak of civil war, so they continued to sift the parliamentarians themselves, both into further parliamentarian factions and tendencies, and, on occasion, into more converts to the king's cause.

MOTIVATIONS

What made a person into a parliamentarian? If we simply mean that a person became aligned with the parliamentarian side—an MP or peer by not leaving parliament to join the king; a gentleman by implementing the Militia Ordinance; a soldier by fighting in the parliamentary armies—then the level of active and chosen commitment to a parliamentarian rather than a royalist 'cause' may have been minimal. Conrad Russell, in a revisionist argument questioning the predictive power of polarization in the parliamentary politics of the 1620s for the eventual taking of sides in the civil war, pointed out that most of those who chose to implement the Militia Ordinance in 1642 became parliamentarians.[3] The competing claims to legality of the king's Commission of Array and the parliament's Militia Ordinance were finely balanced; and the Militia Ordinance, like other parliamentarian statements, claimed to be acting in the king's interests. Perhaps, Russell implied, people could stumble innocently into parliamentarianism with little sense of making a momentous decision about allegiance; a suggestion which the royalist Hyde made of the Earl of Pembroke, who by accepting office from the two Houses in August 1642 'got into actual rebellion, which he never intended to do'.[4] Perhaps; but the agonized pleas of those who hoped to resist the polarization which led to war suggest that such decisions were not taken so innocently. The inhabitants of Cheshire complained in August 1642 that the 'dangerous and disloyal distinccon' between loyalty to the king or to the parliament 'rings twoe lowd in oure eares'.[5] Even if the contours and implications of the developing parliamentarian cause were not entirely clear to those who went along with it, the fact that they had momentous choices to make had become crystal clear by the time Charles I raised his standard at Nottingham.

Those who chose to stand with parliament were united, minimally, by the sense that what had been won from the king in the course of the Long Parliament to date still needed defending, and implicitly by the claim that they were entitled to undertake this defence by raising forces. Distrust of the king was a powerful driver of sustained parliamentarian loyalty, even, potentially, among those who felt that the fall of Laud, Strafford, and others, the Triennial Act, and the renunciation of prerogative courts and non-parliamentary taxation had returned England to its proper equilibrium. The push for further reform in the state and further reformation in the church did not character-ize all parliamentarians; that was why the slogans under which parliament rallied its supporters were so studiously bland.

Distrust was one motivation; but it cannot in itself explain the divergence of those (royalists) who felt that the king had provided enough redress from those (parliamen-tarians) who felt that these gains were not safe. Partly royalists had perhaps discovered greater fears: of popular iconoclasm, for example. Partly, though, the drivers of distrust of the king ran deeper with parliamentarians than with royalists, because they were often locked in to a broader set of beliefs about the meaning of Charles's objectiona-ble policies. These broader beliefs, in the case of many parliamentarians, and often in the case of the most zealous parliamentarians, were beliefs about the struggle between Protestantism and popery. For those who saw the defects of counsel and royal policy as evidence of a popish plot against law and religion, the remedies achieved by the Long Parliament might seem only to relieve the symptoms rather than to secure them against popery for the future.

Who became a parliamentarian, and what kind of parliamentarian he or she became, depended on circumstance and on belief and on motivation. Attempts to find the roots of parliamentarianism by finding criteria which successfully predict or map the distri-bution of parliamentarianism among the political elite or the nation at large have strug-gled to find very significant correlates other than in religion or the culture and politics of religion. Looking at the 1620s, Conrad Russell found that MPs' attitudes to Buckingham did not presage their civil war allegiance, but that hostility to Arminianism, and par-ticularly support of a war against the popish enemy, Spain, did tally significantly with future parliamentarianism.[6] In an influential essay, John Morrill saw attitudes towards the Church of England and further reformation as the key to the divide between royal-ists and parliamentarians, and indeed between the misgivings of more constitutionalist parliamentarians and the urgency of their more 'godly' colleagues.[7] On a larger scale, arguments made by David Underdown about the ecology of allegiance in the civil war have been revised by Mark Stoyle, who has mapped the political allegiances of localities in the civil war onto indicators of their religious culture, finding puritanism a stronger predictor of parliamentarianism in Devon than local or individual opposition to royal policy in the 1620s and beyond.[8]

Some parliamentarians thus understood themselves and the struggle in which they were engaged in strongly religious terms—even if they did not consider it legitimate to wage a 'holy war', they were fighting a war which they hoped God would reward with religious deliverance.[9] The London wood-turner Nehemiah Wallington implored God to 'send help and deliverance to thy distressed children and to prosper they people in battle to the overthrough of thine and our enemies'.[10] He took it for granted that his enemies were God's enemies, and turned his prayers to the external struggle of the civil war as well as to his own internal struggles of faith. The non-combatant Wallington shared his providentialist parliamentarianism with soldiers like Cromwell himself, although they would end up on opposing sides in the religio-political bifurcation of parliamentarianism into 'presbyterian' and 'Independent' later in the 1640s. The protection of true religion and the defence against 'popery' could shape the thought but also motivate and legitimize the actions of parliamentarians of the middling and lower sort, even without explicit parliamentarian authorization, as it did in the case of the 'Colchester Plunderers' of 1642.[11] The mobilizing power of religion—and particularly of anti-popery—enabled a zealous minority to channel a broader Protestant patriotism into the parliamentarian cause.

Religion may have shaped much parliamentarian thought but it was interfused with constitutionalism and other more secular varieties of thought. While some of the most zealous parliamentarians were driven by godly conviction, a circle of radicals around Henry Marten and Thomas Chaloner were noted for their scepticism; Marten himself was (according to Aubrey's *Brief Lives*) 'as far from a Puritane as light from darknesse'.[12] While such scepticism led to a tolerationist position that could place these men alongside other radical parliamentarians who rejected religious coercion, it left no place for the providentialist interrogation of the events of the 1640s which shaped and reinforced the political commitments of many enthusiastic parliamentarians. The secular motivations of such parliamentarians, as well as of more conventionally and moderately religious adherents of parliament, could come to the fore. Here, perhaps, the lawyerly temperament and education of so many gentry and MPs bolstered convictions which could lead men to parliamentarianism, under the aegis of great figures like John Selden and Sir Edward Coke. For many parliamentarians, the force of legalistic arguments about the limits of the king's power was amplified by fears about the future of the church by law established.

Motivation may of course have had other, more circumstantial, elements. Even if 1620s positions cannot be used as a predictor of allegiance in the 1640s, it appears that veterans of the political struggles of the 1620s formed a higher proportion of the parliamentarian MPs than of those who joined the king, whose average age was younger.[13] Courtiers who became parliamentarians, such as the Earl of Pembroke, may have been pushed in that direction by loss of favour at court as well as by conviction. War posed enormous threats to property, and differences within the parliamentarian side, and even defections from it, have been mapped onto individuals' level of wealth as well as the location of their estates within royalist, parliamentarian, or contested areas.[14] The impact of war on individuals' fortunes may have prompted or reinforced their attitudes towards the continuation of war: Bulstrode Whitelocke's gravitation towards the peace party has been linked with his bitter experience of the early months of the war in the sacking of his house Fawley Court.[15] Even for parliamentarians with less personal experience of the effects of war, the benefits to be won by a potential victory had to be weighed up against the physically and socially destructive consequences of the war itself. For early, zealous and prominent opponents of royal policy, calculations of personal risk and benefit might run the other way round, and fear of royal vengeance, as well as principled desires for a more reformist settlement, may have kept them fighting.[16] Even at the greatest crisis of the parliamentarian cause, personal motivation and principle cannot be decoupled: David Underdown's analysis of the eventual revolutionaries of 1649 saw them as a group distinguished from the larger set of political Independents both by the impulses of an intense puritanism and by their less secure hold on gentility and fortune.[17] Principle interacted in complex ways with experience and expedience.

Beliefs and Theories

One of the weaknesses of parliamentarianism was that much of what held parliamentarians together was retrospective: a belief in the king's (or his counsellors') misgovernment in the years before the calling of the Long Parliament. Various discourses could underpin such a claim of misgovernment, and indeed, royalists as well as parliamentarians could subscribe to some of these claims. Notions of good government were rooted in custom and law, in the idea of responsiveness to counsel, and in the platitude (whether expressed in terms of monarchical paternalism or in classicizing analysis of good and corrupt forms of rule) that government should be for the good of the governed. Organic metaphors of the state as a body politic composed of interdependent parts, while hierarchical, still fostered the notion that there was a balance within a healthy kingdom. The participation of the 'members' of that body in ensuring the shared good of the 'commonwealth' was essential, and the distribution of responsibility for government, justice, and counsel across local and national elites has been seen by historians as fostering a kind of participatory republican ethos within a customary monarchical state.[18] Violation of that balance—whether through the diminution of the role of the great peers of the realm in counsel, or through the failure to call parliaments, in which the whole nation was taken to be present—was a threat to the health of the whole body. The law itself bound together and vivified the polity (Fortescue had equated the laws with the nerves of the body politic), so any slighting of legality also constituted an attack on the state itself, as John Pym argued in his case against Strafford. Many parliamentarians would have agreed with Pym that 'The Law is the Boundary, the Measure betwixt the Kings Prerogative, and the peoples Liberty'; law preserved the balance of the polity, and set bounds to the king's, as well as the people's, actions.[19] While many of these assumptions were shared across the political nation, they offered fertile ground for further development by parliamentarians.

Looking back, parliamentarians could agree that royal government had overstepped its bounds. In the present, what they needed to justify was action to remedy this. The key question was on what grounds parliament could act to challenge or remedy the deficiencies of royal government. Royalists who conceded the possibility of royal tyranny argued that it could only be addressed through 'prayers and tears'. Parliamentarians, by definition, argued that it could be actively resisted. Although the classical language of 'tyranny' offered potentially drastic solutions, placing the tyrant outside the protection of the law, in practice, European argument about the right of resistance against princes guilty of misgovernment had been constrained by biblical precepts of obedience to divinely anointed rulers, which if anything had been strengthened rather than weakened in Protestant political thought. When sixteenth-century Protestants had found themselves threatened by Catholic rulers, they had resorted to a mixture of argumentative strategies to justify resistance. They drew on a Catholic heritage of arguments from natural law, in which self-preservation was a duty to God and governments came into being through a process of consent; they fleshed out fictive accounts of their nations' 'ancient constitutions' to demonstrate that power had always been shared, rather than derived from or concentrated in a single ruler; and they argued that part of the function of 'lesser magistrates' was to act as a check on or substitute for chief magistrates who defected from their duties to God or the people. The most extreme of the Protestant resistance theories may have verged on justifications for popular revolution, but the more restrained versions of these theories, hedged around with qualifications and justifications, were more culturally suited to the mainstream of parliamentarian argument—and certainly to propaganda aimed at waverers and royalists—at the start of the civil war.[20]

In some cases, parliamentarian commitment may have sprung from a set of principled beliefs about government, obedience, and resistance; but even where it did not, the perceived need to act against the king needed justification. The parliamentarian cause generated a mass of printed propaganda, from parliament's own published statements and communications with the king, through commissioned propaganda, to spontaneous publications by supporters of the parliamentarian cause. Whatever their evolving differences—and different emphases and assumptions were visible from the earliest stages of the war—parliamentarian justifications clustered round a core of shared or overlapping arguments about political power and the English constitution. Drawing on English versions of the 'ancient constitution', parliamentarians could argue that England was a mixed monarchy or a form of co-ordinate government, in which the king's power was in some way balanced with the (independent) powers of the Houses of Lords and Commons in parliament. Such co-ordination placed the king not above but as one of the 'three estates', and denied him ultimate power in these times of emergency, since 'one is less than three'.[21] Indeed, resistance theory offered precedents for such unfavourable assessments of the power of the king in comparison with his subjects, while still allowing parliamentarians to find room for the king's place at the apex of the constitution. 'It is true,' conceded the parliamentarian propagandist Henry Parker, 'two supreames cannot bee in the same sense and respect, but nothing is more known or assented to then this, that the King is *singulis major*, and yet *universis minor*' (greater than individuals, but less than all [his subjects] together—a tag from the sixteenth-century resistance theorists).[22] This did not, however, mean that parliamentarians envisaged a popular rising of the king's subjects sweeping him from power: parliament, as a 'lesser magistrate', had to lead those people. Indeed, parliament was not just an authority over the people, or even a representative of them: in some mysterious way, it *was* the people, who by an accepted fiction were taken to be present in parliament through their representatives. Parliamentarians subscribed to 'ascending' theories of power, in which political power was either originally the power 'inherent in the people',[23] or was conferred by their 'designation', even if they never held it themselves. If parliament simply *was* the people, then the Long Parliament was in a peculiarly authoritative position in interpreting the constitution created by the original decisions of the people.

Parliamentarians thus agreed that parliament as an institution could in the current emergency circumstances wage a defensive war against the king. However, when they looked to the future beyond the war, their defensive principles could not generate any agreement about how the balance of the polity should be restored and protected. Some parliamentarians simply wanted to secure the settlement already achieved. Thus even a politician associated with the political Independents (though a middle-group 'royal' Independent who recoiled from regicide) could argue that 'we do not hold it lawful to take up Arms, thereby to force the alteration of laws already made, or the making of new'. Rather, he argued that the war had been fought simply to defend the existing balance of the constitution against royal attack.[24] For some parliamentarians, the requirements for settlement were minimal indeed: at the Oxford treaty of the first winter of the war, parliament's proposed terms were overwhelmingly focused on the requirement that all national and local offices be kept by or returned to people acceptable to parliament upon the conclusion of the settlement. In contrast, the provocative Nineteen Propositions of June 1642 had sought to institutionalize such parliamentary control of counsel in a permanent and systematic way which clearly infringed the king's prerogative of choosing his own counsellors. Right from the beginning of the war, then, parliamentarian aims began to fragment, and with them the arguments which were used in support both of those aims and of the war effort itself.

FRAGMENTATION

The tragedy of parliamentarianism was that it generated the oppositional power to fight the king, but could not find the cohesive force to forge a positive settlement. From the earliest months of the civil war, the parliamentarian coalition proved to be fissiparous and undermined by divisions and misgivings. How far such divisions were over matters of deep principle is hard to say. Contemporary rhetoric picked out factions (as modern historians have done) but anatomized them in ways which ascribed mixed motives to their different members.[25] Alongside the analysis of faction itself, contemporaries also saw those who were (at least nominally) parliamentarian as divided by their zeal or lukewarmness: for the parliamentarian poet George Wither, animated partly by his experiences on the much-contested county committee(s) of Surrey, the parliamentarian cause was threatened not by divisions of principle but by 'neuters' who would never be committed enough to bring the war to a successful conclusion.[26] Certainly the experience of war itself provoked both the great and the humble to reassess how far they were prepared to align themselves not just with the parliamentarian cause but with the war effort which brought such destruction and disruption with it.

The parliamentarian coalition had been pushed to breaking point by the time of the regicide, but its fragmentation began early. No sooner had the war begun than a 'peace party' started negotiations with the king; the 'war party' held out for the stronger negotiating position which military success, if not outright victory, might eventually bring. In the course of the war, an amalgamation of perceived political and religious differences led to a binary division within the parliamentarian cause, with the successors of the peace party labelled (political) 'Presbyterians' and their opponents the (political) 'Independents'. Neither group, of course, was unitary (and some historians have identified a 'middle' group who evolved into the more conservative 'royal Independents'); the religious labels given to them were somewhat misleading; and most parliamentarians were not securely aligned with either faction. Nonetheless, much of the parliamentarian politics of the 1640s was shaped by the conflict between them.

In many ways, those who sought an early peace, reluctant to pursue the war against Charles I to its military conclusion, were the most 'conservative' of parliamentarians, least willing to challenge royal authority through war and the expedients of war, and most willing to leave parts of Charles's prerogative intact in any settlement. Some adherents of the presbyterians have even been labelled as 'crypto-royalists' by the time of their failed coup in the summer of 1647. Those, in contrast, who formed the early 'war party' and sought to win the war before negotiating with Charles from a position of strength, were more comfortable with what this entailed (including the more divisive, punitive, and arbitrary measures which parliament used in support of its war effort in the localities), and more likely to want to enact long-term reform of the polity once it was in a position to make peace. To the extent that there were religious divisions between the two groups, they were largely over the question of religious toleration. Toleration for sectarians was alarming to the political Presbyterians, who became willing to accept a modified Erastian form of the presbyterianism advocated by their Scottish allies precisely because it would block such toleration. The political Independents came to be the defenders of a degree of religious toleration, and the champions of the contributions of the sects to the war effort. In rejecting religious coercion, the Independents rejected their former allies the Scots, in spite of their shared desire to restrict the king's prerogative; the Independents' desire for a defiantly English settlement was increasingly provocatively expressed as more radical and anti-monarchical Independents moved towards an English regicide which the Scottish presbyterians could not accept. However, while the two developing factions were generally distinguished from each other by the greater severity of the Independents' demands on the king, both sides could offer relatively generous proposals under the right circumstances (notably the army's Heads of the Proposals in 1647), hoping to benefit from being the peace-brokers; neither side invariably insisted on their typical requirements such as the taking of the Covenant or the long-term removal of control of the militia from the king.

Of course, individuals moved between these fluid parliamentarian factions at watershed moments in the developing politics of the 1640s. Even beyond such changes in factional allegiance, individuals' thought can be hard to place in any simple scheme of parliamentarian tendencies. William Prynne eventually became one of the prime representatives of the political Presbyterian faction, and the most voluble protester against the turn of events which led via Pride's Purge to the regicide. However, his signal contribution to the parliamentarian cause in its early years was his *Soveraigne Power of Parliaments* (1643), which presented to English readers in their own language some of the most forthright arguments for the deposition and execution of kings, particularly those of the sixteenth-century resistance tract *Vindiciae contra tyrannos*.[27] William Lamont suggests that Prynne's argument for parliamentary sovereignty was not a 'solution' to the constitutional problem of the civil war, but (more appropriately for an adherent of the political Presbyterians) 'an interim expedient until confidence was restored in the King'.[28] This highlights the fact that in justifying the civil war, parliamentarians could open the way for ideas which could transform the constitution itself, even if that was not their intention. Prynne was not the only political Presbyterian whose ideas fed into more radical streams of parliamentarian thought.

There are some broad distinctions between the political thought of the Presbyterians and Independents. The political Independents, represented among others by the able propagandist Henry Parker, were more given to emphasizing that political power really did come from the people themselves. However, they were also more likely to insist that parliament was the only legitimate forum through which that power could be expressed and exercised; the king, increasingly, might be seen as a 'chief magistrate' answerable to the people through their parliament, rather than an independent or superior power. The political Presbyterians, on the other hand, gave God a more immediate role in the endowment of human political authority, even if through the designation of the people, and held on with much more conviction to an independent role for royal power within the constitution, which parliament might balance but could not eliminate. A mixed monarchy, as defended by Presbyterians like Philip Hunton, was a delicate and almost paradoxical balance: royal power must be 'not so great as to destroy the mixture; not so titular as to destroy the Monarchy'.[29] For Hunton, this argument led to a disturbing conclusion: parliament could not, after all, claim that the constitution legitimated its war against Charles I. Rather, the constitutional position was a stalemate, and it was the people who would decide, in their own consciences, which of their constitutional masters to obey. Although this argument of Hunton's could be interpreted as radical, he developed it within tight constraints, strenuously avoiding the suggestion that the people had held onto or could resume any kind of original sovereign power. Nonetheless, like some other theorists of coordination of powers between the monarch and parliament, he had opened up a space—in this case, a space outside rather than within the constitution—in which the consciences of the people could start to play a direct part in the political fate of the nation. This possibility was anathema to the staunchest defenders of a new parliamentary absolutism, who were as inclined to defend the authority of parliament against the people as against the king, but it was to be developed by the

Levellers.[30] From early in the war, we begin to glimpse different potential parliamentarian radicalisms; their developments and metamorphoses were to be shaped by the events of the 1640s.

RADICALIZATION

Historians differ over the fundamental character of parliamentarian thought. Parliament, driven on particularly by the 'war party' and their successors, constructed a wartime machinery of central and local administration which violated every provision of the totemic 1628 Petition of Right. Their enemies were naturally aware of parliament's vulnerability on this point, and royalists from early on, and increasingly successfully, depicted the king rather than parliament as the champion of the rule of law. But the extent to which parliamentarians developed political theories which acknowledged and justified such apparently unconstitutional action is disputed. This is partly because even those parliamentarian authors who were most willing to place any kind of arbitrary power in parliament tended to do so within discourses which presented this as an interpretation of the existing role of parliament within the constitution; and partly because the actions taken by parliament—from the simple act of resisting the king to the more blatant disregard for law and appropriation of aspects of the king's prerogative—could be seen as justified by emergency circumstances, potentially allowing the normal constitutional norms to be resumed unchanged once the war was over. In addition, the imperatives of effective propaganda, especially against a king claiming the high ground of legality, might mean that parliamentarians were keen to 'make their case as conventional as possible'.[31] Although accounts like Glenn Burgess's emphasize this resistance to innovation, the very elements which parliamentarians used to construct their arguments could betray them into dangerous innovation. Burgess points out that in striving to justify resistance without overstepping constitutional bounds, parliamentarian theorists raised the disturbing possibility that constitutionalism itself endorsed violence within the state, rather than enabling peaceful resolution of conflicts. Scholars who are more disposed to emphasize the disturbance to, rather than the continuity of, such political thought may place a very different construction on the character of parliamentarian thought. For Burgess, arguments of 'emergency' functioned to allow parliamentarians to defend themselves, in Henry Parker's words, as offering 'Physicke', a mere temporary medicinal treatment, rather than a permanent 'diet' of parliamentary rule which challenged the prerogatives of monarchy.[32] But for Richard Tuck, parliamentarian resort to the language of 'necessity' represents an unmistakable alignment with the most 'modern' European ideas of the time: in appealing to necessity, and to the principle that the safety of the people (*salus populi*) was the supreme law, parliamentarians were aligning themselves with the new 'reason of state', which overrode constitutional niceties to enable effective and often absolutist rule.[33]

During the 1640s, a radical spectrum developed: not unified in its aims, and linked by loose rather than systematic personal connections, it would prove almost as fissile as the broader spectrum of parliamentarianism. More moderate parliamentarian observers could pick out groupings of 'fiery spirits' among MPs, but parliament's more daring adherents were also increasingly visible in an extra-parliamentary politics of print, petitioning, and organizing which could spread particularly effectively through religious networks and through the parliamentarian armies. One part of this developing spectrum was eventually labelled with the pejorative term of 'Levellers', and they can be seen to have clustered round the writing and organizing of a small group of key individuals from as early as 1645. Historians have picked over the connections between Levellers and other radical parliamentarians, helped in making connections by the flow of contemporary rumour and the vagueness with which terms such as 'Leveller' might be used, but hindered by the difficulty of establishing personal relationships between different figures with any certainty. Undoubtedly connections existed, but they were unstable; moments of crisis might unite a wider radical spectrum than just the Levellers, but support could fall away or be diverted when events divided opinion. Consequently, while we can see from sources such as the army-related newsbook *The Moderate* that some people followed the activities and writings of different radical tendencies and saw them as having some common ground, it also makes sense to consider these different tendencies within radical thought and activity in their distinctiveness.

Parliamentarians were radicalized in divergent ways by the events of the 1640s. For some, the increasing conviction that the king could never be trusted was the main driver; for others the main impetus might be the apparently escalating challenges posed by a providence which led parliament victorious through not one but two civil wars. Some were spurred—as was the Independent coalition itself—by a developing dread of the type of authoritarian religious settlement which might be imposed even on England by Scottish brokers of or partners in settlement. To some parliamentarians, the English parliament itself came to seem an overbearing threat. Although many of these impulses might be combined into a recognizable 'radicalism' such as that of the Levellers, they could also pull in different directions.

In broad terms, we can detect a contrast between a populist radicalism and a type of parliamentary absolutism which in itself represented a radical innovation upon the constitutional understandings of the political nation before the civil war. The potential for constitutional radicalism was arguably present from the beginnings of Charles I's troubles in England: John Adamson has drawn a portrait of a godly junto who drove the opposition to Charles, depicting their aims as quasi-republican in character even by the outbreak of the war.[34] Parliamentarian demands such as the Nineteen Propositions mounted a genuine challenge to the royal prerogative, and David Wootton has pointed to the swift emergence (in the first winter of the war) of pamphlets hinting that the deposition even of a hereditary king would be legitimate.[35] Although he was punished in 1643 for his comments on the king, the MP Henry Marten also demonstrates that it was possible to envisage a non-monarchical future early in the war. As the 1640s went on, such 'war party ultraists' on the 'extreme fringe' of the Independent faction, including Marten himself and colleagues including Thomas Chaloner, went on to develop a some-times mocking critique of the prospects for royal settlement.[36] But although this critique overstepped the bounds of mainstream Independent politics, it was aligned with it in its endorsement of parliamentary rather than popular power as the shaper of the new constitution.

A more popular parliamentarian radicalism grew up partly in response to the par-liamentary pretensions of Independent political thought, and partly for the more pragmatic reason of disillusionment with a now long-standing parliament which was offering few or unattractive prospects of settlement, in which faction and corruption were perceived to prevail over principle, and which was instrumental in the imprison-ing of vocal radicals such as the Leveller leader John Lilburne. Seizing on the notion that parliament was the representative of the people, some began to argue that 'to rep-resent . . . doth not import (as some would have it) to be an absolute *Iudge or Vmpire* in all things, (for then he doth not represent . . . but is absolute, and independent)'.[37] If the House of Commons represented the people, it should be accountable to them, and might even be subject to popular recall or armed action if it betrayed its betrust-ers. The Leveller leaders Lilburne and Overton issued an 'appeal to the people' in 1647, despairing of justice from the two Houses; but their faith in the political role of the people was also expressed in Lilburne's argument—later echoed by the army officer Rainborough at the Putney Debates—that 'the poorest that lives, hath as true a right to give a vote, as well as the richest and greatest'.[38] Parliament had justified itself by monopolizing the right to speak for the people, but from its mobilization of individu-als via the Protestation, to its raising of armies, it had also asked people to answer for themselves and act for the good of the people. Radicals could easily appeal particularly to those who had fought for parliament and resented the implication that they were 'a meer mercinary Army'.[39]

Alongside the division between parliamentarian absolutists and more populist radicals, there was a broad division in the religious character of radicalism. Religious toleration was a cause which bound together some radicals—it was one of the cen-tral commitments of the Leveller movement—but which could coexist with a rather constitutionalist and even rationalist approach to political life. For the Levellers, the prohibition on the magistrate exercising coercive power in religion was simply one part of a system of thought about 'self-propriety' and rights, which led them also to outline a civil constitution based on such natural rights. The regicide could only be justified if it rested on the consent of the people and led to such a constitution. For others who we would also call radicals, and who were at the extreme end of the parliamentarian spectrum, for example in advocating or supporting the regicide, the immediate promptings of the spirit and the workings of providence were more important than the more historical or abstract principles of the constitution. At the Whitehall debates, the millenarian Joshua Sprigge argued that rather than rushing to make a new constitution, it was the duty of the godly simply to put an end to the persecution of the saints, and to wait on God, who would 'bring forth a New Heaven and a New Earth'.[40] The radicalisms of the civil wars grew not from a single impulse, but from multiple priorities and possibilities opened up by the events and theories of the 1640s.

CONCLUSION

Parliamentarians were, from the beginning, a coalition of individuals with different motives for committing themselves to the military resistance to Charles I. These could range from the deeply traditionalist, fighting a purely defensive war, via the more creatively constitutionalist, to the brave new world of those who saw a need, or perhaps even an opportunity, to actively reshape the polity. As the 1640s proceeded, the very act of waging such a war—in which parliament took on so many of the king's powers, and negotiated with him about the terms on which he might resume his throne—made more radical thoughts thinkable, and ultimately made possible the desperate act of regicide. But that process in its turn repelled some who had originally committed themselves to parliament, and who were now horrified by what others found thinkable, both in religion and in politics. The paths of parliamentarians crossed and diverged over the years in complicated ways.

I began this chapter with an example from the Leveller leader William Walwyn. The family of Walwyn's Leveller colleague John Lilburne provides my concluding illustration of the complexities of parliamentarianism. It is an evocative commonplace of accounts of the trauma of the civil wars that families were pulled apart by questions of allegiance at the outbreak of war in 1642, with fathers divided from sons and brothers from brothers across the lines of battle. In Lilburne's family, matters were more straightforward: the broader family was parliamentarian, and John and his two brothers, Robert and Henry, all enlisted in the parliamentarian forces. However, as the 1640s progressed, the three brothers took divergent paths which exemplify some of the many strands of parliamentarianism. Henry, the youngest, in a rapid change of allegiance which makes it impossible to judge his motives, declared for the king in August 1648, attempting to hold Tynemouth Castle for the royalists and dying when it was stormed. He was far from the only parliamentarian to find that the circumstances of the later 1640s made him reassess his loyalties; parliamentarian allegiance was far from fixed. John Lilburne—the middle brother—found that his disillusionment with parliament turned him in a different direction from his brother (in spite of his fraternizing with royalist fellow-prisoners); he challenged the existing, corrupt parliament in the hope of a settlement which would enshrine the supremacy of a legitimate new 'Representative', elected annually by the sovereign people themselves. He rejected a regicide enacted without such authority, and saw the new regime as a new tyranny replacing the old. But his older brother Robert Lilburne followed the revolution through to its conclusion, sitting as a commissioner in the High Court of Justice which condemned Charles I, signing his death warrant, and going on to serve the Republic and Protectorate. It was a different kind of radicalism from his brother's, but in many ways an equally revolutionary path through the English Revolution. Within the parliamentarian family, affinities could sometimes persist alongside slow divergences and bitter divisions.

Notes

1. W.P. [William Walwyn], *The Bloody Project* (1648), in J. R. McMichael and Barbara Taft (eds.), *The Writings of William Walwyn* (Athens, GA, 1989), 298.

2. Edward Vallance, *Revolutionary England and the National Covenant: State Oaths, Protestantism, and the Political Nation, 1553-1682* (Woodbridge, 2005), 51–59.

3. Conrad Russell, *Parliaments and English Politics, 1621-1629* (Oxford, 1979), 433.

4. David L. Smith, 'Herbert, Philip, first earl of Montgomery and fourth earl of Pembroke (1584-1650)', *Oxford Dictionary of National Biography*.

5. J. S. Morrill, *The Revolt of the Provinces: Conservatives and Radicals in the English Civil War, 1630-1650* (London, 1980), 159.

6. Russell, *Parliaments and English Politics*, 428–9.

7. J. S. Morrill, 'The Religious Context of the English Civil War', in his *The Nature of the English Revolution* (London, 1993), 65–6.

8. Mark Stoyle, *Loyalty and Locality: Popular Allegiance in Devon During the English Civil War* (Exeter, 1996), chaps. 9–10.

9. Glenn Burgess, 'Was the English Civil War a War of Religion? The Evidence of Political Propaganda', *Huntington Library Quarterly*, 61.2 (2000): 173–201; Rachel Foxley, 'Oliver Cromwell on Religion and Resistance', in Glenn Burgess and Charles Prior (eds.), *England's Wars of Religion, Revisited* (Farnham, 2011), 209–30.

10. David Booy (ed.), *The Notebooks of Nehemiah Wallington, 1618-1654: A Selection* (Aldershot, 2007), 177.

11. John Walter, *Understanding Popular Violence in the English Revolution: The Colchester Plunderers* (Cambridge, 1999), 285–330.

12. Sarah Barber, *A Revolutionary Rogue: Henry Marten and the English Republic* (Stroud, 2000), 71.

13. David Underdown, *Pride's Purge: Politics in the Puritan Revolution* (Oxford, 1971), 224.

14. Andrew Hopper, *Turncoats and Renegadoes: Changing Sides During the English Civil Wars* (Oxford, 2012), 101–4; Lotte Mulligan, 'Property and Parliamentary Politics in the English Civil-War, 1642-1646', *Historical Studies*, 16.64 (1975): 341–61.

15. Ian Gentles, *The English Revolution and the Wars in the Three Kingdoms, 1638-1652* (Harlow, 2007), 159; Ruth Spalding (ed.), *The Diary of Bulstrode Whitelocke, 1605-1675* (Oxford, 1989), 138–9.

16. David Scott, *Politics and War in the Three Stuart Kingdoms, 1637-49* (Basingstoke, 2004), 41–2.

17. Underdown, *Pride's Purge*, 4, 223–56.

18. Mark Goldie, 'The Unacknowledged Republic: Office-Holding in Early Modern England', in Tim Harris (ed.), *The Politics of the Excluded, c.1500-1800* (Basingstoke, 2001), 153–94.

19. *The declaration of Iohn Pym Esquire upon the whole matter of the charge of high treason against Thomas Earle of Strafford, April 12, 1641* (London, 1641), 5. For Fortescue, see Ernst Kantorowicz, *The King's Two Bodies* (Princeton, NJ, 1997), 224.

20. For a classic introduction to Protestant resistance theories, see Quentin Skinner, *The Foundations of Modern Political Thought* (Cambridge, 1978), vol. II: *The Age of Reformation*, Part 3.

21. [Charles Herle], *A Fuller Answer to a Treatise Written by Doctor Ferne* (London, 1642), 3.

22. Henry Parker, *Observations upon some of his Majesties late Answers and Expresses* (2nd edition, London, 1642), 8.

23. Parker, *Observations upon some of his Majesties late Answers and Expresses*, 1.

24. [Nathaniel Fiennes?], *Vindiciae Veritatis* (London, 1654), 33.

25. Jason Peacey, 'Perceptions of Parliament: Factions and "the Public"', in J. S. A. Adamson (ed.), *The English Civil War: Conflict and Contexts, 1640–1649* (Basingstoke, 2009), 82–105.

26. John Gurney, 'George Wither and Surrey Politics, 1642–1649', *Southern History*, 19 (1997): 74–98.

27. David Wootton, 'From Rebellion to Revolution: The Crisis of the Winter of 1642–3 and the Origins of Civil War Radicalism', *English Historical Review*, 105 (1990): 654–69.

28. William Lamont, *Marginal Prynne, 1600–1669* (London, 1963), 117.

29. Philip Hunton, *A Treatise of Monarchie* (London, 1643), 25–6.

30. Rachel Foxley, *The Levellers: Radical Political Thought in the English Revolution* (Manchester, 2013), 51–83.

31. Glenn Burgess, *British Political Thought, 1500–1660: The Politics of the Post-Reformation* (Basingstoke, 2009), 193–4.

32. Glenn Burgess, 'Political Thought', in Laura Lunger Knoppers (ed.), *The Oxford Handbook of Literature and the English Revolution* (Oxford, 2012), 81.

33. Richard Tuck, *Philosophy and Government, 1572–1651* (Cambridge, 1993), 222–3.

34. John Adamson, *The Noble Revolt: The Overthrow of Charles I* (London, 2007), 516–18.

35. Wootton, 'From Rebellion to Revolution', 660–2.

36. Sarah Barber, *Regicide and Republicanism: Politics and Ethics in the English Revolution, 1646–1659* (Edinburgh, 1998), 11–39, quotation at 11.

37. William Ball, *Tractatus De Iure Regnandi, & Regni* (London, 1645), 13.

38. John Lilburne, *The Charters of London* (London, 1646), 4.

39. *A Declaration of the Engagements, Remonstrances, Representations ... from his Excellency Sir Tho: Fairfax, and the general Councel of the Army* (London, 1647), 39.

40. A. S. P. Woodhouse, *Puritanism and Liberty: Being the Army Debates (1647–49) from the Clarke Manuscripts* (3rd edition, London, 1986 (originally 1938)), 134–6.

FURTHER READING

Adamson, J. S. A., *The Noble Revolt: The Overthrow of Charles I* (London, 2007).

Barber, Sarah, *Regicide and Republicanism: Politics and Ethics in the English Revolution, 1646–1659* (Edinburgh, 1998).

Burgess, Glenn, *British Political Thought, 1500–1660: The Politics of the Post-Reformation* (Basingstoke, 2009).

Burgess, Glenn, 'Was the English Civil War a War of Religion? The Evidence of Political Propaganda', *Huntington Library Quarterly*, 61.2 (2000): 173–201.

Foxley, Rachel, *The Levellers: Radical Political Thought in the English Revolution* (Manchester, 2013).

Gentles, Ian, *The English Revolution and the Wars in the Three Kingdoms, 1638–1652* (Harlow, 2007).

Hughes, Ann, *Gangraena and the Struggle for the English Revolution* (Oxford, 2004).

Morrill, J. S., 'The Religious Context of the English Civil War', in his *The Nature of the English Revolution* (London, 1993), 45–68.

Morrill, J. S., *The Revolt of the Provinces: Conservatives and Radicals in the English Civil War, 1630–1650* (London, 1980).

Peacey, Jason, 'Perceptions of Parliament: Factions and "the Public"', in J. S. A. Adamson (ed.), *The English Civil War: Conflict and Contexts, 1640–1649* (Basingstoke, 2009), 82–105.

Sanderson, John, *'But the People's Creatures': The Philosophical Basis of the English Civil War* (Manchester, 1989).

Scott, David, *Politics and War in the Three Stuart Kingdoms, 1637–1649* (Basingstoke, 2004).

Stoyle, Mark, *Loyalty and Locality: Popular Allegiance in Devon During the English Civil War* (Exeter, 1996).

Tuck, Richard, *Philosophy and Government, 1572–1651* (Cambridge, 1993).

Underdown, David, *Pride's Purge: Politics in the Puritan Revolution* (Oxford, 1971).

Walter, John, *Understanding Popular Violence in the English Revolution: The Colchester Plunderers* (Cambridge, 1999).

Wootton, David, 'From Rebellion to Revolution: The Crisis of the Winter of 1642–3 and the Origins of Civil War Radicalism', *English Historical Review*, 105 (1990): 654–669.

CHAPTER 25

....

POLITICAL THOUGHT

....

TED VALLANCE

Liberty in the English Revolution

THIS chapter will argue that the political thought of the English Revolution can be read as a controversy over the meaning of liberty and how it might best be secured. Discussions of liberty in modern political philosophy have centred on Isaiah Berlin's classic distinction between 'negative liberty', meaning only freedom from external constraint, and 'positive liberty', meaning the freedom to be master of oneself, to be in a condition where full self-realization is possible. Central to this chapter, however, is a third, historically grounded conception of liberty: Quentin Skinner's concept of 'neo-Roman' liberty. According to Skinner, in the years before the civil war, a number of parliamentarians, later dubbed the 'democratical men' by their philosophical opponent Thomas Hobbes, propounded a theory of liberty indebted to Roman law and history. In this theory of liberty, the condition of slavery was defined not by actual or threatened coercion and restraint, but by the mere possibility of the arbitrary domination of one individual by another (as through the operation of royal prerogative).[1] Yet, as we will see, classical traditions were not the exclusive source of distinctions between freedom and servitude. There were many other sources which assisted English writers in defining liberty and slavery, foremost amongst these the common law. The peculiarities of English law point towards the cultural aspects of the idea of liberty in this period. Contemporaries identified societies (both ancient and modern) that were conducive to liberty and those that were not. As will be shown, many writers believed that the experience of living in either free or unfree societies could change the character of their inhabitants, allowing those in free states to flourish as virtuous, independent citizens while those governed by tyrants were reduced to cringing, bestial slavishness. These beliefs in turn, it will be suggested, indicate the way in which discussions of liberty and slavery in the seventeenth century were often rooted in lived experience: the nature of servitude could be found written in the welts the size of 'Tobacco-pipes' on the back of the puritan 'martyr' and later Leveller, John Lilburne (whipped by order of the prerogative court of Star Chamber in 1638) as much as it could be identified in works of Roman or English law and history.[2]

In arguing that a struggle over liberty was at the heart of the political arguments of the 1640s and 1650s, this chapter is not reasserting an older view of the civil war as a climactic moment in the establishment of political and religious freedom in England. As J. C. Davis has shown, some early modern understandings of liberty, especially as regards liberty of conscience, were quite different from those defined by modern political philosophers such as Berlin. Rather than being an aspect of 'positive liberty', in allowing the individual to fully realize their own beliefs, liberty of conscience for many seventeenth-century English puritans actually meant the freedom to be able to submit oneself entirely to the rule of the ultimate absolute sovereign, God, unencumbered by interference from any earthly magistrate.[3] Equally, this conflict over liberty was not divided between two distinct ideological camps: the supporters of absolute monarchy on the one side and the defenders of an English mixed constitution of king, lords, and commons on the other. As many historians have pointed out, absolutism and constitutionalism were not the exclusive preserve of either royalists or parliamentarians, nor were these groupings homogeneous in terms of their political outlook. Sources and slogans that were employed by one party could be repurposed for use by their opponents. For example, the Ciceronian axiom *salus populi suprema lex esto* (the people's welfare shall be the supreme law) which Quentin Skinner identifies as an important component of the 'neo-Roman' ideal of liberty, was also deployed by the advocates of absolute sovereignty, most notably Thomas Hobbes.[4] In this way, the reconfiguration of the history of political thought as the study of political discourses or languages offers a very valuable way of approaching these texts by heightening our awareness of these works as exercises in rhetorical persuasion, appealing to both supporters and opponents through the utilization of a variety of literary and intellectual strategies, which were dependent on audience and context as much as the author's political principles.

Rather than proposing that the political thought of the English civil war was characterized by a struggle between those who sought to defend and those who aimed to curtail individual freedom, this chapter argues that all sides agreed that liberty was of critical importance. Division arose not over the value of liberty but over its precise meaning and, crucially, how that liberty could be realized and protected.[5] These distinctions were more profound even than differences over the origins of political sovereignty (whether it derived from the people or whether it originated from God), as very different conceptions of sovereignty could nonetheless result in very similar, for example absolutist, ideas about political authority. These divergent ideas about liberty in early modern England help us understand how a royal government which rarely used force to suppress dissent could be regarded by some of its subjects as a tyranny and, conversely, how some of the Caroline regime's supporters could see the crown's opponents as seeking to undermine and destroy royal sovereignty—in their eyes, the sole guarantor of the liberty of the subject.

LIBERTY AND SOVEREIGNTY BEFORE THE CIVIL WAR

In Thomas Hobbes's *The Elements of Law*, composed during the years of Charles I's personal rule (1629–40), Hobbes considered the factors that provoked rebellion within a commonwealth. One common cause of dissatisfaction was the 'fear of want', caused by 'great exactions', but Hobbes recognized that discontent could also be stirred by men who 'live at ease' but lacked power:

> such men must needs take it ill, and be grieved with the state, as find themselves postponed to those in honour, whom they think they excel in virtue and ability to govern. And this is it for which they think themselves regarded as but slaves.[6]

As Quentin Skinner has noted, this passage reflected the context of opposition to Charles I's rule in the 1620s and 1630s, pointedly attacking the king's noble and gentry critics as driven by ambition and pride.[7] Overall, *The Elements of Law* was far more directed at tackling the threat of *aristocratic* government than Hobbes's later *Leviathan*: as he argued in *The Elements*, democracy and aristocracy were 'in effect but one. For (as I have shewed before) democracy is but the government of a few orators' (Hobbes, *Elements*, 138).

These remarks parodied the pretensions of 'patriot' thinkers such as Thomas Scott, MP for Canterbury, who thought that public office should be restricted to 'religious, grave, learned, wise, and honest men (true to the realme) free from all dependence on those that have other than public and English ends'.[8] Members of parliament such as Scott and before him Sir Thomas Hetley or Hedley, attacked the financial instruments employed by first James I and then his son as direct assaults on the liberty of the subject. Hetley cited Tacitus and Cicero to argue that James I's use of prerogative taxation ('impositions') threatened English 'freemen' with being reduced to the status of slaves. Similar arguments were advanced in response to another royal financial expedient, the Forced Loan of 1627, which Sir Dudley Digges, MP for Kent, argued, if unchecked, would leave Charles a 'king of slaves'. The clearest argument was developed in Henry Parker's *The Case of Shipmoney* (1640)—if the king could arbitrarily impose levies such as Ship Money in this way, the people were completely subject to the will of the sovereign, leaving the English 'the most despicable slaves in the whole world'.[9]

While these arguments were clearly indebted to Roman history and law for their view of slavery as a condition in which the possibility of domination by another existed, this was obviously not their only source of ideas regarding freedom and servitude. As Quentin Skinner himself has noted, these same parliamentarians could also call upon discussions of property and villeinage in medieval English legal texts such as Bracton and Littleton, and some MPs (Hetley) could be found combining Roman and English examples in their speeches.[10] There were similarities in how these English authors defined servitude which meant that classical and medieval traditions could be easily combined. However, the liberty of the subject was also defended in ways that clearly diverged from this 'neo-Roman' configuration. Most clearly, in the 1628 Petition of Right, parliament relied on the idea of the 'ancient constitution', confirmed and restored in Magna Carta, which prohibited the imposition of financial instruments such as the Forced Loan without parliamentary consent, arbitrary imprisonment, 'free quarter', and the use of martial law in peacetime. The 'ancient constitution' then provided subjects with an identifiable set of rights—to property, to personal liberty, to legal due process—and it also placed restrictions on the monarch. In this view, the king was bound by legal obligations, embodied in his coronation oath and by the law of Edward the Confessor known as the 'office of the king'. This stated that

> The king, because he is the vicar of the highest king, is appointed for this purpose, to
> rule the earthly kingdom, and the Lord's people, and, above all things, to reverence
> his holy church, to govern it, and to defend it from injuries; to pluck away wicked
> doers, and utterly to destroy them: which, unless he do, the name of a king agreeth
> not unto him, but he loseth the name of a king.[11]

These sanctions against kings who did not fulfil their office would be explored more fully in the 1640s. What was significant was that 'ancient constitutionalism' connected effective kingship with the defence of the church as well as the liberties of the subject. These connections in turn reflected the interplay between 'patriot' opposition to Charles I's domestic and foreign policy, and 'godly' Protestantism. Thomas Scott, for example, was part of puritan networks in Kent and a close friend of the puritan preacher Herbert Palmer (later one of the co-authors of the important parliamentarian tract, *Scripture and Reason Pleaded for Defensive Arms* (1643)). Scott's denunciations of the government of Charles I incorporated Roman history and the notion of an 'ancient constitution' with the idea of England as a latter-day Israel, beset with its own 'Babylonish monarch'. Significantly, though, Scott's arguments shifted from criticisms of one king to an attack on the institution of monarchy itself as 'the most apt to degenerate into a Tyrannie and lawless soveraigntie'.[12] Scott's arguments were expressed only in manuscript but similarly hostile statements could be found in (unlicensed) print. Alexander Leighton's *Sion's Plea*, published in Amsterdam in 1629, decried Queen Henrietta Maria as the 'Daughter of Heth' (implying she was an idolatress and adulteress), praised the duke of Buckingham's assassin, John Felton, as an emissary of divine wrath, and warned Charles I that he would be deemed an enemy of God if he continued to heed the advice of 'Laudian' prelates. Leighton was punished severely for these remarks: Star Chamber fined him £10,000, his nose was slit, his ears trimmed and his head branded (with the initials S.S. for 'sower of sedition'), and he was imprisoned for life.[13]

The positions of Scott and Leighton may have been extreme, even in godly circles, but they demonstrate the extent of the threat some of Charles I's opponents posed not just to his rule but to monarchy itself. The challenge made to the Stuart dynasty in these arguments was countered in the works of Hobbes and Thomas Scott's cousin, Sir Robert Filmer. Filmer's major work of political theory, *Patriarcha*, was not published until 1680 but large sections of it were certainly written before the civil war and a version of the text was refused a licence for publication in 1632. In response to the rhetoric of 'birthrights' and natural freedom, Filmer instead presented man as a creature born into domination. All authority was derived from the authority of the father over the family which itself was of divine donation. This was the nature of all kingly authority, irrespective of local arrangements regarding royal succession. Royal sovereignty was indivisible and unlimited. Contrary to the arguments of the defenders of the 'ancient constitution', the king was the author of the laws, not their subject, and parliament was summoned and dismissed at his will. These arguments were not peculiar to Filmer and could be found in the writings of his Elizabethan predecessor Saravia and Filmer's contemporary Peter Heylyn.[14] Their currency during the reign of Charles I is demonstrated by the way in which Hobbes felt it necessary to distinguish his own absolutist political theory from the patriarchalists by emphasizing that, in the family, obedience was naturally due to the mother as the giver of life and the provider of protection, shelter, and food (Hobbes, *Elements*, 130–1).

Hobbes and Filmer were equally damning, though, of the rhetoric of liberty espoused by Charles I's critics. For Hobbes, the condition of 'freemen' was virtually identical to that of servants, save only for one difference: that as they had submitted 'uncompelled' to authority, they might expect to be 'better used' by their sovereign. 'Freedom therefore in commonwealths is nothing but the honour of equality of favour with other subjects, and servitude the estate of the rest' (Hobbes, *Elements*, 132–3). Filmer's subtitle to *Patriarcha* contrasted the 'natural' power of kings with the 'Unnatural Liberty' of the people, and within the work the desire for liberty was equated with the fall of Man.[15] Yet, as Cesare Cuttica has argued with respect to Filmer, absolutist arguments were not purely negative—both Hobbes and Filmer sought to convince their readers that actual liberty could only be enjoyed under absolute sovereignty. According to Filmer the 'greatest liberty in the world (if it be duly considered) is for people to live under a monarch. It is the Magna Carta of this kingdom. All other shows or pretexts of liberty are but several degrees of slavery, and a liberty only to destroy liberty.'[16] Though they had very distinct views on liberty in the state of nature (Filmer that it was non-existent, Hobbes that it was complete but also completely insecure), their thoughts concerning liberty under sovereignty were remarkably similar. Both thought that the prime duty of the sovereign was *salus populi* and both contended that monarchical governments were best suited to pursue this because, as Filmer put it, even a tyrant who wished only to enrich himself had a vested interest in ruling a prosperous people.[17] For Hobbes, the public good meant more than the mere preservation of life 'but generally their [the public's] benefit and good'. Within this liberty included a general freedom from interference except 'what is necessary for the good of the commonwealth' (Hobbes, *Elements*, 172–3). This included freedom of movement, of trade, rights to private property, and the expectation that justice would be executed fairly and that individuals would contribute to the upkeep of the Commonwealth in proportion to their means (which in Hobbes's opinion was best achieved by taxes on consumption rather than property) (Hobbes, *Elements*, 173–5). Those who complained that the crown's prerogative levies fatally undermined the right to private property failed to understand that 'without such sovereign power, the right of men is not propriety to any thing, but a community .... Those levies therefore which are made upon men's estates, by the sovereign authority, are no more but the price of that peace and defence which the sovereignty maintaineth for them' (Hobbes, *Elements*, 137).

The contrast between what has been described as 'neo-Roman' and absolutist conceptions of liberty was extreme: in one case, liberty could only exist where even the possibility of arbitrary domination had been excluded; in the other, liberty could only be preserved where sovereignty was untrammelled. These stark divisions sit uneasily with some recent treatments of political ideas in pre-civil war England that have stressed a broad degree of consensus amongst English politicians concerning the primacy of the common law in governing political arrangements. At least in terms of absolutist thought, the very fact that *Patriarcha* remained unpublished has been taken by some scholars as an indication that its content was too controversial for public consumption.[18] Yet these two distinct positions on liberty arguably do tell us something about why it was so difficult to achieve political agreement once the Long Parliament was summoned in November 1640. Both played into established and opposing conspiracy theories concerning the threat to the English church and state. One claimed that the freedom of the subject was jeopardized by the plotting of evil counsellors and 'Popish' prelates around the king—as the Scottish divine Robert Baillie put it—to 'bring in our Church *Arminianisme*, and compleet Popery, and in our State a slavery no lesse then *Turkish*'.[19] The conception of liberty as freedom from the possibility of domination complemented this theory as it urged vigilance against not just actual instances of coercion (the punishments meted out to men such as Lilburne and Leighton) but also the potential for tyranny. It was no coincidence here that 'liberty' was frequently juxtaposed with 'popery', given the commonplace assumption that Catholic states were predisposed to arbitrary rule.[20] Conversely, absolutist thinkers such as Hobbes saw the main threat to the Commonwealth coming from men of ambition, who through 'reprehension of public actions, affect popularity and applause amongst the multitude, by which they may be enabled to have a faction in the commonwealth at their devotion' (Hobbes, *Elements*, 176). Theorists such as Filmer and Hobbes shared with the crown a belief that, for example, the refusal to pay taxes represented neither a principled stand against illegal impositions, nor a limited incidence of civil disobedience but instead a fundamental threat to good government.[21] The particularly corrosive nature of both of these conspiracy theories was that they encouraged contemporaries to see potential threats to be as dangerous as actual ones and, as a result, endorsed taking pre-emptive steps to suppress incipient dangers. They served overall to erode trust and support more radical courses of political action. As Ann Hughes has noted, notions concerning the threat of 'popularity' underwrote Charles I's attempt to arrest the Five Members in January 1642, on the grounds that the MPs had attempted to 'deprive the King of his regal power, and to place in subjects an arbitrary and tyrannical power over the lives, liberties and estates of his Majesty's liege people'.[22] The same attempt convinced many of the king's subjects of the direct and real threat to their liberties posed by his government.

LIBERTY AND PARLIAMENTARY SOVEREIGNTY

The royalist lawyer Sir John Spelman, in a response to the parliamentarian Henry Parker, warned his readers that it was not 'prerogative that is now contending with the Subiects libertie, but libertie struggles with *Othlocracie* [*sic*—Ochlocracy = mob rule]'.[23] Spelman's comments indicated both the desire of the king and his supporters to present themselves as the true defenders of the subject's liberties and their contention that it was now parliament which posed the greatest threat to freedom. The ostensible moderation of royalist political thought received its classic embodiment in the king's *Answer* to parliament's Nineteen Propositions. It cast Charles, not parliament, as the defender of England's 'ancient, equall, happy, well-poised, and never-enough commended Constitution', in which the *Answer*'s authors Lucius Cary, 2nd Viscount Falkland, and Sir John Culpepper, both critics of the policies of the personal rule, argued the crown operated as one of the three estates. These estates offered a tripartite system of constitutional balances which ensured that there was already power enough to prevent monarchy from descending into tyranny, while its democratic component, the Commons, conserved liberty and the 'Courage and Industry which Liberty begets'. This praise for England's mixed constitution was nonetheless combined with the continued assertion that this well-balanced polity was under threat from 'ambitious, turbulent Spirits' who wished to destroy regal sovereignty, and leave Charles 'but the outside, but the Picture, but the signe of a King'. These 'Spirits' would in time make the king of England no better than the 'Duke of Venice' and this 'Kingdom a Republique'.[24] While the *Answer* has sometimes been seen as a propaganda blunder, presenting an opportunity for opponents to argue that, as only one estate in three, the crown could be overruled by parliament, it was largely repackaging established conceptions of the constitution.[25] Its moderate tone was also adopted in many other early royalist works, some of which, such as Dudley Digges's *The Unlawfulness of Subjects Taking up Armes* (1643) did not even deny that some forms of public resistance might be offered to royal commands in certain circumstances, but argued casuistically that this was not the present case in England.[26]

It was also clear that the parliament's Nineteen Propositions would have dramatically altered the powers of the crown: prerogative powers of appointment and over the militia were effectively handed over to the legislature, while royal fortresses were also to be placed in parliamentary control. As the *Answer* noted, the king's position would have been made weaker than that of his meanest subject by effectively taking away from him even the paternal right to decide how his children should be educated and who they should marry.[27] This dramatic seizure of power was in part justified by parliament and its spokesmen on the grounds that the king's continued enjoyment of these prerogatives, especially the exercise of his Negative Voice to veto legislation, left the English people in a state of dependence on his will and therefore effectively rendered them slaves.[28] As the Lords and Commons stated in their own declaration justifying the resort to arms, the Houses' actions were necessary to stop those who sought to 'destroy the Parliament, be masters of our religion and liberties, to make us slaves, and alter the Government of this Kingdom, and reduce it to the condition of some other countries which are not governed by Parliaments, and so by Laws, but by the will of the Prince, or rather of those who are about him'.[29]

The most daring, and most controversial, print intervention in support of this position was offered in Henry Parker's *Observations* (1642).[30] Parker argued that there was indeed an 'arbitrary' power in the state but that this power was lodged in parliament as the representative of the people (Parker, *Observations*, 34). To suggest, as some royalist writers did, that even if power had originally resided in the people, this had been resigned to the monarch, was absurd. It was not possible 'for any nation so to inslave it selfe, and to resigne its owne interest to the will of one Lord, as that that Lord may destroy it without injury, and yet to have no right to preserve it selfe' (Parker, *Observations*, 8). This would be to go against the fundamental natural right of self-defence. It was not the parliament's propositions which eviscerated true sovereignty but the king's *Answer*, for if the Lords and Commons were to be governed at the monarch's will or those of his 'sordid flatterers', the two Houses would become the 'very Engines and Scaffolds whereby to erect a government more tyrannicall then ever was knowne in any other Kingdome' (Parker, *Observations*, 21–2, 44). Rather than complain at the diminution of his power, Charles should extol limited monarchy, for those nations (Venice, the Dutch Republic) were happiest which were governed 'by such Monarchs' (Parker, *Observations*, 26, 40).

The notion that freedom consisted in a state of independence from the possibility of arbitrary domination clearly informed parliament's attempt to almost completely abrogate the royal prerogative. However, these tracts also suggested the potential for even more radical political change. Parker's glowing reflections on European states usually regarded as republics (or at least quasi-republics), as well as his emphasis on the absolute sovereignty of parliament suggested that this pamphlet was rather more than a defence of limited monarchy. Elsewhere in his *Observations* Parker felt it necessary to deny that any 'free Parliament' of England had ever deposed a king (Parker, *Observations*, 32). Yet, in his pamphlet he had also argued that 'Treason in Subjects against their Prince, so far only as it concernes the Prince, is not so horrid in nature, as oppression in the Prince exercised violently upon Subjects' (Parker, *Observations*, 19). Parker also insisted that Charles I's coronation oath showed that the English crown was 'not absolute . . . . but in part conditionate and fiduciary' (Parker, *Observations*, 4), a claim also made in two parliamentary remonstrances or declarations of May 1642.[31] While these declarations also included disclaimers denying a parliamentary right to try the king, they also contained radical assertions of the sovereign authority of parliament as court, against whose judgments there was no appeal and which could not be bound by past precedent.[32] This employment of the coronation oath went beyond denying the king's Negative Voice in matters relating to the safety of the kingdom. Parker's discussion of treason also bore some similarity with the House of Lords resolution on 20 May 1642 that 'Whensoever the King maketh War upon the Parliament, it is a Breach of the Trust reposed in Him by His People, contrary to His Oath, and tending to the Dissolution of this Government.'

The argument that attacks by the king against the realm were a breach of his oath resurfaced in the presbyterian lawyer William Prynne's *Soveraigne Power of Parliaments* (1643), where it was argued that such actions effectively meant that king had ceased to be monarch *de jure* and the people (through parliament) were free to use force to defend themselves.[33] Not without reason did John Milton in his *Tenure of Kings and Magistrates* (1649) suggest that Presbyterian writers had 'unkinged the king' long before the Rump determined in that year to put Charles I on trial and execute him.[34]

Arguments of this kind were, though, primarily used to legitimize parliament's adoption of extensive new powers, including the raising of armies, the imposition of taxes, the regulation of the press, and the direction of religious policy. The use of such extensive powers raised anxieties not only amongst royalists. Parker's argument that there was little danger from the misuse of power when absolute sovereignty was lodged in parliament because the state was effectively the people was less than reassuring (Parker, *Observations*, 22, 34). Indeed, it bore comparison with Hobbes's argument that a man who was imprisoned or punished for rebelling against the state did not suffer an injury because the subject had, through transferring their right to the sovereign, effectively authorized their own punishment.[35] Instead, a number of writers, later designated as 'Levellers', while affirming popular sovereignty, recognized that simply embodying this in parliament threatened replacing the tyranny of one man with the tyranny of many.

For some of these writers, notably John Lilburne, the rights and liberties enshrined in England's 'ancient constitution' and affirmed in documents such as Magna Carta and the Petition of Right, could check the power of parliament as well as king. Other Leveller writers, such as Richard Overton and William Walwyn, were, in contrast, critical of the English law as a bulwark of liberty—Overton and Walwyn dismissed that great emblem of English liberty, Magna Carta as 'but a beggarly thing containing many marks of intolerable bondage'.[36] Lilburne, though, as Rachel Foxley has shown, meant something broader than a specific set of laws when he spoke of the rights of 'freeborn Englishmen'—that 'Englishmen, as Englishmen, had political status'.[37] The core of the Levellers' political philosophy can be found, not in English common law traditions, which they certainly made free use of, but in the idea of 'self-propriety' articulated at the beginning of Richard Overton's *An Arrow against all Tyrants* (1646). Every individual, Overton argued, was 'given an individual property by nature not to be invaded or usurped by any .... For by natural birth all men are equally and alike born to like propriety, liberty and freedom; .... so are we to live, everyone equally and alike to enjoy his birthright and privilege' (*Levellers*, ed. Sharp, 55). Parliament had no right, any more than the king, to invade this 'birthright': the powers of parliament were only delegated from the people—the people were the 'principals' and their representatives only their 'agents'. To exceed their delegated authority or act in ways which threatened the individual's property was to usurp powers that rightly belonged to the people and to oppress their 'just freedom' (*Levellers*, ed. Sharp, 34). Actions of this kind were 'usurpations' because they infringed upon rights which, according to nature, the individual themselves could not resign, specifically liberty of conscience and self-preservation. It was not coincidental, then, that much of the Levellers' political philosophy developed from the engagement of its leading writers, Lilburne, Overton, and Walwyn in debates over religious toleration.[38] However, the Leveller position was distinct from that of radical Independents who also argued for liberty of conscience. The freedom demanded here was not only that to submit oneself entirely to God, to become vehicles for his will. As another leading Leveller, John Wildman, articulated at the Whitehall debates in 1648, it was impossible for men to show what the will of God was and difficult by 'the light of nature' to demonstrate anything more than that some sort of supreme being existed.[39] As Glenn Burgess has described it, for the Levellers, 'to do God's will required involvement in a genuinely *political* world of free human choices, using "the best care and abilities God hath afforded us" '.[40]

The structure devised by the Levellers for protecting these rights from usurpation was outlined in the various versions of the 'Agreements of the People'. Whether these documents represented a completely new written constitution, or envisaged the dissolution of the nation into an effective 'state of nature' before their adoption has recently been contested by Rachel Foxley.[41] What they did attempt to do was to provide electoral and constitutional mechanisms to affirm first, that the people were sovereign and their representatives their delegates, and second that not even this new popular representative could abrogate certain fundamental rights, including liberty of conscience.[42] The franchise was never treated by the Levellers as one of these 'reserved' rights. Nonetheless, Leveller views on the vote were connected to the idea of 'self-propriety' and the denial of voting rights seen as an infringement of the rights of citizens. Philip Baker has shown that the importance of the vote to the Levellers may have been underestimated in recent scholarship, and Leveller support for a broader franchise may, in fact, have been derived from the experience of leading figures in the movement—Lilburne, Walwyn, and Thomas Prince—in the relatively open politics of London wards.[43] Even so, during the Putney debates of 1647, it was the army's proposals, not those from the civilian Levellers which called for adult male suffrage.[44] As Quentin Skinner has suggested, the gulf that is often depicted between the army grandee Henry Ireton, who demanded that only those with a 'fixed interest' (property in land) should exercise the vote, and the Levellers, was narrower than it seemed. Both the Levellers and Ireton were agreed that only independent men, those who had not lost mastery over themselves, should exercise the vote—hence the exclusion of servants and those receiving charity from most Leveller statements on the franchise. The difference lay only in the type of wealth and property that each envisaged as conferring independence: for Ireton, only property in land was sufficient; for the Levellers, a franchise of rate-paying male householders was possible.[45] This common ground, as much as political necessity, may explain why Ireton and the Levellers were able to work together in drawing up a new version of the Agreement of the People in the winter of 1648/9. Though this was tendered to parliament for its consideration (a move which went against the Leveller principle that the Agreements should receive popular approval first), it fell by the wayside as the Rump, redeploying arguments first aired in 1642–3, turned its attention to prosecuting Charles I as a traitor who had waged war on his own people.

LIBERTY IN A 'FREE STATE'

For some historians, the length of time that it took for the new regime to publicly declare itself a 'Commonwealth and Free-State'—nearly four months after the king's execution—was evidence of the absence of any real republican impetus behind either the regicide or the establishment of government without a king. According to Blair Worden, 'The republicanism of the Rump in 1649 was, in fact, a mere improvisation, triumphant by default, unconvinced and largely unprofessed.'[46] If an 'ideology' could be detected, it was the survival of the arguments of the early 1640s for absolute parliamentary sovereignty, as evidenced in the Commons' declaration of 4 January 1649 that the 'Commons of *England*, in Parliament assembled, being chosen by, and representing the People, have the Supreme Power in this Nation'.[47] However, as noted by both Jonathan Scott and Quentin Skinner, if not exclusively 'republican', the public pronouncements of both the Rump and its supporters connected back to the ideal of liberty which had been used to challenge Charles I's 'tyranny' in the 1630s.[48] In fact, rather than being hesitant, the Rump had already begun altering its public style before the king had been executed. An act of 29 January 1649 changed the form of English legal proceedings so that 'Instead of the Name, Stile and *Teste* [authorizing clause in a writ] of the King, heretofore used', all writs, grants, and patents would be the *Teste* of '*Custodes libertatis Angliae authoritate Parliamenti*' ('The Keepers of the liberty of England authorized by Parliament') (*A & O*, I, 1262–3). The act abolishing the kingly office of March 1649 made clear that government by a single person had been found by experience to be inimical to liberty:

> to have the power thereof in any single person, is unnecessary, burthensom and dangerous to the liberty, safety and publique interest of the people, and that for the most part, use hath been made of the Regal power and prerogative, to oppress, and impoverish and enslave the Subject; and that usually and naturally any one person in such power, makes it his interest to incroach upon the just freedom and liberty of the people, and to promote the setting up of their own will and power above the Laws, that so they might enslave these Kingdoms to their own Lust.

The act disclaimed constitutional innovation—by returning to government by the people's own representatives, the Rump claimed it was restoring the nation's 'just and ancient right'—yet it also promised such 'freedom in choice and equality in distribution of Members to be elected thereunto, as shall most conduce to the lasting freedom and good of this Commonwealth' (*A & O*, II, 18–20).

Although this promise was vague, it seemed to connect the establishment of a Commonwealth with broadening political liberties, specifically the franchise. Not only monarchy but also aristocracy was challenged in the act of the same month abolishing the House of Lords. This did not completely exclude the peerage from politics but ensured that only those who 'demeaned themselves with Honor, Courage and

Fidelity to the Commonwealth' would have their 'free vote' in parliament if elected (*A & O*, II, 24). Finally, the act of 19 May 1649 which declared 'the *People of England* [my emphasis] to be a Commonwealth and Free-State', clearly intended more than just to signal the fact that England was now governed 'without a king or House of Lords'. Its title stressed that this was a government founded on popular sovereignty whose officers would work for the good of the people (*A & O*, II, 122). The designation of the new government as a 'Free-State' was more important than its description as a 'Commonwealth'. In contemporary usage, 'free state' was understood to mean not simply a state that was independent and free from foreign jurisdiction, but a polity in which its citizens were free.[49]

The new Commonwealth's promotion of itself as a government which would protect, support, and increase the liberty of its citizens was noted by both sympathetic and hostile observers. John Milton, while devoting most of his literary effort in the *Tenure of Kings and Magistrates* (1649) to defending the regicide also asserted that the death of the king would lead the people to turn away from monarchy as a system, instead heeding the republic's call to 'liberty and the flourishing deeds of a reformed Commonwealth'.[50] No contemporary read as much into the acts establishing a Commonwealth as the Digger leader Gerrard Winstanley. As he argued in a pamphlet urging subscription to the 'Engagement' of loyalty to the new regime, the acts abolishing the kingly office and establishing a free state 'takes away the Tirany of conquests, which is Kingly and Lordly power; and restores *England* to their creation right' and gives 'full liberty to all sort of people that are *English* men'. (Although few of England's new magistrates would have concurred that these acts made 'the Land of *England*' a 'common Treasury'.)[51] Hobbes's *Leviathan*, published in 1651, is indicative of the strength of these positive arguments for popular government. The tone of *Leviathan*, as suggested by Noel Malcolm, is arguably more distinctly royalist than in his earlier political works.[52] Within *Leviathan*, the focus of Hobbes's attacks shifted from the threat posed by ambitious aristocrats to the dangers of democracy. For Hobbes, the opinion that 'they that live under a Popular Common-wealth enjoy Liberty; but that in a Monarchy they are all Slaves' was now what needed to be demolished.[53]

Of course, even before the Rump had declared itself a 'Free-State' the actual degree of liberty its subjects would enjoy had already been put in to question. It was significant that the act declaring a commonwealth had been preceded four days earlier by a new law which stated that anyone who wrote, printed, or said that the 'Government is Tyrannical, Usurped or Unlawful; or that the Commons in Parliament assembled are not the Supreme authority of this Nation' would be deemed guilty of 'High Treason' (*A & O*, II, 120–1). It was an act specifically targeted at vociferous critics of the Rump, such as the Leveller John Lilburne who denounced the men who now governed England and had 'beheaded the King for a tyrant', yet now walked 'in his oppressingest steps, if not worse and higher'.[54] Lilburne was tried for treason the same year. He only escaped a guilty verdict by successfully convincing his jurors that they, the people, and not the new Commonwealth's magistrates, were the true judges of the law.[55]

CONCLUSION

As contemporaries saw it, however, the failure to secure liberty during the Interregnum was at least as much the fault of individuals as of institutions. Indeed, looking at the political thought of the 1630s and 1640s, it is remarkable how few thinkers saw themselves as being in the business of reforming the English constitution. Both absolutists and constitutionalists believed they were describing the English state as it was, not as it should be. Even the Levellers probably conceived of their new 'representative' as fitting within the established frame of mixed government and though they had radical ideas about 'reserved' rights, they created no constitutional mechanism to deal with the consequences of legislative or executive infraction of these rights. Instead, true liberty would be achieved, as Milton put it in his second defence of the English people, through 'the renewed cultivation of freedom and civic life'.[56] The problem was that the English people were accustomed to living under a monarch. The Rump's propagandist Marchamont Nedham contended that, like caged animals who were often too habituated to captivity to leave their lair when liberated, the danger in England was that there were many who, 'by reason of our former education under a monarchy', remained great 'admirers of the pomp of tyranny and enemies to that freedom which hath been so dearly purchased'. Milton showed himself equally sceptical about the readiness of most of the English people for life under a free state in his *History of Britain*, begun in the 1640s but only published in 1670.[57] The answer for Nedham and Milton, both in the employment of Commonwealth and Protectorate as writers, was to engage the English people in a programme of public political education. For other thinkers, such as Gerrard Winstanley and James Harrington, the solution was to develop detailed proposals for a new commonwealth which would ensure that the English people could not return to their old ways. In Harrington's model commonwealth, *Oceana* (1656), however, this left the people with virtually no freedom of action. Like the cats he had observed at a Roman carnival, forced to skim pots, turn spits, and whip up green sauce in a kitchen diorama, the mechanisms of Harrington's commonwealth would compel the people to exercise their freedom in the appropriate manner, each according to their station.[58] Winstanley's vision of 'true magistracy' was even more coercive: those who did not conform to the requirements of his ideal commonwealth would lose their freedom and, like those who had once defied Charles I's Star Chamber, would be whipped 'till such time as their proud hearts do bend to the Law'.[59]

The failure of the English Commonwealth and Protectorate in the eyes of these writers to cultivate freedom offers a reminder that understandings of liberty were grounded in specific historical contexts and informed by political practice and lived experience. England failed to establish a free state not only because of the intransigence and corruption of its governors but also, according to many thinkers, because its people were too accustomed to servitude. These contexts and experiences were not purely domestic either. Just as the examples of modern states both free and unfree were employed in contemporary political discourse, so the existence and threat of slavery gave substance to radical arguments for liberty. Ideas concerning freedom and slavery, however, shaped as much as were shaped by the historical context they inhabited. As has been shown, differing understandings of the threat to liberty encouraged minor challenges and infractions to be read as potentially catastrophic assaults on civil society. In this sense, the English civil war can be seen as a war fought for liberty. Yet it was a conflict in which both sides saw themselves as the defenders of freedom. Arguably, in the mid-seventeenth century what we witness is not the battle between different conceptions of liberty, whether negative, positive, or 'neo-Roman', but a dispute over how best to achieve and secure civil liberty, understood by all thinkers as more than just protection and security but the 'good life' itself. Notionally 'free' states today struggle with problems of inequality, social deprivation, and religious extremism. It is, therefore, scarcely surprising that some of the greatest scholars of early modern liberty have suggested that its rich and deep literature may offer us a similarly instructive political education as Milton and Nedham once felt was necessary for the people of seventeenth-century England.[60]

Notes

1. I would like to thank Mike Braddick, Chris Brooke, and Cesare Cuttica for their help with and comments on this chapter. For this conception of liberty see Quentin Skinner, 'A Third Concept of Liberty', *Proceedings of the British Academy*, 117 (2002): 237–68 and for Berlin, 238–40; see also Quentin Skinner, 'Classical Liberty and the Coming of the English Civil War', in MartinVan Gelderen and Quentin Skinner (eds.), *Republicanism: A Shared European Heritage, II: The Values of Republicanism in Early Modern Europe* (Cambridge, 2002), chap. 1; Quentin Skinner, 'Rethinking Political Liberty', *History Workshop Journal*, 61 (2006): 156–70.

2. [John Lilburne], *A True Relation Of . . . . Lilburnes Sufferings* (1646), 3. For the impact of Lilburne's punishments and imprisonments on his concept of liberty see D. Alan Orr, 'Law, Liberty and the English Civil War: John Lilburne's Prison Experience, the Levellers and Freedom', in Michael J. Braddick and David L. Smith (eds.), *The Experience of Revolution in Stuart Britain and Ireland: Essays for John Morrill* (Cambridge, 2011), 154–71.

3. J. C. Davis, 'Religion and the Struggle for Freedom in the English Revolution', *Historical Journal* [*HJ*], 35 (1992): 507–30.

4. Quentin Skinner, 'Classical Liberty, Renaissance Translation, and the English Civil War', in Skinner, *Visions of Politics*, 3 vols (Cambridge, 2002), II, 308–42, at 326–9. For absolutist use of the same language, Johann P. Sommerville, 'English and Roman Liberty in the Monarchical Republic of Early Stuart England', in John F. McDiarmid (ed.), *The Monarchical Republic of Early Modern England: Essays in Response to Patrick Collinson* (Farnham, 2007), 201–16; Glenn Burgess, *British Political Thought, 1500–1660: The Politics of the Post-Reformation* (Basingstoke, 2009), 213, 217; Thomas Hobbes, *Leviathan*, ed. Noel Malcolm, 3 vols. (Oxford, 2012), II, 16.

5. While 'liberty' could be understood as inferring something more limited—a privilege pertaining to a particular individual or group—in this chapter I use 'liberty' and 'freedom' as synonyms given that the terms were nonetheless used interchangeably in the seventeenth

century and liberty, as the quotations within this chapter demonstrate, was frequently employed in a broad, as well as narrow, sense.

6. Thomas Hobbes, *The Elements of Law Natural and Politic*, ed. John Charles Addison Gaskin (Oxford, 1994), 164–5. Further page references to this work are given in the text.

7. Quentin Skinner, *Hobbes and Liberty* (Cambridge, 2008), 80–1.

8. Quoted in Cesare Cuttica, *Sir Robert Filmer (1588–1653) and the Patriotic Monarch: Patriarchalism in Seventeenth-Century Political Thought* (Manchester, 2012), 68.

9. Quotations from Skinner, 'Third Concept of Liberty', 251–3.

10. Skinner, 'Classical Liberty', 309–12.

11. Quoted in Corinne Comstock Weston, 'England: Ancient Constitution and Common Law', in James Henderson Burns (ed.), *The Cambridge History of Political Thought, 1450–1700 [CHPT]* (Cambridge, 1991), chap. 13 at 386 and see 374–96 for a discussion of early Stuart ideas of the ancient constitution.

12. Quoted in Cuttica, *Filmer*, 65 and for Scott's ideas see 60–5.

13. Edward Vallance, *Revolutionary England and the National Covenant: State Oaths, Protestantism and the Political Nation, 1553–1682* (Woodbridge, 2005), 43. The biblical reference to the daughters of Heth adds weight to Eric Nelson's thesis concerning the radical potential of rabbinical sources: Eric Nelson, *The Hebrew Republic: Jewish Sources and the Transformation of European Political Thought* (London, 2010), chap. 1 and see Cuttica, *Filmer*, 64.

14. For the refusal to license *Patriarcha* see Cuttica, *Filmer*, 65. For a summary of Filmer's ideas and those of his contemporaries see Johann Sommerville, 'Absolutism and Royalism', in *CHPT*, chap. 12, 358–9.

15. Cuttica, *Filmer*, 66.

16. Quoted in Cuttica, *Filmer*, 75.

17. Cuttica, *Filmer*, 69–70; and see Hobbes, *Elements*, 139, 172.

18. For a powerful argument for constitutional consensus see Glenn Burgess, *The Politics of the Ancient Constitution: An Introduction to English Political Thought, 1603–1642* (Basingstoke, 1992); for the debate on *Patriarcha* see Cuttica, *Filmer*, 147–8.

19. Robert Baillie, *The Life of William now Lord Arch-Bishop of Canterbury* (London, 1643), preface.

20. See, for example, John Goodwin, *Anti-Cavalierisme* (London, 1642), 38. For the general association in English anti-popery of Catholicism and absolutism see Peter Lake, 'Anti-Popery: The Structure of a Prejudice', in Richard Cust and Ann Hughes (eds.), *Conflict in Early Stuart England* (Harlow, 1989), chap. 3.

21. For this see Richard Cust, 'Charles I and Popularity', in Thomas Cogswell, Richard Cust, and Peter Lake (eds.), *Politics, Religion and Popularity in Early Stuart Britain: Essays in Honour of Conrad Russell* (Cambridge, 2011), chap. 11.

22. Quoted in Ann Hughes, *The Causes of the English Civil War* (2nd edition, Basingstoke, 1998), 90.

23. Sir John Spelman, *A View of a Printed Book Intituled Observations upon His Majesties Late Answers* (Oxford, 1643) [unpaginated].

24. Text used here is that reproduced in *An Exact Collection of all Remonstrances* (London, 1643), British Library [BL], E. 241[1], 311–27, quotations at 313, 316, and 320.

25. Michael Mendle, *Dangerous Positions: Mixed Government, the Estates of the Realm, and the Making of the Answer to the 19 Propositions* (Tuscaloosa, 1985) and see Alan Cromartie's chapter in this volume.

26. Dudley Digges, *The Unlawfulnesse of Subjects Taking Up Armes Against Their Soveraigne* ([Oxford], 1643), 9.

27. *An Exact Collection*, 319. For a summary of the propositions see Michael J. Braddick, *God's Fury, England's Fire: A New History of the English Civil Wars* (London, 2008), 192–3.

28. Skinner, 'Third Concept of Liberty', 253.

29. *An exact collection*, 497. Skinner, 'Rethinking Political Liberty', 167–8.

30. Henry Parker, *Observations on some of his Majesties late answers and expresses* (London, 1642), BL, E. 153 [26]. Page references to this work are given in the text.

31. *An Exact Collection*, 268–9; *A Remonstrance of the Lords and Commons Assembled in Parliament, or The Reply of Both Houses* (London, 1642), 25–38.

32. *A Remonstrance .... or The Reply of Both Houses*, 13, 52.

33. Vallance, *Revolutionary England*, 74–9, quotation at 77.

34. *The Complete Prose Works of Milton*, ed. Don M. Wolfe, 8 vols. (New Haven, 1953–82) [*CPWM*], III, 230.

35. *Leviathan*, ed. Malcolm, II, 264–6.

36. Andrew Sharp (ed.), *The English Levellers* (Cambridge, 1998), 46–47. Further page references to this work are given in the text.

37. Rachel Foxley, *The Levellers: Radical Political Thought in the English Revolution* (Manchester, 2013), 113 and chap. 3 *passim*.

38. See Foxley, *Levellers*, chap. 4; Burgess, *British Political Thought*, 251–6; David R. Como, 'Print, Censorship and Ideological Escalation in the English Civil War', *Journal of British Studies*, 51 (2012): 820–57.

39. *The Clarke Papers*, ed. Charles Harding Firth, 4 vols. (London, 1891–1901), II, 121.

40. Burgess, *British Political Thought*, 254.

41. Foxley, *Levellers*, 78–81.

42. For the Agreements generally see Philip Baker and Eliot Vernon (eds.), *The Agreements of the People, the Levellers and the Constitutional Crisis of the English Revolution* (Basingstoke, 2012).

43. Philip Baker, 'The Franchise Debate Revisited: The Levellers and the Army', in Stephen Taylor and Grant Tapsell (eds.), *The Nature of the English Revolution Revisited* (Woodbridge, 2013), 103–22.

44. See Edward Vallance, 'Oaths, Covenants, Associations and the Origins of the Agreements of the People: The Road to and from Putney', in Baker and Vernon (eds.), *Agreements of the People*, 28–49. But see also Baker, 'Franchise', 122.

45. Skinner, 'Rethinking Political Liberty', 162–3.

46. Blair Worden, *The Rump Parliament* (Cambridge, 1978), 173.

47. *Journals of the House of Commons*, vi, 110–11 and see also the act establishing the Council of State, *Acts and Ordinances of the Interregnum, 1642-1660* [*A & O*], ed. Charles Harding Firth and Robert Sangster Rait, 2 vols. (London, 1911), II, 2–4. Further page references to this work are given in the text.

48. Jonathan Scott, 'What Were Commonwealth Principles?', *HJ*, 47 (2004): 591–613, at 602–3; Scott, *Commonwealth Principles: Republican Writing of the English Revolution* (Cambridge, 2004), 80; Skinner, 'Third Concept of Liberty', 255.

9. Quentin Skinner, *Liberty before Liberalism* (Cambridge, 1998), 67–8. Eugene Volokh, 'Necessary to the Security of a Free State', *Notre Dame Law Review*, 83.1 (2007): 101–39.

50. *CPWM*, III, 236.

51. *The Complete Works of Gerrard Winstanley*, ed. Thomas Corns, Ann Hughes, and David Loewenstein, 2 vols. (Oxford, 2009), II, 162.

52. *Leviathan*, ed. Malcolm, I, chap. 1; Skinner, *Hobbes and Liberty*, 202–3; for an alternative view, Jeffrey R. Collins, *The Allegiance of Thomas Hobbes* (Oxford, 2005).

53. *Leviathan*, ed. Malcolm, II, 508.

54. John Lilburne, *The Legall Fundamentall Liberties of the People of England Revived* (London, 1649), title page.

55. Theodorus Verax [Clement Walker], *The Triall, of Lieut. Collonell John Lilburne* (London, 1649), and see 60—Lilburne was specifically accused of suggesting that the Rump would reduce England to 'slavery and absolute bondage'.

56. *CPWM*, IV, 556.

57. Marchamont Nedham, *The Case of the Commonwealth of England, Stated*, ed. Phillip Atherton Knachel (Charlottesville, 1969), 112, quotation at 114. Blair Worden, 'Marchamont Nedham and English Republicanism', in David Wootton (ed.), *Republicanism, Liberty and Commercial Society* (Stanford, 1994), 45–81 at 58–9 and see Martin Dzelzainis, 'Conquest and Slavery in Milton's History of Britain', in Nicholas McDowell and Nigel Smith (eds.), *The Oxford Handbook to Milton* (Oxford, 2009), chap. 22.

58. James Harrington, *Political Works*, ed. John Greville Agard Pocock (Cambridge, 1977), 744.

59. Winstanley, *Works*, II, 330.

60. For the impact of slavery and indentured labour on political ideas see John Donoghue, *Fire Under the Ashes: An Atlantic History of the English Revolution* (Chicago, 2013). For the suggestion that modern discussions of liberty might benefit from an awareness of seventeenth-century debates, see Skinner, *Liberty before Liberalism*, chap. 3; Scott, 'What Were Commonwealth Principles?', 613.

FURTHER READING

Burgess, Glenn, *British Political Thought, 1500–1660: The Politics of the Post-Reformation* (Basingstoke, 2009).

Burns, James Henderson (ed.), *The Cambridge History of Political Thought, 1450–1700* (Cambridge, 1991).

Davis, James Colin, 'Religion and the Struggle for Freedom in the English Revolution', *Historical Journal*, 35 (1992): 507–530.

Hobbes, Thomas, *The Elements of Law Natural and Politic*, ed. John Charles Addison Gaskin (Oxford, 1994).

Parker, Henry, *Observations on some of his Majesties late answers and expresses* (London, 1642), British Library, E. 153 [26].

Scott, Jonathan, *Commonwealth Principles: Republican Writing of the English Revolution* (Cambridge, 2004).

Sharp, Andrew (ed.), *The English Levellers* (Cambridge, 1998).

Skinner, Quentin, *Liberty before Liberalism* (Cambridge, 1998).

Skinner, Quentin, *Visions of Politics*, 3 vols. (Cambridge, 2002).

Skinner, Quentin and Martin Van Gelderen (eds.), *Republicanism: A Shared European Heritage*, 2 vols. (Cambridge, 2002).

CHAPTER 26

··

RELIGIOUS THOUGHT

··

JOHN COFFEY

A Theological Crisis

THE English Revolution was a theological crisis, a struggle over the identity of British Protestantism. Thomas Hobbes would later say that 'the cause of the civil war' was 'nothing other than the quarrelling about theological issues'.[1] This was a reductionist analysis, but it contained a kernel of truth. The Church of England and the Church of Scotland had experienced very different reformations in the sixteenth century, but both had been aligned with international Calvinism, or what contemporaries called 'the Reformed churches'. Under Charles I and Archbishop Laud, however, there was a concerted campaign to remodel the British churches. In matters of doctrine, the Laudians rejected the predestinarianism of Zwingli and Calvin, preferring the teaching of the Greek Fathers and the Dutch Arminians who had emphasized the synergy of divine grace and human freewill in salvation. In matters of worship, Laudians sought to infuse 'the beauty of holiness' into Protestantism through choral music, elaborate vestments, liturgical rites, and restoration of altars. Communicants were to kneel at the altar rails, and receive the elements from the priest, thus imbibing a high view of both the eucharist and the priestly office. In matters of discipline and government, the Laudians asserted the authority of the higher clergy over parish pastors, often justifying this by a divine right (*jure divino*) theory of episcopacy that cast doubt on the legitimacy of the ministry in Europe's non-episcopal Reformed churches. These policies involved a fundamental realignment of the *Ecclesia Anglicana*. Instead of identifying with the Reformed churches of Switzerland, France, and the Netherlands, it would discover a unique identity as the purest embodiment of the early patristic church. Finally, in their political theology, the Laudians articulated an exalted conception of kingship—the king's authority came directly from God, not the people, and he had an inviolable and quasi-sacramental status as the Lord's Anointed. It was a vision of hierarchy, order, and beauty that appealed powerfully to Charles I.[2]

The king's Personal Rule (1629–40) was ended by the Scottish Covenanters, who initially rose up against the imposition of a new liturgy, and quickly abolished episcopacy.

They forced the king to recall the Westminster Parliament, and it emphatically reversed the Laudian 'innovations' in 1640–1. But Puritans wanted to do more than turn the clock back to 1625. They had always believed that the English church was 'but halfly reformed'; now was their chance to complete the Reformation. In 1643, the parliamentarians signed a Solemn League and Covenant with the Scottish Covenanters. The first article set an agenda for religious reform. It committed both parties to 'the preservation of the reformed religion in the Church of Scotland' and 'the reformation of religion in the kingdoms of England and Ireland, in doctrine, worship, discipline and government, according to the Word of God, and the example of the best reformed Churches'. They also agreed 'to bring the Churches of God in the three kingdoms to the nearest conjunction and uniformity in religion, confession of faith, form of Church government, directory for worship and catechising'.[3]

The problem was that 'the Word of God' and 'the best reformed Churches' did not speak with one voice. Reformed churches had variously adopted episcopacy, presbyterianism, and congregationalism, and Protestants were often divided over matters of biblical interpretation. While theological tradition still carried great weight, it was relatively easy to legitimize intellectual novelty on grounds of 'further reformation'. The eschatological excitement of the 1640s and 1650s strengthened the hand of innovators. Many puritans believed that they were living in the last days predicted by the prophet Daniel and the Book of Revelation. God was destroying Antichrist, restoring the church, and revealing 'new light' from his Word.[4]

A torrent of religious works poured forth from London presses. Between 1640 and 1661, the London bookseller George Thomason collected approximately 15,000 books and pamphlets. On average, 'explicitly religious titles averaged between twenty and fifty per month', around half the total number.[5] In 1641, for example, more than two hundred pamphlets were published on the subject of episcopacy alone. Root and branch reformers, like John Milton, argued for its abolition, while Joseph Hall and other bishops made the case for divine right episcopacy. Many rejected both extremes, advocating either a return to the Reformed episcopate of the Jacobean years or a 'reduction' of episcopacy on the lines suggested by the patristic scholarship of Archbishop Ussher.[6] No secular issue in that critical year generated this volume of print—it was the first of a series of religious controversies that dominated the book market. Among publications by women, prophecy constituted the single largest genre in the 1640s, Quaker works in the following decade—together they comprised more than half of the printed writings of women during the Revolution.[7] The public appetite for religious debate was voracious. By 1660, hundreds of public disputations had been held between puritan clergy and sectarians like the Baptists and the Quakers, attracting throngs of spectators. England had become a religious marketplace.[8]

Forging Confessional Orthodoxy

This was not supposed to happen. In 1640, parliamentary leaders had no intention of letting a hundred flowers blossom and a hundred schools of thought contend. (Exceptions were Robert Greville, second Baron Brooke, author of *The Nature of Truth*, and Sir Henry

Vane the younger, former governor of Massachusetts, both unusually sympathetic to radical ideas among the godly.) Once the civil war began, parliament called a learned Assembly of Divines at Westminster to make official recommendations for reform of the church. As its leading historian explains, 'To the extent that religion was a cause of the first civil war, this Assembly at Westminster was supposed to be a solution.'[9] It was the last of the major post-Reformation synods and the largest parliamentary committee. Its membership comprised 120 puritan divines, ten members of the House of Lords, twenty members of the Commons (including the formidably erudite Hebraist, John Selden), and a team of Scottish commissioners, both clerical and lay. In hundreds of plenary sessions between 1643 and 1647, these men debated issues of doctrine, worship, discipline, and church government. Scribes recorded the substance of their debates, though a complete transcription of the Assembly's minutes was not published until 2012.[10] What were published at the time were the Assembly's major documents, the ones envisaged by the Solemn League and Covenant: a new confession of faith (the Westminster Confession), Larger and Shorter Catechisms, a Directory for Worship, a Directory for Ordination, and a Directory for Church Government.

Because historians of ideas privilege innovatory individuals, we tend to overlook the role of corporate bodies in shaping intellectual traditions. Synods and assemblies imposed a discipline on theologians. Their task was to identify the teaching of the Scriptures, to work faithfully within the tradition of the best Reformed churches, to seek consensus amidst their disagreements, and to address new challenges and ideas. They could do so using the tools of scholastic logic and humanist learning, and with reference to the Bible, the Fathers, Reformation theologians, and earlier Reformed confessions. By the mid-seventeenth century, the Reformed churches had a mature and highly articulated theological tradition. It was codified in a series of national confessions of faith—including the Helvetic, the French, the Belgic, the English Thirty-Nine Articles of 1563, and the Irish Articles of 1615. It had been solidified at the international synod of Dort which repudiated Arminianism in 1618–19. And it had been expounded at length and in depth by a long line of distinguished Reformed divines—Zwingli, Bullinger, Bucer, Martyr, Calvin, Beza, Musculus, and Paraeus.[11]

Thus the Westminster Assembly was working within well-established parameters, and its Confession was a precise summation of Reformed Protestant orthodoxy. It began with the Reformation principle of *sola scriptura*: 'The Holy Spirit speaking in Scripture' was 'the Supreme Judge by which all controversies of religion are to be determined, and all decrees of councils, opinions of ancient writers, doctrines of men, and private spirits are to be examined' (I.10). To underline the point, the divines provided hundreds of biblical proof texts for every statement in the Confession. This thoroughgoing Biblicism was a key feature of puritan theology in the Revolution, and it placed a question mark against the status of extra-biblical statements of faith. Clergy in the English church had been required to subscribe to the ecumenical creeds (the Apostles' Creed, the Nicene Creed, and the Athanasian Creed) and all three had been used in the Prayer Book Service. But a substantial minority of Westminster divines (whom John Lightfoot dubbed the 'excepters') challenged the imposition of these 'forms', and (by implication) of the Assembly's own Confession. This provoked the synod's longest-running debate, and although the 'creedalist' majority voted that 'the three creeds are thoroughly to be received', later Assembly documents like the Directory, the Confession of Faith, and the Catechisms were silent on the Creeds.[12]

Despite these hesitations, however, the Confession emphatically endorsed Trinitarian orthodoxy, using the conceptual categories of the Council of Nicaea (AD 325) and the Council of Chalcedon (AD 451). 'In the unity of the Godhead', it asserted, 'there be three persons, of one substance, power, and eternity: God the Father, God the Son, and God the Holy Ghost' (II.3). Christ was 'the second person of the Trinity, being very and eternal God, of one substance, and equal with the Father'. In him, 'two whole, perfect, and distinct natures, the Godhead and the manhood, were inseparably joined together in one person, without conversion, composition, or confusion' (VIII.2).

As well as entrenching Trinitarianism, the Confession was designed to defend Calvinist orthodoxy, especially the doctrine of predestination that had come under assault from within the Reformed churches by Arminians. Chapter III was entitled 'God's Eternal Decree', and it taught that 'By the decree of God, for the manifestation of his glory, some men and angels are predestinated unto everlasting life, and others foreordained to everlasting death' (III.3). This had been done 'without any foresight of faith or good works, or perseverance in either of them, or any other thing in the creature, as conditions, or causes moving him thereunto' (III.5).

The heart of the Confession set out classic Reformed soteriology (the doctrine of salvation), devoting chapters to Effectual Calling, Justification, Adoption, Sanctification, Saving Faith, Repentance, Good Works, Perseverance, and Assurance. The divines upheld Reformation principles of *sola gratia* and *sola fides*, but the Confession displayed a characteristically Reformed concern for the role of the law in the life of the believer and the Christian community. Hence the chapters on God's law and 'Christian Liberty', oath-taking, Sabbath-keeping, magistracy, marriage and divorce, the sacraments, and church discipline. In addressing such matters, the divines were determined to leave no room for libertines and antinomians (whom the Assembly's minutes mention twice as often as papists).

The Confession was a meticulously crafted collective statement, designed to give the impression of unanimity. But it disguised years of internal debate on a raft of issues. Protocol forbade the divines from divulging these disputes, but the controversy over ecclesiology did reach the public domain. This consumed a quarter of the Assembly's 1333 plenary sessions, a fifth of its ad hoc committees, and a quarter of its texts. A small minority (the 'Dissenting Brethren' or 'Apologists') issued a public statement, *An Apologeticall Narration* (1643/44), which explained that they favoured a middle way between separatism and presbyterianism—'the congregational Way'. The congregationalists had set up self-governing congregations during their exile in the Netherlands in the 1630s, and they did so again in England in the 1640s. Led by Thomas Goodwin and Philip Nye, they drew inspiration from the New England churches, and especially from the theologian John Cotton. Another minority, the Erastians, included John Lightfoot, Thomas Coleman, and John Selden. They argued strenuously that the power of church discipline (especially excommunication) should rest in the hands of the civil magistrates rather than the clergy, and their position was firmly endorsed by parliament itself. But the majority of Westminster divines favoured a presbyterian form of church government, in which individual congregations were subject to the authority of local presbyteries, regional assemblies, and general assemblies or synods. In contrast to the Erastians, the presbyterians were keen to preserve clerical authority. Against the congregationalists, they were opposed to the gathering of congregations, and firmly committed to the parish as the basic ecclesial unit.

However, this neat three-party taxonomy obscures as much as it clarifies. Recent scholarship has shown that the patterns of clerical alignment shifted in kaleidoscopic fashion from debate to debate. When the Assembly tackled the locus of church authority ('the power of keys') in the autumn and winter of 1643–4, the congregationalists repudiated the populist notion (associated with separatists and radical Independents) that church power was located in the congregation as a whole, insisting instead that it rested with both the people and their elders. The Erastians maintained that the power of the keys was shared by godly magistrates. As for the presbyterians, they were divided. Some, like the Scottish commissioners Samuel Rutherford and George Gillespie, were surprisingly sympathetic to the Dissenting Brethren and keen to accord some power to the congregation. The English presbyterian majority, however, was staunchly clericalist, and located the power of the keys in the presbytery (pastors and elders governing multiple congregations). It was led by two of the Assembly's dominant figures, Cornelius Burgess (the acting prolocutor) and Lazarus Seaman, who ensured that the Scots and the Apologists were sidelined. Moderate English presbyterians like Stephen Marshall and Charles Herle attempted to mediate, but to no avail. Yet close study of the debate punctures several myths about the Assembly. The English presbyterians were not meekly led towards clericalism by tough-minded Scots; the Scots (with the exception of Robert Baillie) were not the polar opposites of the congregationalists; and the congregationalists were less isolated than their critics alleged.[13]

When we examine theological debates within the Assembly, the complexity of alignments becomes even more striking. Reformed divines were divided over the extent of the atonement—did Christ die for the elect alone, or did he atone for the whole of humanity? Hypothetical universalists like Archbishop Ussher and John Davenant had each argued for the latter proposition, and a significant minority of Westminster divines agreed with them. On the doctrine of justification—which Luther had seen as the central dogma of the Reformation—there were heated disputes. Whereas the majority at Westminster believed that justification involved the imputation of Christ's perfect life (his 'active obedience') to the believer, a vocal minority (led by the learned presbyterians Thomas Gataker and Richard Vines) dissented. They worried that this teaching would encourage antinomians. A third issue that divided the divines was millenarianism. The sixteenth-century Reformers had followed Augustine in rejecting the idea of a future millennial rule of the saints on earth, but in the early seventeenth century leading Calvinist intellectuals, including Thomas Brightman and Joseph Mede, had argued that Protestants should expect a coming millennium. This view was endorsed by the venerable prolocutor of the Assembly, William Twisse, and embraced by all the congregationalist Brethren. It was rejected by the Scots and most English presbyterians, though many of them still expected a period of latter-day glory before the Second Coming of Christ. The Confession was worded so that it could be endorsed by divines who took different positions on these issues.[14]

Debating such points and defending Reformed theology against its enemies was a major preoccupation of puritan divines, and during these decades they published hundreds of doctrinal works.[15] But the rise of the New Model Army and the triumph of the Independents ended hopes of a presbyterian national church and also prevented the formal adoption to the Westminster Confession. Nevertheless, the lack of an official confession troubled leading congregationalists like Thomas Goodwin and John Owen, as well as many presbyterians. Through the course of the 1650s, there were a series of further efforts at creed-making and confessionalization.[16] In 1652, Owen and his allies drew up a list of sixteen 'Principles of the Christian Religion' to supplement their Humble Proposals for a new church settlement. These were designed to secure the fundamentals of Trinitarianism and Protestantism, and could have been signed by Arminians, but although the Rump debated the Proposals, they were not formally adopted. The Instrument of Government (1653) called for a new confession, but it also promised toleration for all who 'profess faith in God by Jesus Christ', excluding proponents of prelacy or popery. A parliamentary sub-committee was set up in 1654, chaired by Owen, which drew up A New Confession, a statement of faith with twenty articles which was more explicitly Calvinist. Once again, parliament failed to adopt the confession, and in 1657 the Humble Petition and Advice asked Cromwell that 'a Confession of Faith, to be agreed by your Highness and the Parliament, according to the rule and warrant of the Scriptures, be asserted, held forth, and recommended to the people of these nations'.[17] The following year, Owen and his fellow congregationalists sought to get the process moving by drawing up a major confessional document. Two hundred delegates assembled at the Savoy Palace, making this the largest clerical assembly since Westminster. They relegated their congregational principles to an appendix, and there is a good case for seeing the Savoy Confession itself as a semi-official proposal for the national church, since the meeting was organized by Henry Scobell, secretary to the privy council. Once again, however, political developments ensured that no official confession was adopted.

CHALLENGING REFORMED ORTHODOXY

Thus, despite their hegemony, conservative Calvinists failed to turn England into a confessional state. On the contrary, they struggled to make themselves heard amidst a cacophony of heterodox voices. The years following the regicide saw the publication of an English translation of the Koran in 1649, the 'blasphemous' pamphlets of the Ranters, Thomas Hobbes's *Leviathan* (1651), John Goodwin's full-scale defence of Arminianism, *Redemption Redeemed* (1651), and the anti-Trinitarian Racovian Catechism. Parliament voted to seize and burn copies of Ranter pamphlets and the Racovian Catechism, and presbyterian booksellers mounted a sustained campaign against heretical publications. But while the puritan regime of the 1650s sponsored a draconian campaign of moral reformation, and steadily narrowed the range of newsbooks printed, it had less success restricting the publication of religious thought. England under the puritans was troubled by culture wars and distinguished by extraordinary intellectual fecundity.[18]

The absence of an official confession created genuine confusion about the boundaries of acceptable doctrine. Some of the godly were less than enthusiastic about confessional orthodoxy. Richard Baxter, the bestselling puritan pastor of the decade, had come to prominence with The Aphorismes of Justification (1649), an attack on antinomianism that rejected justification by faith alone. In 1654, Baxter endured a bruising encounter with John Owen and Francis Cheynell in parliament's sub-committee for drawing up a new confession of faith. He accused 'the Over-Orthodoxe Doctors' of seeking to impose their own understanding of the faith, and advocated a more minimalist basis for church unity—the Bible and (if necessary) the Apostles' Creed. Owen's failure to secure a strict confessional settlement allowed figures like Baxter to promote a modified 'neonomian' version of Calvinism that emphasized the necessity of good works for salvation and Christ's death for all mankind not just the elect.[19]

Arminianism had been the bugbear of puritans in the 1630s, but it was now making inroads among the godly themselves. John Goodwin, one of London's leading congregational pastors, forcefully advocated Arminianism (though not under that name) in a series of books and public disputations. Although he attracted a host of hostile rejoinders, he continued to be held in high regard by moderate Calvinists like Baxter. In 1652, he was even recruited to sign John Owen's Humble Proposals for the reform of the national church, which suggested that Arminianism was now a legitimate option among the godly. Later in the decade, the solidly Calvinist Triers would make it difficult for overt Arminians to enter the parish ministry, but opposition to strict Calvinism now extended well beyond the Laudian clergy.[20]

This was particularly evident at the University of Cambridge, where the Cambridge Platonists were increasingly influential. A tense exchange of letters between the Vice-Chancellor, Benjamin Whichcote and the Master of Emmanuel College, Anthony Tuckney in 1651 revealed that loyalties to Reformed orthodoxy were weakening. John Goodwin had dedicated Redemption Redeemed to Whichcote and the College Masters, but Whichcote refused to take up the cudgels against Arminianism, insisting that liberty of private judgement was 'the foundation of Protestancy'.[21] The Cambridge Platonists avoided a direct confrontation with Calvinism, but suggested a profound reorientation of English theology. Turning away from Aristotelian scholasticism they found inspiration in the Platonist tradition. Troubled by the stark predestinarianism of Augustine, they looked instead to Greek Fathers like Origen of Alexandria. Drawing on these sources, they developed a philosophical theology and spirituality centred on the goodness of God and the dignity of man. As rational but fallen beings, humans could be restored through Christ, whose incarnation united deity and humanity, making it possible for humans to be experience 'deification', as 'partakers of the divine nature'.[22]

Among the episcopal clergy, the tide turned against Calvinism even more decisively. A minority of episcopal divines would hold tenaciously to Reformed orthodoxy through the later seventeenth century, and these high church Calvinists would become well entrenched at Oxford University. But the most influential 'Anglican' theologians were Henry Hammond and Jeremy Taylor, emphatically Arminian figures. Hammond championed divine right episcopacy in *The Power of the Keyes* (1647), and produced a massive 1,000-word biblical commentary, *A Paraphrase and Annotations on all the Books of the New Testament* (1653). Most importantly, in his *Practical Catechism* and elsewhere, he articulated a neo-Arminian doctrine of salvation that owed much to Hugo Grotius. Christ's death had not paid the exact debt owed by sinners; instead, it allowed God to uphold public retributive justice while offering generous terms in the new covenant. Justification before God was not unconditional or by faith alone (as Luther had asserted); rather the new covenant offered justification to those who sincerely endeavoured to obey the law of Christ.[23] Justification seemed to follow sanctification, a reversal of Luther's *ordo salutis* (order of salvation). The moralism of Anglican theology was reinforced by a trio of devotional works by Jeremy Taylor that emphasized the imitation of Christ—*The Great Exemplar* (1649), *Holy Living* (1650), and *Holy Dying* (1651). But the most popular exposition of this soteriology was *The Whole Duty of Man* (1657), probably written by Richard Allestree. It was a manual intended to show its readers how 'to behave themselves so in this world that they may be happy for ever in the next'. Heaven was to be reached through dutiful behaviour.

These challenges to Reformed orthodoxy all came from divines, but to restrict our survey to the clergy would be to fundamentally misrepresent religious thought in the English Revolution. Theology in the 1640s and 1650s was far too important to leave to the ordained ministry. This was the great age of lay theologians. In 1644, one of them—the Londoner John Milton—imagined many 'pens and heads' in 'this vast city', 'sitting by their studious lamps, musing, searching, revolving new notions and ideas wherewith to present, as with their homage and their fealty the approaching Reformation'.[24] The lay engagement with theology was extraordinarily intense and creative.

The laity often held particular divines in high esteem, and it would be misleading to set up a false dichotomy between clerical orthodoxy and lay heterodoxy. Reformed orthodoxy was staunchly upheld by various non-clerical writers, including the lawyer William Prynne and the MP Edward Leigh, whose *Treatise of Divinity* (1646) was an able summary of Calvinist doctrine. The President of Cromwell's Council of State, Henry Lawrence, wrote several theological works, including one of the major defences of adult baptism in the 1640s—*Of Baptism* (1646). Like many who advocated believer's baptism, he remained firmly Calvinist in soteriology. The poet Lucy Hutchinson translated the infamous Lucretius, but she also translated a Latin work by John Owen, and her own theological writings reveal someone well versed in Reformed divinity.[25]

Much lay writing, however, was doctrinally unconventional. The Leveller William Walwyn was devoted to the 'antinomian' theology of 'free justification' that circulated in radical puritan circles, and it was eloquently presented in his tract *The Power of Love* (1643). Another Leveller, Richard Overton, rejected the traditional notion of the soul's immortality in *Man's Mortalitie* (1643) on the grounds that it owed more to Greek philosophy than to the Hebrew Scriptures. The leading Independent politician, Sir Henry Vane, one of the Revolution's most powerful politicians, published a major theological treatise, *The Retired Man's Meditations* (1655). Vane had been influenced by the mystical writings of Jacob Boehme, and had taken to expounding Scripture to gatherings in his house on the Charing Cross Road (where he was once taken to task by another socially eminent lay theologian, Robert Boyle). His cloudy mysticism bemused contemporaries, but a Calvinist critic claimed that he had deviated from normative Protestant teaching on 'Adam's Fall, Christ's Person, and Sufferings, Justification, Common and Special Grace; and Many Other Things...'.[26]

Vane's friend, John Milton, was more conventional in his mode of argument, but equally daring in his doctrines. The blind Milton dictated his systematic theology—*De Doctrina Christiana*—to amanuenses in the 1650s.[27] It rejected creation out of nothing, advanced a vitalist conception of nature against body–spirit dualism, denied the immortality of the soul, embraced Arminianism, and defended divorce and polygamy. The treatise was written in Latin and addressed to 'all the churches of Christ ... anywhere among the peoples', but its immediate English context is important. There is evidence that Milton was preparing it for publication in the late 1650s, when the imposition of confessional orthodoxy was a very real possibility. For Milton, implicit trust in clerical guides was a betrayal of the Reformation; to draw up one's own systematic theology was a quintessentially Protestant project.

In celebrating Milton's heresies, much recent scholarship has underplayed his identification with the Reformed tradition. In his own eyes, he was no heretic, but an exemplary Reformed Protestant.[28] He employed the logic of the Reformed intellectual Petrus Ramus, modelled his work on the systematic treatises of the Reformed theologians Ames and Wollebius, and drew his citations from the standard Protestant Latin Bible, the Junius-Tremellius translation. The Bible only was the religion of Protestants, and Milton's work contained no fewer than eight thousand scriptural references. Though not Trinitarian, he still articulated a high Christology. While the Son was not co-eternal with the Father, he was consubstantial, begotten from the substance of the Father rather than created *ex nihilo*, and worthy of worship. In matters of soteriology, Milton gave an Arminian or antinomian twist to certain doctrines, but he also adopted the forensic, penal account of the atonement that was conventional among Lutherans and Calvinists. *Paradise Lost* bears clear traces of his heterodoxies, but they were easily overlooked by generations of orthodox readers.

Others offered a more blatant challenge to traditional theology. The soldier-scholar Paul Best and the schoolmaster John Biddle had little use for the Western theological tradition between Nicaea and the Reformation, and they launched bitter attacks on the doctrine of the Trinity, associating it with the corruption of the church by Antichrist. This aggressive anti-Trinitarianism was intensified by the influence of the Polish Socinians, who combined Biblicism with an aversion to Mystery and a firm faith in the power of Reason. The Socinians denied the pre-existence of the Son; some even refused to worship Christ. But Socinianism was about more than Christology. Its chief theologians had been lawyers, and they saw Christ as the promulgator of a new law, and

Christianity as a revelation of new ethical principles. Christ saved men through his teaching and example; he had died as an exemplar, not as a substitute taking the punishment that humanity deserved. Salvation was achieved as humans exercised their free will by obeying Christ's new law. Such was their emphasis on Christ's new law that they displaced the natural law, denied the innate knowledge of God, and endorsed Christian pacifism against just war theory. The challenge of Socinianism preoccupied a variety of thinkers at mid-century, above all John Owen.[29]

Quakers posed a different kind of challenge. George Fox and the other Quaker itinerants posed as prophets, not intellectuals, and they had little interest in systematizing their thought. The first Quaker systematic theology was Robert Barclay's *Apology*, written in the 1670s. Although the puritan clergy and the baptists held numerous public disputations with Quakers, these were usually exercises in mutual incomprehension. Nevertheless, the early Quakers had some very definite ideas, ones that ran counter to mainstream Protestantism. They rejected doctrines of original sin and unconditional predestination in favour of the notion of the 'light within', based on the prologue of John's Gospel which declared that Christ had enlightened every man who came into the world. To orthodox Protestants, the Quakers' unrelenting emphasis on the inner light appeared to downgrade biblical authority, or even Christ's death and resurrection in first-century Palestine. Avoiding Christological disputes, Quakers were non-Trinitarian rather than anti-Trinitarian, but their disinterest in traditional doctrinal categories caused consternation.[30]

The rise of sects and heresies owed much to the radical potentialities of Protestant Biblicism and puritan populism, as well as to the feverish atmosphere created by the civil war. The notorious Ranters, for example, flourished in the wake of the regicide and emerged from within the puritan subculture, taking its emphases on free grace, the Spirit, and justification to extreme conclusions.[31] But equally significant were the voracious and eclectic reading habits of English Protestants, whether elite or plebeian. Elites eagerly devoured the writings of neo-Platonists, Greek Fathers, Dutch Arminians, and Polish Socinians, turning them against classic Reformed divinity. The new science and philosophy associated with Galileo and Descartes was used to undermine the scholastic categories of post-Reformation orthodoxy. And against the advice of conservative divines, English readers immersed themselves in a range of esoteric and occultic literature. The autodidact and prophet Thomas Totney built his idiosyncratic theology from a *mélange* of Behmenism, hermeticism, angelology, Pythagorean mysticism, alchemy, astrology, heraldry, genealogy, and apocryphal scriptures.[32] In 1640, puritan divines had set out to build Jerusalem; by the 1650s, they could be forgiven for thinking that England resembled Babel.

Scientific and Political Thought

But to focus on orthodoxy and its discontents would be to underplay the reach of religious thought. It spilled out beyond strictly theological debates to inundate other fields of intellectual discourse. As Patrick Collinson observed, the study of 'religious' titles hardly does justice to the influence of religious ideas, for if we turn to almanacs, medical treatises, and cookbooks we find them 'all saturated with pious vocabulary'.[33] A recent study of printed recipe books under the Protectorate confirms the point, noting that early modern recipes were partly inspired by the alchemical thought of Paracelsus, who sought a universal cure that would end disease and thus remedy the effects of the Fall of Adam.[34]

The 'scientific' projects of the Revolution were often devoted to the same end. Francis Bacon had cited the prophet Daniel who foresaw that in the last days 'knowledge would increase', and Baconian experimenters aimed to recover Adamic knowledge of the natural world. There was considerable interest in rediscovering a 'Paradisical language' that Adam had spoken in Eden, one that would provide privileged insight into the natures of things. The circle of 'projectors' around the German Reformed intellectual Samuel Hartlib was strongly influenced by the new Reformed millenarianism, and devised utopian and practical schemes of improvement in education, chemistry, engineering, horticulture, medicine, poor relief, and colonization. Another London-based group in the mid-1640s was centred on clerical intellectuals like the Westminster divine and mathematician John Wallis, the astronomer Seth Ward, and the natural philosopher John Wilkins. In the 1650s, the nucleus of this group was relocated to Oxford, where they were joined by Robert Boyle, who was to become the father of modern chemistry. Boyle was an exceptionally devout layman, who saw natural philosophy as an exercise in doxology—worshipping God by studying the created order. Like other participants in these scientific circles he favoured an irenic Protestant Christianity. Rather than engaging in detailed points of dispute with other Protestants, these thinkers had two major targets: the traditional scholastic philosophy that impeded the progress of the new science, and the materialist metaphysics that some intellectuals (notably Thomas Hobbes) saw as the corollary of the new philosophy.[35]

As for political thought, it arguably had less in common with modern political theory than with what we now call political theology. Although there was a rough division of labour between clerical, legal, and philosophical writers, the languages of religion, law, and philosophy frequently intermingled.[36] Political theory was linked to ecclesiology. In the Middle Ages, the arguments advanced by conciliarists and papalists had been redeployed in the civil sphere by imperialists and advocates of representative assemblies. In the English Revolution too, contemporaries drew analogies between the government of church and state. Richard Baxter heard parliamentarian soldiers debating 'church democracy and state democracy', and he saw a correlation between the populist ecclesiology of the sects and the case for popular revolt against rulers. By 1649, James I's famous dictum, 'No bishop, no king', seemed prophetic.[37]

Clerical writers played a major role in political debates. In 1642–4, clergy rushed to provide theoretical defences of the parliamentarian or royalist cause. Resistance theorists like William Bridge, Charles Herle, and Samuel Rutherford were ranged against royalists like Henry Hammond, Henry Ferne, and Griffith Williams. They debated the implications of natural law theory, with parliamentarians building on the traditional scholastic notion that mankind was naturally free from subjection so that government was created by a contract between king and people. While matters of legality were primarily the domain of lawyers, puritan divines were keen to insist on the constitutional grounds for parliament's war—it was being waged to defend the church by law established.[38] But they also expended a great deal of energy debating precedents from Scripture and church history. Resistance theorists appealed to Old Testament revolts against tyrants and recent Calvinist risings; their critics pointed to the passive suffering of Christ and the non-violence of the primitive church. In political sermons, providential and apocalyptic ideas often came to the fore, as preachers depicted God at work in contemporary events, even bringing history to its climax with the overthrow of the civil and ecclesiastical tyranny of papal Antichrist. Biblical arguments remained prominent in 1649, when regicides cited Old Testament warrants for capital punishment—the Noahic rule that murderers forfeited their own lives (Genesis 9:5–6), and the Mosaic teaching that a land would not be purged of its blood guilt until the 'man of blood' was put to death (Numbers 35:33). In the Engagement controversy that followed the regicide, divines like Francis Rous and John Dury appealed to the doctrine of Providence and to Romans 13 (on obedience to rulers), to justify submission to the new regime.[39]

Theological considerations were also important for the Levellers and their offspring, the True Levellers (or Diggers). The Leveller account of natural equality and freedom had theistic foundations. All humanity had been made in God's image and given dominion over creation. According to Lilburne, this meant that they were 'by nature all equal and alike in power, dignity, authority and majesty—none of them having (by nature) any authority, dominion or magisterial power, one over or above another'. Civil authority was established by 'mutual agreement or consent', and hence subject to strict limitations. Even Leveller women could justify assertive petitioning on the ground that 'we are assured of our creation in the image of God, and of an interest in Christ equal unto men'.[40] The Levellers also stressed the duties of practical Christianity, citing passages from the Hebrew prophets and the Letter of James about justice and mercy towards the poor and downtrodden. Such texts inspired the Digger Gerrard Winstanley too, but his political theology was more innovative in its method. He reconceptualized the Christian doctrines of Creation, Fall, and Redemption from the standpoint of the landless—the earth (he argued) was created as a common treasury; man had been corrupted by selfishness and private property; Christ was now restoring the common ownership of the earth.[41]

The resurgence of republican thought after 1649 also had a significant religious dimension. While republican theorists looked to the classical republics of the ancient world and Renaissance Italy, they also turned to the Old Testament. Historians of political thought have often overlooked works on the Hebrew republic, but Eric Nelson argues that this was among the most important genres of European political writing in 'the Biblical Century'. In the 1650s, English republicans drew on rabbinic commentaries which opened up new perspectives on biblical texts. In the Mosaic land laws and the institution of the Jubilee, James Harrington found a warrant for the redistribution of property. In I Samuel 8, Milton found the basis for an exclusivist republicanism that depicted monarchy as a departure from God's will.[42] In contrast to Harrington, Milton and other godly republicans stressed the primacy of civic virtue and godly citizens. They also incorporated New Testament themes into their political thought. Unlike Luther, Milton argued that the Pauline doctrine of Christian Liberty had political ramifications—Christ came to free mankind from temporal as well as spiritual tyranny. Christian politics must begin from Christ's critique of the 'princes of the Gentiles' who lorded it over their subjects.[43]

The relationship of church and state was a matter of contention among republicans, as it was among their contemporaries. Indeed, the role of the magistrate in matters of religion was one of the most hotly contested issues across the revolutionary era. While Harrington favoured a national civil religion, Milton opposed the very idea of state churches. On this, Milton was out on a limb. Advocates of magisterial reformation— that is, mainstream Protestants—emphasized the necessity of an established church. Magistrates were the 'keepers of both tables' of the Ten Commandments, and responsible for policing offences against God as well as against neighbours. Support for religious uniformity remained strong among the clergy and many laity too. Major treatises were written in defence of religious coercion, including works by the English lawyer William Prynne and the Scottish theologian Samuel Rutherford. But among magisterial Protestants there was a fierce dispute about the relations between church and state. Whereas Prynne was staunchly Erastian, Rutherford was emphatically clericalist—and once again, both penned treatises to prove their case. A similar dispute arose among royalists as the king contemplated reaching a deal with Scottish presbyterians and English Independents. Assertors of exclusive divine right episcopacy like John Bramhall were adamant that the king must not compromise on church government and liturgy. But they were confronted by those who argued that the king's supremacy in matters of religion allowed him to determine the government of the church.

Among these anti-clericalist royalists the most radical, least representative, and most brilliant was Thomas Hobbes. He appears to have written his masterpiece *Leviathan* (1651) in the wake of the regicide. It began as a powerful indictment of rebellion against kings and a compelling argument for the undivided sovereignty of the monarch over civil and religious affairs, though its 'Review and Conclusion' appended conciliatory comments about the new Independent regime, and it has been seen as a contribution to the case for submission during the Engagement Controversy.[44] The first half of his *magnum opus* argued from natural reason, seeking to resolve the problem of religious war by appealing to universal natural laws that required men to submit to their political sovereign, whether they agreed with him or not. The second half (Books III and IV) was devoted to questions of theology and ecclesiology, and here Hobbes presented a sweeping critique of churchly orthodoxies. His radical theology had two principal drivers. The first was his materialist reading of the new science. For Hobbes, the mechanical philosophy was simply incompatible with metaphysical dualism. There were no 'incorporeal substances'—human souls were material and could not survive as disembodied spirits; ghosts were a fiction; angels were not real beings; even God was corporeal. The second driver was political—his single-minded belief in the necessity of undivided sovereignty. This led him to deny the clericalist claims made by *jure divino* papalists, prelatists, and presbyterians. In the past, God had ruled Israel as a theocracy; in the future, he would rule his kingdom on earth; but in the present, the church had no political power. Churchmen might teach if tolerated or authorized by the magistrate, but only rulers could make law. Indeed, legally speaking, the magistrate was the sole interpreter of Scripture, and his subjects must conform outwardly to his religious laws for the sake of peace, regardless of their own religious beliefs. Hobbes had no time for martyrs or conscientious objectors. On this, he went far beyond traditional Protestant Erastianism, and was radically out of step with the Independents whom he praised in his 'Review and Conclusion'.[45]

Although 'magisterial Independents' like John Owen and Philip Nye believed that the magistrate had the power to maintain a state religion, they wanted their own 'gathered' churches to be self-governing. The state should tolerate non-parochial congregations, as long as they were peaceable, Protestant, and Trinitarian. More radical members of the Independent coalition, by contrast, flatly rejected the concept of 'State Religion' and denied the magistrate's regulatory and coercive power in matters of religion. There were pragmatic and philosophical arguments for this position, but biblical and theological arguments were particularly important. Under the Old Testament, reasoned writers like Roger Williams, John Goodwin, and John Milton, church and state had been unified; but in the Church Age, there was to be a 'severing' of church and state. Churches were voluntary associations, supported by gifts not compulsory tithes; the task of magistrates was wholly civil, for it concerned 'bodies and goods' not souls. This view was embraced by Levellers, baptists, and Quakers, but it was an extreme position, and Henry Stubbe admitted that 'Sectarian Toleration' had few supporters.[46]

Legacies

Historians have often pronounced the English Revolution a failure, but the religious thought of the period was to have a seminal influence on later Protestantism. The Westminster Assembly's Shorter Catechism was memorized by generations of presbyterian children. The Westminster Confession was adopted by the Church of Scotland, and formed the basis for later confessions by congregationalists and Particular baptists. For millions of presbyterians (including many in South Korea) it remains an official statement of faith. Similarly, the writings of John Owen became a touchstone of Protestant orthodoxy. Frequently referred to in the eighteenth century, they were republished in twenty-four volumes in the 1850s and then again in the 1960s. Since then, there have been over forty Ph.D. theses written on Owen's theology.[47] Richard Baxter's bestsellers—*The Saints Everlasting Rest* (1650), *The Reformed Pastor* (1656), and *Call to the Unconverted* (1658)—quickly attained classic status and went through countless editions in England, America, The Netherlands, and elsewhere. Among Anglicans, the writings of Henry Hammond, Jeremy Taylor, and the Cambridge Platonists achieved the same kind of acclaim, helping to forge a post-Calvinist identity for the established church.

The neo-Arminian soteriology popularized by Richard Allestree and later restated by Archbishop Tillotson (a Cambridge academic in the 1650s) would become the dominant understanding of salvation in the English parish, where the emphasis on dutiful behaviour crowded out the puritan demand for conversion.[48]

The Revolution's radical religious thinkers had a mixed reception. The theological reflections of William Walwyn, Gerrard Winstanley, and Abiezer Coppe were soon forgotten, and only rescued from obscurity by twentieth-century scholars. Milton's systematic theology was first published in 1820s, and has attracted little attention beyond academia. By contrast, the writings of George Fox (especially his retrospective *Journal* looking back on the 1650s) became foundational for the Quaker ethos. If we consider the critical influence of later Quakers on antislavery, pacifism, and even the early movement for women's rights, it becomes clear that the rise of this sect was one the Revolution's lasting legacies. Radical Protestant questioning of mainstream orthodoxy could feed into the Enlightenment in surprising ways. The Quaker Samuel Fisher, who had written a witty and learned attack on Protestant Biblicism, may have influenced the biblical criticism of Benedict Spinoza, since the two seem to have collaborated on a translation of pamphlets by Margaret Fell. Another Quaker in The Netherlands, the merchant Benjamin Furly, kept a remarkable library of radical Protestant works (many from the 1640s and 1650s) at his house in Rotterdam, where he hosted an intellectual circle that included John Locke and Pierre Bayle. *A Discourse of the Torments of Hell* (1660), a tract by the Particular baptist Samuel Richardson which denied the doctrine of eternal conscious torment, was translated and republished as *L'Enfer Detruit* (1769) by the atheist circle of the Baron D'Holbach. The impact of Socinianism would also persist. John Locke had been educated at Christ Church, Oxford, when John Owen was dean, but by the late seventeenth century Locke's theology would look suspiciously Socinian; for other writers, it was a small step from Socinianism to Deism.

The natural philosophy and political theology of the revolutionary years also proved seminal. The scientific circles of Hartlib, Wilkins, and Boyle were the forerunners of the Royal Society founded in 1662. Wilkins and Ward became bishops, while Boyle emerged as Europe's leading experimental scientist, as well as a lay theologian who wrote works of apologetics designed to reconcile natural philosophy with classical theism. The materialism and heterodoxy of Hobbes's *Leviathan* offered a very different account of the theological ramifications of the new science, and though it came under constant critical fire in the later seventeenth century, the work was repeatedly exploited by Deists and other thinkers of the radical Enlightenment. In political thought, the royalist case against armed resistance weighed heavily with later high church Anglicans, who remembered 'King Charles the Martyr' and insisted that subjects must imitate the passive obedience of Christ. Their principles caused a crisis at the Glorious Revolution—non-jurors left the Church rather than swear allegiance to William and Mary, while others took comfort in the fiction that James II had abdicated. In the American Revolution, high church episcopalians would form the core of the loyalist movement. Their opponents drew on the radical Whig tradition built on the collected works of Milton and Harrington published by John Toland at the end of the seventeenth century. In *Common Sense*, the Deist

Tom Paine even made cynical use of Milton's biblical argument against kingship, knowing it would resonate with his Reformed Protestant readership. Milton's case for the separation of church and state also enjoyed greater success in America than in Britain, and the writings of Roger Williams were rediscovered by American baptists in the later eighteenth century. In the United States, a Miltonic fusion of radical Protestantism, disestablishment, and republicanism would become mainstream ideology. This was the last and greatest of the English Revolution's posthumous triumphs.

Notes

1. Thomas Hobbes, *Leviathan*, ed. Noel Malcolm, 3 vols. (Oxford, 2012), III, 1226–7: 'causam Belli Civilis . . . non fuisse quam dissensionem . . . circa quaestiones Theologicas'.

2. Nicholas Tyacke, *Anti-Calvinists: The Rise of English Arminianism, c.1590–1640* (Oxford, 1987); Kenneth Fincham and Nicholas Tyacke, *Altars Restored: The Changing Face of English Religious Worship, 1547–c.1700* (Oxford, 2007); Anthony Milton, *Catholic and Reformed: The Roman and Protestant Churches in English Protestant Thought, 1600–1640* (Cambridge, 1995); Jean-Louis Quantin, *The Church of England and Christian Antiquity: The Construction of a Confessional Identity in the 17th Century* (Oxford, 2009).

3. S. R. Gardiner, *Constitutional Documents of the Puritan Revolution, 1625–1660* (3rd edition, Oxford, 1906), 268.

4. Christopher Hill, *Antichrist in Seventeenth-Century England* (London, 1971); Bernard Capp, 'The Political Dimension of Apocalyptic Thought', in C. A. Patrides and Joseph Wittreich (eds.), *The Apocalypse in English Renaissance Thought and Literature* (Manchester, 1984), chap. 4; John Coffey, 'The Impact of Apocalypticism during the Puritan Revolutions', *Perichoresis*, 4 (2006): 117–47.

5. David Loewenstein and John Morrill, 'Literature and Religion', in David Loewenstein and Janet Mueller (eds.), *Early Modern English Literature* (Cambridge, 2002), 671.

6. See Alan Ford, *James Ussher: Theology, History, and Politics in Early-Modern Ireland and England* (Oxford, 2007), chap. 10.

7. Mary Prior (ed.), *Women in English Society, 1500–1800* (London, 1991), 268–9.

8. Bernard Capp, 'The Religious Market-place: Public Disputations in Civil War and Interregnum England', *English Historical Review* (forthcoming).

9. Chad van Dixhoorn, 'Reforming the Reformation: Theological Debate in the Westminster Assembly, 1643–52', University of Cambridge Ph.D. thesis, 7 vols. (2004), I, 2.

10. Chad Van Dixhoorn (ed.), *The Minutes and Papers of the Westminster Assembly, 1643–1652* (Oxford, 2012).

11. See two magisterial accounts of the Reformed tradition: Philip Benedict, *Christ's Churches Purely Reformed: A Social History of Calvinism* (New Haven, 2002); Richard Muller, *Post-Reformation Reformed Dogmatics: The Rise and Development of Reformed Orthodoxy, ca. 1520 to ca. 1725*, 4 vols. (Grand Rapids, 2003).

12. Van Dixhoorn, 'Reforming the Reformation', chap. 4.

13. Hunter Powell, *The Crisis of British Protestantism: Church Power in the Puritan Revolution, 1638-1644* (Manchester, forthcoming).

14. See Michael Haykin and Mark Jones (eds.), *Drawn into Controversie: Reformed Theological Diversity and Debates within Seventeenth-Century British Puritanism* (Gottingen, 2011), chaps. 2, 4, 6.

15. For a basic list of works by Westminster divines see: <http://www.westminsterassembly.org/printed-works-catalog-2/> (accessed 3 January 2012).

16. For a useful survey see Ryan Kelly, 'Reformed or Reforming? John Owen and the Complexity of Theological Codification for Mid-Seventeenth-Century England', in Kelly Kapic and Mark Jones (eds.), *The Ashgate Research Companion to John Owen's Theology* (Farnham, 2012), chap. 1.

17. Gardiner, *Constitutional Documents*, 454.

18. Bernard Capp, *England's Culture Wars: Puritan Reformation and its Enemies in the Interregnum, 1649–1660* (Oxford, 2012); Christopher Hill, *The World Turned Upside Down: Radical Ideas during the English Revolution* (London, 1972).

19. See Tim Cooper, *John Owen, Richard Baxter and the Formation of Nonconformity* (Farnham, 2011).

20. John Coffey, *John Goodwin and the Puritan Revolution: Religion and Intellectual Change in Seventeenth-Century England* (Woodbridge, 2006), chap. 7.

21. Benjamin Whichcote, *Moral and Religious Aphorismes*, ed. S. Salter (1753), 56–7.

22. C. A. Patrides (ed.), *The Cambridge Platonists* (London, 1969).

23. See J. W. Packer, *The Transformation of Anglicanism, 1643–1660, with Special Reference to Henry Hammond* (Manchester, 1969).

24. *Areopagitica, a Speech of Mr John Milton for the Liberty of Unlicens'd Printing* (London, 1644), 31.

25. Elizabeth Clarke, David Norbrook, and Jane Stevenson are currently editing a volume of Hutchinson's theological writings for *The Works of Lucy Hutchinson*, 4 vols. (Oxford, 2011–).

26. Martin Finch, *Animadversions upon Sir Henry Vanes Book, entituled* The Retired Mans Meditations: *Examining his Doctrine concerning Adam's Fall, Christs Person, and Sufferings, Justification, Common and Special Grace; and Many Other Things in his Book* (London, 1656).

27. *De Doctrina Christiana*, ed. John K. Hale and J. Donald Cullington, in *The Complete Works of John Milton*, ed. Gordon Campbell and Thomas Corns (Oxford, 2008–), VII–VIII.

28. See Tobias Gregory, 'How Milton Defined Heresy and Why', *Religion and Literature*, 45 (2013): 148–160.

29. See Paul C.-H. Lim, *Mystery Unveiled: The Crisis of the Trinity in Early Modern England* (New York, 2012); Sarah Mortimer, *Reason and Religion in the English Revolution: The Challenge of Socinianism* (Cambridge, 2010).

30. The theological issues are best approached through T. L. Underwood, *Primitivism, Radicalism and the Lamb's War: The Baptist–Quaker Conflict in Seventeenth-Century England* (Oxford, 1997).

31. The best study is now Ariel Hessayon, 'The Ranters', in Laura Lunger Knoppers (ed.), *The Oxford Handbook of Literature and the English Revolution* (Oxford, 2012), chap. 18.

32. Ariel Hessayon, *Gold Tried in the Fire: The Prophet TheaurauJohn Tany and the English Revolution* (Aldershot, 2007). For the wider intellectual context see Nigel Smith, *Perfection Proclaimed: Language and Literature in English Radical Religion, 1640–1660* (Oxford, 1989).

33. Patrick Collinson, Arnold Hunt, and Alexandra Walsham, 'Religious Publishing in England, 1557–1640', in John Barnard and D. F. Mackenzie (eds.), *The Cambridge History of the Book in Britain, vol. IV: 1557–1695* (Cambridge, 2002), 29.

34. Elizabeth Spiller, 'Printed Recipe Books in Medical, Political and Scientific Contexts', in Knoppers (ed.), *Oxford Handbook*, chap. 27.

35. See Charles Webster, *The Great Instauration: Science, Medicine and Reform, 1626–1660* (London, 1975); Peter Harrison, *The Fall of Man and the Foundations of Science* (Cambridge, 2007); Michael Hunter, *Boyle: Between God and Science* (New Haven, 2009), chaps. 4–7.

36. See Glenn Burgess, *British Political Thought, 1500–1660* (Basingstoke, 2009), Part II: 'Political Thought and Religious Revolution, 1640–60'.

37. See especially Charles Prior, *A Confusion of Tongues: Britain's Wars of Reformation* (Oxford, 2012); 'Religion, Political Thought and the English Civil War', *History Compass*, 11 (2013): 24–42.

38. Glenn Burgess, 'Was the English Civil War a War of Religion? The Evidence of Political Propaganda', *Huntingdon Library Quarterly*, 61 (1998): 173–203.

39. On the political uses of the Bible see Christopher Hill, *The English Bible and the Seventeenth-Century Revolution* (London, 1993).

40. A. S. P. Woodhouse (ed.), *Puritanism and Liberty: Being the Army Debates (1647–49) from the Clarke Manuscripts* (London, 1992), 317, 367.

41. See *The Complete Works of Gerrard Winstanley*, ed. Thomas N. Corns, Ann Hughes, and David Loewenstein, 2 vols. (Oxford, 2009), which gives marginal references for his numerous biblical citations.

42. See Eric Nelson, *The Hebrew Republic: Jewish Sources and the Transformation of European Political Thought* (Cambridge, MA, 2010).

43. See his *Defence of the People of England*, chap. 3 in *Milton: Political Writings*, ed. Martin Dzelzainis (Cambridge, 1991), 105–10; John Coffey, ' "The Brand of Gentilism": Milton's Jesus and the Augustinian Critique of Pagan Kingship, 1649–1671', *Milton Quarterly*, 48 (2014): 67–95.

44. On its composition and agendas see Malcolm, 'The Writing of Leviathan', in Hobbes, *Leviathan*, I, 1–100.

45. On the ensuing controversies see Jon Parkin, *Taming the Leviathan: The Reception of the Political and Religious Ideas of Thomas Hobbes in England, 1640–1700* (Cambridge, 2007).

46. See John Coffey, 'The Toleration Controversy', in Christopher Durston and Judith D. Maltby (eds.), *Religion in the English Revolution* (Manchester, 2006), 42–68.

47. Listed in Kapic and Jones (eds.), *The Ashgate Research Companion to the Theology of John Owen*, 326–8.

48. See Mark Smith, 'The Hanoverian Parish: Towards a New Agenda', *Past and Present*, 216 (2012): 79–105.

Further Reading

Burgess, Glenn, *British Political Thought, 1500–1660* (Basingstoke, 2009).

Haykin, Michael and Mark Jones (eds.), *Drawn into Controversie: Reformed Theological Diversity and Debates within Seventeenth-Century British Puritanism* (Gottingen, 2011).

Hessayon, Ariel, *Gold Tried in the Fire: The Prophet TheaurauJohn Tany and the English Revolution* (Aldershot, 2007).

Hill, Christopher, *The World Turned Upside Down: Radical Ideas during the English Revolution* (London, 1972).

Hobbes, Thomas, *Leviathan*, ed. Noel Malcolm, 3 vols. (Oxford, 2012).

Keeble, N. H. and Geoffrey Nuttall (eds.), *Calendar of the Correspondence of Richard Baxter*, 2 vols. (Oxford, 1991).

Lim, Paul C.-H., *Mystery Unveiled: The Crisis of the Trinity in Early Modern England* (New York, 2012).

Mortimer, Sarah, *Reason and Religion in the English Revolution: The Challenge of Socinianism* (Cambridge, 2010).

Nelson, Eric, *The Hebrew Republic: Jewish Sources and the Transformation of European Political Thought* (Cambridge, MA, 2010).

Nuttall, Geoffrey, *The Holy Spirit in Puritan Faith and Experience* (Oxford, 1946).

Packer, J. W., *The Transformation of Anglicanism, 1643–1660, with Special Reference to Henry Hammond* (Manchester, 1969).

Parkin, Jon, *Taming the Leviathan: The Reception of the Political and Religious Ideas of Thomas Hobbes in England, 1640–1700* (Cambridge, 2007).

Underwood, T. L., *Primitivism, Radicalism and the Lamb's War: The Baptist–Quaker Conflict in Seventeenth-Century England* (Oxford, 1997).

Van Dixhoorn, Chad (ed.), *The Minutes and Papers of the Westminster Assembly, 1643–1652* (Oxford, 2012).

Webster, Charles, *The Great Instauration: Science, Medicine and Reform, 1626–1660* (London, 1975).

Woodhouse, A. S. P. (ed.), *Puritanism and Liberty: Being the Army Debates (1647–1649) from the Clarke Manuscripts* (London, 1992).

CHAPTER 27

....

'MAY YOU LIVE IN INTERESTING TIMES':

The Literature of Civil War, Revolution, and Restoration

....

STEVEN N. ZWICKER

'MAY you live in interesting times': the writers who lived through the middle decades of the seventeenth century would have understood the ironies and implications of that supposed Chinese curse. Some raised arms or joined plots or were imprisoned, some lost their lives in those interesting times: Lucius Cary, Viscount Falkland, died at the battle of Newbury; Sir John Suckling died in Paris following his flight from England. Richard Lovelace, John Cleveland, James Howell, and Edmund Waller were jailed; and a number of writers went into exile—Waller himself, Abraham Cowley, Thomas Hobbes, Richard Crashaw, Margaret Cavendish, Thomas Killigrew, Aurelian Townshend, Sir William Davenant, Sir John Denham, Thomas Stanley, Sir Kenelm Digby. Some writers turned from lyric sentiment to state verse, some from poetry to prose; William Davenant put aside plays and masques to try his hand at epic, and one theorist of the state, Thomas Hobbes, exiled in Paris in the 1640s, extended his reach from political philosophy to literary theory.

Waller, Cowley, Crashaw, Killigrew, Townshend, Davenant, Denham, Stanley—a virtual roll call of the Cavaliers, evidence of a culture divided, literally and imaginatively, or so we have been told. Yet if we look closer, the stories of these Cavaliers often turn out to be narratives of accommodation, histories of negotiating and renegotiating political affiliation, perhaps cultural identity, certainly personal advantage. Hobbes was tutor to the young Prince Charles in exile, but in 1651 after the publication of *Leviathan*, he returned to London and made peace with the Cromwellian regime. Waller conspired against parliament, then turned informer on his fellow royalists, was banished in 1643, restored to the realm in 1651, wrote first a panegyric, then an elegy on Cromwell, and in 1660 joined the chorus of poets welcoming the return of Stuart monarchy. Nor does the story of Abraham Cowley read very differently: he wrote satires on the puritans in the 1640s, followed Henrietta Maria into exile, served as secretary to the court in Paris, returned to London in 1654 and published his *Poems* in 1656, and despaired in its Preface over the cause that drove him into exile, and in that volume omitted his satires against the puritans. In 1660 Cowley greeted the return of Stuart monarchy with an elaborate Pindaric, repudiated Oliver Cromwell, and celebrated the founding of the Royal Society whose *History* was written in the early 1660s by his friend Thomas Sprat. Like Cowley, Sprat wrote a funeral elegy for Oliver Cromwell, then dedicated his *History of the Royal Society* (1677) to Charles II, and celebrated the Restoration as a return of arms and arts. And though Andrew Marvell was supposed to have joined Sprat in *Three Poems on the Death of O. C.*, by January of 1659, when the volume was to be issued, Marvell seems to have thought better of offering public obsequies to the memory of the Lord Protector. Like Cowley, Marvell spent time on the continent (1642/3–47), though perhaps less in exile than on a grand tour, and his elegy on Francis Villiers (1648), his commendatory verse for Lovelace's *Lucasta* (1648), and his contribution to *Lachrymae Musarum*—the volume of elegies for Henry, Lord Hastings (1649)—all suggest association with the royalist cause and with courtly aesthetics. But that was neither a stable political nor a fixed literary identity. Marvell's *Horatian Ode* (written in 1650) may seem the very emblem of divided or uncertain loyalties, but his *First Anniversary* (1655)—and without a trace of nostalgia, irony, or ambiguity—declares an undivided (though anonymous) support for the Lord Protector. In the autumn of 1658 Marvell wrote his funeral elegy for Cromwell, withdrew it from publication, got elected to Richard Cromwell's parliament (1659), was re-elected to the Cavalier parliament, wrote scathing, though anonymous, satires on the restored king and his court, then in *The Rehearsal Transpros'd* (1672) made common cause with Charles II over the issue of religious toleration. Was there a more sinuous career than Andrew Marvell's? By comparison, John Dryden seems naïve; he struggled with a turncoat identity over much of his career, a fate that more cautious contemporaries avoided. Shifting loyalties certainly marked the beginning of Dryden's career: first a contribution to *Lachrymae Musarum*; then an appointment in 1657 to the Office of Foreign Tongues where he worked alongside Andrew Marvell and under John Milton; cool and formal quatrains in memory of Oliver Cromwell (*Heroic Stanzas*, 1659), and then couplets celebrating the Restoration (*Astræa Redux*, 1660) and the coronation of Charles II (*To His Sacred Majesty*, 1661). There were of course less compromised careers—John Denham on one side, John Milton to the other—but even Milton's cultural identity is not as easy to fix as are his political ideals; from these he did not waver, but earlier in his literary career Milton seems to have aimed in the direction of what we might now identify as a Cavalier poetics. *Poems of Mr. John Milton* (1645) is marked by its cultivation of aristocratic patrons and aristocratic forms: Arcadian entertainments, a masque, odes, elegies on princes of the church. Whatever we now construe, by backward glance, to have been Milton's reforming impulses in *Poems of Mr. John Milton*, no contemporary of Milton's reading the book in 1646 would have thought this the work of a political or social or aesthetic revolutionary.

Numbers

What emerges from such brief lives is an uncertain picture, one that discloses writers and careers moving across political, geographical, and cultural divides—first London, then Paris, then London again; loyalty to one regime, then to another; pastorals that cultivate Arcadian repose, then poetry in graver accents. Is there a clearer picture to be had? Perhaps a different perspective would sharpen its resolution; looking from a distance, at statistics rather than passports, might yield a more distinctive image.

First, the general frame. Between 1640 and 1670 about 40,000 separate titles were published with London imprints: about 17,000 in the first of these decades, 12,000 between 1650 and 1659, 10,000 between 1660 and 1670, a noticeable decline in numbers of books, pamphlets, and broadsides, though as we glance at these numbers we need to remember that there is a spike in the early 1640s when the licensing laws had lapsed with the elimination of the Star Chamber in July of 1641—750 books in 1640, 2,300 books in 1641, then nearly 4,000 in 1642 (approximately 10% of the total number of books issued over this thirty-year period).[1] And there is a striking move in the opposite direction in the mid-1660s—the number of London imprints drops to a low of 556 in 1666—when war, plague, and fire damaged printed stock, printing presses, and certainly the market for print. From these numbers it seems clear that the civil wars, religious controversy, and social upheavals of the 1640s produced and were reflected by growth in the market for print in that decade.[2] Between 1600 and 1639 the number of new titles rarely went above 500; in 1641 there are 2,300 new titles, in 1642—as we have seen—there are almost 4,000 titles published with London imprints, or almost ten times the average number of titles in each of the preceding years. The next notable spike occurs, not surprisingly, in 1660 when the number of London imprints reaches close to 3,000. And if we glance at the panegyrics issued singly for the event of the Restoration (over 130 separate titles), or the large number of sermons of thanksgiving (more than 100), the driving force behind the large number of imprints is clear.[3] The event of the Restoration, the return of monarchy, and the person of Charles II are repeatedly celebrated in print, constituting a large number of the imprints of the year 1660. In the following years the numbers drop by two-thirds, hovering around 1,000 new imprints a year until the debacle of the mid-1660s. One thing that seems clear over these thirty years is the importance of national political events to the London print trade in general: war and the rumours and reports of war, regicide and restoration, the fate of the national church, and, as we look later in the century, the Popish Plot, Exclusion, and the Glorious Revolution all gave certain definition to the world of print.

Though mid-century writing should not only be identified with print and polemic, its themes and preoccupations often express the deep imprint of polemical controversy and armed conflict. Writers moved into print when the imagining or reporting or representing of events and controversies might allow them to occupy a position in the marketplace of ideas. But their writings also occupied a place in the shops and on the stalls that sold the products of the press, and the quantities of writing at mid-century, the flood of print, and the commercial character of this trade all form a backdrop for any picture that we might want to fashion of literature at mid-century. Milton regretted that the title pages of his works had to compete for the attention of stall-readers, but *Poems of Mr. John Milton* (1645) and *The Doctrine and Discipline of Divorce* (1643) were no less commercial products appealing to readerly tastes and pocketbooks than they were assertions of literary aspiration and spiritual freedom.[4] The commercial character of the book trade may not clarify the profile of individual careers—it does not in the case of John Milton, although Milton in his commitment to the commerce of ideas recognized the importance of the circulation of print, or in the case of Andrew Marvell, most of whose verse, if it circulated at all during his life circulated in manuscript—or the profile of literary coteries which more often depended on manuscript circulation than print publication, or the distinctive character of what we often think of as literary eras. But the commerce of books reminds us that literature was not only an aesthetic and social enterprise but also part of an exchange economy, and that economics and aesthetics though they may in some deep ways be bound together can work by very different overt logics. Aesthetics and social relations provide frames within which to situate literary texts, and of course literature is swept up in the whirlwind of debate over politics and religion, but books are commercial goods and very few books of poems, or artful prose, or playbooks, or meditations came to print without the hope of a return on investment. Print publication of books involved the risk of capital—intellectual reputation but also money; ideas were at stake but so too were profits and losses. And as we calculate the commercial meaning of the trade, it becomes clear that books (like authors) crossed party lines, indeed that at times books hardly recognize those divides. Not all the trade in lyric poetry or prose romance or playbooks went to readers of one party; and prophecies, prayers, and manuals of piety to another. If political ideals and social affinities can shape writing, commerce can reconfigure or blur that shape. Think, for example, of the commerce in romance, that supposedly quintessential genre of royalist literature. High ideals and matters of the heart, hidden identities and allegorical landscapes feature prominently in these at times fantastic stories of knights and ladies. But the commerce in romances, which flourished in the 1650s and almost as much in the 1660s, and the collecting of romances, which found their way into a surprising variety of private libraries, also make clear that it was not only languishing cavaliers who wrote or bought and read these tales, nor was it only royalists who might self-identify with ideals, with loyalty, love, and honour.[5]

If we ask further, of different kinds of books dominating and expressing different eras of political or social or religious life, the trade in books makes definitive cases rather difficult to come by. The fate of the theatre has always seemed to provide the most striking evidence of a divided culture at mid-century: a royalist imaginary of theatre and theatricality crushed by the parliamentary order closing the commercial playhouses in 1642 and reasserted only with the return of Stuart monarchy and the reopening of the theatres in 1660. Surely, to some extent, the characterization is true: the court had sponsored acting companies and supported masque writing and masques—that most extravagant of theatrical genres—and William Prynne's infamous attack on actresses and whores associated Henrietta Maria with both theatricality and whoredom. Milton of course seized on the polemical advantage of identifying Charles I with masquing and more largely with a culture of performance and theatricality. While his own literary career gives evidence of affinity, and perhaps something more, for the theatre, Milton understood that in the aftermath of the civil wars and the trial and execution of the king, the theatre was tainted by royal association, and that association was ripe for exploiting: the theatre and idolatry and ungodliness went together and would be perceived, perhaps by many, as belonging to one another.

But the London audiences that paid to go to the theatre in the 1630s did not form a political unity and the plays of the 1630s did not display a simple political or ideological programme before the civil wars, nor did they, perhaps even more surprisingly, after the reopening of the London theatres in 1660.[6] But as complex as was the life of the theatre over these decades, especially mapped against the fortunes of political causes, when we integrate the life of playbooks into this story the picture becomes even less clear. The publishing of playbooks was not subject to parliamentary strictures against the stage. All through this period plays were published and their numbers do not seem inflected in any simple ways by the fortune of parties: more Shakespeare in the 1630s than in the 1640s, more Shakespeare in the 1640s than in the 1650s, but the number of Shakespeare playbooks hardly rises in the 1660s; overall, as many tragedies were published in the 1650s as in the 1660s though a few more comedies in the first decade of the Restoration than in the previous decade. And while it is true that volumes like William Cartwright's *Comedies, Tragi-Comedies, and Other Poems* (1651) seem a way station for cavaliers whose commendatory verse crowds its antechamber, it is not at all clear who was reading and using the Cartwright volume.

What we must also recognize is that set against the total output of the commercial press, the number of these supposedly distinctive types of books—romances and playbooks, for example—was very small. If the total number of individual titles issued over this thirty-year period is approximately 40,000 and if we assume that the average print run was 1,000 copies, then we are engaging with a large number of printed broadsides, pamphlets, and books[7]—something like 40 million printed texts were issued over the middle decades of the century; the trade was substantial indeed and romances and playbooks form a minuscule element within this trade. And what of the broad character of the book trade? Religion accounts for a very large proportion—by some estimates 50%—of this trade over all three of the decades: bibles and psalters, scriptural paraphrases and commentaries, catechisms, sermons, and treatises on church governance, tracts on worship, ceremony, and vestments, or controversies over confessional practice and identity. And print that addressed or announced matters of state—proclamations and declarations, orders and ordinances, books of politics and governance, histories and true accounts—make up the second largest category of print. But primers and almanacs—what Ian Green has called perennial sellers—these too make up a substantial percentage of the books printed, even if not of individual titles; almanacs, for example, were issued in very large editions, as many as 10,000 copies of an almanac made up a single issue.[8] And these large segments of the trade in printed books identify strains of unchanging or slowly changing taste; that is, they point to the steadiness of the commercial market and the continuities of kind within this sphere: books and kinds of books that sold well one year also sold well the next. And so, despite some significant variation in numbers, the story of books told from a distance is of large numbers and long-term continuities rather than sharp differences and distinctions: romances in the 1650s and in the 1660s, playbooks through these decades, bibles and sermons everywhere. The gross numbers fluctuate, but often the same or similar kinds of books are issued throughout the tumultuous decades at mid-century. Even playbooks, as we have seen, have a surprisingly continuous print life through these decades, as do other genres like editions and translations of classical authors. Does the distant perspective then—fluctuating numbers but long continuities in kinds of books and preoccupations of readers—make more distinctive the image of mid-century print, or do numbers and statistics, in some ways, reinforce that sense of an unclear picture? There are oscillations in the numbers of titles published, but not a very clear association of kinds of books and genres of writings with particular decades, and often what might appear to be major fluctuations when examined against the larger picture dissolve back into near insignificance.

Of course news dispatches from civil war battles do not simply reappear in the years of the Cromwellian Protectorate, and for sure the early years of the Restoration did not see the continued print publication of some of the radical puritans; neither the works of Christopher Love nor of Gerrard Winstanley—widely available in the 1650s—were reprinted in the 1660s. Common sense, though not always the most reliable guide to the past, tells us that this must have been so. And the familiar narratives of literary history with their clarifying sequence of cavalier lyric displaced by a literature of inwardness followed by a return of celebratory song reinforce an assumption—our desire?—that literary eras should unfold rather distinctively one from the other, that a book like Lovelace's *Lucasta* could only belong to the particular experiences of love and loss in the 1640s, that Marvell's *First Anniversary* was distinctively situated in the rhetoric of spiritual and political contest in the 1650s, and that a poem like Dryden's *Annus Mirabilis* which so superbly manages to spin both the rhetoric of dissenting prophecy and the hopeful alchemy of commerce and urban renewal could only emerge from the pamphlet culture and literary ambitions of the early years of the Restoration. For sure these are books that seem distinctively to express the spirit of particular cultural moments, but we need to counterpoint such rhetorical distinctiveness with longer histories, with the stories of literary genres, of readerly protocols, and of commercial instincts that play out not over individual years or even decades but over longer chronologies. In our desire for a clear sense of literary periods we should not ignore the currents moving at other speeds and at more oblique angles; as well we need to acknowledge the ways in which those works that we think of as literary masterpieces often confound partisan and period distinctions, confound even our own desire for political and moral clarity; and we also need to acknowledge that the irony and ambiguity which seem to compromise clear moral arguments and distinct political identities are often the very hallmarks of those masterpieces. What, after all, is the ethical argument or political allegiance of *An Horatian Ode*?

BOOKS

To return for a moment to Lovelace's *Lucasta*, that most famous of Cavalier collections: the banner of high ideals flies over this collection, and its intertexts—the poetry of Ovid and Catullus, of Horace and Anacreon, and the verses of the poet's more immediate contemporaries—suggest the book's learning, its aristocratic ethos, and its literary sociability. But did those ideals and intertexts, even Lovelace's echoes of and allusions to his social and literary circles, fashion partisanship? Of course, poems in this collection honour king and country, but perhaps this is an aristocratic rather than a partisan stance. As a number of critics have suggested, the poetry of *Lucasta* might better be associated with a social order than a political programme.[9] And if we press the volume for a politics, more likely neutralism or disengagement than partisanship characterize Lovelace's stance in poems like 'The Grasshopper', with its invitation to savour the pleasures of secluded friendship and diminished expectations, or the epode 'to Lucasta from Prison' with its mists and occlusions and sense of engulfing isolation. Indeed it seems that something closer to the political ambivalences of Andrew Marvell at the end of the 1640s than to the overt royalism of Herrick's panegyrics in *Hesperides* (1648) characterizes Lovelace, that quintessential Cavalier. And even *Hesperides* has recently been seen as a book 'straddling all divides', in love more with English ways than partisan programmes.[10]

And what of the book itself—its metatexts and its materiality—its printer, its publisher, its commercial life? *Lucasta* was entered in the Stationers' Register in February 1648, licensed more than a year later in May 1649; a second, posthumous, edition appeared in 1658. Like the latter edition, the 1649 volume was a collaborative effort; a number of hands participated in its creation, and it was collaborative not only in the sense that all books are the products of many hands, but also in its echoes of voices, ancient and modern, and in the network of associations that the commendatory verse at the front of the book evokes with compliments by, among others, Lovelace's brother, Col. Francis Lovelace, John Hall, the Independent, the parliamentary officer John Jephson, and of course Andrew Marvell.[11] The commendations are, as scholars have noted, not only from those who supported the king and but also from Independents, members of the parliamentary army and supporters of its cause. As is the case with Marvell's particular (and peculiar) commendation of *Lucasta*, it is difficult exactly to fix the political as distinguished from the social or cultural argument of many of these commendations or of their collective meaning. Indeed, Lovelace's affinities and obligations were more local and particularist than national and ideological. Perhaps what Sir Lewis Namier once characterized as the associational rather than ideological structure of politics in the eighteenth century might also help us to see *Lucasta* as a book not to be defined by binaries—of royalist and Roundhead—but as a collective situated within a network of family relations and social and literary affinities.[12]

Lucasta was licensed in May 1649, and published shortly after that date—Thomason's copy is marked 4 June—that is, fourteen months after it was registered. The delay between the registering of the book and its print publication perhaps was due to

Lovelace's imprisonment or difficulty with censors, and Marvell's commendatory verse alludes to the threats and practices of censorship. But in assessing the ideological character of the volume we need to remember that the writing was produced and the book manufactured at different moments. The defeat of the king's cause hovers over the writing of this collection, but not the polarizing event of his execution. And even its manufacture does not yield a clear picture of political association. The book was printed and published by Thomas Harper for Thomas Ewster. Harper was a busy stationer in the years surrounding the publication of *Lucasta*. Several scholars have argued that Harper's royalist affinities help fix the identity of Lovelace's volume, and those affinities have been asserted on the basis of Harper's printing of pamphlets denounced by parliament.[13] But Harper was printing and publishing pamphlets and books across the political spectrum, including works of puritan divines and prophets as well as of Anglican churchmen, and a variety of books and pamphlets unrelated to matters of church or state; he was a stationer and his business was printing, publishing, and selling books; he published widely and variously and without seeming care for his ideological profile. In that way he resembles many other printers and stationers—their concerns were financial. He was indeed censured by parliament for printing pamphlets that scandalized its members, but the Stationers' Company was also concerned with Harper's printing of 'great quantities of stock books such as the Psalms, the Primer and School book, with the expectation of the Almanacs'.[14] Here the Stationers' Company was looking after its own financial interests and neither Harper's record nor that of the other stationer involved with *Lucasta*—one Thomas Ewster who is associated with only two other books, both published in 1649— help us to discern the political identity of Lovelace's volume. Projecting the partisan identity or ideological position of books from their associations with particular stationers can mislead or exaggerate partisanship since various motives were at play among authors and their stationers.

Consider the case of *Poems of Mr. John Milton* published by Humphrey Moseley in January 1646. The 'royalist' identity of Moseley has been repeatedly cited as an element of, a contribution to, the contradictory nature of the volume. There may indeed be tensions, for example, between the head note that Milton attached to *Lycidas* in 1645 prophesying the 'ruin of our corrupted clergy', and the volume's Latin elegies for Anglican bishops, but they do not arise from dissonance between the royalist Moseley and the reforming Milton. While Milton had a reforming reputation by the time the volume of poems was published, Moseley had hardly any profile at all as a publisher and certainly not as the publisher of elegant volumes of cavalier lyrics—those all postdate the publication of *Poems of Mr. John Milton*. Whatever Moseley may have intended by the template of *Poems of Mr. John Milton*, royalism would not yet have been a discernible element of its design. In the years immediately following the publication of Milton's volume, the emerging character of Moseley's list and the design and format of his volumes may have cast a certain after-the-fact social or cultural aura over Milton's book and perhaps underscored—or perhaps helped to fashion—the poet's and the book's complex identity, but that complexity did not derive from Moseley's identity in January 1646 when readers would first have picked out the volume from among the books on the shelves of the shop at the Prince's Arms in St Paul's Churchyard.

Not that the volume lacked in complexity, even contradiction; those were there in abundance but by the poet's design. And here I refer not to the volume's extraordinary display of linguistic and literary complexity but, in the first instance, to Milton's work as editor of the volume, to his interventions in dating individual poems in print next to or under their titles, and at times to back-dating them. Milton dated his poems to underscore his precocity the trajectory of his career; but at other times he seems to provide dates of composition in an attempt to remove his volume from religious and political turmoil and from dangerous controversy. Such topics as baptism, circumcision, the passion, and the celebration of Christmas were deeply embedded in religious and political conflicts of the civil war years, and Milton's careful dating of his poems on these themes and occasions away from the 1640s puts them at a blurring distance from controversy. It was one thing to celebrate the Lord's nativity in 1629, quite another to celebrate Christmas in December 1645. And further, even though Milton would have been, by the mid-1640s, deeply associated with church reformation and with the radical arguments of his divorce pamphlets, *Poems of Mr. John Milton* conveys a very different social and cultural aura. How indeed do the Arcadian entertainments for the dowager countess of Derby, or the obsequies for the marchioness of Winchester, or the masque written for the earl of Bridgewater and his titled family, intimate associates of Charles I's government and court, fit with the poet's identity as a radical pamphleteer? How do Milton's literary, social, and political identities converge? Indeed, what is the political or cultural identity of *Poems of Mr. John Milton* and which elements constitute it? There are no simple answers and they depend in part on where you stand—at what distance from this volume you ask these questions, and with what intent: to place the volume vertically in the trajectory of Milton's career, to situate it on a horizon of print of the days and months surrounding its publication in January 1646, or to read its poems as extraordinary contributions to the history of genres, of masques, odes, and pastoral elegies. But the meanings associated with the volume derive not only from the angle of our questions, they also derive from the ways—intentional and not—in which Milton seems to deny the book a simple identity or clear allegiance, perhaps even from a conviction that the work of literature is not commensurate with partisanship, that poetry and polemic not only belong to different hands but to different ethical spheres.

This might seem a surprising lesson to draw from John Milton's work, but to set *Poems of Mr. John Milton* within the contradictory and rapidly changing alliances and circumstances of the 1640s might explain its lack of positional clarity. It is difficult to keep your bearings in a whirlwind; and perhaps a lack of positional clarity is inevitable too for a book of poems composed over a number of years—from the time that the poet was fifteen in 1623 and began to write 'On the Circumcision' to the poet's work as editor of the volume at age thirty-six in the autumn of 1645—and in a wide range of genres. But the lack of clear coordinates for mapping the social and political position of *Poems of Mr. John Milton* may also be inevitable for the work of the muses, work that its author is eager to claim as his own.

But what of a book written quickly, issued near to the date of its composition, and bearing the marks of a clear agenda? I refer to *Annus Mirabilis*, the book that John

Dryden published in 1667. As Michael McKeon long ago demonstrated, the very title and an important element of the book's polemical swerve derive from a set of radical prophecies, 'mirabilis annus' pamphlets, published in the mid-1660s which predicted God's vengeance on the corruptions of the Restoration court.[15] Nor did it help that the year of wonders was 1666, that 666 was the number of the beast, that by the middle years of this decade the monarchy was already badly tarnished—the king's and court's sexual profligacy widely rumoured, ridiculed, and denounced—that plague had broken out in the summer months of 1665, that the Great Fire had devastated the city of London, or that the English were engaged in a costly and at points disastrous and embarrassing naval war with the Dutch. The poet had achieved some degree of visibility in the first years of the Restoration. He started out late as a writer—he was twenty-nine when he published *Heroic Stanzas*—but he made up for the tardiness. In 1665, at the outbreak of the plague in London, he removed from the city to the country estate of his father-in-law, the earl of Berkshire, and there wrote *The Essay of Dramatic Poesy*, his masterpiece of literary criticism, and *Annus Mirabilis*, his miniature epic on the disasters of that season of wonders that dissenting critics of the court had already conjured up in their pamphlets. What could possibly be ambiguous or even complex about the identity of Dryden's book?

In answering that question we must first turn to the poem's metatexts: its dedication and its preface. Here Dryden begins to negotiate what turns out to be the book's surprisingly layered programme of argument. The dedication is made to the city of London:

> As perhaps I am the first who ever presented a work of this nature to the Metropolis of any Nation, so is it likewise consonant to Justice, that he who was to give the first Example of such a Dedication should begin it with that City, which has set a pattern to all others of true Loyalty, invincible Courage and unshaken Constancy.[16]

With pleasure—and in rather baroque syntax—Dryden notes his own originality but also the way in which London models loyalty, courage, and constancy. And here already, in the very first sentence of the dedication, trouble begins. In what way does London—that hotbed of parliamentary resistance to the crown in the 1640s, the very foundation of its war effort, and in the 1660s once again a site of plots and intrigues, of jealousies and fears, a city where 'nests of fanatics prayed daily for delivery by the Dutch and French'[17]—in what way does this metropolis model loyalty and constancy? Dryden could hardly have been unaware of stories of disloyalty from the 1640s or in more recent times. All of London had heard of Thomas Venner and his Fifth Monarchists, perhaps of the bills of indictment read against the Quakers and the rest of that 'diabolical crew'. In January 1666 the Common Prayer Book 'was stolen out of Bolton Church [London], torn in pieces, and thrown in the street channel'; on 1 March of that year of wonders it was reported, 'Alderman Reed and Underwood of London are engaged with Col. Inglesby [late lieutenant in Cromwell's Life Guard] and his confederates'. In April information was circulated about a radical rising that would take place in London 'as soon as the general was gone to sea'. And by September 1666 special care had to be taken in the election of the Common Council to ensure that none would be seated who would not take 'the Lord's supper, the Oaths of Allegiance and Supremacy', and swear an oath affirming 'the unlawfulness of taking up arms against [the king]'.[18] The Common Council was explicitly named at the head of Dryden's dedication; it was very much a part of the body politic of that matchless lover—the 'most Renowned and late Flourishing City of London'—yearning to embrace the king, or so Dryden declares in his dedication. He dated the dedication 'Novem. 10. 1666.' and yet a few weeks earlier, the Common Council had to be warned of the 'unlawfulness of taking up arms' against its matchless lover. The dedication—and there are more wonderful ironies that seem to cut against its cheer-leading project—is either an effort to paper over, and to do so in a mood of baroque exaggeration, the difficult relations between the city and the crown, to patch up the strains and dissonances that mark the king's efforts at rapprochement with the city during its times of unprecedented trial, or a deeply knowing and heavily ironic reminder to that metropolis—to those instruments of its civic life named in the dedication: its lord mayor, its aldermen, its sheriffs, and Common Council (a group not noted, in the previous two decades of the city's history, for particularly happy relations with Stuart government)—that the Act of Indemnity and Oblivion had not in fact wiped out the memory of civil war or the reputation of this city and its Common Council, its sheriffs, its court of aldermen, or its lord mayor.

And this wonderful exercise in ambidexterity—of caressing as it were with one hand and provoking, even threatening and conjuring up memories with the other—is followed by Dryden's 'account of the ensuing Poem', addressed, in the form of a letter (signed, dated, and provided with a return address, little touches of realism), to his brother-in-law, Sir Robert Howard. That text is an assemblage of literary learning, a careful, almost pedantic exercise in the discussion of genres enquiring into the distinctions between history and epic and recounting the positions that Virgil, Homer, Lucan, and Silius Italicus might occupy within a debate over the merits and character of historians in verse and epic poets. While Rome (or rather London) is burning, this poet has the leisure to engage with fine points of literary learning and literary history, to discuss spondees and dactyls, the quantities of syllables, the nature of female rhymes. And sprinkled right through these discussions are the names and language of a number of ancient poets along with a smattering of French and Italian exemplars. The whole debate over epic poetry and history in verse hinges on Dryden's desire to call his 'few Stanzas' (304 quatrains!) historical and not epic. This seems a rather small quibble, hardly worth pursuing in the face of the disasters that his poem is burdened with representing, and yet the literary learning of the preface, like the footnotes that Dryden scatters through the text of his poem, is part of an effort to defuse the sense of catastrophe hovering over this year of wonders and conjured up by the radical pamphleteering that was busy predicting the end of the world. Apocalypse is what the texts of this book aim to deny: *Annus Mirabilis* is an un-apocalypse, an anti-apocalypse; it traces its careful ways through literary culture in very different rhythms from those marked by the apocalyptic rush of dissenting prophecy. There is no question that the texts of *Annus Mirabilis* were fashioned by a poet with plenty of ideas and one who had ambitions for court patronage. But its agendas are more complex than those of propaganda or careerism, its aims more ambitious than face-saving for a beleaguered court or the caressing of courtiers who might turn patrons. In the midst of that work, other ambitions drove the poet so that a literary career and a national literature, indeed a distinctively modern literature and a contemporary literary language, might be lifted on the crest of political and patronage efforts. The complexity of alignment in this set of texts is not an effect of the terms of its partisanship but of the terms of affiliation to its audiences and themes: its relation to London, to the court, to ancient poets and modern literature, to the contradictory aims of epic and history—issues counterpointed throughout Dryden's career. And perhaps there is as well Dryden's awareness of his own past written into the sharpness of his ironies against the disloyalties of London; the discomfort of those ironies reveals Dryden's awareness that his own divided loyalties were not so distant, perhaps not wholly invisible.

A Literary Masterpiece

Whatever else one might say of *Annus Mirabilis*—of its ambition and range, its real learning as well as its little touches of pretentiousness, its energy and daring and willingness to risk sentiment, even bathos, and the wonderful and knowing ironies of its dedication and preface, no one, not even Dryden's most ardent fans (and surely not Dryden himself), would imagine this effort a literary masterpiece. *Annus Mirabilis* may be important for understanding Dryden's range and accomplishment early in his career, his grasp of the genres of print and of the complex ways in which one might address various reading publics of the 1660s, but it is not a masterpiece. The poem has its *longueurs*, its patches of verse inducing boredom, though in fact a limited dose of boredom might have been exactly the right prescription for a reading public in a distempered state. But for a true masterpiece, one without a moment of boredom written into its intricate scenes and stanzas, I want to turn to a text that had no print life or for all we know manuscript circulation during its author's lifetime, Andrew Marvell's *Upon Appleton House*.

   At this point in our appreciation of Marvell's work there is no question that it is his masterpiece, though perhaps we are not certain of the ways in which it is a masterpiece. And here I want to make an intersection with the themes of this chapter—the civil wars and the memory and dangers and circumstances of warfare, and the polarities created by these circumstances but as well its dilemmas, even muddles, and the difficulties of allegiance in the face of political revolution—how all these conditions created a set of imaginative circumstances that Marvell was able to capitalize on in a remarkable way. He brought them to life in the landscapes and histories of the Fairfax estate at Nun Appleton, and he created a work of art that in its circumventing of polarities—its denial of certainties, its mazes and wanderings and shifting perspectives, its self-criticisms and its oblique and compromising glances at the career of his patron, and its capacity to acknowledge a future of unknowing—brought into perfect alignment the formal and imaginative strengths of poetry and the enormous complexities of the political and social and religious present tense of this poem, the summer season of 1651. The Lord General had retired from the army and from public life in June of 1650, moved north to his estate in Yorkshire, and hired Andrew Marvell as tutor for his twelve-year-old daughter—his only child and heir, Mary Fairfax. On this estate, and in the summer of 1651, on the verge of her thirteenth birthday when she might be imagined to hold the reproductive future of this family, Marvell wrote his magnificent country house poem.[19]

Here is an uncertain future, a past and present with their own unsteadiness: a country estate founded on the ruins of a religious house; a lovely garden that turns into a military fort; a lush agricultural field endangered by pillaging workers; a deep forest where one may not only lose one's way but also one's identity; a river that promises renewal but also threatens flood; a young girl whose judicious eyes cast a spell of innocence and calm but who is beset by the dangers of sexual ambush. All these tense spaces and conditions are mapped onto the estate and the history of the family and onto the present tense of a time beset with military crises, political uncertainties for the future of the republic, and familial anxiousness over a future dependent on the female heir. These anxieties Marvell both highlights and softens, underscores as brooding presences but half occludes with veils of irony and allusion. And what of the poet's own future and fate? He had in June of 1650 in *An Horatian Ode* half imagined a way forward—he might as a forward youth seize the occasion of the founding moment of the republic, the political climacteric imposed by Oliver Cromwell, and declare on its behalf, engage with the future, brutal and calculating though its foundation may have been. But a year later, and now employed as a tutor by the retired Lord General who had himself stepped away from public commitment and engagement, Marvell seems to acknowledge his own unsteadiness, even, perhaps, his failure of nerve. What would his own future be and the future of his writing? Would the mixed modes of *Upon Appleton House* carry him forward into the republic? These uncertainties Marvell dramatizes and weaves into the shared spaces of the country estate.

The Lord General spans imaginary forts, walks as sentinel of the garden, contemplates the future of his family, while Marvell hides in the shadows of the poem writing himself into a companionship of the Lord General's uncertainty and of the uncertain future of the heir—uncertainty beautifully dramatized at the end of the poem as Marvell turns his verse into a celebration of that heir. There he apostrophizes the thirteen-year-old Mary as the apotheosis of order, justice, and beauty; but he also reminds himself (and whoever may have read this poem) that in the summer of 1651 she is merely at the verge of adulthood, and that the summer is a waiting time—for her, for her father, for the nation, and, ever so quietly, for a poet who can write brilliant celebratory verse, pastorals and georgics, odes and elegies, lyrics and prophetic verse, but who cannot see beyond the edge of the estate and of the poem:

> 'Tis not, what it was, the *World*;
> But a rude heap together hurl'd;
> All negligently overthrown,
> Gulfes, Deserts, Precipices, Stone.
> Your lesser *World* contains the same.
>
> . . . .

> But now the *Salmon-Fishers* moist
> Their *Leathern Boats* begin to hoist;
> And, like *Antipodes* in Shoes,
> Have shod their *Heads* in their *Canoos*.
> How *Tortoise like*, but not so slow,
> These rational *Amphibii* go?
> Let's in: for the dark *Hemisphere*
> Does now like one of them appear.[20]

With its haunting, perhaps comic, surely foreboding imagery, Marvell captures the personal and political un-clarity of that time.

When Marvell wrote *Upon Appleton House* he seems to have lost any clear sense of his own political identity. He wrote his poem for a man who might boast an ancient and distinguished genealogy—whose estates covered vast holdings in the north of England and who had forged a distinguished military career at the head of the parliamentary forces that defeated Charles I, assuring the imprisonment, trial, and execution of the king—but Lord Fairfax's political identity was clouded by his retreat from the future, his stepping away from command and his dissent from the violent end of Charles I on which the republic was founded. That bleeding head Marvell brilliantly rendered in *Horatian Ode* as a token of the future. But what partisan values could now be celebrated in the country house poem that Marvell imagined for this patron? What political passions drove its performance? These questions must be answered less in terms of political ideology than in those of patronage and psychology, but whatever answers we might provide it seems clear that its readers in the early 1650s (if it had any) or in 1681 when the poem came into print, posthumously, would not likely have experienced *Upon Appleton House* initially or primarily or hardly at all in terms of its partisanship.[21] The poem's aims are rather to deny any simple roadmap to political identity, indeed to identity altogether. In that work, the poem is an extraordinary accomplishment.

An Inexact Picture May Be More Useful ...

Marvell would later write of the civil wars, that they had been too fine a cause, 'too good to have been fought for',[22] and whether or not his contemporaries would have understood this retrospective judgement as merely a way of excusing his own inconstancies, the phrase opens a way for us to understand more broadly not only complexity of allegiance but also, and with it, complexity of identity in relation to ways in which we might imagine a history for literature of the civil wars, republic, Protectorate, and Restoration. The title of my coda comes from an often cited expression in Ludwig Wittgenstein's *Philosophical Investigations*, and while I'm uncertain if twentieth-century philosophy of language can truly illuminate seventeenth-century literary history, there is something attractive about the idea that an inexact, a fuzzy picture may be just what we need for imagining these decades at the middle of the seventeenth century—because a more distinct picture distorts political and ethical uncertainties, the blurred cultural alliances and allegiances that writers and readers occupied in these decades of warfare, political revolution, and the unsteady restoration of old forms.[23] That inexact picture is beautifully conveyed by the imagery that closes the *Horatian Ode*:

> But thou the Wars and Fortunes Son
> March indefatigably on;
> And for the last effect
> Still keep thy Sword erect:
> Besides the force it has to fright
> The Spirits of the shady Night,
> The same *Arts* that did *gain*
> A *Pow'r* must it *maintain*.[24]

Here contradictions of feeling are matched by complexities of literary allusion and political argumentation that seem to defy summary: Cromwell as an Horatian figure tinged with humour, Cromwell as Virgilian figure tinged with tragedy; the sword held aloft as a pagan emblem, or upside down as a Christian image, or simply drawn in readiness for battle; the spirits of the shady night emerging from an Homeric or Virgilian underworld and fearing cold iron, or the spirits as the ghosts of soldiers on the English and Irish battlefields who had felt the keen edge of Cromwell's command; the acknowledgement that power seized by the sword must be so maintained as Machiavellian pragmatism, or as the threat of royalist revenge, or as a Shakespearean allusion to the perfidious Scots whose presence demanded a sword drawn to defend religion and the state. The sentiment is also resonant with English writings in the 1640s—writings, for example, of Anthony Ascham who had argued in July 1648, that 'the Usurper . . . will find himself oblig'd to secure his conquest by the same meanes he obtained it'.[25] As Marvell's editors note, Ascham was a supporter of Cromwell. Was Andrew Marvell? Where did those and other allusions and ironies leave the reader (if there had been one) contemplating the contradictory claims of allegiance and authority in the summer of 1650? It may be that an inexact picture is sometimes more useful than a clear one—for Andrew Marvell contemplating the threshold zone between regimes; for us imagining the literary history of these decades—interesting times, indeed.

NOTES

1. These and all subsequent publishing statistics are derived from the British Library ESTC database, <http://estc.bl.uk>. Numbers of print publications surviving from the mid-seventeenth century are always approximate because of the loss rate for ballads, broadsides, pamphlets, and other print ephemera; see D. F. McKenzie, 'Printing and Publishing, 1557–1700: Constraints on the London Book Trades', in John Barnard and D. F. McKenzie, with the assistance of Maureen Bell (eds.), *The Cambridge History of the Book in Britain*, 6 vols. (Cambridge, 1999–2012), IV, 577.

2. Though some scholars have cautioned that while the number of titles increased, the number of printed pages likely remained the same: see, for example, Sheila Lambert, 'State Control of the Press in Theory and Practice', in Robin Myers and Michael Harris (eds.), *Censorship and the Control of Print in England and France, 1600–1910* (London, 1992), 1–32.

3. On Restoration panegyrics, see the electronic database and edition made by Gerald MacLean, *The Return of the King: An Anthology of Poems Commemorating the Restoration of Charles II*, <http://etext.lib.virginia.edu/toc/modeng/public/MacKing.html>; on the Restoration sermons, see Carolyn Edie, 'Right Rejoicing: Sermons on the Occasion of the Stuart Restoration', *Bulletin of the John Rylands Library*, 62.1 (1979): 61–86; see also John Gordon Spaulding's 'Pulpit Publications: 1660–1782', on deposit at the Henry E. Huntington Library.

4. See Milton's Sonnet 11, 'A book was writ of late called *Tetrachordon*', in *The Complete Poetry and Essential Prose of John Milton*, ed. William Kerrigan, John Rumrich, and Stephen M. Fallon (New York, 2007), 147–8.

5. On the numbers and distribution of romances, see Steven N. Zwicker, 'Royalist Romance?' in Thomas Keymer (ed.), *The New Oxford History of the Novel* (Oxford, in press).

6. See David Bywaters, 'Representations of the Interregnum and Restoration in Drama of the early 1660s', *Review of English Studies*, 60 (2009): 255–70.

7. On the size of print runs, see Ian Green, *Print and Protestantism in Early Modern England* (Oxford, 2000), 177ff., and William St. Clair, *The Reading Nation in the Romantic Period* (Cambridge, 2004), 21 and Appendix 1.

8. Green, *Print and Protestantism*, 305ff.

9. See Gerald Hammond, *Fleeting Things: English Poets and Poems, 1616–1660* (Cambridge, MA, 1990), 255–8; Nigel Smith, *Literature and Revolution in England, 1640–1660* (New Haven, 1994), 253–5; David Norbrook, *Writing the English Republic: Poetry, Rhetoric, and Politics 1627–1660* (Cambridge, 1999), 172–8; and Nicholas McDowell, *Poetry and Allegiance in the English Civil Wars* (Oxford, 2008), 112–54.

10. See Nigel Smith's review of Ruth Connolly and Tom Cain (eds.), *Lords of Wine and Oile*, *Times Literary Supplement*, 5682 (24 February 2012), 25.

11. On the commendatory verse for *Lucasta*, see Randy Robertson, *Censorship and Conflict in Seventeenth-Century England* (University Park, PA, 2009), 70–99.

12. Sir Lewis B. Namier, *The Structure of Politics at the Accession of George III* (London, 1957).

13. Most commentary on Thomas Harper follows H. R. Plomer's account in *A Dictionary of the Booksellers and Printers . . . 1641 to 1667* (London, 1907), but see the discussion of Harper in the 'Mercurius Politicus' blog: <http://mercuriuspoliticus.wordpress.com/2010/11/14/thomas-harper>.

14. D. F. McKenzie and Maureen Bell (eds.), *A Chronology and Calendar of Documents Relating to the London Book Trade, 1641–1700*, 3 vols. (Oxford, 2005), I, 73.

15. Michael McKeon, *Politics and Poetry in Restoration England: The Case of Dryden's 'Annus Mirabilis'* (Cambridge, MA, 1975).

16. *The Poems of John Dryden*, 4 vols. (Oxford, 1965), I, 42.

17. *Calendar of State Papers, Domestic, 1660–1661*, 470–1.

18. *Calendar of State Papers, Domestic, 1665–1666*, 270 ff.

19. See the account of the poem in Derek Hirst and Steven N. Zwicker, *Andrew Marvell, Orphan of the Hurricane* (Oxford, 2012), 9–40.

20. *The Poems and Letters of Andrew Marvell*, 2 vols. (Oxford, 1971), I, 86.

21. The approach to this poem and to Marvell's whole career through patronage and psychology is laid out in Hirst and Zwicker, *Andrew Marvell*.

22. *The Prose Works of Andrew Marvell*, 2 vols. (New Haven, 2003), I, 192.

23. Ludwig Wittgenstein, *Philosophical Investigations*, trans. G. E. M Anscombe (Oxford, 2001), 34.

24. *Poems and Letters*, I, 94.

25. Ascham is cited by John Wallace in *Destiny His Choice: The Loyalism of Andrew Marvell* (Cambridge, 1968), 96–7; see also the commentary in *Poems and Letters*, I, 302–3, and Nigel Smith, *The Poems of Andrew Marvell*, ed. Nigel Smith (Harlow, 2007), 279.

FURTHER READING

Bywaters, David, 'Representations of the Interregnum and Restoration in Drama of the Early 1660s', *Review of English Studies*, 60 (2009): 255–270.

Green, Ian, *Print and Protestantism in Early Modern England* (Oxford, 2000).

Healy, Thomas and Jonathan Sawday (eds.), *Literature and the English Civil Wars* (Cambridge, 1990).

Hirst, Derek and Steven N. Zwicker, *Andrew Marvell, Orphan of the Hurricane* (Oxford, 2012).

Lambert, Sheila, 'State Control of the Press in Theory and Practice', in Robin Myers and Michael Harris (eds.), *Censorship and the Control of Print in England and France, 1600–1910* (London, 1992).

McKenzie, D. F., 'Printing and Publishing 1557–1700: Constraints on the London Book Trades', in John Barnard and D. F. McKenzie, with the assistance of Maureen Bell (eds.), *The Cambridge History of the Book in Britain, vol. IV: 1557–1695* (Cambridge, 2002).

Norbrook, David, *Writing the English Republic: Poetry, Rhetoric, and Politics 1627–1660* (Cambridge, 1999).

Robertson, Randy, *Censorship and Conflict in Seventeenth-Century England* (University Park, PA, 2009).

Smith, Nigel, *Literature and Revolution in England, 1640–1660* (New Haven, 1994).

Zwicker, Steven N., 'Royalist Romance?', in Thomas Keymer (ed.), *New Oxford History of the Novel* (Oxford, in press).

CHAPTER 28

....

THE ART AND
ARCHITECTURE OF
WAR, REVOLUTION, AND
RESTORATION

....

TIMOTHY WILKS

ART

....

EVEN as the violent and revolutionary events of the 1640s and 1650s were being played
out, it was well understood that art and architecture were among those matters being
contested. Though they may not have been central to the ideological struggle, neither
were they incidental. In that contemporaneous European conflict, the Thirty Years War,
the location of art treasures was sometimes a consideration in the setting of a military
objective (as with the plundering of Munich in 1632 and Prague in 1648).[1] Yet, in the
English civil war, artworks *in situ* generally came to attention in other ways and for other
reasons. London, with its concentration of monuments, decorated interiors, and royalist art collections, was always under parliamentary control but in contested parts of the
country cathedrals, churches, great houses, and their interior art passed from one side
to the other as part of wider territorial gains and losses. Their subsequent treatment,
however, was often more deliberate than the manner of their acquisition, and on the
parliamentarian side the urge to destroy art was possibly more evident than the urge to
possess it. Even the ordered seizure of the magnificent collections of Charles I does not
fit the familiar model of organized art plunder, as their subsequent sale indicates that the
Commonwealth was unconvinced of art's value to the state.[2]

   As well as considering the material fortunes of art, scholars have also turned in recent
years to the war as conducted within art itself, which continued until the Restoration.
This was a largely a contest of the printed image, whether in the form of crude woodcuts or fine engravings. Between 1640 and 1646, many hundreds of prints appeared

as illustrations in English broadsides or pamphlets, of which roughly half directly addressed political or religious controversies.[3] Parliament's control of London gave its supporters access to some of the best designs produced in the pre-war years for the court, and effective use was made of them. This appropriation of iconography suggests that within art at least, no appreciable revolution took place.

While both printed and painted image was used by each side to disparage the other and to celebrate its own virtues, victories, and leaders, art continued to be dogged by its association with idolatry in the minds of many. The irreconcilability of the beliefs of puritans (of even the more moderate variety) and Laudian Anglicans who accepted the notion of the 'beauty of holiness' may be demonstrated by an elegant restatement by John Saltmarsh, Sir Thomas Fairfax's chaplain, of the Reformed position on the attainment of faith through the senses:

> And further, What is it that is said of grace comming in by the *eye*? This is the way the *Papists* let in *Christ*, having made the *eye* rather the organ for conversion then the *eare*: Now faith commeth by hearing, and therefore all their *Idolarous Pictures*, their *Imagery*; and *theabicall* representations, are all for the *eye*, and bringing in *Christ* by *Optick* or sense, and making *conversion* to be by perspective, and working only an historicall faith.[4]

More strident condemnations of idolatry had already appeared in print, as in Edmund Gurnay's *Towards the Vindication of the Second Commandment* (1639) and, following the breakdown of Archbishop Laud's licensing restrictions, John Vicars's *The Sinfulness and Unlawfulness of making or having the picture of Christ's humanity* (1641) and George Salteran's *A treatise against images and pictures in churches* (1641).

We might contrast Saltmarsh's sight-centred argument with that expressed in *The Nurse of Pious Thoughts: Wherein the use which Roman Catholikes do make of sacred Pictures, Signes and Images, is not Idolatry, or any other misdemeanour*, published in 1652, which declared:

> if you do not permit visible signes, pictures, images, and remembrances of piety, vertue, and the Obligations which men have unto God, and Christ Jesus his only Son, to be exposed to the senses, the windows of their souls, and yet allow of vain, idle and prophane, you shall shut up the door to vertue and gratitude.[5]

Though its author optimistically addressed the entire aristocracy and gentry as well as 'all the free-born people of England', its obvious Catholic origins would have severely limited its readership and it seems directed mainly at royalist exiles—many already amenable to Arminian ideas—in the hope of inclining them further towards Catholicism. There was, in fact, little in this book with which Laudians would have taken issue.

The moderate puritan Saltmarsh's use in some memorably ironic phrases of such words as 'optic' and 'perspective' suggests that he was not uninformed about art. Though he might have been capable of making a distinction between idolatrous imagery and art that did not offend God, there were many other puritans who were incapable. It was their ascendancy that caused a general malaise to settle on art production and the art market in the 1640s. Attributing this merely to the disappearance of patrons and purchasers is to fail to detect the sheer demoralization of those who wished to engage with art. As the rebellion gathered momentum, emboldened puritans found offence in an ever-wider range of imagery. Royalists reminded themselves of their opponents' extremism with stories such as that which told of the pulling down of Charing Cross, when the mob turned its attention to a picture of the Cross on a nearby inn sign, apparently outraged by the mere image of an image.[6] Patrick Collinson has identified a kind of 'visual anorexia' within English Protestantism that had developed from a core concern with idolatry into a suspicion of imagery in general.[7] This interpretation has been challenged by Tessa Watt and others, who find instead a 'secularization of imagery' taking place at this time, explained both as a refocusing onto safer subjects and as a manifestation of the growth of curiosity.[8]

While iconophobia might have been characteristic of puritanism if not Protestantism, an entirely contrary tendency had also appeared before the war and would re-emerge strongly at the Restoration. Contemporaries initially struggled to find words for it; Henry Peacham, in the 1634 edition of *The Compleat Gentleman*, introduced his readers to '*virtuosi*', explaining that such men, through their patient examination of works of art, attained acuity of judgement, connection with the past, and moral improvement.[9] By 1644, John Evelyn was using 'virtuoso' as an adopted English word in his correspondence and, presumably, in his conversation. The term 'lover of art', meanwhile, was committed to print for the first time in 1638 by Franciscus Junius, secretary to the 'Collector Earl' Thomas Howard, 14th earl of Arundel.[10] The new vocabulary signalled the arrival of taste and virtuosity in England along with an influx of high-quality artworks, artists from the continent, and returning early Grand Tourists. This may also have been assisted by a changing European mental outlook, indications of which are detectable among the English though are easier to observe in contemporary Dutch society. This change seems to have had something to do with a projection of the self into the world of perceptions; an essentially phenomenological event, though with epistemological consequences. Harold Cook has found, certainly among the Dutch, a requirement for 'a deep comprehension of the material world combined with, and driven by, the passions' leading to new perceptions resting on 'acquaintance' rather than 'knowledge of casual explanations'.[11] Though his focus is on commerce, science, and medicine, he recognizes that this same attitude also produced the *liefhebber*—a word familiar to cultured Englishmen, who sometimes used it to describe the recently appeared connoisseur of art.

From exile, John Bramhall, bishop of Londonderry, wrote:

> Put a *Liefhebber,* or *Virtueso,* among a company of rare Pictures, and he will pick out the best pieces for their proper value: But a friend or a child will more esteem the Picture of a Benefactor, or Ancestor, for its relation. The respect of the one is terminated in the Picture, that of the other is radicated in the exemplar. Yet still an Image is but an Image, and the kinds of respect must not be confounded.[12]

Answering Catholics rather than his usual puritan adversaries here, Bramhall reveals his awareness that art has internal as well as associative qualities; an insight the bishop probably acquired living in art-saturated Holland. In any case, as Graham Parry points out, 'Laudian fondness for images ran alongside the courtly love of the fine arts.'[13] Indeed, Laudian churchmen, in their desire to recreate the splendour of the Temple of Solomon in England's places of worship, had always paid close attention to the intense engagement of Charles I's court with art and architecture.

It was the early Stuart court and the peripheral, great courtier households of London and Westminster which had led the demand for more sophisticated art, both old and new. This led to the formation of collections that astonished Rubens when he visited London in 1629. In the following decade the visual arts in England would be further stimulated by Van Dyck's appointment as the king's painter. When Charles I left Whitehall in January 1642 cultural life was suddenly stilled in the royal palaces and in many of the aristocratic houses in and around London, though not in all of them. The London art trade immediately fell into a deep depression and artists were faced with three possible courses of action: to follow the court to Oxford, to leave the country, or to attempt to maintain their livelihood in London. Some who chose the last course lingered for a while and then departed, others left and later returned. Most of the leading painters and sculptors, foreign and native-born, however, left England early in the civil war, among them Cornelius Johnson, Henry Stone, Henry Cook, Hendrick van der Borcht, Frans Wouters, John Michael Wright, John Hayls, William Sheppard, Francesco Fanelli, Francois Dieussart, Jean Petitot, Jacques Bordier, and Simon and Isaac Luttichuys.[14] Van Dyck had already died in London in 1641, though not before he, too, had sensed the impending crisis and had begun to look for work in Paris and Antwerp.

In March 1643, two members of parliament, the republican and later regicide Henry Marten, and another extremist, Sir John Clotworthy, led soldiers to Somerset House and set about destroying the lavish decoration of Inigo Jones's Queen's Chapel, where Henrietta Maria, her attendant Capuchin friars and English Catholics had worshipped.[15] The stupendous Baroque art it contained included François Dieussart's soaring sculptural work and Rubens's *Crucifixion* altarpiece, which was ripped to shreds with a halberd. A month after Marten and Clotworthy's orgy of destruction, Sir Robert Harley, another parliamentarian, was tasked with removing all images of the Trinity and of the Virgin Mary from the royal palaces of Whitehall, Greenwich, and Hampton Court, though the remainder of the art was at that time left undisturbed. As early as 1641, parliament had issued an order requiring that idolatrous images be removed from churches and chapels, later extended to include such meeting places as the Guildhall in London. Commissioners were appointed to enforce the order, the most notorious of them, William Dowsing, becoming highly active in Suffolk and Cambridgeshire.

The effects of war and revolution on the visual arts in England may all too easily be assumed to have been entirely deleterious. The view that the very continuance of artistic life (along with much else) had been at stake once fitted neatly into the 'Court and Country' view of a sharply divided society on the eve of civil war and, despite the perceptive criticisms of Malcolm Smuts, it remains the most enduring part of that heavily revised model.[16] According to this view, the court declared its superiority and displayed its self-perceived virtues by the means of a 'court culture' that contrived to be both magnificent and esoteric, becoming, as Charles I's political difficulties worsened, ever more inward looking; its cultural manifestations and productions serving to reassure a courtier elite. To regard the court as the prime driver of artistic activity before the war is also to regard the near redundancy of art as an inevitable consequence of the royalist defeat. Yet, the fortunes of art were never entirely bound up with that of the court and even the Protectorate found it necessary to withhold or buy back some artworks from the sale of the royal collections in order to decorate state rooms.

Notwithstanding the disappearance of many patrons, there remained sympathizers of parliament for whom art and architecture were very important, including the earls of Northumberland, Pembroke, Essex, and Warwick, whose households continued to function more or less normally. Northumberland House, belonging to Algernon Percy, 10th earl of Northumberland, for example, contained a large and important art collection, which unlike the Buckingham, Hamilton, and Arundel collections, remained in place throughout the civil wars and the Protectorate, as its owner had sided with parliament. Similarly, Philip Herbert, 4th earl of Pembroke, who took no active part in the struggle, was able to continue to patronize a few practitioners of the arts in London and at Wilton. Isaac de Caus, designer of Wilton's formal gardens and builder of its south wing in the 1630s, probably did not remain resident for long once war broke out, but new faces entered the Pembroke circle: Richard Gibson, the queen's dwarf turned accomplished miniaturist, and a talented young painter, Peter Lely. In 1648, John Webb, Inigo Jones's protégé, was called to Wilton to survey extensive fire damage to De Caus's wing and to rebuild it to a revised design, which was achieved by 1652.[17] There were, in fact, many who might be described variously as puritans, parliamentarians, or republicans who were sympathetic to art and to artists, Sir John Danvers, regicide and aesthete, among them, who, as John Aubrey put it, 'had a very fine fancy, which lay chiefly for gardens and architecture'.

In Oxford, meanwhile, where the court had relocated, a great English painter emerged. William Dobson died young, in 1646, though not before producing a body of work markedly different in mood to that of Van Dyck's pre-war *oeuvre*. Dobson's portraits—for which he could barely obtain enough paint to cover the canvas—provide the definitive image of the cavalier at war. Recourse to the painter's studio, even in a garrison environment, was for these royalists a self-affirming social custom. These portraits seem to have been painted as much for the moment as for posterity, and sitting for Dobson, no doubt, provided some temporary distraction from the strain of war.

After the fall of Oxford in June 1646, Dobson returned to London, where in the few months before his death his attempt to re-establish his practice throws more light on the state of the art market at that time. The engraver William Faithorne also returned to work in London after his capture at the fall of Basing House, even though remaining in loose custody prior to his five-year banishment to France.[18] Also captured at Basing House were his employer, the art dealer-turned-colonel, Robert Peake, the aged Inigo Jones, and one Rowlett, who was very probably a relation of the royalist print publisher, Thomas Rowlett. These clusters of prominent figures within the English artistic community in Oxford and in one of the last royalist strongholds remind us of their considerable stake in the life of the court and their personal commitment to the ideology of the

Stuart monarchy. A similar, provincial example may be found in the case of John Souch, who had made a good living before the war painting the gentry of Cheshire, Shropshire, and North Wales, and when most of them chose the king's side, he did also, later dying in the siege of royalist Chester.[19]

In London, Faithorne set about engraving three of the portraits that Dobson had earlier painted: the Prince of Wales, Prince Rupert, and the courtier Endymion Porter. It was a venture founded on an old friendship: Faithorne and Dobson had both been apprenticed to Robert Peake's brother William, though at different times, and were also apparently old friends of Thomas Rowlett, who agreed to sell the prints from his shop near Temple Bar.[20] Here, then, is evidence that even in late 1646, when the royalist cause seemed hopeless, there still existed a market in London for images of the principal royalists. This joint venture was brought to an end by Dobson's premature death, a lamented event sufficient to prompt a memorial print etched by Josias English.

English's etching was based on Dobson's self-portrait which was contained in his ambitious, triple portrait of him in the company of Sir Charles Cotterell and Nicholas Lanier, Master of the King's Music and also collector of Old Master drawings, amateur painter, and art adviser to Charles I. Once thought to have been painted at Oxford, the triple portrait is now dated later, to Dobson's last months in London—further indication that small cliques were able to rebuild at the very heart of the new regime a discreet social life enriched with art and artistic discourse.

Josias English was trained at the important pre-war Mortlake workshop, where the highly regarded Rostock-born painter Francis Cleyn had arrived in 1625 to provide designs for the new tapestry works. Cleyn not only taught his sons there but also a number of aspiring English artists, among them Dobson. After the civil war, interestingly, the Commonwealth maintained state support for the tapestry works, though Cleyn and his co-workers found supplementary, private commissions difficult to obtain. Cleyn's loss of income drove him to etching—to the great benefit of English printmaking. Between 1645 and 1646 he produced three allegorical and decorative series for Rowlett and continued to produce many designs for others to etch or engrave.

Only Quakers and a few other extreme sectarians sought a world entirely purged of the visual arts. After parliament's victory, there was some attempt to redirect art but scholarly opinion remains divided as to its intent. Kelsey observes an attempt between 1649 and 1653 to create a new culture of republicanism with a role for pictorial imagery.[21] Sharpe, though, has argued that it proved almost impossible to conceive of art forms owing nothing to the old visual culture, even though that was directed to representing kingly authority, virtue, and piety.[22] Sharpe also observes that after the execution of Charles I the royal image became much more prevalent and potent than it had been throughout the 1640s, the Rump then having to contend with the imagery of two kings: a martyred king and a king-in-exile. Other historians, among them Knoppers, have taken a middle position.[23]

Though the civil war provoked an exodus of artists, there is evidence of some movement in the opposite direction, particularly after Charles I's execution. Jean-Baptiste Gaspars, for example, was a newcomer, proving to be a highly competent etcher prior to becoming one of Peter Lely's principal assistants. Pierre Lombart appears to have arrived as one of a team of French art advisers sent over by Cardinal Mazarin to assess for possible purchase and to copy some of Charles I's confiscated pictures. He is of particular interest because he found sufficient work to stay in London where he became actively involved in printmaking. While a colleague, Ludwig Richer, contributed a few plates to Ogilby's *Virgil* (1654), Lombart was more active and ambitious, even contributing significantly to the iconography of Cromwell. Lombart dedicated his large engraving of *Oliver Cromwell with a Page* (1651–3), based on Robert Walker's painting, to parliament clearly in the hope of winning official commissions. John Evelyn bought a print of it, judging it to be 'accurate'. Lombart proceeded to strike up a working relationship with Walker, engraving a number of his painted works, including *Oliver Cromwell on Horseback* (1655). For a couple of years after the Restoration, he continued to work on the so-called 'Countesses', a series of twelve high-quality engravings after portraits by Van Dyck.[24] This series, which revived memories of the elegance of the court of Charles I, proved popular on publication and was sold both in London and Paris.

Not only Cromwell but also most of the parliamentary leaders and generals had themselves painted. It was left, however, to three non-native artists: Peter Lely, Balthasar Gerbier, and George Geldorp, combining in 1651 to propose a series of large, painted canvases that would have commemorated parliament's memorable achievements. If their proposal had been taken up, it might have gone some way to initiating the new visual culture that the English Revolution lacked, but the inevitable contentiousness of any proposed visual programme probably stifled the idea.

Peter Lely, German-born but of Dutch extraction, was the youngest of the trio and newly arrived, whereas Gerbier and Geldorp had long been resident in England; Gerbier had assiduously served the court favourite, George Villiers, 1st duke of Buckingham in the 1620s, as the keeper of his art collection, but had latterly vilified Charles I and his court in print; Geldorp had long since given up painting himself to become, as the art historian Ellis Waterhouse put it, an 'artistic impresario, art dealer, and pimp'.[25] If any of the remaining London art community were to prosper during the Interregnum it was likely to have been Gerbier and Geldorp. Lely may have been lucky to fall in with them and may even have been persuaded by Geldorp to come to England to work for him, possibly as early as 1643. If the great parliamentary commission had been granted, Lely would have done the painting. Even without it, he soon found his own path to success in inauspicious circumstances.

The way in which Lely adapted to pre-existing trends in English art is both fascinating and revealing. There is some evidence to suggest that he started out painting landscapes and histories, adopting the bold and direct manners of Dobson and Isaac Fuller, the versatile painter of chapels and taverns.[26] In 1647, Lely reappears as a portraitist, having been brought to Hampton Court by the art-loving earl of Northumberland, then Charles I's custodian, to record his brief reunion with his son, the duke of York (later James II). Lely's portrait is unlike any other of Charles I, suggesting the mood and possibly the mind of the king in captivity.[27] Lely, therefore, entered at the highest level of portrait commissions, monopolized by Van Dyck before the war. After the Restoration,

Lely consolidated his position as Van Dyck's successor, adopting his languid manner but using somewhat bolder Baroque settings. His pre-Restoration work, however, may be his finest, when his sensitivity to the seriousness of the times is evident.

In what might be assumed were poor conditions for all parts of the art market, the 1650s saw an upsurge in book illustration, and it was within the covers of illustrated books that much of the visual inventiveness of the decade was expressed. Whether artistic energies and aesthetic impulses were concentrated in this medium as other means of visual expression were closed off, or whether developments in illustrated book production would have occurred at this time anyway, is hard to determine. The influence of the French market, however, is evident. Michel de Marolles's illustrated, folio edition of Virgil (1649) was clearly the inspiration for John Ogilby's *The Works of Publius Virgilius Maro, Translated, Adorn'd with Sculpture and Illustrated with Annotations* (1654): also an ambitious folio edition. It was an even greater printing challenge than Ogilby's early quarto publication, *The Fables of Aesop* (1651) for which Francis Cleyn had etched eighty full-page plates. Cleyn also designed the plates for the Ogilby's Virgil, half of which were engraved by Lombart, Richer, and others, and the other half etched (more quickly and cheaply) by Wenceslaus Hollar. These plates continued to be used for subsequent editions and single-sheets until at least 1709. The entrepreneurial Ogilby built on this success by publishing illustrated folios of his translations of the *Iliad* (1660) and the *Odyssey* (1665), each of which, he claimed, cost him £5,000 to produce, a figure which, assuming he recouped his investment—achieved partly through his innovative subscription schemes and sponsorship of plates—gives an indication of the size to which the market for such works had grown by the Restoration.[28]

Wenceslas Hollar's career serves well to mark the wider fortunes of art in England in the 1640s and 1650s.[29] Hollar, a native of Prague, entered the service of the earl of Arundel in 1636 but did not accompany him into exile in 1642. Hollar remained in London and began to release etchings of Arundel masterpieces, which he had copied before the earl's vast collection was taken abroad; he also released some tranquil views of the continent. Demand for such prints stretched across the political divide and Hollar responded by also etching several stirring images of leading royalists and parliamentarians. These included an equestrian portrait of the earl of Essex dominating a map marking the first battle sites of the war (1643) and an equestrian portrait of Charles I, with the royal army in miniature scale arrayed in battle formation between the king's horse's legs (1644). Also in 1644, Hollar engraved a series of six pocket maps for the publisher Thomas Jenner, who advertised them on the title page as 'Usefull for all Comanders for Quarteringe of Souldiers. & all sorts of Persons that would be informed Where the Armies be'. This relatively undemanding commission for Hollar proved so popular that there were to be post-war editions. Despite these apparent successes Hollar soon afterwards left for Antwerp where he re-established contact with the countess of Arundel and other royalist exiles.

Inevitably, much discussion of the art of the Protectorate focuses upon Cromwell's image. To consider the adaptation of earlier designs derived from pre-war commissions generated by the court of Charles I, in some instances it amounted to the copying of almost every detail save the head, as in Lombart's notorious engraving of Van Dyck's equestrian portrait of Charles I, in which the king's head was replaced with Cromwell's, and in several oil portraits by Robert Walker, in which we recognize poses seen before in Van Dyck's work. This seems to indicate a serious lack of artistic talent available to the Republic. Payne Fisher's *Irenodia Gratulatoria* (1652), a panegyric in Latin verse to the victorious Cromwell, includes in its preliminaries two full-page engravings; the first, a reworked equestrian portrait with an absurdly oversized head of Cromwell newly added; the second, a crude copy by William Trevillian of Lombart's copy of Walker's borrowing from Van Dyck's portrait of Strafford. Small wonder, then, that Fisher wastes no time, as Knoppers points out, in directing the reader away from the imagery to the text: 'Come close readers and be instructed. Why do you gawp at silent portraits (*Icones*) or shadowy likenesses such as these? If you desire to know the invincible Cromwell, you will contemplate not his face but his virtues.'[30]

More recently, attention has been drawn to the variation within the iconography of Cromwell, which was such that his image may be said to have been contested. Here, the war was fought through the presentation of sympathetic and hostile portraits of him; some of the latter taking the form of out-and-out caricature. From his first emergence as an important commander Cromwell became the butt of royalist satirists who mocked his unhandsome appearance; Cleveland's *A Character of a London Diurnall* (1645) drew attention to his 'bloody Beake' and *Mercurius Elenchtus* contrived a particularly vivid insult: 'Now you *King Noll*, with your *bacon-flicht-face* . . .', while *A Case for Noll Cromwells Nose* (1648) carried the disparagement of his features into its very title.[31] Following Charles I's execution and the subsequent growth of the possibility that Cromwell might take the crown for himself, the matter of his appearance, which his enemies had always ridiculed, was adduced to arguments as to his essential lack of kingly qualities: appearance and virtue, as always, somehow being connected in the public mind.

Samuel Cooper's famous, warty miniature of Cromwell, which exists in several versions, confirms that the art of miniature painting continued to flourish throughout this period. The miniature was the only art for which England was praised abroad, and the best practitioners of the 1650s were of the third or fourth generation to maintain its excellence. Cooper learned his craft in the studio of his uncle, John Hoskins, before establishing his own London practice shortly before the civil war. He was already England's leading miniaturist and would remain pre-eminent until his death in 1672. Throughout this period the English miniature continued to evolve and by the Restoration the finest work was both identifiably English and modern, in the sense of being realistic rather than iconic. The modernity of Cooper's work and his early Restoration followers, Matthew Snelling and Thomas Flatman, is very evident when compared with that of Nicholas Hilliard, who was still practising when Cooper was a boy. The difference is a fundamental one between Hilliard's lack of interest in conveying either time or space and Cooper's desire to create images that are convincingly 'present'. Cooper, moreover, conveyed the character of his sitters without yielding to insincerity or affectation, possibly for which reason puritans were equally keen to sit for Cooper. It is perhaps more surprising that Cooper's reputation continued to grow in the reign of Charles II, as his style owed nothing to the Baroque.

Significantly, miniature painting took hold among the gentry at this time, regarded as an acceptable, 'virtuoso' pastime. In 1648/49, Edward Norgate rewrote for publication his treatise, *The Art of Limning* (1627–8), intending it for a wider readership than the courtly circle among which manuscripts of the first version had circulated. Though his death in 1650 prevented this, William Sanderson published his *Graphice*, in 1658, which included a pirated edition of Norgate's earlier treatise, and thereby made hitherto privileged artistic knowledge available. The acquiring of some practical skill and a little theory by a wider section of society, including women, did much to secure a favourable reception for art wherever it appeared in the second half of the seventeenth century.

ARCHITECTURE

The building boom of the 1630s, which followed a decade of bad harvests and costly wars, came to an end in 1642. Work stopped abruptly on several important building projects, as at Stoke Park in Northamptonshire, where the colonnaded wings of this significant attempt at Italianate Classicism were left unconnected, and at Clare College, Cambridge, where the new foundations of the west range would lay bare for twenty years. The rest of the 1640s subsequently became exceptional for the destruction of buildings rather than their construction, which resulted either from military action or by later demolition. Many royalist fortified houses and castles were 'slighted' after their capture; mainly to render them permanently indefensible. The scale of devastation, however, was nothing like that in parts of Germany; only English villages and suburbs unluckily adjacent to a stronghold were likely to be battered or burned. The destruction of defended great houses also rendered a significant number of royalist families and rather fewer parliament-supporting families homeless; many post-Restoration new builds, rebuilds, and relocations were a consequence of this.

At Montgomery Castle, Lord Herbert of Cherbury, after surrendering, hoped that his mansion house, recently built within the medieval walls, might be spared, pleading that it was so indefensible that it could barely keep out the weather.[32] But it was not to be; both old and new structures were knocked down and Herbert's heir chose to build anew after the Restoration at nearby Lymore. At Carew Castle, near Pembroke, the Carews re-installed themselves in its east wing after the Restoration, other sections of the castle having been slighted, but they eventually abandoned it for their Somerset estates. All told during the civil wars, there were more than 300 sieges; some small-scale, others major and protracted.[33] Additional to the loss of life at these sieges, the toppling of fine architecture and even the destruction of formal gardens, as at Raglan Castle, may be considered a cost of war, diminishing the cultural fabric of the country.

Some houses of parliamentarians seem to have directly benefited from the demolition of the castles and houses of their defeated opponents—actual reuse of materials

reflecting local shifts of power; one example being the delivery of large quantities of timber, salvaged from Pontefract Castle, to Tanshelf Court, the main seat of the Wards, a
parliament-supporting family in the West Riding. Turning to the practice of slighting
itself, recent studies have revised the long-held belief that once the army had rendered
captured royalist strongholds indefensible with gunpowder charges, local populations
typically expressed their antipathy towards the former occupants by tearing down and
removing much of the remaining *matériel*. It has now been established that the dismantling of these properties was usually authorized, organized, and efficiently carried out.[34]

The sieges and subsequent fates of isolated strongholds have undoubtedly drawn
attention away from the more significant sieges of entire towns and cities, and the very
extensive damage done to property—Newcastle-upon-Tyne, York, Leicester, Hereford,
Gloucester, Worcester, and Carlisle all suffered heavily. Exeter was doubly unfortunate
in being besieged and captured by both sides in turn; those of its parishes which lay
outside the city walls lay in ruins at the end of the war.[35] Such communities where multiple dwellings, commercial premises, and churches had been destroyed were rebuilt in
the latter half of the century at different rates, some piecemeal, others in more planned
fashion.

Building in England began to pick up as early as 1646, by which time most royalist
resistance had ended. Work recommenced on Southampton House in Bloomsbury
(located inconveniently just beyond London's northern line of defences), begun possibly
as early as 1640 to a design that had probably originated in Inigo Jones's office. Its commissioning owner, the 4th earl of Southampton, a wartime conciliator rather than com-
batant, having compounded with parliament for £9,000, could only thereafter afford
to make slow progress. The house was eventually completed in the first years of the
Restoration, presenting a thirteen-bayed facade, a *piano nobile*, and a further two sto-
reys rising to a hipped roof contained by a balustrade. Extending from it was one of the
new squares of residential properties, constructed by lessees at their own expense.[36] The
once-novel Southampton House was by then being rivalled by more recent designs such
as Sir Roger Pratt's Clarendon House and John Webb's new range at Somerset House.

'Regularity' in new urban developments was, by the 1660s, established as one of the
goals of the most sophisticated architects and their aristocratic patrons. It was exemplified in the very first of the London squares, Inigo Jones's Covent Garden, begun in the
1630s, and also in a much larger development, the enclosure of Lincoln's Inn Fields—a
trend interrupted by the civil war. As guiding principles in English architecture, regularity together with simplicity of design had been advocated on intellectual and aesthetic
grounds, and developers found that they could be adhered to at relatively low cost and
by moderately skilled craftsmen. Astylar, Classicist buildings began to appear in London
in the 1650s. Though such innovation ran counter to widespread artisan conservatism,
enough showpiece buildings were completed during the 1650s and early 1660s for them
to have eventually influenced more modest domestic architecture. In 1666, however, the
Great Fire of London forced the pace of change.

Architectural historians remain divided as to the progress of Classicism in England.
Whereas Worsley pronounces that a 'Palladian consensus' had been arrived at by

the 1660s, Kerry Downes finds 'remarkable diversity ... partly due to the traditional Anglo-Saxon preference for empiricism over fundamentalism'.[37] These differences of interpretation seem to match contrary opinions as to the influence (even the religion) of the dominant figure of English architecture of the first half of the century—Inigo Jones, who died in 1652 at the age of seventy-eight. Jones's contemporary admirers attributed to him the introduction of proper architecture to England, based on principles of harmony and proportion. Though Jones's work owed much to his study of the treatises of Vitruvius, Serlio, Palladio, and Scamozzi, he never wrote a treatise of his own, achieving influence in his lifetime rather by his own work, his mentoring of a few close associates, and the advice he gave to those competent enough to design for themselves. Among these were Nicholas Stone, designer of the Goldsmith's Hall (1635), whose son, John, would provide a Jonesian design for the parliament-supporting Peyto family's house at Chesterton in Warwickshire (c.1655), and Peter Mills who carried Jonesian design to Cambridgeshire, where he built Thorpe Hall (1653) for another parliamentarian, Oliver St John, and Wisbech Castle (c.1658) for John Thurloe, Cromwell's secretary of state. As for Coleshill, in Berkshire, it is still debated whether its owner, Sir Roger Pratt, a returned exile, built it to his own design, to Jones's design, or had merely taken Jones's advice.[38]

English architecture carried into the second half of the century certain indelible characteristics that were Jonesian, leading Giles Worsley to contend that Jones was 'no lonely genius' and that he must have had a significant following among fellow practitioners.[39] Though some architects may have admired Jones, if Mowl and Earnshaw's alternative analysis is correct, a divide existed, nonetheless, between him and the many builder-surveyors unable to fully grasp his message and unwilling to abandon their familiar 'Artisan-Mannerism'. More controversially, Jones has been held responsible by them for so-called 'Puritan Minimalism', though this seems only to appear in the 1650s, a decade in which there was a mildly confident revival of house building but Jones barely lived into it.[40] The new style was characterized by a compact, two-storey, double pile with a basement and a fairly steeply pitched roof, often with dormer windows. Houses built in this style could either be astylar or with pilasters applied to the facade for a modest show of grandeur. They seem immediately 'modern'—certainly when compared to their Elizabethan and Jacobean antecedents, which prompts the question whether their first owners had become similarly modern in comparison to their forebears. Rationality and, arguably, sobriety were qualities required to appreciate such buildings, which were well timed, therefore, for the coming Age of Reason and Science.

Though the puritan mind might also have found such design acceptable for eschewing ornament and excess, Jones and (far more extensively) his followers clearly did not design for puritans because they were puritans. Indeed, Jones's plain Classicism found as much favour with his principal patron, Charles I, as it did with the puritan gentry.[41] A 'Cromwellian style' is still harder to discern. No state building programme to speak of was initiated during the Protectorate—there would be no triumphal arches, no Temple of Glory (as in Napoleon's Paris) to memorialize revolution and sacrifice. On the contrary, the Protectorate spent large sums energetically renovating the Tudor palaces of Whitehall and Hampton Court.[42]

If the various patrons of English architecture between 1642 and 1660 had any common purpose it was to distance themselves from the medieval Gothic—it had become hard to admire buildings that showed scant evidence of classical learning. Accordingly, Charles I had set Jones the very considerable task of disguising the old St Paul's Cathedral, to be achieved with the addition of a Corinthian-columned west portico and gigantic scrolls and obelisks, re-facing much of the exterior, and installing Serlian casement windows along the length of the nave. This considerable undertaking only continued until 1642. The subsequent damage done to St Paul's in the civil war and the disrespect shown to it in the 1650s, however, was provoked less by its architectural styles than by its interior statues and decorations and by the sheer vanity of its conception.

The antiquary William Dugdale later surveyed St Paul's after Christopher, Lord Hatton, appalled at the widespread damage done to England's churches, had asked him to make:

> a speedy view of what Monuments I could, especially in the Principall Churches of this Realme; to the end, that by Inke and paper, the Shadows of them, with their Inscriptions might be preserved for posteritie, forasmuch as the things themselves were so neere unto ruine.[43]

The result of Dugdale's research was his superbly illustrated *History*, printed and published in London in 1658, apparently with little fear of the authorities. Dugdale had the temerity to curse the army, if only obliquely, for its violation of the cathedral, by availing himself of Raleigh's description of Xerxes' army coming to grief for the impious act of desecrating the Temple of Apollo. The publication of Dugdale's *History* suggests that that the once widespread destructive fervour had dissipated. Cromwell died in this same year and was buried like a king in Westminster Abbey—pomp, ceremony, and memorialization returning to sanctified places.

Conclusion

Art in mid-seventeenth century England elicited demonstrations of both devotion and detestation. These extremes of response may be taken as stark evidence of a rift having occurred in English society. Brotton suggests that, after the execution of Charles I, a kind of revolution—the sudden opening of access to art (and, for that matter, architecture)—took place. The seizure of the king's goods led to 'Skinners, drapers, and itinerant poets ... wandering through Whitehall, handling and assessing the most intimate objects and cherished possessions of their dead monarch'. Yet this so-called 'transfer of royal possessions from the palace to the people'[44] hardly amounted to the democratization of art; the more humble purchasers sold on quickly for a profit. The parliamentarian Colonel Hutchinson, iconoclast turned enthusiastic purchaser of Titian's ravishing *Pardo Venus*, was hardly of the common people, spending £1,349 on his new collection.

Those with impeccable puritan qualifications, it seems, could also be aesthetes. Major-General John Lambert was identified at the Restoration by Geldorp as having 'diverse rare pictures' belonging to the king.[45] Lambert's first virtuoso passion was, in fact, horticulture, for which he was satirically depicted on a royalist playing card as 'Lambert Kt of ye Golden Tulip', and he readily exchanged rare bulbs with royalists. Even Cromwell's ability to appreciate and enjoy the visual arts has been noted.[46] He returned to Hampton Court four statues of Venus, Apollo, Adonis, and Cleopatra that Charles I had bought from the court of Mantua, though pressed by sectarians to get rid of them. A Mrs Netheway, a friend of one of Crowell's chaplains, demanded that he 'demolish thos monstres wich are set up as ornaments in prevy garden, for w[h]ils[t] they stand, though you se no evel in them, [y]it thar is much evel in it'.[47] At Whitehall, a Quaker cook took matters into his own hands and attacked statues there with a hammer, inflicting £500 of damage in half an hour before being apprehended while trying to get at Le Sueur's bronze *Antinous*.[48] If society was divided over art, this kind of report might indicate that the divide lay not down its middle but much to one side, between sectarians and the majority. William Prynne had argued that no permission beyond the authority of Scripture was needed to act against idolatrous images: 'every man in such a case being a lawfull Magistrate, without any special warrant'.[49] But such a view encouraged the mob and the fanatic and challenged civil authority; as such it was one of the destabilizing notions that, by the late 1650s, no longer elicited a popular response. In 1660, Samuel Pepys, newly employed as a servant of the restored monarchy, saw at once that settled and propitious conditions called for art and lost no time in buying and commissioning pictures for his house.

NOTES

1. See Ian Roy, ' "England turned Germany"? The Aftermath of the Civil War in its European Context', *Transactions of the Royal Historical Society*, 5th series, 28 (1978): 127–44.
2. See Jerry Brotton, *The Sale of the Late King's Goods: Charles I and his Art Collection* (Basingstoke, 2007), 210–39.
3. Tessa Watt, *Cheap Print and Popular Piety, 1550–1640* (Cambridge, 1991), 159.
4. John Saltmarsh, *The Opening of Master Prynnes New Book* (London, 1645), 17–18.
5. F. P. Philopater, 'Dedicatory address', *The Nurse of Pious Thoughts* (Douai, 1652).
6. Julie Spraggon, *Puritan Iconoclasm during the English Civil War* (Woodbridge, 2003), 86.
7. Patrick Collinson, *From Iconoclasm to Iconophobia: The Cultural Impact of the Second Reformation* (Reading, 1988), 22, 27.
8. Watt, *Cheap Print*, 165.
9. Henry Peacham, *The Compleat Gentleman* (London, 1634), 105.
10. Franciscus Junius, *The Painting of the Ancients* (London, 1638), 353.
11. Harold J. Cook, *Matters of Exchange: Commerce, Medicine, and Science in the Dutch Golden Age* (New Haven, 2007), 72.

12. John Bramhall, *An answer to Monsieur de la Militiere* (The Hague, 1653), 109–110.

13. Graham Parry, *The Arts of the Anglican Counter-Reformation: Glory, Laud and Honour* (Woodbridge, 2005), 96.

14. Edward Chaney, *The Grand Tour and the Great Rebellion* (Geneva, 1985), 57, 319–23.

15. Albert Loomie, 'The Destruction of Rubens's "Crucifixion" in the Queen's Chapel, Somerset House', *The Burlington Magazine*, 140 (October 1998): 680–1.

16. R. Malcolm Smuts, 'Art and the Material Culture of Majesty', in Smuts (ed.), *The Stuart Court and Europe* (Cambridge, 1996), 86–112. Cf. Perez Zagorin, *The Court and the Country: The Beginning of the English Revolution* (London, 1969), 71–2; Lawrence Stone, *Causes of the English Revolution* (London, 1972), 86.

17. John Heward, 'The Restoration of the South Front of Wilton House; the Development of the House Reconsidered', *Architectural History*, 35 (1992): 78–117.

18. Antony Griffiths, *The Print in Stuart Britain, 1603–1689* (London, 1998), 125–6.

19. See Julian Treuherz, 'New Light on John Souch of Chester', *The Burlington Magazine*, 139 (May, 1997): 300–7.

20. Griffiths, *The Print in Stuart Britain*, 128.

21. Sean Kelsey, *Inventing a Republic: The Political Culture of the English Commonwealth, 1649–1653* (Manchester, 1997).

22. Kevin Sharpe, *Remapping Early Modern England: The Culture of Seventeenth-century Politics* (Cambridge, 2000), 223–65.

23. See Laura Lunger Knoppers, *Constructing Cromwell: Ceremony, Portrait and Print, 1645–1661* (Cambridge, 2000).

24. Griffiths, *The Print in Stuart Britain*, 178–83.

25. Ellis Waterhouse, *Painting in Britain, 1530 to 1790* (Harmondsworth, 1978), 66.

26. See M. J. H. Liversidge, 'Prelude to the Baroque: Isaac Fuller at Oxford', *Oxoniensa*, 57 (1992): 311–30; David H. Solkin, 'Isaac Fuller's Escape of Charles II: A Restoration Tragicomedy', *Journal of the Warburg and Courtauld Institutes*, 62 (1999): 199–240.

27. Raymond A. Anselment, ' "Clouded Majesty": Richard Lovelace, Sir Peter Lely, and the Royalist Spirit', *Studies in Philology*, 86 (1989): 367–87.

28. See Griffiths, *The Print in Stuart Britain*, 184–8.

29. See Katherine van Eerde, *Wenceslaus Hollar: Delineator of his Time* (Charlottesville, 1970); Griffiths, *The Print in Stuart Britain*, 87–96, 105–6, 110–15.

30. Knoppers, *Constructing Cromwell*, 32–4, 61.

31. Knoppers, *Constructing Cromwell*, 11–14.

32. *Herbert Correspondence*, ed. W. J. Smith (Cardiff, 1963), 132.

33. See Stephen Porter, *The Blast of War: Destruction in the English Civil Wars* (Stroud, 2011), 14.

34. Lila Rakoczy, 'Out of the Ashes: Destruction, Reuse, and Profiteering in the English Civil War', in Lila Rakoczy (ed.), *The Archaeology of Destruction* (Newcastle-upon-Tyne, 2008), 261–86.

35. Mark Stoyle (ed.), *From Deliverance to Destruction: Rebellion and Civil War in an English City* (Exeter, 1996), 136–41.

36. Giles Worsley, *Classical Architecture in Britain: The Heroic Age* (New Haven and London, 1995), 10–11.

37. Worsley, *Classical Architecture*, 312; Kerry Downes, 'Taking Orders', *Times Literary Supplement* (10 November 1995): 15.

38. See Colin Platt, *The Great Rebuildings of Tudor and Stuart England* (London, 1994), 38–9, 68; Worsley, *Classical Architecture*, 18–19.

39. Worsley, *Classical Architecture*, 1–19.

40. Timothy Mowl and Brian Earnshaw, *Architecture Without Kings: The Rise of Puritan Classicism under Cromwell* (Manchester, 1995), 27–8, 59–71.

41. See Gordon Higgott, '"Varying with Reason", Inigo Jones's Theory of Design', *Architectural History*, 35 (1992): 51–77.

42. Paul M. Hunneyball, 'Cromwellian Style: The Architectural Trappings of the Protestant Regime', in Patrick Little (ed.), *The Cromwellian Protectorate* (Woodbridge, 2007), 53–81.

43. William Dugdale, 'Dedicatory Epistle', *The History of St Pauls Cathedral in London* (London, 1658).

44. Brotton, *Late King's Goods*, 219, 237.

45. David Farr, *John Lambert, Parliamentary Soldier and Cromwellian Major-General* (Woodbridge, 2003), 4.

46. Roy Sherwood, *The Court of Oliver Cromwell* (London, 1977), 135–8; Hunneyball, 'Cromwellian Style', 71–2.

47. J. Nickolls, *Original Letters . . . addressed to Oliver Cromwell* (London, 1743), 115.

48. Francis Haskell and Nicholas Penny, *Taste and the Antique* (New Haven and London, 1981), 31.

49. William Prynne, *Canterburies doome* (London, 1646), 495.

FURTHER READING

Brown, Jonathan, 'The Sale of the Century', in Brown, *Kings and Connoisseurs: Collecting in Seventeenth-Century Europe* (Princeton, 1995), 59–93.

Cooper, Trevor (ed.), *The Journal of William Dowsing: Iconoclasm in East Anglia in the English Civil War* (Woodbridge, 2001).

Fincham, Kenneth and Nicholas Tyacke, *Altars Restored: The Changing Face of English Religious Worship, 1547–c.1700* (Oxford, 2007), 176–273.

Millar, Oliver (ed.), *The Inventories and Valuations of the King's Goods, 1649–1651* (Walpole Society, XLIII, 1972).

Millar, Oliver, *Sir Peter Lely, 1618–1680* (London, 1978).

Norgate, Edward, *Miniatura or the Art of Limning*, ed. Jeffrey M. Muller and Jim Murrell (New Haven, 1997).

Rogers, Malcolm, *William Dobson, 1611–1646* (London, 1984).

Smuts, R. Malcolm, *Court Culture and the Origins of a Royalist Tradition in Early Stuart England* (Philadelphia, 1987).

Thomas, Keith, 'Art and Iconoclasm in Early Modern England', in Kenneth Fincham and Peter Lake (eds.), *Religious Politics in Post-Reformation England* (Woodbridge, 2006), 16–40.

PART V

WIDER PERSPECTIVES

CHAPTER 29

THE LONG-TERM CONSEQUENCES OF THE ENGLISH REVOLUTION:

Economic and Social Development

JOHN MILLER

THE impact of the Revolution on England's economic and social development was considerable, but it is necessary to distinguish between changes for which the civil wars were directly responsible and those which owed more to developments which were happening, or happened, anyway.

THE RULING ELITE

Many historians have tried to explain the origins of the Revolution in terms of social and economic change, so one would expect them also to have considered its economic and social consequences. An obvious model was Marx's 'bourgeois revolution', but applying it created serious problems. According to Marx, shifts in the social balance of power followed fundamental changes in the means of production, but the industrial revolution happened between a hundred and two hundred years after the Revolution of the mid-seventeenth century. Recognizing this, historians from Engels onwards placed the gentry in the historic role of the bourgeoisie. R. H. Tawney's studies of gentry estate management showed some landlords taking a ruthlessly commercial approach, driving up rents and entry fines, and evicting unprofitable tenants. Tawney argued that this enabled the gentry to acquire property at the expense of less commercially efficient landlords, notably the crown and the peerage, who (he claimed) were wedded to old-fashioned habits of hospitality and paternalism. In the Revolution power passed from the 'feudal' aristocracy to the gentry, just as the House of Commons eclipsed the

Lords. Tawney's model generated complex debates. Exhaustive studies of estate management showed no significant difference between the methods of peers and gentry. More fundamentally, social historians questioned whether there was any significant difference (other than formal status) between peers and gentry. They shared a common source of income (land) and a common leisured lifestyle. 'They built—according to their capacity—similar houses; they were buried in similar tombs.'[1] The peers were recruited from among the gentry and their younger sons were not usually ennobled, so were, in effect, members of the gentry. Moreover, about a quarter of peerage families died out every twenty-five years; to maintain the peerage at a viable level they were replaced by new creations, from among the gentry. In 1640 well over half the existing peerages had been created since 1603. This made it hard to see the peerage as socially or economically distinct from the gentry.[2]

The problems of applying the concept of a 'bourgeois revolution' to 1640–60 can be seen in the work of Christopher Hill. Hill was at pains to point out that the concept of a 'bourgeois revolution' did not require that the 'bourgeoisie' should play an active part. Starting with an orthodox Marxist-Leninist analysis in 1940 his approach became increasingly allusive. He found ample evidence of class conflict, with abuses of landlord power on one hand and the protests of independent small farmers and craftsmen on the other; Hill always had a strong sympathy for the underdog. He argued in 1976 that it was a bourgeois revolution because it had the sort of effects that one would expect from a bourgeois revolution. These included the creation of conditions in which 'bourgeois' property and capitalist production could develop. He claimed that the abolition of wardship in 1660 marked the end of feudalism: now landowners had 'absolute property in their estates, freed from arbitrary death duties and dependence on the crown' and they were able to plan long-term to maximize the return on their property.[3] But lands held by feudal tenures had long been freehold in all but name and wardship had become an irritant rather than a serious burden. He argued that the tenure of poorer tenants and freeholders was weakened after 1660, making it easier to dispossess or evict them. Parliamentary legislation was used to protect property, the definition of which was extended by (for example) the game laws, which restricted the right to hunt game to those owning land of a certain value; poorer people could not hunt on their own land. However, much of Hill's analysis of power and class was implicit rather than explicit—underlying assumptions rather than clearly developed arguments. Moreover, he analysed the civil war solely in terms of social change within England. Most historians now see the wars of the 1640s and 1650s as embracing the three kingdoms of England, Scotland, and Ireland, so explanations in purely English terms are inadequate.

A more sophisticated analysis of the workings of power can be found in E. P. Thompson's work on the eighteenth century. Thompson explained social relations in terms of hegemony rather than coercion.[4] The ruling elite wished to protect their property against any threat from 'the plebs', but they had no wish to allow the creation of a strong monarchical state. Experience of 1640–60 made them wary of standing armies and the intrusion of professional bureaucrats into local administration. The need to pay for wars against France meant that they had to accept professional revenue officials, but the revenue was voted for limited periods by parliament. In other respects, local government remained local self-government, in the hands of local men, whose powers of coercion were limited. The gentry protected and extended their interests by passing 'class' legislation in parliament: game laws; laws which endeavoured to keep grain prices up, to safeguard the landed interest; laws criminalizing traditional perquisites of the poor, such as gleaning after the harvest; and enclosure acts, which reallocated the land in a manor or village, obliterating the traditional common rights of the poorer villagers.

Both Hill and Thompson argued that at the Restoration the old ruling elite regained power, which they used to promote their interests and protect their property against the crown and the lower orders. As Hill put it, the Revolution created fissures in the old order which allowed capitalism to thrive unchecked. As food production rose, prices fell. Farmers had to become more efficient if they were to make a living; those who could not do so went out of business. The gulf between rich and poor widened as the poor lost their economic independence: small farmers and craftsmen became dependent on wages. Neither historian seemed concerned to analyse the composition of this ruling elite. Thompson referred to it as 'the gentry', Hill as 'the gentry and merchant oligarchies', or 'the men of property'.[5] Hill saw English capitalism as predominantly rural and added that the aristocracy came to accept the advantages of capitalism, especially when it came to supporting their lavish lifestyle.[6] This might suggest (though Hill denied this) that the Revolution left the social order largely unchanged.[7] Neither Hill nor Thompson showed much interest in the balance of power within the landed elite between the nobility and the gentry. Tawney claimed that there had been a permanent shift of power from the former to the latter, accentuated by the very extensive transfers of land in the 1640s and 1650s. Royalist estates were confiscated and they were invited to 'compound' for them, to buy them back for a proportion of their value. At the Restoration those who had not recovered their lands were often able to do so through the courts. Many royalists suffered financially during and after the civil wars, having raised money for the king's cause or sold land to compound for their estates. Some emerged in 1660 heavily in debt, but few were totally ruined. Mortgages were becoming more easily available, so landowners could raise large sums on the security of their lands. The 5th earl of Worcester, who had possibly the largest landed income of all the peers in 1640, claimed to have spent over £250,000 in the king's cause. His grandson rebuilt the family's fortunes and later built Badminton House and kept the largest aristocratic household in the country.[8] Henry Howard, brother of the 5th duke of Norfolk, liquidated the family's massive debts and spent heavily on building, notably at Norfolk House on the Strand in London, a palace at Weybridge, and the Duke's Palace in Norwich, on which he spent £30,000: in 1663–4 he kept open house there from Christmas to Easter.[9]

In general the nobility re-established their fortunes after 1660 and regained and even enhanced their political power. The House of Lords might have less power than the Commons, because the peers could not initiate money bills, but in other respects the peers' power was greater than the commoners'. They had kin and clients in the Commons (which was sometimes referred to as an assembly of younger sons). They also held most of the great offices of state. After 1689 the crown needed annual grants of taxation from parliament to pay for the armed forces and civil government. With the Commons often divided on party lines, the leaders of the majority party could demand a say in the making of policy and appointments in return for piloting money bills through the Commons. William III and Anne both resisted such pressures as far as they could, but George I allowed himself to be convinced that only the Whigs were loyal to his regime. Occasionally a split among the Whigs allowed him a measure of choice but most of the time the Whig leaders cooperated to put pressure on him to follow their advice and to stick to what had been agreed in cabinet. His son sometimes felt that he was the Whigs' prisoner: 'Ministers', he said in 1744, allegedly smiling, 'are the kings in this country'.[10] The Whig oligarchs used their control over the Commons to manage the king, and used their influence over the king to manage the Commons, demanding the appointments and favours they needed to secure the goodwill (and votes) of backbench MPs. They also used the crown's patronage to influence elections, especially in the many small borough constituencies. In one borough after another, the size of the electorate was reduced to make it easier to manage, with the result that the Commons under George II was less representative of public opinion than it had been under Queen Anne. Between the early sixteenth century and the early eighteenth century the nature of the English nobility changed radically.[11] Under the Yorkists the greatest nobles were still regional warlords, with extensive power over men based on grants of lands, money, and other favours, and on their ability to offer protection against violence and plunder. By the age of the Georges Whig aristocrats had great estates, but no longer possessed significant military or regional power. Instead their power rested on control over the central government and the king: to a large extent the powers of the crown were exercised by aristocratic ministers. Far from the Revolution signalling the end of the landed nobility, under George I and George II it seemed that both crown and parliament had been subjugated by a section of the nobility, defined by political affiliation and ambition.

TRADE AND EMPIRE

In the early seventeenth century England's most important export commodity was woollen cloth. English sheep produced high quality wool, but the types of cloth made from it were limited: mainly heavy broadcloths, practical for English winters, but with limited appeal in warmer climes. The cloth trade was vulnerable: bad harvests depressed demand, wars disrupted it, and foreign rulers placed high tariffs on imports to protect their cloth industries. Other exports included minerals, like tin and lead; imports included luxuries like wine and brandy, but also necessities such as high quality timber, pitch, and tar for shipbuilding. Although such trades could be profitable, for centuries much of the profit had been reaped by foreigners, such as the Hanseatic League. In the early seventeenth century the Dutch dominated the carrying trade of Europe. Their ships were cheaper to build and to man, and they developed the organizational skills to transport the goods of other nations more cheaply and efficiently than those countries could do for themselves. Meanwhile English traders, blinkered by monopolies, concentrated on their well-established trade in cloth to north-west Europe.

English rivalry with the Dutch originated in their respective efforts to muscle in on the spice trade with the East Indies. This was hugely lucrative and both nations were ruthless in their methods. A series of violent clashes led to intense anti-Dutch feeling in the 1650s. The English had been at a disadvantage because their navy was much smaller than the Dutch, but from 1642 parliament built more ships to guard against invasion by the king's continental allies. There was a further surge of naval shipbuilding in 1648–52 after which the English navy was able to take on the Dutch: in the First Anglo-Dutch War (1652–4) it held its own. This new confidence in England's navy encouraged it to challenge the Dutch dominance of the carrying trade. The Navigation Act of 1651 laid down that all ships bringing goods into English ports had to be carried in either English ships or ships of the country of origin: in other words, Swedish iron had to be carried in Swedish or English ships, but not Dutch. The Dutch did not submit to this tamely, and there was much evasion of the Act, but England now had the naval power to police its trade routes more effectively.

Breaking into the Dutch carrying trade was one aim of the Navigation Act. The other was to secure a monopoly of England's growing trade with its colonies in North America and the Caribbean. The first colonial settlements were slow to establish themselves, but by 1651 the plantations, cultivated by slaves from West Africa, were producing significant amounts of tobacco and sugar. Both these commodities were much in demand in England and Europe, creating a lucrative re-export trade. Initially they were very expensive, but as production increased prices fell; the more prices fell, the more demand increased, and the more valuable the trade became. At first England's major competitors in the New World had been the Spanish, who fiercely resisted English attempts to intrude on their monopoly of the region's trade, but the Dutch soon moved in to transport goods to and from both Spanish and English colonies. Meanwhile, as the population of the English colonies grew so did the demand for manufactured goods: tools and metal wares of all kinds, textiles, and (later) porcelain and glass. This demand stimulated English manufacturing, especially in metalworking centres like Birmingham and Sheffield. The more valuable the trade became, the more it was worth protecting: naval power was needed to make the Navigation Act as effective as possible.

After the Restoration, new Navigation Acts built on and refined the old. England fought two further naval wars against the Dutch, the first of which, in 1665–7 was widely seen as about trade: 'What we want is more of the trade that the Dutch now have.' This war was initially popular in England, but the Third Dutch War in 1672–4 was not. England was allied to Louis XIV's France, emerging as the dominant Catholic power in Europe, and many Englishmen were uneasy about fighting with such an ally against a Protestant nation. In the late 1660s France suddenly emerged as a naval, colonial, and commercial competitor more potent than the Dutch. France was a much bigger country, and aimed to establish substantial colonies, producing commodities that would sell well in Europe. The Dutch preferred to establish trading posts and to deal in high-value goods from the East Indies or to carry the produce of other nations' colonies.

Moreover, the French were active in the same regions as the English: North America, the Caribbean, and, increasingly, India.

The Navigation Act and the expansion of the navy—both products of the Revolution—underpinned the spectacular growth of English overseas trade under Charles II. By 1662 the navy had more than three times as many ships as in 1642, and on average they were larger. England's colonial empire expanded: it acquired Jamaica in 1655 and more colonies were established in North America, including the Carolinas and Pennsylvania. This burgeoning colonial trade led to a major expansion of the merchant marine: shipbuilding flourished as England increasingly wrested control of the carrying trade from the Dutch. Other new commodities, such as coffee and tea, offered different tastes and new types of sociability (although a Dutch visitor to Cornwall in 1662 was unimpressed that everyone—men, women, and children—seemed to be smoking).[12] Most people who could afford such commodities, however, saw them as improving the quality of life and many were intoxicated by the increasingly wide range of consumer goods available to buy. Godly people bewailed the materialism of the age, the obsession with the things of this world rather than concern about the next. But the growth in trade, especially colonial trade, brought real changes to everyday lives.

THE FINANCIAL SECTOR

The Revolution saw significant developments in the financial sector. Although credit was necessary for the functioning of the economy at all levels, much of it was small scale and informal: small loans from neighbours, or the pawning of valuables for cash. Notes promising to repay a sum of money at a future date could be assigned to someone else and became a form of paper money. The most important borrower was the crown, but lending to the king was risky: repayment was usually slow and sometimes he defaulted. The royal revenue was unpredictable (and shrouded in secrecy) so provided poor security for lenders. The radical restructuring of taxation in the 1640s made available increasingly predictable revenue streams, while taxes voted by parliament offered better security than the word of a king. As a result first parliament and then the Commonwealth and Protectorate were able to borrow far more money than the crown had ever done. By the later 1650s the government depended on borrowing; new loans were raised to help pay off old and the downward spiral of debt was ended only by the Restoration. In addition, in 1653, 1657, and 1660 the Commons estimated the necessary cost of government and undertook to raise the necessary revenues (the yield often did not match the estimates). With the return of monarchy, government borrowing again depended on the king's credit—generally better than before 1640, but occasionally tarnished. From 1689 parliament began to raise much higher taxes for the long wars against France, which to a large extent were paid for by borrowing. It gradually became accepted that these loans would never be repaid; the national debt became a permanent feature of government finance and a significant proportion of the yield of taxation was devoted to paying the interest on it. With interest rates as low as 3 or 2 per cent, government borrowing enabled Britain to punch well above its weight on the international stage.[13]

There were also significant developments in the private sector. There were few banks in England before 1640 and most were foreign. By the early seventeenth century private individuals, particularly goldsmiths, were acting as bankers. They received deposits on which they paid interest; they made loans, on which they charged interest. They issued paper receipts for moneys deposited and accepted written drafts, or demands for payment. The civil wars increased the volume and speed of financial transactions, with increased taxation, spending, and borrowing. Parliamentary soldiers were increasingly paid in debentures, promises of payment; these were discounted in return for cash, creating a new area of speculation. Many borrowed to raise money to buy confiscated lands or, in the case of royalists, to buy back their own lands. As the land was the security for the loans, mortgages became an important part of the bankers' business; some, like Clayton and Morris, specialized in it. Others, like Thomas Viner and Edward Backwell, made loans to the government. After 1660 the crown sought new sources of loans: the City of London, tax farmers (syndicates who contracted to collect major revenues), and revenue receivers, like the paymaster of the forces, who often had considerable amounts of cash in hand: some of these receivers, like Sir Stephen Fox, also acted as private bankers.[14]

The growth of banking enabled cash-strapped or indebted landowners to raise mortgages on the security of their estates and provided a source of loans for the government and the merchant community. Government borrowing was opened up to a wider public by the foundation of the Bank of England in 1694, while merchants raised capital through joint-stock companies and stocks and shares: from the 1690s there was an embryonic stock market in the City of London. Insurance (another borrowing from the Dutch) began with the first fire insurance office in 1682; Lloyd's coffee house was the venue for what became the world's most famous insurer. The rise of the 'moneyed interest', which does not figure in Hill's discussion of the consequences of the Revolution, was viewed with alarm by contemporaries. In 1709 Lord Bolingbroke wrote that 'a new sort of property which was not known twenty years ago is now increased to be almost equal to the terra firma of our island'. Moreover, it was alleged that the bankers used their financial clout to dictate to the government.[15] The wide availability of credit made possible the increased investment in commerce and manufacturing which was to underpin the industrial revolution.

DEMOGRAPHY AND THE ECONOMY

The most fundamental influence on the overall strength of the economy was the balance between population and resources. A sustained rise in population put a strain on the ability of agriculture to feed the people. Crop yields were limited by primitive techniques. When the population was low, as in the fifteenth century, there was enough adequate arable land to feed the people in most years. If the population rose, there was a temptation to put down more land for arable, leaving less for grazing or hay. Alternatively, cultivation could be extended into less fertile land, barely viable even in an average year. At times, as in the early fourteenth century, the population rose so high that harvest failure brought widespread starvation. With the Black Death, the population of England and Wales fell from as high as six million in the early fourteenth century to as low as two million in the fifteenth. By the early sixteenth century it was rising again, reaching around five million in 1640.[16] This did not bring a demographic catastrophe, but there was widespread hunger, and not just among farmers. Bad harvests and high food prices left consumers with less to spare for manufactured goods. This meant that manufacturing employers, facing falling demand, laid their workers off. For many, the problem was not so much high food prices as loss of income. As one Lincolnshire land-owner wrote in 1623: 'Our country [county] was never in that want that now it is, and more of money than corn.' People had sold all they had and were forced to eat dead horses and dogs.[17] And yet the population continued to rise, partly because of the relative absence of epidemic disease.

From the 1640s the balance between population and resources shifted. The population levelled out and even fell slightly. The death rate, which had lagged behind the birth rate, began to catch up. Some of this can be ascribed to the civil wars. It has been estimated that some 80,000 were killed as a result of the fighting, and another 100,000 from disease: sickness was rife (on both sides) in sieges and the marching armies carried infections with them.[18] There was also a sudden increase in emigration, plus the beginning of transportation of convicted felons or rebels, with a peak of some 70,000 between 1650 and 1659. Death and emigration on this scale had a significant effect, especially as those affected included a disproportionate number of men, and particularly young men. Women found it harder to find husbands; the proportion of people who were still unmarried in their early forties reached over a quarter in the 1690s. Meanwhile, the death rate rose, due to some exceptionally cold winters and increased mortality from infectious diseases, such as smallpox and typhus.

The shift in the demographic balance cannot be explained wholly by the civil wars— they cannot have contributed to the later rise in infectious disease—but that impact was clearly significant. The wars also inflicted much short-term damage on the economy. The loss of so many men weakened the labour force; trade and agriculture were badly disrupted. Sieges could lead to massive destruction; besieged townsmen razed suburbs to the ground so that they could not provide cover for the besiegers. Some of this urban damage took decades to make good, but there were strong signs of economic recovery from the 1650s, notably a growth in overseas trade. Equally important was a substantial fall in food prices, which led to widespread complaints from landlords and farmers from the 1660s. In the century before 1640 the government had tried to protect consumers against high food prices. Now parliament tried repeatedly to prevent prices from falling. The first Corn Law, in 1673, tried to keep grain prices up at home, by paying a bounty on exports and forbidding imports until English prices had risen to a high level. This fall in prices owed something to frequent good harvests, but also to the impact of innovations by farmers to increase productivity, including new crops, crop rotations, and fertilizers. But whatever the reasons, the main beneficiary was the consumer: many farmers and landowners, especially those with modest estates, found the going tough.

Not all consumers benefited. Data on wages and prices suggest that, on average, people had more to spend, after feeding their families, between 1660 and 1720 than they had between 1590 and 1640. Moreover, there is strong evidence that many chose to spend it on consumer goods. People began to buy goods, not because they needed them, but because they wanted them: style became more important than durability. Traditionally, most consumer goods had been produced by artisan-shopkeepers, who manufactured their wares—shoes, or leather goods, or hats—in the back room of their house and sold them in the front. The range of goods that such shopkeepers could offer was necessarily limited. As customers became more conscious of style and fashion, this was no longer good enough. Manufacture and retail began to diverge. Manufacturers began to offer a wider range of goods, employing many workmen in many workshops, producing specialist goods to precise specifications. They sold them to shops which stocked a wide range of goods, which were displayed and sold in a distinct retail environment, with windows to tempt shoppers off the street and mirrors to show them how they looked: shopping became a pleasurable experience. Standards of design improved markedly and advertising brought new items to the attention of the consumer.

The growth of consumerism was predominantly an urban, and above all a London, phenomenon. Larger provincial towns could offer a similar range of shops—a doughty traveller, Celia Fiennes, referred approvingly to Nottingham or Newcastle as 'much like London'[19]—but small market towns could not compete. Skilled workers in successful manufacturing and port towns could afford at least some consumer goods. The families of wealthy landowners and perhaps farmers could go to the nearest significant town to shop, or to London. The growth of consumerism can be traced through artefacts of all kinds—Chinese and English porcelain, furniture, clothes, silver. English glass manufacturing expanded rapidly, which made available not only domestic glassware but cheaper window glass, so that house interiors could be better illuminated and possessions better displayed. Those who could afford it beautified the outsides of their houses, with an emphasis on symmetry and discreet decoration. Those without access to shops might buy from pedlars, perhaps a halfpenny handkerchief, or some ribbon, or a cheap print. But many remained too poor to think of such luxuries. Economic survival was a struggle, a matter of 'making shift': getting by depended on the charity of neighbours and kin, a little help from poor relief, and, in hard times, selling what few possessions they had.[20] The prosperity that came to skilled workers in successful industries did not reach most rural workers: farmers struggling to make a profit kept labourers' wages down. Many farm workers also worked in manufacturing, especially low quality cloth, but the work was irregular and poorly paid. Those living in forest and upland regions had formerly been able to exploit natural resources to help get by, such as timber for building and fuel, nuts, and berries. But as unemployment grew in the arable areas workers migrated to forest parishes which became overcrowded and struggled to support their poor. In Eccleshall, Staffordshire, many people were too poor to make a will. The poorest man who did so left goods worth only £2 1s. He had a bed, but no table or chair, and his clothes comprised two coats, a waistcoat, and a pair of breeches.[21]

It was not only rural areas that suffered from poverty. Towns enjoyed mixed fortunes. The buoyant colonial demand for metal wares meant that Birmingham grew rapidly. Liverpool and Bristol profited from trade with the American and Caribbean colonies. Fashionable spa towns, like Bath and Tunbridge Wells, grew apace, while some county and cathedral towns, like Shrewsbury, Bury St Edmund's, or Winchester, which attracted many gentry, prospered. But others found the going tough. Norwich, heavily dependent on its textile industry, suffered badly from competition from cheap Asian fabrics. Small market towns were eclipsed by their larger neighbours, and many ports suffered from competition from London. Even in London there was much poverty—not so much in the East End, which profited from the boom in trade and shipping, but Southwark and older areas between the City and Westminster. In Bristol the wealth of the merchants contrasted with a shifting population of seamen, transients, and beggars, who came looking for work. The growth of empire, trade, and industry brought prosperity to many, but increased the gulf between rich and poor.

Local Government and the Poor

In the decades after the Restoration there is strong evidence of both a rise in consumer spending and a substantial problem of poverty, especially during the French wars of 1689–1713. The Elizabethan poor laws authorized parish officials to raise compulsory rates for the relief of the poor, and gave magistrates powers to deal with the disruptive and disorderly poor, driven to crime by hunger. The unemployed who travelled in search of work could be punished as vagrants—flogged and sent back to their home parish. Underlying this mixture of relief and punishment lay a distinction between the deserving and the undeserving poor. The former included those too sick, young, or old to work; to these could be added, somewhat reluctantly, able-bodied men who tried to support their families but could not find enough work. The undeserving were able-bodied people who were deemed to be idle, shiftless, and unthrifty, inclined to drunkenness and petty crime; those who took to the road were viewed with particular suspicion, as they became 'masterless', without an employer or parent to keep them in order.[22]

It should be stressed that the poor laws empowered parish officials and magistrates to relieve or punish the poor: they did not *require* them to do so. In the early seventeenth century parish officials tried to keep the poor rates down and often raised none at all. The self-styled 'better sort' often regarded poverty as evidence of moral failings rather than genuine misfortune. Poor people who felt that they had been unfairly denied relief could appeal to magistrates for redress, but initially magistrates were reluctant to intervene. That changed in the 1650s, when they were instructed to supervise poor law administration much more closely. Unlike parish officials, magistrates were not pressured by neighbours to keep rates low. Most disapproved of idleness, but were inclined to treat the 'deserving' poor sympathetically. As a result, the sums raised by the poor rate began to rise, and those denied relief developed the habit of appealing to the magistrates, who became more inclined to listen.[23]

Parliament continued to pass statutes about the poor after the Restoration, notably the 1662 Act of Settlement. Existing poor laws assumed that each parish was responsible for its own poor, but no mechanism had been established to determine who was 'settled' where. The 1662 Act placed this responsibility on the magistrates, who could issue certificates of settlement so that those who travelled in search of work would not be treated as vagrants. To achieve settlement in another parish, a person needed to meet stringent conditions, finding sureties that they would not become a financial burden. Those without such a certificate could, as before, be whipped back to their home parish. Some historians have seen this Act as designed to tie peasants to their villages, creating a reservoir of cheap labour. This assumes that the provisions of the Act were rigorously enforced, but like so much legislation it gave powers to officials to use at their discretion. Many distinguished between ne'er do wells and people genuinely looking for work. Much agricultural employment was seasonal. Magistrates and neighbours showed common sense: incomers were allowed to stay so long as they supported themselves; this was recognized by an Act of 1697 which stated that a person could be removed only if they were a burden on the poor rate.[24] Magistrates had long used discretion when dealing with those on the move: if they judged that they were genuinely seeking work, they moved them on rather than sending them home. After 1660 some vagrants were whipped home, but these had usually been found guilty of petty crime or begging—punishment for vagrancy alone was unusual.[25]

The growing frequency of appeals, and the willingness of magistrates to overrule parish officials, created a sense of entitlement. The sums raised from the poor rate increased from about £100,000 a year in the 1650s to between £400,000 and £600,000 in 1696. Town authorities tried to stem this increase, insisting that pauper families give a statement each year of what each member earned. The increased cost of poor relief was an unintended consequence of the Interregnum government's concern to extend the magistrates' supervision over local government, but the fact that the cost of relief rose most sharply in towns would suggest that town magistrates and officials were coming to accept the principle of entitlement as well. In an inversion of Hill's view of the landed elite ruthlessly oppressing the poor, county magistrates overrode parsimonious parish officials. A decision by a group of Berkshire magistrates in 1795 to subsidize farm wages from the poor rate marked the beginning of the end of the old poor law. It was abolished in 1834 because it was too generous.

RELIGIOUS AND POLITICAL DIVISIONS

Perhaps the most profound and lasting legacy of the Revolution was a society divided in religion and politics. There had been divisions before the civil wars between puritan and anti-puritan,[26] but those of the 1640s ran much deeper and were transmitted through an unprecedented volume of political publishing. Both sides in the civil war appealed in print for popular support and, although a form of censorship was reimposed in 1662, Charles II accepted the need to justify the conduct of his government through the press: something had to be said to the people. Many historians have been reluctant even to consider the phenomenon of popular royalism, but it became increasingly potent as time went on. Charles I was profoundly isolated in 1640. By 1642 he had enough support to fight a civil war and by 1648 a beleaguered parliament was under enormous pressure to settle with him on almost any terms: the king now seemed a more attractive proposition than an oppressive parliament and a domineering army.[27] Charles I's martyrdom was his greatest contribution to the monarchy and his sons encouraged the cult of the royal martyr and exploited popular belief in touching for the king's evil.[28] Anglican royalism, and the rhetoric of the divine right of kings, gathered further strength after the Restoration and reached its zenith in the last years of Queen Anne, when it became clear that the Protestant Stuart dynasty would end with her death.

If in 1640 Charles I was unpopular, the monarchy was not. Similarly, it was Laud's brand of religion that was hated, not the church as such. The puritans might denounce the Prayer Book and its ceremonies as 'popish', but puritans formed only a minority of Protestants, and were proud of it, distinguishing between the godly few and the ungodly multitude. Many Protestants had become attached to the Prayer Book services because they emphasized community—common prayer—and relatively inclusive teachings on salvation. The church's ceremonies added dignity and edification to the celebrations of the Christian year and rites of passage. Laud's innovations were deeply disruptive, but the changes wrought by the puritans—the abolition of the Prayer Book, the drastic simplification of the Christian calendar, the whitewashing of church interiors, the banning of Christmas—proved far worse. After the Restoration, ceremonies were gradually restored: altars began to replace communion tables, congregations gathered money to install organs or to 'beautify' their churches. Many churchgoers deplored these 'high church' innovations, but they were undoubtedly popular and were underpinned by an aggressive demand to revive the authority of the church within society. Under Anne the Church of England, most unusually, became militant.

For nonconformist historians the main legacy of the Revolution were the laws against nonconformity, which led, in the early 1680s, to the most intense persecution of Protestants in English history. Earlier, persecution had been much more sporadic. The greatest sufferers were the Quakers, whose aggressive behaviour in the 1650s provoked violent retaliation. After they had abandoned this confrontational approach, they still suffered violence, but by the 1680s some hard-line Tories came to see the Quakers as deluded but harmless. Judge Jeffreys concentrated most of his considerable venom on presbyterians and occasional conformists, and treated Quakers kindly.[29] This became the norm after the Toleration Act of 1689: Tories hated Quakers, baptists, and Independents less than they hated presbyterians, whom they described as 'schismatics', who had split the church. (They were also a major element in the Whig party.) In the summer of 1715 many dissenting meeting houses, almost all presbyterian, were attacked, and in some cases demolished. The 'loyal mob' of Shrewsbury issued a 'proclamation' warning baptists and Quakers not to allow presbyterians to worship with them, or their meeting houses would be attacked as well.[30]

Violence was equally apparent in political disputes, which tended to occur during elections and civic celebrations. Contested elections had been rare before 1640. They became more common with the political polarization of 1679–81, fuelled by three general elections in two years. Frequent elections kept the political temperature high: following the Triennial Act of 1694, which stated that there must be a general election at least every three years, there were eleven in twenty years. Elections aroused great public interest. Even in boroughs where the electorate was very small, voting was a public act and the unenfranchised could show their approval or disapproval. Electoral patrons and managers exploited conflicting precedents and a partisan House of Commons to broaden their electorate when it seemed in their interest to do so. By 1715 the electorate became larger in percentage terms than *after* the Reform Bill of 1832.[31] As elections became more keenly contested, both sides mobilized all eligible electors (and some who were not). As tempers frayed and beer flowed, violence broke out and was by no means confined to the electors. Whig and Tory magnates gathered large numbers of young men (most of them ineligible to vote), plied them with drink, and marched them into town to do battle. Sometimes the unqualified acted on their own initiative. The Kingswood colliers were famously belligerent. For the 1713 Bristol election the single Whig candidate hired 500 sailors to escort his voters to the hustings, but the Tories ensured that they had to assemble some way away and the colliers, armed with flails, made most Whigs too frightened to vote; the Tory candidates were declared elected.[32]

Party competition spread to days of civic celebration, which should have been expressions of unity. The Whigs exploited traditional commemorations of deliverance from popery, notably 5 and 17 November (Elizabeth's accession day). Effigies were burned, including the pope, the Pretender, and leading Tories like the duke of Ormond. After James II banned bonfires, people put candles in their windows, but when celebrations were appropriated for partisan purposes those who illuminated, or failed to illuminate, might have their windows smashed. This became more common under George I, whose birthday fell the day before Charles II's, so the parties competed to outdo each other's celebrations. Tories set up mocking effigies of George I, arrayed with turnips and horns; Whigs paraded with a warming pan on the Pretender's birthday. In 1715–16 the army took over many celebrations and patriotic days. Soldiers marched to and from church, then back to the inn where the Whigs were celebrating, where they fired volleys into the air and drank loyal toasts.[33] There was rarely any violence on such occasions, but soldiers responded to evidence of 'disaffection' by beating up those responsible. There was no sustained army harassment of suspected Jacobites, but perceptible intimidation. There was more intense violence in London. On celebration days one party displayed their contempt for their opponents, while the other sought to disrupt them. Preparations in Whig mug houses and Tory taverns were often elaborate, as both parties gathered their supporters, armed with cudgels and other weapons. Often each side claimed victory, but the Whigs had the magistrates on their side, so that Tories were gaoled on flimsy evidence and Whigs who wounded or killed Tories went unpunished.[34]

The urban fighting which reached a peak in the 1710s gives a very different impression of early Georgian England to that found in older works, in which the people played no part in politics.[35] Political violence continued sporadically through the eighteenth century, and showed renewed vigour from the 1760s. The divisions of the civil wars, about the nature of the church and the monarchy, remained relevant and emotive in the early eighteenth century: in the 1720s Whig candidates were met by chants of 'down with the Roundheads, down with the Rump'. The Tories' massive election victories in 1710 and 1713 showed that they now had the support of the majority of an unprecedentedly large electorate. Very conscious of this, the Whigs ensured that elections should be less frequent—only every seven years, following the Septennial Act of 1716—and that the electorate of small boroughs should be reduced to manageable size. The Tories still performed creditably in the counties and larger boroughs, but the Whigs controlled enough small boroughs to ensure a majority in the Commons. As the Whig supremacy consolidated, the ideas which linked the royalists of the civil wars to the Tories of the 1710s began to lose their power. A Catholic Stuart over the water could not arouse the same emotional loyalty as an Anglican Stuart on the English throne. The high church continued, but its voice was muted as bishoprics and other leading positions went to Whigs. The 1745 rising came surprisingly close to success, but it also showed the relatively limited support for the Pretender in England. When a new popular politics began to appear in the 1760s it focused on new and different issues.

CONCLUSION

Rather strangely, attempts to explain the Revolution in terms of economic and social change did not result in discussions of post-Restoration England in similar terms. Historians largely agreed that the landed aristocracy remained politically dominant. The mercantile and financial sectors grew, encouraged by developments in the 1640s and 1650s, but successful merchants and bankers bought country estates and tried to merge into the gentry. The nobility and gentry came to terms with the rise of trade and banking, investing in trading companies and seeking the advice of bankers and stockbrokers. Merchants and bankers for their part came to value some aspects as the aristocratic ethos, especially the importance of personal reputation: if a banker's word was his bond, he needed to maintain trust in his integrity.[36] The landed elite seized the opportunities created by the growth of manufacturing, exploiting mineral resources and investing in turnpikes and canals. As the landed elite began to exploit its political power for economic advantage, the gap between rich and poor probably grew, but with the paradox that much more was paid out in poor relief than in the first half of the seventeenth century. But in many ways the greatest legacy of the civil wars were the divisions between Tory and Whig, churchman and dissenter, which remained powerful and often painful into the nineteenth century.

Notes

1. H. R. Trevor Roper, *The Gentry, 1540–1640* (*Economic History Review* [*EcHR*] Supplement, 1, 1953), 6.
2. Tawney excluded 'new creations' from his figures for the peerage, which rendered them largely meaningless: Trevor Roper, *The Gentry*, 4–5.
3. Christopher Hill, *Some Intellectual Consequences of the English Revolution* (London, 1980), 34–35. Christopher Hill, 'A Bourgeois Revolution?' in J. G. A. Pocock (ed.), *Three British Revolutions: 1641, 1688, 1776* (Princeton, 1980), 115–16, 134. Robert Brenner, 'Bourgeois Revolution and Transition to Capitalism', in A. L. Beier, David Cannadine, and James M. Rosenheim (eds.), *The First Modern Society: Essays in English History in Honour of Lawrence Stone* (Cambridge, 1989) discusses the concept of a bourgeois revolution in a wholly agrarian context.
4. E. P. Thompson, *Customs in Common* (London, 1993), especially chap. 2 ('The Patricians and the Plebs').
5. Hill, *Intellectual Consequences*, 1, 11.
6. Hill, 'Bourgeois Revolution?', 113, 121.
7. J. G. A. Pocock, 'Introduction' and Lawrence Stone, 'The Results of the English Revolutions of the Seventeenth Century', in Pocock (ed.), *Three British Revolutions*, 5–6, 55–6.
8. Molly McClain, *Beaufort: The Duke and his Duchess 1657–1715* (New Haven, 2001).
9. John M. Robinson, *The Dukes of Norfolk: A Quincentennial History* (Oxford, 1982), 121–3.
10. W. C. Costin and J. S. Watson (eds.), *The Law and Working of the Constitution: Documents 1660–1914*, 2 vols. (London, 1952), I, 376.
11. For a pioneering discussion of the changing nature of the English nobility, see J. H. Hexter, *Reappraisals in History* (London, 1961), chap. 2. For continental comparisons, see H. M. Scott and Christopher Storrs, 'Introduction: The Consolidation of Noble Power in Europe 1650–1800', in H. M. Scott (ed.), *The European Nobilities in the Seventeenth and Eighteenth Centuries I: Western Europe* (Harlow, 1995).
12. Maurice Exwood and H. L. Lehmann (eds.), *The Journal of William Schellinks' Travels in England, 1661–3*, Camden Society, 5th Series, I (1993), 121.
13. On the financial sector generally, see Henry Roseveare, *The Financial Revolution, 1660–1760* (London, 1991).
14. Christopher Clay, *Public Finance and Private Wealth: The Career of Sir Stephen Fox, 1627–1716* (Oxford, 1978).
15. John Miller, *The Glorious Revolution* (2nd edition, London, 1997), 117.
16. E. A. Wrigley and R. S. Schofield, *The Population History of England, 1541–1871: A Reconstruction* (Cambridge, 1989), 531–533.
17. Joan Thirsk and J. P. Cooper (eds.), *Seventeenth Century Economic Documents* (Oxford, 1972), 24.
18. Charles Carlton, *Going to the Wars: The Experience of the British Civil Wars, 1638–51* (London, 1992), chap. 9, summary on 214.
19. Celia Fiennes, *The Journeys of Celia Fiennes*, ed. Christopher Morris (London, 1947), 72, 210–11.
20. Steve Hindle, *On the Parish? The Micro-Politics of Poor Relief in Rural England c.1550–1750* (Oxford, 2004), chap. 1.
21. Margaret Spufford, *Poverty Portrayed: Gregory King and the Parish of Eccleshall* (Keele, 1995), 62.

22. The outstanding works on poor relief in this period are Paul Slack, *Poverty and Policy in Tudor and Stuart England* (London, 1988) and Hindle, *On the Parish?* The latter is concerned with rural parishes, so for information on the towns, see Slack, *Poverty and Policy* and Slack, *From Reformation to Improvement: Public Welfare in Early Modern England* (Oxford, 1999).

23. Joan R. Kent, 'The Centre and the Localities: State Formation and Parish Government, 1640–1740', *Historical Journal*, 39 (1996): 363–404.

24. Philip Styles, *Studies in Seventeenth-Century West Midlands History* (Kineton, 1978), 189–93.

25. A. L. Beier, 'Vagrants and the Social Order in Elizabethan England', *Past and Present [P&P]*, 64 (1974): 3–29; John Miller, *Cities Divided: Politics and Religion in English Provincial Towns, 1660–1722* (Oxford, 2007), 69–70.

26. On the last of these, see David Underdown, *Revel, Riot and Rebellion: Popular Politics and Culture in England, 1603–60* (Oxford, 1985); Ronald Hutton, *The Rise and Fall of Merry England: The Ritual Year 1400–1700* (London, 1994).

27. For an attempt to follow these developments, see John Miller, *A Brief History of the English Civil Wars* (London, 2009).

28. Anna Keay, *The Magnificent Monarch: Charles II and the Ceremonies of Power* (London, 2008), 190–4, 211–13.

29. John Miller, ' "A Suffering People?" English Quakers and their Neighbours, c.1650–1700', *P&P*, 188 (2005): 71–103.

30 Miller, *Cities Divided*, pp. 283–8.

31. Hill, *Intellectual Consequences*, 30, states, correctly, that the electorate was probably smaller in 1740 than in 1640, but fails to mention that the reduction had occurred since 1715. See Geoffrey Holmes, *The Electorate and the National Will in the First Age of Party* (Lancaster, 1975); David Hayton, *Introductory Survey, The History of Parliament: The House of Commons, 1690–1715*, 5 vols. (Cambridge, 2002), I.

32. Miller, *Cities Divided*, 279; *History of Parliament: The Commons 1690–1715*, II, 214–15.

33. Miller, *Cities Divided*, 288–95.

34. Nicholas Rogers, 'Popular Protest in Early Hanoverian London', *P&P*, 79 (1978): 70–100; J. L. Fitts, 'Newcastle's Mob', *Albion*, 5 (1973): 41–9.

35. The 'discovery' of popular politics in this period owes much to Kathleen Wilson, *The Sense of the People: Politics, Culture and Imperialism in England, 1715–85* (New York, 1995) and the work of Nicholas Rogers.

36. P. J. Cain and A. G. Hopkins, 'Gentlemanly Capitalism and British Expansion Overseas: 1. The Old Colonial System 1688–1850', *EcHR*, 2nd Series, 39 (1986), 501–25.

FURTHER READING

Clay, Christopher, *Economic Expansion and Social Change: England, 1500–1700*, 2 vols. (Cambridge, 1984).

Harris, Tim, *Politics under the later Stuarts: Party Conflict in a Divided Society, 1660–1714* (Harlow, 1993).

Hill, Christopher, *Some Intellectual Consequences of the English Revolution* (London, 1980).

Miller, John, *Cities Divided: Politics and Religion in English Provincial Towns, 1660–1722* (Oxford, 2007).

Roseveare, Henry, *The Financial Revolution, 1660–1760* (Harlow, 1991).

Slack, P., *Poverty and Policy in Tudor and Stuart England* (London, 1988).

Thompson, E. P., *Customs in Common* (London, 1993).

Underdown, David, *Revel, Riot and Rebellion: Popular Politics and Culture in England 1603–60* (Oxford, 1985).

Wilson, Kathleen, *The Sense of the People: Politics, Culture and Imperialism in England, 1715–85* (New York, 1995).

Wrightson, Keith, *Earthly Necessities: Economic Lives in Early Modern Britain, 1470–1750* (London, 2002).

....

CHAPTER 30

THE LONG-TERM CONSEQUENCES OF THE ENGLISH REVOLUTION:

State Formation, Political Culture, and Ideology

....

MARK KNIGHTS

ONE of the first acts of the restored monarchy in 1660 was to pass an act of 'oblivion' which sought to eradicate the memory of the 1640s and 1650s. The act made it illegal for 'anyone malitiously to call or alledge of, or object against any other person or persons, any name or names, or other words of reproach any way tending to revive the memory of the late Differences'. For a period of three years any offender was to be fined. And yet the same act also listed a number of people excepted from its general pardon, including the Irish rebels, anyone who had held traitorous intelligence with a foreign state, and the regicides. As a result, ten signatories of Charles I's death warrant were tried and executed, and a further nineteen imprisoned for life. The post-revolutionary generation thus held a deeply ambiguous attitude to the mid-century events: the yearning for retribution and punishment often outweighed the official desire to forget. In truth, forgetting such a major upheaval proved impossible. Consequently, the mid-century crisis cast a long shadow over the next fifty years, and arguably for a century after that, until the French Revolution provided a more immediate threat, and even then it is striking how resonant the debates of the 1790s were of seventeenth-century ones. This chapter therefore seeks to outline some of the ways in which the memory of the civil wars and Interregnum shaped the political culture of the later Stuart period and beyond.

A key aim of the chapter is to argue that the second revolution of the seventeenth century, triggered by the invasion of William of Orange in 1688, should be seen as conceptually yoked to the first revolution of the 1640s and 1650s. The two revolutions should be seen as part of a linked *process* of revolution that lasted well into the early eighteenth century and which *cumulatively* had a major impact on politics, political thought, and the constitution.

Seeing the two seventeenth-century revolutions as part of a revolutionary process, rather than as two separate 'events', has the advantage not only of analysing themes across the two revolutions—such as partisan divisions, print culture, state formation, and religious toleration—but also of seeing the second revolution through contemporary eyes, since those living in 1688 never forgot the precedent and lessons of the earlier revolution. The argument put forward here is not that the first revolution caused the second; but that, as Jonathan Scott argues, because the 'settlement' of the 1660s failed to settle much, the second revolution addressed many of the issues left outstanding by the first.[1] The chapter also challenges conventional periodization, for the 'early modern' period is often taken to end in 1660 or 1700. Reuniting the revolutions and assessing their cumulative impact requires venturing into the later Stuart period and the eighteenth century.

Nevertheless discussing the two revolutions together runs counter to much of the historiography, which has considered them as fundamentally different and hence treated them separately. For most scholars, the revolutionary credentials of the 1640s and 1650s are seldom in doubt (even if the period before could be termed 'unrevolutionary' by Conrad Russell[2]); but 1688 has seemed to many to be either a 'conservative' or 'moderate' revolution pursued by 'reluctant revolutionaries' or little more than a palace coup, in which James II was replaced by his son-in-law William.[3] Such views are increasingly unsustainable and more attention is now being paid to the revolutionary nature of 1688. Tim Harris's *Revolution* highlights the radical revolutions that took place in Scotland and Ireland in 1688–9, and Steve Pincus's *1688: The First Modern Revolution* forcefully asserts the popular, violent, and divisive nature of 1688 (in England as well as its neighbours).[4] Even so, both works consider the second seventeenth-century revolution as rather divorced from the first. Showing the links between the two, however, may help to reshape how we conceive of both revolutions. From the perspective of the restoration of the monarchy and state church in 1660, the first revolution appears something of a failed experiment; but seen from 1725 or 1750, the cumulative legacy of the two seventeenth-century revolutions seems to have been a transformative one. Nicholas Tyacke's suggestion that we should think of the English revolution as spanning a long seventeenth century, from c.1590–1720, has the considerable advantage of conceptualizing the revolution as a process that played out over a very long time.[5] Just as we now recognize that the Reformation was a process that was ongoing throughout much of the seventeenth century, rather than being a sixteenth-century event, so we should see the revolutions of the seventeenth century as linked and the process of revolution as far more protracted than has previously been allowed.

THE TRANSFORMATION OF THE STATE

One theme that links both revolutions is the transformation of the state. As social historians have pointed out, state power was not simply a top-down series of commands that secured obedience and implementation.[6] As Sir Thomas Smith recognized in his work *De Republica Anglorum* (1583) it was not always easy to tell those who governed from those who were governed: subjects were also sometimes in a position of authority because the state lacked a bureaucracy of paid officials, relying instead on large numbers of voluntary office-holders. Mark Goldie has suggested that perhaps one in ten adult males held office in some capacity.[7] This could either be a structural weakness or a strength, depending on whether the government was attempting to enforce measures with which the majority of that citizen magistracy agreed. Either way, it created a sense of self-government, of a 'monarchical republic' in Collinson's apt phrase.[8] This was particularly strong in the urban corporations, as Phil Withington's work has shown: towns were largely self-governing communities with traditions of citizen participation.[9] They were what Thomas Hobbes and his pupil the duke of Newcastle saw as dangerous commonwealths gnawing at the inside of the monarchical state. Moreover, the extent of office-holding shaped how many Britons conceived of themselves: independent, privileged citizens as well as subjects, with rights as well as duties. And the institutions of the state were not so much centrally located, in Westminster and Whitehall, but were located in every parish and every locality. The state was, for much of the sixteenth and seventeenth century, de-centred, local, and run by unsalaried officers.

That participatory, dispersed state relying on voluntary office-holders persisted for much of the eighteenth century but was nevertheless fundamentally challenged and reshaped by the seventeenth-century revolutions. In part the driver was the need to finance war: both the civil wars of the 1640s and then the wars between revolutionary England and France after 1689 put unprecedented pressures on state finances and on the structures that existed to raise revenue. The regimes of the mid-seventeenth century were able to crack a problem that had bedevilled the Tudor and early Stuart state: how to extract sufficient revenue from a population on whom the state relied for its office-holders. The introduction of the excise, for the first time in early modern history, gave the regime sufficient funds to fight war. These mid-century precedents about how to fight war were not lost, even though during the 1660s and 1670s there was a return to pre-war hand-to-mouth fiscal methods. As John Brewer has shown for the period after 1688, the state was able to raise enormous sums of money to fight foreign wars because of what Peter Dickson called the 'financial revolution' of the 1690s: the creation of the Bank of England in 1694, which loaned money to the state; the establishment of a national debt with interest payments being met by receipts from taxation; the fostering of a stock market in which private investors made their money available to state-backed private enterprises that loaned money to the state; and a series of fiscal experiments, in lotteries and annuities, that again made private capital available to the state.[10] John Brewer calls this resulting state a 'fiscal-military one' because it had the capacity to raise sufficient money to fight large-scale war and to do so on a prolonged and repeatable basis. But it was also a state that harnessed the commercial power of England's precocious economy in return for state-sponsored (rather than royal) monopolies and military protection. Between them, the two seventeenth-century revolutions solved one of the structural problems of the Tudor and early Stuart state, how to fund and fight war.

Yet the fiscal-military state initiated in the first revolution, and consolidated in the second, also aroused anxieties. A graphic satire of 1683 depicted 'The common wealth ruleing with a standing army' as a dragon devouring civil and religious liberties and excreting the numerous taxes needed to pay for this monster state.[11] Concerns about the fiscal-military state endured. As Lois Schwoerer showed, the debates about the necessity of keeping up a standing army were particularly intense during the late 1690s.[12] Hostility to wartime high taxation also featured in the propaganda produced by the Stuarts trying to recover their throne and became associated with a 'Country' strain of thinking that attacked government office-holders and their City cronies for benefiting financially from the pursuit of war and accused them of corruption. The larger resources of the state opened the way to peculation, fraud, bribery, and extortion. The liberation of self-interest, unleashed by the rise of the fiscal-military and commercial state, was thus felt even more strongly to have occurred with the second revolution. As the resources of the state grew, so the temptations to corrupt, self-interested behaviour also grew—or at least, that was the perception. Whereas corruption had, in the sixteenth century, been primarily about the corruption of faith, it was increasingly being seen as fiscal corruption that was linked to the self-interested behaviour associated with the rise of the new state which lacked codes of behaviour, inherent in the restraining and self-regulating voluntary office-holding model of public duty. The two revolutions of the seventeenth century created the system that became known as 'Old Corruption' and which was the target of reformers in the late eighteenth and early nineteenth centuries.

Indeed, 'Country' rhetoric saw the fiscal-military state undermining the 'patriot' ideal of voluntarily and selflessly putting country before private interest. Corrupt behaviour also manifested itself in the type of hypocrisy that politicians had shown during the first revolution, when, to some, the pursuit of a religious war was a veneer for the advancement of power and self-interest. Just as tyranny and hypocrisy seemed fused in the first revolution—literally so in the title of William Walwyn's 1649 tract *Tyranipocrit*—so it also seemed to pervade the political culture of the fiscal-military state enlarged by the second of the revolutions. One legacy of the revolutions was thus the oppressive, tax-levying state that favoured a group of self-interested parasites who fed off it; another was a tradition of protest against this that championed the ideal of participatory, self-governing communities resting on an ideal of disinterested office-holding. That dualistic legacy will recur in subsequent discussion of other themes.

Such dualism was certainly evident in the divided and pluralistic religious culture left by the first revolution, with adherents to the church of England, which was restored in 1660, ranged against a variety of (not always united) Protestant sectarians who scrupled at conformity with it. These divisions profoundly shaped the politics of the later Stuart period and ultimately reconfigured the boundaries between church and state.[13] The restoration of a persecuting state church, the ending of religious toleration, and attempts to repress nonconformity—or 'dissent' as it became known—ensured that the thirty years after 1660 were plagued by the failure to achieve a religious settlement. At the heart of the issue was the demand for some degree of religious toleration for the Protestant sects that had flourished in the 1640s and 1650s, or a relaxation of the church's doctrine and ritual that would allow the re-established church to encompass—or 'comprehend' in con-temporary discourse—moderate dissenters. Securing either toleration or comprehen-sion was nevertheless an intensely political business. Adherents of the restored church mobilized their forces to block attempts at comprehension. And if the king suspended the penal laws enacted in the early 1660s against Catholic and Protestant dissenters—as Charles II did in 1672 and James in 1687 and 1688—it suggested that royal prerogative power was superior to parliament and therefore threatened that institution, placing the king's will above the law. Yet during the 1660s and 1670s toleration was unobtainable in parliament, where Anglican royalism was particularly strong.

It took the second revolution to make a Toleration Act possible, in 1689, and even then the position of dissenters in relation to the state remained a hotly contested issue. In 1709 a zealous cleric, Henry Sacheverell, preached an inflammatory sermon attacking the toleration and the dissenters, whom he represented as seditious, as well as moder-ate churchmen who, he claimed, were indifferent to religion and the fate of the church. Sacheverell was tried by parliament in 1710, an impeachment that produced one of the largest print controversies of the eighteenth century, with over 1,000 titles being pub-lished in 1709–10. Yet the Toleration was never repealed. Religious controversy contin-ued to flourish in the eighteenth century but a dividing line between state and religious power had been achieved. Perhaps as importantly, the zealotry of the puritan revolution became increasingly out of fashion, amid a culture of 'politeness' that prized rational and moderate argument. The biblical and millenarian language used by polemicists in the 1640s and 1650s became much rarer, changing the tone and nature of debate. Although the idea that Britain became more secular is a controversial one, the state was less often conceived in the eighteenth century as endeavouring the type of godly rule favoured by puritan revolutionaries. Indeed, the moral reform movement at the end of the sev-enteenth and early eighteenth century relied on paid informers to bring prosecutions (itself another sign of the evolution of the state).

A physical redrawing of the boundaries of the state was also a long-term consequence of the first and then the second revolution. Whereas a union with Ireland and Scotland had been imposed by force, and formalized in the Instrument of Government, the resto-ration of the monarchy in 1660 dissolved the British experiment in union. Yet a British dimension of the second revolution was striking. More radical than the revolution south of the border, the Scots abolished church government by bishops and instituted the presbyterian kirk. Unlike the English Bill of Rights, which was offered to William and Mary at the time of their coronation, the Scottish Claim of Right was more assertive and radical, stating that James had 'forfeited' his crown. But it was the need to secure the Protestant succession after the death of Queen Anne's sole surviving child that forced England to ensure unification in 1707 with Scotland to form the new state of Britain. Whilst this did not entirely solve the problem of the multiple state—Scotland remained a refuge for sympathizers of the exiled Stuarts who staged rebellions there in 1715 and 1745—the legislative union achieved by the Cromwellian regime was made permanent (at least, until recent devolution). Linda Colley's suggestion that a Protestant national identity was a product of the eighteenth century has been challenged but arguably a distinctive 'Britishness' was a legacy of the first and second seventeenth-century revolutions.[14] This was a Britishness without Catholic Ireland. The Cromwellian, Protestant conquest of Ireland was given renewed energy as a result of James II's military stand there. William III was forced personally to head an army to defeat the Jacobite forces at the Boyne in 1691 and the later 'peace' treaties further eroded Catholic property rights and liberties in favour of the Protestant minority. But instead of union, the Irish were subordinated, with colonial status emphasized by the 1720 Declaratory Act. The union of England, Scotland, and Ireland, temporarily achieved in 1653, had to wait until the creation of the United Kingdom in 1801.

The boundaries of the state were also expanding into a British Atlantic world. Before 1640 colonial expansion had been the result of royal encouragement of noble proprietors with little engagement by the state; but after the first revolution this was reversed, with the state taking a leading role, and the religious tensions that had exploded in England were also key to conflict in North America. By 1660 the Atlantic world was centralized but diverse, religiously divided, polarized, and prickly, with an increasing shift towards black labour. Of course the great migration had begun in the 1630s; and religious divisions already existed; but the first revolution had a profound effect in creating an Atlantic sensibility that linked the colonies. Owen Stanwood has recently shown how the second revolution significantly accelerated this process.[15] Whereas in the seventeenth century the American colonies were plagued by rebellions, he suggests that the second revolution allowed Britain to rebuild its empire into a powerful resource. Just as the fear of Catholic conspiracy had permeated English politics in the 1630s and 1640s, and again in the 1680s, so anti-popery initially helped to trigger revolution in Boston, New York, and Maryland in the late 1680s but then provided an ideological glue that held the emerging empire together. American colonists thus saw themselves as Britons and as part of a potent Protestant union. In that sense the wars of religion of the mid-seventeenth century helped to forge a global empire, though this was one with a labour force drawn not from the white indentured workers who still composed the bulk of Caribbean populations in 1650 but black, African slaves. It is striking how, as William Pettigrew has shown, 'revolution principles' established by the second revolution (such as of liberty to trade) ironically, as he puts it, upheld 'a freedom to enslave'.[16]

Pettigrew's case study, the Royal African Company, also reminds us that the achievement of global trading companies became part of the transformation of the state. Brenner's *Merchants and Revolution* showed the connections between commercial and political power (thereby resuscitating some of the Marxist, social perspective of the revolution), and the struggle in the first revolution between different conceptions of the role of the sovereign vis-à-vis trade. Brenner also sees the seventeenth-century revolutions as a coherent pair: 'The Revolution of 1688 and its sequels not only realised the project of 1640–1641 of the Parliamentary capitalist aristocracy; in so doing, it also realised, in a politically subordinated form, the project of 1649–1653 of its leading allies outside the landed classes, the American colonial and East Indian-interloping leadership.'[17] Steve Pincus has given Brenner's thesis a renewed interest and vitality by suggesting that the second revolution also witnessed a struggle between rival political economies, one based on land and the other on manufacture, rather than a fundamentally religious conflict. Indeed, his *1688* suggests that political economy was a central concern to the revolutionaries. Certainly the revolutions unleashed the trading corporations from royal control (a problem that was to resurface with the East India Company, once significant territorial acquisitions were made from the mid-eighteenth century onwards). But we might also note the ways in which these trading companies, which secured parliamentary monopolies as a result of the second revolution, shaped Britain's interactions with a wider world. The revolution in foreign policy ushered in by the second revolution, reversing Cromwell's decision to go to war with Spain rather than France, ensured a century of rivalry with France that necessarily spilled over into a global theatre. This, combined with the consolidation of the British state noted earlier, fostered the forging of a British national identity. Whilst Britishness owed much to the Reformation it was also fundamentally reshaped by the two seventeenth-century revolutions.

The state, then, underwent long-term change as a result of the two revolutions. It became capable of fighting and sustaining large-scale war, initially at home but then, after the second revolution, abroad. This was in part the result of, and in turn accelerated, a financial revolution that created new forms of public finance that relied on a new notion of public credit that underpinned the state's capacity to raise money and hence necessarily became the focal point of political and public debate. The state also became more geographically unified within the isle of Britain but also increasingly imperial in North America, the Caribbean, and the East Indies. At the same time, clearer boundaries between the state and private religious belief were put in place. As this suggests, these changes affected how the public interacted with the state and the type of political culture that prevailed.

Political Culture

A legacy of both seventeenth-century revolutions was institutionalized partisanship. Partisanship had, of course, been evident at least since the Reformation but in the later seventeenth century it became more formalized and institutionalized with the emergence of party politics.[18] The party labels of Whig and Tory emerged in 1681, when polarization over the succession, toleration, and the powers of king and people reached a height. From then on, to varying degrees of discipline and intensity, something like a party system operated. Yet although this was novel—and it took several generations for parties to be distinguished from factions and for pluralism to be grudgingly accepted as inevitable—it is striking how many observers of the emergence of party politics in the later Stuart period drew the lines back to the divisions of the mid-century revolution. The mapping of Cavaliers and parliamentarians on to Tory and Whig was not, of course, a perfect one, and arguably became rather fuzzy in the 1720s, 1730s, and 1740s.

Nevertheless the identity of the first Whigs and Tories owed a good deal to enduring stereotypes drawn from the first revolution.[19]

To the Whigs and Low Churchmen (those who sought a more broad-bottomed state church with some measure of toleration) the Tories were crypto-Laudians intent on resurrecting the power of the church, magnifying the prerogatives of the monarchy, and denying civil liberties. The Whig version of the Tories thus played on notions of Stuart tyranny and a crypto-Catholic conspiracy theory reminiscent of the 1630s and early 1640s. Indeed a Whig version of the history of the revolution highlighted the growth of popery and arbitrary power. But the memory of the first revolution proved far more powerful to the Tories and High Churchmen (those who upheld a strict notion of the established church with no room for latitude for nonconformists), since the civil war and the Interregnum gave them plenty of ammunition against dissenters. Thus to Tories and High Churchmen, the Whigs were republicans, dissenters, and atheists intent on undermining church and state, just as the puritan revolutionaries had done a generation earlier. The slogan '41 is come again' proved a useful Tory rallying cry during the succession crisis of 1678–82, when it seemed possible that the nation might once again descend into civil war. Roger L'Estrange, the principal propagandist for the Tories, endlessly repeated the claim that the spirit of the first revolution had revived to pose a renewed danger to the country. Indeed, the fear of a return to civil war proved both enduring and an important element of the Tory psyche. The 30th of January became an annual fast day allowing clerics to thunder out warnings about the past and ongoing danger of regicide, and prints of Charles the Martyr were published as further reminders. One image of the High Church cleric, Henry Sacheverell, prosecuted in parliament in 1710, depicted him holding Charles I's portrait, and in his offending sermon Sacheverell had very clearly drawn the parallels between the dissenters of the early eighteenth century and those of the mid-seventeenth. That theme was echoed elsewhere. One early eighteenth-century print, *A Genealogy of Anti-Christ Oliver Cromwel Triumphant, as Head of ye Fanaticks and their Vices, supported by Devils*, showed Oliver at the head of a tribe of dissenters who, it alleged, produced 'strife', 'sedition', 'rebellion', 'discord', and 'civil war'. Indeed, the historical interpretation of the first revolution was in part seen through party lenses, with Whig and Tory versions of the causes and course of the civil war and Cromwellian rule.[20] It is significant that Clarendon's *History of the Rebellion* was published to coincide with a Tory election campaign in 1702, since the memory of the civil war was thought to be an electoral asset.

As that use of the memory of the civil war in electioneering suggests, the bitterness of later Stuart politics owed much to the seventeenth-century shift from relatively consensual 'selection' to partisan 'election' of MPs described by Mark Kishlansky, who has also argued that 1646 marked a key turning point from consensus to competition within parliament.[21] The later Stuart period built on earlier developments but also accelerated trends as a result of frequent elections that occurred, on average, every two and a half years between 1679 and 1716. The first revolution's concern for free and fair elections also endured. The second revolution was in part triggered by James II's attempts to purge and pack parliament and after 1689 a series of measures reached the statute book to try to regulate electioneering. There were also discussions about reorganizing the distribution of parliamentary seats and altering the franchise, and some of these echoed the innovations of the 1650s. The Leveller demand for annual parliaments, for example, continued to be made after 1660, especially when Charles II failed to call a general election between 1661 and 1679. Annual sessions of parliament became the norm after 1689, since the need to raise wartime parliamentary taxation made them routine; and in 1694 a Triennial Act, similar to the one conceded by Charles I in 1641, was passed until its repeal in 1716 in favour of less frequent elections every seven years. The size of the electorate also grew in the later Stuart period, so that by 1715 a higher percentage of the adult male population could vote in an election than at any other time in the eighteenth century and even after the 1832 Reform Act. Nevertheless the systematic recasting of the franchise, envisaged by the earlier revolutionaries, failed to reach the statute book, though there were attempts to introduce a standard scot and lot franchise in boroughs, and even, in 1679, to introduce the £200 voting threshold introduced by the Instrument of Government.[22] The earlier calls for a redistribution of seats were also kept alive by a series of attempts to highlight the disparity between the number of MPs, tax, and population. Even so, it would be almost two hundred years before extensive reform was enacted.

The electioneering of the later Stuart period owed another debt to the first revolution: a free press. Although pre-publication censorship was restored in 1661, it lapsed during the succession crisis in 1679, resulting in a flood of material that matched levels achieved in the 1640s. Control was reimposed by extra-parliamentary measures in 1683 and by statute in 1685 but the second revolution saw the demise of the 'licensing' system of control, with the system being allowed to expire permanently in 1695.[23] This opened the way in the eighteenth century for a market-regulated press that expanded according to demand rather than being restricted by governmental pre-publication censorship. It is clear that the two seventeenth-century revolutions thus achieved a transformation of the press and its role in politics and society.

If we add to that increase in print the improvements in the postal system and the introduction of the coffee house (first in Oxford in 1650 but spreading to most provincial towns by 1700) we could talk about a communications revolution. The implications of that can nevertheless be exaggerated: oral and manuscript cultures were not simply displaced by print. But print did change how the conversations within and beyond the state could operate. The greater availability of print in the 1640s and 1650s helped to change the way in which public opinion was articulated and represented; and the power of this as a force on government was consolidated after the second revolution. One indication of this is the transformation of the periodical. The newspaper was largely the creation of the first revolution but came of age after the second, so that by the early eighteenth century Britain had daily, morning, and evening papers, and, from the 1700s onwards, regional ones. Enterprising publishers experimented with the potential of periodicals to engage and interact with the public. John Dunton in the late seventeenth century thus developed a question and answer format, a printed dialogue between readers and writers, and this was soon adopted elsewhere.

Such developments enlarged what Jürgen Habermas described as the 'public sphere' which he saw as emerging in the 1690s.[24] Although commentators have suggested that this was already in existence by the 1640s, so that we should acknowledge that the later period built on earlier foundations, the 1690s public sphere was both more robust (in part because of the free press established after 1695) and, because of discussions about the fiscal-military state and public credit, slightly different to that of the first revolution.[25] Habermas was clear that the public sphere was a bourgeois one: knowledge about the state was economically as well as politically powerful. As we have seen, the fiscal innovations of the 1690s created a system of public credit that both stimulated discussion about economic issues but also made the financing of the war dependent on public investment. Similarly although notions of 'civility' had permeated much of the sixteenth and seventeenth century, the later Stuart public sphere was also a self-consciously 'polite' one. One of its champions, the 3rd earl of Shaftesbury, was clear that politeness could only flourish in conditions of freedom and hence that it was a consequence of the defeat of tyranny in the second revolution.[26] Yet there is also a sense in which politeness was a reaction against the first as well as the second revolution. Politeness urged reason over passion and abuse, and moderation over zeal; and to that extent (although it remained an ideal far more than Habermas allowed) it was a cultural mechanism for ensuring that the excessive political and religious heats of the mid-century revolution could be contained within civil society without recourse to civil war.

An interesting test-case for the achievement of the seventeenth-century revolutions in changing communicative practices is petitioning. Before the civil war petitions were written in manuscript; presented to someone in authority who was perceived to be in a position to offer redress; and were regarded with enormous suspicion by the government when appropriated as a means of trying to exert popular pressure on the authorities. During and after the first seventeenth-century revolution they were often printed: their ostensible audience was now not only the addressee but also those who read the petition. Printed petitions thus provoked counter-petitions, leading to the type of ongoing conversation that helped to invoke public opinion.[27] Petitions, addresses, and associations became an important way of articulating popular grievances and exerting popular pressure for national campaigns. Although one of the first acts of the newly restored regime in 1661 was to pass an act forbidding 'tumultuous' petitions (ironically modelled on parliament's 1648 restraint of army petitioning), mass petitioning was revived in 1679 to try to force Charles II to summon the parliament that he had prorogued and thereafter subscriptions to petitions, addresses, and associations became an important way of mobilizing public opinion and using it as a political instrument. Although the right to petition parliament remained contested, and the number of petitioning campaigns on national political and religious issues declined in the 1720s, 1730s, and 1740s, the revival of mass petitioning campaigns in the 1760s, early 1780s, and early 1790s was a key means of articulating popular opinion.

The addresses signed in their thousands during the later seventeenth and early eighteenth century to express loyalty to the monarch (on accessions, deaths, military victories, and national threats) nevertheless remind us that an important legacy of the first revolution was popular loyalism as much as radicalism. Allegiance to the church and monarchy survived the experiences of the 1640s and 1650s to flower—sometimes in an aggressive form of Anglican royalism—during the Restoration era and beyond. Robert Beddard suggested that the revolution of 1688 was initially a revolution by those Anglican royalists who resented what they saw as James II's breach of the understanding of the union of Protestant church and state, a revolution that was hijacked in its later stages by those seeking a more Whiggish outcome.[28] Certainly a good deal of the success of the Tory party after 1688 derived from an ardent loyalism to the church of England (though it is true to say that many Whigs were also moderate churchmen). Expressions of duty and loyalty to the monarch were plentiful enough to show what in Queen Anne's reign in the first decade of the eighteenth century bordered on a national cult of monarchy, a collective attempt to exorcize the memory of the regicide. The Sacheverell affair in 1710 also produced an outpouring of loyalty to the established church. Floods of loyalist, Tory addresses in 1710 and 1713, for example, repeatedly attacked the republicanism and atheism associated with the Whigs. Similarly it is clear that popular radicalism on the streets and at the polls was more than matched by popular loyalism. This militant High Church Toryism—a legacy of the first revolution's Anglican royalism—remained a persistent feature of popular politics through to the church and king riots in 1791 and the 'vulgar conservatism' described by Mark Philp.[29] The important point to note is that the two revolutions left a divided political culture and discourse, leaving a legacy both of political, religious, and social radicalism but also an equally powerful adherence to church and monarchy. These conflicting and contesting strands shaped each other and the parameters of political debate and thought.

Political Discourse

Was there a set of revolutionary ideas or a revolutionary language bequeathed by the first seventeenth-century revolution to the second revolution and beyond? Or was there a counter-revolutionary ideology with its own counter-revolutionary language? Given the dualistic legacy outlined earlier, the conclusion that both revolutionary and counter-revolutionary ideologies persisted and competed against each other should not be surprising.[30] Both revolutions of the seventeenth century generated and left rival, antagonistic ideologies that provided a resource of ideas and ways of expressing them that could be invoked by later politicians for their own purposes. It is true that much of the eighteenth-century invocation of the seventeenth-century past focused on the revolution of 1688–9 rather than that of the 1640s and 1650s: revolution societies were set up in 1788 but there was no equivalent in 1742 or 1749. Much of the discussion of the first revolution occurred in histories.[31] Yet there was also a small group of

'commonwealthsmen' who did very consciously seek to keep the commonwealth experiment alive, through republications of mid-century texts or the absorption of commonwealth principles into their writings.[32] This did not mean the survival of republicanism,
if the latter is taken to advocate a state without a prince; there were very few calls for the
abolition of monarchy after 1660. But if republicanism or 'commonwealth' principles
amounted to a set of values and a language of public virtue then a commonwealth tradition did persist.[33] Moreover, although 'revolution principles' were debated after 1689,
their formulation owed a good deal to the first revolution, the memory of which was
never far below the surface of public debate. These points can be illustrated through a
brief sketch of the debate over 'revolution principles' that erupted in Anne's reign, when
party divisions were at their most bitter and came to a head during and after the trial in
1710 of the High Church cleric Henry Sacheverell.[34]

One very important link between the first and second revolutions was the doctrine of popular sovereignty and the right of resistance that it conferred. In the sermon for which he was prosecuted, Sacheverell alleged that those who upheld these
notions approved of 'the horrid Actions and Principles of Forty One'. He saw the
dissenters and republicans of the first revolution as active again: 'the Old Leaven of
their Fore-Fathers is still working in their present Generation' and their 'Poison still
remains in this brood of Vipers, to Sting us to Death'.[35] Yet the Whigs did uphold
a right of resistance which was seen as a key revolution principle. Countering
Sacheverell's attack, Robert Walpole argued that 'to plead for Resistance' was 'to
assert and maintain the very Being of our present Government and Constitution;
and to assert Non-resistance, in that boundless and unlimited sense in which Doctor
Sacheverell presumes to assert it, is to Sap and Undermine the very Foundations
of the Government'.[36] Establishing a right of resistance was so important because a
good deal more flowed from it, including the rule of law as opposed to the arbitrary
whims of monarchs; a Protestant, parliamentary-determined succession; and the
war against France. Denying a right of resistance, the Whig managers of Sacheverell's
prosecution argued, questioned the queen's own right to sit on the throne. The right
of resistance was the most important revolution principle, bearing the weight of the
change of dynasty and acting as short-hand for a series of other positions about civil
governance derived from the people.

A second revolution principle running across both revolutions was religious toleration. The defence of this took several days of Sacheverell's trial. Lord William Paulet
asserted that 'the good Effects of the Wisdom of the Legislature in making that Act
had been seen' and Spencer Cowper insisted that 'Indulgence was requir'd from them
as Christians and as men professing Humanity and Good Will towards one another'.
On the other hand Sacheverell, the doctor's prosecutors suggested, wanted a 'Church
that would destroy all those who brought about, and had since supported, the happy
Revolution. A Church, which upon Anti-Christian principles, profess'd Burning for
Conscience-sake ... A Church that would turn all the Blessings they enjoy'd under the
present Administration into all those Miseries they had got rid of by the late glorious
Revolution'.[37] Such views hardened amongst some into a long-lasting anti-clericalism—a

fear of 'priestcraft'—that also drew nourishment from attacks on all forms of clerical power made in the 1640s.[38]

A right of resistance and religious toleration stood at the core of 'revolution principles', though there were many different ways of grounding these: historically, through an 'ancient constitution', scripturally, or by deriving them from reason or natural rights, natural equality and natural liberty.[39] Other 'revolution principles' flowed from them or were sometimes connected to them: freedom of the press and of parliament.[40] The popular tract *Political Aphorisms*, first published in 1690, was a compendium of revolution principles (including sections of John Locke's *Two Treatises of Government*, which Richard Ashcraft has argued owed a good deal to Leveller ideas).[41] The tract was republished in 1709, during the Sacheverell affair with the fuller title *Vox Populi, Vox Dei*, suggesting (as revolutionaries in the 1640s had) that the voice of the people was the voice of God. The tract set out, as its title page proclaimed, the following principles: that all power derived from and for the good of the people and was the product of a contract between king and people; that resisting tyrannical power was allowed by scripture and reason; and that the High Church Tory doctrine of 'passive obedience', that is to say obedience to all the monarch's demands, was a 'damnable and treasonable' one. The tract, republished in a different form with the title *The Judgment of Whole Kingdoms*, went through at least twelve editions by 1714, making it one of the best sellers of the eighteenth century.

Yet revolution principles were also bitterly attacked by those who sought to uphold notions of a strong monarchy and church. The tract by Robert Filmer for which Charles I had refused a licence, *Patriarcha*, was nevertheless republished during the succession crisis in 1680 in order to restate a doctrine of patriarchal royal authority in which power was divinely given, owing nothing to popular sovereignty, and without any right of resistance. Although Filmerian ideas were dealt a major blow by the transfer of the crown to William III in 1689, divine right ideas did persist and found expression in the Jacobite movement seeking the restoration of the Stuarts. But even if divine right was largely abandoned, the attack on revolution principles was uncompromising. Francis Atterbury, a future Jacobite plotter and bishop in 1713, published a refutation of *Vox Populi, Vox Dei*. Making every individual's will the law for church and state, he claimed, would create 'no other than Confusion' and sully the word of God. 'The Voice of the People is the Cry of Hell, leading to Idolatry, Rebellion, Murder and all the Wickedness the Devil can suggest.' It was, he claimed, 'the Voice of the People, rais'd in frequent Mutinies and Seditions, that began the Rebellion against King Charles the first of England; that maintain'd it for so many Years, that brought him to a Tryal and Murder'd him on a Scaffold.'[42] The history of loyalist political thought has yet to be written but it would be a rich one, linking the two revolutions of the seventeenth century with the counter-revolutionary ideology and popular loyalism of the 1790s, and stressing a high strain of loyalism to monarchy and church. It is no coincidence that John Reeves called his anti-Jacobin society 'The Association for Preserving Liberty and Property against Republicans and Levellers' and that in 1793 it published 'The Fatal Effects of Republican Principles, exemplified in the History of England from the Death of Charles I to the Restoration of Charles II'.[43]

It is of course possible to exaggerate the part played by the memory of the civil war and Interregnum in the century after 1660. The observation of the 30 January fast day, for example, seems to have waned in the first decades of the eighteenth century.[44] In 1710 the decree of Oxford University that had been passed in 1683 to proscribe revolution principles and authors who were thought to enunciate them (including Hunton, Milton, Owen, Baxter, Hobbes, the Quakers, and Fifth Monarchists) was ceremoniously burnt along with Sacheverell's sermon and condemned by parliament. Nevertheless the shadow of the first revolution was a long one, influencing the character and shape of the second seventeenth-century revolution and the ensuing hundred years. The cumulative effect of the two revolutions was to transform the state's fiscal and military capabilities, establishing a framework that would facilitate a global empire. Similarly the two revolutions transformed the public sphere, embedding printed, national discussion and systematic partisanship at its heart and enabling a bourgeois set of investors to acquire a stake in the state, both directly through their capital and indirectly, through public opinion. Finally, the two revolutions left a complex and rich ideological heritage, a dualistic revolutionary and counter-revolutionary set of ideas and languages. The varied set of traditions could be invoked many years later for polemical purposes and in that sense, the civil war never really ended.

Notes

1. Jonathan Scott, *England's Troubles: Seventeenth-Century English Political Instability in European Context* (Cambridge, 2000).
2. Conrad Russell, *Unrevolutionary England, 1630–1642* (London, 1990).
3. The historiography is surveyed by Steven Pincus, *1688: The First Modern Revolution* (New Haven, 2011), chap. 1.
4. Tim Harris, *Revolution: The Great Crisis of the British Monarchy 1685–1720* (London, 2006).
5. Nicholas Tyacke (ed.), *The English Revolution, c.1590–1720* (Manchester, 2007), introduction.
6. The best introduction is Michael J. Braddick, *State Formation in Early Modern England, c.1550–1700* (Cambridge, 2000).
7. Mark Goldie, 'The Unacknowledged Republic: Office-Holding in Early Modern England', in Tim Harris (ed.), *The Politics of the Excluded, c.1500–1850* (Basingstoke, 2001), 153–94.
8. Patrick Collinson, 'The Monarchical Republic of Queen Elizabeth I', in his *Elizabethan Essays* (London, 1994), 31–58.
9. Phil Withington, *The Politics of Commonwealth: Citizens and Freemen in Early Modern England* (Cambridge, 2005).
10. John Brewer, *The Sinews of Power: War, Money and the English State, 1688–1783* (London, 1989); Peter Dickson, *The Financial Revolution in England: A Study in the Development of Public Credit, 1688–1756* (London, 1967).
11. The image can be seen on the British Museum website at <http://www.britishmuseum.org/research/collection_online/collection_object_details/collection_image_gallery.aspx?partid=1&assetid=353388&objectid=3069115>.
12. Lois Schwoerer, *No Standing Armies! The Anti-Army Ideology in C17th England* (Baltimore, 1974).

13. Tim Harris, Mark Goldie, and Paul Seaward (eds.), *The Politics of Religion in Restoration England* (Oxford, 1990).

14. Linda Colley, *Britons: Forging the Nation, 1707–1837* (New Haven, 1992).

15. Owen Stanwood, *The Empire Reformed: English America in the Age of the Glorious Revolution* (Philadelphia, 2011).

16. William Pettigrew, 'Free to Enslave: Politics and the Escalation of Britain's Transatlantic Slave Trade, 1688–1714', *William and Mary Quarterly*, 3rd Series, 64.1 (January 2007): 3–38.

17. Robert Brenner, *Merchants and Revolution: Commercial Change, Political Conflict, and London's Overseas Traders, 1550–1653* (Princeton, 1992), 716.

18. Tim Harris, *Politics under the Later Stuarts: Party Conflict in a Divided Society, 1660–1715* (London, 1993).

19. Tom Corns, W. A. Speck, and J. A. Downie, 'Archetypal Mystification: Polemic and Reality in English Political Literature, 1640–1750', *Eighteenth-Century Life*, 7.3 (1982): 1–27.

20. Mark Knights, 'The Tory Interpretation of History in the Rage of Parties', in Paulina Kewes (ed.), *The Uses of History in Early Modern England* (San Marino, 2006), 347–66.

21. Mark Kishlansky, *Parliamentary Selection: Social and Political Choice in Early Modern England* (Cambridge, 1986); Kishlansky, *The Rise of the New Model Army* (Cambridge, 1979).

22. Mark Knights, 'John Locke and Post-Revolutionary Politics', *Past and Present*, 213 (2011): 41–86.

23. A graph of press output 1475–1800 can be found in Mark Knights, *Representation and Misrepresentation in Later Stuart Britain: Partisanship and Political Culture* (Oxford, 2005), 16.

24. Jürgen Habermas, *The Structural Transformation of the Public Sphere: An Inquiry into a Category of Bourgeois Society*, trans. Thomas Burger with the assistance of Frederick Lawrence (Cambridge, 1989).

25. Peter Lake and Steve Pincus, 'Rethinking the Public Sphere in Early Modern England', *Journal of British Studies*, 45.2 (2006): 270–92.

26. Lawrence Klein, 'The Political Significance of Politeness in Early Eighteenth Century Britain', in Gordon Schochet, Patricia Tatspaugh, and Carol Brobeck (eds.), *Politics, Politeness and Patriotism* (Washington, 1993), 73–108.

27. David Zaret, *The Origins of Democratic Culture: Printing, Petitions, and the Public Sphere in Early-Modern England* (Princeton, 2000).

28. Robert Beddard, *The Unexpected Whig Revolution of 1688* (Oxford, 1991).

29. Mark Philp, 'Vulgar Conservatism 1792–3', *English Historical Review*, 110.435 (1995): 42–69.

30. The two sides are summarized in John Shute Barrington, *The revolution and anti-revolution principles stated and compar'd* (London, 1714).

31. Laird Okie, *Augustan Historical Writing: Histories of England in the English Enlightenment* (Lanham, MD, 1991); Royce MacGillivray, *Restoration Historians and the English Civil War* (The Hague, 1974); Philip S. Hicks, *Neoclassical History and English Culture: From Clarendon to Hume* (London, 1996); Paulina Kewes, 'Acts of Remembrance, Acts of Oblivion: Rhetoric, Law, and National Memory in Early Restoration England', in Lorna Clymer (ed.), *Ritual, Routine, and Regime: Institutions of Repetition in Euro-American Cultures, 1650–1832* (Toronto, 2005), 103–31.

32. Blair Worden, *Roundhead Reputations: The English Civil War and the Passions of Posterity* (London, 2001); Justin Champion, *Republican Learning: John Toland and the Crisis of Christian Culture, 1696–1722* (Manchester, 2003); Caroline Robbins, *The Eighteenth Century Commonwealthman: Studies in the Transmission, Development, and Circumstance*

of English Liberal Thought from the Restoration of Charles II until the War with the Thirteen Colonies (Cambridge, MA, 1959).

33. Blair Worden, 'English Republicanism', in J. H. Burns and Mark Goldie (eds.), *The Cambridge History of Political Thought, 1450–1700* (Cambridge, 1991), 443–75.

34. John Kenyon, *Revolution Principles: The Politics of Party, 1689–1720* (Cambridge, 1977).

35. Henry Sacheverell, *The Perils of False Brethren* (London, 1709, ESTC T164159), 18.

36. *A Compleat History of the Whole Proceedings … against Dr Henry Sacheverell* (London, 1710), 69.

37. *Compleat History*, 110–11, 127.

38. Justin Champion, ' "Religion's Safe, with Priestcraft is the War": Augustan Anticlericalism and the Legacy of the English Revolution, 1660–1720', *The European Legacy*, 5.4 (2000): 547–61.

39. J. G. A. Pocock, *Virtue, Commerce and History: Essays on Political Thought and History, Chiefly in the Eighteenth Century* (Cambridge, 1976), esp. chap. 11.

40. These were, for example, stated in the three 'revolution principles' listed by the Revolution Society in 1789 (*An abstract of the history and proceedings of the Revolution Society*, 1789/90, 14–15).

41. Richard Ashcraft and M. M. Goldsmith, 'Locke, Revolution Principles and the Formation of Whig Ideology', *Historical Journal*, 26.4 (1983): 773–800; Ashcraft, *Revolutionary Politics and Locke's Two Treatises* (Princeton, 1986).

42. Francis Atterbury, *The Voice of the People no Voice of God* (London, 1710), 4, 6, 13.

43. *The Association for Preserving Liberty and Property against Republicans and Levellers* (London, 1793), Part 1, no. 5: 2.

44. Andrew Lacey, *The Cult of King Charles the Martyr* (Woodbridge, 2003).

FURTHER READING

Braddick, Michael J., 'The English Revolution and its Legacies', in Nicholas Tyacke (ed.), *The English Revolution, c.1590–1720: Politics, Religion and Communities* (Manchester, 2007), 27–42.

Burgess, Glenn and Matthew Festenstein (eds.), *English Radicalism, 1550–1850* (Cambridge, 2007).

Champion, Justin, 'Political Thinking between Restoration and Hanoverian Succession', in Barry Coward (ed.), *A Companion to Stuart Britain* (Oxford, 2003), 474–491.

De Krey, Gary, *Restoration and Revolution in Britain: A Political History of the Era of Charles II and the Glorious Revolution* (2007).

Holmes, Geoffrey, *The Making of a Great Power: Late Stuart and Early Georgian Britain, 1660–1722* (London, 1993).

Hoppit, Julian, *Land of Liberty? England, 1689–1727* (Oxford, 2000).

Kenyon, John, *Revolution Principles: The Politics of Party, 1689–1720* (Cambridge, 1977).

Knights, Mark, *The Devil in Disguise: Deception, Delusion, and Fanaticism in the Early English Enlightenment* (Oxford, 2011).

Knights, Mark, *Representation and Misrepresentation in Later Stuart Britain: Partisanship and Political Culture* (Oxford, 2005).

Lang, Timothy, *The Victorians and the Stuart Heritage: Interpretations of a Discordant Past* (Cambridge, 1995).

Miller, John, *After the Civil Wars: English Politics and Government in the Reign of Charles II* (Harlow, 2000).

Pincus, Steve, *1688: The First Modern Revolution* (New Haven, 2011).

Robbins, Caroline, *The Eighteenth Century Commonwealthman: Studies in the Transmission, Development, and Circumstance of English Liberal Thought from the Restoration of Charles II until the War with the Thirteen Colonies* (Cambridge, MA, 1959).

Scott, Jonathan, *England's Troubles: Seventeenth-Century English Political Instability in European Context* (Cambridge, 2000).

Worden, Blair, *Roundhead Reputations: The English Civil War and the Passions of Posterity* (London, 2001).

CHAPTER 31

....

CULTURAL LEGACIES:

The English Revolution in Nineteenth-Century British and French Literature and Art

....

LAURA LUNGER KNOPPERS

CROWDED together, spectators watch an unfolding drama, the unprecedented execution of a condemned king and the reactions of the man thought to have done the most to bring it about. The audience's reaction is mixed, ranging from sympathy to hostility. But the event being watched is not the beheading of King Charles I before Whitehall Palace on 30 January 1649. Rather, the setting is the Queen's Theatre, London, on 21 December 1872, and the audience that 'laughed, hissed, and applauded in turns' is watching a performance of *Oliver Cromwell: An Historical Tragedy* by Colonel Alfred Bate Richards, originally published in 1847 and restaged as a counter-point to a September 1872 production of the fiercely anti-Cromwellian *Charles I: An Historical Tragedy* by W. G. Wills.[1]

While Richards's play could not plausibly claim the status of high art, it provides insight into an important but often overlooked legacy of the English Revolution: its cultural impact as the subject of visual art, drama, and fiction. The Revolution itself, as is well known, prompted not only an outpouring of print but a flourishing and transformation of literary genres, including satire, prophecy, conversion narrative, lyric verse, polemical prose, epic, and dramatic dialogue.[2] Literary and artistic representations also joined the interpretive and polemic struggle over the central figures of the Revolution, variously constructing Charles I as tyrant, Christ-like martyr, or loving husband and Cromwell as Moses, Caesar, brewer, or Machiavel.[3] And in a longer-term cultural legacy, literature and art became a means of remembering, debating, interpreting, and experiencing the Revolution not only in Britain but in a European context.[4] Long after the primary actors had fought their battles in the field and in the public sphere, the Revolution lived on in the representational arts.

The cultural legacy of the English Revolution was by no means a simple act of looking to the past as past. Particularly in moments of reform, crisis, or change, artists and writers re-imagined the English revolutionary past in a kind of 'doubled time' in order to comment obliquely on the present, in turn shaping or pointing towards the future.[5] Late eighteenth- and nineteenth-century Britain and France looked to the English Revolution as a lens upon or analogue to their present-day concerns. The events of the French Revolution and its long aftermath, and England's constitutional reforms and the long reign of a female monarch, prompted an intense interest in English revolutionary history.

Nineteenth-century visual and literary representations imagined, restaged, and constructed a window into the interiority of leading actors of the English Revolution. In turn, the aesthetic genres themselves were remade, from a new synthesis of historical and genre painting, to the historical novel, to Romantic drama in both Britain and France. In a kind of democratizing move, literary works and visual art allowed readers and viewers to see the inner emotions and moral dilemmas of figures of power, to empathize with them as fellow human beings and to interpret and judge their actions.[6] As such, the nineteenth-century literature and art that brought history to a much wider public, and prompted that public to engage in and experience the historical past as the present, constitutes an important and neglected legacy that parallels and extends the opening up of the public sphere during the English Revolution itself.[7]

RECREATING DEBATE IN VICTORIAN DRAMA

The Victorians were obsessed with the English civil wars, seeing in the conflict between parliament and King Charles I the source of their own constitutional monarchy and individual rights and liberties. Mindful of and attempting to stave off the radical upheaval of the French Revolution, nineteenth-century England moved through major constitutional reform, broadening the franchise and expanding parliamentary powers. The Napoleonic Wars prompted England's renewed interest in its own military leaders, while the flourishing of evangelicalism and nonconformity brought interest in England's history of religious liberty. Hence, the century saw the rehabilitation of Oliver Cromwell from villain, tyrant, and hypocrite to pious religious leader and agent of England's successful foreign conquests.[8] At the same time, the marketing of Victoria and Albert and their large brood of children as a loving, domestic unit reached back to representations of Charles I and Henrietta Maria as loving husband and wife.[9] Artistic and literary representations of the civil wars, including fiction, drama, poetry, and history paintings, complemented historiography and great Victorian editions of revolutionary figures.[10]

Indeed, the open-endedness of the civil war cultural legacy may in some ways be seen as recreating the public debate and activist readers of the Revolution itself. Richards's *Cromwell* constitutes a Whig-Liberal response to the Tory rendition of *Charles I*. The two plays, *Cromwell* and *Charles I*, came at a critical time for the monarchy. The late 1860s and early 1870s saw a rising popular republicanism, fuelled by Victoria's long seclusion after the death of Prince Albert in December 1861 and by widespread dislike of the Prince of Wales. In February 1872 Victoria attended a Service of National Thanksgiving at St Paul's Cathedral for the recovery of the prince from typhoid fever, and she thereafter resumed a more public role.[11] At a crucial time in public opinion, then, Richards's *Cromwell* constitutes a late Victorian reworking of civil war narrative into a moralistic family quasi-tragedy, showing the private as well as public struggles of powerful figures. The main political plot draws upon Shakespeare's *Macbeth* and *Hamlet* to dramatize Cromwell's early resistance to Charles I, his civil war victories, and his leading, if conflicted, role in the execution of the king. Cromwell shares Macbeth's ambition, fatal embrace of regicide, and guilt, while Lady Macbeth's torment is projected onto Cromwell's innocent daughter, Elizabeth, who disapproves of the regicide and takes on the guilt of her father. The second, non-historical plot, with some echoes of Shakespeare's Shylock and Jessica in *The Merchant of Venice*, is a love conflict, as the virtuous Florence Nevel tries to resist being forced by her father to marry the villain Basil Walton, who has tricked his virtuous brother Arthur (her true love) out of his inheritance. Florence takes refuge with her old school-chum, Elizabeth Cromwell, hence setting up much dialogue and intrigue.

While the execution of Charles I takes place off-stage in Richards's *Cromwell*, reported with a focus on Cromwell's reaction, one late scene (3.3) merits particular attention. The coffin of Charles I has been placed in Whitehall, the nervous guards (evoking scenes in *Macbeth* and *Hamlet*) standing watch and eager to be relieved of their duty. Cromwell enters alone at midnight and demands that the coffin be opened:

> Stay ... I have need of thee awhile.
> Remove the covering from your dead charge there.
> Quick, fool! Thy mouth is all agape as if
> Thou didst lack tidings. What dost shake thus for?
> [*He advances to the coffin and tears aside the covering*] (3.3)[12]

Cromwell sends the guards away, asking them to 'leave me here alone awhile in prayer'.

What follows is a remarkable apostrophe. Broken, guilty, self-justifying, and haunted, Cromwell advances to the coffin, as a 'test to my soul, to look on him; | To set my living face by his dead face. | Then tax him with the deeds for which I slew him'. His lifting the covering, 'very gently', provokes an impassioned outburst and recognition of the full humanity of the former king:

> O thou discrownèd and insensible clay!
> Stripped 'midst a butchered score or so of men
> Upon some bleak hill-side, beneath the rack
> Of flying clouds torn by the cannon's boom,
> If the red trampled grass were all thy shroud,
> The scowl of Heaven thy plumèd canopy,
> Thou might'st be any one. What art thou, now?—
> How is it with thee, Man! Charles Stuart! King?

(3.3)

Cromwell's stark recognition of the humanity of the corpse in the coffin brings a vivid and horrifying imagining of decay, corruption, and rot in 'gory death': a Hamlet-like meditation on the festering grave and the 'eyeless socket-holes' of the 'poor, weeping skull'. The audience sees Cromwell in a moment of horror and guilt, like Macbeth with the ghost of Banquo, or Hamlet with the skull in the graveyard.

Richards's Cromwell, like Shakespeare's Macbeth before him, recognizes that he will draw the censure of history:

> For I have done a deed in slaying thee
> Shall wring the world's heart with its memory.
> Men shall believe me not, as they are base,
> And knaves shall cry 'hypocrite!' as they dare judge
> The naked fervour of my struggling soul.
> Heaven judge between us! (3.3)

But the steady moment of tragic self-recognition cannot be sustained, and Cromwell turns to self-exculpation:

> I am armed in this—
> Couldst thou have reigned, not crushing English hearts
> With fierce compression of thine iron sway,
> Cromwell had lived contented and unknown,
> To teach his children loyalty and faith
> Sacred and simple, as the grass-grown mound
> That should have pressed more lightly on his bones
> Than ever greatness on his wearied spirit. (3.3)

When the guards return, Cromwell—like Hamlet after having seen his father's ghost—warns them not to speak of what they have seen. The audience sees only the coffin of Charles I, not the body itself, but the stark and macabre scene haunts the rest of the play. Through the language and representation of the drama, the audience experiences the moral dilemma facing Oliver Cromwell, along with pity and fear of his actions.

Indeed Richards's scene of Cromwell brooding over the dead Charles I that so struck the theatre audience was something that at least some Londoners had seen before: in an 1831 French painting of Cromwell gazing into the opened coffin of the dead king.[13] The painting serves to illustrate not only French uses of the English Revolution, but the way in which art transformed the English past into present-time experience, eliciting the very kinds of interpretation and judgement that had been part of the emergent public sphere in mid-seventeenth-century England.

DELAROCHE AND FRENCH VISUAL REPRESENTATIONS

The outbreak of the French Revolution with the meeting of the Estates General and the fall of the Bastille in 1789 had prompted intense French interest in what many saw as the earlier English prototype of their own struggles. As events progressed through revolution and reaction, the execution of Louis XVI and its violent aftermath in the Terror and the Directory, the rise, imperial conquests, defeat and (double) exile of Napoleon, and what would prove the temporary restoration of the Bourbons, the dizzying shifts prompted new and shifting analogies based on the political sympathies of the historian, visual artist, or literary writer.[14]

The coffin scene in Richards's *Oliver Cromwell: An Historical Tragedy* was in fact a 'realization': a *tableau vivant* of the painting *Cromwell and Charles I* by French artist Paul Delaroche (fig. 31.1) that was displayed in London and circulated even more widely in engraving and print.[15] Delaroche produced *Cromwell and Charles I* for the Salon of 1831, the first after the 'July Revolution' in which the constitutional monarch Louis-Philippe had replaced the ageing Bourbon king, Charles X. French painter Eugène Delacroix had executed several historical canvases for the same Salon, featuring panoramas that directly celebrated recent events, including his famous *The Twenty-Eighth of July: Liberty Leading the People*.[16] Delaroche used 'historical and geographical displacement' to comment more obliquely, but no less powerfully, on current affairs.[17] Hence, the striking image of the military conqueror Cromwell, almost certainly evocative of Napoleon, gazing upon the opened coffin and corpse of the recently decapitated Charles I (evoking

FIG. 31.1 Paul Delaroche, Cromwell opens the coffin of King Charles I (1831).

Musee des Beaux-Arts, Nimes, France. Photo Credit: Erich Lessing / Art Resource, NY.

Louis XVI), depicted emotions and trauma of the past as a lens (however ambiguous) on the present and future.

The composition of the life-size painting, with the foregrounded figure of Oliver Cromwell in military dress, gazing intently on the dead King Charles I in his coffin, has a striking immediacy and accessibility, even to a viewer unfamiliar with the history. In contrast to large-scale, panoramic history scenes, the painting pulls the viewer into a highly charged private encounter between two public figures. As art historians have noted, Delaroche's life-size figures and monumental historical paintings are experiential rather than representational: the viewer empathizes, understands, and experiences.[18] The painting's local colour—the detail of Charles's clothing and beard, the chair, and Cromwell's boots and military dress—paradoxically makes the figures both historical and immediate, accessible. The viewer is drawn in, willingly or no. Yet what precisely is that moment that the viewer is, in the words of art historian Beth S. Wright, 'forced to share'?[19]

The painting seems to represent differences and contrasts between the sturdy, stocky vertical figure of the military conqueror, Cromwell, dressed in roughly-textured brown leather jerkin and high boots, and the ethereal delicacy of Charles I, dressed in elegant white-embroidered lace, and whose finely pointed beard and facial features are bathed in light, in a horizontal coffin that recedes sharply into the background. The commoner Cromwell does not remove his hat in the presence of the monarch; as he holds open the coffin, the force of his recent action as well as further potential violence are suggested by the rumpled coffin cloth beneath his feet, in contrast to the still figure of the king.

Even the art historical lineage seems to contrast the two figures. Charles I is drawn from the influential court portraiture of Flemish artist Sir Anthony van Dyck, whose paintings of the king and of his queen, Henrietta Maria, promulgated the grace and majesty of the Caroline court.[20] Van Dyck's Charles, with finely pointed features, elegant lace collar, and George medal (fig. 31.2), was widely circulated in engravings. In contrast, Delaroche's Cromwell seems derived from Northern European art and most closely resembles not the English portraiture of Robert Walker or Peter Lely, but an anonymous equestrian painting of Cromwell, looking much like a Dutch burgher, that also circulated in print (fig. 31.3).[21]

Yet for all of the compositional contrasts between Cromwell and Charles, Delaroche's painting also insists on interconnections and complexity. The figures are not simply opposed with colour, surface and texture, light and shadow, horizontal and vertical lines, but are also paralleled and echoing. Colour links, rather than separates, Charles and Cromwell. The thin red line where the king's head was cut from the body and then reattached, and the plush red velvet of the chairs upon which the coffin rests, are echoed in the red plume in Cromwell's hat and the red lining of his boots. The black coffin correlates with Cromwell's black hat, and the brown of the chair legs parallels the brown of Cromwell's jerkin and books, as well as the brown shadows behind the two men. Light and shadow similarly link, rather than distinguish, the two figures. The light reflects variously on the king's face and upper torso, on Cromwell's right arm and left shoulder,

The High & mighty Monarch Charles by the grace of God,
King of Great Brittaine France & Ireland Defender of if Faith.

FIG. 31.2 *The High and Mighty Monarch Charles.* Portrait of Charles I, wearing lace collar and chain (ca. 1640s).

and on the left side of his face. Nor is the distinction between king and subject wholly marked, as no royal regalia are present, with only a simple 'Carolus Rex' lettered on the black coffin.

Despite the immediate emotional impact and the close-up accessibility of the striking, even macabre, painting, its precise narrative remains stubbornly opaque. Genre does not aid interpretation, as Delaroche moves between classical and Romantic modes of painting, and between history and genre painting in a new mode of 'historical genre' that is full of local colour and precise detail. The work cannot be characterized as tragic or comic, as beautiful or ugly. The private moment is made public. Yet what exactly is that private moment? Cromwell's face is impassive, unreadable. The viewer must supply for him or herself the meaning of the scene.

A popular painter, Delaroche was accused, even in his own day, of pandering to the public, of sensational and even melodramatic representation. A number of his paintings—including the highly popular *Execution of Lady Jane Grey* (1833) and the *Two Princes in the Tower* (1830)—capture a moment of imminent trauma.[22] Yet what is the trauma in the portrait of Cromwell and Charles I? Does the painting represent the king's recent trauma: the off-stage trial and execution? Or, more

FIG. 31.3 *Olivarius Cromwell Exercituum Angliae Reipublicae Dux Generalis.* Portrait of Cromwell on horseback, with the Thames and a view of London in background (c. 1655).

in line with Delaroche's other paintings, does it intimate a trauma to come, representing a moment of recognition that will haunt and even torment Oliver Cromwell? Furthermore, what, precisely, would the obvious parallels—Cromwell and Napoleon, Charles I and the executed Louis XVI—mean as an interpretation of recent French history or present politics? Does the painting on balance guide the viewers' sympathy towards the monarchy? If so, does that sympathy endorse the current French king, the 'usurper' Louis-Philippe, or point back at the now-exiled Bourbons? Or does it simply show nostalgia and recognition of the king's full humanity, while acknowledging the power of might over right? Does the portrait recommend—or warn against—another Napoleon? The portrait pulls a wide audience into history in the present tense, conveying the tension, but gives the viewer the opportunity—or burden—of interpreting for him or herself.

In its refusal of judgement, even interpretation, the painting differs significantly from Delaroche's historiographical sources. Delaroche attributed the source of the composition to French diplomat, politician, and writer François-René, vicomte de Chateaubriand, whose pro-Bourbon historiography *Les Quatre Stuarts* (1828) depicts Cromwell gloating over and touching the head of the dead king.[23] If this is indeed Delaroche's source, he has significantly altered Cromwell's reaction. Another possible source that describes the coffin scene is French Protestant and historian François Guizot's *Histoire de la Révolution d'Angleterre* (1826-7), which depicts Cromwell as even lifting up the head.[24] Both Chateaubriand and Guizot describe the scene to undergird their own political views and bring closure to the revolutionary upheaval and its aftermath in France. For Chateaubriand, the coffin scene with the martyred monarch and gloating Cromwell epitomizes the wrongs of revolution, righted and ended with the restoration of the Bourbons (which had, of course, changed by 1831). For Guizot, the closure came not with the Bourbons but with the constitutional monarch Louis-Philippe, under whom he became chief minister: in Guizot's view, 1640 and 1789 were alike 'Revolutions' against absolutism.[25] But Delaroche significantly resists any such closure.

While the coffin scene may have been prompted by the historiographers, Delaroche's painting has more in common with his predecessors in early nineteenth-century historical fiction and drama—both British and French—on the English civil wars. Delaroche's ideas about Cromwell were quite likely influenced by Sir Walter Scott's historical novel, *Woodstock* (1826), which depicts a moment of startled recognition and guilt for Cromwell (albeit not a coffin scene) that had gained additional prominence in being illustrated by Delaroche's fellow French artist, Delacroix.[26] The portrait resonates, as well, with French Romantic writer Victor Hugo's long unacted drama, *Cromwell* (1827), the Preface to which was an important manifesto for Romanticism. Each of these fictional works reworks historical sources to offer to its readers a complex Cromwellian interiority at a moment of moral crisis. Each uses art to make history present tense and immediate, and each provides an open-ended representation that calls for an active reader, refusing easy answers or black-and-white distinctions.

SIR WALTER SCOTT, HISTORICAL FICTION, AND THE PRESENTNESS OF THE PAST

Through the medium of fiction, the highly influential Scots writer, Sir Walter Scott brought English revolutionary history to a much wider audience.[27] The form of the historical novel not only narrates events, but lets the reader into the minds of characters, including Oliver Cromwell. In the words of one Scott scholar, 'History was conceived as a drama that unfolded as if in the reader's own moment, creating an engulfing illusion of proximity.'[28] Indeed, the particularities of Scott's historical fiction may have cut against its seeming universality in a narrative of British progress and eventual unification; the Stuarts were treated with nostalgia, but ultimately relegated to the past.[29]

Scott's Waverley novels had helped to create and popularize the genre of historical fiction, in no small part due to his reinvention of the Stuarts, from Bonnie Prince Charles or the 'Young Pretender' (grandson of the exiled James II and VII and focus of 'Jacobite' sympathies until his final defeat at the battle of Culloden in 1746) in his first novel, *Waverley* (1814), to *Woodstock* (1824), an account set three years after the regicide. Scott deploys the subject matter of the English Revolution to transform fictional form and genre, and what are usually considered his best works include the long history of the Stuarts. The tensions and ambivalences of the civil war are most fully dramatized in *Woodstock* in a romance between the Presbyterian Markham Everard and Alice Lee, daughter of the fiercely royalist Sir Henry Lee, and in the story of the royalist Wildrake.

Scott's characteristic practice was to focus his novels on a fictional character set in precise historical circumstances, some of which included interaction with real historical personages.[30] *Woodstock* narrates the story of Wildrake, a cavalier, and Markham Everard, a Presbyterian who shields his cavalier friend by letting him act as secretary or clerk. Much of this long and complex novel focuses on the adventures of fictional characters. Yet for all of the sprawling plot and action of the novel, a single private moment stands out. A central revelatory scene lets the reader into Cromwell as a conflicted, complex character caught in a moment of remorse and irresolution, as he looks not into a coffin but at a van Dyck portrait of the late Charles I.

If the genre of historical fiction shapes the character of Cromwell, Cromwell also reshapes the genre: *Woodstock* is atypical of Scott's works in its fast-moving pace, the relatively early introduction of the 'historical' character, Cromwell, and in giving Cromwell a sustained monologue.[31] Scott (whose work precedes and influences Delaroche, Richards, and—as we will see—Victor Hugo) memorably depicts an ambivalent Cromwell who is startled into recognition of his own guilt by inadvertently viewing a van Dyck portrait of Charles I. When the royalist Wildrake seeks out Cromwell in the palace of Whitehall on behalf of his 'master' (but actually friend) Everard to ask that Woodstock be spared from parliamentary sequestration, he prompts a moment of introspection and potential moral crisis. At first, Cromwell impresses the seemingly incorrigible cavalier with his force of character. He reproves Wildrake for swearing and seems to be a stereotypical canting Puritan, with flashes of the ambition with which his opponents charged him. Cromwell doesn't fully trust the Presbyterian Everard, despite Everard's undoubted integrity and strength of character. Hence, he asks Wildrake essentially to spy on his master and keep an eye out for the fugitive Charles II, as the rambling palace of Woodstock would be an ideal hiding place. Wildrake manages to convince Cromwell to overrule his grasping colleagues and relatives, who expect material gain from the palace of Woodstock, on the grounds that the fugitive Stuart's return will be much more likely if the palace is not sequestered but left to its royalist keepers. Cromwell clearly intends to use the issue of control over Woodstock to challenge the power of the parliament, now increasingly at odds with the army.

When Wildrake feigns ignorance and asks how he is to recognize Charles, he inadvertently precipitates a crisis. Cromwell replies: 'A tall, rawboned, swarthy lad, they say he has shot up into. Here is his picture by a good hand, some time since', and he turns around 'one of the portraits which stood with its face against the wall'.[32] But the portrait turns out 'not to be that of Charles the Second, but of his unhappy father', prompting a quite unexpected reaction.

As Wildrake watches, silent and wondering, Cromwell forces himself to look at the portrait, 'as one who compels himself to look on what some strong internal feeling renders painful and disgustful to him' (124), and he proceeds to a kind of 'spontaneous unburdening of his own bosom, swelling under recollection of the past and anticipation of the future'(125):

> 'That Flemish painter' he said—'that Antonio Vandyke—what a power he has! Steel may mutilate, warriors may waste and destroy—still the King stands uninjured by time; and our grandchildren, while they read his history, may look on his image, and compare the melancholy features with the woful tale.—It was a stern necessity—it was an awful deed!' (125)

Deeply moved by the power of the dead king's image, Cromwell nonetheless insists on the necessity of the regicide, but he is unable to bring himself to name the 'awful deed'. He thus reveals his guilt in the act of denying it:

> 'Then, what is that piece of painted canvas to me more than others? No; let him show to others the reproaches of that cold, calm face, that proud yet complaining eye: Those who have acted on higher respects have no cause to start at painted shadows. Not wealth nor power brought me from my obscurity. The oppressed consciences, the injured liberties of England, were the banner that I followed.' (125)

In this moment of soliloquy, the various masks that Cromwell uses throughout to manipulate others fall away. But the reader is left not with clarity but complexity, with a glimpse of differing, even inconsistent motives and feelings within the character himself. Ideals mingle with ambition, and the sublime with the base. Yet the historical figure comes into sharp focus—and into the foreground—only briefly, and Scott soon returns to the adventures of his fictional creatures.

Produced on the stage as a melodrama in both England and France, and immediately translated into French, *Woodstock* (as with Scott's novels in general) had a huge

European influence.[33] Most pertinent for our interests, *Woodstock* also seems to have shaped Victor Hugo's *Cromwell*. Hugo, who read all of Scott almost immediately in the translations provided by Auguste-Jean-Baptiste Defauconpret, expands upon the moral dilemma for Cromwell: and for the reader.[34]

VICTOR HUGO AND FRENCH ROMANTIC DRAMA

We have been exploring how, in an important cultural legacy of the English Revolution, nineteenth-century visual and literary art both represents and continues aspects of the Revolution itself. In a kind of 'democratization' of experience, historical personages are brought close-up to the reader or viewer, who becomes perforce part of the moment of change, decision, and trauma, evoking the activist readers of the English Revolution. That this cultural legacy must be traced not only in Britain, but in Europe more broadly, reminds us as well of the European context—and impact—of the English Revolution.

Through his unacted play, *Cromwell* (1827), Victor Hugo became the spokesman for and prime representative of a French Romantic drama that overturned neo-classical strictures, no longer observing the unities of time and place, featuring a sprawling and multi-faceted (if single) plot, and mingling comic and tragic elements, the grotesque and the sublime.[35] The complex and controversial character of Oliver Cromwell suited or even inspired this bold remaking of genre and form. Indeed, *Cromwell*, with its Preface that set out the new aesthetic principles, became 'the quintessential Romantic rejection of French neo-classical theatre'.[36]

Hugo was not a republican in 1827, although his views may have already been in transition. While he had earlier adhered to his mother's royalism, and was largely estranged from his father, a former Napoleonic officer, Hugo came to admire, even to be obsessed with, the figure of Napoleon, whose imperial victories he viewed as having brought glory to France and as consolidating the achievements of the French Revolution.[37] In 1826–7, with the Bourbons seemingly firmly back on the throne, Hugo could only indirectly explore Napoleonic character, and he found in Cromwell an analogous republican and military leader, who like Napoleon was tempted to take the throne. There is a great deal of external and oppositional action in the drama, but, as we shall see, there is also a central moment of moral crisis—like Cromwell before the portrait of Charles I in Scott's *Woodstock* or (after Hugo and Scott) like Delaroche's Cromwell peering into the king's coffin.

The multi-faceted action in Hugo's *Cromwell* seems to focus on machinations and manoeuvring in the struggle between the conspirators and Cromwell. The conspirators (a temporary and self-serving alliance of puritans and cavaliers) meet in early morning at the Three Cranes Inn to conclude their alliance and plan Cromwell's assassination for the very day that he is to take the crown. The conspirators are largely a craven, self-serving bunch, whether canting puritans (the ambitious Lambert, grasping and avaricious Barebones, duplicitous Davenant) or hot-headed cavaliers (the rake Rochester, who has fallen in love with Cromwell's daughter, Frances, and who plagues the others with his foolish love poems). At the behest of King Charles II himself, the cavaliers launch a second, secret and improbable plot to insinuate Rochester into the Cromwellian household as a godly puritan minister, giving them access by which they can kidnap Cromwell and bring him to the king.

Yet for all of the intrigue and the plotting against him, Cromwell remains in control of the action. With spies both in the royalist and the puritan camps, Cromwell soon learns of the double conspiracy. Substituting the false chaplain for himself in his bed, Cromwell disguises himself as a sentinel to watch and then expose the royalist conspirators. Although forced while in disguise to hear and tolerate all manner of criticism of himself—often with comic effects—Cromwell never seems to be in actual physical danger. He sends the royalists off to prison, to be hung on the day of the coronation.

Thus, despite all the seeming external action, it could be argued that the most profound drama in *Cromwell* is internal. The real struggle is the moral dilemma within Cromwell, analogous to that staged by Hugo for many of his fictional protagonists. As Isabel Roche writes, while the 'universality and ultimate accessibility' of Hugo's works help to explain their wide hold and staying power, yet nothing is uncomplicated: 'For behind the immediate accessibility and the famous use of antithesis lies a world of gray in which spiritual, moral, and political clarity are far from given.'[38] As in the novels, *Cromwell* does not provide any easy answers.

Indeed, the complex figure of Cromwell enables Hugo to articulate a manifesto for a new, Romantic mode of literature that challenges set boundaries and genres. The Preface to *Cromwell* comments on how historians have left the figure of Cromwell incomplete:

> Olivier Cromwell est du nombre de ces personnages de l'histoire qui sont tout ensemble très célèbres et très peu connus. La plupart de ses biographes, et dans le nombre il en est qui sont historiens, ont laissé incomplète cette grande figure. Il semble qu'ils n'aient pas osé réunir tous les traits de ce bizarre et colossal prototype de la réforme religieuse, de la révolution politique d'Angleterre. (78)

> [Oliver Cromwell is one of those historical characters who are at once very famous and very little known. Most of his biographers—and among them there are some who are themselves historical—have left that colossal figure incomplete. It would seem that they dared not assemble all the characteristic features of that strange and gigantic prototype of the religious reformation, of the political revolution of England. (43)]

As Hugo explains in the Preface, heterogeneity and complexity of character link Cromwell with the figure of Napoleon himself. Hugo sees the turning-point for Cromwell at the moment not of regicide but when he seems about to take, and then suddenly rejects, the crown. Why does he refuse it? As Hugo writes, this is a question which no contemporary document answers satisfactorily: 'Tant mieux: la liberté du poëte en est plus entière, et le drame gagne à ces latitudes que lui laisse l'histoire' (80) ['So much the better: the poet's liberty is the more complete, and the drama is the gainer by the latitude which history affords it' (45)].

In addressing Cromwell's refusal of the crown during his single-person Protectorate, Hugo's *Cromwell* provides a much more extensive account than in Scott's *Woodstock* (set under the Republic). Yet Scott's central moment of recognition seems to have shaped Hugo's more complex and darker character.[39] The moment of recognition, of gazing upon the dead king (metaphorically), comes in Act Two, scene fifteen of the drama, when Cromwell is on the stage alone (or so he thinks) for the first time. The setting, significantly, is the Banqueting House at Whitehall, before which Charles I was publicly executed. The rhetorical masks that Cromwell has employed with the ambassadors and when trying to seek information from his spies drop away. The audience sees the man himself in soliloquy, seeming to recognize for the first time the scope of his own ambition. Cromwell speaks repeatedly in the interrogative:

> Que veux-tu donc, Cromwell? Dis? un trône! A quoi bon?
> Te nommes-tu Stuart? Plantagenet? Bourbon?
> Es-tu de ces mortels qui, grâce à leurs ancêtres,
> Tout enfants, pour la terre ont eu des yeux de maîtres?
> Quel sceptre, heureux soldat, sous ton poids ne se rompt?
> Quelle couronne est faite à l'ampleur de ton front?
> Toi, roi, fils du hasard!
> . . . .
> Ta maison,—dynastie! (2, 15)

>   [Cromwell, say,
> What wouldst thou? Is't a throne? Wherefore a throne?
> Is thy name Stuart, or Plantagenet,
> Or Bourbon? Art thou of that race of men,
> Who, from their birth, thanks to their ancestors,
> Have viewed the whole world with a master's eye?
> What sceptre does not break beneath thy weight,
> O fortune-favoured soldier? And what crown
> Is made to fit thy amplitude of brow?
> Thou, King, the child of chance!
> . . . .
> Thy family—a dynasty! (2.15)]

Hugo's Cromwell is so conflicted that Rochester, as he steps closer to listen in, takes him to be a secret royalist. Like Macbeth recognizing that his fatal ambition will drive him to both worldly infamy and eternal damnation, Cromwell recognizes that the throne may be aligned with, even a stepping-stone to, the scaffold. Filled, again like Macbeth, with horror at his own thoughts, he attempts to get fresh air by opening the window through which the king stepped to his death. The window, however, remains shut, as if sealed with the king's blood: 'C'est du sang de Stuart la fenêtre souillée!' ['With the Stuart blood, | The window's marred!'].

The window in Whitehall which ushered the king onto the scaffold serves, like the van Dyck portrait in Scott's *Woodstock*, to bring a moment of tragic insight, remorse, and regret: 'Oui, c'est de là qu'il prit son essor vers les cieux!' ['Ay, thence he took his flight

| Toward heaven!']. Charles is the innocent, wronged figure that we see in Scott or the white-clothed serene figure that Delaroche will later depict in his painting. Cromwell himself attests to the goodness of the king and feels guilt for his own impious deed ('attentat impie'), which like Scott's Cromwell he cannot bring himself to name. Guilt competes with ambition, recognition of the king's virtues with justification of his death. Cromwell's assertion of the king's goodness—'Jamais plus noble front n'orna le dais royal; | Charles premier fut juste et bon.' ['A nobler brow ne'er graced the royal seat. | A good man and a just was Charles the First.']—prompts the listening Rochester to exclaim: 'Sujet loyal!'

Yet, as with Scott's Cromwell, the moment of tragic recognition cannot be sustained, and Hugo's Cromwell turns to self-justification, albeit still in the interrogative mode:

> Pouvais-je empêcher, moi, ces fureurs meurtrières?
> Mortifications, veilles, jeûnes, prières,
> Pour sauver la victime ai-je rien épargné?
> Mais son arrêt de mort au ciel était signé. (2, 15)

> [How could I forestall
> That murd'rous frenzy? Spared I aught of prayers,
> Of vigils and of fasts to save the victim?
> But his decree of death was signed in heav'n. (2.15)]

The 'stern necessity' of Scott's Cromwell finds a dark echo here. Hugo's Cromwell, haunted by remorse for killing the king, shows even more deeply the struggle between lofty ideals and ruthless ambition.

Yet this recognition scene in Hugo's drama is complicated and compromised. Cromwell is misunderstood by Rochester, who approaches him as a fellow-royalist, so that comic mix-ups follow closely upon near-tragic insights. Further, Cromwell himself seems to use the tragic insight gained to dissemble resistance to the crown in the later coronation scene. The tortured questions that in Act Two come from anguish and guilt competing with ambition are used as a cynical political ploy in the final act of the drama.

Hugo's Cromwell brilliantly outmanoeuvres his opponents in the political game. His rejecting the crown in the middle of the coronation that he has himself arranged (Act Five, scene twelve) wins back the praise of the fickle people, who have been complaining bitterly. Cromwell now turns his guilt-filled questioning into political theatre in (seemingly) refusing the crown:

> Arrêtez!
> Que veut dire ceci? Pourquoi cette couronne?
> Que veut-on que j'en fasse? et qui donc me la donne?
> Est-ce un rêve? Est-ce bien le bandeau que je vois?
> De quel droit me vient-on confondre avec les rois?
> Qui mêle un tel scandale à nos pieuses fêtes?
> Quoi! Leur couronne, à moi qui fais tomber leurs têtes!
> S'est-on mépris au but de ces solennités? (5, 12)

> [How now! What means this? Why this crown—to me?
> What would you that I do with it? And who
> Doth give it me, I pray? Is it a dream?

> Is it, in truth, the diadem I see?
> And by what right do ye with kings confound me?
> Who dares into our pious festivals
> Such scandal to import?—Their crown, to me
> Who caused their heads to fall!—Have you mistook
> The purpose of this ceremonial? (5.12)]

Having manipulated the parliament into offering him the crown, Cromwell now feigns surprise and disbelief, still in interrogative mode: 'Mais la couronne royale! | Quand l'ai-je demandée? Et qui dit que j'en veux?' ['But for the crown—when did I ask for it? | Who says that I would have it?' (5.12)]. Seemingly about to take the crown, Cromwell rejects it in an ostentatious show that brings him new acclaim. He then publicly forgives the puritan conspirators, gaining even further power. When the royalist conspirators come in to claim that, given their nobility, they should be beheaded rather than hanged, Oliver forgives them too. Public mercy and forgiveness gain him the people—and even more power than if he had taken on the formal title of king.

Despite the assertion of the Preface, the last Act of Hugo's *Cromwell* does not answer the questions left out by historians. How is the reader to judge Cromwell? Cromwell is not a tragic hero, who makes a mistake, achieves recognition, and pays for it, restoring, though at great cost, his former status. The ending of *Cromwell* is neither happy nor unhappy. And indeed, the refusal of the crown seems to be merely temporary expedience. The drama ends with another question, as Cromwell, left alone on the stage, muses: 'Quand donc serai-je roi?' [When shall I be king? (5.12)]. Hugo sets out to explore the mindset of a highly successful military conqueror whose early support for the Republic turned to self-aggrandizement, leading to an eventual fall. But the present-tense fictionalized history pulls the reader into moral ambiguity.

Strikingly, then, one important long-term effect of the English revolutionary crisis on forms of cultural expression is not the representation of any particular political message, but almost the opposite: a kind of open-endedness and need for interpretation. Hugo asserts in his Preface to *Cromwell* that the fiction writer moves into historiographical gaps. But, as we have seen, such a move raises more questions than it answers, resisting closure and empowering the viewer with aesthetic and moral choices. Looking at Cromwell as he looks at Charles I—whether in a coffin, in a painting, or through a window sealed with blood—the reader or viewer is also drawn into a moral dilemma, forced to react, experience, interpret, and judge. And if, unlike the audience at Richards's late Victorian drama, a twenty-first-century audience may not overtly laugh, hiss, or applaud, we can still be moved and challenged by the figures, issues, and situations of the English Revolution, powerfully recreated in visual art and literature.

Notes

1. 'Queen's Theatre', *The Morning Post* (23 December 1672). This largely negative reviewer of Richards's *Cromwell* pronounces that 'from the dramatic point of view, the play is hopeless', tedious despite its 'psychological value' and 'rhetorical force', but he discloses his royalist

sympathies by commenting that 'regal sorrows prove tenfold more touching than those of men self-exalted'. Contemporary notices and reviews remark on the ideological conflict of the two plays: e.g., *The Graphic*, 'The Theatres', 7 December 1872 ('It is understood that this piece will represent the Puritan view of the times of the First Charles and the Commonwealth, and may thus serve as an antidote to the enthusiastic loyalty of Mr. Wills's *Charles I*. at the Lyceum'). See also the discussion in Martin Meisel, *Realizations: Narrative, Pictorial, and Theatrical Arts in Nineteenth-Century England* (Princeton, 1983), 239–44.

2. Nigel Smith, *Literature and Revolution in England, 1640–1660* (New Haven, 1994); Laura Lunger Knoppers (ed.), *The Oxford Handbook of Literature and the English Revolution* (Oxford, 2012). On the transformative effects of the 1640s crisis on the legitimating languages, rituals, and performances of political culture more broadly, see Michael J. Braddick, 'The English Revolution and Its Legacies', in Nicholas Tyacke (ed.), *The English Revolution, c.1590–1720: Politics, Religion and Communities* (Manchester, 2007), 27–42.

3. See Laura Lunger Knoppers, *Constructing Cromwell: Ceremony, Portrait, and Print, 1645–1661* (Cambridge, 2000).

4. On long-term representations of the English civil wars, see Blair Worden, *Roundhead Reputations: The English Civil Wars and the Passions of Posterity* (London, 2001); R. C. Richardson (ed.), *Images of Oliver Cromwell: Essays for and by Roger Howell, Jr.* (Manchester, 1993). On the Victorians, see Roy Strong, *Recreating the Past: British History and the Victorian Painter* (London, 1978); Timothy Lang, *The Victorians and the Stuart Heritage: Interpretations of a Discordant Past* (Cambridge, 1995); Susie Steinbach, *Understanding the Victorians: Politics, Culture, and Society in Nineteenth-Century Britain* (New York, 2012). On shifting representations of Cromwell in nineteenth-century France, see Beth Wright, 'Delaroche's *Cromwell* and the Historians', *Word & Image*, 16.1 (January–March 2000): 77–90.

5. Beth Wright comments on the 'doubled time' in 'The Space of Time: Delaroche's Depiction of Modern Historical Narrative', *Nineteenth-Century French Studies*, 36.1 & 2 (Fall–Winter 2007): 72–92. On French artists shaping the future by re-imaging the past, see Beth S. Wright, *Painting and History during the French Restoration: Abandoned by the Past* (New York, 1997), 8–9.

6. On the experience of catastrophe, see Wright, *Painting and History*, chap. 4.

7. On the Revolution as an opening up of a public sphere of rational debate, prompting activist readers and expanded political opinion, see Sharon Achinstein, *Milton and the Revolutionary Reader* (Princeton, 1994); David Norbrook, '*Areopagitica*, Censorship and the Early Modern Public Sphere', in Richard Burt (ed.), *The Administration of Aesthetics: Censorship, Political Criticism, and the Public Sphere* (Minneapolis, 1994), 3–33; Joad Raymond, *The Invention of the Newspaper: English Newsbooks, 1641–1649* (Oxford, 1996); Raymond, 'The Newspaper, Public Opinion and the Public Sphere in the Seventeenth Century', in Joad Raymond (ed.), *News, Newspapers and Society in Early Modern Britain* (London, 1999), 109–40; and Jason Peacey, 'News, Pamphlets, and Public Opinion', in Knoppers (ed.), *The Oxford Handbook of Literature and the English Revolution*, 173–89.

8. Steinbach, *Understanding the Victorians*.

9. Strong, *Recreating the Past*; see also Laura Lunger Knoppers, *Politicizing Domesticity from Henrietta Maria to Milton's Eve* (Cambridge, 2011), Introduction.

10. On Victorian historiographers, including the influential Whig Samuel Rawson Gardiner, see Nicholas Tyacke, 'Introduction: Locating the English Revolution', in Tyacke (ed.), *The English Revolution*, 1–8.

11. Steinbach, *Understanding the Victorians*, 156–7.

12. All quotations are from Alfred Bate Richards, *Oliver Cromwell: An Historical Tragedy, in a Prologue and Four Acts* (2nd edition, London, 1873) and are cited by Act and scene number.

13. The most positive review of the coffin scene may have been in an early notice of the play ('Oliver Cromwell', *The Era*, 1 December 1872): 'The soliloquy and the entire business of this scene is dramatic and powerful in the extreme. It is the conception of a true poet and a keen observer of human motives and feelings.' Later reviewers recognized the pictorial source, with differing reactions, e.g., 'The realisation of the well-known picture by Paul Delaroche, of Cromwell gazing into the coffin of the dead Charles, had not the effect that might have been expected. The scene was too dark, and the soliloquy of Cromwell too long' ('Queen's Theatre', *The Standard*, 23 December 1872), or, 'A scene in which (after the picture of Delaroche) Cromwell is seen beside the coffin containing the body of Charles I and which might be expected to revolt the audience was … one of the most successful' ('Queen's *Daily News*', 27 December 1872).

14. On the French Revolution and its long aftermath, see François Furet, *Revolutionary France, 1770–1880*, trans. Antonia Nevill (1988; Oxford, 2000).

15. See the early study by Norman D. Ziff, *Paul Delaroche: A Study in Nineteenth-Century French History Painting* (New York and London, 1977), 105–16 on *Cromwell*; Wright, *Painting and History*, 103–8 on *Cromwell*; Stephen Bann, *Paul Delaroche: History Painted* (Princeton, 1997), 107–15 on *Cromwell* and 111–13 on engravings of *Cromwell* by Henrique-Dupont.

16. On Delacroix's paintings, see Wright, 'Delaroche's *Cromwell* and the Historians'; Wright, 'The Space of Time'.

17. Meisel, *Realizations*, 230–2.

18. For instance, Susan L. Siegfried, 'Ingres and the Theatrics of History Painting', *Word & Image*, 16.1 (January–March 2000): 58–76, writes that the emotionally charged interaction of Delaroche's paintings elicited (as in the theatre) spectators' empathy with the protagonist. Siegfried explains that *Cromwell* stopped people in their tracks: 'people forgot themselves in front of the canvas and entered the drama of history' (70).

19. Wright, *Painting and History*, 81.

20. On van Dyck, see Karen Hearn (ed.), *Van Dyck and Britain* (London, 2009).

21. On Cromwellian portraiture, see Laura Lunger Knoppers, 'The Politics of Portraiture: Oliver Cromwell and the Plain Style', *Renaissance Quarterly*, 51 (1998): 1283–1319; and *Constructing Cromwell*.

22. On the witnessing of catastrophe, see Stephen Bann, *The Clothing of Clio: A Study of the Representation of History in Nineteenth-Century Britain and France* (Cambridge, 1984), 75.

23. Chateaubriand, *Les Quatre Stuarts (1828), in Œuvres Complètes*, 28 vols. (Paris, 1826–31), 22: 182. On Chateaubriand, see Ziff, *Paul Delaroche*, 106; Wright, *Painting and History*, 96–108. The scene is almost certainly apocryphal, although Delaroche likely understood it as having actually occurred.

24. François Guizot, *Histoire de la Révolution d'Angleterre (1826–7)*, 2 vols. (4th edition, Paris, 1850), II, 528.

25. Indeed, it was the French historian Guizot who familiarized Victorians with the idea of 'Revolution' in mid-seventeenth-century England, as his works were widely translated into English. See Tyacke, 'Introduction', 6, and note 30.

26. On Delacroix's illustrations of Scott, see Beth S. Wright, 'An Image for Imagining the Past: Delacroix, Cromwell, and Romantic Historical Painting', *Clio*, 21.3 (1992): 243–63, 256–60. Delacroix would later criticize the lack of emotion in Delaroche's *Cromwell*, and did several studies himself of the coffin scene, see Wright, 'An Image', 253–6.

27. Richard Maxwell, *The Historical Novel in Europe, 1650–1950* (Cambridge, 2009), 3.
28. Maxwell, *Historical Novel*, 4.
29. Murray Pittock, 'Sir Walter Scott: Historiography Contested by Fiction', in Robert L. Caserio and Clement Hawes (eds.), *Cambridge History of the English Novel* (Cambridge, 2012), 277–91.
30. On this practice, illustrated with reference to *Waverley*, see Maxwell, *Historical Novel*, 47–58.
31. I owe these insights to my colleague Robert Caserio.
32. Sir Walter Scott, *Woodstock, or the Cavalier, vol. 21, The Waverley Novels*, 25 vols. (London and New York, 1880), 124.
33. Murray Pittock, 'Introduction: Scott and the European Nationalities Question', and Richard Maxwell, 'Scott in France', in Murray Pittock (ed.), *The Reception of Sir Walter Scott in Europe* (London, 2006), 1–10, 11–30.
34. See Paul Barnaby, 'Another Tale of Old Mortality: The Translations of Auguste-Jean-Baptiste Defauconpret in the French Reception of Scott', in Pittock (ed.), *Reception of Sir Walter Scott*, 31–44.
35. All French citations are from Hugo, *Cromwell*, vol. 3, 1–2, *Œuvres Complètes*, ed. Jean Massin, 18 vols. (Paris, 1967–70). English translations are taken from Victor Hugo, *Cromwell, vol. 3, Dramas*, trans. George Burnham Ives, 3 vols. (Boston, 1909). On the generic mixture and Romanticism in the early novels, see Kathryn M. Grossman, *The Early Novels of Victor Hugo: Towards a Poetics of Harmony* (Histoire des idées et critique littéraire, 241; Geneva, 1986). I am grateful to my colleague Kathryn Grossman for her insightful suggestions on my discussion of Hugo.
36. Albert W. Halsall, *Hugo and the Romantic Drama* (Toronto, 1998), 52.
37. Halsall, *Hugo and the Romantic Drama*. See also Maurice Descotes, *L'Obsession de Napoléon dans le 'Cromwell' de Victor Hugo* (Paris, 1967).
38. Isabel Roche, *Character and Meaning in the Novels of Victor Hugo* (West Lafayette, IN, 2007), 2–3. Roche also notes Hugo's interest in encouraging the reader's 'thoughtful involvement' (8).
39. Keith Wren, 'Cromwell and Woodstock', in A. R. W. James (ed.), *Victor Hugo et la Grande-Bretagne* (Liverpool, 1986), 27–38, argues that Hugo's darkening of the character comes from his antipathy to Cromwell's crime of regicide.

Further Reading

Achinstein, Sharon, *Milton and the Revolutionary Reader* (Princeton, 1994).
Bann, Stephen, *The Clothing of Clio: A Study of the Representation of History in Nineteenth-Century Britain and France* (Cambridge, 1984).
Bann, Stephen, *Paul Delaroche: History Painted* (Princeton, 1997).
Halsall, Albert W., *Victor Hugo and the Romantic Drama* (Toronto, 1998).
Hugo, Victor, *Cromwell, vol. 3, pts.1–2, Œuvres Complètes*, ed. Jean Massin, 18 vols. (Paris, 1967–70).
James, A. R. W., *Victor Hugo et la Grande-Bretagne* (Liverpool, 1986).
Knoppers, Laura Lunger, *Constructing Cromwell: Ceremony, Portrait, and Print, 1645–61* (Cambridge, 2000).
Knoppers, Laura Lunger (ed.), *The Oxford Handbook of Literature and the English Revolution* (Oxford, 2012).

Meisel, Martin, *Realizations: Narrative, Pictorial, and Theatrical Arts in Nineteenth-Century England* (Princeton, 1983).

Richards, Alfred Bate, *Oliver Cromwell: An Historical Tragedy, in a Prologue and Four Acts* (2nd edition, London, 1873).

Richardson, R. C. (ed.), *Images of Oliver Cromwell: Essays for and by Roger Howell, Jr.* (Manchester, 1993).

Scott, Sir Walter, *Woodstock, or the Cavalier, vol. 21, The Waverley Novels*, 25 vols. (London and New York, 1880).

Strong, Roy, *Recreating the Past: British History and the Victorian Painter* (London, 1978).

Worden, Blair, *Roundhead Reputations: The English Civil Wars and the Passions of Posterity* (London, 2001).

Wright, Beth S., 'Delaroche's *Cromwell* and the Historians', *Word & Image*, 16.1 (January–March 2000): 77–90.

Wright, Beth S., *Painting and History during the French Restoration: Abandoned by the Past* (New York, 1997).

CHAPTER 32

THE ENGLISH REVOLUTION IN BRITISH AND IRISH CONTEXT

JOHN MORRILL

THE ENGLISH KILL A BRITISH KING

THE public trial and execution of a king is a revolutionary act by any standard. He was tried by martial law,[1] so there was no indictment, only a 'charge', which began:

> That the said Charles Stuart, being admitted *King of England*, and therein trusted with a limited power to govern by and according to the laws of the land.... yet, nevertheless, out of a wicked design to erect and uphold in himself an unlimited and tyrannical power to rule according to his will, and to overthrow the rights and liberties of the people, yea, to take away and make void the foundations thereof.... hath traitorously and maliciously levied war against the present Parliament, and the people therein represented [eleven military episodes enumerated].... and by divisions, parties, and insurrections within this land, by *invasions from foreign parts*, endeavoured and procured by him, and by many other evil ways and means, he, the said Charles Stuart, hath not only maintained and carried on the said war both by land and sea, during the years beforementioned, but also hath renewed, or caused to be renewed, the said war against the Parliament and good people of this nation in this present year 1648, in [many] Counties and places in England and Wales, and also by sea.... And for further prosecution of his said evil designs, he, the said Charles Stuart, doth still continue his commissions to the said Prince [of Wales], and other rebels and revolters, *both English and foreigners*, and to the Earl of Ormond, and the Irish rebels and revolters associated with him; from whom further *invasions* upon this land are threatened, upon the procurement, and on the behalf of the said Charles Stuart.[2]

A few days later, 59 *English* commissioners signed the King's death warrant:

> Whereas Charles Stuart, *King of England*, is, and standeth convicted, attainted, and condemned of high treason, and other high crimes; and…. to be put to death by the severing of his head from his body…. And for so doing this shall be your sufficient warrant And these are to require all officers, soldiers, and others, the good people of *this nation of England*, to be assisting unto you in this service.[3]

This was, then, an English trial of an English king for being 'the occasioner, author, and continuer of the said unnatural, cruel and bloody wars; and therein guilty of all the treasons, murders, rapines, burnings, spoils, desolations, damages and mischiefs to this nation'. English king, English nation, English trial, English execution. When he brought his subjects from Scotland and Ireland into this unnatural, cruel, and bloody war, they were 'foreigners' and their participation was 'invasion'. But Charles I *was* also king of Scotland and Ireland. Scotland was by January 1649 under the control of the Scottish allies of the English parliament, secured in power by an English 'invasion' just three months previously. Yet on three separate occasions (6, 17, and 21 January 1649) the commissioners of the Scottish parliament vainly protested that not only was the English parliament failing to honour its commitment to introduce a confederal government for church and state in Britain, but that 'applications are made to you for proceeding against the king to take away his life and for changing the government of *this kingdom* [i.e. Scotland]'. There was the rub. The English intended unilaterally to kill the king of a composite monarchy. The commissioners went on to denounce the 'strong endeavours on foot' to 'overturn the whole work of reformation', to 'introduce a toleration of all religions and forms of worship'. In short the Rump of the Long Parliament intended to 'frustrate *all* the ends of the Solemn League and Covenant'. They then reminded the English of all the engagements they were under to work with and not against the Scottish interest and under and through the Covenant: 'wherefore, they concluded, we do expect that there shall be no proceeding against his person'.[4] King Cnut could not have written a more futile injunction against the rising tide of revolution. On each occasion, the Commons voted not to open the letters, let alone read them. Abandoning protocol, on 25 January the Scottish Commissioners caused all three letters to be published; but still parliament snubbed them.[5]

It was all in vain. On 30 January 1649, the English parliament executed the King of Scots without ever having consulted them. They tried to ignore the existence of a Scottish crown. Indeed, an Act was rushed through on the morning of Charles's execution to prevent any successor from being proclaimed and forbade any proclamation of a new 'King of England or Ireland or the Dominions thereof';[6] a form closely followed five weeks later in the Act abolishing the Kingly Office.[7] Similarly the House of Lords, itself ignored by the Commons throughout the period of the king's trial and execution, in a futile attempt to claim some part in the post-Caroline settlement, voted on 1 February to 'consider the settlement of the government of England and Ireland'.[8] As far as all those in power in early 1649 were concerned, the regnal Union of England and Scotland had been severed and Scotland was free to determine its own destiny. It was indeed a foreign country. At the heart of the English Revolution was a unilateral declaration of independence by England, a dissolution of the union of 1603.

But the Scots did not want to be independent. On the day they received news of the Regicide, the Scottish parliament declared that:

> For as much as the Kings Majesty who lately reigned is contrary to the dissent and protestation of this kingdom now removed by a violent death and that by the Lords Blessing there is left unto us as righteous heir and lawful successor, Charles Prince of Scotland and Wales, now King of Great Britain, France and Ireland, we the estates of Parliament of the kingdom of Scotland do therefore unanimously and cheerfully in recognizance and acknowledgement of his just right, title and succession to the Crowns of these kingdoms, hereby proclaim and declare to all the world that the said Lord and Prince Charles by the providence of God and by the lawful right of undoubted succession and descent King of Great Britain, France and Ireland.[9]

They did not proclaim Charles as a new King of Scotland. They proclaimed him as the new King of Great Britain, France, and Ireland. And, knowing as they did, that the Rump was actively considering putting prince Henry, the youngest of Charles I's sons, and a boy in their custody, on the throne in place of his father, they emphatically endorsed primogeniture and hereditary right. This put them on a double collision course with the parliament (and army) of England. The English had implicated Charles Prince of Wales in the treasons of his father and if monarchy was to be recreated it would be in his youngest of his three sons who was in their custody; and they had unilaterally ended the 'Kingdom of Great Britain'. They were now the 'Commonwealth of England and Ireland'.[10]

Scotland's British Problem

What happened in January 1649 shows us in stark detail the nature of Scotland's English problem, Ireland's British problem, and England's little Englander problem.

For the Scots, the Union of the Crowns had been a mitigated disaster. Many at the top of Scottish society and government had acquired positions at a *British* court at Whitehall, along with *English* titles and *English* brides. But Scotland was excluded from trade with England and its overseas colonies and markets; it played no part in the making of war and peace but suffered the consequences of English wars and English treaties. Policy for Scotland was increasingly made in England and the council in Edinburgh was increasingly required to deliver policy it did not make. Nowhere was this more obvious than in religion. Decades of anglic[an]ization of the Scottish church culminated in the promulgation of a prayer book based on English prayer books, one not seen, let alone approved, by any Scottish parliament or General Assembly, by the Scottish bishops collectively or even by the council. The result was the National Covenant, binding the Scots under God to defy the king. It was a national (or at least a Lowland Protestant) strike which would make the king's policies unenforceable. Or so they thought. They had not considered that Charles might use the resources of all his kingdoms (Highland Scots,

Protestant and Catholic Irish, English) to break their Covenant. From the time the Scots mobilized against this threat, they knew they had to achieve two things.

First, they achieved local self-determination under an extreme form of monarchical republicanism, with a king who lost control of policy-making in Scotland, who was constrained to meet parliament every third year without the forms of executive control (the Lords of the Articles) that had controlled the agenda of parliaments in recent reigns, who had to surrender any power over the kirk, with the abolition of episcopacy. It was one of the more unpleasant customs of victors in the great Gaelic and Norse periods, to put out the eyes of the defeated. In a sense in 1640–1 the Scots put out Charles I's constitutional eyes and cut off his ears (ministers who would report back to him) leaving him only with a tongue to speak but not command.

Second, the Scots needed not only a new relationship with their king, but a new relationship with the other kingdoms of their king. When the Scottish parliament sent its commissioners south to negotiate a peace after the second Bishops' War in the autumn of 1640, they issued a set of nineteen 'instructions' on the process of negotiation and seventeen 'groundworks' for a new federal or confederal constitution for Britain. The commissioners were to press for simultaneous meetings of the two parliaments every second or third year in which wrongs done by either nation to the other were to be tried, and commissioners appointed by both parliaments to treat about them. These commissioners were also to try (unspecified) differences betwixt the king and subject, and to take action against 'those who have given bad counsel' or encroached on the king's power or on the liberties of religion and country. Between parliaments each parliament would appoint *conservatores pacis* who would jointly 'try and remedy any wrongs that arise'. No armies were to be raised, no war declared without consent of both kingdoms. No monarch or heir to the throne was to marry without consent of both kingdoms (they did not realize they needed to add, 'or be put on trial for their lives'). And (and this is November 1640) 'a common confession of faith should be made for both kingdoms with mutual obligation to defend it' (and what did 'defend it' mean here?).[11] As it turned out, while the Long Parliament was happy to agree to all the terms set out in the 'instructions' they were no keener on these 'groundworks' than was the king and when the treaty of London was signed ten months later there was a deafening silence about confederation and all the issues raised in the groundworks were kicked into the long grass except the aspiration to 'unity and uniformity of religion' where promises of a settlement 'in due time as shall best conduce to the glory of God, the peace of the church and of both kingdoms' were made, a form of words that left plenty of scope for different interpretation.[12]

The Scots occupation of the north of England in late 1640 and for much of 1641 allowed the Long Parliament to dismantle the instruments (people and institutions) of supposed misgovernment in the 1630s. It allowed the Scots to reform their own parliament, the relationship of executive and legislature in Scotland, the autonomy of the Scottish kirk from the Scottish state, and especially the complete freedom of the General Assembly from royal control or management. But the seeds of English solipsism are also to be found in their failure to negotiate about guarantees that the English would not interfere in Scottish governance, drag Scotland into its wars or treaties, or determine the future of the monarchy by failing to involve them in questions of royal marriage. In essence by the end of 1641 the Scots had created a Scottish monarchical republic, but could not be sure they would cease to be a subordinate kingdom. For the next ten years the Scots were to press for confederation and the English were to make promises they ignored or quickly forgot.[13]

Although the Scots' subsequent decision to become a party to the civil war in England in 1643 was late, divisive, and hesitant, driven overwhelmingly by the belief that unless there was uniformity of religion, based on common ecclesiology, common worship, common confessions of faith and catechisms, *and* by political structures that would guarantee that uniformity, they were far less hesitant and far less divided about involving themselves in the civil war in Ireland. This was largely, of course, because Scottish planters and settlers were being massacred vicariously alongside English planters and settlers in the winter of 1641–2. So a Scottish army was the first to arrive in 1642, some months ahead of the English army. From that time on, the Scots assumed that they would be a party to the making of any post-war Irish settlement. From 1643 to 1648, the Scots included draconian terms for a Protestant settlement in Ireland in their proposals for a settlement in England. The very title of 'A solemn league and covenant for Reformation and Defence of Religion, the honour and happiness of the King, and the peace and safety of the *three* kingdoms of England, Scotland and Ireland' (September 1643) is telling enough; and it opens 'We noblemen, barons, knights, gentlemen, citizens, burgesses, ministers of the Gospel, and commons of all sorts in the kingdoms of England, Scotland and Ireland, by the providence of God living under one King….' and links together 'the deplorable estate of the Church and kingdom of Ireland, the distressed estate of the Church and kingdom of England, and the dangerous estate of the Church and kingdom of Scotland', an interesting choice of adjectives.[14]

The English parliament went along with this, of course, in order to get 20,000 troops to turn the course of the war in England, but very soon English backsliding began. They failed completely to honour commitments to pay Scottish troops in Ireland (and fell far behind with payments for their troops in England) and they pursued an Irish policy without involving the Scots. This set the pattern to such an extent that faced by the betrayals of the Covenant and of political collaboration by the Long Parliament and the army which was increasingly its master, by 1648 that significant minority of the Scots—including a simple majority of the Scottish peerage—who had opposed the intervention in England in 1643 were able to seize power and to agree to restore the king in return for a diluted version of the Covenant and a dramatic commitment to union:

> that His Majesty, according to the intention of his father, shall endeavour a complete union of the kingdoms, so as they may be one under His Majesty and his posterity; and, if that cannot be speedily effected, that all liberties, privileges, concerning commerce, traffic, and manufactories peculiar to the subjects of either nation, shall be common to the subjects of both kingdoms without distinction; and that there be a communication of mutual capacity of all other privileges of the subject in the two kingdoms.[15]

In return for an end to episcopacy and the suppression of 'all blasphemy, heresy, schism, and all such scandalous doctrines and practices as are contrary to the light of nature, or to the known principles of Christianity' (what the Long Parliament preferred to call 'liberty for tender consciences'), a leading group of Scots were willing to consider a much closer form of union than the confederal schemes of earlier years.[16] It was 1707 *avant la lettre*.

Thus, even though no English armies entered Scotland before the autumn of 1648, and even though no English mercenaries or volunteers joined the armies of the Covenant, there was an intensely *British* context to the political, religious, and military dynamics of the 1640s. The English Revolution was driven by a British dynamic; yet when the Rump refused to open letters from the Scottish commissioners in January 1649, they were following custom.

IRELAND'S BRITISH PROBLEM

And so too, only more so, in Ireland. The rebellion which began on 22 October 1641 was intended by those who planned it as a pre-emptive strike, a seizure of Dublin Castle and of forts and castles in the areas of plantation principally in Ulster and the disarming of the settlers. This would allow frightened Catholic members of the elite to negotiate from strength with an English government in turmoil to secure for the Catholics of Ireland what the king had just given to the presbyterians of Scotland: self-determination within a loosely confederated monarchy. By the autumn of 1641, Irish Catholics had already seen direct intervention of the English parliament in the internal affairs of Ireland and they wanted to create watertight guarantees that the English parliament could not legislate for Ireland, or seek to regulate governance there. Whatever Protestants on either side of the Irish Sea believed at the time, there never was any intention of a general massacre of English (let alone Scottish) Protestants. Deep resentments at perceived past injustice, a settling of scores, and a reclaiming of property taken away within the memory of the old and in the imaginations of the young, became conjoined with anxiety-driven pre-emptive action, to produce rebellion but not ethnic cleansing.

Thousands of depositions were sworn by Protestant survivors of the events of the winter of 1641–2.[17] In addition to lists of goods seized and destroyed, a form of insurance claim, they contained two narratives, one in the form of *eyewitness* testimony and another in *hearsay* testimony. Those taking the depositions (Protestant clergy for the most part) were careful to keep them separate. They were aware that sworn eyewitness testimony could be used in the intended trials of rebels, even if the deponent subsequently died or could not be found; hearsay could not be so used.[18]

The eyewitness testimony speaks of a determination of the rebels to strip British Protestants of all that they had, to take away all that was of value and to destroy the rest; and routinely to strip those British Protestants of their clothes, often (perhaps normally) stripping them stark naked, either because clothes have their own value, or surely mainly as a form of ritual humiliation. Thousands of men, women, and children, stripped and humiliated, often more than once, staggered out into the bitter cold and died. Where there was resistance, however, there *was* violence, often resulting in death. The violence was immediate and sought to end resistance: weapons of war (guns, swords, clubs) were used to subdue or to kill. Killing for the sake of it—most famously the mass drowning of scores of Protestants in Portadown—was rare and most often retaliation for actual or rumoured Protestant revenge killing. Violence bred violence, and it bred panic and apocalyptic anxiety in Britain as well as in Ireland. Yet there is very little eyewitness evidence of torture, mutilation, and sexual violence except in the *hearsay* testimony; and violent death is gendered, disproportionately of adult males.

There is an insistent theme in the eyewitness (more precisely the earwitness) evidence that the *English* parliament intended to extirpate Catholicism in *England* and in *Ireland*. Deponent after deponent reported stories that grew in the telling of the hunting down, torture, and killing of Catholic priests in England, of the plans of the English parliament to drive all Catholic clergy out of Ireland and place new draconian burdens on the Catholic population, to supersede the Irish parliament by direct rule not so much from Whitehall but from Westminster. Yet this was linked to the catastrophic claim by Phelim O'Neill, the single most prominent of the 'rebels', that he and his co-conspirators had a warrant under the king's Scottish seal to disarm the Protestants of Ireland. News of this claim spread widely in the north of Ireland, and got back to England where it brought many off the fence and into the camp of the junto of peers and commoners determined, by force if necessary, to place the kind of restrictions on the King of England that he had already accepted on his power as King of Scotland. Thus the Catholic rebels in Ireland, the puritan party in England and the presbyterian party in England all wanted the same thing: a king who was forced to meet 'free' parliaments, to surrender control of the executive to the heroes of the protest movements of 1641, and to accept a religious settlement in their confessional interest. They were all learning from one another. The result would be three monarchical republics, one puritan, one Catholic, one presbyterian, the first an erastian republic, the others theocratic republics. This would have replaced one unhappy dynastic agglomerate by an even unhappier one.

It would not be an exaggeration to say that what was reported from Ireland (much more than what was actually happening there) dominated the course of politics in England in the first six months of 1642. Within weeks of the depositions beginning to be sworn, their contents were being leaked to the English press. In the first nine months after the rebellion more than 250 pamphlets relating to it and to the massacres were published, a quarter of all titles published. In the crucial months of February, March, and April 1642, more than one-third of all titles related to the massacres. And these were the months during which the English parliament was pondering its response. There were several sources of information for these pamphleteers. The first was the evidence of survivors who crossed to Britain and seem to have told tales similar to those in the depositions. The second was the hearsay element of the depositions themselves. Most important was the digest of the early depositions prepared by Henry Jones, dean of Kilmore and seven other commissioners. It had two intentions: to *make the case* for a planned general massacre of the English Protestant communities of Ireland; and to portray the violence in the most extreme form. It drew overwhelmingly on the hearsay testimony. Thus, English responses were based more on misinformation than on a balanced account of what had happened and was happening. In the weeks on either side of Jones's *Remonstrance* we get many pamphlets which draw heavily on the hearsay component of the deposition material, always from the hearsay not the eyewitness; and the hearsay inflamed by echoes of atrocity pamphlets from the Thirty Years War and from Foxe's *Book of Martyrs*. Woodcuts of sadism and sexual cruelty from Germany were brought in to tell an Irish tale, images more distressing and violent than anything we would be allowed to see in the media today.

With England collapsing into civil war and no trust between the king and a majority of parliamentarians, agreement to raise taxes for an Irish expedition was non-existent. And so in March 1642 parliament passed the *Act for the speedie and effectual reducing of the rebels in…. Ireland* (known in modern times as the Adventurers Act).[19] It provided for the raising of loans to deploy an army to protect survivors of the massacre and to repress the rebellion, the loans to be repaid from the confiscation of Irish land. As the first clause of the Act puts it: 'two and a half [million] acres be assigned, allotted and divided amongst them that adventure money in the cause'. The Adventurers Act was both an early exercise in venture capitalism and an opportunity for the puritans to vote with their wallets.[20] A majority of future parliamentarian MPs signed up (something that kept up their radical edge over the decade that followed), many for themselves alone, but others as leaders of godly consortia. Sir William Brereton MP, soon to be Major General in the North Midlands, invested £900. But he was investing on behalf of himself and a group of Cheshire puritans including some key supporters in the years to come and two separatist clergymen. Investing in Ireland was almost certainly one of the things that bonded together what were soon to be syndicates of war party puritans in a war of three kingdoms against Charles I.[21]

The Adventurers Act galvanized the great majority of the Catholics of Ireland, including many who had held back from the original rebellion, to come together as the Confederation of Kilkenny. They were always to describe themselves as 'Your [or His] Majesty's Catholic subjects of Ireland' and they were strongly committed to Stuart monarchy, the legal and institutional framework of the Tudor/Stuart Irish kingdom but under Catholic not English Protestant control and with the Catholic Church not the Protestant Church as the official religion of the kingdom (and Catholic bishops replacing Protestant ones as the first estate in the Irish parliament). This is important: it was religion not ethnicity that defined the Confederacy from its formation in October 1642.[22] One of the articles of the Confederation stated 'that there shalbe no distinction, nor comparison betwixt old *Irish*, and old or new *English*, or betwixt septs and families, or betwixt Cittizens or Townesmen, and Contrymen ioyning in this vnion, on paine of the highest punishment'; and another even more dramatically that

> for the avoiding of National distinction between the subjects of his Majesty's Dominions…. it is ordered, and established…. that every Roman Catholic as well English, as Welsh, and Scottish, who was of that profession before these troubles,

and who will come, and please to reside in this Kingdom, and join in the present union, shall be preserved, and cherished in his life, goods and estate, by the power and authority, and force if need require it, of all the Catholics of *Ireland*, as fully and freely, as any native born therein.... all new converts, born in any of his Majesty's dominions, or elsewhere.... and joining in this cause, shall be accounted as Catholic natives.[23]

If Catholicism was what bound them together, a Catholic oath of association only to be taken after confession heard and communion received was what demonstrated that Catholicity. This was solemn indeed. It is almost certain that the Confederates were echoing the National Covenant in Scotland and the Protestation in England (where the oaths were taken after sermon (and often communion). The arrangements for enrolling and engrossing the returns from every parish reinforced this. The originals (sealed by every parish priest) would be kept in each diocesan treasury but certified copies would be transmitted both to each metropolitan and to the headquarters of the Confederation.[24] The taking of the oath both conferred on those who took it and denied to those who did not, the rights of full membership of civil society.

The oath itself began with a promise that 'I will, during my life, bear true faith and allegiance to my Sovereign Lord, Charles, by the grace of God, King of Great Britain, France and Ireland, and to his heirs and lawful successors' and a promise to uphold his and their just prerogatives, estates, and rights, the power and privilege of the parliament of the realm of Ireland, the fundamental laws of Ireland, and 'the free exercise of the Roman Catholic faith and religion throughout this land; and the lives, *just* liberties, possessions, estates, and rights of all those that have taken, or that shall take this Oath....'[25] That is the rub, of course: what were the *just* liberties, possessions, estates, and rights of Irish Catholics? Did they include those seized in successive waves of plantation over the past 80 years? Of course the Confederates were more divided over this than they could acknowledge even to themselves and it was a fault line which would handicap them across the decade and ruin them in 1649. For many reasons the differences were never spelled out in the years that followed.

By 1643, the Confederates controlled most of Ireland, and had made a truce with the king's lord deputy/lord lieutenant the earl/marquis of Ormond. Their long-term aims were an Ireland under Catholic control with a fully established Catholic Church, with diocesan bishops exercising jurisdiction over Catholics. They were divided over the restoration of church lands, and the rights of the Protestant minority were never addressed. But they all knew that controlling Ireland would not be enough. They needed the king to win the wars in Britain. Almost every Confederate leader was willing to send a substantial Catholic army (10,000 men is the figure most often mentioned) to help Charles. Some would do so in return for only the vaguest promises by the king and Ormond (believing a victorious king would not have the resources or wish to resist their demands), but others wanted guarantees up front, while recognizing that they could not be made public without causing a massive haemorrhage of royalist support in England. All negotiations between Charles and his agents and the Confederates therefore contained secret understandings. But the fact remains that Ormond could not concede as much as most Confederates saw as the minimum needed for a military alliance, and that he was too committed to the interests of the Protestants of Ireland to give the king easy access to an Irish army; that the Catholic clergy headed by a papal nuncio more interested in saving souls than winning wars could not send men to England until the conditions for the full-scale Tridentine reform of the Irish church were in place. The Irish motto was: for God, for king, for the homeland.[26] Both the Protestant King and the Catholic God demanded first place. The British dimension skewed negotiations for an Irish settlement, but the threat of an irruption of Irish Catholics into the English theatre (in 1648–9 as much as in 1644–6) constantly diffracted political choices in England (as, of course, did the fact that the core of Montrose's army was made up of Irish Catholics, transform the Scottish civil wars of 1644–5).

FLAGS AS SYMBOLS OF IDENTITY

My main points can be finally demonstrated in the iconography of war. It would seem that the *English* marched under regimental banners with no ethnic or national symbols. None of the more than 500 battle colours discussed in one study contained a St George cross, for example, or any other 'English' symbol. By far the largest group contained religious images and/or biblical quotation—as with the divine hand of justice brandishing a sword and emerging from a cloud with the words 'for reformation' in a scroll (Captain Copley) and the most frequent slogan being '*si deus nobiscum quis contra us*' [if God is with us, who can be against us], while the most startling is the post-regicidal image of Charles's head dripping bloody and set above the axe that has just executed justice on him encircled by a scroll that reads '*salus populi suprema lex*' [the people's security—or safety—is the highest law]. No English flag proclaimed national identity or recognized a three-kingdom dynamic.[27] In striking contrast, almost all the Scottish battle colours are based on the saltire (blue diagonal cross of St Andrew adopted by the Scots in the sixteenth century), with regimental distinctiveness being found in the symbols at the centrepiece of the cross. But in the four quarters created by the cross is normally written: 'For Religion, Covenant, King and Kingdomes'—both the sequence and the use of 'kingdomes' are striking. And of course 'Covenant' for the Scots meant commitment to a British church and confederal monarchy.[28] Similarly there is a consistency in the flags of the Irish Confederacy: a green base, incorporating a small red cross of St Patrick, a (specifically) Irish harp, and the motto of the Confederacy, '*Pro Deo, Rege et Patria Hibernia unanimis*' [Ireland united for God, King and Fatherland]. Once more the sequence is striking. A contemporary report from a Confederate priest to his Franciscan superior in Rome speaks of standards with a green background, and below the cross of St Patrick, 'vivat rex Carolus' and above it C.R. (Carolus Rex) *et corona Imperialis*. The reference to the (English) imperial crown and its higher status than the life of the current king is again striking.[29] The Scots and the Irish both had a sense of nationhood and a sense of being in a war of three kingdoms. The English had a sense of being in their own civil war over political freedom and religious truth.

NOBLE CONGRUITIES

One of the recoveries of recent years has been the recognition that a (if not the) crucial dynamic of the political crisis of the 1640s was it was a noble revolt, a conspiracy of well-established noble families in all three kingdoms. That knots of senior (and for the most part well-established) noble families in each kingdom, with strong interconnections by blood and marriage, saw it as their responsibility to bring an end to what they perceived as Charles I's misgovernment, is no surprise. How they worked with equally powerful knots of clergy and disaffected lawyers and would-be politicians to place limitations on the king's freedom of action, above all in making senior appointments in church and state, and indeed to replace the hybrid half-reformed churches of England, Scotland, and Ireland is now well established. But the extent of the collusion between the juntos in each of the kingdoms further demonstrates the themes of this chapter.

In 1641 there were just over 300 peers across the three Stuart kingdoms, about half of them barons and viscounts, and the other half earls, with half a dozen marquises and three dukes. About 10% of the upper tier had titles in more than one kingdom (and seats in two of the three parliaments) and many of them were at the heart of Charles's government as the crisis broke. Both the Scottish dukes (Hamilton and Lennox) had English titles (earl of Cambridge, duke of Richmond) and English wives (a niece and a daughter of the assassinated duke of Buckingham). The greatest surviving Gaelic lord in Ulster, Randal Macdonnell, was married to the daughter of the earl of Rutland, and more importantly the widow of the duke of Buckingham. Ulick Burke, 4th earl of Clanricarde, the greatest Catholic land-owner in Connacht, was a half-brother of the 3rd earl of Essex (by his mother, wife of the 3rd earl of Clanricarde and widow of Sir Philip Sidney, and Robert Devereux 2nd earl of Essex, and Elizabeth I's lord lieutenant in Ireland [1599–1601]) and was married to the only daughter of the earl of Northampton. He sat in the English House as Lord Burgh, and then as earl of St Albans. He was a major land-owner in Kent as well as counties Galway and Roscommon. The greatest Catholic land-owners in Leinster and Munster also had English wives or English mothers. So did a simple majority of the Protestant nobility of Ireland, especially the earls, above all James Butler, 12th earl (later 1st marquis and duke) of Ormonde, Charles I's lord deputy, later lord lieutenant throughout the 1640s. His mother was a Gloucestershire heiress and he in turn married the heiress of the earl of Desmond who was Lady Dingwall in the Scottish peerage in her own right and the daughter of a Scottish settler in Ireland. There may have been no British state in the 1630s, but a British peerage was rapidly emerging. Perhaps the ultimate proof that blood-ties mattered for many at least as much as religious affiliation is that Robert Devereux, earl of Essex and soon-to-be parliamentarian captain general, a stern and principled Protestant, persuaded Charles I, as one of his 'bridge appointments' in 1641 to make his Catholic half-brother Ulick Burke, earl of Clanricarde, a member of the English privy council, under his English title, earl of St Albans.[30]

But yet again there are asymmetries. Between 1600 and 1649, 60% of Irish peers took Irish brides (many of course 'Old English' or even second- or third-generation New English or New Scottish), and 40% took brides born in Britain.[31] The figure of marriages of Scottish peers to English and Irish brides has not been so authoritatively determined, but (for earls and above) was probably around 15%. The figure for marriages of English peers to Scottish and Irish brides was negligible, certainly less than 1%. Indeed one of the most remarkable things about the period down to 1688 is that while many English peers gave up their daughters to Scottish and Irish lords, they did not give up their sons even to wealthy Scottish or Irish heiresses.

It is true that a handful of Englishmen acquired Scottish titles (without Scottish lands), the most prominent of whom was the grandfather of Lord General Thomas Fairfax, but this was not a political issue in either country. On the other hand, the swamping of the Irish peerage with Englishmen did have significant consequences. Between 1603 and 1641, fifty-one English families acquired Irish titles. Less than half of these—twenty-two in all—were men without titles in England who had been planters, mainly post-1580 in Munster or post-1590 in Ulster, and they were a solid New English Protestant bloc in the Irish parliament. To them need to be added six peers from amongst the Scottish settlers, Protestant and Catholic.[32] But there were also twenty-nine non-resident English peers. Some of these had some family connection with Ireland (one was the grandson of an Elizabethan lord deputy, and others had fathers who had served with Essex between 1597 and 1601 and who were still owed money. But most were friends or suitors of Buckingham, rewarded or fobbed off with an Irish title).[33] There is some evidence that while many paid good money for their titles, the crown had specifically in mind the building of a Protestant majority in the Irish House of Lords, and the granting by these non-resident peers of their proxies to successive lords deputy became a major grievance of the Old English and Old Irish majority.[34] Indeed there were demands in the parliament of 1634–5, developed in the 1640s, to require the possession of an amount of land proportionate to status (in 1634–5 it was £200 p.a. for a baron, £250 p.a. for a viscount, £300 for an earl) by all peers before they could sit in the Irish parliament.[35]

But the creation of England-dwelling Irish and British-dwelling Scottish peers was also a not-negligible source of grievance in the English House of Lords. As early as 1621, thirty-three English peers protested (in a petition to the king) against the granting of privilege to what it called men with 'foreign' titles, to 'noblemen strangers', an Irish earl being given precedence in processions, for example, over an English viscount and baron. James VI and I was furious, and closeted the thirty-three one by one but to no avail. None would withdraw their protest.[36] This was not just a problem for the Westminster village; it caused problems in many counties. In Cheshire, bitter arguments over seniority between those who had bought Irish peerages in the 1620s and those who had bought English baronetcies a generation earlier were at the root of party conflict before and during the civil wars.[37] In the spring of 1628, so many complaints were pouring in that the English privy council decided to keep Irish and Scottish barons and viscounts off all commissions 'for wronging the English in their places', an interesting choice of words.[38] It was also suggested at the time (by Sir Edward Walker, Garter King of Arms, writing in 1653) that the too-great enlargement of the peerage of all three kingdoms had been a major cause of the conflicts. Certainly the junto of peers identified as being at the heart of the resistance to Charles I was not only predominantly a group of the longer-established peerage families; it was also a group uncontaminated by Irish and Scottish connections. Conversely, those closest to Charles I in each of the kingdoms were precisely the 'Briticized': thus the Catholic peers who delayed longest in joining the Confederation of Kilkenny (Antrim to 1644, Clanrickarde to 1649) were those with English wives and, in the latter case, mother; as were the leaders of the dissident Covenanters who signed the Engagement to restore Charles I on easy terms in 1648 (headed by Hamilton, Lanark, and Lauderdale).

The webs of interconnection put the peerage/peerages of the three kingdoms at the heart of the thesis of this chapter. There is an only-partly written story of the way that agents for Confederate lords networked into royalist headquarters at Oxford in 1643–4 as they tried to firm up a deal to deliver 20,000 troops to England in return for a Catholic constitution for Ireland (just as the Irish exile peers were to play a major role in the exiled court of Charles II in the 1650s).[39] Randal Macdonnel, marquis of Antrim, could imagine the recreation of the ancient Macdonnel/Macdonald Lordship of the Isles in the western Highlands of Scotland and the north-east of Ulster. For this to happen, court contacts facilitated the reorientation of his war effort into sending an expeditionary force to help the marquis of Montrose in what promised to be a Highland clearance of the Covenanters and the destruction of Campbell power in Argyll and the islands.[40] Much has been written about the mission of Edward Somerset, earl of Glamorgan (heir to the marquis of Worcester, the greatest Catholic magnate in the Welsh borders) to make a treaty (behind Ormonde's back) with the Confederates in 1645–6. It is rarely mentioned in these accounts that he was married to Margaret, second daughter of Henry O'Brien, fourth earl of Thomond. Although his father-in-law was a Protestant, his web of connections eased Glamorgan's way into the negotiations. What is more, Lady Glamorgan's mother was the daughter of Lord Creighton of Sanquhar, a key supporter of the marquis of Montrose.[41]

One of the most enigmatic politicians of the 1640s was Murrough O'Brien, earl of Inchiquin. The orphaned child of an O'Brien and a Fitzgerald, he was fostered by Sir William St Leger, lord president of Munster. Despite Murrough's Protestantism, St Leger sent him to learn the arts of war with the Spanish armies in Italy and on his return he was made vice president of Munster. His career in the 1640s, constantly changing sides, was determined by the ambition to replace St Leger as lord president, and by those the king and parliament both incompetently appointed ahead of him to that post: the 2nd earl of Portland, the grandson of the Chief Justice of Ireland who had visited much grief on the O'Briens at the time of the Munster Plantation, and Viscount Lisle, grandson of Sir Henry Sidney, a lord lieutenant even more hated by the O'Briens.[42]

Many of the well over one-third of the Irish and Scottish peers owning land in England felt deeply circumscribed in their political choices. While allegiance for many must have been driven by powerful ethnic, religious, and constitutional preferences, many of them strong, they also had *very* strong self-preservation preferences and the prospect of the escheat of their estates in one kingdom may well have tempered their behaviour in another. This is almost certainly true of the earl of Cork in Ireland or the earl of Lauderdale in Scotland, for example. And in the give and take of negotiations for the surrender of towns in the early 1650s in Ireland, for example, the protection of lands in Britain was often an important negotiating ploy.

For the king and for his supporters in each of his kingdoms, this was a single conflict in at least three theatres. And yet again we find for the English parliament, the Irish and Scottish theatres were subordinate and to be marginalized as far as possible. As final examples of the relentless little-Englander mentality of those running the Long Parliament let us look at two trials that they supervised. Connor Maguire, 2nd Lord Enniskillen, was one of the plotters arrested on 22 October 1641 for planning the violent seizure of Dublin Castle. He was brought to England and incarcerated until early 1645 when he was tried. He demanded his rights as an Irish lord to be tried not by a common jury in England but by a jury of his peers in Ireland. Both the judges and the parliament itself voted to deny him. An Irish peer who had committed treason in the kingdom of Ireland, he was tried as a commoner in England. And to complete the vindictive disregard for his status, he then died as a commoner by hanging, drawing, and quartering not by beheading as his status demanded.[43] Similarly when the duke of Hamilton was taken prisoner after leading a Scottish 'invasion'—the English parliament's word—of England, he was put on trial for treason. How was this possible? He led an invasion but since he was earl of Cambridge in the English peerage, he was a subject of the King of England leading an invasion by the king's Scottish subjects. At least as an English peer, he was subject to the axe not the rope and the knife. It is a very British story of wars that were whatever people wanted them to be.[44]

THE BRITISH REVOLUTION IN THE ENGLISH PROVINCES

This has been a very a top-down account. It has suggested that the choices of decision-makers in England, Ireland, and Scotland were constrained by what was happening elsewhere in the archipelago, even if sometimes, at least in England, they pretended otherwise to themselves and others. They also learned from one another, and they imitated one another, whether in triennial acts, or in specific measures about how to limit the king's freedom to appoint and retain his own ministers, or by bonding of peoples together by solemn oaths. But there is another unrecognized way in which the unfolding crisis in each kingdom influenced what happened. The civil war in each region of each kingdom was different precisely insofar as geographical proximity affected its sense of the war as a War of the Three Kingdoms. For reasons of space we will focus here on England; but the argument applies equally to Scotland, Ireland, or Wales.[45]

Let us consider first the county of Cheshire. The standard accounts of the civil war in Cheshire,[46] the present author's included, have all missed the 'Irish' dimension of a local war. First of all, they have missed the large number of 'Irish' troops serving in Cheshire during the civil wars. Two stick out as especially important. The first was Michael Jones, the son of Lewis Jones, bishop of Killaloe (in Connacht) from 1633–46. His elder brother Henry was the man put in charge of taking the 1641 depositions, and there is little doubt that Michael would have brought detailed knowledge of the massacres with him to Cheshire when he was appointed as Sir William Brereton's deputy in 1644. Michael Jones had served as a major under Ormond in 1642–3 but defected after the truce with the Catholic Confederacy.[47] When Brereton was recalled to London under the Self-Denying Ordnance, Jones managed the siege of Chester, for him a dangerous bridgehead for any army of Irish Catholics the king might seek to bring over to save his neck and also an important bridgehead for the army of English Protestants that Jones hoped would go over from England to settle the Irish problem once and for all.

The second Protestant Irish officer in Brereton's army was Chidley Coote, son of a brutal Jacobean settler who had been provost martial of Connacht, with unlimited powers of arrest and execution under martial law. The older Coote was killed in battle in 1642, but Chidley's older brother Charles was by early 1645 parliament's lord president of Connacht and hence responsible for defending and extending the Protestant interest in the most Irish part of Ireland. *Chidley* Coote was in regular touch with his brother and Brereton's letter books contain many transcripts of letters to Coote reporting on the war in Ireland.[48] It is also striking that one of Brereton's key agents in London, keeping him informed of events as reported there, was Sir Robert King, another defector from Ormond and agent for the pro-parliamentarian forces in Ireland. He was doubtless watching Brereton's Irish interests as well as his supply lines from Westminster to Cheshire.[49]

There was an important Irish dimension to Brereton's feud with John Booth, son of the leading peace party activist in Cheshire. Booth was strongly opposed to Brereton's strategy of seeing the war in larger, regional, North Midlands terms, but one of his key acts of obstruction was to prevent the diversion of moneys raised in the area around his garrison for use in Ireland and Scotland. He also obstructed the efforts of a major Scottish land-owner from Cavan, in conjunction with Chidley Coote, to recruit a regiment in Cheshire for service in Ireland in 1645. The animus against men from Ireland can be seen in the harsh treatment of *English* officers who had served in Ireland in 1642–4 and who had returned under the Cessation to assist the king in England, such as Captain Thomas Sandford. Most of the officers from the English-army-from-Ireland captured after the battle of Nantwich were (unusually) sent up to London and kept prisoner until the end of the war. Intriguingly Brereton wrote to Robert Monroe, commander of the force defending the Scottish settlers in Ulster, offering him the services of many captured soldiers who had crossed over to and from Ireland, saying that they could not be trusted to serve in his army against the king, but that they were willing to serve in Ireland against the Confederates.

So the Irish dimension made significant contributions to the nastiness of the war in Cheshire. It may also have contributed to so many of Brereton's officers volunteering for service in Cromwell's army of conquest in and after 1649, including Robert Venables, who was with him at the sack of Drogheda, and the fierce Baptist Jerome or Hieronymus

Zankey. Brereton himself was obsessed with monitoring what was happening in Ireland, in a way that other regional commanders were not. Norman Dore argued that Brereton planned to lure the princes Rupert and Maurice to Chester where the newly formed New Model Army, the Scots, and his own troops would combine to destroy them. Crucial to his thinking is his knowledge, gleaned from the Cootes and other Irish agents, of the secret negotiations between the earl of Glamorgan and the Confederates that would bring Confederate troops to England. It was in the knowledge that the king wanted a conjunction of his own between Rupert and the Confederates, and hence the necessity of keeping Chester in royalist hands, that lay behind Brereton's strategic plan.[50]

But perhaps the most dramatic illustration of the impact of the Irish war on this English theatre is the so-called and little understood Bartholemy 'massacre' of 23 December 1644.[51] There is no dispute that a royalist force including men returned from Ireland smoked out twenty local men who had taken refuge in Bartholemy church and executed twelve of them in cold blood. This is admitted in a letter from Lord Byron to Ormond, and was widely reported in royalist and parliamentarian newsbooks at the time. What is disputed is whether the men were armed, whether they surrendered on quarter or on mercy, and how they were killed. The royalists claimed that the men were armed, surrendered to mercy, and that twelve were executed *in terrorem* in accordance with the laws of war. The English parliamentarian newsbooks blamed the English commander, Lord Byron, and claimed that the men had surrendered on a promise of quarter and were then butchered. They all highlight the action of Major Connock (*sic*), the senior officer at the scene, in killing the village schoolmaster with one blow of a battle-axe and it was indeed as John *Connock* that he was tried and executed for that murder at the Great Sessions in Chester in 1654. But there is a range of local sources, including the diaries of a Nantwich gentleman and a local puritan minister, which add a significant spin not picked up in the national sources. In these versions, the major is named as John Connaught, that is, he is given an Irish name, a name redolent of an untamed and uncivilized part of Ireland; and he is said to have ordered the prisoners to be stripped stark naked before he ordered them to be killed.[52] This is, of course, the absolutely standard allegation of the thousands of depositions of survivors recorded by Michael Jones's brother Henry Jones, since 1642, and reported in the hundreds of pamphlets about the Irish atrocities circulating in Cheshire as elsewhere. It is difficult to think of anywhere else in the English civil war that looks so like a particular local elaboration based on close knowledge of Irish material. This appears to be clear evidence that in Cheshire, more than elsewhere, the expectation of a repeat of the Irish massacres on English soil informed the way people viewed the war in their midst.

If we move to the north-east of England we find little preoccupation with Ireland, but a great deal of preoccupation with Scotland.[53] Roger Howell's model study of Newcastle in the civil war stressed the essential neutralism and moderate puritanism of the city's rulers in the build-up to civil war, and he carefully chronicles the economic catastrophe of successive occupations by the Scots (1640–2 and 1644–7) and in between those occupations by the marquis of Newcastle (whose own power base, notwithstanding his title, was not in the north-east but in the Trent Valley in Derbyshire and Nottinghamshire).[54]

Yet only a strong sense of the nature and consequences of the Scottish occupation not only of Newcastle but also of all the crossing points in the Tyne and Coquet valleys can explain the nature and extent of the polarization of Northumbrian communities in the later 1640s. A pamphlet published in 1646 and entitled *Truth's Discovery or a Black Cloud in the North showing some anti-parliamentary inhuman cruel and base proceedings of the Scotch army against the well-affected in the North of England* consisted of a number of separate letters by north-easterners alleging tyrannical exploitation by the Scots, impoverishing and brutalizing those who had welcomed them as deliverers.[55] It took a north-easterner in July 1646 to say, from a Congregationalist position: 'consider one thing more, which is that the papists, prelates and Antichristian Presbyters are now linked in one chain and doing one work even opposing the heavenly powers'.[56] I do not think Cheshire men saw presbyterians and papists in bed together in 1646.

The likely author of this is John Blakiston, as staid and conservative a puritan as one could expect to find anywhere in 1640. He was MP for Newcastle in the Long Parliament and we can chronicle his move first to war-party politics and then to magisterial Congregationalist religion as he sought to save his home town first from the royalists and then from the Scots. After the liberation of the city in 1646 he, as mayor, made common cause with the military governor and war-party/Independent activist, Sir Arthur Heselrige, to restore the fortunes of the town. But that meant taking on the fiercely presbyterian leadership of Sunderland, under the leadership of John Lilburne's uncle George (whose money had set John up in business as a brewer in 1641). Sunderland had taken advantage of the high tolls that the Scottish army had placed on coal passing through Newcastle, and had supplied cheap coal to London, and George and others had used their position on sequestration committees to get control of many Durham coalmines. One of Blakiston's allies wrote that 'thus came the Sunderland rats across the water'.[57] In the ensuing power struggle, Heselrige used main force to occupy the collieries occupied by the Lilburnes and killed another of the Lilburne brothers in a skirmish. Blakiston's career was to culminate in his assiduous attendance at the king's trial and signing of the death warrant, enraged as he was by the king's attempt once more in 1648 to bring the Scots into the English struggle. I would suggest that such radicalization needs its local context.

Equally, only the north-eastern and specifically British (i.e. anti-Scottish) dimension can explain the trajectory of Thomas Widdrington, keeper of the Great Seal under the Commonwealth and speaker in the Protectorate parliaments. He was a moderate Puritan MP for Berwick and his first response on hearing of the Solemn League and Covenant and the proposed occupation of his town by the Scots was to desert to the king, so great was his disgust with the Long Parliament. But he soon wearied of ungodly Oxford and began a long steady march to the left and to his key roles in 1649 and in the years that followed, driven once more by a detestation of everything the Scots stood for in religion and governance and precisely because they stood for it.[58]

Blakiston's great enemy was George Lilburne, whose presbyterianism and opposition to religious toleration did not dissolve the ties of blood between himself and John Lilburne. Indeed John's enforced exile on Jersey was a direct result of an intemperate literary assault on George's nemesis, Sir Arthur Heselrige. Indeed only the particularities of north-eastern 'British' origins can explain the very different political and religious routes taken by each of the Lilburne family: George, the Congregationalist town boss; Robert, the Baptist colonel in the New Model Army and uncomfortable upholder of the Protectorate, John the Leveller leader and eventual Quaker, and Henry the presbyterian supporter of a royalist coup in 1648. The career of each needs its north-eastern context to make sense of each and of all of them.

My main argument is thus that Cheshire had a very particular experience and dynamic of civil war because it was so close to Ireland; Northumberland had a very particular experience and dynamic of civil war because it was occupied by Scots who arrived, as so many occupying forces still do, as heroes and left as villains; if there was space for a consideration of, say, Essex we would find that it too had its own very particular experience and dynamic of civil war because it was close to London and far from marauding royalists be they English, Scottish, or Irish (although it did have its fair share of Protestant refugees from Ireland keen to tell their tales). In other words, place matters as much as abstract ideas and we need to factor that into any account of the civil wars within England, Scotland, and Ireland, as well as the wars between them.

Conclusion

In the 1640s, there were civil wars in England, Scotland, and Ireland, but there were wars between the kingdoms too. There were *Scottish* armies in England (1640–1, 1643–7, 1648, 1651) and Ireland (1642–50); there were very different *Irish* bodies of troops in England and Scotland (1644–5) and a large army constantly threatened to descend on England (1644–50); there were *English* armies in Scotland (1647–60) and Ireland (1648, 1650–60). Each war was conditioned by what was happening elsewhere and each war affected each part of each other country in a different way.

Beyond 1649, even the English could see that the Revolution had become a Britain-and-Ireland event. Ireland was conquered and more than 40% of the land was confiscated and redistributed from (Irish) Catholics to (British) Protestants. The costs of conquest and the need to keep anything up to 30,000 soldiers in Ireland to hold it down contributed to the high-tax regime across the archipelago and this in turn was crucial to the alienation of moderate opinion from Commonwealth and Protectorate. The English Commonwealth conquered Scotland, and incorporated Scotland into an enhanced English state. Successive governments strove to make English law and legal processes universal throughout the archipelago, created a single parliament (with small numbers of MPs from Ireland and Scotland, principally drawn from the occupying forces), and proclaimed a common religious settlement based on a very broad religious liberty and an even greater religious equality (there were no religious tests for holding political office) that put enormous strains on the narrow coalition of interests that were kept in power by the army. The Commonwealth, and to a large extent the

Protectorate, remained a vanguard state of godly men governing, as Cromwell memorably put it, 'what's for [the people's] good, not what pleases them' and it was never likely to evolve into a government that rested on consent or hold free elections.[59] The instabilities of the Stuart dynastic agglomerate were replaced by the instabilities of a militarized tripartite Commonwealth which could command obedience but not sufficient loyalty or support. The least-studied part of the greatest of all republican tracts of the 1650s, Harrington's *Oceana*, is its provisions for its three historically distinct parts, representing England, Scotland, and Ireland. It is not surprising that the authority of the state collapsed first in the winter of 1659–60 in Ireland and then through the English occupying force in Scotland throwing in the towel and marching south to force elections that would unscramble 1649 as a British and Irish as much as an English event. England's attempt to solve the British problem by incorporating the awkward neighbours had been a failure. The search had to continue for a stable state system that would never be fully a British state with one law, one church, one sense of nationhood.

Notes

1. I am grateful to John Collins of the University of Virginia for teaching me this, and for sharing with me his forthcoming article: 'For the Safety of the State, Garrison, and Army: Martial Law and the Genesis of the High Court of Justice'.

2. S. R. Gardiner (ed.), *Constitutional Documents of the Puritan Revolution* (3rd edition, Oxford, 1906), 371–4, emphasis added (accessible online at <http://www.constitution.org/eng/conpur.htm>).

3. Gardiner (ed.), *Constitutional Documents*, 380, emphasis added.

4. *Acts of the Parliament of Scotland* (1819 edition), VI, 347–8; printed with minor changes as *A Letter from the Commissioners of the Kingdom of Scotland Residing Here in London to William Lenthall, Speaker of the House of Commons* (25 January 1649), emphasis added.

5. *Acts of the Parliament of Scotland* (1819 edition), VI, 347–8.

6. *Journal of the House of Commons* [*CJ*] for 30 January 1649 (accessed at <http://www.british-history.ac.uk/report.asp>); *Records of the Kirk of Scotland, Containing the Acts and Proceedings of the General Assemblies, From the Year 1638 Downwards, As Authenticated by the Clerks of Assembly; With Notes and Historical Illustrations*, ed. Alexander Peterkin (Edinburgh, 1838 edition), 86.

7. Gardiner (ed.), *Constitutional Documents*, 384–7.

8. *Journal of the House of Lords* [*LJ*] for 1 February 1649 (accessed at <http://www.british-history.ac.uk/report.asp>).

9. 'Proclamation of Charles II King of Great Britain, France and Ireland', 5 February 1649, as in *Records of the Parliament of Scotland* (<http://www.rps.ac.uk—1649/1/71>).

10. For a slightly different take on Scotland and the Regicide, see Laura Stewart's chapter in this volume, 127–8.

11. *Calendar of State Papers Domestic 1640–1*, for 4 November 1640 (accessed at <http://www.british-history.ac.uk/report.aspx?compid=52958>). See also the Records of the Parliament of Scotland, for 21 August 1641: *Act Regarding the Ratification of the Articles of the Treaty* (accessed at <http://www.rps.ac.uk/>).

12. The National Archives [TNA], SP16/471 no. 22; NLS, Wodrow MSS folio series, vol. 67, fo. 3. For a fuller discussion, see John Morrill, 'Three Kingdoms and One Commonwealth? The Enigma of Mid-Seventeenth-Century Britain and Ireland', in Alexander Grant and Keith Stringer (eds.), *Uniting the Kingdom: The Making of British History* (London, 1995), 170–93 at 179–82.

13. For further discussion of these points see Goodare's chapter in this volume.

14. Gardiner (ed.), *Constitutional Documents*, 267–71, quotations at 267 and 268.

15. Gardiner (ed.), *Constitutional Documents*, 347–52, quotation at 351. For a discussion of all the 'British' dimension of the joint Anglo-Scottish negotiations with the king for a peace settlement in 1645–7, see Morrill, 'Three Kingdoms and One Commonwealth?'

16. Gardiner (ed.), *Constitutional Documents*, 347–52, quotation at 348.

17. Now conveniently available and free at <http://1641.tcd.ie>.

18. See the separate discussion of the nature of the 1641 depositions in Cope's chapter in this volume, esp. 83–4, 90–1.

19. The best discussion of the Adventurers Act and of its consequences remains Karl. S. Bottigheimer, *English Adventurers and Irish Land: The 'Adventurers' in the Cromwellian Settlement of Ireland* (Oxford, 1971), esp. 2. But see also Patrick Little, 'The English Parliament and the Irish Constitution', in Micheál Ó Siochrú (ed.), *Kingdoms in Crisis: Ireland in the 1640s* (Dublin, 2001), 106–21.

20. For a separate discussion of the Adventurers Act, see Cope's chapter in this volume, 87.

21. For Brereton as front man for a group, see Bottigheimer, *English Adventurers*, 153–4. Oliver Cromwell invested £600, a sum far beyond his means which suggests to me that he was acting in the same way as Brereton (Bottigheimer, *English Adventurers*, 178).

22. For the alternative views of Cope and Ó Siochrú on the origins and nature of the Confederation of Kilkenny, see their chapters in this volume, esp. 87–8, 140–1.

23. *Orders Made and Established by the Lords Spirituall and Temporall and the Rest of the General Assembly of the Kingdome of Ireland* (London, 1642: Wing 1426A).

24. *Orders Made and Established.*

25. T. W. Moody, F. X. Martin, and F. J. Byrne (eds.), *A New History of Ireland, III: Early Modern Ireland, 1534–1691* (Oxford, 1976), 298, emphasis added.

26. See Ó Siochrú's chapter in this volume, esp. 140–1.

27. Ian Gentles, 'The Iconography of Revolution: England 1642–1649', in Ian Gentles, John Morrill, and Blair Worden (eds.), *Soldiers, Writers and Statesmen of the English Revolution* (Cambridge, 1998), 91–113.

28. A particularly fine example, kept in the National Museum of Scotland can be found at <http://www.geograph.org.uk/photo/1538552>.

29. P. F. Moran, *Spicilegium Ossoriense III* (1884), 18, and more generally Brian O Cuiv, 'The Wearing of the Green', *Studia Hibernia* 17 (1977): 108–10.

30. All references in this chapter from the *Oxford Dictionary of National Biography* [ODNB], 2004; online edition, January 2008 (<http://www.oxforddnb.com/view/article/7566>, accessed 12–20 December 2012) and from J. McGuire and J. Quinn (eds.), *Dictionary of Irish Biography* [DIB] (Cambridge, 2009).

31. Jane Ohlmeyer, *Making Ireland English: The Irish Aristocracy in the Seventeenth Century* (London, 2012), 184.

32. Ohlmeyer, *Making Ireland English*, 35.

33. Charles R. Mayes, 'The Early Stuarts and the Irish Peerage', *English Historical Review*, 73 (1958): 227–51.

34. Ohlmeyer, *Making Ireland English*, 239, 242–3, 247, and 258.

35. Mayes, 'Irish Peerage', 250n.

36. Mayes, 'Irish Peerage', 248–50.

37. John Morrill, *Cheshire 1630–1660: County Government and Politics in the 'English Revolution'* (Oxford, 1974), 32–39; John Morrill, 'Parliamentary Representation', in Brian Harris (ed.), *VCH County of Cheshire II* (London, 1979), 106–7.

38. Mayes, 'Irish Peerage', 249.

39. The fullest recent study is Micheál Ó Siochrú, *Confederate Ireland: A Constitutional and Political Analysis* (2nd edition, Dublin, 2008), 70–3.

40. David Stevenson, *Alasdair MacColla and the Highland Problem in the Seventeenth Century* (Edinburgh, 1980), 102–18.

41. For the mission, see Ó Siochrú, *Confederate Ireland*, 94–109 *passim*; or John Lowe, 'The Glamorgan Mission to Ireland, 1645–6', *Studia Hibernica*, 4 (1964): 155–96. For his ancestry see Stephen K. Roberts, 'Somerset, Edward, Second Marquess of Worcester (d. 1667)', *ODNB*; online edition, May 2006 (<http://www.oxforddnb.com/view/article/26006>, accessed 16 December 2012).

42. Reconstructed from lives of the O'Briens, the Westons, and the Sidneys in *ODNB* and *DIB*.

43. D. Alan Orr, ' England, Ireland, Magna Carta, and the Common Law: The Case of Connor, Lord Maguire Second Baron of Enniskillen', *Journal of British Studies*, 39.4 (2000): 389–421.

44. John J. Scally, 'Hamilton, James, first duke of Hamilton (1606–1649)', *ODNB*; online edition, October 2005 (<http://www.oxforddnb.com/view/article/12087>, accessed 20 December 2012).

45. This draws on my unpublished paper 'The British Revolution in the English Provinces 1640–9', delivered as The Marc Fitch Lecture (Birkbeck College, London, 6 July 2009), which I intend to publish elsewhere.

46. For the 'standard' account, see my *Cheshire 1630–1660*, esp. chaps. 3–5. For this and the following paragraphs I relied mainly on re-reading (a) *The Letter Books of Sir William Brereton*, vol. I, *Jan. 31—May 29th 1645*, ed. R. N. Dore, The Record Society of Lancashire and Cheshire, CXXIII (1984–9); (b) *The Letter Books of Sir William Brereton*, vol. II, *June 18th 1645—Feb 1st 1646*, ed. R. N. Dore, The Record Society of Lancashire and Cheshire, CXXVIII (1990); (c) *The Civil War in Staffordshire in the Spring of 1646: Sir William Brereton's Letter Book, April–May 1646*, ed. Ivor Carr and Ian Atherton, Staffordshire Record Society, 4th series, 21 (2007).

47. Thomas Carte, *Life of the Duke of Ormonde; Containing an Account of the Most Remarkable Affairs of his Time, and Particularly of Ireland under his Government with an Appendix and a Collection of Letters*, 6 vols. (Oxford, 1851), VI, 23.

48. Dore, *Brereton Letter Books*, I, 27–8 and *passim* (index, *sub.* Coote). A particularly gripping account of Ireland in 1645, in a letter from Robert Blakeney to Coote, is in the same volume, 250–2.

49. Dore, *Brereton Letter Books*, I, 285; Patrick Little, 'King, Sir Robert (*d.* 1657)', *ODNB*; online edition, January 2008 (<http://www.oxforddnb.com/view/article/15593>, accessed 11 September 2012).

50. R. N. Dore, 'Sir William Brereton's Siege of Chester and the Campaign of Naseby', *Transactions of the Lancashire and Cheshire Antiquarian Society*, 67 (1958 for 1957): 17–44.

51. Inga Volmer, 'A Comparative Study of Massacres during the Wars of the Three Kingdoms', University of Cambridge Ph.D. dissertation (2006), 141–51; Barbara Donagan, 'Atrocity, War, Crime and Treason', *American Historical Review*, 99 (1994): 1137–66, at 1151–3; Peter Gaunt, 'Bartholemy', *Cromwelliana* (1994), 66–70.

52. *Memorials of the Civil War in Cheshire*, ed. J. Hall, Record Society of Lancashire and Cheshire, 19 (1889), containing the 'Briefe and true relation' of Thomas Malbon and the 'Providence Improved' of Edward Burghall, at 94–5.

53. There was a Scottish dimension to the war in Cheshire, especially when Leven and his army arrived at the Mersey in the spring of 1645. See Dore, *Brereton Letter Books*, I, 11–12.

54. Roger Howell, *Newcastle-Upon-Tyne and the Puritan Revolution: A Study of the Civil War in North England* (Oxford, 1967), esp. chap. 4.

55. *Truth's Discovery or a Black Cloud in the North Showing Some Anti-Parliamentary Inhuman Cruel and Base Proceedings of the Scotch Army against the Well-Affected in the North of England* (London, 1646). The 'several letters' came from 'Northumberland, Bishoprick [i.e. Durham] and Yorkshire'.

56. *Truth's Discovery*, 2.

57. H. L. Robson, 'George Lilburne, Mayor of Sunderland', *Antiquities of Sunderland & its Vicinity*, 22 (1960), 102.

58. David Scott, 'Widdrington, Sir Thomas (c.1600–1664)', *ODNB*; online edition, January 2008 (<http://www.oxforddnb.com/view/article/29358>, accessed 11 September 2012).

59. *The Letters and Speeches of Oliver Cromwell*, ed. Thomas Carlyle and S. C. Lomas, 3 vols. (London, 1904), III, 345.

Further Reading

Burgess, Glenn, *The New British History: Founding a British State, 1603–1714* (London, 1999).

Darcy, Eamon, *The Irish Rebellion of 1641 and the Wars of the Three Kingdoms* (Woodbridge, 2013).

Gentles, Ian, *The English Civil War in the Three Kingdoms, 1638–1652* (Harlow, 2007).

Grant, Alexander and Keith Stringer (eds.), *Uniting the Kingdom? The Making of British History* (London, 1995).

Hirst, Derek, *Dominion: England and Its Island Neighbours, c.1500-1707* (Oxford, 2012).

Macinnes, Allan I., *The British Revolution, 1625–1660* (Basingstoke, 2005).

Morrill, John, *The Nature of the English Revolution* (London, 1993).

Ó Siochrú, Micheál, *Confederate Ireland, 1642–1649: A Constitutional and Political Analysis* (2nd edition, Dublin, 2008).

Ohlmeyer, Jane, *Civil War and Restoration in the Three Stuart Kingdoms: The Career of Randal MacDonnell, Marquis of Antrim* (2nd edition, Dublin, 2001).

Scott, David, *Politics and War in the Three Kingdoms* (Basingstoke, 2004).

Wormald, Jenny, *The Seventeenth Century: 1603–1688* (Oxford, 2007).

CHAPTER 33

KINGDOM DIVIDED

The British and Continental European Conflicts Compared

PETER H. WILSON

THE British civil wars and the Continental European conflicts of the first half of the seventeenth century are widely accepted as important historical markers. Though opinions divide—often sharply—many would agree with one recent analysis that events in Britain between 1637 and 1654 'laid the foundation for English liberty and for British imperial power'.[1] Likewise, Continental conflicts are generally credited with the transition from an international order characterized by fragmented sovereignty and fluid boundaries, to one based on more clearly defined sovereign states. Such an order is widely associated in political science and contemporary discourse with the Peace of Westphalia concluding the Thirty Years War in 1648. Though the characterization as an 'age of absolutism' has recently fallen from favour, historians still routinely identify the years between 1648 and the French Revolution as a distinct period of European history.[2]

Before comparing British and Continental events, it is necessary to narrow our selection of conflicts. As will become clear, this process of identification is far from simple and already entails a significant degree of interpretation as to whether we are dealing with multiple wars, or manifestations of a single, general struggle. This chapter will argue for the former, suggesting that inter-state wars in early seventeenth-century Europe were distinct contests for regional dominance. Those in western and southern Europe had some underlying unity in the common opposition of several powers to perceived Spanish Habsburg hegemonic pretensions. France was Spain's most consistent opponent, alternating between brief 'hot' and more prolonged 'cold' wars until beginning major hostilities in 1635 which lasted until 1659. Spain also faced the Dutch Revolt after 1568 which assumed the character of an inter-state war in its second stage (1621–48), after widespread international recognition of the northern Netherlands as an independent state during the Twelve Years Truce (1609–21). Further revolts followed in Portugal (1640–68), Catalonia (1640–53), and Naples (1647–8), though only the first of these concluded with the (re-)establishment of a sovereign state. Northern and north-east Europe saw a four-cornered struggle for dominance between Denmark, Sweden, Poland, and Russia in which Sweden variously opposed all three powers, while Poland fought Russia and Sweden separately. Poland was also involved in the struggle to control south-eastern Europe which centred on a long-running contest between the Ottoman and Austrian Habsburg empires. Major operations ceased with the conclusion of the Thirteen Years War in a truce between the Habsburgs and Ottomans in 1606 which left both parties exhausted. The Ottomans then turned eastwards against Persia 1623–39, only resuming conflict in south-eastern Europe in 1645 when they opened a long war with Venice (until 1669).

All these conflicts influenced European relations, but the focus of this chapter will be on the greatest and most destructive of all seventeenth-century wars, namely the Thirty Years War which was waged largely within the boundaries of the Holy Roman Empire. The Stuart monarchy was one of the few states to refrain from formal involvement and, along with Russia and the Ottoman Empire it was the only large state not represented at the Westphalian Peace congress 1643–8.[3] However, at least as many Britons and Irish fought on the Continent as did Swedes,[4] while the Stuart monarchy provided considerable financial assistance to several belligerents and fought its own, brief wars against France and Spain, both of which were also heavily involved in the Empire. The cost of these activities, combined with their disappointing outcomes, contributed to the monarchy's domestic problems and thus to the civil wars after 1637. Britons also followed events on the Continent closely through the expanding print media characterizing the early Stuart age. Yet, their view was clouded by their own confessional and political prejudices and few really understood what was going on. Unfortunately, their misconceptions have been shared by many later Anglophone historians who found their reading of seventeenth-century British observers' accounts reinforced by the writings of Protestant, pro-Prussian German historians in the nineteenth and twentieth centuries.[5]

A common problem has been to present the Empire anachronistically as 'Germany'; a practice which tends to interpret it as a failed nation state, rather than more accurately as a successful system of mixed monarchy. Broad comparisons between Britain and the Empire are largely limited to proponents of the General Crisis of the Seventeenth Century, which sees all wars and revolts as expressions of some structural shift, be it socio-economic, political, or environmental.[6] Outside this problematic approach, there has been little exchange between historians studying Britain and those working on the Continent. There are several cases where scholars of one country have 'reinvented the wheel', arriving (often with much effort) at interpretative models already developed and, in some cases, abandoned by those working on another. This chapter intends to address this by outlining key interpretative issues in the Thirty Years War which reflect, or could inform thinking about other European conflicts, including those in Britain. Since most readers will be approaching this from the perspective of British and Irish history, it is helpful to begin by surveying the constraints on Stuart involvement in European politics, before offering a rather more detailed comparison of their interpretations of the British civil wars and the Thirty Years War.

BRITAIN AND THE THIRTY YEARS WAR

Most discussions of Stuart foreign policy approach it as a factor in the crown's worsening relations with its domestic opponents, rather than as an element of early modern European relations. Events are generally viewed as progressing in two stages. In the first, James I sought influence by posing as 'arbiter of Christendom'.[7] Better relations with Catholic France and Spain were balanced by dynastic ties to Denmark, then Europe's richest and most powerful Protestant kingdom.[8] Attempts to refine these arrangements led to the fatal 'Palatine match' in 1613, whereby James's daughter Elisabeth married Frederick V, the elector Palatine. Despite the recent interest in the lavish wedding festivities and associated propaganda, the critical significance of this event is often overlooked. James and his subjects viewed the elector through their own aspirations, variously seeing a reliable ally or a true Protestant champion. Frederick was neither. Rather, he was leader of both a confessional and political minority in the Empire who sought to redress his own principality's declining influence by deliberately enflaming confessional tensions. As a Calvinist, he was not only at loggerheads with his own predominantly Lutheran subjects (who had rebelled in 1592), but was viewed suspiciously by most of the Lutheran princes who refused to join his alliance, generally known as the Protestant Union of 1608, rightly recognizing it as a vehicle for Palatine dynastic interests.[9]

The second stage began after November 1619 when Frederick rashly accepted the offer of a royal crown from the Bohemian aristocrats who had opened the Thirty Years War by rebelling against the Austrian Habsburgs in May 1618. Any Stuart response was pre-empted by Frederick's crushing defeat at the battle of White Mountain, in November 1620, terminating his reign as 'winter king' and consigning him to perpetual exile. Bavarian assistance had been crucial in the Habsburgs' victory. Bavaria was ruled by a rival, Catholic branch of the same Wittelsbach family that governed the Palatinate. Bavaria's price was the transfer of Frederick's lands and titles which were legally forfeit under the mainstream interpretation of the imperial constitution. Bavaria swiftly occupied both the Upper (eastern) and most of the Lower (western) Palatinate. Spanish forces, also assisting the emperor, meanwhile overran the portion of the Lower Palatinate west of the Rhine.[10]

James was faced with only one realistic option: he could only recover the Palatinate by negotiating with the powers in actual possession. Even this was difficult, since Spain only held a small portion and pursued interests which often diverged sharply from those of its Austrian cousins. There was no guarantee that, had Spain agreed to a Palatine restoration, it could have persuaded Austria to accept it. Any approach to Bavaria was pointless, since the Stuarts had nothing to offer as compensation for relinquishing the Palatinate. Negotiations with the emperor were almost equally futile unless England was prepared to replace Bavaria as Austria's most potent and reliable ally. That was practically as well as politically impossible, given England's geographical distance from the war zone, its status as a separate country, and the sheer inability of the Stuarts to raise the necessary resources. The same obstacles prevented any direct intervention in support of the Palatinate, leaving the Stuarts to alternate between piecemeal, indirect assistance and inept efforts to pressure other countries to help. Hopes for an international evangelical alliance were as illusory as the pre-war view that the Palatine-led Union was a committed body of pious Protestants.[11]

PROBLEMS OF DEFINITION I: DURATION AND SCOPE

The historiographical issues are not so easy to disentangle and can be approached several ways. It is important to remember that we are dealing with complex, multiple events and that any discussion must balance a need for clarity with the recognition that many aspects were closely related. The most pressing issue is one of definition which in turn subdivides into three issues. The first task is to define the duration and scope of each conflict. The difficulties are already suggested by the plethora of competing names for Britain's conflicts, which variously suggest singular, parallel, or multiple struggles depending on which label is endorsed.[12]

Historians of Continental Europe have grappled with the same problem, with several rejecting the term 'Thirty Years War'. Earlier presentations of events as a 'German war' gave way in the twentieth century to interpretations of the conflict escalating into an international struggle encompassing much, if not all of Europe.[13] From that it was but a small step to subsuming the conflict in the Empire into a longer-running Franco-Habsburg struggle which, in one extreme interpretation, was stretched across three centuries.[14] The risk with the current fashion for transoceanic 'Atlantic' and other paradigms is that the undoubtedly costly and important colonial activities of European powers will be woven into a global interpretation of that continent's seventeenth-century wars.[15] A more satisfactory approach is to return to the contemporary understanding of events. The overwhelming majority recognized a distinct Thirty Years War which began with the Defenestration of Prague in May 1618 and continued, with some substantial breaks in 1624 and 1629–30, until the Peace of Westphalia in October 1648. This was seen as separate from other wars elsewhere, despite the participation of several countries in more than one conflict simultaneously.[16]

PROBLEMS OF DEFINITION II: CIVIL OR INTERNATIONAL WAR?

Britain's conflicts have always been recognized as 'civil wars', even if the precise nomenclature has varied. Other powers were not indifferent to British events, but the turmoil simply confirmed their general view—in sharp contrast to that of many historians—that

Britain was a peripheral power, rather than on the cusp of acquiring a world empire. By contrast, the Thirty Years War is generally regarded as an inter- rather than intra-state conflict. This is particularly entrenched in Anglophone writing which, like some current German interpretations, refuses to see the Empire as a state.[17]

The general view informs the popular four-phase model widely used to simplify the complex course of events. The initial outbreak in Bohemia is accepted as a revolt against Austrian Habsburg rule, but most accounts already stress an international dimension through the presence of foreign auxiliaries and subsidies, as well as the Palatinate's decision to accept the Bohemian crown. The conflict then appears to widen in concentric circles, with each successive stage identified by the appearance of an ever larger foreign power. After a Danish phase 1625–9, we have one associated with Sweden following 1630, with French intervention in 1635 usually taken to define the last, longest, and supposedly most destructive stage. This four-stage model does chime with a contemporary lament that Germans were innocent victims of foreign aggression, as well as later German nationalist condemnation of the Empire as incapable of acting as a viable state.

Careful re-examination of how foreign intervention was facilitated and legitimized reveals that the Thirty Years War was actually a civil war over the Empire's political and religious balance.[18] What divided the Empire in 1618 essentially still fuelled the conflict in the 1640s. All intervention was justified in relation to one or other of the competing interpretations of the imperial constitution. That intervention was only possible thanks to the support of those already involved in the imperial civil war. Intervention was not altruistic, since foreign powers were concerned lest adjustments to the Empire's internal balance affect their interests. Thus, Spain backed Austria in the hope that a stronger Habsburg position within the Empire would enable the emperor to redirect German resources against Spain's enemies elsewhere. The Dutch and French intervened to effect precisely the opposite, hoping to distract Spain by prolonging the Thirty Years War. Denmark and Sweden invaded to safeguard their respective interests in northern Germany, but only because they perceived these as threatened by the growth of imperial power following Habsburg victories in the 1620s.

The Dutch Republic never became a full belligerent, sending only modest indirect aid to Bohemia and the Palatinate.[19] Their presence at the Westphalian congress was because their own conflict with Spain was included in a general effort to settle Europe's major wars. Their Peace of Münster of May 1648 was entirely separate from the Franco-imperial treaty signed in the same town which helped conclude the Thirty Years War five months later. Spain intervened in its capacity as a constituent part of the Empire thanks to its Burgundian possessions, sending troops to pacify the Empire according to Austria's interpretation of its constitution. The re-entry of Spanish forces in 1633 after a decade's absence did not entail war with Sweden, even though they contributed significantly to the major Swedish defeat at Nördlingen in 1634. Likewise, Sweden's alliance with France did not make it party to that country's support for the Dutch Revolt or war against Spain after 1635. Indeed, Spain remained a major Swedish trading partner throughout the first half of the seventeenth century.[20] This point could be elaborated further with reference to Denmark,[21] but the general points remain the same. Each power wished to keep its involvement in the Empire distinct from other conflicts it might be engaged in. Each wanted to promote the interpretation of the Empire's constitution best suited to its own interests. Each relied heavily on soldiers and resources provided by imperial princes and others already engaged in the Empire's civil war or, like Frederick V, saw foreign intervention as the only way of recovering lost lands.

Polish and Transylvanian intervention is less well known, but still important. Unlike the other countries, neither legitimated involvement by reference to the imperial constitution, but both saw events as struggles over the Empire's internal balance, rather than an inter-state war. Poland provided auxiliaries to Austria on the basis of a pre-war dynastic pact to oppose rebels in each country. Like Spain, Poland hoped the emperor would assist in its separate conflict with Sweden in the 1620s, but help proved unforthcoming except in 1628. Transylvanian intervention (1619–24, 1644–5) was intended to enhance that principality's precarious autonomy by exploiting the Habsburgs' difficulties with their Bohemian and Hungarian subjects. A major factor in Transylvania's general failure was the Ottoman sultan's decision to renew the 1606 truce with the Habsburgs, primarily to attack Persia instead. Formally, the sultan accepted the Habsburg interpretation of events as a rebellion and even offered military assistance at one point. The Ottomans' decision not to exploit Austria's difficulties was a major factor in the Habsburgs' ability to overcome the crisis after 1618.

Foreign intervention prolonged the war, but did little to shake its basic character as a struggle over the two-fold balance at the heart of the imperial constitution. The Empire was a mixed monarchy, rather than a core–periphery system of imperial dominance. Though the Austrian Habsburgs ruled about 30% of the Empire directly as hereditary principalities (mainly Austria and Bohemia), they shared management of the Empire as a whole with the various princes and magistrates of imperial cities who collectively held the other 70%. These magistrates and princes (including the Habsburgs as Austrian archdukes) were 'imperial Estates' (Reichsstände), each with varying degrees of representation in imperial institutions. Powers were distributed unequally across the long status hierarchy stretching from the elite group of seven electors (including Bohemia) with exclusive rights to choose each emperor, through a variety of different princes down to the magistrates of the imperial cities whose delegates were segregated into an inferior 'college' in the imperial diet (Reichstag). Cutting across the electors and princes was a division between secular hereditary rulers, and elected clergymen ruling the smaller, but more numerous ecclesiastical principalities forming about a seventh of the total Empire. Possession of these church lands was a primary bone of contention in the struggle at the imperial level during the war.

However, hostilities started at the secondary, territorial level of the individual imperial Estates with the Bohemian Revolt. Politics at this level partly replicated that at the imperial level, with each prince sharing the exercise of key functions with representatives of his own nobility, burghers, sometimes clergy, and (very occasionally) peasants as territorial Estates (Landstände).[22] As we shall see, events at this level come closer to those of the British civil wars, with disaffected Bohemian and Austrian nobles and burghers opposing Habsburg measures, notably attempts to restrict crown appointments to

Catholics.[23] The Habsburgs' decisive defeat of their opponents in their hereditary lands drove many of their subjects into exile and, often, into the arms of foreign powers. Moreover, consolidation of Habsburg authority in these areas was perceived by others as a threat to the Empire's internal balance, since it appeared the dynasty would translate its success into stronger imperial rule.

Whereas conflict at the territorial level can be presented as a (relatively) straightforward clash between monarch and domestic opponents, that at the imperial level was far more complex. The threat of 'imperial absolutism' was more apparent than real, but nonetheless encouraged opposition to the Habsburgs, both from within the Empire and through foreign intervention. In fact, Emperor Ferdinand II (r. 1619–37) was extremely reluctant not to compromise his legitimacy by exceeding what he regarded as his proper authority, despite being repeatedly urged to do so by his more impatient supporters during the almost unbroken run of Habsburg victories in the 1620s.[24] His son and successor, Ferdinand III, was likewise determined to uphold what he regarded as his rightful prerogatives, but proved more flexible in adapting to the more adverse environment following Swedish intervention in 1630.[25]

A factor in the Habsburgs' relative success during the war was that imperial politics were never a simple dualism of emperor against 'the princes'. The numerous imperial Estates differed considerably in their conception of the Empire's proper constitution. The majority were primarily defensive, wishing to avoid commitments which threatened to over-burden their fragile governmental structures and often meagre resources. Mainstream opinion was represented by Lutheran Saxony which wanted to preserve the internal distribution of power achieved in the middle of the sixteenth century.[26] Others, like Bavaria and the Palatinate, wanted to adjust this in their favour, but invariably saw change as singular, not a sweeping revision which would have benefited other imperial Estates. Only the counts at the very bottom of the princely stretch of the hierarchy envisaged something more akin to general change, wishing to curb the influence of the electors and more powerful princes by levelling status distinctions amongst imperial Estates. Sweden and France came to support this 'aristocratic' interpretation of the imperial constitution, since it would have emasculated the Habsburgs and rendered the Empire's already cumbersome decision-making mechanisms almost inoperable.

PROBLEMS OF DEFINITION III:
A REVOLUTION?

Discussion of political objectives points to the social dimension and raises the question whether events can be classed as revolutionary. This issue is common to both the British civil wars and the Thirty Years War, but has only really been addressed for the former. As with any term not employed by the historical participants, the utility of 'revolution' depends on how it is defined. Over the last three decades, this concept has been freed from doctrinaire interpretations and instead defined by the presence of 'genuine radicalism', conceived as challenges to the existing social distribution of political and economic power.[27] To qualify as a revolution, the outcome must involve more than simply changing who ruled, or reversing some unpopular measure.

The Thirty Years War obviously does not meet these criteria, but it is worth exploring whether some events at the secondary, territorial level might offer interesting parallels to the English/British revolution(s). The most obvious case is the Bohemian Revolt which culminated in the formal confederation of the five provinces comprising that kingdom, plus their allies in Lower Austria in August 1619. Like virtually all early modern movements, the Confederates presented their actions as restoring their liberties to their 'proper' state. Many of the arrangements were naïve, conservative, or both. The Bohemians also lacked the geographic, economic, and political advantages which eventually enabled the Dutch to make a success of their similar experiment in state-building two decades earlier. Nonetheless, there is no denying that the Confederation was a radical attempt to fashion a new kind of state based on property-owners incorporated as provincial Estates.[28] The Act of Confederation was agreed prior to deposing the current Habsburg king of Bohemia and electing Frederick V instead. The timing reinforced the point that the Estates, not the monarch, were now in charge. The leading participants were also fully conscious of indigenous radical traditions: the decision to throw the Habsburg regents from a window in Prague castle was deliberately staged in remembrance of a similar act at the start of the Hussite insurrection two centuries earlier.

However, if revolutions are defined by the extent of popular support, the Bohemian Revolt fails the test. The leadership singularly failed to connect with the broad mass of the population. The so-called 'militias' which appear in secondary accounts as Confederate forces were in fact mercenaries hired by the provincial assemblies. There is a danger, however, of over-emphasizing the socially conservative character of these events. Despite all the criticism of Whiggism, there is still a widespread assumption that the distinguishing feature of British history is a story of the rise of individual liberty, whereas Continental history is an account of the growth of state power. The latter appears particularly to apply to Germany and the rest of Central Europe. It is compounded by the persistence of the view that imperial politics were primarily princely and aristocratic, that the Empire was not a state, that its inhabitants did not identify with it, and—most perniciously—that 'real' history was made at the level of the territories. The Thirty Years War plays a central part in these narratives, being generally held responsible for ending any chance that the Empire would survive as an effective framework, as well as ushering in an age of princely absolutism at territorial level characterized by a steady process of 'social discipline' reducing Germans to obedient subjects.[29] These issues are too wide to be addressed satisfactorily here, but it is worth noting that the Thirty Years War saw widespread protest across much of western and southern Germany, including major revolts in Upper Austria (1626, 1636) and Bavaria (1633–4) which represented the largest popular movements in these areas prior to 1848. There were also numerous examples of local resistance to all armies similar to the Clubmen of the English Civil Wars.

It is also worth reconsidering print culture which is a fertile area of current research on the British civil wars, fuelled by the 'linguistic turn' in history since the 1980s. This has, quite properly, identified transatlantic links and explored the subsequent impact of the seventeenth-century language of liberty on the American Revolution of 1776. This should not, however, overshadow British and Irish reception of, and engagement with European debates. Indeed, the desire for news from the Continent was a major factor stimulating British print culture. Historians are increasingly aware how perceptions of Continental events shaped attitudes and behaviour into the civil wars.[30] This issue offers a fruitful field for future study which might shed more light on the differences and similarities between British and Continental print culture in terms of both medium and message. The Empire in fact had a highly developed news media that was, in some respects, more advanced, diverse, and sophisticated than that of the British Isles.[31]

THE ROLE OF RELIGION

Religion was a major issue in public discourse on both sides of the Channel. The Thirty Years War has long been regarded as the last and greatest of an entire age of 'religious wars' beginning with the Protestant Reformation, and some have recently restated this.[32] The same label is now being applied to the British civil wars following a resurgence of interest in this aspect after several decades of comparative neglect.[33] The trend seems general and includes attempts to 'put religion back into the French Wars of Religion' (1562–1629), as well as to unearth a religious dimension to international conflict in the supposedly more secular age after 1648.[34]

This trend is clearly related to the widespread disillusionment with Marxist histori-cal materialism by the 1980s, which contributed to a decline in more overtly social, economic, as well as political explanations. It is also difficult not to see it linked, albeit unconsciously, with current world events and the media preoccupation with Islamic extremism. A controversial statement of this approach is Samuel Huntington's *Clash of Civilizations* which locates major conflicts in diametrically opposed cultures, with those outside the West defined primarily by religion.[35] Many find this approach unsatisfactory, not least for its rather loose definition as to what constitutes 'religion'. Several German historians have addressed this by reserving 'religious war' to denote clashes of civiliza-tion, such as that commonly held to have taken place between Christian Europeans and the Muslim Ottomans, and to designate intra-Christian disputes as 'confessional wars'.[36]

The emphasis on confession began in the 1950s and has evolved into the concepts of 'confessionalization', denoting the process of forging a distinct community of believers, and the 'confessional state', identifying the alliance of throne and altar as the primary means to achieve this.[37] The concept's original purpose was to bridge the confessional divide in historical writing by finding a common language for scholars of all faiths to study the Reformation. Irrespective of their doctrinal differences, sixteenth-century reformers and their supporters employed broadly similar methods to proselytize, encourage orthodoxy, promote morality, and combat dissent. Studying these aspects moved religious history from the realms of theology and church organization, and examined it as a social and cultural phenomenon. Like all good ideas, this approach prompted extensive research, some of which undermined the validity of the original concept.[38] Perhaps more seriously, further development of the idea eroded much of its distinctiveness and left it looking remarkably similar to Huntington's 'civilizations'. According to one prominent proponent, confessionalization structured European relations between the end of medieval universalism and the rise of an international order based on sovereign states. In the process, 'Christian fundamentalism' caused not only the Thirty Years War, but the entire General Crisis.[39] This interpretation expressly endorses the division of seventeenth-century Europe by the Czech historian Josef Polišenský into a historically progressive Calvinist–Puritan block of north-western states pitted against a reactionary Catholic consortium headed by Spain, Austria, and Poland.[40] All this comes perilously close to warming up 1970s notions that the British civil wars and Dutch Revolt constituted 'early bourgeois revolutions' which, in turn, reflected an underlying shift from feudalism to market capitalism supposedly responsible for the General Crisis. It is particularly difficult to apply such ideas to Central Europe where, in contrast to Britain and the Netherlands, Calvinism was primarily an elite phenomenon represented by Bohemian and Hungarian magnates, and lesser German princes and counts.

Nonetheless, the confessionalization thesis does illuminate one important characteristic of early modernity. The fragmentation of western Christendom into distinct communities forged new connections across geographical, linguistic, and social barriers, encouraging people to identify with others with whom they previously had little or no contact.[41] These connections are now being explored, revealing the significance of shared military service, university education, and experience as exiles, alongside the more obvious role of trade and commerce.[42]

The crucial question for all approaches emphasizing religion is how to explain the link between belief and action. All too often, historians analyse the extensive evidence of sectarian polemic, but fail to demonstrate how this affected behaviour, let alone whether it precipitated violence or war. To remedy this it is perhaps worth reconsidering doctrine more closely without losing sight of the importance of the social and cultural dimension of religious history rightly noted in the confessionalization thesis. The big, perhaps insurmountable, problem is how to do this without descending into the 'blame game' of trying to portray one faith as more inherently belligerent than others—something which bedevils much of the discussion of religious violence in the contemporary world. A potentially fruitful approach is to identify certain tenets of faith which might have encouraged risk-taking, or resistance beyond the point where others might have given up. Providentialism is an obvious example and was found in subtly different forms across several confessional groups though, importantly, was not shared equally by all members.[43] The overriding message from most pulpits in the Empire was one of repentance, rather than calls to arms. Regardless of confession, the official line was that Germans had brought the calamity of war upon themselves through their own sinfulness. The true path to victory lay in purging their souls and, indeed, there is little evidence that the undeniably high level of violence during the Thirty Years War owed much to sectarianism.[44]

The preceding suggests we should identify militants and moderates, rather than distinguishing between solid confessional groups supposedly so polarized they could only communicate through violence. Militants believed that religious goals were within their grasp, regarded setbacks as tests of their faith, and were more likely to take risks in the conviction that God was on their side. For them, the war represented a struggle between good and evil: neutrality was not an option (even for co-religionists in other countries). By contrast, moderates generally denied that there was a valid theological basis to claim that God personally summoned individuals to do his bidding. They were more pragmatic and flexible and saw conflicts as distinct, generally opposing calls to intervene elsewhere purely on religious grounds. It is important to recognize that this is not a distinction between religious and secular views. The war was not fought by a mob of fanatics, with secularists seeking peace. It was waged by moderates and militants alike. Moderates were also religious: they differed primarily in regarding religious goals as longer-term objectives, generally unobtainable in their own lifetimes. Moderate and militant positions were not fixed, and an individual's views could shift depending on circumstances. Moderates were in the majority, including amongst those in authority, while militants tended to be clergy, observers outside the main war zone, and/or those on the losing side, especially those driven into exile. However, militants usually generated more 'noise' than moderates, as their words dominated the public discussion of events and consequently influenced historical interpretations.

The importance of the preceding becomes clearer when we place religious issues in their political context, since this allows us to move beyond examining individual attitudes and behaviour, to see how belief could have wider, more significant results. Several studies have noted that the collective nature of Christian worship means that political outcomes often have less to do with differences of theology than the precise relationship each community has with higher authorities.[45] The final part of this chapter will explore this through the three elements of political power: legitimacy, executive authority, and infrastructure.

Politics I: Legitimacy

The shift from medieval ecclesiastical monoculture to early modern multi-confessionalism forced rulers to pick between the competing varieties of Christianity. Making such a choice represented a vast increase in political authority, which in turn sharpened ideas of sovereignty and promoted the formation of more clearly distinct states. Rulers assumed the right to decide not only between doctrines, but also to determine far more than previously matters like public morality, church organization, ritual, and the clergy's role and status. The assumption of such powers defined the confessional state, identifying political authority with a particular faith. Problems flowed from the fact that at least some subjects and neighbouring powers believed particular rulers had made the wrong choice and, consequently, their extension of authority over church and society was illegitimate.

Far from representing an exception, Britain followed the European norm by impos-ing a monarchical solution to the anxiety following the Reformation. The crown approved a single, supposedly definitive doctrinal statement and asserted supervision over a church structure intended to enforce orthodoxy. This immediately equated dis-sent with political subversion. To believe something different than the monarch was to challenge royal authority. Debates on the right of resistance sharpened as some dis-senters claimed allegiance to 'higher' authorities, not merely the pope in the case of Ultramontane Catholicism, but often asserting that their conscience before God took precedence over political obedience.[46] Opposition was stirred not only by persecution, but also by failure of established authorities to fulfil expectations to do 'the right thing', including in the early Stuarts' case, not aiding the Palatine cause with sufficient vigour. Dissenters invariably identified themselves with 'the godly', lending a moral edge to existing court–country tensions as those outside the charmed inner courtly circle criti-cized unwelcome policies as immoral.[47]

This situation was replicated in the Empire at the secondary level of the imperial Estates where princes and civic magistrates identified themselves with a particular con-fession and promoted conformity through all the usual methods associated with confes-sionalization. The situation for the Empire as a whole was radically different. In place of the unambiguous association of the crown with one confession, the Empire tried to defuse tension through dissimulation.[48] A cornerstone of this process was the so-called Religious Peace of Augsburg in 1555 which deliberately avoided defining doctrine and instead employed vague terms to enable Lutherans and Catholics to coexist within the same political system. This was a fundamentally different approach to that in Britain, France, Poland, and other countries where dissenters were licensed through char-ters like the Edict of Nantes. These identified dissenters as legally distinct and inferior groups whose protection rested solely on privileges granted by the crown which was free to revoke them. By contrast, the settlement in the Empire rested on a treaty negotiated by the imperial Estates, binding all regardless of faith within a common legal and politi-cal framework. Lutherans remained concerned at the in-built Catholic majority within most imperial institutions after 1555, but this was simply a consequence of there being more Catholic than Protestant imperial Estates, not that the Catholics had superior rights. Whereas dissenters elsewhere in Europe were defined in relation to their mon-arch's established church, the Empire had no official faith beyond a deliberately unspeci-fied Christianity.

Unfortunately, this solution contained the seed of future problems, though it did not make it inevitable that major war would follow sixty-three years later. Dissimulation did become harder as the Empire moved from a 'culture of personal presence' to one based on writing.[49] Personal presence had ensured that politics usually remained open-ended. Face-to-face interaction helped demarcate status, signal cooperation or enmity, but the absence of a written record enabled the players to reinterpret events later if it suited new circumstances. Written culture grew in response to the 'free rider problem' of ensuring all parties stuck to agreements and so increasingly closed politics which were now intended to have a single, unambiguous outcome. The problems of written culture were manifest in the Reformation where the major doctrinal statements emerged from position papers prepared by theologians prior to colloquia intended to resolve differences and preserve Christian unity. Writing things down merely made the differences more obvious and so promoted confessionalization. The Empire's political problems arose from the same desire for precision as interested parties argued their interpretation of ambiguous points was the only one valid.

POLITICS II: EXECUTIVE AUTHORITY

Much has been made of the composite character of the Stuart monarchy, comprising not just three kingdoms, but also overseas colonies and pronounced localism everywhere. In European terms, however, it was a highly centralized system for taking decisions. Though each kingdom had its own parliament, that in Ireland rarely met. Consequently, outside Scotland, the entire monarchy was essentially ruled from London, despite all the acknowledgement we must make to the significance of localism. London was the recognized capital and location for the only permanent royal court. With executive authority clearly held by the crown, the main question was how far the monarch should share key decisions with the vested interests represented in Parliament. Thus, whereas the Empire's problems derived from its ambiguous constitution, those of Britain stemmed from an all-too-clear clash between the crown and its opponents. Charles I's enemies sought to curtail his powers and, ultimately, remove him altogether. By contrast, conflict in the Empire fragmented as each party tried to assert its interpretation of the constitution whilst also improving its status within the hierarchy of imperial Estates. With the partial exception of Sweden, the Habsburgs' enemies were not trying to depose them from the imperial title: Frederick V's representative even voted for Archduke Ferdinand II in the imperial election of 1619, while his master was in the process of contesting possession of the Bohemian crown.

The greater complexity of imperial politics becomes still more apparent when we examine the Empire's framework for decision-making. The Thirty Years War is often presented as a breakdown of the imperial constitution, because the pro-Palatine group amongst the Protestant imperial Estates walked out of the Reichstag meetings in 1608 and 1613, after which that institution did not reconvene until 1640–1. Nonetheless, the Empire still functioned, albeit imperfectly, because it resembled an animal with multiple organs; when one stopped functioning, another usually took its place. There were two supreme courts, while the range of alternatives to the Reichstag for collective decision-making included various imperial deputations, electoral congresses, regional assemblies (*Kreistage*), and ad hoc summit meetings. These institutions emerged stronger from the war. Disputes persisted over the precise function and jurisdiction of each element, but virtually all parties regarded the constitution as the moral high ground, especially because it was not clearly associated with any particular confession.

More significant changes occurred at the secondary level of territorial politics where the 'Bohemian alternative' to princely government was decisively defeated. The provincial and territorial Estates certainly remained important after 1648 and continued to influence domestic affairs in various principalities, in some cases into the 1830s. However, constitutional changes enacted at Westphalia in 1648 removed earlier ambiguities and denied these institutions any say in key areas of sovereignty, such as external relations and military policy, all of which were reserved expressly for the princes.[50] Still more significant were the changes in personnel that ensured that the Habsburgs only needed to issue 'renewed constitutions' to their provincial Estates, rather than abolish them after the rebels' defeat in the early 1620s. The confiscation of rebel property led to an unprecedented transfer of assets to Habsburg loyalists, consolidating social and economic power in the hands of families who owed their influence to their close association with the dynasty.

Politics III: Infrastructure

The other factor eroding the influence of the territorial Estates was their inability to cope with the burdens of war. The Estates traditionally saw their task as assisting their ruler in 'extraordinary' circumstances. The usual practice worked *ex post facto* as Estates voted taxes to amortize debts incurred by their ruler in tackling an emergency, such as war or natural disaster. Debt amortization was the primary means employed by the Protestant group in the Habsburg provincial Estates to extort religious and political privileges from the 1560s. Such concessions were similar to those granted to dissenters in France and elsewhere and likewise depended on how far the Habsburgs were willing or obliged to continue them. Ferdinand II lost little time in revoking them after 1619, on the grounds that these were particular rights granted to selected members of the Estates who had forfeited their privileges by taking up arms against him.

More generally, it proved impossible to sustain the old pattern of ruler–Estates relations as it became obvious that war was not temporary or distant, but permanent and immediate after 1618. By 1625 most principalities had moved over to a system generally known as 'contributions', whereby they stopped trying to pay for war by channelling tax revenue through central treasuries, and instead licensed military units to take resources directly from local communities. In short, war funding was adjusted to the actual level of infrastructural development. The really robust early modern institutions were the networks of local officials in towns and villages who knew where resources were and how to extract them. This method ultimately boosted princely power rather than that of the Estates, because it was the prince, as war lord, who legitimated the system through an increasingly sophisticated rhetoric of 'necessity'.[51] The resumption of prolonged warfare against the Turks and French after 1662 ensured that war remained the norm, not the exception, and prevented any return to pre-war fiscal practice.

Central European experience in this respect contrasts with the usual interpretation of how the British civil wars strengthened the Westminster Parliament, either as a guardian of individual liberties in the Whiggish historical tradition, or as a fiscal-military powerhouse in more recent accounts. However, the general conclusion of this chapter is that the differences were a matter of degree rather than stark divergence. Above all, research has posed remarkably similar questions and suggested approaches which can be fruitfully applied to both Britain and Continental Europe.

NOTES

1. James Scott Wheeler, *The Irish and British Wars 1637–1654: Triumph, Tragedy and Failure* (London, 2002), 256–7. For reasons of space this chapter will not reference works on British or Irish history unless directly relevant to particular points. Similarly, readers seeking more information on events in Central Europe are referred to my *Europe's Tragedy: The Thirty Years War* (London, 2009). I would also like to thank my colleague Charles Prior for his helpful suggestions.

2. A recent example is Robin W. Winks and Thomas E. Kaiser, *Europe from the Old Regime to the Age of Revolution, 1648–1815* (Oxford, 2004).

3. Franz Bosbach, *Die Kosten des westfälischen Friedenskongresses* (Münster, 1984). This work is more comprehensive than its title suggests and gives an excellent overview of diplomatic representation at the congress.

4. An aspect which cannot be explored here. See Steven Murdoch (ed.), *Scotland and the Thirty Years War, 1618–1648* (Leiden, 2001); David Worthington, *Scots in Habsburg Service, 1618–1648* (Leiden, 2004); R. A. Stradling, *The Spanish Monarchy and Irish Mercenaries: The Wild Geese in Spain, 1618–68* (Dublin, 1994). Total numbers and further references in Wilson, *Europe's Tragedy*, 321–2. Rather fewer, but still significant numbers of Continental Europeans fought in the British civil wars: Mark Stoyle, *Soldiers and Strangers: An Ethnic History of the English Civil War* (New Haven, 2005), 91–109, 213–21. The full impact of British–Continental military links remains to be investigated.

5. For these see Kevin Cramer, *The Thirty Years War and German Memory in the Nineteenth Century* (Lincoln, NE, 2007).

6. Geoffrey Parker and L. M. Smith (eds.), *The General Crisis of the Seventeenth Century* (London, 1997); Theodore K. Rabb, *The Struggle for Stability in Early Modern Europe* (New York, 1975); and the special issue devoted to the concept by *American Historical Review* [*AHR*], 113(4) (2008). Space precludes further discussion of this concept which I have addressed in 'The Causes of the Thirty Years War 1618–48', *English Historical Review* [*EHR*], 123 (2008): 554–86. This article also reviews the important contribution of German historian Johannes Burkhardt who seeks to explain early modern wars as consequences of structural deficits in European state development. English-speaking readers can access Burkhardt's interpretation through his 'The Thirty Years War', in Ronnie Po-chia Hsia (ed.), *A Companion to the Reformation World* (Oxford, 2004), 272–90.

7. Christoph Kampmann, *Arbiter und Friedensstiftung. Die Auseinandersetzung um den politischen Schiedsrichter im Europa der Frühen Neuzeit* (Paderborn, 2001).

8. Steven Murdoch, *Britain, Denmark-Norway and the House of Stuart, 1603–1660* (East Linton, 2000).

9. Magnus Rüde, *England und Kurpfalz im werdenden Mächteeuropa (1608–1632)* (Stuttgart, 2007); Albrecht Ernst and Anton Schindling (eds.), *Union und Liga 1608/09. Konfessionelle Bündnisse im Reich—Weichenstellung zum Religionskrieg?* (Stuttgart, 2010). English-speaking readers can consult Brennan C. Pursell, *The Winter King: Frederick V of the Palatinate and the Coming of the Thirty Years War* (Aldershot, 2003) which offers useful insight into his mentality while accepting perhaps too readily his assertion that Palatine policy was intended to preserve the imperial constitution.

10. Bavarian policy has been extensively studied. The best, if somewhat daunting starting point is Dieter Albrecht's monumental biography of *Maximilian I. von Bayern 1573–1651* (Münster, 1998).

11. The best overview of Stuart policy in this period remains Simon Adams, 'Spain or the Netherlands: The Dilemmas of Early Stuart Foreign Policy', in Howard Tomlinson (ed.), *Before the English Civil War* (London, 1983), 79–101.

12. For discussion of this issue, see Braddick's introduction to this volume, esp. 4, 7–11.

13. Geoffrey Parker (ed.), *The Thirty Years War* (London, 1987); Christoph Kampmann, *Europa und das Reich im Dreißigjährigen Krieg* (Stuttgart, 2008).

14. Nicola M. Sutherland, 'The Origins of the Thirty Years War and the Structure of European Politics', *EHR*, 107 (1992): 587–625. More restrained, if equally controversial views in S. H. Steinberg, *The 'Thirty Years War' and the Conflict for European Hegemony, 1600–1660* (London, 1966).

15. It is worth remembering that even the mighty Dutch East India Company only contributed 10% of the Republic's GDP; a figure matched by Dutch arms sales in Europe. North Sea fisheries and the Baltic grain trade were far more significant economic factors than colonial activity.

16. Geoffrey Mortimer, 'Did Contemporaries Recognize a "Thirty Years War"?', *EHR*, 116 (2001): 124–36; Konrad Repgen, *Dreißigjähriger Krieg und Westfälischer Friede* (Paderborn, 1998), 21–105.

17. Further discussion of the Empire as a state in Peter H. Wilson, *The Holy Roman Empire, 1495–1806* (2nd edition, Basingstoke, 2011).

18. Further elaboration in Peter H. Wilson, 'The Thirty Years War as the Empire's Constitutional Crisis', in R. J. W. Evans, Michael Schaich, and Peter H. Wilson (eds.), *The Holy Roman Empire, 1495–1806* (Oxford, 2011), 95–114.

19. Josef Polišenský, *Tragic Triangle: The Netherlands, Spain and Bohemia, 1617–1621* (Prague, 1991).

20. Enrique Martínez Ruiz and Magdalena de Pazzis Pi Corrales (eds.), *Spain and Sweden in the Baroque Era (1600–1660)* (Madrid, 2000).

21. See Paul D. Lockhart, *Denmark in the Thirty Years War, 1618–1648* (Selinsgrove, 1996).

22. R. J. W. Evans and T. V. Thomas (eds.), *Crown, Church and Estates: Central European Politics in the Sixteenth and Seventeenth Centuries* (New York, 1991).

23. A good starting point in the extensive literature is Karin J. MacHardy, *War, Religion and Court Patronage in Habsburg Austria: The Social and Cultural Dimensions of Political Interaction, 1521–1622* (Basingstoke, 2003).

24. Thomas Brockmann, *Dynastie, Kaiseramt und Konfession. Politik und Ordnungsvorstellungen Ferdinands II. im Dreißigjährigen Krieg* (Paderborn, 2011).

25. Lothar Höbelt, *Ferdinand III. (1608–1657)* (Graz, 2008).

26. Saxon policy has been repeatedly misunderstood. For an exceptionally clear discussion, see Dominic Phelps, 'The Triumph of Unity over Dualism: Saxony and the Imperial Elections 1559–1619', in Evans, Schaich, and Wilson (eds.), *Holy Roman Empire*, 185–202.

27. Glenn Burgess, 'On Revisionism: An Analysis of Early Stuart Historiography in the 1970s and 1980s', *Historical Journal*, 33 (1990): 609–27 at 625.

28. Joachim Bahlcke, 'Modernization and State Building in an East-Central European Estates' System: The Example of the *Confoederatio Bohemica* of 1619', *Parliaments, Estates and Representation*, 17 (1997): 61–73.

29. Critical appraisal of the traditional views in Matthias Schnettger (ed.), *Imperium Romanum—Irregulare Corpus—Teutscher Reichs-Staat* (Mainz, 2002). Peter Blickle has waged a sustained critique of the authoritarian view of German history, but still concludes that the period after 1648 was largely characterized by a loss of liberty: *Obedient Germans? A Rebuttal. A New View of German History* (Charlottesville, 1997).

30. Ian Roy, 'England turned Germany? The Aftermath of the Civil War in its European Context', *Transactions of the Royal Historical Society*, 5th series, 28 (1977): 127–44; Barbara Donagan, 'Codes of Conduct in the English Civil War', *Past and Present [P&P]*, 118 (1988): 65–95.

31. Wolfgang Behringer, *Im Zeichen des Merkur: Reichspost und Kommunikationsrevolution in der Frühen Neuzeit* (Göttingen, 2000); Johannes Weber, 'Strassburg, 1605: The Origins of the Newspaper in Europe', *German History*, 24 (2006): 387–412.

32. Notably the series of articles by Axel Gotthard including, 'Der deutsche Konfessionskrieg seit 1619. Ein Resultat gestörter politischer Kommunikation', *Historisches Jahrbuch*, 122 (2002): 141–72. Further discussion and critique in Peter H. Wilson, 'Dynasty, Constitution and Confession: The Role of Religion in the Thirty Years War', *International History Review*, 30 (2008): 473–514.

33. Glenn Burgess and Charles W. Prior (eds.), *England's Wars of Religion, Revisited* (Basingstoke, 2011).

34. Mack P. Holt, 'Putting Religion Back into the Wars of Religion', *French Historical Studies*, 18 (1993): 524–51; David Onnekink (ed.), *War and Religion after Westphalia, 1648–1713* (Farnham, 2009).

35. Samuel P. Huntington, *The Clash of Civilizations and the Remaking of World Order* (London, 1996).

36. Excellent introduction to the debate by Franz Brendle and Anton Schindling, 'Religious War and Religious Peace in the Age of Reformation', in Evans, Schaich, and Wilson (eds.), *Holy Roman Empire*, 165–82. Fuller discussion in Franz Brendle and Anton Schindling (eds.), *Religionskriege im Alten Reich und in Alteuropa* (Münster, 2006).

37. Wolfgang Reinhard, 'Pressures Towards Confessionalization? Prolegomena to a Theory of the Confessional Age', in C. Scott Dixon (ed.), *The German Reformation* (Oxford, 1999), 169–92; Anton Schindling and Walter Ziegler (eds.), *Die Territorien des Reiches im Zeitalter der Reformation und Konfessionalisierung*, 7 vols. (Münster, 1989–97).

38. For example, the work summarized in Marc R. Forster, *Catholic Germany from the Reformation to the Enlightenment* (Basingstoke, 2007).

39. Heinz Schilling, *Konfessionalisierung und Staatsinteressen 1559–1660* (Paderborn, 2007), esp. 6–14. Quotation from p. 78. English-speaking readers can access this interpretation through Schilling's shorter essay which comes even closer to Huntington, *Early Modern European Civilization and its Political and Cultural Dynamism* (Hanover, NH, 2008).

40. Schilling, *Konfessionalisierung*, 398–9. It is not clear how far Polišenský believed his own view, given the need to please Czech Communist censorship. See R. J. W. Evans, 'A Czech Historian in Troubled Times: J. V. Polišenský', *P&P*, 176 (2002): 257–74.

41. Schilling, *Konfessionalisierung*, 108–19. For a suggestive integration of this insight into a broader reappraisal of early modern relations, see Daniel H. Nexon, *The Struggle for Power in Early Modern Europe: Religious Conflict, Dynastic Empires and International Change* (Princeton, 2009), esp. 3–4, 265, 289.

42. For example, Graeme Murdock, *Beyond Calvin: The Intellectual, Political and Cultural World of Europe's Reformed Churches* (Basingstoke, 2004), esp. 31–53.

43. A good example is the extent to which Frederick V's Providential beliefs may have encouraged his acceptance of the Bohemian crown: Pursell, *Winter King*, 76–80.

44. See the excellent regional study, Holger Berg, *Military Occupation under the Eyes of the Lord: Studies in Erfurt during the Thirty Years War* (Göttingen, 2010).

45. Mary Fulbrook, *Piety and Politics: Religion and the Rise of Absolutism in England, Württemberg and Prussia* (Cambridge, 1983); Philip S. Gorski, *The Disciplinary Revolution: Calvinism and the Rise of the State in Early Modern Europe* (Chicago, 2003).

46. Robert von Friedeburg, *Self-Defence and Religious Strife in Early Modern Europe: England and Germany, 1530–1680* (Aldershot, 2002).

47. Peter Lake, 'The "Court", the "Country" and the Northamptonshire Connection: Watching the "Puritan Opposition" Think (Historically) about Politics on the Eve of the English Civil War', *Midland History*, 35 (2010): 28–70.

48. The classic assessment of this process is still worth reading: Martin Heckel, 'Autonomia und Pacis Compositio', *Zeitschrift der Savigny-Stiftung für Rechtsgeschichte Kanonistische Abteilung*, 45 (1959): 141–248.

49. Barbara Stollberg-Rilinger, *Des Kaisers alte Kleider. Verfassungsgeschichte und Symbolsprache des alten Reiches* (Munich, 2008).

50. Ronald G. Asch, 'Estates and Princes after 1648: The Consequences of the Thirty Years War', *German History*, 6 (1988): 113–32.

51. Michael Behnen, 'Der gerechte und der notwendige Krieg. "Necessitas" und "utilitas reipublicae" in der Kriegstheorie des 16. und 17. Jahrhunderts', in Johannes Kunisch (ed.), *Staatsverfassung und Heeresverfassung in der europäischen Geschichte der Frühen Neuzeit* (Berlin, 1986), 42–106.

FURTHER READING

Asch, Ronald G., *The Thirty Years War: The Holy Roman Empire and Europe, 1618–48* (Basingstoke, 1997).

Asche, Matthias and Anton Schindling (eds.), *Das Strafgericht Gottes. Kriegserfahrung und Religion im Heilgen Römischen Reich deutscher Nation im Zeitalter des Dreißigjährigen Krieges* (2nd edition, Münster, 2002).

Burkhardt, Johannes, *Der Dreißigjährigen Krieg* (Frankfurt am Main, 1992).

Bussmann, Klaus and Heinz Schilling (eds.), *1648: War and Peace in Europe*, 3 vols. (Münster, 1998).

Kaplan, Benjamin J., *Divided by Faith: Religious Conflict and the Practice of Toleration in Early Modern Europe* (Cambridge, MA, 2007).

Parker, Geoffrey (ed.), *The Thirty Years War* (London, 1987).

Schmidt, Alexander, *Vaterlandsliebe und Religionskonflikt. Politische Diskurse im Alten Reich (1555–1648)* (Leiden, 2007).

Wilson, Peter H., *Europe's Tragedy: The Thirty Years War* (London, 2009).

Wilson, Peter H., *The Thirty Years War: A Sourcebook* (Basingstoke, 2010).

Index

Note: page numbers in *italic* indicate illustrations.